OTHER WORLDS

TORKOM SARAYDARIAN

Visions for the Twenty-First Century®

ISBN: 0-929874-04-8 (Hardcover)
ISBN: 0-929874-05-6 (Softcover)

Library of Congress Catalog Number 89-51506

Printed in the United States of America

Cover design: *Fine Point Graphics,* Sedona, Arizona

Printed by: *Delta Lithograph, Co.* Valencia, California

Published by:

T.S.G. Publishing Foundation, Inc.
Visions For The Twenty-First Century
P.O.Box 4273
West Hills, California 91308
United States of America

NOTE: The meditations and prayers contained in this book are given as guidelines. They should be used with discretion and after receiving professional advice.

Dedicated to M. M.

published in memory of

Robert M. Patton

with blessings

Torkom Saraydarian

Table of Contents

Diagrams

Do not believe on the strength of traditions even if they have been held in honor for many generations and in many places; do not believe anything because many people speak of it; do not believe on the strength of sages of old times; do not believe that which you have yourselves imagined, thinking that a god has inspired you. Believe nothing which depends only on the authority of your master or of priests. After investigation, believe that which you have yourselves tested and found reasonable, and which is for your good and that of others.

Buddha

Introduction

Why write about the "Other Worlds," especially at this time when people are able to walk in Space, when laser beams are capable of solving many obscure problems, when man is able to destroy life on the planet?

Despite all these achievements, man has not yet met his True Self. His present achievements are insignificant in relation to the vision that he will discover in the Other Worlds. The knowledge of the Other Worlds will not only help man use his scientific knowledge for the advancement and liberation of humanity, but it will also expand the consciousness of humanity to such an extent that the present life of man will seem to him a nightmare in comparison with the new dawn.

The Other Worlds are the worlds of causes which will be recorded not through our microscopes, telescopes, and lasers but through our astral, mental, and intuitional senses. We are the prisoners of our physical senses. The knowledge of the Other Worlds will prepare our emancipation from such a slavery and will reveal a new understanding of balance between what we are and what we can be.

Every expansion toward a new dimension is achieved through crises and joy. Both of these factors are expressions of accumulated karma. A crisis is the moment when your past karma reaches its maturity and creates a whirlwind in your life. A joy is the moment when your past efforts for Beauty, Goodness, Righteousness, Freedom, and Gratitude reach their maturity and disperse the clouds for a new dawn. The knowledge of the Other Worlds will condition your life in such a way that you will sow beauty and harvest joy.

The Other Worlds existed before the existence of the material world in which man is stuck. All Sages are conscious inhabitants of the Other Worlds. Whenever man loses his awareness of the Other Worlds, he falls into "sleep" and "dreams." This is what our life has been. The Other Worlds are a call for a new awakening.

I wrote this book knowing that many people will think I am hallucinating or dreaming. But this book may change their whole outlook on life. If a dream could make my life more beautiful, creative, useful, and real, I would cherish that dream. Actually, our civilization has gone too far away from such a Teaching and has found itself stuck in crimes of all sorts.

Do not read this book if you are an earthbound person and if your university degrees satisfy you. This book is written for "spiritual fools"— those who have not just a sophisticated and mechanized brain but also a heart and an intuition. What the brain cannot sense, the heart sees. This book is written for those who are mature souls, those who have a great amount of experience, labor, and tolerance. It is written for those who really love all living beings.

Do not read this book if you are going to be irritated because of your narrow-mindedness, fanaticism, dogmas, and doctrines. This book is written to give people hope and aspiration and to direct their eyes toward the future, toward what they can be. It can be read by those who know that they will one day die, by those who are ready to prepare themselves to die, and by those who know that they are immortal.

This book synthesizes many experiences, traditions, and Teachings of the East and West. It is not written to create a field of argument but to help people see the beauty of eternal life, the beauty of the continuity of life. Especially at this time, when humanity is in grave danger of extinction, this book will give some hope and even some courage to try to change the life of the planet.

Before you proceed, it will be helpful if you know the definitions of certain words.

The *Subtle World* is equivalent to the astral world. It is next to the physical-etheric plane. When it is used in the plural form, as *Subtle Worlds,* it refers to all planes or worlds beyond the physical.

The *Fiery World* refers to the higher mental plane, the Intuitional Plane, and still higher planes... into Infinity.

The *ego* is the human soul attached to his bodies, glamors, illusions, and vanities — either with one or with all of them.

The *human soul* is the developing Divine Spark, aware of his independent existence as a spiritual, immortal being.

If you still have difficulty in your mind regarding the Subtle Worlds, let me say that the physical world is the concrete earth. The astral or Subtle World is water, or steam. The Fiery World is the air. Beings of various kinds live on earth, water, air, and beyond. This analogy may help you find your footsteps on these rocky mountains.

This Teaching has its sources of inspiration in the Higher Worlds. It is given to humanity to make people understand that every minute and every event of life must be used to prepare oneself for the Higher Worlds. A teaching that is not related to the Higher Worlds is nothing else but a blind alley.

All instructions given to man are formulas to be used to harmonize his steps with the Cosmic Visions.

Some people, while living on this earth, think that this is their home base. When they pass away, they expect to return and continue their life on earth. There are even people who plan for their next life. There is nothing seriously wrong in such a concept except that these people think about earth as if it were their home to which they eventually will return.

The fact is that their Home is in the Higher Worlds. The truth is that we live long periods of time in the Higher Worlds and return to earth for short periods to help the evolution of the world, walk on the path of perfection, and return Home where greater plans, projects, and labor are awaiting us.

Some great Saints realized this fact as their last days on earth approached. They felt very joyful and enthusiastic as they knew they would be returning to their *natural* life, back from a short mission. The disciples on earth must begin to think about their earthly life as a short mission which they must accomplish with honor. Most earthly occupations have originated from the Higher Worlds. Conscious workers try to actualize on earth the creative life they had in the Higher Worlds.

To actualize our creative ideas and put in action our skills on earth is not an easy matter. People are one-hundred percent more creative in the Higher Worlds than on earth, where they are trapped in glamors. It is true that, originally, all creative efforts started in the Higher Worlds, and must do so. Every time man passes away, he develops and multiplies his labor in the Higher Worlds, provided that he is in light, in love, and in beauty. Such a man, when he takes new incarnations, tries to bring back his higher realizations and work them out on the earthly plane.

It is through such a conscious work that eventually the bridge between the two worlds is built.

In the Higher Worlds an awakened man is a source of creativity, and there is no limit to his creativity and expansion. That is why, when the time of incarnation arrives, many beings in the Higher Worlds fall into anxiety and even try legally to postpone their incarnation; that is, they try to manipulate the Law.

A great Sage states that before an incarnation one falls into a real loneliness. But the actual departure is joyful because, first, you have your consciousness; second, you are re-engaging yourself in tasks which are waiting for you.

Some people live a double life. They carry on the labor and responsibilities of their earthly life, but when they sleep they continue their work in the Higher World. Thus for them, awakening is going into sleep, and sleep is a real awakening in the Higher Worlds!

This can happen consciously or unconsciously. It happens consciously if the *golden bridge* is built. In this case the labor on earth is the continuation of the labor of the Higher Worlds, and the labor of the Higher Worlds is the continuation of the earthly labor.

We are told that such people are rare, but their number will increase as the unfoldment of the human soul continues.

From the angle of the Higher Worlds, earthly life is either a mission or a karmic confrontation. Those who learn their lessons on earth and clear their karma are not subject to the Law of Reincarnation. They work in the Higher Worlds and expand their consciousness in the Cosmic Home.

In contemporary life, man is extremely busy with the problems of life, with his routine business, with his desire for more comfort and pleasure; but he has only a few minutes, or none at all, to think about the Higher Worlds. We must develop a love for the Higher Worlds.

People may wonder how a love of the Higher Worlds can be developed if one has no information about or experience with the Higher Worlds. A love for the Higher Worlds is not the result of knowledge or information, although such knowledge and information exist in the Ageless Wisdom and within our inner chambers. But such a love is a cause which makes us strive toward the Higher Worlds.

The reality of the Higher Worlds evokes such a love and reflects in our hearts, if our hearts are cleaned of hatred and separative thinking. The seeds under the ground do not need to know about the Sun, but the Sun's rays activate them and make them grow until the Sun shines on their petals and leaves. Those seeds which are eaten by various elements and are paralyzed cannot respond to the Sun and grow to see the Sun.

Man is like such a seed. If his heart is healthy, he will grow in love toward the Higher Worlds and increase in his experience of the Higher Worlds. Such a love will be a healing and uplifting experience in his life.

As one increases in his love, he gradually fuses with the Law of Attraction and manifests certain higher qualities inherent in this law. The Law of Attraction is the Way by which the Cosmic Magnet functions. The Cosmic Magnet, like our Sun, stimulates love in each "seed," and love turns into the Path leading one toward the Sun — toward the Cosmic Magnet.

Thus, love leads man toward the Higher Worlds. When a person feels a love toward the Higher Worlds, he must involve himself in the labor of constantly developing such a love. Many factors may interfere and try to prevent such a labor. The daily routine and problems of life may interfere, but the one who felt the first urge can conquer all hindrances if he daily contacts for a few minutes the initial feeling of love for the Higher Worlds. In that immediate feeling is hidden the whole power to conquer all obstacles antagonistic to his love for Higher Worlds.

We are told that it is not education or learning but love that carries us to the Higher Worlds. The increase of our love for the Higher Worlds must be proven on the battlefield of life. Every day, on every occasion, our love will be tested, and we will eventually recognize that the Path to the Higher Worlds passes through the heart of every living form.

One cannot have a real love for the Higher Worlds without, in the meantime, having love toward all those who share the life with him on this planet. True Teachers and Healers are those who inspire and encourage such a love for the Higher Worlds.

What are the Higher Worlds? All true religions speak about Higher Worlds. All true Teachers have given us maps of Higher Worlds. They have called the Higher Worlds:

Heaven
Paradise
The Kingdom of God
Nirvana
Bliss
Higher states of consciousness
Other dimensions
The realm of Light
The realm of Beauty
The realm where the Immortals live and function
The Cosmic Planes beyond the physical plane
The worlds in which one sees the Face of the Creator

They have also called the Higher Worlds the realm of angels, archangels, and great *devas* who show us the Path to climb toward the Mount of the gods.

Teachers have said that purity of heart is the foundation on which are also found sincerity, simplicity, enthusiasm, and love for all beings.

They said that a sacrificial and heroic life dedicated to the Common Good is necessary in order to walk the Path toward the Higher Worlds. They said that Beauty, Goodness, Righteousness, Joy, and Freedom are doors on the Path and that one cannot open them unless he becomes the embodiment of Beauty, Goodness, Righteousness, Joy, and Freedom.

They said that the Path cannot be trodden without inclusiveness and without developing the sense of synthesis. They said that the Path to the Higher Worlds disappears if one does not exercise the principle of detachment and renunciation of all that slows or stops his steps on the Path.

They said that all virtues are lights on the Path, especially the virtue of discrimination; but these virtues must be tested in the winds, turbulences, and on the battlefield of life before one is able to carry these lights on the Path.

They said that the compass on the Path is the Intuition — faith — which must be developed by all means, especially through meditation, fasting, and prayer.

The Ageless Wisdom is the depository of all philosophies, religions, and sciences. It is given to humanity to guide us toward the Higher Worlds.[1]

One must study this information in order to increase his love of the Higher Worlds.

Human striving starts with a sensitivity to the attraction of a higher force or higher magnet. Striving is the response to the attraction. As the striving becomes pure, the power of attraction increases.

It is through the tension produced between the striving and the attraction that creative manifestation begins. During the contact with a higher attraction, the human soul becomes radioactive and gradually lets the Glory within manifest.

The magnets of attraction have various magnitudes and various forms. Ideas, visions, and calls are forms of magnets in different magnitudes. These come from the center of beauty within our sphere of consciousness.

There are other magnets, such as the images of Great Ones, great Teachers, or Planetary, Solar, and Galactic Magnets, toward which the human soul feels attraction.

The progress of the human soul starts the moment that he registers the currents of attraction and continues through his striving toward the source of attraction.

---

1. For further information, see *The Ageless Wisdom.*

After attraction, there are other phases through which the human soul passes:

1. Contact with the energies of magnets
2. Saturation
3. Creative radiation

Then a new cycle starts on a higher spiral, and the human soul radiates in greater beauty.

1

The Other Worlds

The majority of people have no conscious communication with planes or worlds that are different from the physical plane or the physical world. These people have cut their communication, either because of strong attachment and identification with the material world, or because of their selfish life and accumulated dark karma.

It is true that the human soul comes from higher realms to live in the material worlds for a long time. As he descends into matter, he develops his physical senses and etheric centers. The unfoldment of the senses and centers of his higher bodies starts from the physical plane. This is the ground in which the seeds are planted and from which they must grow. But the descent to the physical plane should not mean severance from higher worlds. It is possible to keep communication with the Higher Worlds as one descends to lower worlds, and vice versa.

Cleavages come into being due to attachment and karma. Attachment is the result of a limitation of consciousness and a preoccupation with the forms of a given plane. Karma is the result of the violation of laws on the physical plane.

The human soul is destined eventually to live on all planes simultaneously with full consciousness. This will be possible when the human soul progressively develops the power of detachment and when he purifies his karma.

Detachment and purification of karma will open the doors to higher planes, and the human soul will build the communication line between all worlds. This communication line is the continuity of consciousness.

Detachment allows the increase of psychic energy, and purification of karma enables man to use the psychic energy constructively or goal-fittingly. A person of human, or earthly, consciousness cannot penetrate into the strata of higher dimensions unless he detaches himself, frees himself, from his karmic burdens and has a great amount of psychic energy in his possession.

When we speak about higher dimensions, higher planes, or the Higher Worlds, we refer to spheres of fires. As we go to higher and more subtle worlds, we realize that we enter into fire, which increases in its intensity and power as we penetrate deeper. This is why the Teaching says that we must not take with us combustible materials when we leave our physical body, as they will burn and scorch our subtle bodies. Sometimes these materials are called "trash." They are actually the images of forms to which we are attached. The attachment can be physical, astral, or mental; it does not make much difference.

Attachment creates greed, violence, crimes, habits, vices, identifications, vanities, glamors, and illusions. All these are inflammable materials which must be left behind, if one wants to have a pleasant journey toward higher worlds.

Those who carry with them large amounts of inflammable materials will be caught in flames until the trash is burned to a certain degree and the human soul can carry the rest as his burden into the Subtle Worlds. Of course, the burning of the trash leaves scars in the subtle body, and souls are differentiated by their scars.

Man in his Core is a fire. That fire can be released and put in contact with the spatial fires. The release of fire is accomplished through developing virtues, through striving toward the highest, through renunciation and sacrificial service.

When the Core-Fire is released and spreads throughout our mechanisms on all planes, it purifies them, burning all the trash accumulated throughout ages. When all the trash is consumed in fire, the human soul consciously and in great joy traverses the earthly planes and enters into higher worlds in ecstasy and bliss.

Increasing the Core-Fire throughout our nature protects us from various diseases and attacks and makes it possible to contact higher spatial fires which carry psychic energy, wisdom, higher visions, and the beauty of the Cosmic Heart. Increasing the fire in our nature makes possible occasional flights toward higher centers. It strengthens the currents of our thoughts and makes our entire aura attractive to higher impressions.

Psychic energy has a very peculiar quality. Being in itself a current of fire, when it comes in contact with burning and consuming fires, it neutralizes them; it takes the scorching and destroying elements out of them. This means that psychic energy can counterbalance any kind of fire, especially subtle fires, fires from the Earth and Space. As psychic energy accumulates, the trash in our nature is exhausted and higher striving is established in our life.

re: fire(s)

After the physical plane, there are other worlds. In the Teaching they are called:
—The Subtle Worlds, which include the etheric and astral planes.
—The Mental World, which is the world of thoughts.
—The Fiery World, which is the abstract levels of the mental plane and the Intuitional Plane. Beginning with the Intuitional Plane, one actually deals with intensified fire.

In the Ageless Wisdom, fire is called the guardian of the doors. Between all planes, even between all Cosmic Planes, one confronts intensified fire. The Spark advances through these fires until It is stripped of all that is not the highest fire. When all is stripped, the Spark becomes one with the source of fire, with the Cosmic Self.

There are many fiery phenomena. For example, the etheric centers progressively emanate fire and flames in various colors. The heart especially has its glorious fires, which are the greatest healing agents. It is the fires of the heart which link the man to Cosmos and to the Cosmic Heart.

Then we have fiery, creative thoughts which, like flames and comets, traverse the worlds.

Let us not forget the twelve-petaled Lotus, a rare beauty, and the thousand-petaled Lotus, with glorious hues.

A still higher fire is manifested through the Spiritual Triad. Like a pyramid of fire and like the head of an arrow, it opens the gates of the most Subtle Worlds.

Then we have the fire of the Monad, the beacon on the Path of the ocean of life on all dimensions.

Then we have the Self, the Divine Fire, the pure essence of man, the only fire which can penetrate into the sanctuary of the Cosmic mysteries. This is often called the Blue Star.

When these fires are lit, the Path is seen and crossed in great joy and glory. On each plane one needs a greater light, a greater fire. The psychic energy glows within all these fires and intensifies them with Cosmic tension and Cosmic direction.

The ancients used to symbolize these fires as a boat sailing upon the water of lower worlds, which carries the human soul to Higher Worlds. The boat is the symbol of fire. It is possible to travel in the Subtle Worlds only in a "boat" of fire.

In ancient Teachings, those who possessed psychic energy and lit their fires were called "carriers of fire." They experienced the fire in their nature as the fire of enthusiasm, creativity, purity, immunity, and invincibility. They were also called "fiery comets" which bring new cultures, new civilizations, new visions, and new dimensions to the consciousness of man.

These "carriers of fire" are the heroes in any field of human endeavor. They are fire-bearers. As they dedicate and sacrifice their lives for humanity, they multiply their fires to a great extent and light the fires of thousands of people living in many dimensions. Such fire-carriers are also called "living flames" or "living torches."

Life progresses and advances only through the pressure of such "carriers of fire." They not only influence the population of the world, but they also enlighten and release millions of souls tied in the astral and other worlds. Their fire purifies and releases these souls to let them proceed on the way of Infinity.

At various times the Ageless Wisdom has recorded that when certain advanced souls were leaving their bodies, there occurred severe thunderstorms and even earthquakes. These phenomena of Nature are called *intensifiers of fires*. They literally amplify the fires of the human soul and help him cross the threshold easily, smoothly, and powerfully, as if filled with a stronger wind in his sails.

We are told that certain minerals such as potassium, magnesium, iron, and sulfur intensify the fires of the centers as well as the higher fires of the subtle planes. Some trees, such as the pine, deodar, eucalyptus, and oak (as also their extracts) increase the subtle fires in man.

Certain people use alcohol or drugs to intensify their fires, but, in reality, alcohol and drugs destroy the centers of fire in the human nature and make man incapable in the future of absorbing fiery energies from Space.

Fire in the human nature is increased, regulated, and used properly through meditation. Regular meditation accumulates a great amount of fire in our system which is used for many creative purposes. That fire is also used when the human soul is crossing the threshold to the Subtle World.

Fire is the protective shield, especially in the Subtle World where many dark forces are ready to attack the human soul. Fire not only burns the bodies of dark entities but also destroys their various arrows aimed at the human soul.

2

Thinking and the Higher Worlds

After one leaves his body, he realizes that all that he had is taken away from him. Such an awareness often makes him feel that he is left totally unprotected, like a leaf that has fallen in the currents of the air.

When this feeling passes, he realizes that the Law of Karma is a firm foundation on which he can rest.

Following this realization, he can see that his aspirations and interests give him certain directions. He eventually realizes that it is his thoughts that he can depend on. In the Subtle World, man communicates with thought. Man receives and gives through thought. Man protects himself and fights with his thoughts. Man finds his way toward Higher Worlds through his thoughts.

Those who develop pure thinking and creative thinking will have greater facility in the Subtle World. Almost anything done in the Subtle World is done by the power of thought. For example, things are created, moved, put in motion, and destroyed by the power of thought. Integration, alignment, and synthesis are achieved by thought. Sublimation and transmutation are achieved by thought. All communication within the Subtle World and other worlds is carried on through thought. Those who do not have the ability to think will toss in the dark sea of the subtle planes like a little boat on the stormy oceans.

In the Subtle World, thinking is related to the eyes. There are those who live as blind people live. There are those who can see, but their eyesight is damaged. There are those who can see in certain conditions. And there are those who have good eyesight.

Our vision is the direct result of our thoughts. This is even true on the physical plane. Those who misuse their thoughts will have a hard time in the Subtle World. The misuse of thought upon earth destroys the mechanism of vision in the Subtle World.

Thought is energy, and this energy must not be used to hurt people, to exploit them, to enslave them, to create unbearable conditions for other living beings, to create cleavages, or to pursue selfish interests.

The worst thoughts are intentionally and consciously misused thoughts. Thoughts affect vision, sometimes to such a degree that one lives as a blind person in the Subtle World and then incarnates blind. If one could examine the past incarnation of such people, he would see that through their thought they violated the Law of Light and Love.

Devotion to a great cause, sacrificial service, and meditation elevate our thoughts and clear our eyes, not only our physical eyes but our astral and mental eyes as well.

The greatest weapon against the dark forces is thought charged with the fire of the heart. Thought can use the fiery currents of the spatial electricity and transmit them through the eyes. Thought uses the eyes to direct the currents of fire to combat the forces of darkness.

These forces are transmitted through the eyes as beams of light in various colors. There are beams that search for and burn away the vehicles of dark forces and repel their dark currents. There are beams which bring illumination and healing. There are beams which purify and uplift. There are beams which communicate and receive communications given from higher realms.

In addition, there are beams which serve as paths for souls. There are beams which bring help from higher realms. There are beams which absorb wisdom and resound the Cosmic Directions.

All these beams are used by thought through the eyes. This is why it is so important to develop a high standard of pure, clear thinking.

Thinking and vision build the bridge between the worlds. This bridge is the continuity of consciousness by which man travels from one plane to another without interrupting his consciousness or awareness of impressions reaching him from various sources.

Every human being must strive to achieve continuity of consciousness before he passes away. His unfolded eyes will provide the light, and his thought will direct the way.

Thinking must be directed to the invisible and higher spheres of life. One must think and study about the Higher Worlds, about the future, and about Infinity.

Thinking about the Higher Worlds establishes a line of communication with the Higher Worlds, and through this line new impressions reach the consciousness, causing enlightenment and expansion.

Thinking about the Higher Worlds makes a man a citizen of the Higher Worlds, and when he enters into the Higher Worlds, he is not considered a stranger.

Entrance into the Higher Worlds is possible through sleep, through withdrawal of consciousness, or through transition. But these methods can be surpassed by thought. Thought can penetrate into the Higher Worlds. It can bring impressions and inspirations from the Higher Worlds, enrich the creativity of the thought, and strengthen the direction of the life.

We are told to think about the Higher Worlds daily. How can we think about the Higher Worlds if there is no corresponding element in our consciousness? What, exactly, must we do, if we are encouraged to think about the Higher Worlds?

We must realize that within our consciousness there are many memories of the Higher Worlds, concealed under the layers of worldly impressions. These memories will slowly release themselves if we continue thinking about the Higher Worlds. We must relax and think about the beauty, harmony, and creativity of the Higher Worlds; about the advanced Souls in the Higher Worlds; about Their labor on behalf of humanity; about Their striving toward Infinity.

When this is done for a long period of time, the snow of the memories will begin to melt and come to the field of your consciousness. You will be able to recall certain impressions, feel certain presences, and interchange telepathic thoughts with them. We are not referring to mediumistic activities. We are referring to conscious communication with the Higher Worlds, without falling into the traps of self-delusion and self-deception.

In a few decades, new disciples will be born who will establish close ties with the Higher Worlds. Such disciples will give us leadership and direction, and they will introduce cooperation between the Higher Worlds and humanity.

The definition of the Higher Worlds can be given as follows: The Higher Worlds are those spheres of consciousness where beauty and creativity exist in harmony with the currents and fires of the Cosmic Magnet. In these Higher Worlds live great Masters of Wisdom, great heroes and Initiates, and great specialists of many fields. The wisdom of the Higher Worlds can be used as a beacon of light for our darkening world and for suffering humanity.

The disciples of the Higher Worlds are not so-called mediums, channels, and "psychics." These disciples are true Initiates whose consciousnesses are truly enlightened, whose hearts are purified, and whose characters have been tested in their lives, in social and national service, and in many fields of human endeavor.

These disciples have the highest records of honesty, sanity, creativity, and nobility. They have the highest degree of mental development and are endowed with the highest virtues.

Before such great messengers of the Higher Worlds appear, the number of mediums, channels, and "psychics" will increase, and they will create future hindrances and difficulties for those real Initiates who will come after them. But this will be a test for humanity to prove if it has enough discrimination and is worthy enough to profit from the revelation of Initiates.

These Initiates will never make claims but will give us deeper wisdom, deeper revelations, and greater beauty. Through their fruits, we will know them.

These Initiates will put their main emphasis upon the transcendental values of life, upon the virtues of the heart, upon renunciation and sharing. They will not occupy themselves with the personality problems and interests of people but will reveal to us the Path and the mysteries of the Path leading us to higher states of consciousness and into the Higher Worlds. They will not be fortunetellers, past-life readers, or aura readers; but they will reveal to us the great future and encourage us to strive by all means possible to achieve that future.

They will bring us beauty from the higher realms, beauty which not only will give us joy but will also evoke the Sleeping Beauty within our hearts. They will not be the merchants of separatism but the prophets of synthesis and unity.

It is possible for each of us to achieve a close contact with the Higher Worlds through meditation and contemplation on the Higher Worlds.

Greater achievements are not accomplished in one lifetime. We must start striving toward greater achievements so that, year after year, life after life, we come closer to our goals and become more able to actualize our dreams.

We must direct our thoughts toward the Higher Worlds as if we were entering a sacred temple of beauty in all reverence and solemnity. Our thoughts weaken and the contact with Higher Worlds suffers if we are burdened by suspicion and disbelief or by personal curiosity. Our thoughts gain energy and strength if our motive is charged with love, joy, the expectancy of beauty, service, and the fire of striving toward higher spheres of existence.

We have many friends, co-workers, and Teachers in the distant worlds. Our thoughts can reach them and find them. It is possible to establish communication with them. In thinking about them, we will slowly realize that we are the children of Infinity and that the Cosmic Space is our true Home.

While watching the midnight sky, send your thoughts, salutations, greetings, and blessings to your distant friends. One day you will meet them once again on various planes and in various conditions. But remember that thought communication will eventually develop to such a degree that, like a big eagle, the thought energy will propel you toward distant worlds.

The joy of existence increases as you expand your consciousness toward distant worlds.

The _power of synthesis_ must be developed in the consciousness of each human being. Synthesis is a very mysterious power. Through synthesis you see things from all directions, and every direction provides for you a way of approach.

Synthesis does not crystallize your thoughts in one direction. It gives you mobility and enables you to orient yourself to any note in the synthesis, as if it were a symphony. Thus your mind is not trapped in a certain note, but is free to chose any one of them and use it as a basis for your approach to the symphony of life.

The power of synthesis makes man able to adapt himself and his mind to any conditions rapidly and without strain or friction.

Events and currents upon the earth flow very slowly in comparison to the speed of the events and currents in the Subtle Worlds. Things change there without the slightest indication. It is very difficult to predict the next phase of an event in the Subtle World.

Those who did not develop the power of synthesis lack adaptability and lose many opportunities of ascent in the Subtle World. This adaptability must often be so fast that one cannot measure time by the standard of time on earth. In spiritual discipline on earth, one must train himself in the art of adaptability, with rapid or even instantaneous motion. Many games are created in the world to develop such a power of quick discernment and action to adapt oneself to a new condition. Slow and delayed action brings continuous failure in the Subtle World, as it does on earth.

This power is called mobility of spirit. Only a watchful, free, and striving spirit can develop such a power. We learn such a mobility of spirit even on our freeways and congested streets, in the handling of our cars with extreme watchfulness and mobility. Those who do not have this mobility of spirit live for a long time in the Subtle World as totally confused fools, or as corpses.

Watchfulness is recommended by all great Teachers. Watchfulness can be achieved only through developing the power of synthesis in our consciousness. Every element of synthesis is a path and an inspiration for mobility — either for modification or adaptation.

In synthesis all directions are harmonized. The power that holds all directions, all "notes," in synthesis is the common purpose of the direction of each "note." The manifestation of such a power can only come into existence when each direction, each "note," works to release the power and beauty of the other "notes."

Those who develop such a synthesis in their consciousness and make their life a note in a greater symphony can enjoy the conditions of the Subtle World immensely.

Recall how your dreams change every second to something else, how a life event condenses within a few seconds. These experiences give you some idea of how fast time runs in the Subtle World, and, because of its speed, people do not notice the existence of time at all in the Subtle World.

Only an awakened consciousness can see the flow of time because, due to the ability of continuity of consciousness, he can relate the three worlds and measure them with the time concept gained on earth.

3

Activity and the Subtle Worlds

People think that action belongs to the earthly existence. But the human soul acts and works on various levels simultaneously or separately.

Some actions are three-dimensional. An action works on three levels simultaneously. The originating source of action can be either on the mental, the astral, or the physical plane. One can be involved in a certain action on the mental plane, while this action is also reflected in his astral and physical worlds like echoes.

Every action performed in the mental world manifests in other worlds. Similarly, every action performed on the physical plane has its corresponding action on the other planes. But people seldom realize this.

A conscious action originates from the plane where the focus of consciousness is.

We sometimes have a faint idea about our actions carried on in the dream state. Sooner or later people come to the realization that, though their body sleeps, they remain active on certain planes and they create effects on the physical plane.

People often have the experience that they leave the body and do things somewhere else. It is even possible that the human soul engages himself in multidimensional work. This refers to the actions that the human soul conducts through his physical, emotional, and mental bodies, independently directing each of them toward certain activities.

All actions of the soul on various planes, simultaneously or separately, create their effects, and all these effects are cumulative. If actions are taken in harmony with the Law of Love and Light, the cumulative result of each action turns into a step of a ladder leading the human soul into more enlightened spheres of existence. It is through our actions that we conquer all obstacles on our path. This is why we are told that each one of us must build his temple through his "hands and feet" and "take refuge in his Self."

Each action must be performed under the light of a clear consciousness. Vices and the waste of energy not only benumb or obscure our consciousness, but they also put us in contact with lower astral entities. Lower psychism is a means of communication with these entities, who eventually obsess the person and pollute his consciousness. Upon entering into the Subtle World, a polluted consciousness is attracted by the same entities to which he was related.

Clarity and purity of consciousness must be achieved before one leaves the earthly plane. If it is impossible to perform a creative, benevolent action on earth without a clear consciousness, it will be a hundred times more difficult to live a creative, benevolent, and progressive life in the Subtle World without having a clear consciousness in the subtle planes. Self-deception is one of the factors which destroys the integrity of the consciousness.

The power of synthesis of the consciousness conducts all activities on all planes, coordinating them in such a way that contradiction and waste of energy are avoided and the road is paved toward the Higher Worlds.

People usually live in the physical dimension. A small percentage live in the physical and astral dimensions. An even smaller percentage of people live in three dimensions.

In the physical dimension people may live mechanically, semi-consciously, or consciously. Those who live in two dimensions, physical and astral, live consciously or semi-consciously. One must be conscious on the physical plane in order to be at least semi-conscious on the astral plane. One must be conscious on the physical and astral planes in order to be semi-conscious on the mental plane. Unless a man becomes conscious on three planes, he cannot penetrate into the fourth dimension.

In actuality, we live on all levels simultaneously but not consciously. Our actions spread to the astral and mental planes immediately but not consciously. The goal is to be conscious of the correspondences of actions on the astral and mental planes.

Integrity between these three planes is reached if an action corresponds to emotions and thoughts, or if a thought corresponds to actions and emotions. Cleavages are created among those dimensions when the action does not correspond to thoughts, or the thought does not correspond to emotions or actions. Such kinds of disunity on the three levels lead a man toward disintegration and health problems.

The Ancients said, "Let your mouth talk out of your heart; let your heart be in harmony with your thought; and let your actions be the flower of your heart and mind." This is what sincerity is, and it is a great virtue for health and happiness.

Almost all discoveries on earth are reflections of the discoveries in the Subtle World. The Subtle World is far more advanced in scientific discoveries than our earth. When the formulas and designs of the machinery of the Subtle World pass through the atmosphere of the earth and through the human brain, much is lost, and sometimes only a distorted reflection remains. This is why it is so important that our scientists develop continuity of consciousness so that they can see the prototypes of their discoveries in subtle planes and make needed changes and adjustments in their discoveries.

We are told that in the Subtle World machines are operated by psychic energy, condensed in and transmuted by the human soul. The machines are not noisy, and they are extremely simple compared to the correspondences here on earth.

We are told that in the Hierarchy the Great Ones have apparatuses created in higher spheres because They are totally conscious on higher spheres. But They cannot yet present them to the world because of the world's karma.

There are three factors that help one to penetrate into the Subtle World:

1. Striving toward the future with the joy of the heart
2. Sacrificial service rendered to humanity without complaint or expectation
3. Purification or settlement of karma

If these three factors are carried on intelligently and progressively, very soon the gates of the Subtle Worlds will open, and we will be able to bring down to earth all that they have there. Then we will be able to unify both worlds.

The wisdom and knowledge of the Subtle Worlds have two sources:

1. The Fiery World, from which the Ray of the Teaching is transmitted to the Subtle World and is received in accordance with the level of the inhabitants there.
2. The earth, where great human beings carry with them their experiences, knowledge, wisdom, and dreams.

There are many great minds on this planet who know how to create new forms of machinery, but they do not have the ways and means to do it because of their own and humanity's karma. They are like seeds which flourish and grow into actualization in the Subtle World because all conditions of achievement exist there. If you developed your thinking power and creativity on earth, you will present a great opportunity for those who strive to manufacture new discoveries.

It is your power of thinking and creativity started here on earth that will be used and advanced to a very high degree in the Subtle World. But if you pass away without the power of thinking, creativity, and the fire of the heart, you will be a burden in the Subtle World. All germinations of talents and enterprises in the Subtle Worlds start here on earth.

Continuity of consciousness must be built from two shores. First, in our earthly life we must develop total continuity of consciousness and awareness of the Subtle World and Fiery World. Then, on the subtle levels and fiery levels we must build a corresponding consciousness of lower levels. It is through this two-dimensional awareness that a person begins to live a conscious life.

The important thing is to remember that this two-way bridge must be built while we are in physical existence.

Continuity of consciousness is a progressive expansion of awareness over greater and greater areas of the subjective and objective worlds.

Some people are only aware about the events of the lowest stratum of the Subtle World. A small number of people fall asleep when they penetrate into the middle sphere. There are very few people who are aware of the higher levels of the Subtle World. Fewer still are those who penetrate and are aware of the Fiery World.

People may be educated or in high positions in science, politics, or finance, but if they deny the existence beyond the physical life, after their departure they will fall into a state of unconsciousness in the Subtle World and in a very short time will be drawn again into incarnation. When anyone denies the existence of the Higher Worlds, his denial turns into his own prison.

Those who return to earth in a short time do not receive the blessings of the Subtle Worlds. In the Subtle World we pass through a process of transformation; our accumulated true knowledge is digested, assimilated, and turned into spiritual energy and wisdom.

The structures of future visions are constructed in our soul. Distant possibilities are sensed by our subtle centers and are tuned to these distant possibilities.

When one comes back almost immediately, he not only misses all these opportunities, but also, because of the lack of nourishment, his bodies come back distorted and weakened and cannot stand the pressure of life.

The human mind cannot function in a balanced way if a part of the mind is not occupied with the supermundane realities because, in reality, a man lives in two worlds. As there is night and there is day, there are also physical realities and superphysical realities. A conscious realization of these two worlds keeps the mind in balance, and continuity of consciousness eventually becomes a fact.

Continuity of consciousness is a great asset for creative work because it transmits instantaneously whatever idea, meaning, or experience is needed from any plane to any plane. Creativity is a way to bring out all that exists in our inner treasury and change it into sound, music, movement, color, or form.

All our experiences are collected in the inner recorders. Painful or joyful, no matter what they are, they can turn into a flow of diamonds through the magic of creative fire.

Thus the storehouses of our memories, the lower mind and the astral plane, are vacated and their contents are used for creative purposes. This is why creativity brings release and is an act of transmutation.

While living in his physical body, man can function in the Fiery World where he creates through his thought. But this creativity is not the highest or most inclusive creativity until his thought acts in a sphere of pure love. The woman with whom the man is in love can provide such a sphere with her love. As a pure electrical sphere, this love reaches the Fiery World and nourishes the creative thoughts of man, revitalizing, strengthening, and unfolding the higher fiery centers in him. This sphere of love is only created if the two persons share a true love with each other.

All great creative people are inspired by the love of a woman or a man whom they love and who loves them. If the love does not continue with one person and frequently changes to different people and turns into a pursuit of sexual satisfaction, the sphere of love cannot be formed and higher creativity cannot take place.

In the East when they see a great, creative man they say, "Someone loves him deeply." It is important that leaders, teachers, and elevated artists are surrounded with a sphere of love to render a better and deeper creative service for others. Love provides substance to their creative thought so that it can take form and manifest on earth.

Thought-creativity degenerates and even turns into hostile currents toward life as a whole when a creative person or a creative leader destroys the formation of the sphere of love of one person and tries to build another sphere with a new arrangement. Disintegrated love-spheres are as dangerous as decomposing food in your environment.

Life passes and the child-minded people run after the satisfaction of their sex, without forming a permanent relation and building their love-sphere which, in the future, would be the source of inspiration of both parties.

The love-sphere created is not only favorable for the creativity of men but also for women. The highest centers of women open, and a great source of inspiration streams into women when they realize that they are truly loved. Such people can have advanced children because at the time of their fusion, their antenna reaches higher spheres where advanced souls dwell. They also provide a strong love-sphere for the children, who bloom and flourish in that atmosphere.

Most of the problems of children originate from broken homes where there is the absence of love and the presence of much irritation, hatred, fear, and remorse. In such a sphere, even advanced children feel suffocation and do not open their flowers. The karma of those who do not care for their children and do not meet their responsibilities is heavy.

Children must be provided with a loving home. The children of a loving home are much healthier than the children of homes without love. A home that is full of love provides a great opportunity for children not to fall into their former habits. Love nourishes their bodies and keeps the forces of their auras in circulation. In a flowing aura, habits do not form. Only in stagnated, inhibited auras do habits begin to form.

During the journey toward the Subtle World, man leaves behind his habits, which are patterns in his etheric, astral, and mental aura. When he incarnates, he is free from his habits; but he inherits the habits of his parents, to a certain degree, and develops new habits from his family, school, and environment.

Of course, the seeds of his habits may still be found in the permanent atoms, and according to their records, the structure of the bodies is formed along certain tendencies. It is also possible that habits, being mostly physical, vanish after death.

We must discriminate between habits, desires, and ways of thinking.

A habit is the repetitious way you express your desire. A habit is the repetitious way you express a posthypnotic suggestion. But a habit is not a desire; it is the mechanical and repetitious way of manifestating a desire. Desire continues in the Subtle World in a greater or lesser degree, but a habit is dropped this side of the grave.

Thinking patterns still exist, but they dissolve when the Fiery World is approached, or when the consciousness is put in contact with Higher Worlds.

The newborn baby is free, as far as his former habits are concerned. Many years in the Subtle World erase habit patterns from the subtle bodies, and he comes with new subtle bodies which are easily affected by the conditions of the bodies of the parents.

In every incarnation, a new chance is given to the baby to start a new life. Consequently, right education is very important so as not to let the children fall into habits.

People sometimes ask, "What about good habits?" If so-called good habits are mechanical, they are as bad as bad habits. This is because those who are caught in habits cannot unfold their essence.

In a home where the sphere of love is pure and strong, habits seldom form.

People who have freedom of thinking, feeling, talking, and acting — think, talk, feel, and act goal-fittingly. Thus, love nourishes not only creative thought but also freedom. In freedom, original and creative thinking become possible. Our emotional centers provide the most lofty emotions when they are activated by love. Heroism, a totally sacrificial life, dedication, devotion, loyalty, and endurance are the flowerings of the higher astral centers. Such qualities are conceived and reach maturity in a sphere of love. When such qualities are developed, they are an affirmation that the ascent toward the Higher Worlds will be a joyful one.

The act of love is not a physical act only; it is also an emotional and mental act. The pure act is an act simultaneously in the astral and mental planes; but, in general, this act does not manifest itself simultaneously on the higher astral and higher mental planes but reflects only on the lower astral planes.

One or both parties may be engaged in lust and worship of the body. Such an act is reflected in the lower astral plane because the act has no idealism or love in it. The higher astral and mental planes are not reached; therefore the act is partial, lower, uncreative, as well as exhausting and degenerative.

When the act is repeated simultaneously on three planes, it evokes the higher emotions from the higher astral levels and the higher thoughts and ideas, nourishes them, and builds a channel from the higher mental centers to the throat center to make the thought manifest creatively.

Prostitution and rape stay in the physical plane only, and the counterparts in the higher bodies of the sexual centers react violently and close their petals in order not to be affected by the lower forces. Thus, instead of opening their petals, the higher centers close their petals. This is why the Great Ones in every cycle warned people about the degeneration of sex. They also emphasized love and called marriage "sacred."

Of course, no marriage is sacred if there is no true love and mutual respect and dedication toward higher ideals.

Children born in love will spread love and become the creative people of the future.

In the lowest astral plane, sex is expressed in its full measure as lust, with all the miseries, pain, and sorrow associated with it. Kidnaping, rape, and crimes are common at this level. When sex is manifested as lust, there is no satisfaction, no fulfillment. During the sexual act, instead of an orgasm, a man and a woman feel sharp pains of burning. Every memory of lust in the lowest levels of the Subtle World causes inflammation in the mind and heart, but people continue running after sex, with all its accompanying misery.

Those who incarnate from this lower astral level find corresponding conditions on earth and proper places to exercise their lust.

In the middle astral plane, sex cools down, loses its fire, and turns into a purposeful act. Astral bodies fuse within each other, with the expectation to rest, sleep, and forget all about existence. On this plane, generally, the sex act starts but is never completed because, during the act, if one imagines or thinks about anything else, he becomes involved in it and the sex act disappears. The dominant note on this plane is relaxation and deep rest.

In the middle astral plane, people are not male and female but demonstrate androgynous characteristics. This creates some problems and difficulties and ends with rejections. If sex is desired, polarity must be created. One must either be male or female. But it often happens that people start sex without a polarity, and they try to mate as if they were female or male. The origins of homosexuality take place from this sphere, if these people enter into incarnation.

On the third level of the astral plane, sex is totally left behind. There is strong friendship and heart-love, like a feeling of strong admiration and gratitude. Here talents are used in full measure, including music, dancing, and painting. There is a widespread, dominant feeling of oneness and synthesis. People begin to see each other's hearts.

The sex center in the astral plane, like other lower centers, is purified and creates no desire whatsoever because the glamors of desire are consumed. There is the spirit of creativity which penetrates into each heart. They look to all forms in the Universe as sources of creative impulse, joy, and admiration.

In the Fiery World there is no sex at all as we understand it, but there is a process of unification of creative currents of spiritual energies. There is the spirit of cooperation and striving. People have no egos. They do not have the urge to have, to own anything. This glamor is gone. All are engaged in great creative efforts in which everyone's creativity has a part. This is the beehive of creativity.

Some people in the Fiery World are dedicated to exploring the energies and rays of the Cosmos. Some of them study color and sound and their effect on spatial electricity. Some of them are engaged in the study of psychic energy. Others are engaged in training people for spatial battles against dark forces.

Almost everyone is aware of dark forces and prepares himself to be a great warrior. There is no hatred or fear, but the dark forces are attacked as if they were a collective sickness in the Universe.

We are told that great warriors on this plane see the Hierarch any time they so desire. Each warrior is equipped with electric weapons. Their centers glow like suns; their thoughts flow like rivers of fire. Fiery Angels, great Devas, and Ray Lords occasionally appear on this plane for instructions.

One second of penetration into this sphere will give an earthly man a great amount of expansion of consciousness. His values will change; he will feel as if he were awakening from a nightmare of earthly horrors.

On this plane there are great contemplators who are on the verge of breakthroughs to the next electric field, the Fiery Intuitional Plane. These souls transmit the supply of intuitional energy to be used for spatial battle, for expansion of consciousness, and as a guide for striving. Those who return from this plane are those who bring great changes in our civilization and culture. They are almost Avatars. Compassion, joy, and freedom are the three notes of this plane.

If humanity understands the scope of the danger of the dark forces and sees their plan for the destruction of all that was built along the lines of evolution, they will unite and make every kind of effort to wipe out the seeds of evil from the planet. This will be the greatest victory of the human spirit.

We are told that the intention of the Great Warrior of the Tower is to create a united front with the earth's, astral world's, and the Fiery Worlds' humanity to defeat the Forces of Evil on this planet and in the three spheres. Only ignorance of the danger of the dark forces is keeping the planetary humanity in the glamor of animosity, separatism, hatred, exploitation, crime, and destruction. When this ignorance is removed and people become aware of the danger of the dark forces, the New Era will dawn on this planet.

4

The Fiery World

The Fiery World is beyond the thought sphere. We are told that it is a world of beauty, revelations, music, and harmonious chords. It has many levels that one may penetrate after he traverses the astral plane and the thought world. In some rare cases, one can directly enter the Fiery World.

On each plane our senses go through a period of readjustment. On the mental plane the correspondences of our five senses slowly unfold and adjust themselves to new conditions.

People experience the Fiery World through their mental senses and according to their development. For example, if the sense corresponding to hearing is developed, the Fiery World is experienced as sound, music, bells, chords, melodies, and symphonies. If the vision is developed, it is a world of beauty of geometrical formations never imagined in the world.

If the touch is developed, then the Fiery World is experienced as sensation, such as cold, heat, motion, tides, currents.

We are told that in the Subtle World the corresponding senses of smell and taste have a difficult time unfolding and adjusting themselves. When smell or taste is developed highly on the physical plane, one will not have too much difficulty unfolding them in the Fiery World. For instance, an advanced soul can smell a man or a woman miles away.

We are also told that when taste is unfolded in the Fiery World, one can sense the taste of metals and rare substances found in the Fiery World.

When these senses are highly developed in man, the Fiery World opens to him in its supreme grandeur. Man awakens to the existence of any plane as his senses unfold and put him in contact with the life on that plane.

Of course, after the senses are opened, one must develop different qualities to use them properly. For example, in the world not everyone uses his eyes in the same way. The eye or the ear of a genius is not the same as the eye and ear of an average man.

The qualities to be developed are discrimination, pure observation, the ability to synthesize, and the ability to discover new dimensions in the experienced objects. This means that the life of the Fiery World has its many gradations, just as there are in the physical world.

When the senses in the Fiery World are developed to a great extent, they can be used to observe and experience the lower worlds, even the physical world.

With our physical senses we deal only with physical realities, but if the mental senses are used to explore and understand the worldly life, they reveal the mental correspondences of all that goes on upon the physical plane. An element is seen not only physically but also astrally and mentally. An event is observed not only as a physical event but also as an astral and mental event. A plant or an animal is observed as a mental reality, too.

Not everyone can have such unfoldment and experiences when he is in the Fiery World.

Each soul goes back to the wheel of incarnation to start once more his schooling on our planet. All seeds of future developments are planted in our nature, here on earth. Also, all our achievements in the Subtle Worlds are tested and verified here in our earthly life.

When a person stays for a cycle in the Fiery World, the Divine Seed in him is nourished, and beauty is impressed in his heart. In addition, all future possibilities are planted in his soul.

Man carries all these treasures and slowly plunges into darker and darker worlds. Eventually he is imprisoned in the baby-flesh. The little brain cannot come in contact with the planted treasures in the Chalice, and after he is seven years old, the memories of the Higher Worlds fade away and the muddy waves of the ocean of the worldly life take over.

We are told that man has many opportunities to come in contact with the treasures of the Higher Worlds impressed on his consciousness. The duty of man is to find these treasures, these seeds of great future possibilities, and bring them into actualization and manifestation with his own labor and devotion. Almost all beauties in all fields of human endeavor are the result of manifestation of these seeds in the consciousness of man.

The deeper is the memory of going into the Subtle Worlds, the greater is the creativity of the human soul.

When people learn how to sleep and then fly to Higher Worlds, as well as maintain continuity of consciousness, they will bring unimaginable revelations from their inner being, or from the Subtle Worlds. In our contemporary life it is not easy to have a deep sleep and develop wings to fly to the Subtle Worlds. Renunciation from the ego and our possessions is a dependable guard on this flight.

Communication with Higher Worlds will make people understand the sacredness and the endlessness of human relationships. People will realize that faithfulness, trust, and friendship are sacred virtues which bring great help to everyone on the long journey toward Home.

There is almost no one whom we can get rid of. All are travelers on the same road toward perfection. We will meet again and again to solve our problems or work together to reach our destination. How much our social life will change if we look at each other as fellow travelers on the same Path.

Those who took things away from you will be forced to give them back. Karma rules on all planes with pure justice, and no one can escape from any of his violations. This is why Sages have always emphasized goodwill, friendship, peace, understanding, and sacrifice. These are the milestones on the path of a better life.

We are told that nothing enters the Fiery World which is not as pure as fire itself. Before entrance into the Fiery World, the astral body disintegrates or is left out. All remains of astral glamors are evaporated from the advancing soul, and joy and love radiate out of it. At the gate all illusions are destroyed. Anything that is not in harmony with the Fiery World is cast away. The things that remain in the soul are daring, purity, joy, and love.

Thoughts in the Fiery World travel like lightning, with a mighty power and light. The human soul, like a flame, enters the gates of the Fiery World and senses the power of his thoughts.

We are told that all striving and daring in the lower worlds prepare us for the moment in which we enter the Fiery World. Highest daring is necessary to create that fiery tension which will enable a soul to enter the gates of the Fiery World, the gates of Beauty.

We not only prepare ourselves for the Fiery World on earth, but also in the Subtle World. Actually, the earthly life is a life of schooling, in all its phases; but the Subtle World is the major testing ground, especially for our thoughts. If the schooling is done right, the needed principles are built into our nature and the needed virtues are developed within us. Then the Subtle World will be a world of challenge where one will successfully pass subtle tests and prepare himself for entrance to the Fiery World.

When the vision of the Fiery World is grasped, then life on the earth changes its course. It will not stand as a place of suffering, pain, greed, possessions, self-interest, selfish pleasures, and crime; it will be a place where one learns the art of progressive life toward a fiery future.

People lose a great amount of time and invite much pain and suffering upon themselves because of the delay in learning their lessons. Similarly, one may lose a great amount of time in failing the tests in the Subtle World. But if one realizes that he must reach the gates of the Fiery World, he begins to live a life that helps him reach his destination. Such simple truths are not taught in the centers of higher learning, but the arts of competition and self-interest are taught and are used to build the foundations of the pitiful life of the students.

Help reaches us from the Subtle and Fiery Worlds in the form of signs, symbols, and hints. One must try to decipher them, decode them, and understand them. The reasons for such methods of communication are many:

1. The Higher Worlds do not impose any Teaching or advice. That is why advice reaches us in the form of hints or symbols. It is up to us to understand and apply them, if our karma permits it.
2. Abstract thinking, which will be very necessary, can be developed if one tries to understand signs, hints, symbols, and parables. Straight advice may create karma, prematurely expand the consciousness, or make people lazy and passive. One always must work for his own salvation with his own efforts.
3. Symbols, signs, and hints not only create striving but also enable man to contact the intuitional fires.

When the Ancients had special classes to cultivate observation, vigilance, and attentiveness, they intended to prepare students to understand fiery signs, symbols, and hints from Higher Worlds. A mechanical life generally kills such a spiritual vigilance. The Ancients had many kinds of games to keep vigilance on fire; they had many games to cultivate observation, concentration, and attention. All these were preparatory steps leading eventually to the Fiery World.

Thus, the Fiery and Subtle Worlds send many signs and many calls, but most of them are lost in the tumult of daily life in the great cities and in the storms of human thoughts and emotions.

In the not too distant future, children will be taught about the Fiery World and the Subtle World, and they especially will be instructed about the Hierarchy and the Masters. In universities, courses will be given on how to cooperate with Masters and with the Hierarchy and penetrate consciously into the Subtle and Fiery Worlds.

All this will happen once the fundamentals of life are understood and the vision of the future is made clear.

The Fiery World can communicate with the physical world through those individuals who pass through the experience of Transfiguration. During the short process of Transfiguration, the mental body is purified by the fire of spirit to such a degree that it turns into a pure flame. Man walks on earth like a living flame, like a fiery transmitter of the wisdom and energy of the Fiery World.

Such people continuously live in the Fiery World while they are in their physical bodies. During the night they live in the Fiery World and meet their responsibilities and labor. Thus they live a double life. On one side, they live the mundane life and energize their spheres with the fire of the Higher Worlds. On the other hand, they present human problems to the Fiery World and try to find solutions.

When fiery beings occasionally come in contact with the astral and mental worlds, they bring many changes there. When they descend into the astral worlds, the astral corpses are inflamed and immediately burned. In addition, the astral bodies of those who are ready to pass into the mental plane disintegrate and vanish.

The descent of fiery beings into the middle and lowest strata is very rare. They cause intense burning and suffering to the inhabitants if they visit there. The astral bodies of those who are in the higher spheres pass through a process of purification.

If the bodies contain fiery elements, which means if their centers are unfolded and radioactive or charged with the energies of spiritual realms, they glow. But if they are full of the trash of lower desires, crimes, and diseases of various kinds, they disintegrate and vanish.

We are told that while on earth we must charge our bodies with fiery energies. Fiery energies are those energies which come from our Inner Guide, from the Hierarchy, from still higher Centers, and from the Core of the Sun. These energies express themselves as virtues, sacrificial service, heroism, creativity, and beauty.

The descent of Higher Fiery Beings into the mental world prepares the inhabitants of the lower strata to move into the higher realms. The fire of these Higher Beings makes the atoms that compose the bodies of those who inhabit the lower strata of the mental plane more radioactive and pure. It is only the increasing purity and the fiery elements that enable the inhabitants of the Fiery World to move forward into higher realms.

The inhabitants of the Fiery World live in an ocean of electrical fire, which they can use as we use the air. They do not live in an ocean of flame, but in an ocean of light. Their bodies are fiery and transparent, and, through each action, rays of flames are projected from their bodies. They are like fiery angels on a gradient scale.

We are told that viewed from the Subtle World, the inhabitants of the Fiery World appear as if they were armed with rays and beams of various colors which emanate from their heads, arms, and feet. Some of them look like radiant five-pointed stars. These rays are fiery energy flames which emanate from the inhabitants of the Fiery World and penetrate into the higher astral plane. Among these emanations there are also the emanations of fiery thoughts which are used to communicate, to destroy, to create, to fight, and to transform.

In the esoteric Teaching one is advised to develop fearlessness in each incarnation, on any level of achievement, because one can enter into the Fiery World only through extreme fearlessness. Fearlessness is developed as one becomes more spirit and less matter. Spirit is fire.

Those who approach the Fiery World in their consciousness while living on earth must develop a pure understanding of justice and live in justice — in thoughts, words, and actions. Justice is the ability to harmonize oneself with pure light. No one can understand the truth unless he is righteous and all his life is based on justice.

The absence of justice creates those shadows in one's aura which become inflammable and extremely painful when one approaches the Fiery World.

The law may be used for injustice, but those who live in justice live a life which is beneficial for all beings. The suffering of those who are martyrs of justice builds their fiery bodies and makes them ready for fiery communication with the Fiery World.

Those who are preparing for the Fiery World must also cultivate moderation, a moderation which is fiery and balanced. Moderation is the ability to sustain balance within the polarities of various forces and objects. Moderation regulates the ascent of the human soul to the Fiery World.

There are other virtues which are highly needed for the Fiery World. They include courage, friendship, and patience. Those who want to come closer to the Fiery World must cultivate fiery courage, a courage that consumes the hindrances on the Path with deep patience. Friendship is a sacred tie. If it is based on trust, sincerity, and the firm ground of commitment, then it kindles the fires of the heart which illuminate the Path of the ascending soul.

5

The Mental Plane

Man has a mind. Without the mind, man cannot do the things he is doing in all fields of human endeavor.

The planet also has a Mind, and it is doing things man cannot do. All of nature, with all its kingdoms, is the result of the operation of the Planetary Mind. Crystals, gems, flowers, bushes, trees, fish, birds, animals, and human beings — what a creative mind the planet has!

Human minds are little whirlpools in that ocean of the Planetary Mind. Actually, we live, move, and have our being in the Mind of the planet. As our cells and organs live in the sphere of our own mind, man also lives as a cell in the sphere of the Planetary Mind.

But our minds are not yet in fusion with the Planetary Mind. Our minds are individualized, and they form densified spheres in the ocean, like bubbles which are in the ocean but also separate from the ocean. As we advance we communicate with that Mind, and, according to our capacity, we draw knowledge and wisdom from it.

In general, people have no contact with that Mind, and they are limited within their own minds. Their minds are like a closed bottle floating on the ocean of the Mind. Sometimes this bottle is half-empty, sometimes full; but it does not make any difference as long as it is sealed.

One of the greatest tasks of the human being is to learn to communicate and fuse with that Great Mind. All human discoveries and achievements are breakthroughs into that Mind. Every thinking person, according to his interests and needs, penetrates into that Mind and brings out many discoveries and creates many inventions. But if this breakthrough is done for the interest of the individual or for separative interests, greed, and supremacy, the personality of the individual distorts the thoughts received through the contact and uses the results for his separative ends.

We are told that the law of the Planetary Mind severely punishes all those who steal knowledge from the Planetary Mind and use it for selfish interests.

The Planetary Mind has all Solar knowledge. This knowledge will benefit people, make them superhuman beings, and allow them to develop the latent powers of the soul and live in many dimensions simultaneously — and consciously — if it is used for the benefit of all living forms. Knowledge used through the power of separatism, hatred, greed, and exploitation will lead our Planetary Life to a process of total cleansing, which means total disaster for humanity.

Our minds are charged by the substance of the Planetary Mind. This is why it is possible to communicate with it. Communication with the Planetary Mind is *thinking*. Once a person starts to think, he either becomes a transmitter of light between humanity and the Great Mind; or, through his ugly, selfish, destructive, hateful, fearful, and separative thoughtforms, he becomes an agent of pollution in the Planetary Body, as a degenerating cell does in the human body.

Man's mental body coordinates with the brain, or with the physical body, when the bridge between the mental unit and the mental permanent atom is built via the twelve petaled lotus. Then the fires of matter, traveling through the etheric spine, fuse with the mental fires. When this is accomplished, a great amount of spiritual energy pours down from the highest head center and electrifies the entire body.

Thinking is also a process of eliminating from the mind all those elements which prevent contact with the Great Mind. As one opens his mind to the Great Mind, the influencing light either nourishes all the flowers and seeds of greater creativity, or it nourishes all the weeds and vices and makes them grow out of control.

The real Teaching makes a person able to surpass and transcend himself and fuse his mind with the Planetary Mind in such a way that he becomes like a pump which pumps the most delicious water into a pool and distributes it for the regeneration and progress of all people everywhere.

The fusion of minds is not a fairy tale. It is possible to fuse your mind with the mind of a friend and create a common mind used by two persons. It is also possible to fuse your mind with the mind of humanity and with the mind of the planet, just as the Planetary Soul tries to fuse Its Mind with the Solar Mind.

Mention must be made that the Planetary Mind is the inherent intelligence of our planet. The mental plane of the Planetary Logos corresponds to our Atmic Plane. For the Planetary Logos, our physical and emotional planes do not exist, or as we are told they are under the threshold, or they form the *subconscious Mind* of the Planetary Logos.

To penetrate and live in the Mind of the planet or in the mental plane, you need to have an organized mechanism, which is called a body. Like your physical body, the mental body must be conceived and then eventually born. It must grow and develop its seven senses. When the soul no longer needs that body, he discards it in order to use a higher mechanism to communicate with the Universal Reality.

We exist only because we can communicate. The greater our communication, the greater is our success, achievement, joy, and fulfillment of purpose. The less communication we have, the less we exist.

The mental plane can be entered in sleep, in a trance state, or in deep thinking, providing one has a mental body. Not too many people have a mental body. It is true that the mental bodies of people are in the process of being built, but, in general, only twenty percent of the people presently have their mental bodies completely built.

Mental bodies vary from each other as do people's physical bodies. There are baby mental bodies, even though they belong to adults. There are mental bodies whose senses are not yet developed. There are mental bodies whose senses are partially active. There are mental bodies in which some of the senses are damaged. There are mental bodies in which the senses are used by dark forces.

There are also mental bodies which are healthy and have very well-developed senses. There are mental bodies in which the light of the Inner Guide is shining and the intuitional element is increasing. They are all in various stages of development or degeneration.

One must try to enter the mental plane with a healthy, well-developed, and pure mental body. The seven senses of the mental body must be developed in order for the human being to be able to communicate with the mental plane.

The process is exactly the same as for the physical senses: If you want to hear things, you must have the ear to hear. If you want to feel, you must develop the ability to touch. If you want to see, you must be able to see.

The mental senses can be developed while we are on the earthly plane. In the mental plane, the seven senses have different names. The senses of the mental body correspond to the senses of the physical body, but they are far superior:

1. Higher Clairaudience
2. Planetary Psychometry
3. Higher Clairvoyance

4. Discrimination
5. Discernment
6. Response to Group Vibration
7. Spiritual Telepathy

If we have these senses active and unfolded, the mental plane will be a great field of experience and adventure. If we do not have them developed, it will be a dark cave for us, even if we enter it.

Just as we communicate with the forms existing in the world, we also communicate with the mental forms found in the mental plane. The bird has a special body. Man has another kind of body. The fish has still another kind of body. Likewise, each different plane needs a proper body. A person is destined to have seven bodies and seven senses for each body, making a total of forty-nine senses.

Man and Cosmos are created like each other: "As above, so below." We do not know what the Cosmos is because we do not know what man is. And we do not know man because we do not know what the Cosmos is.

The mental body grows naturally and beautifully if a person does scientific meditation and learns how to think. If a person does not learn how to meditate and think, life's problems, difficulties, and complications of relationships will eventually teach him how to think.

The human mental body has seven levels. The lowest levels are the seventh, sixth, and fifth. The middle level is the fourth. The higher levels are the third, second, and first. In meditation, our consciousness climbs from the lowest to the highest levels of the mental plane, if meditation is done in the right way. If we continue thinking and meditating, eventually our meditation focuses on the higher levels and draws thoughts from the corresponding levels of the Planetary Mind.

The language in the mental world is *thought*. Thoughts are the words on the mental plane through which people communicate. This is why meditation, education in colleges and universities, and life's troubles are very important. They teach us how to think. Those who do not know how to think cannot communicate on the mental plane. They stay on the seventh or sixth level of the mental plane, *if* they are pure-hearted.

It is observed that people start to think when they are in a crisis. The Planetary Mind creates those conditions in which man begins to think when he is in suffering and pain. Life will be a field of greed, exploitation, revolutions, and wars until man begins to think and learns a few fundamental lessons.

Those who learn how to think eliminate from their lives many unnecessary anxieties, troubles, and problems. Because they cooperate with the Mind of the planet, they are not involved in the drastic steps that Nature takes to make people think.

The mental senses unfold as you think better and better. As your consciousness expands, your understanding becomes deeper. In the meantime, you need to manifest compassion and love through all your expressions. If you do not have a developed heart, the mental senses do not develop naturally and in a balanced way. This turns into a great cause of failure and pain in your life.

There are many mentally defective people in the lower levels of the mental plane, but as you go up, the mental bodies shine like stars surrounded with rainbow colors.

The first sense of the mental body, as listed above, is **Higher Clairaudience**. When the first sense begins to develop in your mental body, you start hearing voices in the mental plane which are originated by thought-currents. On the seventh, sixth, and fifth levels, you hear all mental conversations between people of those levels, as well as those who are on earth, and are able to converse with them mentally.

In the mental plane, a higher clairaudient hears the sound originated from thought. The same thing happens on the physical plane. If you are mentally clairaudient, you can hear the thoughts of your Teacher or the thoughts of those with whom you have relationships.

The *sounds and colors* of higher thoughts build a shield around the person. This prevents the noise from the astral and physical planes from reaching him there. Thus the more advanced a human soul is, the more peace and silence he has.

On the highest level of the mental plane, the Initiates make their thoughts emanate color in geometrical forms but without sound. Sometimes they are so in tune with each other that they do not need any form of expression to communicate.

It is not the vocal cords that create sound on the mental plane but thought. Thought speaks with the aid of visualization. Every thought not only creates sound but also color.

Color reveals the motive, the intention, and the depth of the being. Sound reveals the meaning and the purpose of the communication. The geometry of colors indicates the degree of coordination of the centers and their relationships to Higher Centers in the Universe.

The Masters walk as a symphony of sounds and colors.

People think that sound or voice creates the color. It does. But the factor which creates color through sound is the energy of motive and intention. If the intention or motive is good and lofty, the color is pure and translucent; but if the motive is bad or mixed, the color is pale and even repulsive.

The difference between colors is the vibration of thought and sound. It is possible to have the same note but different tones of the same color. For example, if the sound is blue for the physical eyes, it is deep blue for the astral eyes, translucent blue for the mental eyes, and a flowing electric-blue flame for the higher eyes.

Colors are changed not only because of the planes but also because of the motive and intention put behind the thought.

Sound and thought are creative forces. Man's life and what he is physically, emotionally, and mentally are the result of the sounds which he has heard and which he has made with his voice. It is also the result of his own thoughts and the thoughts of his environment.

Thought decides the quality of the atoms. Sound accumulates them in certain forms. When a sound is concentrated and focused, it can produce decisive results in the human organism for regeneration or for disintegration. Thought does the same thing. Change your conversation and sound or change your thought, and you will be a different person.

Once a king had a son whose voice was feminine in quality. The boy acted like a girl. The king had a certain surgery done on his son's throat which changed his voice. In a few months' time, the behavior of the son changed and he acted in a masculine and commanding way.

Sound and thought cause substantiation. They make certain forces tangible and materialize them. Sound and thought build relationships and become agents for the flow of energy. If sound and thought are focused, they can stimulate or damage centers found in our vehicles. They build barriers or bridges, according to their quality.

Between each stage of development, there is a barrier which can be overcome by organized sound and thought. Certain music builds such a barrier. Certain thoughts build such a barrier, but certain other music and certain other thoughts can also remove them.

The solar system, as well as the constitution of man, is built by sound and thought. We are the result of our thinking and talking. Imagination is emotional talking; thinking is mental talking; thoughts are mental words charged with meaning.

One must create a way of thinking and a way of talking to regenerate himself. The etheric, astral, and mental vehicles are full of patches of crystallizations. Such crystallizations block the free circulation of energies coming from higher spheres to regenerate the body. If this happens, the aura as a whole loses its integrity and equilibrium and responds to the incoming impressions in distorted ways.

When the aura is free of crystallization, the energies of higher spheres circulate and keep the aura healthy and balanced. A healthy and balanced aura registers impressions accurately and does not cause confusion in the owner of the aura.

Crystallizations in the aura turn into a hotbed of various germs and destructive seeds of habits, glamors, illusions, vanity, ego, and fanaticism. A crystallized aura is the greatest barrier for right human relations.

The conditions in the aura control the judgment, decisions, and understanding of man. If the aura is full of crystallizations, such as maya, glamors, and illusions, the person translates all incoming impressions according to the crystallizations. Pure understanding or feeling becomes impossible.

The aura cannot receive the light of the wisdom of the Sun or the light from the Solar Angel unless it is purified by the presence or help of a Teacher who cares for the person. Often the thoughts and sound of the Teacher melt away many crystallizations.

Communication with average dead people on the astral plane will not give us a great advantage to solve our problems. If people are of no help when alive, how will they help when dead, since they are one and the same?

Instead of communicating with the dead, one must communicate with those who are beyond the planes of the dead, namely, beyond the etheric, astral, and lower mental planes. These are the members of the Hierarchy and the Christ. We must design the device to concentrate our thoughts, reach Them, and wait for answers. Of course, we will experience many hoaxes, many messages coming from astral dwellers. Eventually we will formulate the signs of true communication with the Masters.

Only the Hierarchy can lead us and show us the way of salvation.

Communication with the dead will solve one problem: that a person is still living, in spite of being dead. This may create positive results or bad results. Suppose the members of the United Nations suddenly die, and a few months later we establish radio communication with them. What results will we have?... the same as are going on now!

Dying does not make people enlightened. The dead have the same psychology as they had on the physical plane. The difference is that, instead of living in their physical bodies with their habits, urges, and drives, they are now living in their astral bodies with their glamors and illusions, sometimes amplified to a greater degree.

Radio communication with those who are in the higher mental plane can be beneficial because some of them had formulas and inventions which were not put on the market, due to fear, resistance, or lack of facilities of many kinds. Some of them started their inventions on earth and completed them in the higher mental plane. Such inventions in medicine, physics, space-science, and astro-science can be beneficial if they are received by the right people on earth.

Some of these inventions will be very premature for us now, since a period of one to two thousand years is needed for the manifestation of the right period in time so that correct use can be implemented. Some of them will be put to immediate use, for good or bad, just as our knowledge of atomic science can be used equally for constructive or destructive purposes. If we are able to contact these higher scientists or leaders, will they trust us to impart their secrets accurately?

Great Ones are ready to give us Their inventions, but They say that human beings, especially those whose intellects are highly developed at the expense of their morals and virtues, will misuse them and bring chaos upon humanity. The problem is, if we develop the communication system with the higher planes, will people in these planes trust us? Will our karma be violated? Will the recipients guarantee that the knowledge or energy will be used only for the evolutionary development of humanity? These are serious questions!

We have on earth great Teachers and great Teachings, but how many of us follow Them. How many actualize or practice the Teaching? What is the use of new instructions if the former ones are not understood nor put into practice.

The Great Helpers of humanity have huge problems:

—How to enlighten humanity without violating its karma?
—How to release new formulas and new energies without enabling totalitarian forces to get to them?
—How to lead humanity without violating its free will?

These questions are, of course, very serious ones for Them, but we think that They do not help us because They cannot. Will communication bring a change in such a situation?

The logical conclusion is that man must first learn to contact his Soul and the Soul of humanity, the Christ, if he is searching for the path of universal salvation.

Thinking leads a person to many fields of responsibility and sacrificial service. People like to learn thinking in order to be successful in life, or to conquer those who do not know how to think. But this kind of thinking is selfish, and the Mind of the planet leads selfish people into painful conditions where they gradually learn how to think for the good of others.

Those who know how to think, but do not like to learn how to think for the good of others, eventually vanish from the history of the earth.

Many people believe that they know how to think, but most people, including many scientists, do not know how to think. This is why we see the pollution, crime, and poisoning of the planet. The real thinker is a person who works for your survival, who prepares the way for a happy life, and who builds those steps on which you can travel toward closer contact with Higher Worlds.

In thinking the right way, we increase the substance of the mind and refine it day after day. This reservoir is accumulated throughout the ages in striving toward spiritual values and in dedicating oneself to the service of humanity. It is this substance that is used by the human soul to build the mental body. This substance is wasted when a person is occupied with malice, slander, treason, and idle speech. The reservoir of mental energy is also wasted in daydreaming and fabricating facts.

In the mental plane there are the schools, colleges, and universities of the Masters, but not many people attend them because in earthly life the aspiration toward enlightenment was not in their hearts. Masters do not teach in these institutions, although They occasionally appear among teachers and students. Their advanced disciples on the mental plane teach in these institutions. There are also teachers from the earth who teach classes during their sleep, saving the time and energy of those who have more urgent duties to carry out.

The Black Lodge finds its agents in the lower levels of the mental plane and organizes them for new attacks on humanity. This is done in a dream-like state because in the lower levels people's senses are not yet developed. Instead, people on these levels receive hypnotic forces and sometimes try literally to obey their evil teachers after they reincarnate. They are born according to their attraction to those places where they can bring greatest harm. Even in these conditions, the Hierarchy tries to help them and gives them an opportunity to reverse their path by directing them toward the light.

In general, on the lower mental plane — levels seven, six, and five — are found the following types of people:

1. Intellectuals crystallized in their ideas and knowledge
2. Inventors attached to their theories and plans
3. Architects and mechanics
4. People dedicated to physics and chemistry
5. People who are bound to their special logic and reasoning
6. Dogmatic politicians
7. Lawyers bound to the letter of the law
8. Dogmatic preachers
9. Those who are occupied with legislation
10. Those who are occupied in organizational labor
11. Accountants
12. Materialistic philosophers

All these people are there because of their limited vision and crystallization of mental matter.

On the higher mental plane — levels, three, two, and one — are found the following types of people:

1. Those who sacrificed their lives for others and for the welfare of humanity
2. Great lovers of living forms, nature, and beauty of all kinds
3. Composers, artists, and scientists who have an expanding mental horizon and spiritual vision
4. The cream of all the fields of human endeavor: politicians, educators, philosophers, artists, scientists, spiritually oriented people, financiers

The higher mental plane is for those who are inclined to expand, synthesize, and become more inclusive.

A detailed look at the mental plane shows that on the seventh and sixth levels the following kinds of people are found:

1. Those who arrived from the astral plane for temporary rest before they go to the level they are ready for
2. Those who lived a materialistic life; who were greedy, selfish, separative, nationalistic but not hateful
3. Those who are the agents of dark forces, fishing for those who may fall into their traps

On the fifth level of the mental plane are found scientific people, such as chemists, physicists, doctors, and other specialists in many fields of science and humanities. Also found are dark brothers, wandering about and hunting the innocent.

On the fourth level of the mental plane are found psychologists, psychiatrists, humanitarians, financiers, white magicians, and many creative people. The agents of dark forces seldom come to this level.

On the third level of the mental plane are found educators and teachers.

On the second level of the mental plane are found philosophers, philanthropists, peacemakers, and heroes.

On the first level of the mental plane are found esotericists, initiates of first, second, and third degrees, and those who live a life of sacrificial service.

The seventh, sixth, and fifth levels are sometimes called the "furnace." When people have vanity, ego, and selfish separatism while on these three levels, a highly flammable element is produced which takes flame and burns their mental body. This continues until they learn the reason for their burning and renounce their vanity, ego, and separatism. This is very difficult for people to learn if they have had these vices while living on earth.

On the mental plane are also found many fiery beings and fiery devas of extreme beauty of form and radiations. They are not human yet, but they communicate on the mental plane with human beings. They can even teach people certain sciences. Solar Angels are frequently there, helping people climb the ladder of perfection.

On the higher levels of the mental plane, people directly and visually communicate with their Solar Angels. When they are born, they actually know about their Solar Angels as a faint memory. Very often Masters visit the higher levels of the mental plane, and the knowledge of the Hierarchy is a fact there.

In the mental plane you can find mental flowers and birds. It is very interesting that animals are not found there. Flowers are the works of devas. Devas create a thousand times more beautiful flowers and more colorful birds that we see on earth. Such birds are often devas in bird-form.

Music in the mental plane is heavenly because one can see every color of the notes. The colors do not fade away but form the most fantastic color structures. Often, composers come in contact with these structures, according to the level of their beingness, and compose their music.

On the other hand, the seventh and sixth levels of the mental plane are very noisy because the earthly noises create continuous thunder there.

The mental plane is the sphere in which the path of higher beauty begins. It is there that one firmly understands the secrets of beauty, its effect on life, and its purpose in the Universe. Beauty is felt there as a living Presence penetrating into every form. This Presence becomes more and more beautiful as one moves upward from level to level. The colors and sounds of the mental plane cannot be compared with the colors and sounds on earth.

Those who have mental clairaudience, psychometry, and higher clairvoyance can bring to the physical plane a certain degree of the music, the colors, the motions, and the forms that they experience in the mental plane. Geniuses in the fields of art have been on these levels and are impressed with the beauty there. That is why their art moves mountains and brings bliss to humanity.

When great inventors pass away, they work in the mental plane to perfect their discoveries made while in the physical body. However, often the karma of the world prevents them from transferring advanced formulas to earth humanity. Also, they seldom find someone to whom they can convey their new discoveries. They are able to communicate with those who have developed at least three of their mental senses. But, more often, people have distorted astral senses instead of developed mental senses. Developed mental senses are rare.

Similarly, when a great creative artist passes away, he does not wait in the grave or lie asleep in the air. He goes to his level — the *mansion* in the mental plane — and devotes himself wholeheartedly to the sake of beauty and creativity. Many great artists are handicapped because of physical conditions, but in the mental plane they have complete freedom to create and enjoy beauty. That is why, for certain people, the higher mental levels are spheres of heaven or paradise.

To be able to bring great beauty and knowledge from Higher Worlds, one must have his Antahkarana built. The Antahkarana is a communication line between the lower and higher mind, and also between the brain and mental plane, if the person is on the physical plane. A person who has his Antahkarana built can communicate with the mental plane to renew the charge of beauty and the flower of higher inspirations. Only those who have built their Antahkarana will be trusted by advanced souls.

Those who try to contact Higher Worlds through mechanical means, without having the needed psychic energy and purity of mind, will mislead themselves and humanity through their works.

Communication with Higher Worlds during sleep becomes impossible if people sleep with hatred, fear, anger, jealousy, and feelings of revenge in their hearts. Such factors create inflammable materials, and the human soul instinctively keeps himself away from the fiery spheres.

The second sense is **Planetary Psychometry**. In the mental plane, this sense enables you to touch any form and know the life story of that form, with all its relationships. Actually, in the mental world, thoughts turn into objects. When a person with this sense hears a voice, he can psychometrize the voice and see the whole story connected with the originator of the voice.

In the higher mental plane, this sense makes privacy obsolete and nonexistent.

The third mental sense is **Higher Clairvoyance**. This sense enables a person to see the causes of things happening in the mental plane. One can then see what goes on upon earth.

On the higher levels of the mental plane, people use their power of clairvoyance to watch the dances of the stars and the life going on there. They observe the radiation and energy waves of stars, solar systems, and galaxies — with their colors, their rhythmic interactions, whirlpools, spirals, and so on. They also watch the prototypes of living forms. For example, we are told that the prototype of a rose is a thousand times more beautiful and fragrant than its shadow on the earth.

When many Great Ones penetrated into these spheres consciously, They made a very interesting statement: "There are no words or concepts to describe what we have seen or heard."

The fourth sense is **Discrimination**. On the mental plane this sense makes a person aware of whether or not his thoughts are in harmony with the Cosmic Purpose. Whatever is inharmonious within you and around you is immediately recognized by this straight-knowledge. Thus, this sense keeps you in line with the destiny of your soul.

The fifth sense is **Discernment**. This helps you discriminate between the causes of all phenomena on the mental plane. The remaining senses, namely **Response to Group Vibration** and **Spiritual Telepathy**, further expand the contact of man with the Universe.

Discipleship is preparation for the higher mental plane. People from higher levels of the mental plane are anxious to serve humanity. Usually, they do not stay very long in the mental plane, and they are born voluntarily in difficult conditions so as to bring better changes into the world.

People from the lower levels of the mental plane may stay there two to three thousand years, sometimes, in order to avoid reincarnation when the karmic laws invite them to do so.

When a person incarnates, the hidden, painful records filed in the mental plane, life after life, come to the surface like multiple personalities. These control the person. Each past, painful experience appears as a different person, as if one were a different person in each life, though the human soul is the same one. One person in him says, "Mother killed me." Another person in him says, "They buried me." Another person speaks about injustices done to him. Another says, "They imprisoned me." These are the cores around which the life of each personality in the person is built.

In a milder form, one can experience the surging out of powerful experiences when one is extremely tired or under the pressures of guilt. Such experiences are not necessarily the symptoms of possession. However, in the case of multiple possessions, the person totally loses his sanity because the human soul is entirely impaired by the entities occupying the various departments of his nature.

If problems with multiple personalities are the result of past memories, they can be solved when the filing system is put in order or new locks are created for a period of time.

Recordings of past lives are securely safeguarded in the files of the Chalice and in the subconscious, but it is possible that these recordings escape and pour down into the brain consciousness when artificial methods are used to make people remember their past lives. Most of the recordings do not escape the files in past-life discoveries. But, once the direct line between now and past lives is established, first they manifest occasionally, and then they slowly express themselves regularly with distressing results and effects.

When such painful records gradually imbue the personalities and guide them as their own, the human soul loses his control over his mechanism. He can no longer protect it from the attacks of entities who try to possess a "divided house" and use it for their contact with the physical world.

CHAPTER

6

Friendship and Brotherhood and the Subtle Worlds

On the physical plane, man has an illusion of being alone. But in the Subtle World this illusion vanishes. Many relationships established throughout ages reveal themselves gradually as the human soul penetrates into the higher strata of the Subtle Worlds.

Throughout ages man builds better and better relationships with other souls; as husband and wife, children, parents, teachers, and students; as close, dedicated friends; as business partners, associates, and co-workers. None of these contacts or relationships disappear. They continue in both worlds. Sometimes they fade away slowly. Sometimes they are strengthened with a new supply of love, dedication, and labor.

Thus, throughout ages, we create a network of friends on earth and in the Subtle Worlds.

In the Teaching, friendship is highly recommended, especially friendship based on labor and sacrificial service. A great task done for the love of humanity, for the service of the Hierarchy, builds strong ties of friendship which can last forever.

The relationship between a teacher and a student is also very sacred. It lasts many ages, or forever. The bond created in such a relationship turns into a source of everlasting joy and inspiration.

Not all friendships endure. Sometimes a friendship is shattered because of personality interests, blind attachments, possessive attitudes, treason, malice, slander, and destructive criticism. Every time that a relationship is broken violently, it creates heavy disturbances in the network of relationships in earthly and subtle spheres and brings a limiting, irritating reaction.

Unity is considered sacred, and life advances through unity and unification. Disunity is against evolution, and it is the source of retrogression, pain, and suffering. Unity leads to improvement and toward the path of perfection.

Scattered throughout the earth and the Subtle Worlds, friends hold the threads of relationships. It is so inspiring and so encouraging to know that though one is alone on earth, he is related to hundreds and thousands of friends scattered all over the world and throughout the Subtle Worlds.

Loneliness is an illusion. At any given time, we have friends who are either around us or thinking about us, or actively participating with our labor, either in visible or invisible forms. Our life can bring joy or sorrow to them; it can bring inspiration or depression to them. We live in their presence.

The physical body gives us the impression that we have a private castle in which we can hide or isolate ourselves. This is an illusion. All our friends in the Subtle Worlds can watch us and communicate with us. All our friends who are in incarnation in different parts of the world, within different nationalities, and in different colors and sexes are also with us on subjective levels when we sleep and become active on subtle planes.

Due to our ignorance and the insufficient development of our continuity of consciousness, we do not realize this fact, and we do not affirm our relationships. That does not imply that such relationships do not exist.

One of the goals of the human being is to build good friendships on solid foundations and increase the number of such friendships. A solid foundation is very important. It can be built between people who are dedicated to the following:

1. Improving and transmuting their consciousness
2. Serving the One Humanity
3. Bringing in unity, prosperity, and health to Earth
4. Paving the way for the externalization of the Hierarchy and the reappearance of the Christ
5. "Sealing the door where evil dwells"
6. Bringing Beauty, Goodness, Righteousness, Joy, and Freedom to humanity
7. Building a bridge between subjective and objective worlds
8. Revealing the Inner Glory in each human being
9. Cleansing illusions, glamors, maya, and pollution in the world

Relationships built upon such foundations last forever.

Souls related in ever-increasing joy advance on the Path of perfection. Their relationships become increasingly more conscious and sensitive, and as they progress, they care and sacrifice more for each other. This is how the armies of Light are formed everywhere, in any stratum of existence.

Such a realization takes away the illusion of loneliness from your mind and opens the horizons of unlimited friendship. You slowly realize that you are not alone in your efforts, failures, successes, striving, and labor. Many visible and invisible friends help you with their thoughts and with their aspiration, striving, and active help.

Once you develop faith and trust in your invisible and visible friends, you live as a group, as an army of friends who cooperate and help each other in all their efforts, labor, and service based on solid foundations.

Good friends, especially in the subjective planes, do not like to participate in activities that lead to ugliness, crime, disunity, and embarrassment. Actually, you lose some of your friends if you follow the dark path. For a long time your true friends try to help you, to pull you away from your dark path. They try to reach you through your heart, through your mind; and, if you do not hear them, they feel real pain and sorrow, especially those who tried to lead you into the right direction.

In losing a good friend you gain a dark friend.

You have had and you still have many "friends" who, for many reasons and throughout many incarnations, have hated you, wished ill for you, and created many obstacles on your path. You also have souls who wait for the opportunity to attack you. When a disunity is created within the network of your good relationships, they feel extremely happy because it gives them an opportunity to infiltrate into your network and take possession of your friends for future disturbances and attacks. You can lose your friends if you try to stop them or hurt their spiritual evolution and lead them into darkness, or if you do the same to yourself.

There is an artificial unity between enemies of mankind. There are many networks of those who follow the path of darkness and destruction. Each member retards the evolution of the others, leading them into deeper and greater darkness and into greater pain. Such relationships are based on individual interests, and the threads of the network are weakened by fear and hatred. It is very unhealthy to be in such networks because they accumulate the worst karma and their destruction is very painful on earth. It is even more painful in the Subtle Worlds.

There are people who come into incarnation with serious mental and nervous problems and become burdens upon society. One must be careful not to be caught by such a network of evil.

We are told that there are five major ways through which humanity falls into the traps of the enemies: malice, slander, treason, separatism, and exploitation. Good friendships are built with very sensitive threads. There are things that can sever these threads and make relationships difficult or impossible for a long period of time. Major reasons for cleavages between friends are

1. Criticism
2. Intruding into the personal affairs of others
3. Trying to possess your friend
4. Gossip
5. Unfaithfulness to your promises
6. Stealing
7. Creating cleavages between a friend and his friends
8. Hurting his friends
9. Not meeting your responsibilities toward him or his friends
10. Using his power or reputation for your selfish interests or goals
11. Sending negative thoughts or emotions to him
12. Attacking his freedom and the objects of his devotion and worship

There are a few rules given by the Ancients which can be used to heal cleavages, or to avoid them altogether. In case of any cleavages between you and your friends:

1. Never gossip about them. Never utter an ugly or belittling word about them.
2. Remember that the shared and personal life of friends must be safeguarded and not betrayed.
3. Send blessings often to your friends. Do not carry any remorse in your heart.
4. Remember that an enemy can be the best friend in the future. A lost friend can meet you again at the crossroads of your life in your most critical moments and extend his hand to help.
5. Remember that all cleavages are temporary and are meant to serve as lessons. The sooner we learn our lessons, the better will be the network of our friendships.

When you become more and more aware of the network of your friends, you live a life based on subjective cooperation in which there is mutual help. Thus, every member in each network of friendships inspires, encourages, and helps the others throughout centuries. Often they incarnate together and carry on great works of service for humanity. It is possible that they may not recognize their past relationships or present subjective relationships. Nevertheless, they dedicate themselves to the same goal, for the same vision. Dedication and labor for the same vision are solid proofs of their past relationships.

Advanced souls anxiously watch every field of existence to see if the tapestry of friendship is building, if the electrical lines of the networks are forming. With each formation they pour their blessings and wisdom into the souls of dedicated friends.

In the Higher Worlds, friendship eventually turns into a brotherhood. There are many brotherhoods in many strata of existence. They proceed toward greater light, like fiery flowers.

As we have many friends in our earthly relationships who cause us troubles and bring complications into our lives, we also have invisible friends on the astral plane and friends unknown to us on the physical plane who cause troubles and complications in our lives without any conscious planning or intention. Fortunately, the number of such trouble-making friends decreases as we exhaust our karma with them. They are those whom we have hurt unknowingly and misused unconsciously. We are now repaid through their actions and attitudes.

We find such "friends" on our path on earth and in the Subtle Worlds who, in the name of friendship, create disturbances in our lives. It is possible to put them on the path of a right relationship with us. Or, it may be necessary to postpone our relationships with such "friends" for a long period of time, until conditions are right and the growth of our soul gives us an opportunity to build better relationships.

Such kinds of "friends" are not as dangerous as those who enter the network of our good friendships, masquerading as friends. They are very difficult to uncover on the physical plane but easy to expose in the Subtle Worlds. The problem is due to our lack of continuity of consciousness, and our inability to use on the earthly planes the revelations received in the subtle planes.

When we pass into the subtle planes, these "friends" cannot reach us while they are in the physical body. But if they also pass away, they clearly see their hypocrisy and stop acting against us as enemies.

If we do not dwell on the lower astral plane, they cannot reach us. Animosity cannot go beyond the lower levels of the astral plane. If they also graduate, they do not continue their animosities.

We attract these people though our past karma. Hatred, revenge, and exploitation produce such undercover enemies. Harmlessness is the great virtue which karmically prevents the approach of these people.

The enemies of the Great Ones are the agents of dark forces. This has nothing to do with the karma of these Great Ones. The dark forces follow the steps of the Great Ones life after life to hurt Them and, if possible, to damage Their work. But, fortunately, all their intrigues end with the victory of the Great Ones.

Invisible Helpers

There are human beings who have learned the science of leaving their physical bodies and are able to travel with their astral and mental bodies. In some cases, they even know how to travel with their etheric bodies and densify themselves.

Invisible helpers do this by the following:

1. They withdraw out of their physical body during the day or night, and their physical body falls into sleep.
2. They go to places where there is pain, suffering, grief, sorrow, and distress.
3. They find the people who need help and give them joy, happiness, release, hope, freedom, and healing.
4. They lead lost people to safe destinations.
5. They protect people from wild animals and accidents.
6. They create peace between people or between nations.
7. They protect people from dark forces.

The invisible servers are trained in specific fields of service and, in general, they do only that for which they are trained.

Sometimes they help certain people meet each other for mutual interests or for a future service.

Sometimes such people even appear to travelers and to children to guide them, and then they disappear.

It is also known that invisible helpers influence certain people to make them stop others from doing harmful things. For example, if a man is going to climb a tree and fall down and die, an invisible helper sends a neighbor, and the neighbor in some way prevents him from climbing the tree.

The invisible servers help within the limit of karma. They can approach people if their hearts are pure, sensitive, and harmless. They can approach those who invite them through their prayers, gratitude, hope, and trust to invisible powers.

They can approach those who are in despair and lonely. Of course, the number of invisible helpers is very small in comparison to the number of human beings, and their hands are full every time they are out of their physical body.

Invisible helpers have enemies who try to prevent their service and often heavily damage their bodies, paralyzing them and preventing them from performing any service.

Often their etheric, astral, and mental bodies are heavily damaged along with the corresponding parts in their physical bodies. Even in psychic realms they are beaten wounded, and chased away by those who do not want them to help others. But of course they are also trained to fight back and protect themselves and those who they want to serve.

Some of these invisible helpers are conscious of what they are doing because they have developed continuity of consciousness. There are some who serve subjectively but are not aware of their service in their waking consciousness. It is their inner urge to help and serve that subjectively controls their activities in the Subtle Worlds. Usually such people learn how to use certain methods to protect themselves from negative and involutionary forces.

In the ranks of the invisible servers, there are those who are specialists. Some of them illuminate people, connect people with higher sources, pass wisdom to them, and teach them how to see their errors and free themselves from such errors.

Every human being, before he reaches Mastership, must demonstrate his service in the invisible world and prove that his motive is to serve. Once he is qualified in his service, his evolution proceeds rapidly, and eventually he finds himself in the ranks of those who are preparing themselves for higher initiations.

Some of the specialized ones are occupied with teaching people in the subjective world. They teach mostly principles, laws, and rules and try to expand the consciousness of people.

There are also those who inspire higher visions and ideas by which others can live a more creative life.

There are also peacemakers. These individuals try to eliminate all the thoughtforms, vanity, illusion, and ego which prevent peace, understanding, and cooperation. They are often successful in relation to individuals and families, but are handicapped in relation to nations because of the accumulated walls of hatred, anger, jealousy, and fear. They try to dispel such accumulated poisons and pave the way for understanding and cooperation. But they do have enemies who impose fear, anger, jealousy, and hatred and bring frustration in their peacemaking efforts.

As in the physical plane, the lower astral and lower mental planes in general are battlefields, and spiritual warriors sacrificially offer their lives to help humanity in these levels as well.

Spiritual servers also have their Commanders, Masters, and advanced Initiates Who protect them as far as They are able.

We are told that as we approach the New Age, the number of invisible helpers will increase, and among them will be found very powerful individuals who will organize greater labors of service for the liberation and emancipation of the entire humanity.

Brotherhood in the Subtle World is a very sacred idea based on a very sacred relationship. It originates from the awareness that each soul, in his essence, exists in the One Self and that his future is in the Cosmic Self. This awareness is not a concept or idea but a fact which manifests in the special principles and laws with which we come in contact in the Subtle World.

There are seven principles related to the idea of brotherhood:

1. Harmlessness
2. Goodwill
3. Trust
4. Fusion of consciousness
5. Striving toward beauty
6. Freedom
7. Harmony

Harmlessness is a way of living through which you do not prevent any living form from advancing on the path of spiritual evolution.

Goodwill is an active service to encourage, inspire, and strengthen your brother, to make him achieve progressively higher manifestations of Divinity.

Trust is the intuitional awareness that your brother is part of your True Self and that he will stand by you, by all possible means. Trust is also a way to impart psychic energy and illuminate the path of your brother.

Fusion of consciousness makes the members of a brotherhood fulfill the plan presented to them, according to each one's talent, time, and position. Fusion of consciousness is a state of awareness of the group through which the leader inspires, leads, and organizes the entire labor, as if everyone were listening through his inner ear to the commands of the leader. Fusion of consciousness cannot be achieved until the ego is dropped from our soul.

Striving toward beauty is the daily labor of each brother. Only by increasing beauty will one keep the inner ties and eliminate any ugliness. Unity only exists in beauty. Ugliness is the signal of disturbance and destruction.

Freedom is the understanding that no one in a brotherhood can force his own will upon another. One does not try to impose himself upon a brother by thought, moods, words, or any other actions. A brother has total freedom to be himself and follow his own heart. The principle of freedom is a great teacher in brotherhood. Whoever does not violate it in any way rises to higher responsibilities in brotherhood.

Harmony is the result of law and order. People have the opinion that brotherhood can exist in anarchy, disorderliness, and lawlessness. Actually, brotherhood is based on law and order. Every action, emotion, word, and thought is used in such a way that each creates harmony or does not distort the harmony. Harmony comes into being when the consciousnesses of the individual brothers fuse and create one focal center of consciousness. This center directs the life of each brother according to individual need and according to the need of the body of the brotherhood. It is the same as the human consciousness controlling and putting into action every part of the body, in harmony with the body as a whole.

Such an understanding comes to brothers only after they experience the Higher Worlds.

CHAPTER

7
_____

Drugs and the
Fiery World

There are wrong methods to penetrate into the Fiery World. People use drugs or alcohol to make a breakthrough into the Fiery World. These methods not only build a layer of illusion in their consciousness but also create obstacles which remain on the path of their ascent for a long period of time.

Those who use drugs are damaged to such a degree that they cannot do advanced spiritual work and intensified service on various planes, even if they stop such use. Drugs damage the subtle centers, distort the senses, and waste the psychic energy. To repair the damaged subtle mechanisms may require many lives on the physical plane.

When one uses drugs, he may penetrate into certain levels of the Fiery World, but because his vehicle was not purified enough to stand in the fire, the fire rushes into him and burns very precious formations in his mental body. If at a later time an attempt is made to penetrate into higher spheres, he will not be able to do so, due to the burned centers. Sometimes such people are described as birds whose wings are burned. They try very hard to fly, but they cannot.

Those who use drugs may also register certain phenomena while they are in contact with the Fiery World. If so, they cannot translate these contacts in an accurate way. Thus they build great amounts of illusion concerning the experience. After the illusion is built, dark forces use it to control the users and lead them into various vices and crimes.

The keynote of the power of penetration into the Subtle World is purity. The astral and mental vehicles must pass through a long period of purification before it becomes safe for them to contact the Fiery World. A premature attempt may lead them to destruction.

Those who enter the Subtle World after they pass away will suffer immensely if they carry with them their addictions to drugs and alcohol. The fire of the Subtle World will scorch them heavily, and the dark forms of the astral world will have access into them. This is described as a type of hell in various literatures. The attacking fire burns away parts of the person's astral body and makes him prey to obsession. When the astral body burns badly, the person dies in the astral plane prematurely, and as a consequence finds it very difficult to enter the higher planes. If he enters these higher planes, he finds that for a long period of time it is very difficult to adjust himself. This is how souls are delayed on the path of perfection and are confronted with unnecessary suffering by fire.

We are told that when a man is ready to enter into the astral plane naturally, his astral body is either left in the astral plane, as a snake leaves its skin, or it bursts into flames, giving a great sense of liberation to the soul.

The damage in the astral body does not disappear when the astral body is discarded. The permanent atoms carry the record. When the human soul returns to earth, the scars of the burns in the astral body are still seen in the aura. It is these scars which are the weakest points in the vehicles of man, and they can be the sources of many psychological and physical troubles in the future.

There are other reasons for deformities in the human being. Many children are born with animal-like bodies. Sometimes their head, arms, or legs are like those of animals. Such babies do not live long, and the medical profession puts them to death in some way or another. We are told that the true reason for such deformities is as follows:

Those base human beings who pass away with their strong animalistic character, with their carnal desires and habits, directly fall into the world of animals. The animal principles take possession of them, and they are born with animal urges and drives and with an animal-like form. Life slowly teaches them how to free themselves from such forms, if they have a chance to live. This is why people have been always attracted to refined and beautiful forms. Animal-like people have been rejected because of their appearance and their animal appetites.

Thus our thoughts, emotions, and deeds collectively shape our future forms. As we have greater thoughts, purer emotions, and more selfless deeds, we will have more beneficial, handsome, and healthy forms.

Great Teachers are sometimes called the Fair Ones. They are free from dishonesty and injustice. Their appearance is extremely fair, beautiful, and handsome. It reflects their consciousness and their spiritual achievements.

There are many animals in the lower levels of the astral plane. They do not remain there long because their forms fade away. Some immature and polluted human beings, criminals, or those who are lost in their vices enter into the same level as the animals have entered. Sometimes they are so full of revenge and have such a strong urge for crime that they feel they cannot satisfy their animal instincts unless they take animal forms. They turn into tigers, lions, wolves, or other animal forms and attack their horrified enemies and chew them alive. There are many such animal-like human beings in the lower astral plane.

When these people incarnate, they bring back the animalistic impressions with them and act the same way as they were acting in animal forms in the lower astral plane. Sometimes one can see how certain children act like various kinds of animals.

Education, in the future, will also deal with this aspect of life.

History has records of hundreds of animal-like births, sometimes totally in the form of animals or half-animal-half-man, with tails, ears, or legs of animals. The cause of these births cannot be found in the genes but in the lower astral plane. The animal form was so strongly impressed in the mind of the being that he could not help but be born in such a form.

To minimize the attacks of dark forces and defeat them on this planet, the three worlds must coordinate their efforts, which is not presently the case. Coordination between the earth, astral, and mental forces must take place through those people who develop continuity of consciousness and act as coordinators and synchronizers between the worlds. These forces can be united only in formulating a common cause, a common purpose, which will be based on the foundations of Cosmic principles and laws.

The common enemy of the Earth must be recognized. All countries must coordinate their efforts within the three worlds to fight the enemy in the name of Light, Love, and Divine Power. This mobilization of forces must take place before it is too late.

The purpose of the enemy is not only to stop the process of perfection of humanity on this planet but also to retard the progress of humanity living in the Subtle and Fiery Worlds.

The plan of the enemy involves the inhabitants of the Fiery World. It is a remote possibility that the inhabitants of the Fiery World can fight against the enemy. But those who presently dwell on earth can evoke the help of the Fiery World and involve them in the battle against dark forces. This means, exactly, that the personality of the planet, which is composed of the physical planet, the planetary emotional body, and the planetary mental body, must become integrated and, as one unit, engage in the assaults against the dark forces. People may think this is a wild dream. The reality is that humanity will never reach its Cosmic destination until the forces of darkness are defeated.

Thus humanity can reach the stars. The Galaxy may open its secrets and lead humanity into a greater and greater glory of self-actualization and unification with Cosmic Beauty.

One of the conditions of progress and self-actualization is the existence of obstacles in our life upon the physical, emotional, and mental planes. As we confront these obstacles, we realize our own situation, our level on the Path, and our weaknesses, powers, and possibilities.

Obstacles exist as part of Nature, and in conquering them we expand our consciousness. Without expansion of consciousness, self-actualization is impossible. Because expansion of consciousness is progressive, so also is self-actualization. In whatever degree we overcome our ignorance and weaknesses, in that same degree we conquer our obstacles.

Obstacles also have no end. They grow as we grow.

8

The Subtle Worlds
and Departed Ones

Departed ones can enter various levels in the Subtle Worlds. In the etheric plane, the following are found:

1. Those who committed suicide
2. Earth-bound souls
3. People killed instantly in wars or accidents
4. Those who deny immortality or life after death
5. Cannibals and people who have committed murder
6. Certain animals
7. Reflections of disastrous events occurring in the world

The astral plane is divided into three sections: higher, middle, and lower.

The lower plane is the habitat of drunkards, drug-users, traitors, criminals, selfish and greedy people; those who are separative and destructive to right human relations; those who are full of hatred, anger, revenge, slander, and malice; those who exploit people and sell their souls to Satan; those who are fanatic, animalistic, pleasure seeking.

We are told that a great horror and groaning can be heard by those who pass by the lower astral plane. It is stated that "the torture from such burns of the subtle body surpasses bodily sufferings. The horrors of the lower strata of the Subtle World defy description...."[1] It is also stated, "Whoever has heard even once the roar and groaning in space has a conception of the lower layers over Earth."[2]

---

1. Agni Yoga Society, *Letters of Helena Roerich*, 2 vols. (New York: Agni Yoga Society, 1967), vol. 2, p. 499.
2. Agni Yoga Society, *Heart*, (New York: Agni Yoga Society, 1982), para. 290.

Thus the lower astral plane is full of agitation and full of the forces of desires, glamors, and negative emotions. The dramatization of all these forces creates a chaotic condition.

The lower astral plane is a jungle of low emotions and pain and suffering, perpetuated by imagination. Imagination is used on these planes to satisfy the eight negative elements accumulated in our astral body.

The lower levels of the astral plane are often identified with hell as, through imagination, people instantaneously create those conditions in which they can exercise hatred, fear, anger, jealousy, revenge, slander, and treason to cause suffering to others and to themselves. Every harmful action you take on this plane causes intense burning in your astral body.

We are told that human vices create greater horrors in the astral world than on earth. On earth we see only one aspect of crimes, but in the Subtle World the images of our crimes are dramatized with all the emotions, thoughts, and motives that are associated with the crimes. They appear there with all their layers, colors, and intensity.

People forget that all that we do on all planes is photographed or impressed in the subtle layers of Space. All these recordings are held together, due to the sympathetic frequency, and form our life-film. The inhabitants of the Subtle World are horrified by these recordings, as are those who, after leaving their bodies, see the consequences of their crimes.

The existence of dark forces in the lower astral plane creates another kind of horror for new arrivals. These new arrivals include those who pass away as well as those who enter into the Subtle World in their sleep. The dark forces try to attack and annihilate all the particles of Beauty, Goodness, and Truth which are sometimes brought by the newcomers.

Those who sleep with hatred, malice, and criminal plans generally enter lower levels, and they receive strength from the dark forces. Dark forces not only uproot any sign of goodness in them but also encourage them to carry out their criminal plans. Most of our nightmares are created through contact with these levels.

We must always check ourselves after awakening to see if seeds of harmful urges have been planted in our nature. Early morning meditation, prayer, and worship greatly help to clear these seeds and put our heart in the right direction.

The attacks of dark ones and the dramatization of earthly crimes in the astral world impress the human soul very strongly, especially at times when one is irritated, disturbed, or in a state of confusion and imbalance. The dark ones also succeed in planting dark seeds during the times of spiritual, moral, and physical weakness. The ongoing dramatization of crimes in the Subtle World contaminates those visitors with the same drives and urges them to act on them.

The lower astral plane is very similar to our physical plane. As a matter of fact, many people who enter there do not realize that they are dead, and they continue their life as it was. Even some educated people are caught in this illusion, and certain people must help them and make them aware that they are dead. Sometimes it is very difficult to convince such people because they cannot see any difference, except the fact that they can move faster in the Subtle World.

Some people carry their habits into the Subtle World and try to exercise them as if they were on the physical plane, but they are surprised that they cannot find any satisfaction. If they awaken and realize that they are in the astral plane, they begin to obsess people and urge them toward those vices which give the obsessor the satisfaction desired.

Usually the inhabitants of the lower astral plane live a dream-like life, as if they were on the physical plane. The power of thinking can pull these people away from such traps.

One can send strong currents of thought to departed ones and help them awaken. It is also possible to visit them and make them realize that they are no longer on the physical plane and that they can now leave behind all their concerns for the physical life. These thoughts can affect them and awaken them and make them proceed on the path upward to Higher Worlds.

It is very important to speak good about those who have left their bodies. Even if they had very little good in their life, it must be emphasized and anything else must be forgotten. This is because the remembrance of dark records of their life either reimpresses them or gives them intense suffering. In addition, they must be forgiven by those who are still alive. Forgiveness releases them from many chains. Thoughts can reach them instantaneously, and they hear our thoughts and think we are directly talking with them. This is why our thoughts and words must carry blessings, forgiveness, and wishes for the future happiness of the departed ones.

It is very good to repeat the following mantram any time the memories of the departed ones come to our mind:

> *May their soul be blessed,*
> *and may they proceed on the path of enlightenment.*

Such a mantram, if pronounced with sincere desire and love, blooms on their path as lilies of light.

We must give them as much love as we can and suggest that they exercise all the virtues that they possibly had while on earth. The vices of the departed ones must not be discussed or even mentioned because such conversations stimulate the seeds of their vices, especially if they are on the lower strata of the astral plane.

Great help can also be given to the departed ones if their friends or relatives labor to correct the wrongs done by the departed one. For example, if he hurt anyone, they can take the necessary steps to heal the wounds. If he stole anything, the living friends or relatives can pay it back for him. If he had debts, they can be repaid.

It is also very noble to take care of those who were left behind by the departed one, such as parents and children. In the Holy Qur'an we read the following about the care of orphans:

Those who unjustly
Eat up the property
Of orphans, eat up
A Fire into their own
Bodies: they will soon
Be enduring a blazing Fire![3]

Our thoughts about the departed ones' vices and our negative and revengeful feelings about them create ugly reactions, especially if their consciousness is of a low order. These ugly formations delay their progress and subjectively influence us. Often the hurt souls attack the living ones who use gossip, malice, slander, or speak about their vices.

Such attacks have various forms. Some nightmares are of this origin. Mental suspension, absent-mindedness, and periodic emotional distress are other forms of attack. Our health can also be attacked, failures brought about, and relationships disturbed.

With our negative and hateful attitudes, we may turn the departed ones into evil.

All departed ones must be blessed, and only good things must be spoken about them.

Those who are living can render a great service to departed ones by reading for them literature about beauty, words of wisdom, joy, and everlasting life. One can read such literature as if reading to a friend.

First you can mention the name of the departed one and ask him to listen to something you are going to read for him. Then imagine that he is sitting by you and listening. *The Bhagavad Gita* is one of

---

3.   *The Holy Qur'an*, translated by A. Yusuf Ali, Sura 4, section one, para. 10.

the books you may use for your reading. The holy scriptures of any nation may be read, choosing those parts which you like the most.

The departed ones will listen to your words with intense attention and, very often, suddenly awaken and choose the higher path of spiritual development. You must remember that they have the same consciousness, but because of the new out-of-body experience, they are more ready to listen to the words that reveal the future to them.

It is wonderful to read for them about the Law of Reincarnation and about how vices and harmful actions delay them on the path by creating karmic obstacles.

In the future, various groups will be established to help the departed ones by reading, thinking, and wishing a better life for them.

Most churches have Requiem services performed for the departed ones. *The Tibetan Book of the Dead* is another example of such a service. But all these must be brought up-to-date.

Such groups will not deal with any kind of necromancy. Their work will be based on the Law of Telepathy, and they will only instruct the departed ones to advance on the path of beauty, goodness, and righteousness. Those who passed away loaded with their vices can be helped by special programs and classes organized for them. Intelligently, scientifically, and also esoterically, these groups can explain to departed ones the origin, development, consequences, and karmic liabilities of vices, as a doctor speaks about microbes, germs or viruses, and suggest that they not use them any longer in the astral plane.

Such an activity will be a great service for the coming generations. Most of the children of the future will be born subconsciously prepared against those thoughts, emotions, and activities which prevent their success and achievements and cause great harm to others.

When man lost his etheric and astral vision, he fell into the illusion that departed ones evaporate. Actually, they are more real and present in our life than living ones. Being so, they can be advised, educated, trained, and prepared for the greater journey toward Infinity.

Many Initiates have such responsibilities after they sleep or withdraw from their bodies. They have classes and centers of teaching in the Subtle World. Sometimes they are called "invisible helpers." One can begin training to be an invisible helper by helping people before they depart through one's thoughts, words, feelings, and actions. Later, advanced Teachers will teach us how to carry out similar activity in the subtle planes by counseling, teaching, training, and leading the departed ones.

Most of the time while sleeping, we are active in the Subtle Worlds. Our colleges and universities at the present do not have courses about such training, but very soon teachers will make a breakthrough and these subjects will be openly and seriously taught in universities.

Those who do regular meditation and are trained in creative and scientific work will be the best candidates for invisible helpers.

Of course, in helping departed ones, one not only needs a trained mind but also an unfolded heart. Actually, the heart leads in subjective service. Future servers must develop their hearts, minds, and willpower to carry on successfully their assistance to the departed ones.

We must remember that all our endeavors to help their souls will be directed especially to those who were caught in the network of vices. Those who are advanced souls can also be helped by advanced, subjective Teachers. The immediate need, though, is to release the enslaved souls in the lower strata and let them proceed on the path.

It is evident that some reactions and even attacks from such souls can be expected, and the best protection is *group work*. The help must be given to them after meditation and prayer, so that psychic energy prevents any attacks and protects the participants from the negative forces coming from the departed ones.

The Ancients spoke about purgatory, where man passes through a process of transmutation to enter a higher sphere. In esoteric literature, purgatory is the middle astral plane, where a degree of purification takes place before the human soul enters the higher astral plane.

In the higher astral plane there are various kinds of people, such as

1. Goody-goody and harmless ones
2. Romantic lovers
3. Innocent people
4. Nature lovers
5. Peacemakers
6. Art lovers
7. Artists dedicated to beauty
8. Joyful people
9. Philanthropists
10. Those who want to use any opportunity to serve people

In this level, imagination is used to its fullest to create a pleasant and highly creative atmosphere. This is one of the reasons why the inhabitants of this sphere want to extend their time and stay as long as possible.

Of course, this plane is full of pleasant glamors of all kinds. In this plane people have difficulty realizing that all that is going on there is maya or an illusive phenomena.

From the higher astral level, the human souls can enter another state, which in ancient literature is called *Devachan*. Some human souls do not enter Devachan and incarnate on the physical plane to continue their service and leadership within humanity.

In the middle astral plane, people must realize all the wrongs they did in their physical life. There is a high possibility there for them to review their past physical life and note all thoughts, words, and deeds that were not in line with higher principles. Through close examination and deep aspiration, and with an honest decision not to repeat the errors made in the physical incarnation, they will speed their evolution and gracefully pass into the higher levels of the astral plane.

This is the process in purgatory which actually corresponds to the times in our life in which we do a thorough review of our daily life and try to correct our faults and errors with sincere aspiration. The time in purgatory can be very short if a person exercises an honest review every night before sleep.[4]

Devachan is beyond the astral plane. It is a place of rest and bliss, where the human soul is recharged to come back for another round of labor and service. Before entering the state of Devachan, the astral body is left behind or burned away and the human soul uses his mental body to enter there.

When we say that people go from the astral plane to the mental plane or from the etheric plane to the astral plane, we do not mean that people go all the way from the etheric plane to the highest level of the astral plane or the highest level of the mental plane. They may reach only the second or third level of the astral plane and go to Devachan and, after their time is over, come back. Devachan is not beyond the mental plane; it is a special state for rest. One can enter Devachan from the middle level of the mental plane. Those who cannot pass beyond the lowest levels of the astral plane do not go to Devachan.

The correspondences in the astral body of our physical genes keep the record of our health conditions while we are on the earth.

When a man passes away and remains only in the lower and middle astral planes, he keeps these astral genes, and when the moment of

---

4. For further information, please refer to *The Psyche and Psychism*, pp.791-800.

reincarnation comes, these genes create the old patterns in the physical genes of the new body.

Many children are born with various sicknesses. There are many reasons for this. Accidents, various physical and emotional pressures, alcohol, and drugs can affect the embryo.

Radiation is also a major source of infection in the health of children.

Also, if the parents are healthy, it may be that the sick baby is inheriting the genes of his ancestors.

But, according to the Teaching, the main cause of the illness of a newborn child is in his own past life, in the past records of the astral and physical permanent atoms.

If a man subjected himself to moral and spiritual degeneration in a past life, his subtle centers will show signs of decomposition. Such a decomposition continues sometimes life after life, on each occasion creating a different form of illness.

Sometimes in a certain incarnation one can stop the process of degeneration with intense labor, dedication, and heroic sacrifice. Conversely, the process of decomposition may be increased through a life based on malice, slander, hatred and treason, or by drugs, alcohol and sexual diseases.

There is a possibility that a man can get rid of such records with intense striving and service for humanity. Such a sacrificial and highly aspirational person can make a breakthrough and enter, after he passes away, into higher astral planes. There he burns away the past records in the astral genes.

When such a man is ready to incarnate, he chooses his parents, according to his own karma and past relationships or future goals, and inherits the genes of his parents. His life becomes conditioned by his choice and the conditions of health of his parents.

But, in general, those whose centers are in the process of decomposition can penetrate only into the lower and middle astral planes and take their incarnation from there. In this case their astral genes remain as they were, and in their new birth the people continue the illnesses of their past life, either to exhaust them or to continue to carry them as their karmic tail.

We are told that there exists a great abyss between the astral and mental planes, and no one can traverse this abyss if his mental body is not formed and if its centers are not unfolded or awakened. Many souls try to cross this abyss but instead fall down into the astral world.

The mental body is not built and formed by information or knowledge alone but primarily by fusion with beauty, truth, justice, and fiery creativity. The deeper the fusion of the mental body with the will of the human soul, the greater the formation of the mental body.

Our mental body weakens and even darkens when it is used in vanity, hypocrisy, malice, slander, and exploitation. These factors even cause many complicated diseases to develop in the mental body. When the higher centers are awake because of fiery elements and the higher senses are in the process of unfolding, man has a great opportunity to cross the abyss and enter the Fiery World.

Conflict in the mental body weakens it. This is why a virtuous life and pure thinking are like vitamins for the mental body. A weak mental body cannot dissipate the astral body when it is left in the astral plane. In the name of the owner, this astral corpse floats for a long time in Space, pollutes the astral plane, and may even serve as a vehicle for a dark force.

Every time our astral body does not dissipate itself, we are affected by its slow disintegration or by its misuse by dark forces.

The mental body is developed and unfolded in the best way if it is used in regular meditation and for the actualization of great ideas in the practical world.

There are cases when the human soul departs from the personality and enters the Subtle World. In these cases, insanity results. The personality lives without a soul, activated by the records of lower permanent atoms and auric accumulations. The personality receives energy from the human soul living in the Subtle Worlds but is not controlled by it. The personality is like a car which runs for a while without the driver. Strong impressions accumulated in the centers and nerve cells still control him.

Dark forces may temporarily occupy such an abandoned mechanism and commit many crimes.

It is very rare that some entity occupies it for a long time because entities do not want to be limited by a distorted mechanism if it does not serve their purpose. It is more probable that such an abandoned person is used like a motel room. Many entities play with him or use him for a short time.

Such a case sometimes is called "losing one's own soul." Of course, this is not a correct expression because the soul does not lose himself but abandons the personality for serious reasons.

If the soul leaves the personality in childhood and reincarnates a few years later, it is impossible to bring back the soul to the personality and heal it. If the body is occupied by successive guests, it is also impossible to heal the situation. But if the soul is still in the Subtle

World, a great Master can call him back to his home, after cleansing him from the intruders.

Thus, insane persons or dangerous criminals either have lost their souls or are occupied by dark entities.

The departure of the soul takes place in one of the following circumstances:

1. When life is loaded with heavy crimes against spiritual values, the soul may leave.
2. During a state of deep hypnotism, the soul leaves and never comes back. This is not a rare occurrence.
3. In a somnabulistic trance, when the subject is violently awakened, the entrance is closed and the soul cannot re-enter, although it automatically sends energy to the body left behind.

The souls that desert their bodies during somnabulistic shocks or in a hypnotic state create a very dangerous condition for their bodies. Usually such bodies are occupied permanently, and because of their relatively healthy conditions, they provide a long service for those forces who need time to study human life and plan attacks intelligently.

In such cases only a few people notice the changes in the owner of the bodies. The rest of the friends or family members cannot perceive it, and thus they may even assist the new owners to carry on their destructive work more efficiently.

Similarly, souls of armies may collectively leave their bodies. This occurs as a result of the desire to resist the orders of their commanders. They see the destruction brought about by their actions, and because the conditions force them to proceed with their destruction, they leave their bodies. It is on such occasions that the fighting becomes bestial, in which no one can find the presence of the human element. The human souls suffer in the Subtle World in great distress. When their bodies die, they feel relieved. It is mostly these souls that try to escape from the Law of Reincarnation.

Some of them, after losing their bodies, attack the enemies and possess them temporarily or permanently. After wars, one can see an epidemic of obsessed soldiers which gradually becomes the burden and problem of society.

There are advanced human beings who have dedicated their lives to humanity. Some of them have been assassinated, burned, or poisoned. These people do not fall unconscious immediately after death because the Invisible Guides explain the situation to them and take them to the higher planes where they belong.

Such people have highly organized astral bodies and do not need the same preparation as an average man needs for his astral body. All the sacrificial services that they render nourish the flame of the heart. In the case of an assassination, the flame of the heart lights their path through the Subtle Worlds, led by the protective care of the Guides.

9

Changes of Consciousness

It is important to have an expanding consciousness before we enter into the Subtle World. It is only through an expanding consciousness that we can enrich our life in the Subtle World and assimilate the gifts of new conditions.

One of the ways to expand our consciousness here on earth is to create a certain tension in our life and establish communication with a consciousness that is far more advanced than ours. Tension increases our mental receptivity. Communicating with a higher consciousness awakens in us the buried seeds of treasures accumulated throughout ages. Generally, these seeds turn into spiritual urges in the subtle planes and propel us to higher achievements.

After such an expansion, whenever we enter into the Subtle Worlds, through sleep or meditation, we expose ourselves to a greater light and to very unusual conditions. These things strongly affect our consciousness, and when we return to our earthly habitat, we immediately notice an expansion of consciousness which remains strong for a few minutes or hours, then fades away.

Such periods of expansion of consciousness are very valuable because they provide **new possibilities, new viewpoints, new measures,** and **new visions.**

New possibilities: In expanding we see new goals and feel that we can achieve them. It is in such moments that the foundations of a new life are built.

New viewpoints: We see things from different viewpoints than the usual ones. This makes us see things more clearly and arrive at better conclusions.

New measures: Certain things in our life are very precious to us. Certain things have no value. But after a visit to the Fiery Worlds, our measures change. The world no longer stops at the tip of our nose. Things glow with different values. Relationships are established based upon different goals. Things that we were identified with lose their value and lead us to freedom. Things that we did not appreciate gain new favor with us.

New visions: After returning from the Subtle World, one brings with him new visions. His horizon becomes larger. In view of these new visions and new horizons, he feels greater humility and greater gratitude. Part of the vision turns into new spiritual urges and strivings and greatly expands his field of service.

Every visit to the Subtle Worlds is an opportunity for contact with those whose dimensions of thinking are beyond earthly measure. People penetrating into the Subtle World also come in contact with new types of energy and are charged with them. Many of the etheric centers are kindled because of such contacts.

Very often one receives courage and new inspirations. His spirit of humility and forgiveness grows. He develops a better sense of righteousness.

As we go deeper into the Higher Worlds, we sense a deepening harmony with the great principles of Beauty, Goodness, Righteousness, Joy, and Freedom. As we stay in the Higher Worlds, our consciousness goes through new adjustments and new refinements. Our ideas, thoughts, decisions, and motives are distilled, and only the pure essence remains in our consciousness.

The Higher Worlds are visited not only after our sleep, but also through our daily meditation, contemplation, and ecstasy. In such moments we penetrate into Higher Worlds and gain a new courage to walk on the path of perfection.

It is possible to inspire people by speaking about the Higher Worlds, but one must experience the Higher Worlds and register the effects of the visitation in his daily life. Unless this experience is gained, the effect of such speaking slowly fades away. People must develop pure observation to see such interactions, so that the experiences are evaluated rightly and the striving is charged with a new energy.

It is possible to share the moments of flights of other people. Such people must be sought and observed, and their new standards of value must be appreciated. Many people around us gear their life to a new speed and shift toward new directions. It will be very instructive if we observe them and see how the touch of Higher Worlds transforms them.

Visitation to Higher Worlds is like visiting an architectural grandeur, attending an outstanding symphony, visiting a great gallery or museum, flying at a high altitude, coming in contact with real values, taking a bath after a heavy labor, awakening in a rose garden, finding a dear friend lost for a long time, entering into light from a dark night, experiencing freedom after a long imprisonment, entering into a new rhythm, running in a new direction. One can explain his experience in the Higher Worlds in many different ways, but the basic conclusion is that the Higher Worlds transmute, transform, and transfigure your consciousness and its expression — your life on earth.

Let us always remember that our life reflects the true essence of our consciousness.

We are told that often the consciousness of people is petrified or ossified under the pressure of worldly attachments, greed, exploitation, and hatred. When a consciousness is ossified, the link between man and the Subtle World breaks away. The consciousness no longer registers any impression from higher spheres. This is sometimes called "falling from grace."

It is possible to regenerate such a consciousness and cause a great transmutation in it, if one creates cooperation between his three vehicles under the inspiration of a higher vision or under the pressure of a great need or labor. Thus, in such cases an integration and alignment occur between these three vehicles, and the fire of the personality increases, causing regeneration and quickening in the consciousness.

Every time one uses his Divine Will with the fire of his heart to strive toward higher achievements, he creates a whirlpool of energies, which is often called a vortex. This vortex is highly magnetic, and it attracts spatial energies according to its intensity.

The creativity of man is nourished through such vortexes. A progressive soul uses these energies to build his future and contribute to the future of humanity. The path toward the Higher World is built by the energies attracted to the vortexes.

Speech is not used in the Subtle World. The mechanism of speech is too coarse for it to be used. It is very slow and inappropriate. Instead of speech, people communicate through their thoughts. This does not mean that there is no sound in the Subtle World, but sound is used for singing, for music, and for chanting hymns of gratitude.

Just as the inhabitants of the earth see the lightning in space, the inhabitants of the Subtle World also see the lightning of the Fiery World. This brings them currents of new energy and new hope and builds new paths between the worlds. Such lightning is a stream of energy used to raise the standards of the inhabitants of the Subtle World and keep them aware of their future. Without such reminders, the inhabitants of the Subtle World may slumber on the Path.

In the Higher Worlds, such as in the Fiery World and beyond, it is possible to share each other's consciousness and even lend it to each other. This seems strange, but it is possible to lend your consciousness to a friend and make his consciousness expand in great measure to perform a great task. In the Higher World one meets many unexpected things.

There is an experience which can be explained as the "experience of extension." We can understand this in our daily life when we recall how we plug in an extension cord and bring the electricity twenty-five to fifty feet from the outlet. Such extensions are also usual in the subjective world.

Often you, as the human soul, can be "here" and "there" simultaneously. You can be busy with your daily routine and in the meantime participate in a meeting in a far-off place. You can even participate in many meetings through your other "extension cords." This is not exactly being somewhere with your thoughts, or thinking in your mind about things going on in other locations. This is an actual being "here and there" simultaneously.

In the early stages of such acts of "extension," you feel suddenly exhausted of all your energy. You feel that your focus of consciousness is gone and that you are nowhere. The brain does not register the mission, but the "extension" does its job.

People go through such experiences often, but they consider them the result of being hungry or tired or of lack of sufficient sleep. But, in reality, this experience is not related to any of these factors.

People have many subjective responsibilities. Their hearts are tied to many hearts which they do not remember. People often are needed for a rescue. There are many calls for emergencies and for help.

The human soul has higher ears to hear such calls, and he hastens to meet the need and the challenge. He "extends" himself to such locations, which can be anywhere on earth or in the Subtle World. These are the moments when your body feels suddenly exhausted. But it does not last too long, usually only three to five minutes. Then you feel an inner joy, an inner satisfaction for having responded to a call and having met a need.

Later, such experiences will be conscious. One must be able to know from where the call originated, where the location was, and why one was called to an emergency service. Thus, some people serve subjectively, even during the hours of their tea, while they were busy writing a letter, while repairing their car, or while giving a lecture.

10

Light and the Subtle World

The lower levels of the astral plane are called levels of twilight. They are not completely in the dark, nor completely in light. They are also called levels of dense fog, mist, and haze because the visibility is limited to a great degree.

As one climbs to higher planes, the light increases. All that we have is the light of the Sun, but this light has three phases. We have the physical and etheric light of the Sun; we have the light of the Sun of the astral plane, and we have the mental light of the Sun.

Objects on the physical plane are seen by the physical light of the Sun. Objects in the astral plane are seen by the light of the Sun of the astral plane. Objects in the mental plane are seen by the light of the Sun of the mental plane.

The light is always there. In the subtle planes one can see according to the development of the correspondences of his physical vision. The eyes on the astral and mental planes must be open to see things as they are on those planes.

Curiously enough, the light of the Sun can make things visible on the subtle planes only if the light in man fuses with that light. The fusion of these two lights makes light possible on the subtle planes.

Once the eyes can see on the subtle planes, man can create with his thoughts on the subtle planes. Thus, thought-creativity is directly related to the development of the eyes and the increase of light.

As the light of the soul, or the consciousness, shines, things become increasingly visible to the man; and as things are more visible, he can create through his thought.

Thought-creativity is a strange expression. It means man can actually create the objects that he wants to have in the mental or astral worlds. Thought immediately substantiates, materializes, and comes into existence as the human soul thinks. This has its dangers as well, since, when you create wrong forms, you cannot annihilate them for a long time and they turn into hindrances and distorting factors in the mental world.

This is why the Great Teachers suggest we activate and develop the art of thinking, cultivate control upon our thoughts, create pure and lofty thoughts, and eventually master the mechanicalness of the mind. Once these things are learned or achieved on the physical plane, they can be used on higher planes. They will bring great success to us because all is carried out in the subtle planes through thought-creativity.

Thought-creativity is like a language that you use in a foreign country; if you do not know the language you may have a difficult time.

Meditation, concentration, and contemplation develop the higher counterpart of creative thinking.

Our university studies and all branches of science develop within us the power of thinking. Sometimes we learn thinking best in our life's tensions, problems, sufferings, and crises. All these will be considered favorable experiences once we realize that they help us learn thinking.

In the Subtle World everybody is recognized by his or her radiance. Some very Advanced Ones, using Their thoughts, create very beautiful clothing for Themselves. The beauty of the clothing, its color and design, make people aware of the level of His thought-creativity.

You can create almost anything in the Subtle World. The lower inhabitants live in semi-darkness, and they live with the ugliness of their thoughts. They think in terms of crimes, and crime takes shape according to their thinking. This is why in the lower sections of the Subtle World we see a horrible life everywhere. People on this level bring all their bad habits and bad thoughts into the Subtle World and try to perpetuate them there. Only the light of thought can burn them away and create forms that help people proceed on the Path.

The light of the soul paves the way.

We are told that cycles rule in the physical, the astral, and even the mental world. This means that the years of your life on the physical plane are counted. Similarly, the years of your life in the astral and mental worlds are counted. You have only certain time durations in these worlds, and, when the time comes, the law pushes you into the next plane, whether you are ready or not. You can make rapid progress on any plane, but you cannot ascend before your time arrives.

This does not apply to those who have committed themselves to the Hierarchy or who are high degree Initiates. They proceed straight through such planes and return, if necessary, after a very short time.

One does not enter the Fiery World because of a fixed date. You must strive to enter there; you must prove that you are ready and fit for the Fiery World.

One is mechanically moved from one world to another, but this does not apply to the Fiery World.

Those who enter the Fiery World are only those who have developed the fiery shield or the fiery armor, those who shine with the light of their soul, and those who have complete mastery upon their thought.

Our real destination is the Fiery World. One cannot know when he will enter there because it depends on how one dedicates himself to the path of service and perfection. Often the Fiery World seems an infinity, but those who are awakened see that the Fiery World is not only attainable but also exists within their souls.

We are told that the Fiery World is the world of Beauty, and nothing can be compared with it in the physical, astral, and thought worlds. There are fiery singers, musicians, and artists in the Fiery World who reflect the grandeur of beauty of the Fiery World. It is only after penetration into such a world that one can create beauty within the lower worlds.

But all these are related to the inner light. As the inner light increases, one gets closer to the Fiery World. As he gets closer, the higher counterparts of his vision become active, and, through the light and his unfolding senses, he experiences the unimaginable beauty of the Fiery World.

In the Subtle World one is also recognized by his shadow. Any dark element within our astral and mental bodies obscures the light and produces a shadow. The bigger the shadow, the more loaded is the soul with unnecessary burdens.

Shadows in the lower astral plane can be mile-long tails behind people. In the middle astral plane they are much shorter. In the highest level of the astral plane, you still see traces of them. But in the Fiery World shadows completely disappear, as the Inner Flame radiates out from every part of the body and makes it a living torch of beauty.

The colors of the shadows also indicate the content of the pollution existing in the subtle bodies.

Crystallization or ossification of certain centers also casts various shadows, and one cannot hide his shadow.

There is always light in the Subtle World; hence, one cannot hide. It is a terrible situation for those who have many things to hide.

Love increases the light of our soul. All occasions in which we acted in and expressed love are occasions in which more light was accumulated within us. As love increases, we slowly release ourselves from dark shadows and tails.

Those who live in love, live in light.

Advanced astral bodies are transparent. Those which are loaded with earthly moral pollution look dark. Some astral bodies look exactly like black charcoal with red eyes. In the astral world, people are recognized by their light and darkness.

As your body turns into light and becomes more transparent in the Subtle World, the Guides and Teachers come closer to you and give you more responsible tasks in the battle, or They help you in instructing inexperienced souls on the Path.

Those who are on earth and already have pure astral bodies are assigned to various jobs immediately after they sleep. This is why we are advised to sleep in peace and in purity of heart. It is suggested that we record our experiences in the Subtle World, whether they are our dreams, visions, or direct contacts. Many valuable conclusions can be achieved by reading such recordings throughout the year.

One must sleep with the love of service, as if one were released after the daily routine and felt free to do the things he loved. Such a spirit will immediately engage himself in a new service or continue the service he left the previous night.

Your light attracts the attention of Great Ones Who in various ways try to help you to help others and proceed toward Higher Worlds.

11

Auras in the Subtle World

In the Ageless Wisdom, teaching is given about the auric egg. The auric egg is the egg-shaped sphere around the body composed of the radiations or emanations of the seven vehicles of man:

1. Divine
2. Monadic
3. Atmic
4. Buddhic
5. Mental
6. Astral
7. Physical/Etheric

The center of this auric egg is the Monad, or the Self, which penetrates every part of the aura and nourishes it with the fire of life.

The auric egg is the most sensitive apparatus in the world. First of all, it registers all that we do, speak, feel, think, wish, desire, or will. The entire life's records are found in the auric egg. It is the book of our karmic records on all levels, registered while we were in physical incarnations.

In the average man, only the lower mechanisms exist. The higher ones are not formed yet because of the lack of development of the consciousness.

The auric egg is sometimes considered as being formed layer after layer, like the layers of an onion. But actually each sphere of the aura is composed of millions of atoms with their specific frequency, interpenetrating each other but keeping their own distinct frequencies, in an egg-shaped form around the body.

The auric egg is used for spatial journey during sleep, during a trance, or after death. After death the lowest sphere, which is the etheric sphere, remains with the physical body until the flesh disintegrates or is cremated. The human soul travels through the sphere of the vehicle which is the most developed. For example, if the astral body has enough development, man travels to the astral world and reaches the level where he fits according to his karma. If his intuitional or higher mental body is developed, he penetrates into the Fiery World or the abstract mental or the Intuitional Plane.

The Great Ones travel in Their intuitional, atmic or monadic bodies, as if They were in the physical body. After They leave their physical body, They do not go to Devachan or other spheres, but for a few days or months they rest in Their auric egg in Space. Then They take incarnation to serve humanity. It is possible that They even appear through an illusory body, which appears as if it were physical but is not.

Each sphere of the auric egg has its nourishing fluid which circulates in the whole sphere and nourishes the atoms of its own vehicle. For example, the nourishing fluid of the physical body is the blood. The etheric body has its prana. The astral body has its astral light. The mental body has mental fire, which is called solar fire. The intuitional body has its own blood, which is called pure electric fire, or pure light. The atmic sphere has pure love. The monadic sphere has will energy. The divine sphere is nourished by the fire of the Spark.

The auric egg also has another function. It registers all that is going on in our Solar System on seven planes. These registrations are not conscious at the beginning. As man proceeds on the Path and reaches a certain stage of perfection, he begins to be conscious about things going on progressively on all planes.

When the human soul leaves the physical world, he also leaves his physical body. When he leaves behind the astral world, he leaves his astral body. When he leaves behind the mental world, he leaves his mental body, until he reaches a state in which he has no need for a body, but only shines his flame. The radiation of the flame appears as a fiery sphere in the worlds of fire.

It is from this auric egg that the future Master, the future Avatar, or the future Archangel is born; and it is from this auric egg that future personalities are born. Also, it is from the auric egg that the illusory body is made for those who live in the Devachan. And it is also from the auric egg that the illusory appearance, or form, of a Master is built to appear among men.

The illusory body is not a correct or proper name because all vehicles are illusory. In a sense, higher bodies are more real than denser bodies. It is a matter of viewpoint. If we assume that this physical body is a "real" body, then the astral body will be illusory.

If we assume that the buddhic body is "real," then the physical body is a mere shadow.

In Sanskrit literature the seven kinds of "bloods" of the seven spheres of the "egg" are called:

1. Adi tatva
2. Anupadaka tatva
3. Akasha tatva
4. Vayu tatva
5. Taijasa tatva
6. Apas tatva
7. Prithivi tatva

Our auric sphere, the seven ductless glands, the senses, and the etheric, astral, and mental centers act according to the force available to them. The forces or "bloodstreams" repair the bodies, maintain the health, harmony, and integration of the spheres, nourish them, make them unfold and grow, and put them in contact with their universal correspondences.

Each sphere of the auric egg has its nucleus, which in the Ageless Wisdom is called the seed or permanent atom through which the force originates and circulates in the spheres. Each sphere can form a conscious link between the Self and the corresponding sphere of the Universe through development, unfoldment, and purification.

Through all these spheres the consciousness must expand, and the brain must eventually register all the experiences of expansion through which man passes. The future of man is glorious.

In the mental plane, man has a center which is called the Chalice, the twelve-petaled Lotus, the causal body, or the "Temple not build by hands." This Chalice contains three seeds which are called the three permanent atoms. It also contains the Eternal Fire, the Jewel, the Spark, enveloped by three petals called sacrifice, love, and knowledge.[1]

In the subjective planes, no matter where the man is, he has these petals with him until he reaches the pure fiery state of the Third Cosmic Ether, or the Atmic Plane. Once a man penetrates this sphere, he does not need the Chalice any more because his Inner Divinity is released.

In the higher astral plane or in the Fiery World, this Chalice provides the impulse to go forward with a sacrificial life, with love, and with knowledge. In primitive man this Chalice is like a bud of a

---

1. For further information, please refer to *The Science of Becoming Oneself,* pp. 63-75.

lotus with twelve petals. In average man the first layers of the petals are unfolded. As man increases his sacrificial service, dedication, and knowledge, other petals begin to open. According to the unfoldment of the petals, man enjoys greater communication with the life of his planes.

In the auric egg this Lotus shines as does a diamond with many colors, in either the subjective or objective life. In the birth process, the permanent atoms in the Lotus, with the auric sphere, prepare the birth of man, producing his astral, etheric, and then dense bodies.

In the higher levels of the Subtle World, the auras of advancing people appear in very harmonious colors. They do not shine as do the auras of angels, but they have luminosity and the radiance of a rainbow. The auras of advanced ones appear as the sacred vestments of the inhabitants of the Subtle World. An advanced one is recognized through the size, color, luminosity, and intensity of his aura.

It is interesting that you cannot change your aura through your thoughts and appear as if you were an advanced human being.

The auras in the lower Subtle World are very inharmonious, cloudy, patchy, and unpleasant. You can even see formations of dark colors and reflections of criminal intentions.

In the mental world the auras of progressing people look gorgeous. They bring a great amount of light into the mental world. The auras of the inhabitants of the mental world often fuse with each other. They even share their consciousness.

In the Fiery World the individual aura is almost invisible because of the fusion of all auras, as if all the inhabitants of the Fiery World had only one aura. Instead of having edges, their auras flow into the aura of all. The communication between people on this plane is instantaneous. Their bodies are luminous fires of orange, yellow, and blue. One can also see that their Chalices are in a state of supreme beauty.

People return from the Fiery World as carriers of fire and divine enthusiasm to bring beauty, harmony, and higher striving to the world of human beings. The fire builds slowly in every human being as he strives and lives a virtuous life. But this fire can also be taken away by robbers.

Robbers are of various kinds. They are those who

1. Bring irritation
2. Lead others into dishonesty
3. Give themselves over to the arms of inertia
4. Do not stay vigilant

5. Betray higher principles of Beauty, Goodness, Righteousness, Joy, and Freedom
6. Wander on the path of lesser values and non-essentials
7. Work against Hierarchy or betray the Teacher

Each human being is born with a sacred fire. It is this fire that must be increased, developed, and expanded. It is this fire that builds the Path toward the Fiery World. It is this fire that weaves the *shield* of fire. It is this fire that opens the gates of the Fiery World.

The command to Zoroaster to keep the perpetual fire burning forever was a reference to this fire which should be kept alive. Day after day, the power and intensity of this fire must increase in dedicated watchfulness and a sacrificial life. It is this fire that eventually illuminates and harmonizes the substances and colors of the aura as man ascends to the Fiery World.

This fire remains with man in spite of karmic burdens. At each step on the Path, it silently inspires the heart to go forward, toward the greater fire.

Those who incarnate have many beautiful memories from the higher levels of the Subtle World, even from the Fiery World. We are told that until the age of seven these memories wander in the corridors of the consciousness, and if not nourished from the environment they disappear, though their echoes remain in our hearts.

This is why it is imperative that people converse with their children about the Subtle Worlds. They must help the child keep these memories in his consciousness as long as possible because it is his memories which guide him toward eternal values. Once these memories are kept alive, the child climbs higher and higher, despite many obstacles.

Many children pass through spheres of temptations victoriously. When they think about how they were protected, tears come to their eyes. Because their auras were imbued with fire, they find the way through the jungles of human traps and temptations, through the attacks and assaults of dark forces. It is also seen that the auras of these children change the negative hearts of people and make them positive, loving, and compassionate.

Even some criminals, seeing the possibility that children may fall, help them to continue their ascent. A story is told of such a child who, frustrated and tired of his life, went and knocked on the door of a prostitute.

"What do you want?" asked the prostitute of the young boy.

"Well, I need love."

"You are too beautiful to fall into the trap of a prostitute. You had better keep going toward greater beauty."

"But I will pay for you."

"One more word and I will kill you. Go!" She said, slamming the door in his face.

The boy felt very humiliated, but the fire in him was strengthened, and he never in his life turned back to the world of darkness.

Thus, the souls of fiery people are guided by those who are good, while others are guided by those who are followers of the dark path. The aura in the Subtle World exposes to the observer how many battles were lost and how many battles were won.

Esoteric groups are formed in this age to make possible the spiritual growth of their members. If the members are trained according to higher principles, they will silently protect each other from any failure. If they see the decrease of fire in any member they will lend their fire and not let the fire of their friend decrease.

There are many times when our fire decreases and its flame even flickers. There are days of depression, failure, self-judgment, exhaustion, psychic attacks. It is in these days that the group members demonstrate their love and give fire to such a failing brother and make him stand on the Path. Lending fire does not mean fanatical action, imposition, or forcefulness. Rather it means understanding, non-judgment, giving inspiration, giving courage, giving examples of victory and heroism, explaining possible causes of troubles, and most of all giving the fire of their hearts.

It is after receiving the fire of his fellow members that the failing brother once again steps on the path of dedication and commitment. Usually, those who pass such dark nights of the soul become warriors on the Path and leaders in the groups.

It is essential always to have fire to be able to give fire and enrich the auras of one's brothers with the energy of fire.

12

Subtle Experiences

People often witness or experience higher psychic events. For example, they hear beautiful music; they sense a fragrance; they see visions. Some people experience miraculous healing, miraculous guidance; they receive some unexpected help, or are miraculously protected from a real danger.

Some people suddenly feel or know the words they must speak, the command they must give, the direction they must take. People have many such experiences every day, but most people take very unusual attitudes against such experiences:

—Some of them reject them.
—Some of them ignore them and try to forget.
—Some of them are afraid to talk or write about them.
—Some of them even lie about them.
—Some people immensely distort them.

Only a few people understand the importance of such experiences and use them as proof of the existence of higher realms.

We are told that such experiences are gifts of Higher Worlds, and if they are not accepted gracefully and gratefully and used in solemnity, sincerity, and accuracy, they disappear and seldom revisit our shores. The deplorable thing is that any denial or distortion of higher gifts forms ugly obstacles in the Subtle World. These obstacles block our path when we try to enter, in due time, into the Subtle World.

The Subtle World makes its existence felt through very simple things. For example, one feels the touch of a finger on his ribs; one hears his name and awakens at the right time. One even hears bells ringing. Inhabitants of the Subtle World even use perfumes or fragrance to indicate their closeness.

Sometimes strange noises are heard or objects are moved. Sometimes one hears a strange note in his ear, which he thinks originated from a physiological cause, micro-electrical waves, etc. All these causes can be true, but it is also true that the Subtle World communicates with certain notes to warn you or to cheer you.

Sometimes the note is a call for readiness to receive an impression of great importance. My Teacher used to say that whenever I had such an experience I should direct my whole attention to the note and wait for impressions.

People sometimes feel great joy in their entire being, a sense of exultation or bliss. Such feelings have a great significance because they come from higher sources, or from the elevated beings who send us such gifts. During such periods one must experience the exultation with deep gratitude and humility. Such moments are sometimes called the contact of fiery beings, and they have a special meaning.

Every kind of pure exultation unfolds the higher centers and builds greater communication lines with higher forces. They purify and magnetize our aura and make us more radioactive. Sometimes a man is used to spread certain higher energies in certain places. This moment of transmission is the moment of exultation.

It is also noted that little incidences totally change the destiny of a man. Apparently insignificant words and events give a totally new direction in our life. It is known that such insignificant incidences were controlled by friends in the Subtle World who, knowing our true destination and readiness, helped us fall into line.

People have many such experiences in which a small incident changed their lives.

We are told that many friends from the higher levels of the Subtle World wish to help us, but they are confronted with the barriers of our fears and prejudices. Fear repels them, and prejudice distorts their currents. To be able to receive their help, one must develop fearlessness and cast out all kinds of prejudice.

A gift from the Higher Worlds can be a sign of appreciation for our labor, an act of encouragement and inspiration offered to us, or a proof of higher realities.

Sometimes the Higher World sends us warnings of coming storms. But people hesitate to share or witness such spiritual experiences. Thus they not only deny the gift or the warning, but they also deny their own worth.

Are we insisting that every psychic stand on the housetops and shout about his experiences? Certainly not. We have enough claims from lower psychics, mediums, and channels. We are suggesting instead that people must be alert and observant and consciously record higher and genuine experiences, understand their origins, try to refine their mechanisms to be able to record more subtle experiences, and if necessary share them with others. Many great executives, leaders, presidents of huge corporations, teachers, physicians, lawyers, and striving disciples and initiates often have such experiences. This does not mean that an average citizen cannot have psychic experiences. But generally such people cannot understand the true meaning of the experience. They are not able to interpret and present them in a way that the presentation of the experience is able to draw the attention of highly cultivated and responsible people.

Unfortunately, the bazaars are full of psychics who turn off all those who want to approach things with reason, logic, and intuition. Such a condition makes it more difficult for advanced intellectuals to stand on the witness chair. But this is the actual test and challenge: to announce the truth amidst the tumult of lies; to emphasize the reality in the fields where unreality has blocked the ears of the people; to demonstrate courage where courage is condemned.

This is why Christ and other great Teachers asked Their disciples to stand as witnesses of Beauty, Goodness, Righteousness, Joy, and Freedom. Without going through the tensions of standing as a witness within the chaos of the world, one will never be able to cross the threshold of the Fiery World. Higher realities can spread and grow in the world only if they have fiery witnesses.

Some people are fascinated with automatic writing. There are even people who teach others how to do this. All such experiences must be recorded in a spiritual diary because these records can help us see if we are advancing on the path or are caught by our illusions, glamors, vanities, or by invisible entities.

Automatic writing is a sign of lower psychism. It happens when an entity found in the astral or lower etheric planes obsesses the person and uses his hand for writing. The person does not know the entity; he has no conscious communication with him, and he does not know what the entity is going to write. Such communications are very average and mediocre, and even worse when charged with inferior motives.

There are other forms of communications which are mistakenly placed in the category of automatic writing. For example:

a. It is possible that your Solar Angel inspires you and urges you to write certain instructions which are far more advanced than you can imagine. This happens when you are approaching the Third Initiation.

b. It is possible that, with your own permission, an advanced Initiate uses your hand to convey some advanced instructions.

c. An advanced Initiate can, with your permission, use your hand by telepathic remote control to give certain instructions.

One must judge by the fruits. If the conveyed instructions are a highly organized and advanced Teaching, with clarity and simplicity, or an urgent message to meet the needs of the moment, or a proper and accurate warning, it can be considered to be from higher sources.

There is also the method of *overshadowing*, mentioned by Alice Bailey in *A Treatise on Cosmic Fire* as follows:

...This threefold overshadowing will manifest as:

First. An impression upon the physical brain of the man or woman, of thoughts, plans for work, ideals and intentions which (emanating from the Avatar) will yet be unrecognized by him as being other than his own; he will proceed to put them into action, unconsciously helped by the force flowing in. This is literally a form of higher mental telepathy working out on physical levels.

Second. The overshadowing of the chela during his work (such as lecturing, writing, or teaching), and his illumination for service. He will be conscious of this, though perhaps unable to explain it, and will seek more and more to be available for use, rendering himself up in utter selflessness to the inspiration of His Lord... it is only possible when the fifth petal is unfolded.

Third. The conscious co-operation of the chela is necessitated in the third method of overshadowing. In this case he will (with full knowledge of the laws of his being and nature) surrender himself and step out of his physical body, handing it over for the use of the Great Lord or one of His Masters. This is only possible in the case of a chela who has brought all the three lower bodies into alignment, and necessitates the unfolding of the sixth petal.[1]

It is very important to understand the third case clearly. Unless the Great One can occupy the mental body — the lower and higher levels — of the disciple, it turns into lower mediumism. Any entity that can occupy the etheric, astral, and lower mental bodies is not of

1. Alice A. Bailey, *A Treatise on Cosmic Fire* (New York: Lucis Publishing Co., 1977), pp. 756-757.

higher order. Also, a person who cannot vacate the whole mental body is not an advanced or purified personality.

The Great One actually occupies the causal levels of the mental plane, or levels one, two, and three. How to differentiate between those who possess a personality and those who temporarily occupy it for an important mission...? One must observe the following:

1. The quality of the message or the quality of the work done under occupancy
2. The purpose and the technique used to achieve the purpose
3. The degree of harmony of the teaching or the acts with the great Teaching given by the Great Ones
4. The work the person had done in the past and his associations
5. The universality and clarity of the message
6. The demonstrated humility and selflessness of the psychic
7. The power of the message or action
8. The depth of the person's creativity

It is known that the Great Ones are great and busy Executives, and They do not waste their time and energy with an unprepared person for average instructions or messages. They follow a rule: to spend energy and time for the most essential.

At present, the bazaars of the world are full of pseudo messengers who are creating chaos in the minds of the ignorant and leading them into confusion.

We are told in the Teaching that it is possible to observe the Subtle World while awake on earth. One needs fiery eyes that can see in the astral plane. Such observations are very valuable in the sense that one can understand them through earthly measures and compare them with the events taking place on earth. One must have developed sight, purity, and an expanded consciousness to be able to make such observations.

We are told that in some strata of the Subtle World people think entirely about their own ego and for their own interest. These people are those who, while on earth, ran after their own interests. In these strata of the Subtle World, the weaknesses and vices multiply their power and reach destructive measures. On higher levels of the Subtle Worlds, the vices disappear and the virtues operate in full measure.

Self-interest creates a prison-like environment for people, and they cannot expand their consciousness and fuse their souls with the light of others. Such people come again to earth with full greed and self-interest. It is only continuous pain and suffering that eventually releases a few of them from the prisons of their egos. When egocentricity is continued for a long time, it manifests through physical, emotional, and mental diseases because it does not allow the harmony of the One Self to reverberate within the person's whole system.

In the Subtle World these people pursue all that they were engaged in on earth, but with greater involvement and zeal. The blindness of their egos holds their lives captive in the petty labor of accumulated trash.

There are also those who aimlessly wander. They have no goals or interests, and they pass long periods of time in the Subtle World with no interests. The Higher Worlds are closed for them. They feel the vanity of the lower existence, and they live in a state of desperation.

The self-centered ones live in a hell-like life because they push themselves on others continuously and hurt each other. But they always stay together to spread the venom of their egos in each other. And imagine, this continues for at least one thousand years, measured in earthly time.

Egocentric ones rebel against the higher laws and try to find ways and means to avoid them, as we do when we speed on highways. But sooner or later the Law of Reincarnation brings them down for another chance to correct themselves. Most of those who are thrown into pralaya belong to the egocentric groups. Sometimes it takes many millions of ages to prepare a new planet for them to give them a new opportunity to evolve.

A great number of people are egocentric. A major part of humanity thinks that our globe is the center of the Universe. Because scientists cannot verify life in our and other galaxies, they think this globe is so special that eventually we can own all abandoned galaxies as our properties!

There was a time when people were shocked to discover that the earth was not the center of the solar system. There will be greater shocks when humanity discovers that man on this planet is a member of the universal life-form. Man is engaged in a great labor to liberate the consciousness of every atom and make it the citizen of Cosmos.

As we prepare to enter into the Subtle and Fiery Worlds, the fact of the universality of life slowly dawns in our hearts, and we become the co-workers of great Lives and Laws which carry the wheel of evolution onward.

Many events in the worlds are the manifestation of the events conceived in the Higher Worlds, but an event conceived in the Higher Worlds cannot manifest in its entirety at once in the world. Like pieces of a jigsaw puzzle, it takes form here, there; and gradually one sees the formation of the picture.

Those who know how to read the events and relate them in the right way gradually perceive the formation of the picture. Prophecy is the ability to read single events, then relate them, and then intuitively see *the image* that is in formation. If such a reading and intuition are not clear, one can be easily misled.

The accuracy of seeing the coming world events is based upon the fact that the *seer* is able to be conscious in the higher and lower worlds simultaneously. He has the facility to see what portion of the event is in manifestation, the measure of acceleration of manifestation, the formation of the links between manifested events, and the Conceived Event in the Subtle Worlds. Such an ability to be in both worlds gives accuracy to the seer and to his prophecy.

After this is understood, people will learn that the "Higher Worlds" within a human being also conceive the destiny of that person, and this Conceived Image begins to manifest in the life events of the person, life after life. If the person is advanced enough, he cooperates with the Conceived Image and creates no friction between the Image and his life's events. Thus, he strives to facilitate the manifestation of the Image conceived in his higher realms.

An intelligent person will know that this Conceived Image in his higher realms cannot immediately manifest, but it takes time as the conditions of his life become more favorable through his striving and karma.

The conception of Images has two sources. One source is the Higher Intelligences who, like architects, conceive the best structure they wish to build to guarantee the liberation of the Divine Sparks. The other source is the karmic accumulations. When these accumulations reach a certain degree of saturation, they program the events to come and purify the Space, restore harmony, and give a chance to human beings to see the consequences of their thoughts, feelings, actions, and motives, and help him live a life more harmonious with the laws of karma.

Those who pass through the conflagration of karmic flames often perceive the Image conceived by Higher Lords and strive toward it, creating better conditions of life.

There is also a source of conception which tries to distort the manifestation of the previous two sources. That source is the dark lodge. The dark lodge conceives world events which have the programming to distort the conceptions of the Great Lords and the understanding of the manifestation of karmic law. This creates immense confusion in the minds of people. Often people fail to see the Image created by the Great Lords, the benevolent action of the karmic laws, and the interferences of the dark lodge.

13

Vivisection and the Astral Plane

Vivisection is condemned by the Teaching because it is absolutely cruel and because it contaminates the Subtle World.

When an animal is in pain and suffering, he is already functioning on the astral plane, and all his pain and agony spread over the astral world.

When an animal is under vivisection, he emanates some sort of poison which is attractive to every kind of subtle germ. This poison is released in this world and in the astral world, contaminating both.

An animal cannot understand why he is used in cruelty, why he is cut, injected, operated on. The fear and rejection that he expresses toward the cause of suffering create psychic poison.

Those doctors who are busy with vivisection will have a terrible time in the Subtle World, no matter what motives they had in their mind. In the Subtle World, the end does not justify the means. Those who caused suffering to animals will pay a high price for their cruelty in both worlds.

The cruelty in the lower astral world is intensified when animals under vivisection pass away. Their subtle bodies carry into the astral world a great amount of agitation, irritation, and poison. When such animals incarnate, they carry a deep hatred of humankind. Often they carry dark forces within their subtle bodies to hurt and harm people through obsession. During vivisection their agony attracts those entities who are protectors of the animal kingdom. Very often these entities attack those who practice vivisection on animals. This attack starts on the mental plane, then spreads into the astral, etheric, and physical planes. The destructive result sometimes takes seven to twenty-one years to manifest.

Because animals are weaker than human beings, their rights must be protected more intensely that the rights of human beings. For example, we protect the rights of children more than the rights of adults.

When animals are treated in the right way, they emanate certain vibrations which increase our joy and open our hearts. A good friendship begins to be established between the man and the animal, which grows into Infinity. We must remember that animals are our little brothers, and we have the responsibility to take care of them.

Hunting for sport is as cruel as vivisection. On the astral plane, the animals killed for sport give their hunters a terrible time. The evolution of many hunters is blocked because of the cruelty they exercised toward animals.

Astral entities are attracted to the emanations of animals as they go through suffering. Their urine, blood, and other secretions radiate dark red and brown colors and invite those entities who nourish themselves on these emanations.

Undesirable entities also gather when decomposition of the animal body takes place after death. Stagnant water, trash, rotten fruit, and dead flowers attract similar entities. These entities put the person or family in contact with the lowest level of the astral plane.

Blood is very inviting to lower astral entities. Purity of the body and home is especially recommended. Those places where vivisection is performed; slaughterhouses; and places where rotten fruit, flowers and food, stagnant water, or blood are found are charged with astral entities and negative forces and are contaminated by the emanations of both the entities and the objects to which the entities are attracted.

We are told that any conscious killing shakes the entire surrounding atmosphere. This is not a mystery but a fact. A living animal or human being establishes a regular pattern of relationships with the surrounding field of energy and with objects and other living forms. He becomes part of the fabric of life. When any portion of that fabric is destroyed, it shakes all the threads of energy and creates disturbances in the entire pattern which extend through the Subtle World up to the mental world. Such disturbances create a flow of excess energy or prevent the energy flow. In both cases, the disturbances extend to the Subtle World and, like strong waves, carry destructive results there.

By the same token, people who die prematurely through the cruelty of others cannot adjust themselves to the Subtle World for a long time. This is due to the pollution and disturbances carried there by the departed one. This agitation of the network of energies and pollution echo and re-echo for some time before the harmony is restored once again.

There are also advanced human beings who have dedicated their lives to humanity. Some of them were assassinated, burned, or poisoned in various ways. These people do not fall into unconsciousness immediately after death because the Invisible Guides explain the situation to them and take them to the higher planes where they belong.

Such people have highly organized astral bodies and do not need the same preparation an average person needs for his astral body. All the sacrificial services that they render nourish the flame of the heart. In the case of assassination, the flame of the heart, along with the protective care of the Guides, lights their path in the Subtle Worlds.

Blood attracts low-level entities which, like vultures, accumulate around people who die in bloodshed. Thus, surrounded with horrifying forms, the departing ones carry with them such entities into the Subtle World.

Those who kill their enemies here on the physical plane also prepare ferocious enemies in the Subtle World who wait to take their fiery revenge.

Those who commit crimes, destroy life, and run after malice and slander appear in the Subtle World with terribly deformed subtle bodies, as seen and observed by inhabitants of the Subtle World. Each negative and destructive feeling and each criminal thought create disfiguration and deformities in the subtle body. Often such deformities require much time to be repaired. Each deformity in the subtle body gradually affects the physical body, disturbing the flow of incoming energies, and the body continuously manifests various symptoms of diseases.

These deformities can only be cured with the help of the Fiery World and through purification and expansion of consciousness.

People want to appear beautiful. They dress well, they use make-up and other means to look beautiful, but sometimes they do not realize that when they leave their bodies they appear in the Subtle World exactly as they are. It is possible to hide oneself in the physical world, but it is impossible to hide oneself in the Subtle World.

The fire from the Higher Worlds may restore the beauty of the astral body, if one attracts that force by the purity of his heart. But the heart cannot be purified if cruelty dwells in it. Cruel people, in trying to be victorious and successful, totally disfigure their subtle bodies and lead themselves toward spiritual destruction. We are told that cruelty creates its ugly mask, which sticks to your face, and you cannot take it away. In the Subtle World you always appear with that mask, and all inhabitants can see and observe you that way.

What suffering descends upon one who cannot free himself from his own ugly image!

This image is formed by your thoughts at the time of the crime and by observing and feeling the victim. Your mind mechanically photographs what you see, hear, and do. If you are breaking the Law of Love, the image exactly reflects the event and impresses it on your astral body. This is why we are told that human actions affect a person's own image before affecting others.

A desire is presented on the astral plane as a performed act. Low-level desires create distorted images; high-level desires show also, with their many colors and beauty.

When a desire is in line with the laws of Nature, no matter what obstacles exist in life, it slowly materializes. Devas work on it and make it more substantial and magnetic, until one day the desire materializes on the physical plane. Often low desire also materializes, but it does not manifest beauty and brings with it disturbing forces.

Imagine two rooms. In one room are your parents, grandparents, and your many teachers and friends. In the other room you live with your immediate environment. There, you engage in low-level desires and crimes. When the image of your actions dramatizes itself in the next room full of your beloved ones, don't they immediately become disturbed and shocked by seeing you totally disfigured and deformed? This is exactly what happens in the Subtle World. In addition, the low level desires and crimes stimulate all those who have a tendency toward them.

Those who have healthy and beautiful bodies are those who in their past incarnations did not commit serious crimes, malice, or slander and lived a life of service, culture, and higher striving. When the consciousness is purified, transmuted, and expanded, it creates beautiful bodies, faces, and eyes.

Ugly bodies are mostly the result of the violation of the Law of Love and Unity. Astral bodies and etheric bodies are highly disturbed when one enacts the roles of criminals and killers. Such actors develop many emotional and mental complications in their old age and reincarnate with defective bodies. Imitation and acting put a strong impression in the astral body especially. The images of such people in the astral world look very mixed and diffused.

When animals die naturally or by accident, they do not experience fear as man does. They do not lose their consciousness, and they feel that they are still alive on the physical plane. They keep living in their owners' homes and keep them company, as if they were still alive.

Animals incarnate from the astral plane to the physical plane without leaving their astral body because the astral body is permanent for them within the two worlds. Man dies on the astral and mental planes as well as on the physical plane, but animals do not.

Regarding the initiation of animals into the human kingdom, Master D.K. states that cats, dogs, elephants, and horses will be initiated. When? The date is not given. It is thought that this is their destiny because He states that they served the human race, not their own race or nation!

There are people who believe that a person can be possessed by the animal spirits existing in the lower levels of the astral plane. They think that some of the members of their race are possessed by serpents, dogs, wolves, hyenas, pigs, crows, vultures, etc. In fact, the similarity of the animals' characteristics to that of the possessed one attracts such creatures to him and makes the creatures use the human body for a while for various reasons.

Those who slaughter animals for sport or vivisection bring on the attack of these animals for the reason of revenge upon those who took their lives.

Exorcists usually have power over such animal spirits, and they send the spirits to their proper species as, for example, Christ did when He sent certain spirits to the swine who then threw themselves into the water to get rid of the spirits.

People think that such possessions occur to those individuals who have little education and are lower class citizens. This is not true. Sometimes persons in very high positions are possessed by animal spirits. Their deep hatred and lack of a drop of compassion attract cannibal spirits into their aura. One day, history will prove that people such as Herod the King, Nero, Sultan Hamid and his close associates, Hitler and his associates, as well as many others in the history of humanity were possessed by animal spirits.

It is noticed that some animals do not possess a man continuously but intermittently, as the man and his life's events provide opportunities for them to act. This possession lasts sometimes one hour in a given month, or two hours a day, or twice a year for the entire day. Possession may occur at crucial moments when big decisions are to be made in which the destiny of many thousands are involved.

There is also partial possession, for example during sex, during the eating of food, drinking, or during a war. Sudden animalistic influences can be observed in both sexes during such periods. Men or women "turn" into animals, and when the period of activity is over, they regain their normality because after satisfaction the animals leave them.

Many rapists who attack little children are caught by animal spirits. It is not possible to cure them by punishment or medicine. Unless the animal spirit is cast out, they will repeat their crimes over and over. The only thing that can throw the spirit out is the light of a person who has an aura charged with psychic energy. The animal spirit cannot stand the psychic energy which radiates with extreme brilliance.

In asylums, in mental hospitals, one can see examples of such possession. I saw a man acting exactly like a dog, another one like a pig. They were not imitating but actually acting like animals in human form.

Of course, a person must be out of the sphere of protection of his inner Guardian and involved in the works of darkness to fall into such a calamity.

Animals possess people during eating, prostitution, gambling, and criminal activities. People are possessed by animals especially on battlefields where blood is shed. Such people lose all their human dignity, compassion, and logic. They kill, destroy, burn, and annihilate each other. Those who have been on the battlefield can easily recognize such kinds of possession.

Many causes of insanity, mental imbalance, and confusion in those who survive the battle can be traced to possession by animal spirits.

Those who fight a battle because of the principles of freedom, beauty, and justice do not fall into such traps. Their sacrificial spirit for the human cause stands as a shield of protection. But fights, killings, and genocides which are motivated by animalistic instincts do not provide protection for any fighter.

Possessions occur also near the slaughterhouses where so many animals are killed. Some of them take revenge on their killers and possess them.

Such possessions are sometimes gradual, until the person passes away and enters into the lower levels of the astral plane. If his virtues are too weak to transport him to higher levels, the animal gets him and possesses him. Such people cannot easily incarnate, and when they do incarnate, they demonstrate strong animal tendencies.

People believe that possessions by animals are very rare, and that the majority of disorders in the human character are the result of nervous and glandular disturbances. But if one searches further, one will ask, why did such disturbances occur in the first place?

One opens the carburetor of his car and finds some parts broken. He changes the parts, and a few days later the same problem occurs.

One cannot repair things by repairing the effects but by repairing the causes.

Presently, diseases and illnesses are treated as such. In the future, the physician will investigate the moral life of the patient. The moral life of the patient will give the physician greater clues for a right diagnosis than do X-rays.

Before any possession, serious mental, nervous, or glandular disorders occur. It is very probable that the person has violated many moral laws or submitted himself to the fever of fanaticism. The accumulation of such violations leads up to the crisis of possession or illness.

On the Path toward the Higher World, one must be cautious not to be caught by animal spirits because they will delay your progress, cause you embarrassment, and load you with heavy karmic liabilities.

One can stop such dangers by developing a pure heart full of love and compassion and a readiness to meet the needs of the people.

14

Organ Transplants

Each human being is charged by what he thinks, feels, and does, and no two human beings are alike. Their organs are the exact mirror of their consciousness and the sum-total of their sphere of vibrations or aura.

To take an organ from someone and plant it in the body of someone else is a dire mistake. This is because that organ carries the weaknesses and the virtues of the person and gradually creates chaos in the physical, emotional, and mental bodies of the surviving person. If the transplantation is successful for a short period, it may change the personality of the victim in the long term.

The transplanted organ carries to the person not only the physical germs of the dead person but also the astral and mental germs, plus the karma of the person and the defects of his subtle bodies.

Very soon people will realize that transplantation can become a hot business, and behind the doors of hospitals people can be butchered to take their organs and sell them for a great price. Greed has its own ways. How will one know if a patient was not killed intentionally to make certain his organs are available for the secret bazaars of the hospitals?

If a person is killed deliberately for his organs, his soul knows it, and after he dies he will want to punish the doctor and the person who paid for his organs. This punishment works by way of obsessing or possessing the recipient and the doctor. Such an act will also delay the evolution of the obsessor, the one whose organ was used.

If one gives his organs deliberately, after he passes on he will be etherically attached to the person who has his organ because his etheric body will be stuck to the live organ in the person. Such an attachment will cause confusion in the consciousness of the person who received the transplant. Eventually he will lose his personality because the etheric body of the donor will come and attach to his etheric body. As a result, the evolution of the one who gave his organ to another person will also be delayed.

The attachment of the etheric body of the dead with the living person will create various complications in the chakras and eventually in the corresponding organs. For instance, there is a silver thread between the soul and the heart. In changing the heart, the thread links the new person to the soul of the previous owner. This linkage attaches the released soul to the problems of the new owner. The medical profession will see astonishing changes in the psychology of the survivor. These changes will work against the evolution of both the new owner and the one who gave the organ.

When an animal heart is transplanted, the patient will either die within a short time or his Chalice will be damaged by the new animal heart. Being the product of an animal-consciousness, the animal heart will exercise great pressure on the opening Chalice and delay the person's spiritual evolution for many incarnations. A karmic debt to the animal concerned also adds to the delay.

The most hideous transplantation is related to the heart, animal or human. The heart is the physical organ of the Chalice, and every Chalice has its own development. Some petals are unfolded; some are dormant. When the Chalice is more unfolded, it releases greater energy to the heart, which either assimilates it (if not damaged by the strain of negative emotions and evil acts) or is disturbed by it, developing various organic troubles.

Physical hearts cannot be interchanged because of the uneven development of Chalices. If you transplant a heart that cannot transmit the pressure of the Chalice, the transplanted heart will not survive.

The heart controls the memory. It is the heart that kindles the brain and creates consciousness. In transplanting the heart, one creates chaos in the mechanism of consciousness. When the life thread in the heart contacts the consciousness thread in the brain, memory and consciousness are produced on the physical plane. In transplanting the heart of another person, you are putting in a differently set mechanism whose life thread is in the Spark of the departed soul. What will happen?

If the heart survives, the Spark of the patient will try to withdraw his life thread from his dead heart and plant it in the new heart. The heart will have two life threads, two flows of life energy, which will overload the heart and develop confusion in the memory and consciousness. In addition, the living one will be affected by the experience through which the departed person's soul is passing.

This will be a psychological mess.

The visible human heart is surrounded by an etheric and astral heart. The heart is not only a piece of flesh, but it also has a sphere of subtle energies which are connecting links between man and spatial centers. Medicine is very ignorant of all of this, and with a hammer and a shovel it is engaged in repairing the most delicate mechanism existing in the world.

The heart can be regulated and cured by working to develop virtues and paying the debts of karma. The heart can be regulated and cured by increasing the psychic energy and using it creatively. The heart can be protected by decreasing the poison in the air, food, water, and earth. As long as pollution and fear are increasing in the world, transplantation of the heart is like the effort of a fly who thinks he can push a dead car on the road.

Medical people know only the physical body and the physical world. They have no idea of the subtle bodies and the Subtle Worlds. That is why the vivisection of animals and now the transplantation of organs have become twenty-first century businesses.

Any organ taken from a body has an etheric and astral counterpart. When a new organ is replaced in a certain body, its etheric and astral organs will reject it, as it is built by the influence of a different psychology. That rejection will cause death to the person, but will not affect the income of the hospitals and doctors!

Instead of transplantation, science must try to find the causes of diseases and eliminate them. Presently, science is digging its own grave.

It will not be surprising to see surgeons on the battlefields digging for the organs of wounded soldiers and trying to rush to the big hospitals in the world to receive their rewards. Consider the serious implications.

CHAPTER

15

Art and the
Subtle Worlds

Beauty in any branch of the arts transfers into the Subtle Worlds a great amount of harmony, energy, joy, love, and ecstasy. People in the Fiery World feel uplifted, inspired, and encouraged by the radiations of beauty.

Our creative thoughts make the gardens of the Subtle Worlds bloom. Our joys give the inhabitants of the Subtle Worlds the energy of striving. Our love increases their understanding. Our energy helps them achieve.

Creative artists live very close to the Subtle Worlds. If their inspiration originates from the Fiery World, they render a great service to the astral world, creating a better bridge between the two worlds through their art.

Advanced astral entities and entities from higher realms love music, painting, sculpture, dance, and other art forms and fill the location of such art with the fragrance of their hearts. Some art galleries and music centers often have very elevated visitors from higher realms. They bring psychic energy, healing, and love to everyone attending such centers.

One thing that the higher entities hate is applause. Applause destroys the auric formation of the audience and the energy patterns of psychic emanations of higher visitors. Most artists feel highly rewarded by applause, but they do not realize that it destroys eighty percent of the influence they wanted to create for the audience.

A better form of appreciation is group singing. Suppose the audience loved the performance. They can begin singing a song that expresses gratitude and love for the performers. For example, they can sing:

May your beauty
shine more and more.
May the current
of your inspiration
flow day and night.
Accept our gratitude
for the beauty and
energy you gave us.

In the future, a composer will create music for these words and publish it all over the world, and, instead of applause, it will be sung in great centers of art.

At the onset of applause, the visitors fly away with great regret; whereas, when the entire audience sings the above blessings, the invisible hosts will join the audience and inspire the artist with the spirit of striving for higher achievements.

In the earthly plane, people think that they exist only if they take something or ingest something. Havingness is a great disease on this planet which manifests as ownership and belonging.

In the lower astral plane, this disease is inflamed to its highest degree, and consequently the pain and suffering and all associated problems from ownership are greater than on earth.

In the middle stratum of the Subtle World, people build their feelings of security, existence, and sharing.

In the higher astral plane, people feel that they exist only if they offer, give, and sacrifice for each other.

In the Fiery World, giving is the major note. Giving is an intense participation with the creative striving of the whole Fiery World. No one thinks about himself. The ego is totally left behind. People are anxious to merge into the One Self as part of a symphony. In the Fiery World, you exist only if you exist in others.

Music in the lower astral plane is very similar to rock, acid, or disco music, but louder. These inflame passions, causing delirium and burning pain.

In the middle stratum, music is mostly melodic.

In the higher stratum, it is chorus-like, with magnificent tones and beauty.

In the Fiery World, it is symphonic, with related colors and fiery forms. Music or sound is used in the Fiery World for different purposes, for example:

1. As an expression of fiery gratitude
2. For the construction of a fiery, protective net
3. For the synchronization of all strivings and creative efforts
4. For communication with higher spheres

Each note and form of music is a channel for new creative impressions.

On earth we reflect daily, through our actions and creations, the level of our contacts with the Subtle Worlds. When people have contact with a certain plane or level in their sleep, they bring down to earth certain impressions and act upon them. The higher they go, the greater is the expression of their life. Enthusiasm, nobility, and honesty are fragrances which we bring from the Higher Worlds.

On our earth, people collect physical objects. They have various pleasures. They learn and accumulate knowledge. They keep all that they collect.

In the Subtle and Fiery Worlds, things are different. There, whatever you give is what you really have. This is a very important law and very difficult to teach humanity.

The Subtle and Fiery Worlds collect for you whatever you give to others on earth. The only energy you will have around you and in the space available for you in the Subtle Worlds will be the energy which you either have released from your Core or have transmitted to Nature after transmuting all that you received from Nature.

The correspondences of any object that you gave to others, such as properties, money, or jewels, will appear on your path when you enter into Higher Worlds. Each sacrifice you did for others will build your future fiery body. Any wisdom that you gave to others, you will have. The only knowledge that you will have is the knowledge that you gave to others or that you used to uplift others. If you love, you will have love. If you were a man of gratitude, you will find great treasures. Therefore, in the Subtle World all that you will have are the things which you gave to others while on earth.

This is why great Sages have always emphasized the spirit of giving, generosity, and sacrifice. We are told that even a cup of water given to a thirsty man will not be forgotten, and we will be rewarded for it. Conversely, all that we take from others is registered in our account as debts. The poorest people (with all that this entails in meanings) in the Subtle World are those who accumulated great wealth on earth by exploiting others and robbing them for their own advantage.

To those who gave will be given, not only in the objective world but also in the subjective world.

The highest way to share yourself with others is to create beauty, to let your inner resources manifest in forms of beauty. The higher you penetrate, the deeper your creativity becomes. Those who can penetrate into the sphere of beauty turn into creative artists who light torches and build the path toward the world of higher beauties.

We do not live forever in the Subtle Worlds, but we come back again and again until a certain stage of perfection is achieved. We come back and we either continue the things we were doing in the past or we engage in new activities, dreams, and thoughts.

The quality of our actions and creativity increases if we enter the Subtle Worlds consciously and observe the effects of our past actions in the Subtle Worlds. This gives us a unique opportunity to come back to earth and improve the quality of our life as a whole and the quality of our particular line of action.

Life after life, we improve our ways of living by observing in the Subtle World the prints of the snapshots of our life. This is how we can introduce conscious changes into the field of our creative endeavors.

When we develop continuity of consciousness, we can compare our creative efforts done in the past while on earth with the creative efforts carried on in the present.

One writes a book ten lives in the past. In each succeeding life he writes about the same topic in greater beauty and depth, and one day, when he becomes conscious of his past lives and deeds, he may collect all the books that he wrote in past lives under different names and titles and compare them to see how his soul unfolded, at what speed he unfolded, what obstacles were overcome, and what virtues were developed in each life, contributing to a better creativity.

In the creative process, one can charge his work with psychic energy through using lofty emotions.

People think that thoughts are the best communicators through words and speech. But there is an entire language of emotions which is expressed through sounds. Human beings use this language when words are inadequate to express the state of their consciousness.

Complicated and heavily charged contacts with Higher Worlds often cannot be expressed by our limited language. Often they need emotions, voice, or sound to be expressed. In the creative process, one can heavily charge his expressions through thoughts, emotions, and voice or sound and build a form that can be really understood. Thoughts sometimes limit our minds, but if they are associated with emotions and voice or sound, psychic energy enables us to grasp these expressions in their real meaning.

Lofty emotions are currents of intuitional substance which bring timelessness and Infinity into your creative work and make your thought-expressions multidimensional. This is why you must try to feel your thoughts and your visualizations, and you must try to understand the depth of your emotions and find ways to express your state of consciousness through a form which lives, expands, and unfolds as people try to understand it.

16

The Interrelationship Between the Three Worlds

There are astral books, or scrolls, in Space. These books were written by those living on earth. These books were either never published and the manuscripts were destroyed; they were published and destroyed; or they were published and used throughout the centuries.

No matter what happened to them, the astral counterparts of these books exist in Space. People can study them in their sleep or after they die and enter into the astral plane, provided they are prepared for such a task.

Often when the writer of such a book incarnates, he attracts the book to his consciousness through his past association and literally copies it or develops it further and publishes it.

There are books which are written for the future; they are ahead of their time.

The astral counterparts of books that do not contain reality, or are written for personal interests and do not carry the fire of wisdom, disintegrate in Space. On earth, people lose interest in those particular books.

At times, after the astral counterpart dies or vanishes, the physical part continues to be printed. However, it loses its influence or becomes a corpse infecting the consciousness of people. It can also turn into a destructive tool in the hands of the agents of dark forces.

Important books which carry a condensed reality and were inspired from higher sources have a radioactive correspondence in the Subtle Worlds. Such books shine with a great glow and draw the attention of advanced souls.

It happens that, as the advanced souls study these books in the Subtle Worlds, they charge them with their psychic energy and multiply the radiation of these books in the Subtle World. This affects the physical correspondence of the books, which draws more and more readers and turns into a source of guidance for them.

Similarly, when a published book is read by advanced people with deep interest and devotion, its higher correspondences attract more readers in the astral plane and inspire people to read it astrally, or physically after they return to their waking state on earth.

Precious manuscripts must not be given out to be read by those who are any of the following:

1. Skeptical of the book
2. Antagonistic
3. Not in a good state of mind
4. Full of fear, anger, or irritation
5. Have a dispute over the ideas presented and thus try to change them

All such states of mind and emotions create disturbances in the astral correspondences of the book before it is published. It is the disturbances that make the book difficult to sell. Also, when the book is read by antagonistic people before its publication, that book cannot have an attractive power when it is published.

It is possible to correct such a situation by finding a few faithful friends and having them read the book with deep sympathy, understanding, and devotion. Such an action, if strong enough, can restore the original magnetism of the book in the astral world and magnetize the physical book in the world.

There was a Russian book translated into English. The translated manuscript was a distortion of the original. Someone found the original Russian text and translated it again. After the correct translation, the astral correspondence of the bad translation was corrected. As a result, first, the astral correspondence of the true translation became in harmony with the original Russian astral counterpart of the book. Second, further distortion and confusion were prevented in the minds of the astral readers.

The distortions in various interpretations of the same book take place when something is not translated correctly. This happens not only on the physical plane but also on the astral and builds what we call *illusions* in the minds of people. Sometimes different translations of the same book cause people to quarrel for centuries in order to solve the problems of their illusions.

Books charged with a heavy wisdom and beauty have their own protection. Either their astral correspondences are not available to dark forces living in the astral plane, or, if the astral correspondences are available, the dark forces see the radiation of the book and they escape from this radioactive appearance.

These same dark forces may become aware of such high level books through their agents on the physical plane. Whenever their agents read these books, the dark forces of the astral plane hear them or see them and try to distort the contents of these books.

The dark forces create a distorted copy of any book they hate and distribute it to their followers on the astral plane. Such a forgery creates bad consequences for the book on the physical plane by making the dark agents on the physical plane attack such a book with distorted and palatable interpretations or translations. The usefulness of many valuable books has been hindered by such methods.

Fortunately, the righteous ones here on earth and in the Subtle World take action to combat such a pollution or distortion.

Astral books survive in the Subtle Worlds if they are charged with Beauty, Goodness, Truth, Joy, and Freedom. If any of these elements are defective or lacking, the astral book will gradually degenerate and vanish, unless the agents of darkness try to perpetuate it to use for distorted purposes.

Books, letters, or any documents we write are visible for those in the astral and mental planes who have an interest in them.

Contracts are as important there as they are here. Breaking a contract or forging it or falsifying it or misinterpreting it creates violent reactions from the original astral correspondences. These violent reactions attract those who are guardians of rights, and they often punish those people who violate their promises or contracts.

This is why oaths, vows, verbal promises, and contracts were considered very sacred. People who were foolish enough to break their promises, vows, oaths, word, or contracts were considered by the ancients to be the most miserable traitors.

Once we understand the ways in which Nature works, many mysteries are revealed to us. For example, we think that man lives only on the physical plane. But just as man lives on the physical plane, he simultaneously lives as if reflected in mirrors in the astral and mental worlds. Astral and mental plane inhabitants continuously observe him in his astral and mental reflections. All that he does on the physical plane is reflected in other planes. All his beauty or ugliness is seen there with all its details.

Here on earth you can conceal your emotions or thoughts. Concealment is impossible in the Subtle Worlds. All that you feel and think is observed there by interested parties, and especially by those who in some way or another were related to you in life and have passed away.

A person's life on the physical plane affects many, many people in astral and mental planes because he lives in these three planes simultaneously. He causes the inhabitants in the Subtle Worlds either joy or grief. He either helps their progress or becomes an obstacle to them. He either guarantees their cooperation and blessings or creates rejection and indifference toward him.

Those in the Subtle World who love you want to see you living a life of Beauty, Goodness, Righteousness, Joy, Freedom, striving, and sacrificial service. Of course, there are those in the lower astral plane who rejoice over your crimes. In the meantime, they pity you, knowing the future awaiting you.

People have divided life into a life for those who have a physical body and a life for those who have left it. Such an error has had very drastic consequences upon the human consciousness. Life is one. Every action is an action that echoes on all the planes. There are "mirrors" in which all our actions are observed from the remotest star.

In the future a new science will be given to humanity. This will be called the *Science of Visibility*. This science will teach human beings the fact that they are always visible to the Higher Worlds in terms of their actions, emotions and thoughts, and intentions or plans.

Learning this science will help develop a three dimensional consciousness in human beings by which they will be conscious, not only of their physical actions and physical life but also of the correspondences in the emotional and mental planes. Thus, they will be able to cultivate a threefold vision through which they will see their actions manifested on these planes simultaneously.

The future leaders of humanity will be elected from those people who have that threefold vision.

An act that is accepted on the physical plane but rejected by the heart and feared by the mind will be refused.

A decision that is accepted by a physical level committee but rejected by the emotional plane committee and totally unapproved by the mental plane committee will be discarded immediately.

People agree on the physical plane but often disagree on higher planes. But, when pressed, they agree with a physical plane decision.

Whenever a man or a committee is divided within, there will be no success, only increasing problems.

Through the Science of Visibility, man will learn the true meaning of integrity.

Healing and health problems can be approached from the same perspective. Physical health is related to emotional and mental health. **Any unhealthy condition in the physical plane eventually creates similar conditions in the emotional and mental bodies.** Though the physical body dies, the astral and mental bodies may carry the sickness into the Subtle World, especially if the sickness of the astral and mental bodies is not exhausted through the physical illness.

The astral and mental man may suffer a sickness in the Subtle Planes until his astral or mental body is healed, vacated, or disintegrated in the corresponding planes.

In the next incarnation the human soul still carries the seeds of the illness in the lower three permanent atoms. These seeds provide the tendencies toward the same sickness. After the human soul is born, he develops the same sickness or has the tendencies toward it, especially if the permanent atoms are not purified in the mental world. Purification of the atoms is a possibility if the man has advanced toward the higher mental plane.

There are very advanced doctors in the astral and mental planes who use various methods to heal people. Also, people use their imagination and discrimination to heal themselves. If the physician on the physical plane has developed his psychic centers and has a reservoir of psychic energy, he can consciously cooperate with the physicians of the astral and mental plane in trying to heal a person of his diseases.

This is why it will be imperative in the future that psychiatrists and physicians are chosen from those who have higher psychic abilities.

In the future, physicians acting on all these three planes will cooperate together to cure a physical problem. Gradually it will be clear that most of the sicknesses on the physical plane have their origin in the astral and mental planes.

Astral and mental maladies will be diagnosed by physical plane doctors. They will check in detail the emotional behaviors or the emotions of the patients and the way they think.

People's emotions and the way they think clearly reflect the defects they have in their corresponding bodies. For example, the existence of fear, anger, hate, revenge, and jealousy are clear symptoms that they have corresponding diseases in their astral body. These may manifest physically. Egotism, vanity, greed, and separatism are signs of mental diseases, which may manifest as complicated physical diseases.

In the future it will be possible to diagnose such conditions with specially programmed computers. Actually, the next phase of the development of the computer will be the ability to analyze the sickness patterns of these bodies and synthesize them into certain conclusions.

There are veils between the physical, astral, and mental planes. These veils will slowly be withdrawn, and human beings will see that life is a continuous, simultaneous process on the three planes.

This three-plane life is called the Wheel of Karma. People must eventually prepare to escape from this wheel and enter into a higher plane, the Intuitional Plane, at which gate all the causes of all kinds of disorders are exhausted. The human soul will thus enter into the realm of light as a point of light.[1]

---

1. For further information regarding this subject, please refer to *The Psyche and Psychism.*

17

Desire and the Subtle World

Every time you desire something, you build the forms of the desire around you. They follow you day and night, affecting your thinking, emotions, and actions; but you cannot see them. When you enter the astral plane, you see all the forms of your desires hanging around you.

Imagine how many kinds of desires you had in one life and how many different forms these desires took. All these desire-forms follow you like your little children and create great confusion and loss of energy in you. They follow you to continue their existence, sucking your energy. They follow you to be used and enjoyed.

These desire-forms hang on you, creating a hell-like condition for you. You now have all that you desired, but they are not in harmony with each other. They have conflicting existences, and you cannot harmonize them nor can you destroy them until they exhaust the energy with which you built them.

The delay of a person on the astral plane is due to such desire-forms. Some of them are really ugly and shameful; some of them are very selfish, even destructive. The trouble is that all your desire-forms are visible to all astral entities — your friends, relatives, and enemies — just as your furniture is visible on the physical plane. Often, great embarrassment falls over the face or life of a victim, due to shameful or destructive desire forms.

Desires are of many kinds:

1. Accumulation
2. Enjoyment
3. Transformation
4. Service one can render
5. Wishing well for others
6. Group desire
7. Global or universal desires

The first and second desires are the ugly ones. They are related to greed and exaggerated pleasures, money, sex, possessions, crimes, and positions. Your desires, amplified by your imagination, follow you like a noisy and agitated crowd.

The third is a noble desire. You want to transform yourself. In your elevated moments you visualize yourself and desire to be very beautiful, heroic, courageous, successful, etc. Actually, such a desire acts as an aspiration and pushes you forward on the path of your evolution.

The fourth desire is a deep wish to serve other people: to know, to have, and to be, so that you can render greater service to other people. This is also a noble desire, and it helps you go forward.

Number five is wishing well for others, for children, relatives, friends, so that they have a good, successful, and healthy life.

The sixth form of desire is for groups or nations. For example, one wishes and desires deeply that his nation becomes a healthy, prosperous, and victorious one and that it stands for the benefit of all nations.

The seventh desire is a universal desire for all kingdoms and nations. An example is the desire to have a world where peace, understanding, progress, and right human relations are established.

These noble desires, originating from the person, do have a link with him. But the difference is that he is not imposed upon and controlled by them. They have a more impersonal basis. They are related to all of humanity, rather than to the ego of any single person.

In the Ageless Wisdom it is suggested that we "kill out desire." Here, desire refers to those emotional and mental forms which hinder our path of freedom and sublimation and weaken our willpower and control upon outer forces.

Desire is an expression of willpower used for our physical, emotional, mental, or spiritual interests. A spiritual interest includes the benefit or welfare of a great number of people and nations. It is a holistic desire to see things favorable for all humanity.

The desires that are related to greed and self-satisfaction are examples of the use of willpower which is self-destructive and at the expense of the freedom and welfare of others. Identification with forms and considering oneself as the center of the universe express themselves as greed. This greed can expand itself onto many objects, such as sexual license, gluttony, use of alcohol, tobacco, drugs, etc., to satisfy the physical senses without considering the end results.

Such greed is called the abuse of willpower. In the Subtle World, the habits formed by such abuse bring the worst suffering to man and keep him imprisoned on the same level for hundreds of years.

We are told that the seeds of progress, the urge and drive to progress, always begin from the physical plane. Nothing originates in the subtle planes unless the seeds of it are planted and have germinated in the physical plane. If something such as a habit, glamor, or illusion is hindering your path, you must incarnate and conquer it and get rid of it here on earth. It is impossible to destroy a habit in the Subtle World. If on the physical plane you have taken serious steps to destroy your hindrances, there is a chance to destroy them in the Subtle World. In the subtle plane, you can increase your urge to destroy the hindrance and take a great progressive step.

We are told that we do not create karma in the Subtle Worlds; instead, we pay for our karma which was created in the physical incarnation. Our physical, emotional, and mental actions carried on upon earth condition our life on the corresponding planes in the Subtle World. Most of our actions are fused with thought, emotions, and physical action. Thus, we see how our actions on earth condition our life in the Subtle Planes simultaneously.

Our karmic debts are paid in various ways. We can change them, burn them, or balance them. We can change them through evening review.[1] We can burn them through greater aspiration. We can balance them through greater spiritual striving and achievements. We can conquer our karma through self-renunciation, by living for the good of all, and by being dedicated to the battle for beauty, goodness, and light — in deep joy and freedom.

Karma extends to all three planes — physical, emotional and mental — and desires create heavy karma. Karma created by your actions must be paid on the physical plane. Karma created by your emotions and thoughts must be paid in the astral plane.

One must be cleared of his karma to penetrate into the Fiery World.

All the wrongs that you do on the astral plane are nothing but a way of self-punishment. All that you do toward others on the lower astral plane is the working out of your astral karma. The lower astral life is the programmed performance of the physical life. The higher astral life is the blooming of a programmed plan on earth.

---

1. For further information about this subject, please refer to *The Psyche and Psychism*, Chapter 80.

We must remember that no one can violate our karma. One can change his own karma and even erase it through fiery striving and tuning in with Christ.

Often our dreams and visions are ways to help us see the future, but they are given only in such a degree that they will not infringe upon our karma.

In the Subtle World, before our incarnation, we see what the consequences of our past karma will be on the coming life. With that knowledge we once again return to earth.

There are two ways for evolution to take place. One is karma. The other is conscious striving for improvement. Those who do not have an unfolded consciousness need karma to evolve. Karma moves them forward as their deeds or actions warrant promotion. If the consciousness is awake, the karmic pressure is decreased. Karma is there only to make us stand on our own feet and consciously evolve in the right direction.

Simply stated, those who obey the law do not need the law; those who live according to the law do not need enforcement of the law.

Consciousness slowly replaces the actions of karma until a time comes that the man is totally conscious, lives according to the laws of the Cosmos, and never violates those laws again.

18

Eight Steps for Contact with Higher Worlds

In order to facilitate the contact with higher dimensions of consciousness and beingness, we need to do the following:

1. *Observation* is the first step. We must daily observe if we are under a good or bad influence. A good influence is when we feel joyful, energetic, creative, full of gratitude, and peaceful. A bad influence is when we feel depressed, tired, irritable, revengeful, hateful, or forceful. The second step in observation is to find answers to the following:

    a. Why am I under such an influence?
    b. What is the element in me which is attracting the bad or good influence?
    c. What is the reason for my reaction?

During the day observe your thoughts, words, actions, and relationships and see what influences you are operating under. These influences can come from various sources, for example:

    a. The weather
    b. Electrical turbulences in the air
    c. Cosmic sources
    d. Disturbances on the earth caused by typhoons, tornadoes, earthquakes, volcanic eruptions, floods, etc.
    e. Psychological conditions of nations or great masses of people, such as despair, violence, revolutions, wars, epidemics, feelings of victory, joy, peace, success
    f. One's own physical condition
    g. Chakras, as they awaken or go through petrification
    h. Contact with the Inner Guide
    i. Posthypnotic suggestions

j. Contact with the Master or higher sources, or contact with dark forces and their representatives on earth

k. Thought accumulations in Space

l. The Subtle World

All these and many other sources influence our moods, body, emotions, mind, and relationships. We will achieve a great victory over our vehicles when we clearly see the source which is affecting us, positively or negatively, and then find out the element which is conducting the influence to us. In this way we may be able to cause many changes within our nature and try to contact better and higher sources throughout our life.

It is very important to have a diary so that we can keep the records of our psychic or spiritual life. A spiritual diary will increase our power of observation and bring us closer to our Self.

The influences coming from various sources cannot always affect us, if we do not welcome them or key in to them.

Once when I was playing with my dog, he suddenly ran toward a man who was crossing the street in front of us and began to attack the man's pocket. I hurried to pull my dog back and asked the man, "What is in your pocket?"

"A piece of meat."

I understood why the dog wanted so much to reach the man's pocket.

If there is "meat" in our physical, emotional, and mental pockets, the "dogs" will attack. We will invite special influences according to what we have in our "pockets." If one has a piece of hatred, fear, anger, or a criminal thought in his pocket, the bad influences will rush to him. If one has good thoughts in his pockets, good influences will be attracted to him.

Usually our physical, emotional, and mental actions and thoughts condition the influence under which we live. What else can one expect if he is a "tasty dish" for dark forces, carrying in his "pockets" malice, slander, gossip, and treason!

Good influences will make us healthy, successful, and creative. Bad influences will prevent us from contacting higher sources of inspiration and higher spheres of light and guidance.

One must remember that he cannot free himself from bad influences if he has "meat" in his pockets.

2. Daily register if you have had any *experience of guidance*. Ask the following questions:

a. Why did this guidance come to me? What did I do that such a guidance was given to me? Is this guidance an invitation for a new responsibility?

b. How was this guidance given to me? Directly, indirectly, subjectively, or objectively?

c. Who is the one guiding me? My Guardian Angel? My Master? Another being?

It is as important to know the source of guidance as it is to know who sent you some money.

Guidance can be given with wrong intentions as well. One must ask what and who the source is. Many people are "guided" by spirits and astral entities. Is it safe to follow their guidance?

These are the questions you must have in your mind in order to be able to cooperate with or to reject the source of guidance.

3. Write in your diary your *dreams* and see if they are some sort of *communication*. The questions to be asked are these:
   a. What is the source of this dream?
   b. Why did I dream it?
   c. What can I do with it?

In dreams, the important items are the causes of the dreams, *not the dreams* themselves. Once you know the causes, you can handle the dreams in the right way.

For example, a friend hates you, and he imagines a disaster coming to you. You pick up his imagination as a dream and feel horrified. If you do not find the source of the dream, then the dream will influence you. But if you know the source of it, it will not have any serious influence upon you.

Your dreams may come from astral entities wishing you evil. Your dreams may come from your bad stomach or excited sex center, or from a pain in a part of your body. They may also come as a symbolic message to you for teaching or warning. Try to find the source and ask why. In trying to find the source, you clear your consciousness, or you raise your consciousness to higher spheres.

4. Try to be aware of the *thoughts* that come to your mind:
   a. What is their source?
   b. Why did they come to you?
   c. What can you do with them? Ignore, obey, fight, or transform them?

The source of thoughts are many: friends, enemies, objects, entities, your Guardian Angel, your Master, the Hierarchy, Solar

Sources. How should you discriminate among them? Ask yourself if they come from your lower centers or higher ones? Can you exercise a certain control over them, stop them, or welcome them?

The spiritual life is built through experiments, experiences, and discoveries. When you find the source of your thoughts, you can exercise conscious control over them, either directly or through the type of responses you make. If the source of the thought is lofty, then you can build better ways to expand the lines of communication and enrich your life and the field of your service.

It is important to know that your future is conceived at the point where you meet the incoming thoughts. The differences in your future are the result of the way you responded to your thoughts.

Every thought is a test and a challenge. Through every thought you purify or pollute the Space. People receive your thoughts as blessings, tests, challenges, or pollutions. Such an observation eventually will enable you to develop a filter in your mind which accepts good thoughts and rejects the trash.

Development is impossible until you gain victory over incoming and outgoing thoughts. You must be very careful not to release an arrow which is destructive because every destructive thought returns and hits the originator. You should also be careful not to formulate certain thoughts when you are not sure if they will be used constructively.

Highly charged thoughts are very dangerous if they are given prematurely. One must even be able to slow the flow of highly charged energies, if he has no facility or ability to assimilate, express, and use them.

All such experiences and discoveries lead you toward the Higher Worlds.

There are many people who have opened themselves to incoming thoughts which were beyond their capacity to hold. As a result, they turned into zombies. Our capacity to hold a greater amount of creative thought can be expanded through the development of virtues, purity, and refinement. Our capacity for reception and our capacity for assimilation increase in proportion to our refinement and discipline. Discipline is related to the process of cleaning the thoughts that build a certain false image about oneself. This image acts as a transmitter of similar, unworthy thoughts and builds one's ego.

In a certain Sufi school, a surgeon presented himself to the Headmaster and said, "I am a surgeon. I know six languages. I am well educated in many universities...."

"That is very good and very bad," said the Teacher. "No matter what you think you are, you are going to clean the bathrooms for six months until you can advance to higher classes."

The surgeon was very unhappy, but he performed his job for a while, cursing every time he cleaned the bathrooms. Once the Head Sufi called him and asked, "Why is it that you curse continuously with irritation and anger and pollute our bathrooms with your emotions and thoughts?"

"Well, I didn't come here to clean bathrooms."

"But you came here to transform yourself. You will not advance if you do not free yourself from your ego, or the false image of yourself, and reach a level of humility. After you clear yourself from such a formation, you can work on a higher path."

Then he called the guards and told them to take the surgeon to the gate and let him out. His last words were, "We do not keep here those who worship their own self-made image."

Those who cannot control their words and emotions cannot control their thoughts. Any thought that comes into our mind is a guest, which can turn into a friend, an enemy, or a relative. In the future, mankind will develop a system of filtering, so that no wrong thoughts will enter the sphere of their minds. At present we can control them through discrimination.

There was a very pretty girl who met a wealthy man. He wanted her to be a nude model in a certain magazine and promised her a great amount of money. The girl accepted, and her photograph appeared in the magazine, month after month.

Six months later she came to see me. She could not understand why she had begun to feel an extreme urge for sex, almost to a degree that no one could satisfy her.

"What do you expect," I asked, "when millions of people are looking at your picture and sending you their thoughts of desire and lust?"

"Do these thoughts affect me?"

"Why ask? Look at the result."

It is not easy to resist massive thoughts directed at you. Thoughts of hatred, destructive thoughts, or thoughts of lust eventually weaken your resistance and make you follow paths you never dreamed of taking. You can almost make a man a criminal by hating him.

People will use their minds more and more, and they must start learning the mechanics of thought.

Transformation of thought takes place in many ways. Suppose a thought of harm to a person comes to your mind. You can, through visualization, think about the welfare and the future of that man, and what to do to make him beautiful. Thus the visiting thought is responded to in a constructive way, and it evokes good thoughts from you.

When your heart is full of love and wisdom, the bad thoughts come and serve as catalysts to put your good intentions and ideas into motion.

When a negative thought comes from one who is antagonistic to you, try to transform it and send it back with thoughts of forgiveness, respect, and appreciation. Such thoughts can easily penetrate into his mind and create changes there. People are very receptive to our good thoughts when their bad thoughts are mixed with our thoughts. Your good thoughts penetrate better into the minds of those who have an antagonistic attitude toward you. Hence the importance of enemies: they help distribute your thoughts. The greatest friends in the future will be your present enemies because of your good thoughts. A negative or destructive incoming thought, when sent back with similar thoughts, generates hundreds of more ugly thoughts in the mind of the originator. The best way to make ugly thoughts impotent is to meet them with beautiful thoughts.

Thoughts that come from higher sources inspire and enthuse you for a greater and heroic service. These are the thoughts which build the Path for you to enter the Fiery World. Such thoughts must be welcomed, and the necessary labor and sacrifice must be offered to actualize them.

People do not realize that thoughts are like objects of the physical world. If you know the nature of an object, you handle it intelligently. For example, if a man tells you to open your hand and grasp a burning coal, you do not do it because you know it will burn your hand.

Similarly, if you know the nature of the thought, you handle it in such a way that it is beneficial for you and for others. The important thing is to know the source of it, then the quality and purpose of it, and then to handle it intelligently.

To communicate with the Subtle Worlds, one must develop mastery over thoughts and fearlessness. Fearlessness is identification with your immortal being. Fear is identification with your mortal being. Those who are identified with the Divine part of themselves can penetrate into the Higher Worlds.

5. Note any *apparitions* or *appearances* and ask the following questions:
   a. What are they?
   b. How do they operate?
   c. Why did I register them?

    d. What did I do today?
    e. What did I eat today?
    f. What did I speak today?
    g. Is it a warning?
    h. Is it a responsibility?
    i. Is it an encouragement?

People have many experiences of seeing images, of hands writing on the walls, of heads smiling and talking, of eyes looking at them, of the whole person sitting and talking with them, or of seeing symbols, geometrical forms with colors, etc. The annals of history contain many such experiences, some of them with heavy historic consequences. Of course, one must know that there are also many fabrications and hallucinations, in addition to the genuine experiences.

Those who are striving toward the Higher Worlds must learn how to discriminate between these experiences by asking the questions noted above. Without such a questioning mind, one cannot find the right path either to cooperate with the source of the apparition or to ignore it altogether.

Self-deception is very common in this field. It leads one farther away from the Higher Worlds and develops superstition, prejudices, and illusions in the self-deluded person. Higher contacts cannot be granted to those whose discrimination is not active and whose mind is not clear.

Every contact produces a new chemistry within your aura and body. Some contacts heal you. Some contacts lead you into illnesses. It is important that one welcomes good contacts and avoids bad ones.

The sources of apparitions are many: physical, astral and mental sources; disembodied human beings; Teachers, angels, or higher forces; masqueraders, dark forces, etc.

Once your psychic nature begins to be sensitive, you must know about the experiences you may have, always using the method of questioning referred to above. The most important approach to any apparition is to search for the right translation and for its exact effect upon you. Recording such experiences in your spiritual diary will give you the chance to see the process of their development, cycles, and effects.

    6. Learn to *feel the presence of entities*. Ask yourself:
      a. Are they good?
      b. Are they bad?
      c. Are they indifferent?
      d. What does the presence want to convey to me?

    e. Does it present to me a new duty or responsibility?
    f. Does it challenge me?
    g. Does it flatter me?
    h. Does it give me information?
    i. What kind of information?
    j. Why do I feel the presence?
    k. Is it real?
    l. Is it the result of imagination?
    m. Is it a guide, a helper, or an enemy?

Such questions will help you handle the situation better.

Of course, we must remember that we attract those elements which have a certain interest in us, or we attract "dogs" because we have "meat" in our pockets. We must also remember that the Guardian within us can project images and symbols to establish a dialogue with us. Such images and symbols can be highly instructive and charge us with a great amount of energy and inspiration. Often such images and symbols are ensouled by beneficent entities, whose presence we feel through the images and symbols.

It is also possible that a bad thought projected from someone toward us can be occupied by a dark entity and carry its presence to our rooms. There are also vacated astral bodies which we feel around us. They sometimes disintegrate with bad odors; sometimes they are carried away by invisible servers and burned.

We must try to find out why such corpses were attracted to our location.

    7. Try to register *contact with your Inner Guide*. Ask the following questions:
       a. What is the importance of the contact?
       b. Why is this contact happening?
       c. How can I increase and clarify my contacts in the future?
       d. What is the message of contact?
       e. How can I know that I had a contact with my Guide or Solar Angel?

There are a few signs by which you can be sure that a contact is one with your Solar Angel. Such a contact always leads toward Beauty, Goodness, Righteousness, Joy, Freedom, and Sacrificial Service.

Meditation and evening review can establish closer contact with your Guide. The Inner Guide can even appear to you in human form, or in any beautiful form. It may call you by name, and you may recognize its voice as the voice of an old friend. It mostly directs your eyes toward your future achievements, gives you courage, and inspires in you the spirit of daring.

8. You must also record in your spiritual diary *the action of karma* upon your life by asking the following:
   a. Why did such a thing happen to me?
   b. What was the cause?
   c. How could I avoid it?
   d. Why did I do it?
   e. Why did such help come to me in my depressed moments of life?
   f. Where did it come from? Through whom? In what way?
   g. How should I face the arrow of karma?
   h. How can I get the highest wisdom out of these events?

The gears of karma operate in our subtle nature. Studying our karma gives us a chance to come closer to the subjective side of our nature and learn the ways to find our freedom from all that we did against the karmic laws.

Through these eight steps one can find the best way to approach the Subtle Worlds and establish a better and a conscious contact with these worlds.

19

Astral Contacts

Some people, when their astral body is sufficiently formed, enter the astral plane with their astral body during sleep or while on earth through withdrawal from the physical body. We are told that interesting phenomena occur in the astral world when one visits there. One can observe that certain fiery beings visit the astral plane, and certain fiery beams traverse its atmosphere.

Those who have inflammable materials in their astral bodies hurt their bodies when coming in contact with such currents or fiery beings. Literally, our astral body can be permanently or temporarily hurt, burned, or badly damaged because of such beings or currents. But if the psychic energy is abundant in our astral body, our astral body becomes energized and strengthened by them. Such a charge manifests itself on earth as enthusiasm and a more purified feeling. Also, certain physical illnesses disappear when the astral body is charged by astral contact.

Many of our failures on the physical plane are the result of astral congestions, inflammations, and disturbances. When they disappear through higher contacts, the mode of our relationships with other people changes to a better one. Our prosperity and health improve, and we feel more balanced in our thinking.

It is important to create an astral health care system in which people consider the necessity of having a healthy emotional body and life, and of cultivating those elements in their emotional life that will secure the health of the astral body, not only on the physical plane but also in the astral plane.

Of course, we are not referring here to astral corpses but to astral bodies with living souls in them visiting the astral plane, as their living physical bodies are on earth.

Many virtues provide psychic energy to the astral body and make it immune to astral attacks or accidents, for example:

—The feeling of gratitude
—Complete forgiveness and compassion

—Fiery aspiration
—The spirit of sacrificial devotion to meet human needs
—Detachment
—Renunciation
—Peacefulness

As the astral body is refined and the polluting elements of hatred, anger, irritation, fear, jealousy, revenge, treason, slander, and malice disappear, it naturally enters into higher spheres and contacts higher and fiery beings who electrify the astral body.

The electrified astral body is used on earth as a distributor of benevolent forces. The person becomes a fiery servant of the race, charged with enthusiasm, devotion, and dedication to the human cause.

A purified astral body develops the higher part of the solar plexus, makes the person a healer, develops the heart center, and makes the person come in contact with currents of intuitional energy.

This is where the powers of Saints come from. Their heart center radiates, bringing them the most valuable light and guidance of the Intuition. Their presence causes healing, and they become an uplifting, protecting force in nature.

Emotional disturbances and problems must not last too long because they wear down the astral body. That is why the Great Lord advised us to solve our disputes before sunset. One must enter into sleep with a serene and peaceful heart.

Any harmful action against others deeply damages the astral body. One can record many victories over others through slander, exploitation, and unjust attacks but pay a very high price in the astral world for such transgressions.

It is observed by Great Teachers that some of our degenerative diseases are the result of accumulated astral inflammation, injustice, hatred, conscious manipulation of others, and especially of premature astral plane flights.

Some people are targets of hatred, and if their astral bodies are not sufficiently charged with fire, they can easily and permanently be damaged by such currents of hatred. If they are shielded by fire, all of those who attack them very severely hurt their own astral bodies and pay for their ugliness with many physical illnesses.

In the not too distant future, great Teachers will organize colleges and universities for astral training and discipline. Elements of such Teaching already exist in the religions and myths of the earth. They must be compiled and with new light be presented to the people of the world.

After the astral body is trained and tested, human beings will use their astral bodies as the best communicating device. It will even be possible to visit other planets. Such visitations will replace those false claims which some average people do under hypnosis, insanity, or because of inflammation of their brain cells.

An enormous amount of knowledge and experience will flood the earth because of genuine astral travels, and a great revelation will be offered to people of the earth.

The real science of astro-physics will begin. Higher astral contacts will not be the domain of mystics and religious people but the domain of true scientists, esotericists, occultists, and artists. This will start in a few hundred years, if we do not destroy the planet with pollution and insane actions.

People who have real interest in such a subject must start using the power of their observation and closely examine the result and effect of their emotional life on others and on their own health, creativity, and reasoning. They must especially record when they feel either depressed or exalted after awakening in the morning.

On certain mornings we are depressed and sick; on other mornings we feel joyful and enthusiastic. By observing such feelings and relating them to our previous day's feelings, thoughts, and actions, much revelation comes to our path. We can also closely observe our dreams because certain dreams reveal the astral events taking place in the astral world as a consequence of the previous day's attitudes.

We can observe, also, other people's negative emotional attachment to us and gather much information about astral or emotional life and its effects on life.

A life directed toward beauty, prayers directed to the Most High, and sacrificial labor offered for others also have tremendous effects in our subjective life.

In the near future, the veil of the astral plane will be lifted. People must now start preparing themselves for this great opportunity.

20

Sleep

There are three ways to sleep, each one leading to a different sphere of existence.

The first way leads to the etheric plane, which is the plane closest to earth. This sleep occurs when the etheric body partially disconnects itself from the glandular system. In average people the etheric body never leaves the body, but if one is advanced, he can travel thousands of miles away from the body and still keep the glandular system operating through the electricity of a silver cord anchored in the solar plexus.

In the second way of sleep, the astral body disengages itself from the spine or from the spinal cord. The human soul can travel through the astral body, keeping the body running through a silver cord anchored in the etheric heart center. Of course, one must have a well-formed astral body and astral senses to travel consciously and with a purpose.

In the third way of sleep, the human soul consciously disengages the mental body from the brain and from the three glands in the brain and moves in Space using the mental body. If the mental body is sufficiently built and the mental senses are in order, the time passed in sleep can be used for various kinds of service, for learning, or for teaching.

In the first case, you are not truly sleeping. We call this kind of sleep, "dog-sleep." In this case you may dream, but your dreams are distorted translations of the impressions and stimuli coming from inside and outside sources. Nightmares and attacks usually occur in this phase of sleep because you are closer to the etheric plane, where many *backward* human souls dwell, along with various entities and even animals.

In the second way of sleep, you enter the lower or higher astral plane. You enter the lower astral plane if you are totally occupied with your desire nature, with your glamors, sex, greed, and negative emotions. The higher astral plane is reached through intense aspiration, abstract thinking, contemplation on beauty, and so on. Singing and playing great music before sleep is helpful to ease the withdrawal.

The mental plane is entered if you are totally absorbed in scientific, political, educational, or economic interests.

It is very good to enter sleep with serious questions in your mind, questions upon which you are doing research. These questions will lead you into spheres where you either find the answers yourself, or the answers will be given to you.

The clearest moments of registration of your experiences on the subtle planes occur when your mental body starts to engage itself with the brain, or when your astral body engages itself with the etheric body and the spinal cord. This happens a few minutes before you awaken. You should keep paper and pencil ready to record impressions immediately upon opening your eyes because, when the subtle body further links with the desire body, some of the impressions from Higher Worlds evaporate or mix with the clamor of the denser bodies.

While we sleep our brain is still active, dealing with the body and environment and also with recording impressions reaching us through Space. The brain is very sensitive to the thoughts, plans, and feelings related to us. We draw such impressions and our mind-brain tries to translate them for our benefit as a warning or as good news.

If the person is more advanced, such impressions are registered also in the astral and mental centers, which again are translated through the brain.

Some of our dreams are combinations of such impressions, mixed with our anxieties, worries, and expectations.

The higher our consciousness is, the clearer are the registrations of impressions, and the more exact is the translation of these impressions.

The brain receives the impressions as they come. The astral centers register the emotional parts of the impressions, but if the consciousness is on the mental plane, according to its level, it filters and takes only those impressions which are other than wishful thinking, momentary feelings, and contradictory intentions and plans.

The consciousness on the mental plane registers the facts and real plans, thoughts, and feelings related to us. The brain can do a better translation job if the presented data is clearer, systematized, and free from confusing imagery.

One must know that being in his astral or mental body does not mean that he is in the astral or mental plane. One can be in these spheres only if his subtle bodies are sufficiently built and their senses operative.

It sometimes happens that because of strong emotions and thoughts a person can enter the astral or mental spheres. When this happens, he is either suddenly bounced back to his physical body or he floats in these spheres as an unconscious corpse. Unconscious entrance into the subtle planes begins when the subtle senses of the astral and mental bodies gradually begin to unfold.

When you are in the etheric body, it is possible that some of the astral events going on upon the astral plane reflect in your etheric body, giving you the impression that you are in the astral plane. When you are in the astral body, mental events may reflect in your astral body, giving you the impression that you are in the mental plane. When you are in the mental body, higher events may reflect in your mental body, giving you the impression that you are in higher spheres. Many illusions are formed through such experiences.

Our etheric, astral, and mental bodies must grow, develop, unfold, and reach maturity if we want to function in corresponding planes consciously. We must remember that sometimes in the Subtle Worlds we are very advanced disciples who do a marvelous service in those planes, but we do not remember anything. How does this happen? There are several possible explanations:

1. In past lives we worked very hard in the abstract levels of the mind and dedicated ourselves to certain fields of service, thereby gaining the right to function on higher planes. But we did not build the lower part of the bridge between the mental unit and the mental permanent atom.

2. In the past, we advanced in achievements and service, but when we were incarnating again, our Solar Angel deliberately cut certain connections between the higher planes and the brain, either to urge us to be active in higher planes without remembering our service, or to develop certain needed characteristics on the physical plane which could not be developed if we were aware of our functions on higher planes. Our Inner Guide has very special reasons for taking such an action, such as to protect us, or urge us for our holistic development, or to make us cultivate certain qualities, such as humility.

One may ask how a person can pass into higher levels if his lower bridges are removed. The answer is that at the time of sleep, the Solar Angel offers Itself as a bridge for the human soul to enter higher planes. In the higher planes, the human soul remembers his humble life, but when he returns he cannot remember the experiences he had in higher planes. This continues for a while, through a few lives, until the Solar Angel gives the person an opportunity to build once again his lower bridge. Once this is accomplished, the human soul suddenly realizes how advanced he is and was. This is why for certain duties and certain needs the disciple is led to develop certain higher senses before he develops the lower consciousness.

Everyone who knows how to sleep in the right way becomes a bridge between higher and lower worlds and brings down great beauty, ideas, and directions. It is very important to notice how or in what state you are awakening. If upon awakening you are angry, irritated, depressed, unhappy, or feeling dull, it means that

    a. You were in the lower worlds
    b. You were in conflict either with negative forces that you put into motion or with low-level entities
    c. You invited dark attacks on yourself
    d. You lost energy
    e. Your subtle bodies were wounded

If you sleep well, you will be awakened with joy, with expanded consciousness, and with an urge to work, create, and serve. In observing all these things, you can slowly eliminate all those factors which create negative results and cultivate those factors which will have positive results.

One idea you must plant firmly in your consciousness is that *sleep is sacred*; nothing must interfere with your sleep because sleep puts you in contact with Higher Worlds. In sleep, you can help thousands of people, giving them a message of peace, beauty, cooperation, and synthesis. No one can violate your freedom there. During sleep you have a great field of service, greater than you have in the physical world.

During sleep one needs protection. If your relationship with your Inner Guide is good, you do not need protection from any other source. Remember that Solar Angels work under the command of Christ. To have a good relationship with your Inner Guide, you must

    1. Live a virtuous life
    2. Be noble and honest
    3. Be sacrificial
    4. Follow the path of Beauty, Goodness, Righteousness, Joy, and Freedom

If one lives a life which is against such principles, he creates cleavages between himself and his Solar Angel. It slowly withdraws Its protection, and the person becomes prey to physical and subtle attacks.

Attacks can also occur when a person has sexual relations with the wrong person, when he is unfaithful to his partner, or when he creates cleavages in families. Remember that the Subtle World is totally aware of what each person does.

One can improve his sleep if he sleeps in a room that is very simply furnished, one that has the least amount of furniture and objects. Thoughts, emotions, and entities in Space disturb one's sleep. In addition, thoughts, emotions, and emanations attached to objects and furniture can also do the same. For higher flights, all preparations and precautions must be taken, and small matters must not be neglected.

When people are sleeping in the first stage, or when they are only withdrawn from the physical body into their etheric body, they are very prone to posthypnotic suggestions. Conversations, music, and events occurring around them enter their consciousness as post-hypnotic suggestions.

Most of the patients in hospitals are in such a state of sleep, and the conversations of doctors, nurses, other patients, and visitors enter into them as post-hypnotic suggestions. People may form various habits after an accident or sickness which resulted in a hospital stay because they have gathered commands in their state of sleep while in the hospital. Later, they begin to obey these commands and habits. These habits vary, but they control people's personality lives until these habits are weakened or removed.

A habit is a command given to a person who is in a hypnotized state of mind. It is easy to remove the command from the person, but it is almost impossible to remove the "associates" of the command which are gradually gathered around the command during the hypnotic state.

As a simple example, if the command is "You must smoke," the person obeys the command to smoke. But in order to obey the command, he must first buy cigarettes, matches or a lighter, which means he must have money. He must sit in a certain place to smoke, and he must hide his smoking from certain people. A hypnotist may be able to prevent the man from smoking, but the associated chain of commands still remains in the mind of the person, tempting him, and then forcing him to smoke. Then because another command exists not to smoke, a conflict starts within his consciousness. He is urged to smoke and is commanded not to smoke. Thus, hypnotic suggestions generally result in inner conflict, even if the attempt is made to remove them.

Associated elements of hypnotic suggestion are not always as simple as the ones given above. Sometimes they are so complicated that no one can see or discover what they are. Addicts are hypnotized persons whose associative chain penetrates into astral, or emotional realms. One can knock the head off the devil, but the moment his head is removed, another associate takes its place as the head.

Addicts and victims of various habits must be treated in a location different from their usual environment and among different people, to separate them as much as possible from those objects which feed the "associates" and their core or source.

Becoming "de-hypnotized" is the path of self-discovery. Every great Teacher is a "de-hypnotizer," one who strips people of their glamors, illusions, vanity, and ego, and makes them sense the Self. In most cases, the presence of the Teacher dissolves the hypnotic core and its associates.

One must remember that our glamors, illusions, vanities, and egos are mostly layers of "associates." An associate is a link to the core of the habit. Sometimes great calamities, personal failures, pain, suffering, and loss destroy the core and its associates.

In the second stage of sleep, it is difficult to plant hypnotic suggestions from the physical plane. In the third stage of sleep, it is an impossibility. As one sleeps more deeply, the human soul becomes more and more awakened. A person is out of the body, but his astral or mental elemental is with him and no one or nothing can fool them.

The weeds of hypnotic suggestions are planted within us when we are in a state of shallow sleep, when the human soul is in a lethargic state. The hypnotic suggestions planted in this state can grow in immense complexity, and their cure is almost impossible due to this lethargic condition of the victim.

The science of sleep must be studied because it has great hidden treasures. Children from an early age must be educated in the science of sleep and warned about how to respect the sleep of others so that they are careful around those who are sleeping.

In the future, people will create insulated rooms where noise or conversations cannot reach those who are sleeping, and where forms cannot create rings of association. In the future, one of the most sought after sciences will be the science of sleep.

Sleep has seven stages, a few of which are known to average people. First of all, let us describe what the state of sleep is.

When the human soul steps out of the pineal gland or withdraws its anchorage from the pineal gland, we say that the person falls asleep. This withdrawal makes the etheric body detach itself from the gland; the astral body detaches from the spine; and the mental body detaches from the three glands in the head.

As stated, the first stage is etheric sleep; the second stage is astral sleep; and the third stage is mental sleep. Only initiates of higher degrees can travel beyond these three stages. The fourth stage is intuitional sleep; the fifth stage is atmic, followed by monadic and divine sleeps.

People often associate sleeping with a state of unconsciousness. This is true only in relation to the physical world, up to the fourth stage of sleep.

In the first stage of sleep, the human soul enters the etheric realm, though advanced individuals pass through this stage very quickly and enter into astral sleep. Less developed people and morally degenerate people enter only the first stage of sleep and sleep in a state that is half-sleep, half-awake, between the material and etheric planes. For them, sleep is nothing more than a physical recharging process.

Average people enjoy the astral plane in various forms of dreams related to the sense organs, pleasure or pain, suffering or happiness.

Mental sleep is a fairly advanced stage, divided into two sections — lower and higher mental planes. In the lower mental plane, the person is mostly related to karmic law and its various divisions, and occupied with worldly difficulties, obstacles, and problems. In the higher mental plane, sleep provides an experience of rare phenomena, esoteric beauty related to the human being and Nature, instructions given by Teachers or advanced Beings, deep visions or revelations, solutions or keys to solutions of world problems, and instructions related to the human soul, immortality, and others.

In the fourth stage of sleep, the human soul transcends mind and brain contact and enjoys higher experiences related to the Self, the mystery of Life. Often when the human soul enters such a state, he does not record his experiences in his mind and brain and when he becomes conscious on the physical plane, he remembers absolutely nothing. This happens because of the following reasons:

a. The communication line between the mental plane and the Intuitional Plane is not built yet, and the mind has no "language" with which to translate higher experiences.
b. The human soul thinks it is futile to register such experiences in the computer of the mind.

c. The human soul does not want to bring higher instructions, secrets, and mysteries into the mind so as to prevent those who could sneak in and take the information away to use it for self-interest, or to use it for other destructive purposes. The dark forces and their agents eagerly wait on the mental plane to steal a secret which is passed down by the human soul.

In this fourth level of sleep, a person establishes close contact with the Ashrams of the Masters and with the Hierarchy. Ashrams are mostly occupied with the Plan and with higher wisdom.

The fifth, or atmic, level of sleep is much deeper, and often Great Ones leave Their bodies for days or weeks to be there to attend to higher studies, disciplines, and service. This level and the one that follows (monadic) are mainly concerned with issues of the Cosmic Self and Divine Will.

The seventh, or divine, stage of sleep brings one into the presence of still greater Beings.

The advanced stages of sleep, from the fourth through the seventh levels, are not considered sleep but a progressively awakening state of consciousness. The higher you go while asleep, the more awakened you become. This is why "sleep" is a science. People must learn how to sleep, where to sleep, and what to avoid before going to sleep.

Science has not yet learned about the deeper layers of sleep and does not have any formulated instructions on how to sleep, where to sleep, or under what conditions to sleep. For example, animals, stagnant water, certain odors, electrical wiring and machinery, noise, certain motions, certain trees and flowers must be eliminated from areas where we sleep. Light binds the soul to the earth, except in the fourth and higher stages of sleep. Electrical and magnetic storms create heavy hindrances to the soul. In such cases, one finds it difficult to pass from one plane to the next while "asleep."

There are also emotional and mental hindrances which make it extremely difficult for the human soul to penetrate into higher realms through sleep. Fear, anger, hatred, jealousy, revenge, and slander create heavy obstacles for the human soul. Arrogance, pride, ego, greed, vanity, separatism, and certain posthypnotic suggestions do not allow a soul to pass to the higher mental plane.

Another powerful hindrance in sleep is attachment. Before sleep, one must daily exercise the discipline of detachment. Before sleep, a person must realize, or remind himself, that all that he has is perishable and can be taken from him or becomes useless if he does not return to his body.

Throughout ages, we have been told that attachment to worldly objects is considered a grave sin, especially when one causes pain and suffering to others because of his attachment to material values. We are told that those who are attached to material objects and try to hold onto them, who develop jealousy, hatred, hypocrisy, pride, deceit, greed, anger, and revenge, and try to perpetuate them, will have very painful experiences in the Subtle Worlds and will find it very difficult to sleep well.

The ancients advised us to develop detachment from all kinds of material objects and to realize that one day all will be taken from our hands. We are advised that such objects are totally useless in the Subtle Worlds. If a person does not develop detachment, he carries with him the desire for objects, and these desire-objects become hindrances on his path in the Subtle World, torturing him constantly. We are told also that those who are attached to their possessions and who think that they cannot exist without them resemble a dethroned king when entering the Subtle World.

A person who continuously breaks the law with his crimes and then is caught, brought to justice, and imprisoned is more fortunate than one who escapes the law and justice and then enters the Subtle Worlds. There he passes into the heaviest thunderstorms because the light of the Subtle Worlds reveals all that he is, and he pays a heavy price for all that he did by breaking the Law of Love.

There is a very interesting verse in the Qur'an which is related to the Subtle Worlds. It states, "We have taken away the veil from thee and thy sight today is keen."[1] We are told that after one leaves his body (the veil), if the eyes of the astral body are open, he sees himself as he is, as well as seeing all his actions in his immediate past. If his astral eyes are closed, Nature removes the veil from his eyes, and for a short time he sees his past and exactly what he is. Then he continues an unconscious life in the Subtle Worlds, just as he lived on earth.

It is interesting to note that our state of consciousness or unconsciousness depends upon the life we live on earth. There are things which obscure our consciousness; there are things which clear our consciousness. For example, every time we say something that is against our conscience or against the Laws of Love and Unity, we cast a veil upon our consciousness. These veils accumulate and eventually blind the eye of our consciousness. Then we wander in this and the next world as blind men — semi-conscious or totally unconscious of

---

1. *The Holy Qur'an*, Sura 50, verse 22.

our environment. This is why, in referring to one who has died, we sometimes say, "He slept."

Semi-conscious and conscious people feel suffering according to the degree of their identifications and attachments. The greatest punishment for people who enter the Subtle Worlds as sleeping corpses is that they do not have a chance to see the consequences of their transgressions and they do not learn any lessons until they incarnate. Thus they lose a great amount of time and continue their dark paths, accumulating heavier karma and evoking heavier punishment on earth.

Relatively speaking, to be able to suffer consciously in the Subtle Worlds is a sign of advancement, compared to being an unconscious corpse. It is the semi-conscious or blinded state of beingness that registers the most intense pain. These are "lukewarm" people or "flickering lights."

In the future, schools of preparation for departure to the Higher Worlds will be established, and people will be trained to detach themselves from all that is not-Self. Unless we cultivate such a power of detachment, we will either waste time in the Subtle Worlds, or we will be caught in a self-made web of suffering and pain.

Knowing the above, people may ask how we can live in this modern world without possessions. Can't the best products of human labor be used to live a more efficient life and create greater opportunities for us to dedicate ourselves to spiritual service? Of course one must have the best body, the best car, the best airplane, the best house, the best tools or equipment, the best furniture. But one must also

a. Be *somebody* to use them for a greater service
b. Not be identified with them and be ready to renounce them at any moment — with joy
c. Consider that they belong to Nature and are given to help increase spiritual creativity and service

Once you think that such objects are yours, for your personal pleasure and enjoyment, and once you identify yourself with them, you penetrate their existence and carry them with you as explosives into a sphere of fire.

It is possible for the human soul to pass into the higher mind or the Intuitional Plane without building the Golden Bridge between the lower mind, the higher mind, and the Intuitional planes. This happens in rare instances when the Solar Angel takes the human soul to deeper layers of "sleep" in order to

a. Give the human soul special instructions
b. Reward him for service performed for others

c. Prepare him for future opportunities or crises

In such cases, the human soul remembers his experiences because he uses the communication line of his Solar Angel. When the human soul can consciously and deliberately penetrate into the Intuitional Plane during sleep, he can go to any level of sleep and be conscious on that level or plane. But always, when the human soul enters the lower levels, his intention is to serve on those levels, rescue people, experience new forces and energies, and shed light.

One may ask: What is the difference between the etheric, astral, mental, or intuitional levels of sleep, and the conscious withdrawal of the human soul into those planes during waking consciousness? There is no great difference if the person is able to withdraw consciously without cutting his communication line with his brain.

Conscious withdrawal creates heavy pressure on the physical mechanism. Withdrawal in sleep is more natural, if the Antahkarana is built. In conscious withdrawal, the human soul often is still anchored to the pineal gland, but through his antenna he is aware of what is happening on higher planes. If the human soul in waking consciousness withdraws into higher planes without the Antahkarana, he loses brain consciousness. This happens when the Solar Angel carries him to the higher planes.

If the person is advanced, he can vacate his body and let a higher Being use it to transmit help to humanity. This is not mediumship, as a medium is limited to the astral plane and often is the circus arena for astral entities.

When a person "sleeps" by his own will and with the help of the Solar Angel, he usually penetrates into the higher mental plane or the Intuitional Plane and transmits his knowledge, experience, or wisdom through his brain in the sleeping body via the Antahkarana of the Solar Angel. This is why one who has an experience of being in a trance does not remember anything. But those people who are waiting around his body will record the delivered instructions.

The deeper one goes into sleep, the more wisdom he collects. His life becomes blissful, energetic, enthusiastic, noble, and creative. All beauty, grace, and wisdom are gained in the higher planes through the experience of sleep.

Sometimes we awaken at night and are not able to go back to sleep. At such times we must occupy ourselves by reading books of the Teaching. The reason for such awakening is that conditions in the Subtle Worlds are sometimes injurious to our astral body, and the human soul hurries back to protect the subtle vehicles. We participate in certain battles against the dark forces, against those forces which try to degenerate human life in various ways. We stand against such forces of ugliness, injustice, and heartlessness.

Sometimes the battle becomes very heavy for our subtle body and the human soul withdraws into the physical plane. We do not always remember such battles, but the tension of the subtle body passes to the heart, and the heart shows abnormal functions. This sometimes forces the human soul to withdraw from battle. This is not a sign of defeat, but a period of rest so that the battle can be continued with greater fierceness.

This is why one needs to strengthen himself by reading from the Teaching and, with that energy and renewed strength, once again enter the field of battle. It is through such battles that our subtle muscles become stronger, and gradually we learn the art of battle.

After such battles, many disciples feel exhausted when they return to their bodies. Sometimes, because of their victories, they bring a great amount of joy and energy to their bodies. It also happens that when the dark forces feel that they are losing a battle in the subtle planes, they will make the warrior return to the physical plane by causing certain tensions in his physical body. Dark forces cannot do this easily if the place where the body is sleeping is clean, if there are no animal emanations, and if there is a purifying fragrance of eucalyptus, peppermint, or a pure olive oil lamp.

The waking periods must be filled with meditation, prayer, and reading, until the soul feels that it is time again to depart to the Subtle Worlds.

Sleep and the Solar Plexus

...the solar plexus corresponds in rotation with the sun; therefore, each rotation of the solar plexus establishes a link with the Cosmic Magnet.... Therefore, it is most essential to protect the solar plexus from tension after sunset. [2]

This is the reason why Christ said that before sunset you must settle your conflicts and forgive each other.

Hatred and thoughts of animosity continued during the night reverse the rotation of the solar plexus, and this creates various negative consequences, such as:

---

2. Agni Yoga Society, *Infinity II* (New York: Agni Yoga Society, 1957), para. 300.

1. Digestive problems
2. Liver and pancreas problems
3. Problems in the prostate and generative organs

To keep the rotation of the solar plexus normal, a person must do the following:

—cleanse the poison with which he loaded his system
—avoid negative and hostile thinking
—forgive and have loving understanding
—compensate for all the damage he caused to others
—take hot baths with a small amount of wormwood oil added

Most people exit from the solar plexus during sleep. When the rotation of the solar plexus is reversed, the sleep of a person is disturbed. The person will thus have difficulty departing and difficulty returning and will carry negativity into the subtle and earthly spheres.

When the solar plexus is reversed, it puts strong pressure on the heart and head centers and thus disturbs the balance of the human being. It is most probable that the person will start thinking and feeling in negative ways.

The solar plexus is a central station for most human beings. It has higher and lower sections. Most of the healing energies come to the body through the higher part of the solar plexus. When the rotation of the entire solar plexus is reversed, there is no way to receive healing energies.

When the reversed rotation of the solar plexus continues, the health of the person slowly deteriorates, and in addition his relations with people become negative, harmful, and regretful.

You can see the reversal of the solar plexus in the eyes of people. You can see it in their manners and conversations. Such people are called "reversed" people. They reverse things that they hear and use in a reversed way all that they learn. One must observe these people to learn about the effects of reversal.

Our solar plexus temporarily reverses itself when we listen to slander and gossip, and if we engage in such behavior ourselves, the reversed condition becomes permanent.

While asleep, such people experience tension and "reverse" dreams in the Subtle World. If other centers start reversing themselves, such people experience nightmares, sometimes continuously.

There are many ways to remove such a condition of reversal. But when you are already in reverse rotation, it is as difficult to save yourself as it is to save a boat that is close to a waterfall. However, prayers, heavy labor, wormwood, massage, and healthy companions can minimize the danger.

There are two important factors which make our life richer and happier. One is forgiveness; the other one is good memories.

Forgiving is one way by which you may save your life and the life of others. Good memories are like automatic lubricants that oil your machinery and make them function properly.

The solar plexus lubricates a vast area in the human body, and if it is reversed, the lubrication does not do its job.

Good memories are like sunshine, food, joy, and energy on the path of our life.[3]

When we increase our good memories, we help all our centers to rotate in their natural way. Good memories are sources of joy, and there is no better food for the centers than joy.

Bad memories deprive us of joy, and when they are mixed with the spirit of unforgiveness, they slow down the rotation of the centers and can even reverse their rotation.

The more good memories we have, the brighter will be our thinking, the more joyful will be our emotions, and the more vital will be our physical body.

It is very interesting to realize that good memories have a deep relation to the spirit of forgiveness. Life is very tough, and we pass through the thorns of life unharmed only through the spirit of forgiveness.

Centers in our bodies are distributors of life energy. If they are in proper rotation, they bring in the life energy. If they revolve in reverse, they exhaust the life energy, just like certain pumps which remove water when they are turned in reverse and fill an area with water when they rotate properly.

During the process of death it is observed that centers begin to rotate in reverse. The reverse motion starts with the solar plexus. When centers are rotating properly they bring the fires of the spiritual Core of man to vitalize the vehicles and create a state of balance between internal fires and the fires of Space.

Through striving and meditation we direct these fiery energies, brought in from our Inner Core, to the fields of our service.

Our overall mechanism needs the energies of love, joy, and prana, and the currents of these energies are interrupted by bad memories,

---

3. See *Joy and Healing* for specific exercises on joy.

harmful actions, and revengeful tensions. All these cause the centers to reverse their rotation, starting with the solar plexus.

21

Flights

Those disciples who are ready to experiment with certain flights within the Subtle Worlds go through certain disciplines to learn how to leave their body consciously.

There are many kinds of flights:

1. Around the world, which is called flight within the earth sphere
2. Within the astral world of the planet
3. Within the mental world of the planet
4. Travel between our world and other planets
5. Travel within the Intuitional Plane
6. Travel beyond the Solar System but within the galaxy
7. Travel between galaxies

For each flight, a corresponding body is used. For each flight, corresponding centers and senses are prepared so that the human being properly contacts and registers his contact with the sphere and transfers it to his brain.

If the bridge between the brain and higher bodies is not built, one cannot remember any out of body experience.

Such flights are not taken by oneself. Solar Angels or Guides teach their students how to travel. Everyone has his own Guide.

There are many rules and laws of travel that one needs to learn. The subjective flights have resemblances to the flights of airplanes. Flights have special rules and laws: they need weather information, and they must be guided by radio communications with their towers. Subjective flights have similar needs.

In the Subtle Worlds there are serious conditions which must be considered, for example:

1. Electromagnetic storms and varying pressures
2. Strong currents of energies
3. Explosions and radioactive currents crossing each other
4. Solar and galactic winds charged with fire

5. Layers of accumulated negative and lustful thoughts
6. Tides of human emotions
7. Armies of dark forces

The flight must be carried on in safety, knowing all these possible conditions.

Some people who try to take flight without preparation burn their astral and mental bodies and suffer for years in their physical bodies. Most of the physical illnesses are the result of various shocks, wounds, and burns that people's subtle bodies received in their premature flights.

Premature flights are common. Excessive aspiration, excitement, extreme desire, and an urge to be out of the body make people prematurely face subjective conditions for which they are not ready.

Some people are wounded by their enemies, even by dark forces. Some people are totally burned by the fire of Space. Some people are heavily damaged by energy currents, and they slowly experience physical, emotional, and mental disorders but never think that their causes lie in subjective flights.

Some Teachers even suggest that people can be contaminated during their etheric and astral flights, if they are caught in storms and contact areas of the planet that are contaminated in various ways.

Some of our physical plane enemies who do not dare approach us on the physical plane sometimes demonstrate power, energy, and superiority in the subtle planes. They attack us in various ways and hurt us to such a degree that very soon our physical body shows the signs of various sicknesses or diseases.

This is why Teachers advise us to solve our problems before sunset so that we do not have confrontations in the Subtle Worlds.

M.M. says, "Urusvati was restrained several times from undertaking extremely dangerous flights. The Teacher must protect one from over-courageous investigations. The higher spheres scorch like the heat of the sun. The lower spheres are oppressive for the higher consciousness, and it is impossible to fly through all the spheres, for the subtle body would be consumed. The flight to the higher spheres must be gradual."[1]

There is special training to prepare people for subjective flights. Such training is graded in the following steps:

---

1. Agni Yoga Society, *Supermundane,* unpublished writings.

1. Physical, emotional, and mental purity and increasing compassion
2. Demonstration of sacrificial service for a long time
3. Knowledge about the Higher Worlds
4. Strong devotion, dedication, and striving toward Hierarchy
5. Control over emotions and mind in daring conditions
6. Fearlessness
7. Total trust in the Guide or Teacher
8. Obedience to details
9. Patience to follow instructions, again and again
10. Perseverance, stability, and courage

When the lessons of these ten courses are learned, the Guide urges the person to develop continuity of consciousness. Then the training for the flights begins.

First, you learn how to withdraw consciously from your body.

Second, you learn to visit places of esoteric learning, groups, schools, and Ashrams.

Third, you learn how to visit places where you can bring consolation, love, friendship, forgiveness, understanding.

Fourth, you visit places hit with natural calamities or wars to save those you can and console those who need consolation.

Fifth, you learn to travel to higher planets... and your training never ends as you prepare to contact higher spheres for study and service.

Of course, all these travels are not without danger.

Remember that enemies are everywhere, equipped not only with earthly weapons but also with astral and mental weapons which can cause extreme damage to your subtle bodies if you are not protected, or if you are not an experienced warrior.

We are told that nothing can be achieved without courage and daring, without effort and striving. Sooner or later we must learn how to travel in Space and fulfill our higher destination. If such is the case, why not start our training now?

The applicants for the art of flight must consider that it is not their knowledge and information that urge them to flights, but it is their heart.

They must learn how to make their knowledge change into feeling and fill their heart. Except the heart feels like flying and wants to take risks and be ready for heroic actions, a person cannot do anything. The mind, with all its knowledge, cannot be ready for flights. That is why most of the encyclopedic minds are earthbound, and they stay around their beds, or books, all night in their sleep. It is only the heart that prompts them to expand their space and come in contact with higher spheres. Knowledge and information must transform into feeling and fill the heart to the brim. It is from that moment on that the urge and daring to fly begin in the soul of man.

Most people do not know yet that feeling is not emotion. Feeling is a mixture of knowledge, subjective awareness, identification with the greater Universe, and a response to the high calling of the Soul.

One of the most important things to mention is that spatial flight needs certain sensitive centers within our astral and mental bodies to measure the intensity of light during the travel. The most damage can come to our bodies in exposing ourselves to the intense lights of the luminaries.

This is why we need a Guide who will be able to lead us through paths that are not flooded with intense light.

Certain lights in Space can permanently damage our subtle centers, senses, and organs, which immediately or slowly affect their corresponding organs in the physical body.

Such lights in the Subtle World can also alter our genes and DNA very considerably. Research work in the future will prove that some changes in our DNA occur after certain flights in our sleep.

Some lights can be beneficial if we are exposed to them in such a way that we receive the right dosage of light. Light especially affects our brain, sensitivity, consciousness, and creativity. Teachers take extreme caution when they prepare us for spatial flights. They choose the moments in which the planets, luminaries, and constellations are in a special configuration. They also consider a person's sun sign and rising sign for spatial flights because such factors make them choose the proper time for flight. This means that some special flights are not always permitted or pleasant. Sometimes to find the right time for flight for a person takes sixty to seventy years. But as the person learns the art of flying and trains himself in perseverance to conquer hindrances, his wings grow — so to say — and he can try more dangerous flights gradually until he becomes a "space traveler."

One of the victories that a human being must achieve is victory over space. As years go by, people will understand more what it means to conquer space and why it is imperative to conquer it.

22

Interest in the Higher Worlds

It is very important to think, meditate, read, discuss, and accumulate information about the Higher Worlds and to accustom ourselves to the conditions of the Higher Worlds; but the most important thing is to expand our consciousness so that it always orients itself toward the future and enables us to understand our contacts and experiences related to the Higher Worlds. Information without an expanded consciousness is like eating without digestion.

Expansion of consciousness is related to the unfoldment of the higher centers and senses. When these centers and senses are dormant, one cannot appreciate and understand higher contact. He cannot experience the beauty and significance of the Higher Worlds. Expansion of consciousness can be achieved when the information collected with discrimination is put into experimentation and practice.[1]

When the consciousness expands, it leads you toward the future; it contracts if you look toward the past. In looking toward the past, you become trapped in the values of the past and miss the higher correspondences of the values of the future.

We are told that daring is a great virtue and that without developing daring one cannot contact the fires of Space and enter the Fiery World. Daring is the ability to bypass the fears of the personality and penetrate into the world of the unknown. This virtue can be developed throughout many lives, if the human soul achieves fearlessness and uses his will to penetrate into the unknown.

Daring is the combination of the ray of fearlessness, the ray of the purposeful will, and the ray of humility. Without humility there is no true daring. Humility provides balance and equilibrium on the path of

---

1. For further information regarding higher centers and senses, please refer to *The Psyche and Psychism*, Chapters 12-15.

ascent. Through each step of daring, we expand our consciousness and appreciate the beauty of the Higher Worlds.

People have the heritage and the privilege to enjoy the Higher Worlds, but they sell their heritage for worldly pleasures. Pleasure seeking people change as soon as they come in contact with the beauty of the Fiery World. The beauty of the Fiery World fills their whole nature with joy, and life turns into an experience of joy.

People sometimes think that it is impractical and useless to speak about the Higher Worlds. They say that it does not increase their income. But we spoke and thought about the possibility of traveling to the moon and other planets long before we took practical steps toward it. Faith is an intuitive awareness of things that exist beyond our mental reasoning. First we must create the vision toward a goal which we feel exists.

The object of our faith and hope must be sensed as a vision. Before this vision is achieved, we must orient all our thoughts and aspirations toward the vision and create a great energy field of interest and expectation. It is this field of interest and expectation which will attract those elements and conditions which will enable the vision to be actualized.

The Higher Worlds are within us. We must come in contact with them by tuning in our frequency to the frequency of the Higher Worlds.

It is very possible that when people speak, read, and think about the Higher Worlds they feel a tremor in their hearts, a joy in their hearts. They see a new horizon in their mind. These are called the messengers of the Higher Worlds which reach us and encourage us to keep on toward the Fiery Worlds.

A group of students in our school were impossible to control and could not keep their consciousness focused on any object. They were too wild, too scattered, and too disinterested in what the teachers wanted to teach.

When this fact came to my attention, I felt that it would be possible to create a focus in the class through talking about the Higher Worlds. As the principal, I went to the class and at once said, "Did anybody in this class ever leave his body during the night and have any dream experiences, or contact, or anything?"

There was a great silence.

"Do you know," I said, "that we can fly after we leave our bodies in sleep? Do you know that we are not bodies? Do you know that space is not empty? Do you know that we will live in Higher Worlds when our bodies die?"

There was no movement. All were looking at me as if they were filling their hearts with a new hope.

"Well, why not investigate?" And while we were talking about the Higher Worlds, a teacher knocked at the door and informed me that the other teachers had been waiting for two hours.

A miracle happened at that moment. The class in one voice shouted, "No, we want to continue!"

The next day when we had a teachers' meeting they asked me what I had spoken to the students about that was able to hold their attention for two hours.

"I spoke about the Higher Worlds."

"Higher Worlds!" asked the mouths of all the teachers there.

"Yes, the Higher Worlds. What is wrong with that? If you cannot get their attention with the objects of the lower worlds, I can get their attention with the Higher Worlds."

"But what are the Higher Worlds?" the teachers asked.

I repeated my speech to the teachers as I had given it to the class. When our conversation was over, it was late, the classes had ended, and the students had departed for the day.

This event brought important things: enthusiasm, endless questioning and discussion, and a very unexpected harmony and respect in the school.

When one speaks, thinks, and reads about the Higher Worlds, the energy of striving, harmony, and enthusiasm fills his soul because the soul is a pilgrim longing for his home. The regeneration of consciousness and the strengthening of the spirit of striving can come only through information about and experience of the Higher Worlds.

CHAPTER

23

Fire in the
Subtle World

After one crosses into the Subtle World, the presence of malice in him blinds the vision and breaks the possibility of communication with worthy spirits. We are told that malice emanates a black fire which consumes the network of communication and the accumulations of psychic savings.

Slander is another impediment which attracts elements of fire from the Subtle World and burns away many precious centers in man. This is why, throughout the ages, malice and slander were condemned by great Teachers.

When one enters into the Subtle World, he will see the tongues of fire awaiting him. This is actually a form of hell into which many people enter and burn their wings, until a drop of goodness remaining from the past in their hearts awakens and urges them to proceed out of the fire.

We are told that thoughts of slander and malice attract numerous low-level elementals which hang around a person, preventing him from coming in contact with the forces of freedom or liberation. [1]

Most depressions, anguish, and irritation are caused by the thoughts of slander and malice as they burn the network of *nadis* [2] which are the instruments that collect drops or waves of joy and bliss. One cannot cure a person from depression, irritation, and anguish until the possibility of malice and slander is annihilated in him. The fire created by these two vices burns the roots of many future possibilities.

There are also the fires of virtues, which, as they accumulate, increase the glow of the aura and make it a sphere of fire of many

---

1. Further information about the elementals can be found in *The Psyche and Psychism*, Chapter 17.
2. *Nadis* are the etheric counterparts of the nerves.

harmonious colors. This fire not only protects the man but also nourishes and strengthens every seed of beauty and every center in the various vehicles. The fires of virtues build a network of communication with Higher Worlds and expel any dark attack from lower elementals.

There is also the fire of renunciation. Renunciation generates a violet fire which builds a direct path toward the Fiery World. This path turns into a channel of blessings which pour from fiery spheres.

Every form or act of renunciation, no matter of what size, increases your internal fire. Eventually at the Fourth Initiation it destroys the Chalice[3] and releases the jewel,[4] the True Self. Such a liberation can never be achieved without accumulating the fires of renunciation. This is why the Fourth Initiation[5] is called the Initiation of Crucifixion, or the Initiation of Renunciation.

The fires of the elements try to destroy the construction of the advancing spirit. The fires of the spirit not only annihilate the fires of the elements, but they also build the path of ascent. Psychic energy is the sumtotal of spiritual fires.

The fires of the elements build the ego and lead man into separatism. The fires of the spirit annihilate the formations of the ego and bridge all cleavages.

Every ego is a condensation of a destructive fire.

Every unity, every synthesis is the result of the labor of the fires of spirit.

An ego cannot pass beyond the threshold of the lower astral plane. Before one climbs into the mental plane, he leaves behind his ego, but unfortunately the ego waits to stick with him when he is on the way back to reincarnation. Upon return, the man hates his ego, but it sticks to him nevertheless.

During the worldly life the ego, step by step, creeps along with the man. Chances are given to the person to destroy his ego and liberate himself or to make his ego the prison of his soul and an instrument of destruction.

Those who occasionally enter into the Fiery World see the uselessness of egoism, and they take higher measures to destroy that dark formation. One can fight egoism and extinguish its dark fires by dedicating oneself to the service of humanity and the Hierarchy. Unless

---

3. Please see Chapter 12, *The Science of Becoming Oneself.*
4. *Ibid.*
5. Please see Chapter 12, *Christ, The Avatar of Sacrificial Love.*

the fires of egoism are dissipated, the expansion of consciousness will be an impossibility.

One must also observe those who are the builders of egos. Mothers, fathers, various kinds of friends, political parties, and groups are sometimes dedicated to that unworthy cause: building the ego. Man can be exploited very easily when the ego is built in him. To punish a man and make his life and his future miserable, build an ego in him.

Groups and nations are not destroyed by attackers of various kinds but by the growth of individual, group, and national egos. For the forces of darkness, this is not a secret.

The Subtle World is divided into three spheres:

a. Lower sphere
b. Middle sphere
c. Higher sphere

The lower sphere is often called the valley of pain, suffering, horror, and crime. The lowest stratum of this world is called the satanic sphere, where the light does not penetrate. Decomposing astral bodies which emanate heavy odors exist there. Such odors sometimes even reach the physical nostrils, and people smell them in various locations where heavy decomposition takes place.

One must be prepared on earth not to enter or be trapped in these spheres.

In the lower stratum of the Subtle World there are the most ugly formations and constructions of evil emotions, glamors, and crimes. In critical times the Forces of Light attack this fortress of evil and destroy it to enable the aspiring soul to proceed forward. This creates its effect on earth, and dark forces intensify their attempt and try to take revenge on those who are associated with the Forces of Light. But those who stand in beauty, goodness, and justice have the protection of the Cosmic Power.

The abolition of lower astral forms is done by the fiery rays of the warriors. A massive destruction takes place in the Subtle World which cuts the energy flow from the forces of darkness to their agents on earth.

Fire is a purifier, and in the Teaching the possibility is given to purify this earth through the fire of the Teaching. If the fire of reason and love fails, purification by the fire of destruction will take over. Let us remember Sodom and Gomorrah!

People on earth can hasten their progress by destroying specific constructions before they enter into the Subtle World and thus pave their way to the higher strata of the Subtle World. These constructions are thoughtforms, plans, motives of various crimes; hatred, treason, revenge; vanities of various kinds; and glamors of many colors. If these constructions are cleared before a person enters into the Subtle World, he will not be trapped in the lower strata.

Volcanic eruptions are part of the battle in the Subtle World. When the fire hits certain locations of the astral sphere to wipe away many obstructions, the corresponding fire from the earth rushes up to join in the battle and burn away the falling debris of the destruction. Thus, volcanic actions are controlled by the principle of purification.

The devas of the mountains are fiery devas, and they participate in the battle against dark forces.

Earthquakes are also used to clear away many obstructions created by the human hand. They are evoked by the destructive thoughts of human beings.

Hurricanes are controlled by mental entities, and they use hurricanes to clear away many thought formations; or they accumulate them in certain locations to burn through the power of lightning and thunder. This will seem like superstition to our scientists for a long time to come.

Cataclysms in the Subtle World are recorded on seismographs, just as our emotions and thoughts are recorded by the lie detector.

In essence, all three of these worlds — the physical, emotional, and mental — are closely interrelated with each other. On any plane you can find evidences of events going on on any other plane.

The decomposition occurring upon the lowest stratum of the Subtle World contains very contagious germs and viruses which can be brought down to earthly bodies through mediums and necromancy. Epidemics are astral phenomena. If careful research is done, one will find out that the infecting source came through one who was in contact with the lowest spheres through necromancy or mediumistic activities.

Sometimes great explosions take place in the Subtle World. These explosions create pressures in different layers of the atmosphere and even change our climate in the same way that emotional "explosions" change our blood pressure, our body temperature, the secretion of our glands, etc.

People think that bad weather, droughts, famines, and tornadoes originate from physical causes, whereas their causes lie in the lower levels of the Subtle World.

The middle sphere of the Subtle World can be called the sphere of recovery and rest. After the continuous nightmare in the lower stratum, the human soul eventually finds his way into the middle level.

The higher sphere of the Subtle World is the sphere of harmony, joy, and beauty, where the human ego totally dissolves. Many artistic souls are found there, with their music, colors, and dances.

The human heart is very sensitive to the Subtle World. Those who have an unfolded heart are sensitive to the higher strata of the Subtle World. Those who have a petrified heart are sensitive to the lower strata of the Subtle World.

The heart registers many subtle attacks. Sudden, irregular heartbeats may be the result of attack from the Subtle World, or the result of an attempt to pass energy to the person from the Subtle World.

Many moves and events in the Subtle World which are related to the person noticeably change his heartbeat. When there is a sudden obsession from the Subtle World, it affects the pulse and may even stop it.

Fiery communications expand the joy and love of the heart. The pulse regulates itself during such experiences, as if a burden is taken from the heart.

The increase of heart disease is also a sign that the lower sphere of the Subtle World is infecting the planet.

Beauty is the Path leading toward the Higher Worlds, beauty in thoughts, words, forms, manners, and relationships. Any expression which runs in harmony with the principle of progressive perfection is beautiful. Beauty is the process toward perfection. Ugliness is a disturbance, a distortion, and a retrogression on the Path of life.

The Teaching warns us about the lower sphere and suggests special caution by those who are on the Path to avoid having any communication with that sphere. This is the sphere with which mediums generally come in contact and where the egos are built.

We are told that the inhabitants of the middle sphere do not like to have any contact with earthly dwellers because they remind them of the earthly life, and they feel very irritated. The emanations from the astral bodies of the visitors upset and disturb them. They do not like to give any subjective help to those who approach them. They want to rest from the horrors of the world and the lower planes.

The higher sphere has many beautiful souls who manifest beauty, rhythm, and great aspirations toward the Fiery World, but they are not ready to offer anything to earth dwellers.

One can contact these spheres and see the beauty of communication and the standards of value existing there, but he cannot use the dwellers for his petty problems.

It is not impossible to establish telepathic communication with the dwellers in the Fiery World.

There are many signs of communication by which we feel that relations between the two worlds are achieved. First, when an inhabitant of the higher spheres begins thinking about us, we feel a tremor in our heart; an uplifting, joyful sensation; an expansion of Space; and very often a burning or cold icy ring around our head. We may feel a great silence, as if we were suddenly cut off from all audible and inaudible noise. Sometimes we smell a fragrance of rare quality which penetrates into our bones. Or we may see light in many formations. Our skin and hair may respond with a special sensation of approaching energy.

Various centers can be the focus of communication. Our heart center may respond, or the head center may be the one receiving impressions. If we observe carefully, we will have many discoveries and revelations about our centers and how spatial communications affect them.

Some higher souls can even project their image and in rare cases make their voice audible.

Along with these communications, when one is etherically and astrally loose or disconnected, he experiences many unfortunate interferences from dark forces and from the inhabitants of etheric and lower astral spheres. These forces imitate the signs of the higher contact and lead a man into confusion and destruction.

It is possible to contact the Fiery World from the earth level or from the Subtle World. It is also possible to ascend into the Fiery World from the Subtle World.

We are told that when the time comes for a soul to enter into the Fiery World he passes through a transformation. A great Teacher calls this "the most beautiful transformation." On the higher astral planes, the subtle body of the soul goes through a process of purification. As a result of such a purification, the subtle body shines because of the increasing fire radiating within the Core of the soul. The fire slowly spreads all over the subtle body, and slowly the subtle body falls away and turns into ashes.

Those astral corpses that exist in the astral world belong to the inhabitants of the lower and middle strata.

The human soul, like a radioactive flame, proceeds into the Fiery World. In the beauty and light of the Fiery World, the newcomer, the human soul, enters as a dim light, as a candle in the light of the Sun. This candle does not stay a candle, but gradually greater light is released from the soul's Core, as a response to the fiery colors, beauty, and glory of the Fiery World.

The Fiery World is also divided into many "mansions" — lower, middle, and higher. On each level dwell great sources of light, great creative spirits, in divine rhythm and beauty.

The bodies of the inhabitants are built of green, blue, and red lights. Green is the color of the etheric and lower astral planes. Blue begins after the lower astral plane ends. The blue turns into silvery, sky-blue in the higher astral plane. In the beginning of the mental plane you see pure violet, orange, and red. Red then turns into crimson or ruby red, with all other colors scintillating around the aura.

The consciousness in the Fiery World is extremely pure and clear. In the Subtle World the consciousness begins to awaken until it approaches the Fiery World. In the Fiery World total awakening of the consciousness takes place. Because of such an awakening, the field of contact of the human soul expands to a considerable degree. The Chalice opens in full, and the essence radiates out like a rainbow mist.

Communication in the Fiery World is instantaneous, and if the inhabitants want, they can see and hear all that is going on upon the earth.

Every thought that we create will exist in Space for long ages, and we will meet our thoughts after we leave the astral world. Between the astral world and the Fiery World exists the thought world, which is a sphere by itself. In this sphere every human being has his own thought which is related to him through his particular frequency.

Those thoughts which do not correspond to Beauty, Goodness, and Truth, and are against Joy and Freedom are called *barrier-thoughts*. After you leave the Subtle World, you are drawn into the web of such thoughts. You literally smite yourself against your own thoughts. You are even caught in them for a long period of time, until you find ways to release yourself. This is a kind of purification process in which you learn serious lessons and decide to be very careful not to repeat the creation of *barrier-thoughts*. Thus, at the gates of the Fiery World you pass through a great humiliation, as you realize that all your thoughts on earth which were ugly, non-compassionate, and false are against Joy and Freedom in the Higher Worlds. This causes a delay on your path.

This delay can be not only long but also extremely painful to your mental body, which has been preparing itself to carry you to the Fiery World. So many noble souls are delayed at the gates of the Fiery World because of their unhealthy, inharmonious, and superficial, as well as their low caliber, thoughts. It is after the burning of the parts of this web that the spider or human soul liberates himself and enters into the Higher Worlds, often in great humiliation.

Of course, you may also have magnificent thought formations in the thought world which encourage and cheer you, but you also feel the trap of being caught in your own thoughts. The interesting thing is that this is a period in which you do not condemn anybody else for your condition. You clearly see why, how, and when you worked hard to build the trap in which you are caught.

In the Subtle World and the Fiery World, the highest keynote is constant labor, endless and untiring labor, and absolute fearlessness. The great Teachers advise us to develop these qualities always, everywhere, as much as possible, and to be ready for the Higher Worlds. Thus one must never have a time when nothing is done. The Teaching even refers to rest as a changing form of labor and not as inertia or laziness. One must develop the love for endless labor, rejoice over each opportunity for labor, and develop fearlessness.

In some esoteric schools, people pass through many frightening tests in order to develop fearlessness. We are told that only the highest self-control and readiness for danger can prepare one for the Fiery Spheres.

From childhood one can gradually be prepared for self-control and for fearlessness.

At the gates of the Fiery World, one must radiate the shield of fearlessness and wear the helmet of self-control, if he wants the fiery gates to open for him. Thus, before it is too late, people must prepare themselves for the future.

When this Teaching becomes part of the consciousness of humanity, people will be saved much suffering and pain, and they will have a better world in the future. Such a Teaching does not present you with an image of horror and despair, but rather presents things as they are and challenges you to achieve the great joy of meeting the challenges and victoriously going forward on the Path of Infinity.

With fearlessness and Self-control, with the joy of victory and future, one can overcome all barriers and meet the great Light-Bearers in the Higher Worlds.

24

Battle and the Subtle Worlds

According to the Ageless Wisdom, there were many "wars in heaven." The first one occurred before our solar system came into existence. This was between forces who intended to build this solar system out of the matter of Space and those who did not want it to be built.

Those who did not want the solar system to come into being were forces of dissolution and chaos; they did not want the objectivity and condensation in Space to hinder their free flow.

The second "war in heaven" occurred when angels and devas wanted to incarnate in human form to help educate and take care of the condensing human beings. This happened in the Third Root Race, the Lemurian Race, when the sexes were divided into male and female. The ethereal beings of the Third Race were condensing and becoming material, losing their freedom to a certain degree, and trying to adjust themselves to the similarly hardening globe, our Earth.[1]

The third "war in heaven" happened during the time when the great entities began to organize the Center called Hierarchy.

These three subjective wars are echoed in our worldly wars, the first one of which was the war between Atlantis and the "Sacred Island."

The second war began in 1914 and ended in 1945 when the Forces of Light and Christ defeated the forces of darkness with His army in 1943-1945.

The third global war may destroy this planet, if the Higher Forces from the Stronghold do not interfere.

---

1. For further information on this topic, please refer to *Cosmos in Man*, Chapter 1, and *The Legend of Shamballa*.

There is a legend of the three swords. This legend is engraved in the form of three swords on a stone in the Himalayas. The legend indicates that these three swords refer to the three global wars, which are the most critical moments in the life of the planet. If humanity can pass these three periods, then Nature will open its doors and man will achieve undreamed of glories.

The next major global war may be the third one of the legend, which may be a war of fire and flame during which all civilization and culture may be wiped away. It is possible that no one will survive this war, and the planet will be removed from the chain.

These are the "fairy tales" of the Ageless Wisdom which seem to be more scientific than any other forecasts. If humanity prevents such a war, or if by higher intervention it is stopped, a new life will start on this planet in which people will strive toward the stars and toward spiritual perfection.

People have the opinion that beyond the physical world nothing exists, or that there are either pleasures or hell. However, they forget that the subtle planes are often fields of great battles where human entities fight against each other with great zeal, or fight against those forces which try to stop the evolution of humanity.

The fight between human entities takes place only upon the lower astral plane, but the fight against the dark forces takes place in the Fiery World and even in the higher astral plane and on the physical plane as well. Many departed ones are engaged in these battles. In addition, many of the people on the physical plane are engaged in these battles during their sleep and often during their waking hours.

People on the physical plane sometimes have more difficult tasks. When sleeping, they fight against dark ones on the subtle levels, and they fight against evil human beings on the astral plane. In their waking consciousness, they fight against the representatives of dark forces on the physical plane. In esoteric literature such people are called warriors who, in their love for humanity and its future, dedicate their lives to battle against all those forces which bring degeneration, corruption, crime, retrogression, inertia, hatred, and desire for matter and separatism.

No battle is an easy one. Once you are a warrior, you can be under continuous attack by dark forces — who carefully watch all your steps. This is why you must arm yourself with weapons of the spirit to conquer your enemies. These spiritual weapons are your

—Discipline
—Pure and powerful thoughts
—Pure aspirations, goodwill, and spirit of right human relations

—Courage, daring, and striving
—Sense of unity and synthesis
—Integrity, honesty, and nobility
—Sincerity and simplicity
—Love, dedication, and devotion to a great cause
—Spiritual maturity
—Good Karma
—Silent mouth
—Harmlessness
—Watchful spirit
—Sensitivity and magnetism

You use all these weapons to dispel the darkness, hatred, revenge, ignorance, separatism, and inertia. Of course, your army is formed by millions and backed by the Hierarchy of Light and the Tower of Shamballa, the Lord of which is aware of everyone who fights in the name of Beauty, Goodness, Righteousness, Joy, and Freedom.

Battle is battle. War is war. People die in battle; people are wounded; people lose some of their organs, limbs. They become unconscious; they suffer and pass through intense psychological disturbances. This happens not only in the worldly battles but also in the battles of the Subtle Worlds.

In the subjective battles the most important thing to realize is that you are a pure light in your essence; you are an indestructible immortal spirit, and no one, nothing, can kill you or wound you or destroy you. If you reach such an awareness through many experiences, you are a warrior whom no one can conquer. But if you identify with your body, with your astral and mental bodies, you can be wounded or even killed, until one day you realize that it was not you but your body that was wounded or killed.

Realization of your supreme Self as an immortal, imperishable being is the strongest weapon in your hand. Captains and commanders of the Armies of Light choose their warriors according to the consciousness of the warriors.

Not everyone can fight against organized and highly trained forces of darkness. Those who are not ready for such fights do other work to make the real fighters do their job. Promotion in the spiritual work does not mean letting you have more pleasures in the gardens of the subjective world and sing psalms during all eternity while watching those who are burning in hell. On the contrary, promotion on the Spiritual Path means making you a greater warrior in greater and more dangerous wars. This is why Teachers suggest that those who are in training for spiritual life learn how to dare, how to be courageous, how to be fearless, how to keep equilibrium in the presence of horror. All these are preparations to validate you to be a warrior in the Subtle World.

When a person is still on the physical plane and he takes part in the subjective battles, he manifests certain signs, even if he is not yet conscious about participating in the battle in the Subtle Worlds. People engage in battles long before they become aware of them. They participate in battles because of their intense sense of righteousness, freedom, honesty, nobility, and beauty. They stand for these values, and their hearts lead them into battle to protect and perpetuate these values. All wars, all battles on the physical plane, are first won in the subtle planes. The outer victory is only the echo of the victory achieved in the subtle planes.

What are the signs of one who is fighting in the subjective battles? They are as follows:

1. Insomnia. Those who take part in the battles of the Subtle World may strain their astral body to such a degree that on the physical plane they cannot use it for some time to re-enter into the astral plane — which is where sleep is.

It may be that the astral body is in shock; it may be that the warrior is afraid to enter into the astral plane because of the astral enemies. It may be that the protective hand is withdrawn because of some reason. It may be that he was defeated badly. It may be that he abandoned the field. All these and other causes make one unable to sleep.

There is another kind of insomnia which is the result of an immense victory over dark forces and an intense joy. In this case, insomnia does not weaken the body, and in a short time the warrior is again called for the battle.

There is also insomnia caused by forces which reject the soul who is entering the Subtle World. One of the reasons is that they wish to protect him in certain moments when the battle is really intense, and he is not considered to be ready at that moment to participate.

It also happens that if one insists on passing into sleep, he may never return again if he is caught in the whirlpool of the battle.

2. Weakness of body, inertia, mysterious pains. When the astral body is wounded, the corresponding part on the physical body feels the pain. Inertia comes into existence when the subtle body is beaten very badly. Weakness is the result of exhaustion of the astral body.

People can overcome their symptoms through meditation, prayer, rest, good food, herbs, and taking vacations in the mountains. All these accumulate psychic energy once again, which repairs the astral body and makes it ready for fighting once more.

3. Mental disturbances. Some people are good fighters because of their good heart qualities, and they fight on the astral or etheric planes with success. If these people are exposed to certain drugs, because of the fire of the drugs they decide to fight on the mental plane. Because of their ignorance of the higher techniques of war on the mental plane and because of their unreadiness for battle, such warriors hurt their mental nature very badly.

Drugs hurt their nervous system and brain. The battle on the mental plane wounds their mental body, and the results are

a. Mental disturbances
b. Insanity
c. Severe damage of the mental body which cannot be healed by any physical means

This is why people must be introduced to the Teaching very slowly, and no more Teaching should be given to one who cannot live the Teaching he has.

In its pure reality, the Teaching is the training instruction for war and battle against hostile forces.

An aspirant, a disciple, an Initiate, and a Master are actually army officers. This army fights only for Beauty, Goodness, Righteousness, Joy, and Freedom.

Those who are full of vanities, self-interests, hatred, jealousy, revenge, and separatism are not qualified to enter into the Army of Light. Often such people fight by the side of the Forces of Light, trying to cause great damage and disturbances in the actions of the Forces of Light.

In the Teaching, Christ is the Commander of the Army of Light. Melchizedek is the King, the greatest Warrior on this planet. The great Army is divided into forty-nine wings, and on each wing a Commander is appointed. These commanders are Sixth and Seventh Degree Initiates. Most of the Initiates have a fiery sword on Their forehead which directs the flow of energy beams of intense power.

4. Various physical sicknesses. These are of astral origin and mostly related to the lymphatic system: the glands, circulation, and blood. They must be treated medically and psychologically.

5. Continuous irritability. This is the result of damage to the astral body. The cure is rest. The use of wormwood, musk, and eucalyptus are also helpful.[2]

6. A certain kind of depression. This originates from facing astral enemies, being overwhelmed by the power they present, and feeling that one can do nothing against evil. Such a depression can be cured if the person is led to certain victories, and self-confidence is cultivated in him. It is also possible to give certain visualization exercises in which imaginative battles are won very successfully. Depression consumes many elements in the brain, but self-confidence and courage produce these very elements.

Very often man does not remember these battles because of the lack of continuity of consciousness, but as he continues to fight, gradually his entire attitude in life changes. He begins to fight in society for the rights of people. He tries to annihilate social injustice, to improve living conditions, to protect people who are under heavy exploitation. Such people are the jewels of society, but opposing dark forces hate them and eventually kill them. Martin Luther King, Gandhi, and Abraham Lincoln are in this category, as well as many other reformers in many nations on earth.

The fight for Beauty, Goodness, Righteousness, Joy, and Freedom must start on the physical plane, and the fighter must prove that he can handle complicated situations with wisdom and balance before he can enter into the Army of the Lord and learn the subjective counterpart of the art of war or battle. Great Masters were warriors in certain of Their incarnations and had heavy responsibilities on Their shoulders.

It is the forces fighting for Light that keep the living Spark continuing on the Path of Perfection.

It is very probable that dark forces, through various methods, influence and even obsess family members, group members, and others to create problems and conflict in that family, group, or nation. They use the methods of bribery, flattery, separation, criticism, slander, and malice to get rid of someone who is holding the family, group, or nation together. Often they succeed, but, on the other hand, the Forces of Light increase their warriors and through them create unity and synthesis.

---

2.   For information on irritation, please refer to *Irritation, The Destructive Fire.*

7. Drowsiness. This occurs when the astral body remains far away from the body for a long period. Those who have continuous drowsiness must be awakened during the night at least five times to make them come back to their bodies. Valerian is very good in such cases. It must be taken after consultation with a physician.

It is also good to make such people sleep near waterfalls and rivers.

Whenever there is irregular noise, the astral body remains close to the body, except in cases in which one consciously uses it for various purposes.

We are told that enmity does not survive above the lower astral world. In the middle and higher astral worlds, people see the uselessness of worldly hostility or enmity and discard it totally, but war continues against dark forces to a greater and greater extent as one advances from one world to the next higher world.

To know the scope of the enemy, one must remember that they exist on the Cosmic Astral Plane, and we are advised to prepare ourselves to face the battle to the end.

Every battle carried on in the name of Beauty, Goodness, Righteousness, Joy, and Freedom multiplies our strength and harmonizes all our energy currents; every battle expands our consciousness and prepares us for higher initiations.

On the subtle planes one does not fight to destroy because one can never destroy a spiritual essence. One fights to release the spiritual essence by destroying the prisons in which the essence is caught. On the physical plane, where there is intense hatred and animosity, people fight to destroy the enemy. These two vices open the gates for various diseases and obsession. Certain people do not understand the difference between the ego and the right evaluation of Self. The ego is a selfish, separative, aggressive, destructive, self-centered formation. The ego is the blinded Self. Even sometimes the ego is a mental and astral formation and is independent of the Self. This is often called an "ego-shell" which runs the show without letting the Self interfere.

The Self is inclusive, selfless, loving, sharing, constructive, and creative. Once egoism is burned away through the light of the releasing Self, man appropriates himself as a definite note in a symphony, aware of his individual worth and the worth of all the notes in the symphony.

Egoism is often called a psychic tumor, and it attracts many destructive forces around it and infects the Space. Egos prevent understanding, cooperation, the common good, and humility. Actually, humility is the absence of ego. As one empties himself of his ego, he advances in the virtue of humility. Humility is the awareness of absolute Oneness. In this awareness, the ego disappears.

Animosity is the manifestation of the ego seeking its interest at the expense of others.

Battles in the subjective world are carried on by the Forces of Light, not with animosity but with the love of Beauty, Goodness, Righteousness, Joy, and Freedom. These are battles fought not for the ego and its interests but for the common good and for Cosmic principles.

Sometimes there are other forces which attack you. The attackers are those who are living and those who have passed away. Those who attack can be categorized in the following manner:

1. The ones you have hurt attack you with their feelings and thoughts here on earth and from the lower subjective planes. When people pass away, their animosities do not go beyond the lower astral levels. But those who are still on earth, and who keep their animosity intense, affect you and force you to recall the powerful memories of the past, no matter where you are located in the astral plane.

2. The friends of those you have hurt also attack you the same way as above.

3. If people you have hurt are low-level people, the dark entities who support them or associate with them also can attack you.

4. Your own friends and teachers attack you if they feel hurt when you hurt other people for your own selfish ends. Especially in the subtle planes, you cannot hide and fabricate excuses for your actions.

5. People attack you subjectively if you live a dishonest life. Advanced people see a potential danger in you and dislike you. Though they may continue their association with you, they gradually feel repulsion and distrust.

6. As we have our circle of friends on the physical plane, we also have a larger number of people in subjective planes who expect honesty, beauty, nobility, and other qualities from us. We often disappoint them and make them leave us alone.

Every attack, dissatisfaction, or grief from our friends and enemies in the subjective world affects our life. It weakens our creativity and limits our horizons. It weakens our resistance to dark forces or to attacks by natural elements. To a certain degree we lose our emotional balance and mental focus. We become irritable. We open the window of our nature to obsession from dark forces.

People think that all events on earth originate from the earth. This is a deception. Our weather changes under the pressures of changes in the Sun, even by the pressures coming from the disintegration of remote galaxies, by the meteoric dust in the air, by the chemistry of various rays in Space.

Similarly, the changes and events in the Subtle and Fiery Worlds create corresponding political, religious, educational, and economic changes upon the planet. Even psychological changes come into being. Many revolutions, wars, and reformations have been and continue to be the human psychological responses to the pressures of the events occurring in the Subtle Worlds.

Certain changes in the Subtle World may create good results, if the released energy is met by advanced centers of human beings or responded to by the higher human nature. If the released energies mix with our glamors, illusions, and blind urges and drives, they lead the world into destruction. This is why, in the very far future, a group of people will form an organization to explore the changes occurring in higher realms and educate people about how to appropriate themselves to these changes.

The changes start from the Fiery World, and the released energy penetrates into the Subtle World. There it creates intense conflict, if the majority of souls cannot assimilate the energy and adjust themselves to it. These conflicts create various events in the Subtle World, the waves or energies of which reach the human shore. There, waves of energies face great opposition and negativity and create complicated upheavals. Eventually a part of these energies are absorbed by a few people, who in turn cause beneficial changes on the planet.

Conflicts occur because of the lack of preparation and transmutation and the delay in our evolution.

In the future it will be easier to hear the keynote of the Fiery World and create melodies, songs, and symphonies on that note on subtle levels, as well as on earth, without painful and bloody conflicts. This is the same as in the individual nature. When the fiery realm of man contacts fiery energies, it produces great tension in the emotional and physical systems and in the environment. This process can be used through creativity only if the person has purified his vehicles, increased the fire of his heart, and transmuted his consciousness.

The battles in the lower levels of the Subtle World are mostly related to the earthly problems which people bring with them. Commanders, kings, and soldiers are gathered there in opposite camps, and they try to continue their earthly battles and take revenge on each other. These people are as ignorant as they were on earth. They have not become enlightened about the possibilities of the Higher Worlds and about the stupidity of their problems.

These people create weapons through their imagination or thought and fight with their thoughts. Those whom they strike fall into sleep. For a long time afterward they feel they are dead, and the strikers also think that they have killed them. Thus, the animosity rages on the lower astral level with greater revenge than on earth, creating emotional and mental pollution, disturbances, and destructions.

It is often such battles that influence the psychology of people on earth, and they mechanically try to repeat all that is going on in the subtle planes. Of course in due time, after much suffering, pain and destruction, those engaged in battle awaken a little and realize the futility of their hatreds, revenge, and fears. They try to raise themselves to a higher level of the astral plane. These people engage themselves in a higher labor so intensely that they forget about their life in the lower levels. In still higher spheres, the thoughts of evil, revenge, hatred, and fear evaporate, and people see the light that is shining in higher spheres.

Those people who develop faith and trust in higher forces eventually come under the influence or power of the Cosmic Magnet and are drawn to higher levels of the astral plane.

When special courses are prepared for people on earth about the Subtle World, many miseries will be eliminated before people arrive there. We must not only learn about life in the Subtle World but also about the science of leaving the physical, astral, and mental bodies, and about the contents of the Space through which we will pass.

The inhabitants of the higher spheres of the Subtle World advise us not to pollute the planet, to create right human relations, and especially to free ourselves from our habits and vices. They know that these three factors, based upon a clear knowledge of the Higher Worlds, will not only bring happiness, prosperity, and health on earth but will also prepare for us a greater future in the Subtle Worlds.

We are told that habits and vices delay our evolution not only on earth but also in the Higher Worlds. We are sometimes intelligent enough not to carry our furniture with us while climbing to the top of a mountain, but we are not intelligent enough to avoid carrying habits and vices with us into the Subtle Worlds where they will not only be inflammable materials but also heavy obstacles on our Path.

Those who live long in the lowest stratum of the Subtle World develop a kind of willpower which can be called *destructive will*. Such a will is transmitted not only through their actions but also through their words and especially through their eyes. The origin of the evil eye is the destructive will.

In the presence of such an influence, one feels a slowing down, a disturbance of mind, difficulty in creativity, and difficulty in the expansion of goodwill. Such a destructive force produces some kinds of paralysis, disturbances, and distortions around it. Even beautiful objects are cracked and healthy people fall sick because of such an evil will.

The person full of evil will spreads thoughts and feelings of negativity, denial, and pessimism. Children especially must be protected from such persons because their force is very injurious to the subtle centers of children.

There are many legends in which we read how the Higher World sends a call to heroes in the subjective world to prepare themselves for a new incarnation in order to face heavy crises in the world. Most of us think that such legends have no foundation, but if one does enough study about the Higher Worlds, he will discover that such legends actually are real.

The Higher World sends those who, in certain critical times, can reach higher positions of power and stop or crush the assaults of the evil forces. Sometimes these heroes come in groups; they are born in different nations and occupy high positions. They also come with their associates from different corners of the world who support their success and victory. If human history is read in the right manner, people will find numerous examples of these heroes.

In the Higher Worlds, they know exactly in what condition they will live, what difficulties and crises they will face, and what will happen to them. They see these clearly and knowingly decide to take birth. Most of their information in the Subtle World fades away during the descent to the lower worlds. Only a strong urge remains in their heart to fulfill their responsibility and labor. Of course, beams of revelation sometimes shine on their path, but in most cases they carry on their responsibilities as if they had no previous knowledge about these responsibilities.

Sometimes, some of their associates do not incarnate but keep close ties with them in the subjective world. In critical times they help them telepathically and, in dangerous times, possibly even save them.

When forces of darkness sense a preparation taking place to send a hero to the world, they immediately organize and train those agents who will incarnate during the same period to bring great hardship into the lives of the heroes and prepare the ways and means to annihilate them.

Both parties protect their servants and are eager to fight to the death to bring light or darkness, construction or destruction. But the labor of the Sons of Light always emerges victorious. The Forces of Light arrange things in such a way that even the defeat or death of a hero brings for a long time afterward a great victory for the Forces of Light.

The appearance of a dark force for every hero of Light is itself a triumph. In the presence of a dark force, the psychic energy of a hero multiplies many times. It sharpens his consciousness; makes him more wise, more courageous, more daring; pushes him closer to his inner records or memories of his supreme task, closer to the co-workers in the Subtle Worlds; and gives him tremendous experience with the techniques, plans, and movements of the forces of darkness. In the presence of evil forces, the real hero feels a greater challenge to serve humanity and to bring out greater resources of wisdom hidden within him.

Dark forces do not improve. They change their cunning ways, but always in their essence they feel their defeat.

The Higher Worlds not only send warriors but also great scientists, artists, and financiers who work as a team, especially in critical times.

The destruction of land through earthquakes and other natural means is not planned by the Higher Worlds, nor by the Hierarchy. The cause of such disasters is found in the population of the earth. Insane and criminal living and indifference toward the calls of the Higher Worlds disturb the fiery forces in Nature. Nature tries to restore its equilibrium through natural calamities. The Almighty Presence is Love. It is man who breaks the Law of Love and falls into miseries.

The Higher Worlds even send disciples to restore the balance of forces in certain areas to avoid calamities and safeguard people. But their help cannot go over a certain limit, especially when people decide to "commit suicide" rather than to live.

We are told that at this time in human history thousands of heroes are preparing themselves for a new birth for the sake of humanity; but in spite of all their sacrifices, if the karma of humanity is dark, heroes can bring only limited help to people. The greatest success of these heroes can be guaranteed when the general public hears the call, faces the danger, and organizes themselves against human insanity, crime, and self-destruction.

The coming years will decide if humanity will continue to live on this planet, or if the planet must be burned to allow a new harvest for the future.

For many, many years we have polluted and poisoned our earth without realizing that pollution will spread into the Subtle Worlds as well. Poisonous gases and all kinds of pollution not only contaminate the Subtle World but also create those conditions in which our earth and solar system can be drastically affected. Disturbances noticed in the motion of our earth and of the other planets are the result of pollution, explosions, and human disunity. A fool will laugh at these remarks, but a true scientist is aware that our solar system lives according to the principle of balance.

Pollution, explosions, and human disunity create imbalance in Nature. Every pollution affects the circulation of the subtle energies, rays, and currents in Space. Every explosion disturbs the balance of forces. Every disunity not only indirectly affects the life of the planet as a whole but also directly disturbs the forces of Nature, due to negative and malicious emanations from the emotions and thoughts of man.

Man still does not realize that a thought can be either poisonous or beneficial and fragrant. An emotion can pollute the Space or cleanse it. Pollution, explosions, and disunity brought the planet to the verge of the abyss, to the possibility of an unprecedented disaster. Typhoons, tornadoes, earthquakes, fires, and social disturbances are the effects of the accumulated pollution, explosions, and disunity. Humanity has become blind and suicidal and has trapped itself through its egocentric mind. Humanity can not only destroy this planet; it can not only create great catastrophes in the solar system; but it can also create a condition in the Subtle World which will be worse than the hell that is explained in the New Testament.

If we kill humanity, we will all be living in the astral plane, and the astral plane will be a state of continuous nightmares, suffering, pain, and fire. Can the reason be found why humanity chooses hell instead of joy?

All humanitarians must find a way not only to stop war but also to stop all kinds of test explosions and war games. All humanitarians must find a way to stop the pollution of the air. If they want to survive, they must emphasize one world and one humanity.

The disaster of the earth can come suddenly, and the planet may be totally roasted when the gases around the earth inflame, or when the electromagnetic forces are disturbed beyond their capacity to stop a massive earthquake, submergence, or flood.

We are now in a state in which not even one shot of a gun must be tolerated because the equilibrium of the energies are very much disturbed and can bring final disaster to our globe.

Heroism can be a conscious act or an unconscious urge. In both cases the foundation is the same. Heroes are subjectively predetermined individuals who in the Subtle World have committed themselves to future heroic activities. They have come to earth with a strong impression and the drive to carry out their commitments under any conditions. Some of them remember their commitments; they even remember the encouragement of their Teachers. Some of them do not remember at all, but they feel an irresistible urge to live as heroes for the love of humanity and for the service of the Hierarchy.

Such heroes are not alone. Thousands of known and unknown co-workers, thousands of visible and invisible friends in many spheres help them carry on their heroic life to the end. They send them courage; they inspire them with ideas and vision. They send them thoughts of fearlessness, stability, and serenity. They pour their love into the hearts of such heroes.

Thus a hero does not stand as an individual. He has many assistants, co-workers, friends, and admirers who visibly and invisibly surround him. This is why a real hero moves masses of people, creates great movements, and brings transformation, unity, liberation, and a new level of consciousness to humanity.

It is true that the lives of some heroes end in tragedy, but in the light of the joy which they receive when they immediately pass into the Subtle World, their tragedy turns into a banner of victory and joy.

The spirit of heroism, like a magnet, also attracts the thoughts of the heroes living on earth or acting in the Subtle World. Thus a real hero does not fight alone, but he lives and fights with the cooperation of the numberless heroes. Heroes form a bonfire of flames marching as a group within both worlds.

There is also a kind of hero who is neither conscious nor unconscious but is preparing himself to enter the path of heroism. These kinds of people have a great amount of inspiration. They see the need in life, and they wholeheartedly respond to it, but they do not have any conscious contact with the Hierarchy. They do not even think of, or believe in, the Hierarchy. Their Solar Angels guide them because of the love that these people have for humanity.

Some of these heroes perform a few heroic deeds with far-reaching effects; then, when the difficulties and persecutions begin, they turn into average people. But whatever they did remains in the records of the Hierarchy, and in their next incarnation they work harder. In the subtle planes they begin to see their role and their stature. When they return to earth, they act as heroes again, not remembering the commitments made in the Subtle World.

Conscious heroes not only work on the physical plane but also in the mental plane with their thought energy and through wisely prepared and built thoughtforms. These heroes fight in the mental sphere and protect groups and individuals from destructive thoughtforms which occasionally attack people to prevent the advancement of the spirit. These dark thoughtforms lead humanity into degeneration and crimes.

Heroes fight in the mental sphere to stop these thoughtforms and seal off their originating sources. Many sicknesses are transmitted by thoughts through a distance. Thought can not only carry germs, but it can also plant germs in the auras of people.

Mental suggestion is a fact. Suggestions can weaken one's resistance and impress the image on him. Once the image of a sickness is impressed on the person, he absorbs it and develops it into the actual sickness.

Dark thoughts, thoughts that carry sickness and destruction, eventually turn back to their originating source and hit the source with fiery, destructive blows. Most of our sicknesses are the result of our thoughts returning back to us.

Heroes on the mental plane try to sacrifice themselves to save individuals and groups by destroying the accumulated darkness in Space. They destroy those currents which carry sickness, those currents which carry disunity and chaos. The most beautiful part of the nature of these heroes is that they remain totally unknown, and people are protected because of their sacrifice, without knowing the one who helped them.

Heroes who fight in the subtle planes to protect humanity, whether in the body or out of the body, create their weapons through their thoughts and apply them through the energy of their thoughts. Among their many weapons are electrical rays, flames, arrows of energy, and beams of fiery currents. All these are used against the captains and leaders of darkness.

Some of these heroes lose their vehicles or are hurt very badly, but they accomplish their task and protect humanity or certain leaders of high importance.

The astral and mental bodies are as vulnerable as the physical body. It is true that by physical means we cannot hurt them or knock them down, but the weapons in the Subtle World are different. The energy in Space is used and turned into many kinds of weapons which cause widespread explosions, which burn and evaporate subtle bodies, which paralyze and poison them, and which make the user of the form useless for a long time after.

They are heroes who fight the black assaults of dark ones.

It will be possible to end war on this plane with education and enlightenment in five principles:

—Unity
—Brotherhood
—Progress in Infinity
—Synthesis
—The Cosmic One Self

The battle of Initiate-heroes is to increase light, education, culture, beauty, freedom, and joy.

Destruction of the bodies is not accepted as the best way to deal with evil, but if there is no choice the hero fights and destroys the mechanisms of the dark ones to secure enough time for the progress of the Army of Light.

Not all wars or battles are fought against evil. Most of the battles carried on upon the earth originate from self-interest, vanity, greed, hatred, and exploitation. Such battles not only pollute the Subtle World but also perpetuate the misery in the world. Again and again, **those who raise the sword fall by the sword,** no matter how long it takes karma to program the date.

In all esoteric literature we are told that people in Higher Worlds are aware of those people in the world who

1. Spread the pure Teaching
2. Create great movements of beauty and education
3. Suffer for the Teaching
4. Demonstrate heroic deeds
5. Do not give up the propagation of the Teaching in spite of all difficulties

In our world, the news broadcasts the names of those who perform outstanding labor for humanity. Similarly, in Higher Worlds, the people see and hear all that is going on upon this physical plane.

There are also cases in which all those who are related to you in various ways feel extreme joy over your spiritual success and fall into grief when they see and hear things that are not in line with honesty and nobility.

Those people who try not to bring shame to their family and friends but make them proud of their deeds and achievements innately know that the Higher World is watching them.

The Higher World is very close to our daily life. Sometimes we see how a great multitude gathered in stadiums applaud and cheer an

Olympic athlete. A more fiery excitement circulates in the Higher World in the ranks of those who become aware of a great deed that their family and friends performed on earth. Such an excitement sometimes comes to us as a river of energy and blessings after we perform an act of gratefulness and nobility.

Christ once said, "There will be greater joy in Heaven over one sinner who repents." Also, "There is joy among the Angels of God over one sinner who repents."[3]

Many are those who watch our life closely. Sometimes we bring them shame; sometimes we make them feel proud of us.

War on the earth could eventually be ended by a great catastrophe, or by loving understanding and negotiations in a sense of unity.

The Hierarchy considers that the most powerful weapon is light or *illumination*. Any weapon on earth or in the Subtle World will only make the enemy retreat temporarily. But if the hearts, the minds, and the souls of people are enlightened by the vision of unity, brotherhood, progress to infinity, synthesis, and the Cosmic Self, the power of the Cosmic enemy could be destroyed. This is why esoteric education is so important for future victories.

It will not be possible to end wars on this planet with more wars. True heroes are those people who sacrifice their lives to bring to humanity the understanding of unity, brotherhood, progress to infinity, synthesis, and the Cosmic One Self.

---

3. Luke 15: 7, 10.

25

The Subtle World
and Devotion

In the higher astral world, everyone belongs to a group. Each group has a Guide or Teacher. The astral plane is the plane of deep and pure devotion to the Guide or Teacher. The Teacher demands such a devotion in order to increase the fire of aspiration of the soul and to prevent him from being swayed by the glamors of the lower levels.

This is difficult to understand. However, if we remember that in the astral plane our glamors materialize with all their colors and create a network to trap young and inexperienced souls, we can understand the role of strong devotion.

That is why devotion and worship are very important disciplines on earth. They become useful in the Subtle World as well. Devotion creates focus, accumulation of energy, and a magnetic rapport with the image, idea, or vision of devotion.

Devotion sublimates the forces of the centers; aligns, integrates and charges the aura; and creates a flow, a current which helps the man in his ascent.

People have disgraced devotion toward teachers, husbands, or wives, identifying it with a kind of slavery. It is just those types of people who have demonstrated the worst kind of slavery. They have become slaves of matter, body, sex, ego, and have used every type of crime to safeguard their slavery. Unfortunately, so-called democracy encouraged such steps and eventually created chaos.

Devotion to a teacher, a guru, a saint, or to a great humanitarian vision creates the most beautiful forms and colors in the Subtle World. The inhabitants of the Subtle World feel great joy when the flowers of devotion reach their shores. Devotion is a decisive procession toward a supreme beauty. Devotion creates those elements within us which make possible the transformation of the devotee into the image of devotion.

Prayer is one of the best expressions of devotion. It is through prayer that one keeps the flame of his devotion alive and directed toward the Forces of the Higher Worlds. When prayer is continuous and sincere, it turns into aspiration.

Prayer is more than a religious activity; it is actually a scientific phenomenon. Prayer means the ability to fuse your consciousness with the consciousness of the Cosmos. When you pray, you raise your vibration or your frequency higher and higher until eventually a fusion occurs between your consciousness and the consciousness of the Universal Presence. You absorb the light, love, and power of that Universal Presence.

Prayer is an effort to melt yourself into that Universal Presence. When that melting point is reached, you make a contact. That contact brings light, love, and power into your consciousness.

We do not pray only with our words. There are many kinds of prayers which are more powerful than words.

The first kind of prayer is *a good life*. By living a good life, you raise your frequency and your level to such a degree that you become acceptable to the Great Power. A good life means that physically, emotionally, mentally, and in all your relationships you stand for the Common Good, for the welfare of every living form.

By living such a life you create a fusion with the Universal Consciousness, and your life becomes a manifestation of radioactive goodness. This is one of the goals of living: to be all-giving, all-joyful, radioactive; and to manifest the Divinity existing within you.

The second way to pray is through *aspiration toward perfection*. Perfection means to reach the highest that you can reach. Whenever you aspire to perfect yourself physically, emotionally, mentally, or spiritually, you come closer to that Almighty Consciousness.

In the course of striving toward perfection, you try to eliminate everything in your nature which is ugly or imperfect. The urge toward perfection makes you see your faults and mistakes more clearly and strive to get rid of them.

God is an all-aware, all-conscious Presence. If you say, "God, I am beautiful," but you do ugly things, your words mean nothing. God does not always need to hear your voice. He sees your actions, and whatever you do is a prayer.

The third kind of prayer is *service to others*. A life of service to humanity is a great prayer. Through your service you help the children of God and you try to bring the great Plan of God into manifestation. Service is a practical form of prayer.

The fourth kind of prayer is *service to the Plan of the Hierarchy*. The Hierarchy is formed by Christ and all those disciples who have achieved conscious immortality and who are working to bring greater light and beauty to humanity. The Plan is simply the activities and functions of love and light; the Plan is to increase light and increase love in the world. If humanity has more light and more love, humanity is closer to the Kingdom of God.

You can serve the Plan by trying to increase light and love in the world. You can increase light by trying to bring greater wisdom into all fields of human endeavor, such as science, philosophy, politics, education, economics, and others. You can increase love by continuously trying to create right human relations between people, between families, between nations. Love manifests itself through right human relations.

When a man is loving, he is stable and synthesized — physically, emotionally, and mentally. When he begins to hate or create cleavages or separatism, he becomes ill. The same is true for families and nations. When a nation loves, it is united.

The Plan is love and light. Those who serve love and light are actually serving the Plan, and through their actions and behavior they are praying.

The fifth and more advanced form of prayer is *contemplation.* Contemplation is sometimes called "samadhi" or fusion with the consciousness of God. In contemplation you withdraw your consciousness from physical, emotional, and mental realms and focus yourself in the light of God and communicate with Him. We are told that all great Ones spoke with God or with that Almighty Presence through this method.

Prayer results in the following changes in one's life:

1. Prayer increases your light. Prayer means to bring light to direct your life. When you bring light into your nature, you see more clearly; you have discrimination and right choice; you see the right and the wrong; you have long and short-term vision. You see your interest for the future and your interest for the present. Light helps you conduct your life in a better way.

2. Prayer brings healing. Many scientists have documented miraculous cures which have occurred as a result of prayer. These cures were called "miraculous." They are actually not so. Prayer is a method of fusing yourself with a power station which raises your vibrations and creates harmony within yourself. When you create harmony in yourself, you are healed. Health is harmony. Health is a condition where there are no disturbances or distortions. When you are synthesized within yourself, you are healthy. That energy, which is

sometimes called the psychic energy of God or of the Spirit, cleans and purifies all distorting factors that you have within yourself.

3. Prayer gives you a synthesizing consciousness. A small man always thinks in terms of his own limited interests. When you pray and expand your consciousness into that great Consciousness, you no longer think in terms of separative interests; you include everything within your consciousness; you think in terms of the ALL. All formulas, all great secrets of Nature, come from that great Mind. When you contact that Divine Mind, it makes your mind inclusive, universal, and Cosmic so that you do not use the treasures that are given to you for your own personal ends.

4. Prayer purifies your heart. Once when Christ was asked how people should pray, He stated that before you pray you must first forgive everyone for everything.

God is a unit. When you hate one part of Him, when you hate one man, you hate a part of God. This is why Christ said you cannot love God if you do not love your brother; if you hate your brother you are hating God.

Before you pray, forgive those who have hurt you, or toward whom you have bad feelings. Then you can say, "Lord, I have taken a shower. I can stand in Your presence with my beautiful garments of love, purity, and beauty."

5. Prayer creates a relationship between you and the invisible world. There are hundreds of angels, spirits, and living beings whom you may not be able to see. With prayer you create a friendship with these invisible hosts. This is because prayer creates *light* and *perfume* around you. Pray in all sincerity for one-half hour and then smell yourself. You will see that your odor has totally changed; your radiation has changed; the secretion of your glands has changed; even your hearing and eyesight have changed.

6. Prayer keeps dark forces away from you. Dark forces are yours and other people's ugly and criminal thoughts. When you pray, you radiate your light to such a degree that these dark thoughts cannot come close to you.

There was a man who was very angry with me. Every time I passed his house, I knew this man was thinking evil about me. I would be reading and suddenly his bad thoughts about me would come to my mind.

I began to pray, and suddenly I saw that these dark thoughts weakened and then went away. Later, when the attack came again, I prayed and again it went away.

You are going to increase your frequency to such a degree that it does not allow any wicked or distorted frequencies to penetrate into the field of your electromagnetic energy.

7. Prayer creates optimism in you. There is a heavy pessimistic cloud sitting over humanity at this time in history. Many people think the world is about to be destroyed, that war is coming, that famine is on the way. Like lightning, prayer destroys this pessimistic cloud. Prayer gives you optimism because you see that you are standing with God, and with His help everything is possible.

We were once in a train which was going eighty miles per hour. Suddenly we heard over our radio that a bridge two miles ahead was destroyed, washed out by a flood. There was no way we could stop our train within that short a distance. One mile before the bridge, something happened to the wheels and the train suddenly stopped and ground to a halt. This experience showed me that everything may seem bad and cloudy, but as suddenly as lightning everything may be turned around.

8. Prayer brings you faith. Faith is an intuitive awareness that something good is going to happen; it is not wishful thinking.

We are going to build our lives in such a way that we are always in contact with the higher forces in the Universe; eventually our whole life must turn into a prayer.

The following is a list of times when one should pray:

1. Whenever you do anything wrong. Whenever you do something ugly, nasty or evil, it is a seed thrown into your nature and into the laws of karma. Everything difficult in your life is nothing else but the growth of the seeds you scattered in the past. You must bring these seeds out and remove them before they germinate, and this is done through prayer.

To remove these seeds, you are going to fuse with the Almighty Consciousness in the Universe through prayer. When you are in tune with God, you do not do wrong things.

2. When you have great joy, you must pray. Some people wonder why they should pray when they are successful and happy;

they think they have everything and do not need anything else. But our greatest failures come at the moments when we are very successful and joyful. We forget the source of all our joy. If we forget the source, no matter how rich, beautiful, or joyful we are, all our successes will work against our spiritual interest.

Immediately when you have any success, pray, so that you do not become proud and vain and you keep your honesty and humility before God. A wise man once said, "In front of every defeat, pride walks." Whenever we are really successful, pride comes to our mind. To destroy that pride we must give credit to that Almighty Source.

3. Whenever you need direction, pray for it. Your decision can be partial; God's decision is inclusive. It may seem illogical, but it is always the best decision.

One day three young boys went into a garden and stole a basketful of fruit. They were so happy that they had plenty of fruit to eat.

But as they were leaving one of the boys said, "We stole it. What are we going to do? Let's pray about it," he continued, "and see what answer will come."

The little boys knelt down and said, "God, what do You think about our basket of fruit?"

They opened their eyes. The first one said, "He told me to take it back."

The second one said, "He told me to take it back, too."

The third boy said, "Yes, we must take it all back. But how can we take it back without being caught?"

The first boy said, "God told us to take it back, so let's take it back."

The boys went to the owner's door and returned all the fruit to him. When the man saw how the boys returned the fruit, he invited them in and gave each of them more fruit, a jar of honey, and some bread. "Wow," said one of the boys, "God's way is really the right decision!"

4. When people hate you, pray for them. Whenever you feel that someone does not like you, send light and blessings to him. You can also pray that you find the ways and means to improve your relationship with a person.
5. When people love you, pray. Love is a greater trap than hatred. In love, people can misuse each other. But if you pray, you can use that love in the right way without being trapped in it.

Every time someone wants to help you or to love you more, make a contact with that Almighty Consciousness and ask Him what He sees in the situation. This will save you lots of trouble.

Christ once said, "Ask and it shall be given. Seek and you shall find. Knock and the door shall be opened to you." With prayer we knock on that door with our whole life and soul. And if we keep knocking, the door will always be opened.

In conclusion, we may say that prayer builds the bridges between the earth and the Higher Worlds.

26

Possessions and the Subtle Worlds

Knowledge and experience of the Subtle World change our consciousness, and certain worldly values assume a different light or may even disappear. For example, the sense of possession changes, and man easily renounces his possessions and makes arrangements to distribute them for worthy causes before he passes away.

Such an action brings great joy to the inhabitants of the Subtle Worlds. Every detachment and renunciation is noted in the Subtle World because the inhabitants there know that the progress of the human being depends on detachment and renunciation. Those who are attached to their possessions and do not use them for a great cause give the inhabitants of the Subtle World deep grief, like the grief of a man who from the mountaintop sees people trapped in the barbwire of a field below.

It is important to have the fruits of our labor, but these must be left behind to those who can use them for the common good. When people turn fifty years of age in certain places in Asia, they distribute their possessions to their young family members, relatives, and friends. Then they begin to prepare for departure from the earth. They devote themselves to meditation and prayer. They visit Sages and build the bond between themselves and the Subtle World. Sometimes great wealth is distributed to people as a sign of victory over possessions and as a gift of labor to human beings.

Those who die attached to possessions will have a very difficult time progressing in the Subtle World. Their possessions will hurt them continuously and attach them to the earth. Ghosts are seen wandering around jewels, money, and other belongings. This is called the blindness of the human spirit. Every human being must renounce himself from the beautiful things he leaves behind him.

Once I was talking with an eighty-nine year old man. He had a very beautiful house and was building garden walls out of stones. I said, "Don't you think it is time for you to rest a little?"

"No, no, no," he said. "Time is going on and I must leave this home in the best shape for those who will use it after me."

We must leave behind us beauty, our creative labor, and the best memories of ourselves.

Detachment from earthly objects helps us progress faster in the Subtle and Fiery Worlds because each attachment creates karma. We must leave things behind, as we leave our motel rooms after living in them for a few days.

We are told that people in the Subtle World see the objects with which we are identified.

Almost all the objects that we carry with us in our thoughts and emotions are totally useless there. The money concept is totally absurd. You do not need your furs or cars. What are you going to do with them?

People not only carry objects with them, but in their folly they create such objects with the power of their imagination and build a life exactly like the life on earth. It will be very difficult for them to understand the new situation in the Subtle World, and they will do all that they can to perpetuate their old life there. But the wheel will turn, and they will be forced to leave the astral world, once again, through the pain of detachment.

There was a lady who used to collect various art objects. Her home was like a museum. Once in conversation she said, "I tried to collect all these beautiful objects under one roof, so that those who have no means to collect them or see them may enjoy and study them after I leave my body."

She used to remind me of the old man who planted trees for future generations.

In contrast, our scientists and politicians have planted atomic bombs and poisonous wastes for the future generations.

There are many funny stories about the Subtle World. It is said that one day a man passed away and entered the Subtle World, dressed in an expensive coat and carrying with him a purse full of money.

An inhabitant of the Subtle World asked, "What are you going to do with that currency which has no value at all?"

"But how can I feed myself?"

"You will never be hungry in the Subtle World, and, by the way, why are you dressed in that heavy coat?"

"I want to feel warm."

"In the Subtle World your body radiates heat when you imagine you are cold, and cold when you imagine you are hot."

Thus, people will spend much time adjusting themselves to the entirely new conditions in the Subtle World.

Those who learn their lessons in the Subtle World and reincarnate carry the memories of the conditions of the Subtle World with them, and they try to create changes on earth which will facilitate the journey of the departing ones in the Subtle World.

The power of discrimination is achieved when the awakening human soul observes the objects or events from the viewpoint of the three worlds. An object on the earth has a value, but the same object has a different meaning in the Subtle World. In the Fiery World no one even thinks about that object. Discrimination is the ratio of these three viewpoints. The relative value of the objects and events are measured with a three-dimensional outlook by a soul whose consciousness is focused in the Fiery World.

Through discriminative observation one can understand the real value of objects and events. Through the power of three-dimensional observation one sees how a thought manifests as a motion, as a tone of voice, as a gesture. One also learns how to inspire people to change the expression of their lives.

In the Subtle World, as on earth, if people's consciousness lives in earthly darkness, they lose not only objects but also their children, relatives, and friends. Here, people mourn for those who depart, without realizing that they are still around them. The same thing occurs in the Subtle World; people depart from the Subtle World to the Fiery World, and their friends mourn for them.

It is suggested that we develop the sense of ever-Presence to be able to see that our friends always exist and that communication with them is always possible by thought power.

The fear of death paralyzes people here on earth as well as people existing in the Subtle World. Fear of death is a sign that the human soul still thinks that his existence depends on a vehicle and is measured by time and space. When this concept is dissolved, fear will disappear. Man was, is, and will be; and the beauty is that the human soul can exist in any condition, using any condition as a language of communication.

Before one passes away, he must be impressed with the following thought in order to have the right direction: **Nothing in the Subtle World will retard my progress toward greater light, greater perfection, and greater awakening.**

Discrimination is the light of our Core. If things are seen through the light of the Core, no object, no event, and no force will be able to deceive us and retard our progress toward the light of the Core of the Universe.

Upon entering the Subtle World, one may fall into great perplexity, despair, and confusion; but if he is charged with *direction*, everything will slowly clear away. He will not be trapped by the habits he used to have on earth, but adapt himself to new conditions.

When I was student in a monastery, the leaders used to send us to the city for special missions. My leader used to say, "There are many things to see in the city; there are many traps and temptations. But remember, your destination is to go and find the person and give this letter to him, and then bring the answer directly to me."

This instruction works on any plane. When the destination is clear, one has less of an occasion to be trapped in different glamors and illusions. The destination is very clear: to proceed toward more light and strive toward perfection.

Another thing that is experienced in the Subtle World and even more so in the Fiery World is the absence of secrecy. All that one feels and thinks is visible, as if they were external actions. Our thoughts are audible, and almost nothing can be hidden from others. The earthly consciousness tries to create all types of privacy, but eventually one discovers how ridiculous these efforts are.

A Great One said, "Blessed are those who do not have to be ashamed of their heart's accumulations."[1]

We are told that total justice rules the Subtle World, and one must prepare oneself to receive according to his merits.

We are told that in the Subtle World love is the key to all kinds of locks. Upon entering the Subtle World one slowly sees things as they are. He sees friends and so called enemies who carry many associations from the earthly life. But if his heart is open, he manifests love and exercises his loving understanding in all circumstances. Love not only creates harmony in the Subtle World, but it also calls forth all that is beautiful in the hearts of all the inhabitants of the Subtle World.

In advanced or higher levels of the Subtle World, people know that revenge, offense, bitterness, hatred, egoism, and vengeance are really worthless burdens on their hearts. They do not even like to feel them. Such kinds of base emotions reek in the Subtle World, spreading psychic pollutions.

---

1. Agni Yoga Society, *Fiery World*, vol. 1 (New York: Agni Yoga Society, 1969), para. 660.

Love opens the way to higher levels. This is why Great Teachers emphasized love so much. Love is very important in the Subtle World.

Just as you possess things and have difficulty letting them go, there are also cases when others possess you and do not leave you free. Possession begins with obsession. In possession, you are possessed by an entity. In obsession, you are caught by an urge, drive, emotion, thought, or direction which you obey against your will.

Obsession is an etheric, astral, or mental inhibition. A posthypnotic suggestion is a kind of obsession. Obsession on the etheric level is a mechanical habit which causes distortion in the nerves and the corresponding etheric body.

Emotional obsession is an emotion caught in the emotional plane which controls other emotions. Such an obsession can be local or isolated, or it can have roots in the emotional body of society, from which it derives its power. Accidents and events charged with a strong emotion can be imprinted like a photograph on the astral body. They turn into obsessive neuroses.

One does not need to be in the astral plane to be obsessed. One can attract astral or dark entities into himself through anger, hatred, etc. When you are angry, you tune in to the lower astral plane, and you start channeling the current of anger. If your anger turns into a thoughtform, due to certain planning to satisfy your anger, an astral entity enters your thoughtform and uses it as a destructive mechanism.

When there is massive anger, massive fear, or massive hatred, the masses become channels of such forces which collectively exist in lower astral levels. It is after such a process of channeling that obsession takes place and mass insanity comes into being. At the present we see how many people in the world are acting insanely and living an insane life. This is a phenomenon which is very dangerous to the survival of humanity.

Thus, through anger, fear, hatred, greed, and revenge, one becomes a channel for the pollution of the astral plane. This is why in all religions these five are considered sins and are condemned. Those who are filled with these five will enjoy neither earth nor the Subtle Worlds.

In the mental plane, obsession is an inhibited, trapped thoughtform, with or without entities related to it. Generally, such a thoughtform is part of another massive thoughtform.

Possession is different. Possession is done by an entity who possibly has many obsessions and tries to occupy the nature of a man on the physical plane, partially or completely, as a mechanism of his expression. Thus, a possessed person is occupied not only by an entity but also by the obsessions that the entity has.

An advanced case of possession occurs when more than one entity possesses a person, and they locate themselves in certain etheric, astral, and mental centers according to their level and intentions.

Obsession can be carried on at a distance, when a powerful person controls another person through his etheric emanations, emotions, or thoughts. Some people easily fall victim to such a kind of obsession. At a distance, the person controls his victims as if he were in them. Such obsessions occur only if there is a karmic tie or psychological resonance between the two persons. For example, the sexual act opens the door for such a possession on multiple levels.

There is a kind of possession that occurs when an astral corpse is the possessor. The method is as follows:

When a person emotionally loves another person, such as the mother, wife, husband, child, or even an animal, he creates an emotional tie with the person or animal. When this person or animal dies, the same emotional affinity exists with them. No possession takes place until the departed person or animal leaves his astral body. When the astral body is left behind, the person on earth attracts that astral body, which slowly penetrates his own astral body and contaminates it in a decaying process. The person first feels he is closer to his beloved one, but he gradually realizes that some force is acting independently in his body. Animals, because they live simultaneously in the astral and physical world, see the astral body of a departed owner, and think he is always with them.

Astral bodies all have emotional recordings in them, and they pass all these recordings to the living person. Besides filling his emotional life with confusion, the astral bodies begin to decay, causing unusual emotional problems and heavy depressions.

A contaminated astral body cannot be cured by any orthodox methods. To avoid such a disaster, people must not be attached to their beloved ones. Real love serves and sacrifices, but never attaches. When the beloved one leaves, real love exercises total joy and detachment. Many husbands and wives are obsessed through their attachment. This is the reason why, when one of them dies, the other passes away soon thereafter.

Emotional attachment cannot be translated as a sense of responsibility but as a chemical fusion between two astral bodies. When the person departs, he takes part of the astral body of the devoted one with him. The departed portion of the devoted one's astral body is used as an element of comfort by the departed one, and it is translated by the living one as a deep longing and a sense of depression.

It is this departed portion of the astral body that serves as a link between the two beings. When the power of the departed soul over his astral body weakens, as he leaves it on the astral plane and steps to the mental plane, the living portion of the astral body of the living person is magnetically drawn back to the astral body of the living person. The astral portion of the living person in the astral body of the departed person always nourishes itself by drawing the energy of the living person.

Emotional attachment between two living persons is also not beneficial because the emotional elements, glamors, desires, confusions, and anxieties of each person flow into each other's astral vehicle, creating disturbances, tensions, and irritations. Such a transference is accomplished through the solar plexus center, which eventually becomes super-active and damages the organs connected to it.

A similar thing also happens between mental bodies if, first, the mental centers are unfolded and developed; and second, there is close mental affinity between the two persons. Mental-body obsession is mostly positive when the higher mind is involved. Inspirations and higher impressions may pass down from a departed mental body if the soul is on the mental plane and the living one is active in his higher mental plane.

When the lower mind is involved, the result is very disturbing and negative, as the living one shows all the anxieties and problems of the departed one, if there was a close association between them.

Mental body obsession is not frequent because the higher mental body usually lives for centuries and the lower mental body disintegrates in a relatively short time when one leaves the lower mental plane.

Attachment to objects poses another kind of problem. When the objects disappear or when the owner dies, he becomes stuck with the image of the object which is astrally built. That astral image of the object establishes a link with the real object and influences the owner of the object, almost to the degree of obsessing him. This is why the ancients were very careful not to buy stolen objects or objects whose owners were identified with them but were forced to sell them. Every time they would buy an object from a private owner, they used to ask him to bless the object and wish that the buyer would enjoy it fully.

Also, the ancients were very careful not to buy objects, such as jewels, antiques, carpets, and other things from the house of a departed one who was identified with his belongings.

The Teaching suggests that we learn to develop detachment from any object that we own. We must act as custodians and then pass our objects on to our friends without any attachment, as we do when we go to hotels, using everything in the room and then leaving without any attachment.

Detachment is a special condition of the aura. The aura of a detached person is radiant. It is not like a bottle but like a radiating fiery sphere which insulates the emotional body from the emotional elements of other people, especially from their glamors and hang-ups. It is very healthy to have a radiant aura because it protects you from various negative influences and makes any obsession impossible.

People think that detachment and loving kindness or compassion do not live in the same consciousness. But in reality, a detached person has deeper love and higher commitments than an attached person. In attachment there is always self- interest, ego, and personality; and love cannot exist in its essence with self-interest, ego, and personality concerns. Most of our love is an effort to limit the freedom of our "beloved ones" and use them for our interest, whereas in true love there is no self-interest but the renunciation of self and ego.

Man lives as a soul when he learns to detach. Attachment to objects or persons annihilates the possibility of true love. Attachment is a stage of obsession; detachment is freedom from obsession.

One may ask, if what is said is true, then are worshipers of Great Ones obsessed beings? This is not true because, first, those who have passed the Fourth Initiation do not have astral bodies. Second, the astral body of a second or Third Degree Initiate disappears in the fire immediately when he leaves it on the astral plane. The emotional body of a true worshiper is nourished by the intuitive substance of those who are Fourth or Fifth Degree Initiates.

Any pollution on any of the three planes — physical, emotional, and mental — affects the other planes. If the pollution is on the physical plane, it spreads into the astral and eventually the mental plane. A similar thing happens when pollution is found on the emotional or mental plane.

If our body is polluted, the pollution extends to our emotional nature and gradually penetrates into our mental body. This is why it is so important to stop any pollution on any plane. A lie, a deception, a hatred, or a feeling of revenge manifests itself in various disorders in the physical body.

It is also possible that purification of emotional or mental pollution can eliminate certain disorders and symptoms from the physical plane. Integrity in all the planes makes a person strong, healthy, happy, loving, and creative.

Similar things happen on a large scale in the world if mental deception, exploitation, and criminal and destructive ideas rule the mental sphere of the planet; in such a case, physical plane disturbances and destructions will be inevitable. On the other hand, when man pollutes his physical environment with various poisons and radioactivity, it will affect the mind of humanity and will eventually lead to mass crimes.

Thoughts and feelings are as substantial as physical objects, and they are related to each other as ice, water, and steam are related to each other. A clean environment conditions clear thinking and clear emotional relations.

It is observed that the cases of obsession are multiplied due to the pollution of the air, water, and earth. Pollution weakens the resistance of the vehicles of man and prepares the way to obsession. For the sake of prosperity, luxury, and even sanitation, our modern civilization created poisons in such abundance that, in the future, the survival of humanity will be impossible if outstanding measures are not taken by humanity as a whole.

Obsession is psychic pollution. Poisonous gases, chemicals, radioactivity, and radio waves affect our mental, emotional, and physical natures. Obsession in conjunction with outer pollution has the most destructive effect on all life forms. Pollution on any plane is the seed of obsession. When our threefold personality is purified, obsession and possession become impossible.

There are also invisible entities who either cheer us or lead us into depression. Some people are very sensitive to those invisible guests who visit them occasionally for certain reasons. Such guests are of various kinds. There are those who bring inspiration, courage, energy, and hope. There are those who bring depression, who sap energy, and who slow down the motion of the higher centers. There are also those who temporarily or permanently possess people and use their mechanism.

Most cases of depression are the result of gray entities who come and enter our aura and consume our energy, but generally we attribute our depression to other causes. These entities not only sap our energy, but they pull the focus of our consciousness from higher centers to lower centers and fill our higher centers with hopeless thoughts and feelings, curtailing the vision of the future.

The ancients told us that when one feels the approach of depression, he must invoke joyful thoughts and visions and keep himself extremely busy in order to prevent the settling of the gray entities in his aura. Some inspirational readings, invocations, prayers, and certain songs can push away such entities whose intention is to use man as their food.

Illusions can also facilitate possession and obsession. Illusions are in many forms. They are essentially thoughtforms of truths, facts, and events which have been distorted. They are also distortions of the image of a human being and related facts. For example, a woman intensely attached to her teacher creates his thoughtform to such a degree that she sees it around her. This thoughtform speaks to her and even answers questions, as it is connected to the mental reservoir of her teacher. The mental thoughtform is not really her teacher but an illusion.

She may fall into despair when suddenly the thoughtform begins to give wrong or negative messages to her. This happens when an advanced mental entity from the Dark Lodge occupies this thoughtform and functions in it and through it. For the devoted woman it will have the same form, but the instructions coming out of the thoughtform will be contrary to that which she used to receive.

Such a case is not rare. If the real teacher is an advanced Initiate, he can destroy the thoughtform. If not, he becomes a source of many confusing thoughtforms built by devotees.

It may also happen that the Solar Angel utilizes such a thoughtform built by devotion and love and contacts the personality and guides it on a righteous path. The Solar Angel may answer questions and help the person solve his problems until he learns to utilize his mind.

In such instances, the Solar Angel, using the image that the devotee was attached to, evokes a striving toward perfection from the person. No matter how the person lives, he still feels that he must aspire to perfection. Through such a form of action, the person is always led into the right direction.

When the person reaches maturity, the image slowly dissolves, and the person feels a spiritual loneliness. He often asks, "Why have you forsaken me?" But in the depths of the person, the Solar Angel watches him, subtly inspires him, and encourages him toward the goal of the mastery of life. This is why, since ancient times, devotion to the Teacher was encouraged and the tie between the Teacher and the student was considered sacred.

As long as the person lives a life of purity and one-pointed devotion, it will be impossible to be obsessed or possessed by dark forces. The danger starts when the devotee follows the path of lower pleasures, develops greed, uses alcohol or drugs, or enjoys various vices. The dark forces notice such a change and occupy the thoughtforms or illusions and lead the person into destruction.

This is why all back-sliders were warned gravely in religious circles to be extremely watchful, as they would fall into the hands of dark ones.

It is often noticed that when a devotee or a student of wisdom withdraws from discipline and falls into the pools of his pleasures, very soon a degeneration process takes place in his nature. It starts in his feelings, spreads to his thinking, and gradually manifests in various diseases in his body.[2]

In times past obsession and possession were considered the only source of all diseases. That is why in all ancient temples and religious circles people had various dances, ceremonies, and rituals to exorcise the evil spirits and heal the sick person.

---

2. See Chapters 33, 34, *Challenge For Discipleship*, pp. 265-286.

27

Karma and the Subtle Worlds

People have the opinion that immediately after passing away they are free from the consequences of their deeds or karma. Karma creates results in the earthly spheres and continues into the Subtle and Fiery Worlds. The conditions of our existence in the Subtle Worlds depend on our karma created while we were on earth.

Our deeds create results on earth. Our emotions create results in the Subtle World. Our thoughts create results in the Fiery World. We become the victims of our actions on the three planes. All the seeds of karma are planted while we are on earth.

It is easier to see the results of our karma from the Subtle or Fiery Worlds. In these worlds, we see clearly the consequences of our karma affecting us in the three worlds, as well as how the rest of our karma will manifest in our next incarnations.

People do not realize the seriousness of karma while they are on the lower astral planes. Those who are on higher planes see the consequences of the Law of Karma, but when they return to earth, they do not consider it seriously.

It is important to realize the dimensions of the effects of our actions. Our actions in the world create results in the Subtle and Fiery Worlds. They affect people, animals, and plants around us and around the world. It is impossible to see the end of the effects in Space. Such a recognition would force us to develop a sense of responsibility in the highest degree and have a pure watchfulness over our thoughts, words, and actions.

We do not create karma in the Subtle World perhaps because in that world all that is active and decisive is the result of the causes we put into motion while on earth. We are controlled totally by the *effects*, whether good or bad. If we do things creatively and advance, it is because we set in motion all the causes of it on the physical plane.

We are told that "it is impossible to acquire in the Subtle World those qualities that we have disregarded in our earthly lives."[1] It is, therefore, almost impossible to acquire a new consciousness in the Subtle World, but if we had seeds of aspiration, they may turn into knowledge. It is possible to see the consequences of our vices and, with the help of a Teacher, to realize that in coming incarnations they must be worked out and cleared away.

If a man is serving, striving, and helping people in the Subtle World, it is because he collected such urges and aspirations within his soul while living on earth. In the Subtle World they are put in action, and they create results. Action in the Subtle World is the extension of one's efforts on earth.

Other actions which are produced by semi-conscious beings on lower levels do not create karma because they are motivated or caused by glamors and illusions, not by the man himself.

People who live on earth and work in the Subtle World create karma, bad or good, because the origination of their actions is the earthly existence, the field of causes and effects.

Those who have learned to work on earth, not for the results but for the labor itself, will advance to higher positions quickly when in the Subtle World. You labor not for yourself or for the result; you do your labor because it is right to do it. The energy and urge of that labor originated from the earthly life.

Most of our actions have immediate results in the Subtle World, whether we are stationed there or here on earth. But if our actions are motivated from the earth, they have long range as well as immediate effects.

Our habits and vices go with us into the Subtle World. They stay with us and then return with us to earth. But if we consciously penetrate the higher strata of the Subtle World, we can clear them away. Our vices and habits grow and spread if we retain them every time we pass away and enter the lower strata. The strongest measures must be taken to eliminate them while we are in our physical bodies. By increasing our spiritual labor, striving, and sacrificial service, we uplift ourselves into the higher strata. When we pass away and see the futility and danger of vices and habits, we return with a clear impression and an urge to make ourselves free from them.

Another way to eliminate vices is sincerely to aspire to higher values, follow the Teaching as far as possible, and be anxious to serve

---

1. *Letters of Helena Roerich*, vol.2, pp. 343-344.

and help people. During sleep such a person will raise himself to the higher strata of the Subtle World and there understand the uselessness, the futility, and the future dangers of his vices and habits. The process of understanding takes place through dramatic and symbolic dreams in which he can see how his vices and habits are affecting others, how people look at him subjectively, and how he creates various contradictions and conflicts in his life between how he wants to appear and what he is in essence. Such experiences in the Subtle World strongly impress his mind and the person slowly drops his vices and habits.

It is also possible that during sleep one visits people who are caught in various emotional, mental, and other character traps, educates them in symbolic or dramatic ways, and frees them from their traps. It is possible to do such things in the Subtle World while one is in the physical world, but one must know how to do it and have enough protection so as not to be contaminated by those one tries to help.

Contamination is a real problem in the lower strata of the Subtle World, and while trying to help others eliminate their vices and habits, many well-intentioned people develop the symptoms of vices and habits of those whom they want to help. Every server is subject to such attacks, but if he is strong in psychic energy, the flame of his heart brings an immediate cure.

It is also seen that if a person wants to help another person in the Subtle World be free from those vices or habits that he himself has in his own nature, two kinds of results appear. In trying to help the other person, he may also help himself and eventually conquer them. This is due to the fact that he uses his rationality and raises himself above the level where the vices live and germinate. Also, it is possible that his vices and habits grow and become stronger while he is trying to help a person with similar defects. This happens when his consciousness is focused on the same level as the vices and habits and when his subconsciousness is restimulated, while because of his goodwill he *wishes* to help.

The important point in helping others is to communicate with them from a higher level.

It is necessary to release our Real Self from the traps of our ego. Many incarnations are wasted and many loads of karma have accumulated because of our ego. As the ego gets bigger, it becomes more difficult to annihilate it.

One cannot become free from his ego until he sees the scope of the effect of his deeds.

The value of each thought, word, and action can be determined only when a person comes in contact with the Subtle and Higher Worlds. One can develop a standard of values only when he comes in contact with the values of the higher astral and Fiery Worlds. Those who live only for their egos do not have a developed sense of values. Those who are in contact with the Subtle Worlds love beauty and those values which are more universal and help the progress of humanity.

It is only after coming in contact with the Higher Worlds that we develop a new orientation toward greater values because we see or sense the effect of our whole life in the various strata of life. We distinctly see that those actions which have originated from our ego are the ones which limit our progress, cause us suffering and pain, and make us less free to choose our own path.

It is also interesting that in the Subtle World one cannot develop new vices. It is on the earth that vices are germinated, developed, and used. One can continue his vices in the lowest levels of the Subtle World, but as he climbs higher, they look stupid and non-interesting.

To overcome our vices, we need to fight against them while we are on earth. It is only on the physical plane that we can develop the energies to overcome our vices. It is interesting to know that though we may carry our vices into the Subtle World, we cannot find satisfaction in them. One can never gratify his vices in the Subtle World because gratification of the vices is felt mostly by and through the physical vehicle. Each vice exercised in the Subtle World creates a flame which burns the astral vehicle, causing much pain and suffering to the soul.

The danger in carrying vices into the Subtle World comes from the fact that the carriers of vices try to come in close contact with low-level human beings whose consciousness is asleep on earth. They try to stimulate them and direct them to similar vices, in order to feel their satisfaction through their vices. Easier access is given to such spirits when alcohol is used; when one goes to sleep with the thoughts and feelings of malice, slander, and greed; or when one sleeps near slaughterhouses, whorehouses, or places where there is moral pollution, stagnated matter, or rubbish. Cleanliness is a great help in rejecting such nightly visitors from our homes.

Blood also attracts such visitors. One of the factors that greatly helps them is a foul mouth, a loose mouth, or a mouth that pours out filth, curses, and blasphemy. Such emanations radiate certain signals to the carriers of vices from the Subtle World.

Human vices and habits continue to exist throughout many incarnations. It is possible for them to grow and become stronger.

Vices or habits can be eliminated if the will is activated and used strongly to destroy them.

If the person succeeds in climbing consciously to the highest strata of the Subtle World, he can dissolve the accumulations of vices and habits in his astral body. Each vice or habit originates from a force formation in the aura, and this subtle tumor is not easy to destroy.

The higher harmony and fires of the highest levels of the Subtle World can dissolve them. They can also be dissolved if strong will is exercised on them while one is still living on earth.

We are told that humanity must be very careful not to contact the lowest stratum of the Subtle World. This is so because

1. The lowest stratum provokes the world into war, revolutions, crimes. It is only in such conditions that the inhabitants of the lowest stratum of the Subtle World feel satisfied.
2. Mass obsession can take place within armies and populations, and degeneration of morals can spread within the fighting nations and then throughout the world when people contact the lowest stratum.
3. The lowest stratum of the Subtle World is flooded by the newcomers loaded with various crimes. Contact with them can have fatal results.

Crimes on earth draw a great amount of force around the criminal. This field of force carries the image of the crime within it, and, like a videotape, the crime plays in the Subtle World continuously until the tape wears out and the force field is exhausted. Thus, every criminal not only continuously experiences his own crimes but also his own execution of them. Many of our nightmares are patches of such experiences in the Subtle World.

In the battlefield where the blood of millions is shed and is in a state of decomposition, numberless entities from the astral world are attracted. The emanations from decomposed blood and the associated emotions, horrors, and thoughts are the food by which low astral entities live. Thus, all kinds of bloodshed bring the lower astral world into contact with the earth.

We are told that these astral entities are attached to the auras of those who eat meat, who work in graveyards and taverns, and who consume alcohol and drugs. The first sign of such an attachment is a feeling of vampirism in which all your energy is suddenly exhausted. After your body adjusts itself, you feel emotional and mental depression; then the degeneration of your morals starts.

On the other hand, those who pass into the Subtle World full of striving toward the Hierarchy continue their striving in the Subtle World and make great progress in learning the pure Teaching. These souls attract the attention of the great Initiates, who come directly and teach them the things they need most. Many greater servers in various fields of human endeavor are thus inspired and educated in the Subtle World. They return with the fire of enthusiasm and are charged with the vision of the Plan, ready to sacrifice their lives to actualize the Plan on earth.

When we consider the effect of our actions, we must realize that certain actions create more karma than others. For example, killing an average person and killing a great prophet do not create the same karma. In killing a prophet, one may create national karma, instead of individual karma. A prophet is the result of age-long striving, labor, sacrifice, and achievements. His benefit to the world and his possible service are not limited to a few individuals but extend to millions of people. Destroying a stone is not the same thing as destroying a fruit-bearing tree. Karma takes into consideration all these factors.

All kingdoms are traveling toward developing a selfhood, and each member gradually develops it as he enters higher kingdoms. For example, in the mineral kingdom, the spirit is locked and it advances through the fire of Nature. In the vegetable kingdom, each plant and tree is ensouled with the spirit not yet individualized but, rather, in a state which can be explained as follows:

All vegetable forms, bushes, and trees are like dewdrops which, when they evaporate, become parts of a cloud. This cloud has many gradations. The huge pine tree and the grass do not go to the same level, but they do go to the same chemical formation and come back and produce a new plant. The important point to realize is that the gradations of the cloud advance and develop as a whole, not as individual trees, bushes, etc. A part of the cloud comes again and forms another tree, but the essence of this tree is not of any individual, particular tree.

For example, I have two hundred bottles of water. Each of them contains the same water. I pour them into a barrel and again fill my bottles with the water; it does not make any difference.

But if each time a tree is exposed to different influences, the essence of the tree develops, and so does the "cloud." This is why, when we eat plants, we do not retard the individual process of development. When eating them fresh, we give to their essence the experience of a higher form of existence.

But the case of animals is different. The animal spirit is not a cloud, but it is separated into stable forms. In eating an animal we stop its progress as a separate being and retard its evolution toward higher kingdoms.

Killing a man is a greater crime because the human spirit is not only separated from the mass spirit but also individualized. In the animal stage, the spirit is functioning on the astral plane and is still not completely a self. In the human stage, the human soul is himself; all Cosmos is within the soul as a microcosm.

Karma heavily strikes those who shed human blood because they retard not only the progress of individuals but also the progress of those with whom those individuals were connected.

The human soul has his time limit on every plane of the astral, mental, and Fiery Worlds. When the time is over on one plane, the wheel of the law carries him to the next plane. After he completes his time with the lower mental world, he either passes to the Fiery World or begins to descend, level by level, to the physical world.

Each soul has his own time table according to his unfoldment, responsibilities, rays, etc. Some people stay two thousand years on one plane; others stay only ten days, or even less. But all move under the Law of Karma and the Law of Reincarnation.

If a human soul needs further education, he returns to the earth. He descends from the mental plane to the astral and then to the etheric-physical plane. During his journey down to earth, he puts on heavier and denser vehicles.

Karmic law distributes the souls to the right locations, to the right parents, and into certain conditions where their karma must be met and their progress will be guaranteed. Karmic law has one intention: to position human beings in those conditions where they can meet their karmic obligations and progress on the Path of Perfection. Every human soul is born in the places for which he actually prepared himself in his past lives.

People complain about the conditions in which they are, but they forget that their present conditions are exactly the result of how they lived.

Advanced souls bring many memories or impressions from the Subtle Worlds. Those who are not unfolded yet in their consciousness *feel* that they just came into existence. They do not have any past and perhaps no future impressions.

Actually, there are people who are stuck to material possessions, and they have no relation with the Subtle Worlds and spiritual values. They live and try to enjoy life, but when life presents problems to them, they are surprised and think that some injustice is done to them by people. They react violently toward those who try to show a path toward greater and more inclusive values.

The lowest level of the astral plane is full of criminals, suicide victims, and victims of wars. Because of wars, millions of people pass away into the Subtle World before their predestined time and carry with them all the pain, suffering, and agony of their lives. Most of them are full of revenge and hatred, and they often psychically pollute, with their hatred and revenge, millions of people where they were killed. Very often they sneak into incarnation through those people who use drugs or have fallen into various vices because they look for those who can support and amplify their feelings of revenge, crime, and hatred.

This is why the Elders of the human race have always suggested that we be very serious when bringing children to earth. Special ceremonies were given in the *Upanishads* to raise the consciousness of a couple desiring children to such a degree that they attracted only advanced souls.[2] If such a preparation is not done and conception takes place under the influence of drugs, in the corridors of movie theaters, or in cars, it is very probable that lower astral human souls will sneak in. People who are under the influence of drugs or alcohol or contaminated with venereal diseases are often obsessed before they attract low level beings into conception.

Karma is the law that brings equilibrium whenever the Law of Love and Light is violated and power is misused for personal ends.

Often karma is painful, disciplinary, and imposing. But, of course, behind karma stands the Cosmic Love.

Grace has a close relationship with forgiveness and bliss. Grace is the accumulation of interest from all the actions done on the physical, emotional, and mental planes to increase light, love, goodness, harmony, beauty, and energy. It is a savings account in your Chalice.

All good actions bring their own results or effects, and we call such effects *grace*.

Grace is not something you receive for which you did not labor. It is the answer to your love, sacrifice, and beauty, planted seed by seed in Space throughout your incarnations. The flowers of these seeds bloom on your path without your expectation. Help reaches you, a

---

2.   For information on attracting advanced souls, please refer to *Sex, Family, and the Woman in Society*.

light shows the way, a touch heals you, sunshine wipes away your tears, and, like a bird, joy visits your heart.

We live in a Universe of cause and effect. Not a single seed of beauty that you planted in Space will be lost. Age after age it will accumulate. In the dark hours of your life, it will knock at your door.

Of course, grace will pay your debts of karma, and it will protect you from the violent blows of karma. It will create endurance, patience, and joy in you to meet the unpaid karma.

Just as we have Karmic Lords, we have also the Lord of Grace, which is the Chalice of the Hierarchy as a whole in which is accumulated all drops of love, light, and beauty.

Christ serves as the distributor of Grace. He does not judge but heals with Grace, and if necessary He receives the arrows of Cosmic evil to protect humanity from suffering.

28

Departure to the Subtle World

We are told that during the moment of transition into the Subtle World, one experiences the sensation of dizziness or fainting. If the consciousness is purified and transmuted, the astral senses begin to function and put the soul in contact with the astral world. But if the consciousness is blocked because of denial or rejection of a life-after, or because of karmic reasons, one feels as if he is losing his own reality.

If the departed one is a criminal or a person without merit, his suffering, we are told, is inconceivable. When the departed one is full of fire, which has accumulated in him through sacrificial service, heroic dedication, and daring, after the transition the fire makes all the senses function, and the consciousness soon adapts itself to the new situation. The fire in the heart lights the path and leads him toward higher levels of the Subtle World. The fire in the heart, which is sometimes called Agni, leads his soul toward great Beings on the higher astral levels where They visit to care for the departed ones.

The Path leading to the Fiery World is opened only through the increasing fire of our Chalice. This fire increases as the result of our purity, dedication, selflessness, and sacrifice for humanity.

Before one enters into the Subtle World, the glamor of possessions makes a strong attack on the subject. For a short time he feels that all he had is lost. At this moment, the memory is so clear that man recalls all that he has. The Teachers warn us to prepare for this point, and before death learn that all possessions belong to the earth; we must understand that all we had was not ours. Such a state of detachment must be ours before we pass away.

In various esoteric organizations this attitude is exercised in many ways. All that people have belongs to the community, and they have no attachment whatsoever. The world will slowly develop such a consciousness if it advances on the spiritual Path.

The soul faces the crisis of attachment to possessions, and if he was prepared to let them go, he finds himself upon higher levels of the astral plane. Those who attach mentally to their possessions enter a phase of intense conflict and anxiety. They do not want to let go of their possessions. Upon entering the Subtle World, they even duplicate all their possessions through their thoughts and feel comfortable. But this immensely retards their progress in the Subtle World.

The conflict becomes fiery when the time nears to leave the lower levels of the Subtle Worlds for the higher ones. Thus, the sense of possession turns into a curse and a chain from which the attached soul cannot release himself.

Fortunately, there are helpers on these levels who teach people how to get rid of possessions, but not many people want to listen to them until their intense conflict begins.

In the Subtle and Fiery Worlds people are in continuous striving toward the Cosmic Mysteries. Many experimentations are in progress. Mostly they try to develop their own senses and use them for research. The Fiery World for them is a great sphere of research.

Whenever a chaotic state is created on earth, such as revolutions, wars, genocides, destructive upheavals of emotions and thoughts, it affects and threatens the Subtle World. Even the explosions on the earth penetrate the Subtle World and carry much destruction and many disturbances there. We are even told that the pollution of the air forces many benevolent spirits to leave and depart from our atmosphere. Thus man, with his own hand and for his own greed and hatred, not only destroys the beauty of our earth but also causes irreparable damage to heavenly orders, thus working against his own future.

If the world increases in its pollution, future souls will have a difficult time incarnating into such a world. They will not find conditions in which to continue their schooling on earth.

How can one develop detachment from the past and from his possessions? This is accomplished only if man develops his future visions. For example, instead of accumulating money, he gradually develops a state of beingness in which he does not need money. He becomes like an angel; he does not need to eat, to dress, to have a house. He shines with colors and lights. The Universe is his home; he can travel like a beam of light; he does not need a car; he does not need gas. He does not even need protection because his aura extends for miles and burns any adversary.

Such ideas must be presented to the public in the form of stories and fairy tales in order to help them detach their consciousness from the state of slavery to possessions. Greed is strongly condemned in the Teaching, not because it creates pain and suffering in the world, but because it prevents the transformation of the consciousness and does not allow people to penetrate into the higher spheres of the Subtle Worlds.

The greedy man suffers extremely in the Subtle World. This is because in the Subtle World the more you want to have, the less you enjoy your life. Each possession becomes a new burden on your shoulders and a new trap on your way. The emanations from greed are very inflammable, and they burn your astral body. Greed blinds you totally and makes it impossible for you to realize that you need nothing in the Subtle World but deeper wisdom, greater detachment, and renouncement. The more you detach from the things you do not need, the more you begin to awaken.

But people are too busy building houses and opening businesses to make money in the Subtle World. You do not need a house there because it is only good if you have a physical body. You do not need money either because you can have anything you want. But as long as you keep yourself busy possessing things, your consciousness remains an earthly consciousness; it does not make a breakthrough into new conditions.

Some people lose hundreds of years going through all the horrors of building and making money. There are others in the Subtle World, as there are on earth, who want to destroy whatever others build and steal whatever others make. In the Subtle World there also occur occasional electrical storms which often wipe away many forms made through imagination, leaving people who are attached to possessions in deep desolation.

People must understand that our future is in beingness, not in havingness. Havingness cannot provide beingness, but when one *is,* he will have all that he needs.

People used to worship the golden calf, and still we continue to do so. Instead, Teachers have given the vision of a future, free from matter and possessions, which will not only minimize our suffering on earth but also prepare us for the Subtle World, where one cannot enter with the golden calf. A sudden shock will teach humanity how useless it is to be attached to possessions and how useless to perpetuate the spirit of greed.

On each level of ascent one confronts the following:

    a. A new substance
    b. A new way of communication
    c. A new adjustment

Each plane has a different substance, and it is not easy to adjust oneself from one substance to another without losing consciousness. But if the fire of the heart is aflame, the transition from one substance to another becomes a challenging joy.

On each step, the fire of the heart opens one's consciousness to deal with the new way of communication. On the way to the Higher Worlds, we also have our Guide who advises us to proceed in a certain manner. Sometimes It is called the "most patient one." Often It sees how we wait on the path for a long period under the burden of worldly memories, interests, and concerns.

There are many exciting formations in the higher levels of the Subtle World. There exist great beauties of colors, dances of beams of lights, and formations of visible waves of joy, love, and gratitude. All these waves, colors, and rays fill Space, giving a great delight to the inhabitants of the Subtle World. Then there are fireworks of the flames of the hearts which create the most beautiful symphony of colors in Space. There is the beauty of the Shining Ones, with Their fiery robes and wings. There are also impressions coming from the Fiery World which bloom like huge flowers in Space.

Everything beautiful in the human soul blossoms and becomes visible in the Subtle World. This is how the sense of beauty challenges one to go toward the Source of Beauty.

We are told that there is conflict not only between the Subtle World and the earth, but also between the Fiery World and the Subtle World. The conflict between the Subtle World and the earth originates from the fact that the earth pollutes the Subtle Worlds through air pollution, noise pollution, micro waves, radio waves, blood and hatred, and many other things.

The conflict between the Fiery World and the Subtle World originates from the fact that inhabitants of the Subtle World oppose fiery rays penetrating into the Subtle World and disturbing their comfort. Fiery thoughts evoke a higher state of formation, a higher state of orchestration of life, and the Subtle World cannot cope with it without fiery renunciation and greater expansion of consciousness.

The Fiery World also rejects all the poison that arises from certain strata of the Subtle World. This poison is generated by those thoughts which still carry within them certain amounts of negative emotions, separatism, antagonism, judgment, criticism, and greed. Such uses of energy create poison in the Subtle World, the waves of which reach the Fiery World and create strong reactions.

The principles presented in the Subtle World for ascent are the same as the ones on earth, but with deeper implications. They are

—Detachment or freedom
—Harmlessness
—Joy
—Love
—Gratitude

These are the five steps upon which a wise soul ascends toward the Fiery World. Those who strive from the earth and make the needed adjustments in their consciousness eventually penetrate into the Subtle World. Those in the Subtle World who are able to create a fiery, striving tension welcome all the rays from the Fiery World and proceed onward. The inhabitants of the Subtle World must eventually find the ways to transmute the worldly chaos reaching their shores. Those who have fiery hearts in the Higher Worlds use that fire for the transmutation of those elements which create conflict and change them into useful elements to be used for various constructions. When the flame of the heart purifies the fire of thought, the links between the worlds are established.

Joy is another way to approach the Fiery and Subtle Worlds. We are told that joy not only nourishes the consciousness but also preserves it. The joy of beauty is one of the highest flames which destroys many hindrances on the Path of ascent. Those who have beauty, and the joy of beauty, slowly find their way to the gates of the Fiery World. The Fiery World is a sphere of beauty and joy.

It is important to prepare oneself for the departure from earth. The mental body, together with the astral body, withdraws itself from the physical body. On the Path of ascent, the astral body burns away, if the person is advanced and if he is ready to enter the Fiery World. But if his destination is the astral plane, the astral body serves as a vehicle of contact with the astral world through its centers and senses. Later, if man advances out of the astral sphere into the fiery sphere, the separation between the astral and mental bodies occurs. The mental body must be inflamed with the fire of the Intuition to be able to penetrate the Fiery World. Thus, step by step, the human soul unites himself with the Higher Worlds, leaving, stage by stage, the bodies which cannot be used in higher spheres.

The last hours of the departure from the physical realms to the Higher Worlds are considered sacred. These are hours in which the departing one, as much as possible, must concentrate his light on His Master or on Christ and joyfully relax himself in order to float out of the sphere of the body. Total silence and the feeling of joy and gratitude must fill the sphere of the room. If it is night, dim candlelight is proper, with some sandalwood and rose oil. It is also possible to have some soft music or singing of hymns.

People think of the moment of departure as a sad moment. This feeling must be reversed and the moment looked upon as a moment of great joy and liberation. An advanced soul is even anxious to depart, to experience the great beauty of the higher spheres.

The resurrection of Christ on the third day is an action of law which repeats itself in many forms and in many dimensions. In general, on the third day the soul awakens, and, with the help of his Guardian Angel, is led to the Subtle Worlds. For two days the astral body adjusts itself, and the human soul comes into a clear consciousness after the dark days of sickness, fears, and sorrow. On the third day, with the help of his Guardian Angel, he traverses the sphere of the material world. The soul is then led to the lower astral level, or the middle, or the higher, or even to the Fiery World, according to his merit.

The ascent of advanced souls is sometimes faster. After they leave their bodies and if they have developed sufficient detachment, they enter directly into Devachan or the Fiery World, according to their unfoldment and merit. Some very advanced souls wait longer if they have certain labors to do on lower planes. Some even enter the Fiery World for only a few days and reincarnate for a greater mission on earth.

People on the lowest astral plane want to incarnate as soon as they can, and often they sneak in before their time. People on the middle levels do not want to incarnate until the call arrives from their Guardian Angel. Often they disobey the call to avoid incarnation, knowing the difficulties and problems facing them in the physical life. They do not want to disturb their peace and bliss.

It is very important to realize that the ascent to the Higher Worlds passes through layers of fire, pressure, and intense currents of energy. We are told that to cross such layers one needs not only an expanded consciousness but also a purified and flaming heart. It is the heart that gives power to the consciousness to move ahead through fire, pressure, and intense currents of energy. The consciousness and the heart must move together to conquer heights.

After one leaves the physical heart, the heart center, like a golden chalice, remains with the human soul. The power and the light of the heart are conditioned by the unfolded petals. Advancing souls are like comets propelled by the heart.

As one progresses toward perfection, his consciousness and his heart merge, and he turns into a fountain of wisdom. It is important to expand our consciousness; but without an awakened heart the layers of fire, pressure, and intense currents of energy cannot be crossed, and the human soul stays in lower layers, like a bird whose wings are cut.

The simplest way to refine the heart is through the discipline of giving. The heart must learn to give good thoughts, courage, hope, trust, wisdom, guidance, love, compassion, understanding, psychic energy, fearlessness, vision, and Infinity. The gifts of the heart are endless, and the heart gives without expectation.

The expanding consciousness overshadows the steps of the heart and sees that every drop of the gifts given reaches its right place. The simplest way to expand our consciousness is to dedicate it to the service of the Hierarchy. This is not easy to understand, but one who has a living heart will know that the service for the Hierarchy means service for Beauty, Goodness, Righteousness, Joy, and Freedom. Through these five principles, the Plan of the Hierarchy is fulfilled. The layers between the Higher Worlds are crossed only by a giving heart and by a consciousness that has served the Hierarchy throughout many lives.

There is a legend that states that when conception takes place, the invisible devas engage themselves in labor to build the physical body of the human being, but they do not dare to build the heart because they know that the heart is a link between the Higher Worlds and that it must be sent to the person as a gift from the higher realms. The physical heart is just the outer shadow of the gift planted in each human being. This most precious gift is the Holy Communion given to each "departing one" as a permanent link leading back Home.

There is also another reason why some people delay their incarnation and stay longer in the Subtle Worlds. These people are highly advanced people, and they have certain specialized knowledge which can be used in the Subtle Worlds more than on earth. The appreciation of their knowledge may be premature or highly dangerous for earth humanity; therefore they choose to stay and apply their knowledge in the Subtle Worlds instead. Usually when they take an incarnation, for the purpose of safety, a large part of their knowledge is buried in the depth of their being.

It must be known that in the Subtle Worlds there are very advanced specialists in every field who are a few hundred years ahead of us. The animosity existing between the people in the world and the physical and moral pollution prevent the specialists from coming in contact with earth.

There are also highly advanced souls who prefer to work subjectively with specialists rather than in the physical body. They are the ones who impart new formulas of highly technical subjects and new ways of thinking. Their presence on earth with the abilities they have in the Subtle Worlds would create hatred and animosity from the world. They work all over the world, simultaneously with many nationalities, to facilitate new ways of thinking, instead of attracting attention to their personalities on earth. Of course, they can delay their incarnation for a while. Then the wheel of karma brings them down to earth where they do their best and sometimes risk their lives in leading the work in many fields of human endeavor.

Because of their karma, some of the advanced souls in the Subtle Worlds can have a comfortable, easy, and joyful life on earth, but they choose to go into dangerous conditions at critical times to offer their help and wisdom. These people have a great amount of heroic spirit. Some leaders who bring great changes in critical times of human history belong to this group. Because of their sacrifice, they penetrate the higher levels of the subjective world as a reward for their selfless and dedicated labor for humanity. The Hierarchy sometimes chooses them when they see that such souls are ready for incarnation. They prepare them for different missions and show them what may happen to them, but such warriors prepare to help the Hierarchy rather than to live a normal, happy life.

Progress on the Spiritual Path is not gained by easy, luxurious living but by dedicating oneself to a great goal and striving toward it through many obstacles, difficulties, pains, and suffering. Those who sacrifice more enter into greater light and pass the borders of the earthly spheres more quickly. All such heroes and self-sacrificing people are fiery souls heading toward the Fiery World.

Those who were able to live in the higher strata of the Subtle World charge their nature with a deep joy which expresses itself as endurance, striving, courage, steadfastness, and perseverance in labor, especially at the times of crisis and tensions. The higher strata of the Subtle World are full of joy. Joy shines there as the sun shines in the summer on a clear day. People who are able to penetrate into the higher strata of the Subtle World during their sleep or contemplation also charge themselves with joy and express it in their daily life. The source of the energy of some dedicated workers is the joy with which they fill their hearts while in the Subtle World.

Joy also expresses through them as creativity and wisdom. From the Subtle World one can easily see the futility of certain attachments, fears, and physical conditions and develop a sense which chooses the most essential and sees the reality beyond the forms or events on earth. "Joy is a special wisdom," said a Great One.

In the Subtle Worlds people see the transience of worldly possessions. Those who go to higher levels of the Subtle World do not carry with them their worries about their possessions. And if they leave their bodies, they do not depart carrying greed and worrying about what they left behind. This is the reason why they enter the Subtle World with joy. Joy makes them welcomed by the refined people in the Subtle World.

Joy is the song of heroes on the road to perfection. Such heroes increase their joy by engaging in dangerous battle which continues through Infinity. Joy increases in our heart when we grasp that the Light within us will never allow us to retreat from battle and run our life in the darkness of self-interest and self-existence.

Attachment to our former states of consciousness and worldly forms does not let us expand our soul toward the Higher Worlds. The departing one knows that he will return, except when he is totally blinded by the doctrine of eternal damnation, or if he continually thinks that man never returns but goes to heaven or hell. Such people go through a very hard time when they discover that the wheel of the law will carry them back to incarnation. Many of them refuse to go back; many of them delay the date; many of them return with great terror. It is so important to know about the Law of Karma and the Law of Reincarnation before one leaves the world for higher spheres. Many tensions and horrors can be eliminated if people travel consciously and in harmony with the Laws of Nature.

It is also true that many souls know about incarnation even though they do not talk about it or teach it. In the future, direct instructions will be given to disciples about how to plan for their future life and how to cooperate closely with the Law of Karma.

The Law of Cause and Effect rules the whole Cosmic Physical Plane. Man lives on the physical plane, but all his actions on any level create specific reactions from all planes. The Law of Karma follows us on all planes. The best success, achievement, and victory must be based upon the right causes. Once we create the right cause, we will receive the effect in due time.

It is also possible to change our karma through intense striving toward the Hierarchy. Advanced disciples not only bear their own karma but also voluntarily share the pains and sufferings of others. Sometimes the suffering of advanced disciples is not because of their own karma but because of the expenditure of psychic energy they use to help people directly or indirectly. A great expenditure of psychic energy may cause a very painful life for the server, but such suffering greatly helps his quick advancement in higher planes. This shows that karma is not necessarily responsible for every pain and suffering, but karma is definitely responsible for every joy, success, and bliss that comes to a person.

On the Path to the Higher Worlds such reflections help us to know the events of life.

On the Path to the Fiery World, one must develop a new way of thinking. A new way of thinking consists of seven factors:

1. Synthesis
2. Future
3. Transformation of life
4. Transmutation of consciousness
5. Purification of the Teaching
6. Preparation for the Fiery World
7. Purification of the planet

If our thoughts are inspired by these factors, then we may say that our thinking is constructive and in harmony with the New Age. On the Path to the Fiery World these seven factors must be developed in our thinking. Thoughts inspired by these seven factors will build the bridge between our earth and the Fiery World.

It is impossible to reach the Fiery World without refining the life on earth. Those who destroy the life on earth will not inherit the Fiery World. One can penetrate the Fiery World only when he remains faithful to the laws of the earth.

Purification of the world is a process of building a Path toward the Fiery World. This purification, synthesis, transformation of consciousness on earth, and other factors are understood when thinking power is cultivated with all sincerity and dedication.

When these seven factors serve as a foundation of our thinking, we have already built the body to travel to the Fiery World.

There is a widespread misunderstanding that all people enter the astral plane when they sleep. The fact is that not so many enter the astral plane after they sleep. Many people wander on earth in their etheric bodies and visit places to which they are attracted because of their urges and drives or because of their desires and interests. Most people linger around their bodies. The majority of people are sensitive to astral vibrations, which cause them to dream or to register various directions given by astral entities.

To be in the astral plane is not the same thing as being in contact with the astral plane in some degree. For example, we are in contact with the Sun, but we are not in the Sun. It is a small percentage of people who enter the astral plane consciously.

Also, there are those who are unconscious in the astral plane; they are nowhere. In the esoteric definition, you do not exist if you are not conscious; you do not exist on a plane where you are not conscious. If someone enters a room where scientific formulas are being demonstrated and people are talking about them in scientific terms but he has no idea about such formulas and discussions, in reality he is not even in the room.

Your vehicle can be anywhere, but if you are not conscious about where you are and why you are there, you are not in that sphere. It is your consciousness and awareness that condition your existence and presence, not your vehicle.

On the other hand, it is possible to be anywhere through your awareness of it.

When one leaves his body in death, he is naturally drawn to the astral plane. This is why there are some advanced souls who work in the astral levels and who are called Invisible Servers.

There is also another point to be considered. One who still lives with his physical body can be in his own astral body but not in the astral world. He can be in the astral world if his astral centers and senses are active. This is not the same as receiving impressions or recording vibrations from that certain plane.

It is possible to appear on the physical plane with your body, but in the meantime to be in the mental plane with your mental body.

After one passes away, if he is not ready to enter the astral plane, he wanders for a while. But in a few days, according to the laws of Nature, he enters the level of the astral plane where he fits in. This is why there are many unconscious men and women in the astral plane who are physically dead, but there is no unconscious human being in the astral plane who still lives in the physical body.

Those who are advanced and still live in the physical body are those who can only be in the astral plane consciously.

Christ explained the mystery of being present and absent in a plane, or in a level of a plane, with the following story: A rich man was giving a party. He saw that there was a fellow there who did not have the proper dress for the party. He called his servants and told them to take the man out.

The man had sneaked into the party, but in actuality he was not even there because he did not have the vehicle for that plane.

The first steps to penetrate into the subtle planes or higher strata of consciousness are

1. Prayer
2. Meditation

3. Sacrificial service
4. Deeds of heroism
5. Silence

Through these five steps one can gradually tune into the Hierarchical frequency and be guided into the Subtle Worlds.

1. Prayer. Daily one must establish a rhythm of prayer. Prayer is not a way of asking for things but a way of fusion with the Almighty Presence in the Universe.

2. Meditation is a technique to cooperate with the Plan of Higher Beings in the Universe. Meditation also dissipates the ego and brings in humility.

3. Sacrificial service. One must find a field in which he can work for a lofty purpose without expectation and self-interest. He must prove this through his endurance as oppositions, complications, and dangers face him in his life.

4. Deeds of heroism are concentrated, planned, and orchestrated deeds which benefit all of humanity, deeds carried out with courage and daring unto death.

5. Silence. One can create a great amount of energy through silence. Silence is achievement of mastery over the disturbances and activities of our vehicles. Silence leads into peace because it harmonizes all elements of our nature. Silence is achieved when the noises of our vehicles are quieted. Most of our speech is an expression of these noises. Relaxation in the body is a form of silence.

Silence is not the absence of sound and movement. It is the harmony of sound and movement. Peace in your heart, serenity in your mind, and bliss in your soul are forms of silence. Harmony between the three vehicles and the Self is silence. Labor, worship, and concentration of the mind on a lofty subject are ways to create inner silence.

Prayer, meditation, sacrificial service, heroic deeds, and silence create some sort of an element in your aura which, when you pass away, turns into a fuel which propels you toward the Higher Worlds. Earthly attachment, memories, identifications, and duties pull you down to earth. To overcome that pull, you need the fuel created by these five steps which will propel you higher and higher until you reach the plane where you fit.

Actually, virtues, which are the result of these five steps, are energy sources in your aura. A virtue is a power; it is an energy. This fuel begins to activate itself immediately when one leaves his etheric and physical bodies. In a sense, it disengages the astral body from the etheric body and propels it up toward the Higher Worlds.

We must know that after death there are various obstacles which try to hinder our journey. Symbolically and collectively they are called the *dark angel*. They are

    a. Accumulations of our wrongdoings, wrong thoughts, and wrong words
    b. Astral attacks
    c. Electromagnetic disturbances in the air
    d. Collective pollution of human immorality
    e. Cosmic Rays
    f. Fear

All these obstacles are overcome by the energies created through the five steps given above. Criminals cannot go higher than the lowest level of the astral plane because they lack the needed "fuel."

When you pass away, the five beneficial elements in your aura are used to create the following in you:

    a. Increasing awareness
    b. Balance in your flight
    c. Increasing speed in your journey
    d. Protection from certain attacks
    e. Right direction in your journey

If you read *The Egyptian Book of the Dead,* all these phases of the journey are symbolically given. These five steps also expand your consciousness, increase your willpower for creativity, and synchronize you with the frequency of the Hierarchy. Such a synchronization with the frequency of the Hierarchy makes you realize that everything personal is transient and that you need to offer yourself in total dedication to service. It also creates an urge in you toward self-renunciation and humility.

One cannot raise himself to higher levels of consciousness and contact the Hierarchy unless he is *humble*. Humility opens the gates to trust, knowledge, and position. Lack of humility means that one is trapped in personal vanity, pride, and illusion. In such a condition one cannot approach the Hierarchy. Our ego is built by our vanities, pride, illusions, and glamors. It is just like a millstone hanging from our necks, preventing our ascent.

29

Cooperation
Between the Worlds

Cooperation between the inhabitants of the higher astral plane and the Fiery World should be mutual. Departed ones must cultivate the means to reach the Fiery World, and those of the earth must cultivate means to reach the Higher Worlds. In both worlds there are advanced souls who can help each other until the time comes when the three worlds will function as one field in full cooperation. Our humanity is destined to reach such a stage of development if it does not hinder its own path through ignorance and self-deceit.

Throughout centuries the Hierarchy has kept this link between the worlds. They usually live on this earth, but They have complete access into the Subtle and Fiery Worlds. Of course, Their consciousness penetrates into very high spheres for greater inspiration and advancement.

We are told that Satan is an actual force, and he has numberless assistants. His purpose is to destroy this world so that the incarnation of human beings would be impossible for millions of years. After the destruction of the world, Satan will concentrate his forces in full measure on the Subtle World. We are told that the Forces of Light and the Hierarchy are in fiery labor to prevent such a catastrophe and to enable the evolution of humanity to continue on earth. For this purpose the Hierarchy created many centers of observation in the great Ashram itself, and many forces are collected to oppose the hordes of Satan.

The Hierarchy sends Its call to humanity to stand vigilant, to create cooperation between all nations, and to increase Beauty, Goodness, Righteousness, Joy, and Freedom in the world. Every little labor for such a vision is greatly appreciated by the Head of the Hierarchy.

Communication with the Fiery and Subtle Worlds is not beyond human ability. The easiest path is the purification of the heart and the development of harmlessness. As the heart is purified and its flame shines through all the expressions of man, he comes closer to the

Subtle and Fiery Worlds and communication becomes natural and harmless.

The Fiery World must be convinced that the communicator will not waste the given energy and wisdom, that he will not misuse it for his personal ends but will use it for the benefit of all humanity, with extreme caution, co-measurement, and a pure sense of timing. All of these qualities cannot be achieved in one day, but they are the flowers which bloom with the labor of ages and under the flame of the heart.

As one purifies his heart, greater and greater help is given to him by the Hierarchy and greater opportunities and challenges are opened for him.

There are many things that create cleavages between the worlds:

—Materialism
—Totalitarianism
—Doubt about the Higher Worlds
—Denial of higher principles
—Degeneration of morals
—Separatism, hatred, revenge
—Treason, malice, slander
—Action or words against the Hierarchy
—Karmic accumulations
—Unreadiness
—Involvement with the trash of life
—Dishonesty

All of these things and many others prevent the reception of higher calls and keep man earthbound.

Life has morality. The foundation, the growth, and the culmination of life forms are controlled by moral laws, namely, the Law of Unity, the Law of Synthesis, and the Law of Progressive Unfoldment of Beauty and Glory. All other true moral laws are branches of these three laws.

Treason, for example, is a violation of these three laws, and it is the worst attack on the Core of the human being. We are told that when a traitor passes away, he is immediately caught by a storm of chaotic forces in which he loses all life-giving energy and is in danger of total disintegration.

In the Teaching we are told that when one is drawn off by chaotic forces, he experiences the deepest pain and suffering because all his vehicles begin to disintegrate. The victim feels that he exists, but all the supports of his existence slowly fall away. It is even possible that his individuality dissolves into the elements and the Self evaporates in

Space. The traitor infects many people around him with poison. We are told that he can even destroy the happiness of an entire country.

Every type of treason blocks the path of ascent of the traitor. It is possible for a leader or a Teacher to save some traitors from ultimate destruction, if the leader uses great courage and daring at the start of the treason.

Treason starts in the mental plane, in the mind. Those who can penetrate into the mental plane are able to observe the roots and branches of growing treason. Often one cannot remember the details, but the impression remains in the heart of the observer, and whenever the traitor is contacted, his heart warns. Sometimes traitors have mental obsession, and it is not easy to help them. Only one who has continuity of consciousness can expel the obsessor and free the man from the trap of treason.

Often traitors follow certain Initiates in an attempt to cause failure to Their work. They follow Them life after life until they can fulfill their intention. It is after they commit the crime that they are caught in the forces of chaos.

There have been many traitors in the history of humanity. Their treason was directed at millions of people in their own country as well as the world.

Almost all nations come into being by the will of Shamballa. Those who act against the highest interest of their nation through treason act against the will of Shamballa. The fire of Shamballa strikes all traitors. Such people do not even enter into the astral world but are caught in the currents of chaos.

In order to avoid treasonous behavior, one must try to do the following:

1. Serve people with self-forgetfulness, harmlessness, and right speech.
2. Cultivate the heart and have compassion.
3. Learn pure thinking, inclusiveness, and synthesis.
4. Avoid all old-fashioned tools, such as hypnotism, magic, Hatha Yoga, necromancy, etc.
5. Meditate and learn contemplation.
6. Learn to keep silent.
7. Do not interfere with the karma of others.
8. Radiate joy, peace, and serenity.
9. Carry in one's heart the image of the Master.
10. Learn how to sleep.

There are, of course, other steps which need not be mentioned. Once the flame of the heart is kindled, all the rest will come to light.

A person who is full of creative ideas and cannot apply them on earth sees great opportunity to put his ideas into application upon entering the Subtle World. Thus, the possibility of increasing his service and creativity is increased. The Subtle World gives great opportunities for creative people to exercise their talents and to exhaust all of their creative tensions. But one must remember that creative aspiration must exist in the soul before one enters into the Subtle World.

During the flight toward the Subtle World, it is the stage of consciousness and the depth of aspiration that decide the level the soul will reach. If the consciousness is refined and the aspiration is deep and strong, the soul will be led to higher levels of the Subtle World, and he will enter them in great joy. In many esoteric schools much work is done to refine human feelings, to deepen human aspiration, and to expand human consciousness. These three are great guides leading toward the Subtle World.

There is a mysterious point in karmic law. One can pay his karma on earth and release himself, but in the Subtle World one can release himself only through his aspirations. Aspiration is the annihilation of the separate self. Through aspiration the universal Self takes root within us. Through aspiration man is drawn toward the highest. Aspiration is the magnetic current which raises the soul toward higher levels of the Subtle World. In the Subtle World the energy that puts the soul in action is his aspiration.

There will be many hindrances in the Subtle World, but they can be overcome if man has spiritual energy within.

We are told that there are several kinds of people in the Subtle World:

1. Those who work hard and want to stay there longer.
2. Those who want to stay longer in order to avoid incarnation and worldly burdens.
3. Those who want to stay because they love the Subtle World and want to enjoy it all the more.
4. Others who make every effort to return to earth as soon as possible. They too have various motives. Some of them want to continue the service they were rendering to humanity. Some of them want to be rich and re-discover all that they left behind. Some of them want to pay their debts and correct their misdeeds.

In religious literature we read about purgatory. This is a very noble idea if one understands it esoterically. Purgatory is a state in which refinement and sublimation take place and the soul is purified from the dross it has accumulated in its life.

In esoteric literature we read that purgatory begins in the earthly life and extends to the Subtle and Fiery Worlds where the soul eventually purifies himself and becomes ready to pass into higher states of consciousness and beingness. The soul cyclically comes back to pay his karmic debts and unfold his Divinity here on earth. All events in life can be used as a means for the purification of the human being. Then he passes on to the Subtle World where he can refine himself even more. In the Fiery World, the purification process is more intense.

Purgatory, therefore, is composed of the following spheres:

—The earth
—The Subtle World
—The Fiery World

On earth man must reach Transfiguration by going through many fiery purifications. In the Subtle World his astral body must reach a high degree of purification. In the Fiery World all that is unworthy of the mental flames must be burned away. Thus, through purgatory, the soul once more sees the ideal toward which he must strive.

But the karmic law pulls him back again to earth for trial and for payment of the dues forgotten years ago.

People must learn to detach themselves on earth from all earthly attachments and not carry husks with them into the Subtle World. We are told that "any superfluous husk causes inexpressible pain in the Subtle World."

On earth we must try to adapt ourselves to the requirements of the Subtle and Fiery Worlds, accepting the idea that this earth is a refinery and a purgatory. This is why the Sages have insisted that the fire of the heart must purify all our thoughts, emotions, and actions with the fire of renunciation.

Great help can be given to people by teaching them how to detach themselves from the earth. Many experiences are needed to reach such a state of renunciation, and it is possible to create conditions in which people are not tied to their possessions and bodies. The Teaching can help people easily break the tie with earthly life by demonstrating to them the beauty of the Higher Worlds. Meditation and the occasional discipline of renunciation will provide great help for the future ascent.

It is observed that often after the soul has broken the link with the physical body, people around the subject try to bring the person back to the body. This is carried on especially in hospitals with various mechanical means. People must help the departing one to break his ties easily and joyfully with appropriate mantrams, prayers, and words. Sometimes the delay of departure causes many complications.

For example, immediately after the link between the soul and body is broken, the astral body begins to build itself rapidly. A speedy integration, reorganization, and formation takes place. But when people draw the soul back to the body, by machines or by emotions, the formation of the subtle body is disturbed, and it is badly wounded.

A similar thing occurs when a fetus is forced to take birth before it is ready for it.

Delayed departure also causes great suffering for the person and anxiety for those who are waiting to receive him in their spheres.

The inhabitants of the Subtle Worlds who live upon the higher levels want very much to help humanity. This help is not carried on through mediums, channels, aura readers, or past-life readers, but by direct telepathic impression.

Of course, many lower psychics will say that they are receiving telepathic messages from Masters or entities living in the Subtle World, and they believe this; but the quality and the color of their communication will reveal their sources.

First of all, one must have a pure, developed heart as well as experience about the nature of psychic energy and spatial fire. It is not easy to communicate with real helpers because so many entities want to masquerade as them, and so many atmospheric hindrances exist in Space.

The absence of irritability is another condition for real communication. Harmlessness and selflessness are other requisites. With all of these qualities the communicator must have a very purified and transmuted consciousness. Only fiery people who have already demonstrated their beauty in sacrificial service will be able to take the most fiery task of communication upon their shoulders.

One can communicate with the Subtle World through thought. A thought without words is far superior to a thought expressed through words.

We are told that such thoughts must originate from the heart. Thoughts originated from the heart are charged with fire.

It is also possible to communicate with the Fiery World through our thoughts, but this is more difficult. To have such a communication, the mental centers must be unfolded to a great degree and synchronized with the fire of the heart.

The Teacher warns us, saying that every direct contact with the inhabitants of the Subtle World is very dangerous, except when one is highly trained for it. We are warned, also, that it is very dangerous to have people from the Subtle World visit us for guidance. Such events must be very cautiously avoided so as not to fall into the traps of the dark forces.

30

Past Experiences
and Past Lives

It is good that we do not remember our past lives or past experiences in the Subtle Worlds. They all belong to the past, and we are urged to proceed toward the future. In our Chalice exists the essence of our experiences of the past, which can be used if we develop continuity of consciousness.

Premature recollection of the past hinders our development of the physical body and the physical brain and makes us depend on the past or on astral experience. Life demands that we develop the physical mechanism to such a degree that eventually it will be possible to make the brain function in three dimensions. After such an achievement, man will be able to participate in things going on upon three dimensions.

The past memories of our life on any level can be a hindrance before we are mature. Our goal is to proceed toward the future, without the memory of the past, and intuitively to utilize all that we have achieved.

There are two ways to function. One is that you remember the rules and regulations learned in the Subtle World and live accordingly. The second way is that you do not need to remember them because *you are*, and you act out of your beingness, not out of your memory.

When you remember your previous lives prematurely, the memories create great pressure on your brain and glands. Sometimes all the pain and suffering, joy or horror, with all their associations, come and pressure your consciousness and mind. You begin to feel attracted to those whom you knew and to run away from those who hurt you, even if they are now your closest associates. To build your future life, you must detach from and cut the former ties and build new ones; otherwise you distort the plan that life has presented to you. But if you pass through a certain expansion of consciousness and are not disturbed by your past and clearly see your future, then you will be ready to review your past if necessary and with detachment.

Life wants you to go ahead and not renew past memories. If your karma organizes your life, the best way is to follow your karma and leave the past behind.

Most past-life readers bring hindrances, complications, and suffering into your life. Most of what they say is not the truth, but you believe it; and even if it were supposedly true, it does not work to your advantage.

There was a man who, through the method of regression, discovered that his brother's wife killed him in a past life. This impressed him so much that gradually it poisoned his entire life. Then one day he killed her. Many tragedies happen when a man looks back at his past. Nature knows what it is doing. When the time comes, you will know and you will be ready to handle it.

Some writers give the impression that when a human soul passes away he enters the astral plane, then the mental plane, then he comes back to the astral plane, and then incarnates. This was the general instruction. In reality, not everyone goes from the astral to the mental plane. Some people go to the etheric plane and then incarnate without ever entering the astral plane.

Some people enter the lowest astral level and return if they cannot proceed further. Some enter the higher astral level and return if they cannot pass to the mental plane in a given karmic cycle. Some people directly enter the mental plane and return directly to physical incarnation. They appropriate astral matter into an astral body.

Those who are far more advanced enter the Intuitional Plane via the higher mental plane and, if they want, do not return. It is possible to pass into the Intuitional Plane while one is on the mental plane, but those who cannot make it into the Intuitional Plane incarnate again and again until they prepare themselves to such a degree that they are able to penetrate into the Intuitional Plane. Those who can penetrate into the Intuitional Plane while they are on earth are called *Arhats*.

The goal in our incarnation is to cultivate the ability to penetrate into the Intuitional Plane while bypassing all other planes.

Those who return from the Fiery World into incarnation remember their past lives. Those who come back from the Intuitional Plane not only remember their past lives on earth but also their past lives in the astral and mental worlds. Their continuity of consciousness is build to such a degree that the entire thread of their lives becomes an open book for them.

To function on the subtle planes, one must develop healthier bodies in each incarnation. The correct foods are very important for the astral and physical bodies. For the mental body, the best nourishment is virtues, pure thinking, strong aspiration, and devotion.

A vegetarian diet builds the subtle body. If one eats predominantly vegetables for seven years, his entire system changes and he develops a new astral body.

Meat damages the astral body: the influence of blood passes into it, inviting low entities which surround and impress low animalistic urges, drives, and actions into it.

We are told that in the lowest level of the astral plane animals are formless, or they have "foggy outlines." People are often horrified when seeing animals around themselves in that plane. If a man slaughters many animals, he will be extremely sorry in the Subtle World because the animals will surround him with great horror. Fortunately, most animals do not remain long in the Subtle World and pass into the physical plane before their victim arrives in the Subtle World.

Killing has been forbidden. This has a very esoteric meaning, but people do not think about the future. Similarly, criminals who have killed thousands of human beings will live in the lowest level of the astral plane in a hell-like condition, sometimes for thousands of years. This is why we read, "Vengeance is Mine."[1] Karma will take care of those who kill.

Animals seldom penetrate into the higher astral plane but go into the lowest level of the astral plane. Often they even recognize their masters and render useful service in the astral plane. In the Teaching we read that it is good to have our little friends around us in the astral plane.

Those who have a clear and pure consciousness will have good sight in the astral plane. Such people will see all astral animals clearly. But those who do not have clear sight, which is the case of those who find themselves in the lower astral plane, will notice that the animals around them have foggy features.

Once you begin to stand in the light of the Inner Presence, you no longer desire to know about your past lives because you feel that you cannot endure in the presence of the Inner Guide with the memory of the past. You feel the shame of the past. You cannot stand your failures, transgressions, and lies. You cannot bear the pain you caused others with your love or hate, consciously or unconsciously. The light of the

---

1. Romans 12:19

Inner Presence makes you see all the details of your past. This is very important to understand.

A child hates one who comes and tells his parents about his nothingness. A student does not like his parents to complain about him to the Teacher in his presence.

The transformation of your being does not take place if the "movies" of your past failures are still playing in your consciousness. You should like to offer the best of you to your Inner Presence. Memories of past lives are not worthy to be brought into the presence of your Inner Lord. The Inner Lord is interested not in your past but in *your future*. The only reason that the Inner Lord is with you is for your future.

The Inner Lord does not want even to think about your past so as not to impress you with Its thoughts. Only on rare occasions and in critical moments of your life, in order to give you hope for the future, It may show you from your past the cause of the present crisis.

If your Inner Lord continuously impresses you with your past, you will not be able to grow. Your Inner Lord tries to impress upon your mind the importance of the future. On rare occasions It even loans you Its eyes in order to make you see the future.

Suppose you had failed at something in the past, and you saw your life as it was. Seeing your past life's "movie" will not help you see the cause and eliminate the similar causes in this life, but it will impress you with the image of failure and with all of the sensations of failure.

A cause of failure is not eliminated because you know it to be the cause of your failure, but it can be eliminated by an expanding consciousness. Expansion of consciousness cannot take place through the knowledge of the cause but by striving to a new level of being. As long as the old picture of failure is hanging onto your tail, you cannot climb toward new heights. This is why nature blocks your past from your consciousness and gives you a new opportunity to strive for new achievements.

This will not be easy to understand until you realize that knowingness and beingness are two different things.[2]

People who are enlightened do not want to be occupied with the past because they do not want their present labor to be disturbed by past failures or even by past pleasures. Progress is possible only if one can detach from past actions, emotions, and thoughts. Mother

---

2. For further information, please refer to *The Ageless Wisdom*, pp. 36-41.

Nature has lovingly arranged such a procedure in which you naturally do not remember your past.

There will come a time when you will be able to see your past. At that time you will be so sublimated that you will not identify with any of the "movies" of your past lives.

We live in a moment of time which does not provide imagery of the past lives. However, the past is always with us through its effects. It is very important to watch our life and understand where we have failed or made progress in the past.

For example, if at present you are an ordinary person, then you did not strive strongly enough in the past to advance yourself. If you are an above-average person, you can see where you focused your labor. And if you are above average but have many obstacles on your path, you will understand how many obstacles you put on the paths of others.

Using the Law of Cause and Effect, do some research on the past and you will be able to understand yourself and learn your lessons. Often, people cannot even handle the memory of a crisis they have passed through recently. How can they then handle the crises they passed through and experienced in the past, when they were less mature and had darker hours in their lives?

Man lives between the past and the future, in a steady motion out of the past and into the future. This is a chronological move, not spiritual progress or advancement. Development and perfection are achieved only when you use the flow of time as a means for your spiritual transformation. It is possible, however, that you try to move toward the future but your consciousness remains in the patterns of the past.

It is very advantageous to think about the future and program your life in such a way that you actualize your future in time and space. Instead of occupying yourself with the past, penetrate into the future. The best future can be actualized only if you create enough cause for it. Thus, your future vision programs your life and makes it transform itself. No transformation is possible without a vision of the future.

The future does not mean only the future in this present life. The future extends to your life in the coming thousands of years.

People plan for the next week, the next month, and the next year, but there are few people who plan for the next incarnation or for incarnations to come. Planning for the future is the groundwork for the actualization of the *future*. The past will one day be revealed when you become able to balance the failures and pains of the past with the successes and joys of the future.

The future must be more real and more significant for you than the past. In involving yourself with the past, you are tuning on switches and releasing currents of energy which you will not be able to handle at the present stage of your evolution. Sanity, in a sense, is the absence of the interferences of the past and stability in the vision of the future.

How do you explore the future? The answer is very simple: by thinking in terms of the future, by speaking on the line of the future, and by working as if you were constructing your future.

Actually, people build their future by the many ways they live. A future that is consciously contemplated and worked for is indeed rare. In building the future, the safest engineers to use are Beauty, Goodness, Righteousness, Joy, and Freedom. One cannot regret his future if his future is built by such engineers who are working for him.

The Ancients used to say that the beginning of righteousness is the fear of the Lord. Esotericists translate this idea differently. For them, God is love and no one should be afraid of Him, although the Law of Karma is one of the major laws of the Universe. One must know that all of his thoughts, words, and actions not only affect others but also his own future. Whatever one sows, he reaps. Cause and effect follow each other like the wheels of a car. Thus, one must think about the Law of Karma.

Righteousness develops only when people realize this law and are careful not to break the Law of Love. Righteousness is a state of life in which you do not hurt others, not because you are afraid of the civil or criminal laws but because of your understanding of the greater laws. It is a state of consciousness which functions according to the Law of Karma. To be righteous means to live in such a way that you do not create bad karma for you and for others. You are righteous not because of fear but because you know the consequences of your actions.

Righteousness is not limited to one life but operates for all future lives. To be righteous means not to violate the Law of Love.

"The fear of God" can be translated as the understanding of the Law of Karma. Fear is not necessary if there is no violation. If one is in violation, he needs to approach God. How can one approach God in fear? Unless one loves God there will be no connection between them. Fear does not transform your being. Righteousness built under fear evaporates when the object of fear is ignored or bypassed.

Righteousness is a flower of the transformed consciousness. It is a state of beingness in which man is righteous not because of fear but because he cannot be otherwise.

Fearlessness is not a denial of the future consequences of your harmful actions of the past but a state of consciousness in which you try to take positive action to change the consequences of the past and create a new future.

Focusing yourself on your past failures and weaknesses will weaken the vision of your future. Focusing yourself on the vision of your future and synchronizing your life to that vision will make you fearless and loving.

People repeat their mistakes because in their past lives they did not try to be righteous for the sake of righteousness but forced themselves to be righteous because of fear.

Vanity is as bad as fear. Both must be overcome before a person is able to see the "movies" of his past. Vanity acts as a hindrance to the progress of a human being as soon as he sees the achievements of previous lives. If upon seeing past failures one reacts in fear, his future progress is hindered.

Vanity and fear are states of consciousness for which nature does not reveal the past so as not to burden the person's progress.

In each life a new store of psychic energy is given to every person to start a better life. As days and years go by, people will become more interested in their future lives than in their past lives.

There are therapists who use the technique of having their clients speak of the past failures, weaknesses, mistakes, sufferings, and difficulties in order to try to bring a change in the lives of the clients. In the coming years, one will not occupy himself with the trash of the past but with the possible achievements of the future, with the joys and beauties of the future. Such a procedure is not like day dreaming but is an act of inquiring, a concrete effort to plan a future and program oneself to actualize such a future.

One may ask whether the future consists of a specific occupation, position, or wealth. The answer is that the future is a state of consciousness which operates in line with Beauty, Goodness, Righteousness, Joy, Freedom, harmlessness, and striving. Once you achieve such a state of consciousness, you can be in any occupation, position, or financial condition, and you will always be in joy, health, beauty, labor, and in harmony with the Cosmic Laws. This is what is meant by the statement, "Seek ye first the Kingdom of God, and all else will be given to you."[3]

You do not need to plan to be a musician or an engineer or a scientist in a future life. You do need to be creative and full of knowledge and have a clear mind and a healthy body. Once you have

---

3. Luke 12:31

such instruments in your possession, you can decide what to do on your return, according to the demands of life and according to the influences of the long forgotten karma.

On the Path of their evolution, people live for long periods of time through the concept of the past. The past controls their actions, emotions, thoughts, and even their plans. When they graduate from this phase, they enter the state of consciousness which can be called "a life controlled by the present." The present moment controls their thoughts, feelings, and actions. They live for the day. Their life becomes a *present*. There is no past and no future in it. They block their consciousness from the past and do not show any interest in the future. The future for them is the moment in which they live.

As they evolve further, they develop another aspect of their apparatus. They begin to see the future and live in the future. We call such people dreamers, visionaries, or idealists who ignore the past and present and live the future of their dreams.

But in reality, these three phases of time are always there, as the undercurrents in the ocean of life. They are fused with each other. In different levels of consciousness they appear differently. For example, for an advanced consciousness, the future is registered as the past, the past as the future; or the present becomes a mirror on which their past and future fuse.

These kinds of reactions are all the result of the way the apparatus in man is formed. If one has control of the apparatus, he can use the three phases of time and make them the reflection of the "eternal now." In this manner the past-present and the future lose their differences and become interchangeable. The past reflects the present and future; the present reflects the past and the future; the future reflects the past and present. And all of these exist in the consciousness as the "eternal now."

Things are observed by the light they reflect. People for a long time have not thought that actions, emotions, events, words, and thoughts *are things*. Again for a long time, people have thought that there is only one kind of light, which is the light of the sun. But as the human soul develops, he becomes aware of the many kinds of light. Just as we have light on the physical plane, we have a more intense light in the astral and mental planes. There is light on still higher planes, but our physical eyes are not developed enough to see it. More developed eyes are necessary to see this light and the objects they reflect.

This opens a new horizon for us. Astral light reveals astral objects; mental light reveals mental objects. Astral light is faster than physical light. Mental light is much faster than astral and physical light. Because of the speed of these kinds of light, things appear differently. For example, physical light reveals an event, the present. Astral light reveals the past of the event in the present. Mental light reveals the future in the past-present event. Intuitional light fuses them together and makes you see things in the "eternal now" and in relation to the whole. Thus in our dreams, the astral or sometimes the mental light is in operation, and events are seen as the past or as the future.

In esoteric books we are told about seeing the events of our life, emotions, and thoughts on the Path of our journey to the Subtle World. We are told about the Akashic Records, read in the "eternal now." All objects on any plane are seen through the instrumentalities of various forms of light.

Experience shows that a present event is the reflection of an event which happened thousands of years ago; it shows that a past event was the reflection of a future event; it shows that an event either in the past or future is in the "eternal now." A physical event is processed by the speed of physical light. If the same event is processed by the speed of astral light, the consciousness looking at it upon the astral plane will see it as a remote, past event. If the event is processed by mental light, it will be seen in its future complexity, acting as if in the present time.

The intuitional light will approximate the reflections of the physical, astral, and mental light and synthesize them as an "eternal now" in which the three lights will reflect the three facets of the same event.

It is all the game of light, but this game can only be played by an unfolding consciousness.

On the path of our journey, events repeat themselves. There are events which are seen only by physical light and impressed as physical events on our consciousness. Physical light reflects the events again and again, as long as we can register the events reflected by physical light.

When we begin to operate the center in our consciousness which registers the events reflected by our astral light, the physical events do not repeat themselves any more in our physical life, but their emotional counterparts still repeat themselves in our astral life.

When we operate the center in our consciousness which registers the mental counterparts of events, the events repeat themselves in the mental sphere of our life. In the mental sphere, the physical events turn into concepts and knowledge. In the astral sphere, they turn into joy or pain. In the intuitional sphere they reveal the laws by which

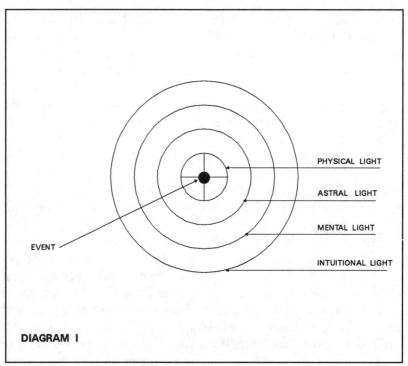

PHYSICAL LIGHT

ASTRAL LIGHT

MENTAL LIGHT

INTUITIONAL LIGHT

EVENT

DIAGRAM I

Concentric Light Table

they operate. After an event is revealed in the intuitional light, one can use the same laws to detach himself from the event, after which there is no longer any recurrence of the event in the physical, emotional, and mental spheres. This is how karma ends, and this is how the Law of Reincarnation is controlled and man lives in the "eternal now," above the tides of the changing times.

The word "feeling" is often related to emotional reactions. This is not correct. Esoterically, "feeling" is a general term referring to a certain registration of impressions coming from the physical, emotional, and mental realms.

One feels cold and heat. One feels the joys and pains of other people. One feels their thoughts. One feels his own thoughts. For example, one can say, "I feel I am right." This is not a figure of speech but a fact. One can feel that his decisions, conclusions, and motives are right. These elements can be felt.

There are also higher feelings. Such feelings transcend intelligence because feeling is done by the aura. It is almost an instantaneous response and registration. It is after such a response and registration that the message goes to the brain, which, according to its content and development, gives its decision. But until it gives its decision, the feeling is registered and responded to already. And if the decision of the mind is contrary, you witness a conflict in human nature.

Feeling is related to understanding. Knowledge is the accumulation of data and not necessarily the understanding of data.

Feeling is a fast and direct approach to Intuition. On the line of this approach, understanding transcends the data accumulated in the mind and reaches its destination before the mind has a chance to reach a conclusion.

Feeling bypasses logic and reasoning, though often logic and reasoning come back to the decision made by the feeling and try to overrule it. Successful people depend upon the response of their Intuition rather than their logic, which often can be used to verify the response of the Intuition.

One can feel physically, emotionally, and mentally and respond according to the feeling. The conditioning factor of the decision of the feeling is the Intuition or the past registrations. It is interesting to note that feeling is seldom conditioned by the past registrations. It generally evokes an immediate response from the Intuition because of its speed. Past registrations may respond and try to modify the intuitive response, but this sometimes takes a long period of time to make the person aware of it.

Feeling is also a phenomenon which is controlled by light. The faster the speed of light, the faster the response. This is why if one wants to free someone from the claws of the past, the best method is to train him to register the impressions coming from the faster light. This is done by raising the focus of the consciousness of the person from lower to higher planes. The focus of consciousness is the determining factor of registration of the reflections of light. Reflections are the images of events on any plane of existence.

There are many means of communication:

—Movement
—Sound
—Light
—Thought energy
—Feelings

Communicating by impression is higher yet than any of the above means. Esoterically, impressions travel faster than feelings, thoughts, light, sound, and movement. These impressions are everywhere, within and without. One needs to prepare the apparatus to register them.

Emotions and thoughts, with their counterparts of actions, are impressed on the substance of the Second Cosmic Ether.[4] The Second Cosmic Ether, which is sometimes called the Akashic Plane, acts in the Solar System as the most sensitive film and keeps these impressions as permanent records. These impressions are accumulated by the special frequency of a human soul. They are arranged in the Cosmic Computer in a systematized manner as the records of that soul.

An advanced Initiate has easy access and in some degree can read the records of the soul extended over many millenniums, if he has permission to do so. To be able consciously to contact these records, reflected on the astral plane, one must pass the Fourth Initiation and have his consciousness focused in the Fourth Cosmic Etheric Plane, the Intuitional Plane.

These records reflected on the astral plane are often like the reflections on running water of the trees and bushes found on its banks, mostly distorted and mixed with other phenomena. An Arhat can read these reflections. Whereas, an average person can tune in to such reflections and express his contacts as various moods, desires, thoughts, actions, aspirations, dreams, and tendencies. These expressions are mechanically carried out through the motive power hidden in the records.

Some people are anxious to know about their past. Others have an intense fear of their past. Actually, our past is always reflected in the life we live at the present. If we observe our present thoughts, emotions, and actions scientifically, we can gain certain accurate information regarding our past.

Lower psychics and mediums have access only to the astral reflections of the records. Their information is not accurate; it is distorted and misleading. The higher, exact records are not available to average people until they develop scientific thinking and the ability to detach themselves from the possible effect or influence of the past events.

As the human soul advances into Arhathood, he feels the necessity of studying his past in order to lead his steps toward higher achievements. The study of the records is done only to develop understanding of the Law of Karma. During the Fourth Initiation the

---

4.   For further explanation of the planes of existence, please refer to *The Ageless Wisdom*, pp. 277-278. Also see Chapter 60 of this book.

astral body solidifies itself like a mirror and the Arhat sees his past lives in that mirror, reflected from the Akashic records. These records are not always available to an Arhat, due to atmospheric and subjective storms. Near the end of the Fourth Initiation, the Arhat's astral body is totally destroyed along with the Chalice.

Conscious progress toward the Higher Worlds is possible only when the traveler on the Path begins to understand and apply the Law of Karma. As he ascends higher, he feels a greater need for understanding the Law. Until one totally understands the operation of the Law, he can make no conscious progress on the Path.

Besides these records in the Second Cosmic Ether, the impressions of our emotions, thoughts, and actions circulate in the astral substance on earth, affecting many life forms. People are responsible for these effects. Karma records the effects, and the Karmic Lords study the records impressed on the Second Cosmic Etheric Plane and their effect on living forms.

We are living in a photographic universe or a sensitive universe where all that is thought, felt, spoken, and done is recorded in a four-dimensional way: as an action, a feeling, a thought, an effect, and amplified with color and sound. If a Chohan — a Sixth Degree Initiate — has permission, He can play back your records registered not only in your human stage but also the records while you were in the animal kingdom.

Higher initiations are taken after studying these records with a far more advanced Initiate Who is designated by the Great Lodge to be your Guide.

31

Akasha

Akasha is the Second Cosmic Etheric Plane, which is also called the Monadic Plane. This is the "hard disk" of the Planetary Life on which is recorded all that transpires on this planet. This is also called the fiery sphere all around the solar system.

Some students of wisdom think that Akasha is the astral light or the astral plane. Actually it is not. Let us study the following illustration:

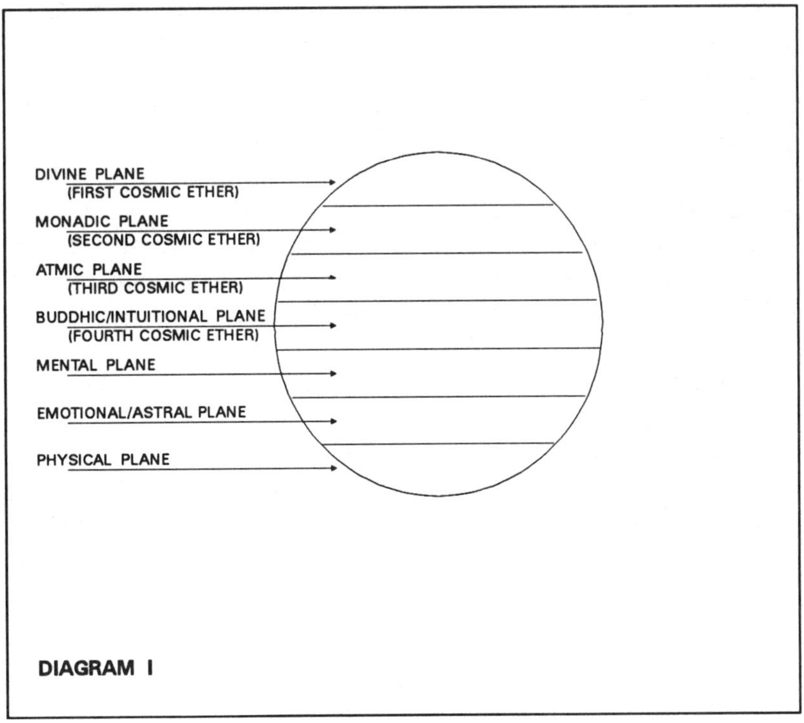

DIVINE PLANE
(FIRST COSMIC ETHER)

MONADIC PLANE
(SECOND COSMIC ETHER)

ATMIC PLANE
(THIRD COSMIC ETHER)

BUDDHIC/INTUITIONAL PLANE
(FOURTH COSMIC ETHER)

MENTAL PLANE

EMOTIONAL/ASTRAL PLANE

PHYSICAL PLANE

DIAGRAM I

Cosmic Physical Plane

The astral plane is related to the Monadic Plane and reflects all that is registered on the Akasha of the Monadic Plane. The astral plane is full of the forms of all kinds of imagination, desires, and glamors of nations, groups, and individuals. It is a real trap to those clairvoyants who cannot penetrate beyond the astral plane because all that they see is mixed with reality and unreality in such a way that it is impossible to discriminate between or separate the real event from the imaginative event. It is this astral reflection of the Akasha that misleads people, making them think that it is the Akashic Records.

Often the so called "akashic records" received by mediums or psychics are the readings of reflections on the astral plane of the Akashic Recordings, misleading and confusing all those who believe these recordings. The true Akashic Recordings can be reached only by those whose consciousness lives and functions on the Atmic Plane. The consciousness of most psychics does not pass beyond the astral or lower mental planes.

The majority of our dreams are reflections of the astral plane. Very few of our dreams are like a beam of light radiated out from our Monadic Plane and transmitted to us by our Solar Angel.

In certain esoteric literature you read that Akasha is called also "sidereal" or "astral light." This is correct if we add that sidereal light and astral light refer to our Akashic Plane — not to the astral plane.

It is better if we call it Star Light, as the Monad, the Star, and the real Monadic Plane are the source of the Star Light.

In human nature there is a portion of Solar and Planetary Akasha which is our Monadic Plane. Our Monadic Plane reflects the records of Planetary and Solar Akasha, and this reflection can reach our astral plane.

In sleep or in waking consciousness we can feel these reflections as our dreams or feelings, but they are all mixed with our emotions, anxieties, glamors, desires, and imaginations — except in the moments that our astral body is in real peace, is focused through a pure aspiration, and can transmit certain amounts of recordings from Akasha.

Clairvoyance has three stages:

1. Etheric clairvoyance
2. Astral clairvoyance
3. Intuitive clairvoyance

Etheric clairvoyance can be a great help to humanity because it shows the etheric counterparts of objects existing in nature.

Astral clairvoyance is the most misleading power.

Intuitional clairvoyance develops when the eye of the human soul opens. These are the *true seers,* those who not only can see what happened in the past but what will happen in the future. The future is the ratio of past events and karmic law. Their eye, relating the past and the Law of Karma, presents them with the image of the events to come.

Any akashic readings done by people who do not yet have intuitional awareness, or if they are not Arhats (Fourth Degree Initiates), are misleading and, in a high percentage, erroneous. Only the readings done by a person who has Christ-consciousness or intuitional awareness are dependable.

In some literature, Akasha is called also the "Light of God."

It is true that a great amount of entities live in the astral plane. Also, a great amount of astral corpses exist in that plane, and these astral entities and astral corpses reflect the Akashic Records, but add to it and disturb it with their nature and contents.

On the other hand, many highly advanced entities live in the Monadic Plane who are true reflectors of such recordings. Like huge mirrors they reflect certain parts of the Akashic Records into Space to provide certain information to those Great Beings who use it for certain tasks on lower planes.

In *A Treatise on Cosmic Fire,* [1] eight different names for Akasha are given:

1. Undifferentiated cosmic substance
2. Primordial ether
3. Primordial electric entity
4. Akasha
5. Super-astral light
6. Fiery serpent
7. Mulaprakriti
8. Pregenetic matter

Also we are told that when Akasha is differentiated, it is called

1. Astral Light
2. Sea of fire
3. Electricity
4. Prakriti
5. Atomic matter

---

1.   *A Treatise on Cosmic Fire,* p. 43.

6. The serpent of evil
7. Ether, with its four divisions, air, fire, water, earth the Second Etheric Plane.

Akasha is found in the highest layer of each plane. Also it is found in the Second Cosmic Ether (Monadic Plane) and in the Fourth Cosmic Ether (Intuitional Plane).

Akasha is reflected on the first, or highest layer of each plane, especially on the Monadic or the Second Cosmic Etheric Plane, and on the Intuitional or the Fourth Cosmic Etheric Plane. The astral plane as a whole has the distorted reflection of the above planes.

Thus, the Akashic Records in man and in the Universe can reflect on all these planes in relative accuracy or in total distortion.

Man has the network of Akasha all around and within him, and this Akasha, as an electrical current, has various functions in the constitution of man.

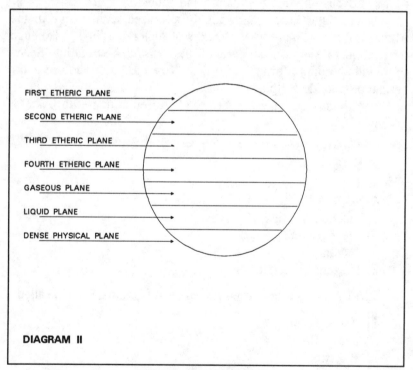

FIRST ETHERIC PLANE

SECOND ETHERIC PLANE

THIRD ETHERIC PLANE

FOURTH ETHERIC PLANE

GASEOUS PLANE

LIQUID PLANE

DENSE PHYSICAL PLANE

DIAGRAM II

Human Physical Plane

If one tries to see certain relationships between Akasha and other planes, he can detect that the astral plane, or desire, triggers the akashic currents. Any strong desire sets will energy into action, which builds various forms in the astral plane. These forms eventually manifest on the objective plane. The phenomenon of building astral forms in the astral plane is called imagination.

Any picture or form built through imagination is a mixture of Akashic Records and the *future results* of Akashic Records.

But both imagination and the future image are distorted because of the agitated and polluted state of the astral plane.

In creative imagination the Astral Plane is involved, but it is the mental plane that is used to build images — and these images are related to the "future," or to the result of the Akashic Records.

Also we must remember that when we speak about Akashic Records, we do not mean only the photographic imagery or the records of life events.

Great Ones read the records in four dimensions:

—the actual event
—the strata of emotions
—the strata of motives and thoughts
—the circuit through which the events, emotions, motives, and thoughts circulate

We must remember also that in the Akashic Records are kept all the treasures of wisdom of super-human, Planetary, and Solar Beings, and those who are able to establish the communicating lines between atomic substances (the highest level of each plane), the heart, the fifth ventricle of the brain, and the Monadic Plane can relatively contact such treasures in Akasha and bring them down through their visualization, creative imagination, and meditation to cause great changes in the Planetary Life.

We must not forget that the Core of man, the Monad, has direct access to the Akashic Plane and the Akashic Records.

For the planet, the point of contact with Planetary and Solar Akashic Records is Shamballa. In the Solar System, it is the Central Spiritual Sun.

We are told also that the Akashic Plane, as all the rest of planes, breathes.

The Akashic Plane inhales and exhales. In inhalation the work of recording is done; in exhalation the precipitation of the treasures takes place in the Solar and Cosmic Space, and those who were able to build their communication system can contact such treasures and bring them into the world.

Every Great One, every great Center in the Planet and Solar System, benefits from this out-breathing because the elevated Beings on this Earth in Planets in the Solar System absorb such radiations. Each Being, on its own level, catches the treasures of the Akasha. All truly creative artists are parts of the network of absorption of the treasures of the Akasha.

Actually, our life thread and our consciousness and creative threads are built of akashic substance found within our constitution.

Astral Light is the depository of all events happening on earth. We are told that all that exists outside of us, in the spheres, also exists within us. Through certain associations, the recordings of the Akashic Records are continuously reflected on the corresponding akashic layers within us; and the person, group, and nation are totally controlled by this reflection. Thus we understand that man conditions his future by the way he lives in the present, and all men everywhere share the common pool and are conditioned by it. This is why everyone of us is responsible for all that is happening to people. Once this fact is understood, people will be educated as citizens of the Universe.

There are cycles in which Akashic Records directly control human life. History repeats itself and no power can change the current of events on earth.

These cycles are periods of balance and equilibrium, and also an opportunity for humanity to see how Nature gives back what men gave to Nature.

The Akashic Records also have all the images of the inventions of past civilizations. These images cyclically are projected to the human consciousness through waves of impressions and inspirations, and past discoveries come again and again to the field of human life.

For example, the Atlanteans had speedier planes than we have now. For many thousands of years these models or inventions were hidden in the Akashic Records. Later they were projected into the human mind, and first a primitive plane was invented; then slowly it was improved as the records impressed human minds more clearly and as men became more sensitive to the records.

Akashic models are not the archetypes. Archetypes are found on the Cosmic Mental Plane. These archetypes stand behind the models and are not accessible to the human mind until man learns to use them for the good of all.

It is the power, gained by using the invention for the common good, that opens the door of human intellect to receive the impressions of the archetypes behind the models.

Every invention can cause the life to progress or retrogress. Progress is caused when the invention is used for the benefit of all and in harmony with Nature.

Retrogression occurs when the invention is used for greed and separative interests and in violation of natural orders.

Man receives that which he gives. Evil ones receive evil from the Akashic Records, which impress them and force them to follow evil paths.

Those who purify their nature and learn precious lessons through their own experiences begin to draw magnificent recordings from the Akasha, and they also add to the Akashic Records their share of beauty.

It must be remembered that Akasha, when condensed, eventually becomes matter. In each atom of matter there is a capacity to register all that is going on on the Earth in its three planes of existence.

We have learned the structure of the atom, but we do not know yet how the energy formation of each atom reflects all that exists in the Akasha.

The Prophet Mohammed said that, on the day of judgment, your clothing or shoes will stand witness for you or against you. What a profound statement that was, and how intuitive He was to see such a truth.

The fact that matter is condensed, intensified Akasha explains the mystery of the interrelationship of spirit, mind, emotions, and body and how they affect each other. Also, it explains the fact of continuity of communication among all that exists in the Universe. Akasha is the bridge in all manifestation.

In the human being, the closest correspondence to the Universal Akasha is the Auric Egg. The Auric Egg is pure Akasha, and we are told that when a baby is born he is born with an Auric Egg which is very small and is white in color.

It is the Auric Egg that connects man to the Cosmos, and all that man does on any plane is directly transmitted to the Akasha, the Second Cosmic Plane. Thus the recorder and the transmitter are born with man.

After death the Auric Egg still continues to exist. In each incarnation people have a more developed Auric Egg. The past registrations always remain in the Akasha and in the permanent atoms. It is possible to make the Auric Egg grow and be used as a mechanism of conscious contact with the Akashic Records.

The purity of the Auric Egg stays until the child is seven years old. Then, either his personality or the lower mind or even his Soul influences it and changes its color or even the shape. The Auric Egg is found around the human soul as a bridge between the personality and the human soul.

The Auric Egg is not the aura, as the aura is the radiation of the physical, emotional, mental, and higher bodies if they exist. It is also not the etheric body. The etheric body is the electrical system of the entire physical body.

Akasha is also found in the brain ventricles, serving as sensitive recorders and transmitters until death.

32

Children and the
Subtle World

More and more children are conscious about the Subtle World. Some of them are able to see subtle forms. When they find mockery and indifference from adults, they slowly suppress their visions.

From a young age children must be told about the Subtle World, the human soul, and the immortality of the soul. Death must be presented as it is in reality: leaving the body and becoming aware of another dimension which is more free and beautiful, providing a good life was lived on earth.

They must learn from a young age about the Laws of Karma and Reincarnation because these are two fundamental laws which will make their life much more beautiful, orderly, and constructive.

We will try always to do our best when we know about the Law of Karma. We will always strive to live a better life in order to have a better incarnation. The Law of Reincarnation will plant in us the hope of the future; it will expand our horizon and make us understand the events occurring on earth.

Children rarely learn from the civil laws. Given any opportunity, or if they think they can escape from the consequences of their misdeeds, they will repeat their mistakes.

The Laws of Karma and Reincarnation will not be taught to them as laws of punishment and retribution, but as laws which execute justice in all aspects of life and open all gates of opportunity for them to strive for a better life. The Law of Karma and the Law of Reincarnation will not only change the behavior of a child but will also transform his consciousness and his being.

When a law is part of one's consciousness, he does not need reinforcement because he will always act according to what his consciousness suggests, according to the Laws of Karma and Reincarnation.

Children must know that whatever they think, speak, and do are just like seeds planted in the ground: the flowers or fruits of the particular seeds will correspond exactly to those seeds. If they think good things for themselves and for others, good things will come to them. If they speak in Beauty, Goodness and Truth, then beauty, goodness and light will come to their path. They will be trusted, and the great laws of the Universe will give them exactly what they gave to others.

They will know that all that is beautiful is so because someone thought in beauty, spoke in beauty, and acted in beauty. They will know that we are the fruit of our own tree which we planted in the past. If we want to have a beautiful life in the future, we must plant seeds for it.

All these ideas can be given to children in the form of stories, movies, and fairy tales, instead of filling their minds with the images of crime and violence.

It is imperative, especially at this time, to teach children about the journey of the soul toward the Subtle World and the Fiery World, and as much as possible to give them the general ideas given by the Sages in all ages.

Children have more impressions from the Subtle Worlds than adults. When people speak to them about the Subtle Worlds, these impressions will awaken and prepare them to accept the information. They will accept the stories of the Subtle Worlds, not because their reasoning and logic is as yet undeveloped but because they unconsciously remember certain events from the Subtle Worlds. They will love to listen to stories about it.

Children love fairy tales because fairy tales are the things which remind them most closely of the Subtle Worlds. Some adults may reject such stories or information, not because they do not have subjective memories but because their logic and reasoning have petrified their consciousness.

Note how a nonreligious man or an unbeliever — about such things as the soul, immortality, and the life-after — suddenly focuses his attention when a dream is related to him. He not only shows interest in the dream, but you can also see changes in his facial expressions and color. I once had a friend who was very materialistically oriented and who would never lose an opportunity to speak against the soul, immortality, the life-after, religion, etc. He was extremely clever, and to me it seemed impossible to reach him through logical means.

One day I dreamed that he had an auto accident, and he was very badly hurt. Early in the morning when he was leaving for his job, I said, "If you need my help today for any reason, call me."

"Why would I need your help? What is the matter?"

"Well, I dreamed that you had an accident."

"You dreamed about me? What can dreams do? Tell me exactly what happened...."

"You had an accident. Drive carefully. That is all."

He went to his car and came back. "You know," he said, "I don't believe in such superstitions, so I can't understand why I am concerned."

"Drive carefully. That is all you need to do."

He left. Three hours later a nurse called me from the hospital. While opening the trunk of his car in a parking lot, he was hit by a car. His left knee was crushed.

"What happened to you?"

"It is what you dreamed."

My friend's leg was amputated. He totally changed. He dedicated his life, as he used to say, to the "dream" life. He found more reality in dreams than in actual life. One day in a conversation he said to me, "All that you knew was a dream to me. Now all that I know about dreams is real to me... and about the world where dreams form!"

Children love dreams. They love visions. They love the future. They love the future because, in reality, they know that they have a future. Those who remember or feel or are impressed by the memory of the Subtle World *know* that that was their future; that they once again will have a future when they pass away — a future in the Subtle Worlds and a future on earth.

Children must be taught how to sleep. The fundamentals of good sleep are as follows:

1. No food should be consumed and no water drunk after sunset.
2. The body must be washed one hour before sleep, and all waste must be eliminated.
3. Before sleep, no television should be watched. Instead, one should read uplifting and inspiring stories, fairy tales, or have a beautiful and loving conversation.

Children must know and experience that in sleep we repair our physical, etheric, and subtle bodies. In the subtle sphere there exists a vivifying substance which can only be assimilated in sleep, or in a conscious withdrawal from the body. This substance is not named, but I like to call it *vitastral*. This is a substance that emanates from the higher astral plane and, as a perfume, radiates within the astral sphere.

Vitastral literally regenerates our worn-out astral, etheric, as well as our physical bodies, providing we go into a deep sleep. When one simply rests, he does not assimilate this substance. One must sleep in the right way.

Children must be encouraged to speak about their experiences or their memories of the Subtle World. The dreams, visions, and psychic experiences of children will open a new road of research into psychic realms, and much guidance can be given to children if they are free to talk about their experiences. From childhood the ties with the Subtle World must be strengthened.

Also, a child's life and consciousness will be balanced by the reality of physical life. Such things as sports activities, domestic work, gardening, the study of natural history and world events, the construction of various items, and work on mechanical devices keep the minds of children balanced. We must remember that children must meet life realistically and keep contacts with the Subtle World in the same realistic spirit.

33

Various Uses of the Subtle Bodies

One may not only develop and organize his astral body, but he can also loan it to someone dear to him or replace his own astral body with the astral body of an Arhat. Thus it is possible that the highly developed astral body of a living Initiate can come and fuse with our own astral body. Like an eagle, such a fusion often uplifts us and leaves us on the summits of higher aspirations and devotion. Sometimes it creates in us a strong sensitivity toward beauty and urges us toward new breakthroughs in the field of our creativity.

After the mission of the advanced astral body is achieved, it can be withdrawn back to the owner.

Other phenomena can be observed in the history of humanity. Sometimes the physical body of a person is salvaged by a great Initiate who needs to work on the physical plane. This happens when a young person leaves his body and departs due to an accident or to extreme fear. The Initiate takes over the body, regenerates it, and uses it for a great service.

The family or friends of that young person do not notice any change until the "body" becomes 18-21 years old. Then the genius of the new occupant slowly appears.

We do not call this possession but *tulku*. Tulku is the occupancy of the body by a Servant of Light to further the evolution of humanity. Tulku also happens when a minor Initiate consciously vacates his body and offers it temporarily for the use of a great Initiate.

There is another side to the story. Sometimes dark forces attack unprotected children or adults, sever their life thread, and occupy the body, forcing the real occupant eventually to leave. This is possession.

Higher bodies can also be loaned or offered for service in certain cases. For example, the intuitional body of a very advanced Initiate may be given to another high-level Initiate who can use it. A Tibetan sage says that when Buddha was leaving His intuitional body to use His atmic body, He hid it in a safe place in order to offer it to Christ to be used at a later date. In addition, we read in the Bible how the mental body of Elijah was given to Elisha.

Higher vehicles have a rare beauty. They are highly organized and capable of putting the person in contact with the Higher Worlds. One must have a very fiery and pure nature and a developed intellect in order to be able to wear such a body without danger and use it with great benefit for mankind. We are told that only very advanced Initiates can do such a thing to render a great service in a very critical moment.

We must remember that our vehicles are like our garments. They are highly organized tools. It is possible to let another person use them if we know how to live without them, how to loan them, and to whom to loan them. It is also important to know from whom to receive them.

There is also evidence that dark forces can loan their astral vehicles to those who have a strong inclination toward crime. Their astral bodies will provide the needed cruelty and evil to carry on their criminal plans.

It is clear that the loaning of higher bodies is accomplished when one is pure enough to handle the presence of the higher bodies, and when there is a natural or global need for a great service.

Evil forces can attack a person through emotional and mental currents, but they cannot vest him with their bodies unless the subject attracts them and makes himself receptive through vices and crimes.

To eliminate the arrows of dark forces and reject their bodies, one must try daily to build his own bodies with the highest substance possible.

The astral body is mostly built through loving affection, harmlessness, a clear conscience, high aspirations, and by passing through certain earthly and subtle tests.

The mental body is built mostly through creating beauty, through meditation, honesty, sacrificial service, and through certain tests.

There are four tests which are given to disciples when they are ready to try spatial experiments. These tests are called tests of earth, water, air, and fire.

In sleep or in a conscious out-of-body state, the neophyte is challenged to pass through closed doors or barriers of rocks or mountains. If he thinks in earthly terms and hesitates to pass or thinks it is impossible, then he fails the test.

Water tests are also in various forms. One is tested to walk through a river, dive in the ocean, walk on the surface of the water, etc. If he is frightened and awakens, he did not pass the test.

Tests of the air are more difficult and related to the thought world. One is taken to high places to jump or to walk near the edge of the roof of a building a hundred feet in height, or to fly in the air. If he thinks in terms of earthly measures, he will immediately react and, due to his fear, he will awaken.

Tests of fire are even more serious. They are related to explosions, forest and house fires, being in flames, etc. If one realizes that fire cannot burn him and that he can be in fire, walk in fire, inhale and exhale fire, he passes the test.

In certain schools of wisdom the neophyte is prepared to take these tests through imagination and visualization exercises, to be ready for the real tests in his dreams.

There are several outcomes of these tests. First, they make you aware that this life is a preparation for a higher life, and one cannot meet the requirements of that higher life by lingering on various lower planes; thus one fails and creates delay in his evolution.

The most important thing they do is awaken you in the Subtle and Fiery Worlds. They make you aware that you are functioning in different spheres, with different measures. They eventually make you realize that each sphere is different from the other. Once the consciousness grasps these facts, liberation from the lower worlds will be easier.

An organized and healthy body can reject most of the attacks of lower forces. It can reject any astral corpse from sticking to the astral body.

The weakness of the astral and mental bodies awakens the desires of dark forces to loan their vehicles to the person. Highly developed and advanced vehicles can be loaned only to those who are called for a spiritual service at a time of a special crises.

Loaning of higher bodies is also used to carry a worthy warrior to higher planes or higher centers, to give him a panoramic view of the situation, or to put him in contact with higher centers to encourage him and create trust in himself. In such cases the advanced vehicles are used for protection and also for transportation toward higher spheres.

We need higher vehicles to travel through the Higher Worlds. These vehicles are called *spatial vehicles*. All vehicles needed for travel are within us, but they are mostly in their potential state. They need to be developed and prepared for future flights.

In esoteric literature we read about co-measurement. Co-measurement is the result of the ability to be conscious in many dimensions or planes and to balance your life, wherever you are, according to the laws and principles of all planes of which you are conscious. For example, you live in the physical plane, but because of your continuity of consciousness you are aware of many planes. This awareness of many planes gives you the privilege of conducting your life on the physical plane in such a way that you not only live according to the laws and principles of the physical plane, but also you do not violate the laws and principles of those planes of which you are aware.

This is real co-measurement. This is how one can have a really balanced life. Thus, whatever you do on any plane does not contradict the laws and principles of any other plane.

The Teaching given to humanity in the Scriptures of the world is, in reality, a Teaching to bring such a balance and co- measurement into our lives. For example, the life we live on the physical plane *appears* to be very fitting to the physical laws and principles, but the majority of people live in the physical plane in such a way that they violate the laws and principles of the subtle or spiritual planes. This is how pain and suffering come into being.

A life lived according to the principles of co-measurement will enable us to live a more healthy, successful, creative, and joyful life and will prepare us to be the citizens of all planes. The Scriptures of the world teach us the steps toward such an achievement.

Co-measurement is also the name of an inner apparatus, the seed of which was inherited by man during the Cycle of Manifestation. Through this apparatus the Creative Forces in Nature have guided humanity and gradually taught them how to use it consciously to guide their own lives in the world and in the Higher Worlds.

Some philosophers have called this apparatus the "Antahkarana." It needs to be built. A Great Sage calls it "synthesis." Actually, this is a symbolic way to explain the process of the conscious mastery of an apparatus which is potentially in existence within man. This apparatus, which at present is called the Antahkarana, is the "co-measurement" which enables man to be conscious on many planes and conduct a holistic life, a life which is in harmony with the laws and principles of all planes.

The seed of this apparatus is found in every individual. Let us not forget the fact that this apparatus within each of us is a portion of the apparatus which exists in the whole manifestation as one complete apparatus. The unfoldment and development of this apparatus in any living form contributes to the better functioning of the one apparatus in all living forms. The roles of this apparatus are as follows:

1. To make man aware of the principle of survival within each human being

2. To register the guidance or directions of the Central or Cosmic Magnet, and to be in harmony with Its directions in the manifested Universe
3. To register the laws and principles of all planes
4. To register beauty
5. To register the One Will beyond all manifestation

This apparatus has been damaged throughout the ages, and man lives like a pilot whose aircraft has fallen to earth and who has a radio transmitter which is either heavily damaged or does not work at all. This is the world problem. How did this damage come about?

Every act that humanity has committed against Beauty, Goodness, Righteousness, Joy, and Freedom has evoked a violent reaction from Nature. Thus, natural and man-made catastrophes have come into being. Through each catastrophe — earthquakes, floods, fires, volcanic eruptions, wars, revolutions, genocides — the central apparatus was damaged. Great damage was also done during the Lemurian and Atlantean disasters.

One may ask, why does humanity live against the guidance they have in their apparatus? The answer is that in addition to this apparatus, humanity has another which is called free will. Free will is like a knob on a radio; it acts as a device to tune in to, or to shut off, the central apparatus.

Man was given the opportunity to prove himself worthy of the apparatus of the Antahkarana[1] and make progress through using his free will. In the Scriptures, this central apparatus was called the ability to discriminate between evil and good. The fraction remaining from this central apparatus is called the conscience.

Free will is the power of man which can be used for good or for evil. Those who have used their free will to tune in, through the central apparatus, to the direction of the Cosmic Magnet have become the Initiates, Masters, and Hierophants of the advancing Army of Light, and They have entered higher evolutions. Those who have misused their central apparatus are still here on earth or in the astral plane, swimming in the mud of human problems, pain, and suffering.

One thing that is noticeable in life is that, in comparison to the large numbers of humanity, very few people have a direction. The majority live without a direction, goal, or purpose, or they live under manipulative hands and interests.

---

1. For more information about the Antahkarana, please refer to *The Psyche and Psychism* and *The Science of Becoming Oneself.*

One may ask, is it possible to repair this apparatus? The answer is yes. This is what the process of building the Antahkarana is. But if one is not under the supervision of a real Teacher, he can be misled by his own half-built or half-damaged apparatus. This creates many glamors and illusions in which the man begins to live.

For example, if your television set is not an up-to-date model, it may project many kinds of distortions and noises. If you become foolish enough, you will begin to enjoy these projections as if they were the ones you were expecting to see. This is how people begin to be "prophets," "apostles," "channels," and "Christs." Many such false "Christs" are now here, serving the special glamors and illusions of people.

There is also the fact that a damaged apparatus can begin functioning if the owner comes in contact with an advanced person. People say, "When I visited that sage or that teacher, many psychic powers awakened in me...." This often happens. One of the reasons that great Teachers do not live in cities is that They do not want to lead the masses into glamors and illusions. If They appear in cities, They take strong measures to prevent, to a certain degree, the stimulation of damaged apparatuses.

On the other hand, the dark forces enjoy stimulating apparatuses which are found in a damaged condition.

People think that the astral body cannot act as the physical body does, but there are cases which show that the astral body, while out of the physical body, writes, sings, or paints.

Many letters are written by astral hands. Many pictures and symbols are produced by astral hands, and an astral voice is heard on many occasions.

If the mental body is disciplined and in control of the astral body, the astral body can be used almost like the physical body.

In the astral world, astral bodies act as if they were physical bodies.

One can learn how to use his astral body through projection or in sleep, after some discipline and training.

Some advanced Initiates can use Their astral hands to move objects or write a letter in front of an audience. People think this is magic, or that it is performed by unseen forces. In reality, man can use his invisible astral hands and perform many actions.

The astral hands can penetrate into the body without damaging the body and perform a certain kind of surgery. To do this, higher clairvoyance and complete control over the astral hands and fingers are needed. Such people appear as if they were motionless, but their astral hands are in action.

People from the Fiery World can descend into the astral and physical worlds and perform many miraculous operations on the human body. They can even stop machines and cars, if they see great dangers in them, or transport various objects from great distances.

It is also reported that they can catch bombs and place them safely on earth before they explode. There is a group of astral servers who are organized to minimize the dangers of the war games which humanity plays so seriously and with great hatred and animosity.

34

The Age of the Human Soul

In esoteric literature we read about young souls and old souls. This is a symbolic way to reveal some subjective facts. The difference between the souls is the difference of experience, consciousness, and will.

One who learns his lessons and returns ten times sooner than another is called an older soul because he has experienced more, learned more, expanded his consciousness more, and developed his will more. Young souls are those who have spent their time and energy and have not learned their lessons. They repeat their "classes" until they learn their lessons.

Old souls are those who, in harmony with the cycles, keep peace and move forward into greater wisdom. They do not waste time and energy. They try to cultivate group virtues and group talents. Every time they appear in the world, they are richer and more beautiful in wisdom than before. For example, we learn that in order for one to attain complete fearlessness, he must cultivate fearlessness for thousands of years.

While the wise one cultivates virtues and talents, the foolish one dances until morning and wastes his energy in the dark corridors of life.

Young souls stay much longer on the lower or middle subtle planes than older ones. Incarnation after incarnation, older ones speed their return. A time comes that they stay only a few days in the subjective world and return to continue their service for humanity.

Young souls run after the accumulation of money or properties. They run after excessive sex, fame, reputation and power, and they imprison themselves with the resulting karmic ties. Young souls create so much karma that they lose their goal in paying off and fighting against their karma.

Old souls try to decrease their karma. As they decrease it, they gain more control over their life and future. They even choose to be in the problems of the world more than being in the peace of the middle astral plane. They sacrifice the beauty of being in the Higher Worlds to meet the needs of a suffering humanity.

As the soul gets older and older, his willpower and psychic energy become great tools in his hand. This enables him to bring greater improvements in life and to create greater resistance to the forces of evil.

Older souls have a greater field of consciousness. Younger souls have a very narrow and sometimes even a decaying consciousness. An expanding consciousness is a blessing, both on earth and in the Subtle Worlds. An expanding consciousness creates a harmonious relationship with the energy system of the Universe. Such a relationship brings greater wisdom, prosperity, and health to the owner of the consciousness.

When the consciousness does not expand, it retreats and contracts. A dying consciousness is like a lamp in which the oil is almost finished. Such a consciousness will not lead the way to other worlds but will fall into the hands of the thieves in the Subtle World.

An expanding consciousness tries to settle problems existing between friends, relatives, and enemies. We are told that by all possible means we must create understanding, harmony, and right relations with those with whom we have problems, difficulties, and tensions because those problems cannot be solved in the Subtle World, and their tension weighs heavily on our shoulders.

The Subtle World is the field in which we reap the things we sowed here on earth.

There is a beautiful story about Mohammed (may peace be with Him) as He was passing away. He remembered that He had borrowed a chicken from His neighbor and had forgotten to replace it. He called a faithful friend and asked him to take a chicken to the neighbor.

In many places on earth there are still people who try to settle their problems with others before they pass away. Our Teacher used to say: "Miserable are those who enter the Subtle World with the baggage of old arguments and problems." This is why the Teaching regarding forgiveness is given. Forgiveness means not to take your problems with you, but to solve them and settle them on earth as soon as possible, as beautifully as possible.

When we ponder on these ideas, we live a life in which we try initially not to cause problems, and when we do cause problems, we then try to solve them.

Harmlessness in our relationships gives us great courage and joy as we step onto the Path to the Subtle Worlds.

Young souls, like certain little children, are harmful and destructive. Older souls are very careful, and they do not destroy anything that is created by human labor, unless it becomes an obstacle on the Path of perfection.

Elderly souls have a will of steel. Throughout ages they have confronted difficult problems and obstacles with courage and daring. Their wisdom has evoked the power of will, which eventually becomes a Ray of Power to be used for the upliftment of humanity.

Older souls accumulate a great amount of treasure in their Chalice, while the younger ones leave their Chalice empty. Older souls have a greater amount of patience, understanding, and tolerance. These are three jewels which adorn their crown. Older souls are those who still try to save this planet and make it an Ashram of wisdom.

It is said that once Timurlane went to Armenia to destroy many towns and villages. One day he came, with his entire army, to a beautiful and prosperous village and surrounded it. A day later he sent a messenger to the village and asked to see the head of the village.

The head of the village was a twenty year old young man. When the messenger brought him into the presence of Timurlane, the Conqueror looked at him with surprise and asked, "Well, you don't even have a beard yet. Why are you the head of the village?"

"Great commander," said the young man, "if you want the leader with a beard, I will bring him to you immediately."

"That is what I want," said Timurlane.

The young man went to the village and came back to the Sovereign with a goat, which had a beard.

"What is this, young man?" asked Timurlane with anger.

"My lord, I wanted to let you know that wisdom is not in the beard, but in the soul."

Timurlane was very pleased with this answer. Taking him to the tent, he gave him many valuable gifts and gave his army the order to withdraw.

The village was saved by this old soul in a young body.

Most men, when loved by a woman, act like children, and eventually the woman or wife becomes their mother. Man, consciously or unconsciously, manipulates a woman by becoming a child. He does many naughty things, knowing that he will be forgiven and loved. He exaggerates things, nags, forces his will, ties her to him with pity, and uses her like his slave.

Just as this is common among men, it is also common among women. Some women live as teen-agers. They stick to their teen-age ways to feel that they are still young, energetic, and beautiful. They stick to that age to allow themselves to behave exactly as teen-agers do. No matter how old they are, such women generally become more adolescent as they grow older in order to create those conditions in which they feel free. Some women stop maturing in their childhood and never grow up. They marry as a child; they work in an office as a child; they relate as a child. They even love and cry like children.

Some men love this kind of women because they can make these women do whatever they want or play with them however they want. Men usually deceive them, manipulate them, and use them for their self-interest and pleasure.

Certain men who look for co-workers and companions cannot live with such "children," and if they intend to leave, they are forced to face all the mischievousness and tantrums that these children can construe. Such women react very irrationally, with revenge and hatred, and never want to negotiate or solve their problems. If they are taken back, they act like spoiled children — demanding, forcing, breaking, screaming, and hating.

It is very important to educate people to mature, to teach them the importance of not stopping their psychological growth on the path of progressing years. Every age has its beauty and its traps, its shortcomings and problems, but they must be left behind and new challenges must be met in each new round. It is very important to destroy the psychological crystallizations on the path of life and proceed toward maturity.

It is also experienced, after growing up normally, that at a certain age or under certain conditions, a person may temporarily regress to the age of a child or teen-ager. Such moments most often occur at times of deep excitement, illness, or crisis. When we become hooked by the past, we dramatize our psychological age of the past in the present event or relationship.

Many do not stay in such traps for long, but the duration in which a person acts like a teen-ager or child becomes quite disturbing to relatives, co-workers, and friends, especially when important decisions are to be made by that person. Such "backsliders" sometimes lose hours, months, or even a few years.

By observing ourselves closely, we can see if we are playing a drama, reverting to our younger years, or if we are really living in the present with our true psychological and physical age, taking actions to prevent ourselves from sliding backward.

There is another phenomenon, which is not as widespread as the previous one, in which some people live older than their years. Some children appear as if they were twenty-five or thirty; some teen-agers live like old men or old women and miss the fun of their physical age.

It is very difficult to live with such people because they are not fun, and they do not cooperate with those who are living their right psychological and physical age. Most of the time they belittle and criticize people. They look down on others and do not enjoy the company of others, creating many problems in social and group relationships.

There are also those rare people whose life is open; there is no blockage or trap in them. They can move into any psychological age when called upon to communicate, have fun, and cooperate with people of all ages. Such people are usually successful in their marriages and business and social circles because they can adjust themselves to the level of any psychological age.

It is interesting to note that sometimes people meet others who have the same psychological age. They enjoy each other and form groups together.

It is also observed that some people, after age sixty five, regress to a younger age; for example, they act as if they were twenty-five years old.

On the other hand, some young people try to live psychologically in an old age, pretending that they are sixty or seventy years old. The interesting thing is that these two types of people may meet each other along the way at a certain point, and for a while they enjoy each other's company until they once again begin to move either backward or forward to their real age.

Life is like a highway. Many cars get stuck. Many are north bound, while others are heading south. Some of them stop along the way, then proceed. Some of them go straight to their destination.

The cause of being retarded in some period of your age is that one of your subtle bodies did not grow at the same pace as your physical body. In most cases, your astral body starts growing when the physical body is five or six years old. At that moment, a shock, grief, deep disappointment, anger, psychic attack or fear can paralyze the energy system of the astral body, and it does not grow anymore. Accidents, death of the parents, or failure may also stop the growth of the astral body. This creates many problems. You grow physically, but emotionally you remain immature.

The emotional body is the body that controls human relationships, protects a person from emotional attacks, and resists possessive intentions from people who want to dominate. If the emotional body does not mature, as a consequence the person cannot have good emotional rapport with people, cannot sense or translate their emotions, and always has a gap between himself and other people. Emotional immaturity often creates embarrassing situations for those who are closely related to the person.

Emotional immaturity makes it difficult for a person to receive intuitive impressions because Intuition communicates with a person through the heart center of the astral body. As a result, the person acts under physical urges and mental perceptions which lack the appropriate emotional counterparts. Thus, the person may seem too "dry" to others.

There is another case that can be called "delayed birth." Some people's emotional nature is born or activated late in life, and it acts in immature ways which embarrass the person.

Visualization

To make the emotional body grow, life presents many crises which may hurt the person for a long time. The best way to help the emotional body grow is to cultivate the arts, acting, poetry, music, and dancing, and to do the following visualization exercise:

1. Visualize your emotional body standing in front of you as a transparent body with a silver color.
2. Feed that body from your heart center through a golden thread through which life-giving psychic energy flows and gives nourishment.
3. Visualize the emotional body growing into maturity.

A similar situation can occur when the mental body is retarded in its maturity. The mental body can be activated when the physical body is sixteen to twenty-one years old, or at age thirty-five. Sometimes a person is seventy, but thinks like a thirty-five-year-old. When the mental body is retarded, the person mostly lives a mechanical life, controlled or guided by others.

There is another situation which is more serious. It often happens that our physical, emotional, and mental natures grow simultaneously and in a satisfactory way, but the human soul remains a baby. Sometimes the soul is not even born. To be born means to be anchored in the pineal gland and in the mental body.

When the human soul is retarded, the person may have a good body, developed emotions and mind, but he will use them for his ego, a pseudo-self which he creates to have an identity of his own and for society. This kind of person lacks a sense of direction, sensitivity to his Solar Angel or to the Plan, and all his life is dedicated to self-interest, materialism, or totalitarianism. He has no innate urge for Beauty, Goodness, Righteousness, Joy, Freedom, sacrificial service, and striving toward perfection. Such personalities can become a menace to humanity, according to the level of their position and power.

In such a case the growth of the human soul can be promoted by hard and heavy labor, voluntarily carried out under the supervision of a Teacher, and by scientific meditation, again supervised by a Teacher.[1]

---

1. For information on meditation, please refer to *The Science of Meditation* and *The Psyche and Psychism*.

35

Dream Experiences

There are many cases in which a person dreams about a stranger, and a few days or weeks later he meets him. This is a very perplexing event for those who have never thought about the Subtle World, but for an esotericist it is very simple.

We meet people daily in the Subtle World, and often we agree to live together for certain reasons, or to work together for a project. It is possible that we forget the details of our dreams, but we remember the stranger when we actually meet him.

Each one of us has many friends in the Subtle World, not only those we know in earthly life, but also those whom we have never met in this life but have met in other lives. Some Teachers have thousands of subjective friends, and occasionally they meet them in various countries and nationalities. When some Teachers go to speak in other countries, through their dreams their unknown friends are informed to go and listen to these Teachers whom they know subjectively.

I have seen many cases where people have looked for a particular Teacher and upon seeing him exclaimed that they saw him in their dreams. Some people dreamed about their Teacher years previously; eventually karma brought them together.

It is also known that some group members on the earthly plane resign from the group if their subjective tie with the group is terminated in the Subtle World. Or, if they secretly violate the trust of the Teacher on the physical plane, the Teacher expels them from the subjective group. Immediately when they are expelled from the subjective counterpart of the earthly group, even if they do not remember their rejection, they feel very uncomfortable in the group and slowly disappear or resign, giving various reasons.

No group stands strongly and harmoniously if the members are not in good rapport subjectively. As long as people live in the state of hypocrisy, bigotry, and superstition, they cannot build good friendships and cannot enter into the group spirit or the spirit of brotherhood.

On the Path to the Higher Worlds, those who are slaves of these three enemies of light cannot penetrate into the worlds of beauty, harmony, and goodness.

In ancient monasteries, which were the centers of advanced Brotherhoods, people were tested to see if they were hypocrites or had fallen into bigotry and superstition. If so, the leaders knew that the candidates should go into the world and spend many years or lives in the refinery of life, and then come and knock on the door of the Brotherhood.

Hypocrisy, bigotry, and superstition can manifest through many forms and in many colors, and an experienced eye can detect them. An experienced eye is one that has seen the beauty, goodness, harmony, and joy of the Higher Worlds.

It is possible to start friendship both from the earth and from the Subjective World. The friendship that starts from the Subtle World during our sleep is more lasting and beautiful than the friendship that starts from the earth. There are many interests and motives involved in earthly friendship. But subjective friendships which begin in the higher levels of the astral or mental planes are only destined to work for great plans and projects in the world.

Because such a relationship is impersonal, it lasts long, sometimes through incarnations, manifesting as friends or family members dedicated together to great global service.

It is also known that in the Subjective World a person can protect a friend from certain dangers or repel attacks directed to him. Such a subjective event acts as a practical protection also for the same friend living in the physical world.

Healing is very prevalent in the Subjective World. Once a doctor in his physical body was trying to heal one of his patients. The prescription he used did not help the patient. One day the doctor dreamed he was going to the patient with a medicine which he never thought of in his earthly consciousness. A few days later he called the patient and suggested the use of that certain medication.

"Well," said the patient, "you already told me about the drug yesterday in my dream, and I am using it with good results."

The important thing is to know that we are every day in the Subjective World, and we live, move, and have our being in the Subjective World.

It also happens that things lost on the physical plane can be found in the subjective plane and then re-discovered on the physical plane.

Once our consciousness begins to function in both spheres, we can use our subjective consciousness to render great services to others and to ourselves because we see the reality behind the appearances and the motive behind the expressions.

We are told that one cannot be conscious in the subjective planes until he cultivates his heart and compassion. The heart and compassion prevent one from using his information for either selfish purposes or to attack others.

People sometimes think that it is possible through drugs and various other mechanical means to penetrate into the higher astral and Fiery Worlds. They even think that one can develop certain thought patterns and yogic powers and penetrate into the Subtle Worlds.[1]

People must know that the higher astral and Fiery Worlds are surrounded by electrical spheres through which one cannot pass until he develops enough psychic electricity to balance the fiery spheres. The higher spheres are protected by the energy of the Hierarchy to keep out those who want to enter through the windows instead of the doors. One can have many experiences of a kind in which he is immediately thrown out when he gets closer to the higher spheres. Some of the "jumping" or startled responses one may have during sleep have a close relationship to this fact. People "fall down" and awaken with a "jump" or a startled feeling.

It would be very dangerous if people were permitted to penetrate into these spheres before they were ready, especially those in whose hearts darkness dwells. They would be able to bring great disasters to the world if they could penetrate into Higher Worlds. In such cases, the Higher Worlds would provide the light by which these people could have all the information and tools to increase darkness and destruction.

In addition to the protection of the Higher Worlds by electrical spheres, the Ashrams of the great Masters and Their disciples are also protected. One must be worthy or ready to attend these Ashrams or classes before he enters. The qualities required are many, but the foundation is purity, compassion, devotion, love for the Hierarchy, and the urge to serve and sacrifice. These are the lights which lead one to the Path of higher learnings.

One must first accept that the Higher Worlds exist. This acceptance is not a blind acceptance but the sign of one who has had experiences in the Subtle World.

Actually, when we speak about faith, we refer to the subjective knowledge which cannot be proven by objective means. For example,

---

1. See *The Fiery Carriage and Drugs. Talks on Agni* presents information on various yogas; see especially Chapter One.

in the Fiery World one sees that his work on earth is going to be protected and inspired by the higher forces and that he will become very prosperous. This is knowledge and direct information in the Fiery World. But when one awakens, the information or knowledge is expressed in the memory as *faith* because by earthly logic one cannot prove that these things related to his work will occur on earth.

Great people live with faith, and their faith always actualizes. Faith is the shadow of manifesting reality. Those who do not have faith are those who have no convictions about the Higher Worlds. Their lives are one-dimensional, mechanical, often artificial, and based on earthly measures.

There are worlds within worlds hidden within Nature. Beyond the physical dimension exist the domains of the emotions, the mind and still higher realms — each a world in itself, just as the physical world is. Because these worlds lie beyond the range of the five physical senses, they are called the Subjective Worlds.

Man is a replica of Nature. The world of feeling and emotions, sometimes called the astral world; the world of the mind, sometimes referred to as the consciousness and the subconscious, or the higher and lower mind; and also the Higher Worlds beyond these exist, hidden within man as they are hidden within Nature.

Dreams are our communication with the Subjective Worlds. If the ability to register impressions exists in the brain consciousness, then we remember our dreams. Without this ability, we dream but do not register the impressions in the brain. The mental world is the field of communication between the emotional world and the brain consciousness, as well as a link between the collective mental world and the brain consciousness.

The ability to register impressions also determines whether or not there is communication with the subconscious mind. All those experiences which have been buried for ages in the subconsciousness can come to the surface or make a contact with the brain, via some association, in the form of an impression which may later be translated as a dream.

The mental world also acts as a field of communication with the higher center within each of us which we call the Soul or the Inner Guide. Sometimes through dreams we may have communication with this creative center, from which all beauty comes.

There are still other sources of communications in dreams. We do not know them directly, yet we come in contact with them. For example, a thoughtform is a common source of impressions in the Subtle World. If ten people concentrate on an idea, the frequency of their thoughts accumulate in Space. This becomes like an entity: it has identity and existence. If the thoughtform contacted is one of love, beauty, and goodness, then those energies are transmitted to you.

There are also great minds in Space. Human beings are not simply born on earth only to disappear altogether. The Ageless Wisdom teaches that consciousness never disappears, nor does the human soul suddenly vanish. We always exist, either in Space or on earth. People who pass away do not cease to have existence. Since much evidence has already been accumulated about this truth, very soon this continuity of existence will be scientifically proven. Through the realm of dreams, we may come in contact with these great minds continuing their existence in Space.

Communications may occur with the Subjective Worlds in many ways. For instance, in a dream you may see your father and hear him tell you to visit the doctor for a checkup. When you do go to the doctor, you find that something was seriously wrong. Your father may have been a symbol, or a thought coming from your subconsciousness, or may really have been your actual father. It does not matter: it is a contact which is guiding you.

Sometimes in dreams someone may give you information which you could have no way of knowing previously. For example, after you moved into a new house, someone in a dream told you that there is a treasure hidden behind a certain wall. In the morning you look, and the treasure is there. There are millions of dreams of this nature beyond disputation. Where do they come from? They cannot come from the subconscious mind because that information was not ever known. Somehow, someone communicated with you.

There also exist other forms of communication which we may consider to be hallucinations, yet we see them. A truly scientific mind does not deny any possibilities and does not dismiss evidence before very thoroughly researching and investigating it in an unbiased manner. Those who deny any possibility outright, without serious inquiry, are not scientific. The unprejudiced, scientific attitude results in the persistent investigation of any phenomena until either it is understood and revealed for what it actually is, or is proved to have no existence.

If Edison had stoutly denied the very possibility of generating electrical light through the light bulb, he would not have invented it. He failed to make the bulbs light up two hundred and seventy-two times, but because he was a scientist, he persisted in uncovering the causes of his failures and on the next try, he succeeded. A scientist not only uses his brain, but also he uses his Intuition.

It is the Intuition which tells you that there is something beyond the wall and you must search for it. The "finder" is the consciousness. The existence of the Intuition cannot be proved physically, emotionally, or mathematically, yet it is there and is known by its effects. In dreams it is possible to communicate with these Higher Worlds.

It is also possible in dreams to communicate with Great Entities such as Those we know as religious leaders, like Christ, Krishna, Buddha, Mohammed, and Moses. They have not disappeared. Nature does not build such beautiful creations only to discard Them. Nature functions with immense beauty, wisdom, knowledge, and economy, and has created us in such a way that we continue developing throughout eternity and never disappear. The Law of Economy is such a beautiful thing; nothing and no one in the world is ever thrown away.

This is a very shocking realization. Each and every word that is spoken will not disappear but will continue to create its effect. Christ said that at the Judgment Day we will have to pay for every ugly word we spoke, and He also said if we give even a cup of water in His name, it will not be forgotten.

He was not speaking in merely religious symbolism but in scientific and actual terms, referring to the fact that once it is created, nothing in the world ever disappears. Even thoughts continue to exist. And if all these effects continue to exist, what about the causes? We are the causes of all that is done, and if the effects do not disappear, then we, the causes, must also continue to exist.

Thus, according to the Ageless Wisdom and to the experiences of human beings, Great Ones do exist. In the face of all ignorance, refusals, rejections and denials, the Ageless Wisdom teaches that there are Great Beings in existence who are interested in guiding humanity just as we guide our young children. If, as an example, you were on the top of a mountain and perceived below you a group of children going down the rapids of a river in a dangerous way, you would call out to warn them to slow down or change direction. In exactly the same way, the earth and humanity have great Leaders, great Watchers Who guide, protect, and warn us.

In ancient religions They are sometimes called Silent Watchers Who watch the destiny of humanity and try to eliminate or modify the bad results of human foolishness and to create good results. Sometimes communication with Them comes through dreams. There are countless examples in the histories of all nations of such dream stories. There are examples of leaders in every field receiving important instructions in dreams, in actual history and in religious texts and mythologies of the world.

Thus we see that dreams are communications with Higher Worlds, with Subtle Worlds. If the contact is with a higher source of goodness and truth, then your dreams are beautiful. If, on the other hand, you are contacting the wrong people and the wrong situations, then you are receiving degenerative dreams.

The quality and depth of your contact depend on your mechanism. The mechanism includes your brain, nervous system, etheric brain, and the electromagnetic sphere around your brain; it also includes your emotions, thoughts, and the contents of your mind.

A very clear analogy can be made with atmospheric conditions. If there is stormy weather, the sun does not shine clearly. You see faint impressions of the sun; then it is lost again behind the clouds. The same thing happens in your mind. If you make a contact in the subjective world but there is agitation around and within you, in your mind or emotions, or even in your physical body, then the impressions you receive are either distorted or very faint. In these cases, impressions cannot reach you because of unclear conditions in your mechanism.

For instance, if you see something while you are in great pain, the translation of that impression will be distorted in your brain because of the condition of your mind. The mind acts as a filter. If there is a red light outside and your window glass is blue, you will see purple light. The mind is a window through which the brain receives impressions.

Your total overall condition, then, is a very important aspect of your dreaming process. Whatever your overall condition is at the time of your dream, it will affect the results of your dream and how you see it. For this reason, in the ancient Temples disciples were cautioned to enter into the dream state in the correct way.

Most of us do not know how to enter the realm of dreams. To enter into sleep in the right way is a great art. First the body, emotions, and mind must be purified, and then you must focus yourself in higher realms, in beauty, goodness, and truth, and then consciously enter into sleep.

Ordinarily we go to sleep in the atmosphere of all our conflicts, greed, hatred, jealousy, excitement, and irritation. In such a condition what can we expect to contact? It will be impossible to contact anything constructive because all these negative impressions will act as parasites and as static during the night. And in the morning, when we awaken, we are exhausted because all night long our wiring and electrical system was working, spending energy to try to clear the short-circuits.

In sleep we should be assimilating energy. If we do not know how to sleep, then in the morning we are more tired that when we went to bed. When people have fights with family members, when there is hatred, when drugs or alcohol are used before the time of sleep, then the sleep state will be very stormy and the dreamer will attract different kinds of attacks from lower forces.

You must enter into sleep with the realization that your aim is to enter into a higher level of consciousness. Beautiful things may be learned if sleep is entered in the right way. As you guard your life and direct it in better ways, you can receive abundant wisdom from the Higher Worlds. There are wondrous creative sources within you which you cannot reach if your bridge is not built for continuity of consciousness.

Sexual excess is another reason dreams are not remembered. It has been proven that the memory is clearer when sexual energy is economized. A useful experiment is to abstain for two months and see how clear your dreams will become.

In the old monasteries our Teachers advised us to refrain from sex for four months and not even to think about it. Our dreams became so beautiful and clear. When people returned to their regular sexual habits, the clarity of their dreams decreased.

In the ancient temples it was taught that sexual energy is a very precious substance that the body builds strictly for creative purposes. We use it lavishly now for our own amusement. It is not that sex is bad, but if you are thinking about communicating with higher spheres of consciousness in higher dimensions, then you must prepare yourself for these contacts.

Worry, grief, and depression are very bad as well. Worry destroys the sensitivity of your mind, but depression causes the greatest damage of all in blocking contact with Higher Worlds. Joy increases the sensitivity of your brain. Joy is not the same as happiness. Happiness is a temporary condition of your personality, but joy is much deeper and more serene. When you are really joyful, you increase the sensitivity of your brain to the point that you can register your higher contacts accurately.

Suppose, then, that your brain is clear and that when you go to bed you are peaceful and purified physically, emotionally, and mentally. The next factor to be considered is your level of evolution. Are you developed physically, or physically and emotionally, or even physically, emotionally, and mentally? Where are you on the evolutionary scale in terms of development and integration? How much have you advanced spiritually? To what degree have you become a human being? People imagine that because they have two eyes, two hands, two feet, and can talk that they are automatically human beings. But there are bipeds walking around who are lower than animals.

You need to examine yourself honestly to discover your actual stage of evolution. What can you tell about yourself? Are you really human and all that this implies? Are you superhuman? Are you entering the next phase of your evolution, and if so, what is it?

According to what we know about evolution, we were once minerals, then vegetation, then animals. Now we are human beings, or working on it. Are we going to stop here? If we are going to cease to evolve all of a sudden, then the Creator is a fool. If all evolution abruptly came to a halt at a certain point, then the Creator would not know what He was doing. But we know that He is not playing with us. We are progressing from level to level, higher and higher, infinitely. Who knows where creation ends? The great Persian poet Rumi wrote:

> *I died from the mineral and became a plant,*
> *I died from the plant and reappeared in an animal;*
> *I died from the animal and became a man.*
> *Wherefore then should I fear, when did I grow less by dying?*
> *Next time I shall die from the man,*
> *That I may grow the wings of an angel.*
> *From the angel too I must seek advance;*
> *Once more shall I wing my way*
> *Above the angels, becoming that which*
> *entereth not the imagination.*
> *Verily unto HIM do we return.*

You can observe evolution even in the human kingdom. There are people in front of whom we are like chickens, in purity, in consciousness, in achievement, in science, in depth and breadth. For example, when I was in the Royal Air Force, I learned the ABC's of the science of weather — how to direct airplanes and how to make charts and maps. When I had finished my courses, I really thought I was somebody and that I knew everything about these subjects. Then one day a scientist came and spoke to us for half an hour. I became smaller and smaller by the minute. Finally I said, "I don't want to know anymore." He asked why and I said, "Because your mind is so vast that it is challenging me to know more."

He was an encyclopedic man, but even he is a "chicken" in front of others greater than he. There are beings who are ten million years ahead, and that is the beauty of life. There is no stopping on the Path of Infinity. When I learned that, I said, "Thank God! Now I am happy that I was born because there is no end to progress."

At what stage in evolution are you, and are you progressing? You can tell where you are from the level into which you are able to penetrate and make a contact. Your contact is limited or conditioned by what you are. A common soldier cannot contact the President of a country, but the President's personal secretary or his cabinet members can because they are close to him. You can contact the level where you are — physically, emotionally, mentally, morally, and spiritually. If you are becoming more beautiful on all these levels, if you are living a life of beauty, goodness, and truth, you are raising your consciousness and penetrating into higher spheres of human development.

Dreams are very different in higher levels. If you are stuck in the mud of the valley, all you can see is the mud, but from the mountain top you can see for miles around. Now you can see where you are going and decide what you are going to do when you get there. This is a completely different experience from being bogged down in the lower levels. As you expand your consciousness and beingness, your contacts with higher forces and higher guidance become clearer and higher.

When I was a child I climbed to the top of a mountain and wondered, "Where is the door through which I can enter into the presence of God?" Later I went to my Teacher and asked him, "Is there any door I can go through to find someone who will tell me something that is beyond this life?" He looked at me and said, "If anyone else had asked me, I would tell him he was crazy. But you are intelligent, and I know you are really searching. You are not crazy." He knew that I wanted to find a door to make a contact with the subjective worlds. And I found out that dreams can be doors through which you can enter into the Higher Worlds.

In most of your dreams you go out of your body. It is important to understand what happens when you go to sleep. If you are an average man, you only go one or two feet from your body when you sleep. A clairvoyant can see that you are sleeping very near your body. If you are a little more advanced, you go miles away from your body. If you are really a disciple or an Initiate, you do not dream; you consciously leave your body and consciously visit Higher Worlds. At this point in evolution, dreaming ends. Your door to the Higher Worlds stands open because you have achieved continuity of consciousness. Now everything that happens to you is a real, factual experience.

There are classes held at night on the subjective planes that you can attend. You can sit there and take notes, and in the morning when you return to your body, you can write a chapter or a book on what you heard in class.

Where are these experiences coming from? These classes are called _Ashrams_. Ashrams are classes on the higher mental plane or on the Intuitional Plane. If you are a disciple and you have a question, you can take it to the Teachers on these planes. You make your frequency higher and higher until you can penetrate into those spheres and attend those classes where your question will be answered.

Let us say that you are a student of physics and you are doing important work for the progress of humanity. There are groups in the subjective world that specialize in physics. You may go to their classes, and when you awaken in the morning, you feel inspired, even if you do not remember where you have been. Your mind has expanded and you find that you have many new ideas to develop.

It is also possible that your impure wishes, urges, and drives take you to places where you can satisfy them. If, for example, you are desiring to drink a glass of whiskey in a nightclub filled with pretty girls, you are there at night because your wish will take you there.

Sometimes a contact from the subjective world will come to you. This is especially true of telepathic messages. Someone thinks about you; then you receive the thought and decipher it, and you have the answer. The question and the answer can work both ways.

If you sleep in the same room with other people, their dreams are not imposed on you, if you are on different levels. It is much like having five different instruments playing in the same room. If you are sensitive, you can listen to all of them, but if you are really on a higher frequency, their frequencies do not affect you. You only tune in to the station which is in harmony with your own frequency. Dream frequencies act like a radio: turn the dial a little and you tune in to one station; turn it more and you find a different one, and so on.

When you turn the dial, you change the frequency. If your frequency is higher than your roommate's, you do not have associative links with him and his dreams will not intermingle with yours. As soon as you go to sleep, you go to your own level immediately, and he goes to his. Of course you are in a real mess if your frequency is equal to your roommate's and you are sharing a common level. In this case, sometimes your dreams will exactly reflect his; you may see his dreams and he may see yours. This is an interesting study.

There are also exceptional dreams. I was living in Los Angeles when there was a big earthquake. Two days before the earthquake I saw my neighbor in a dream. He and his family were traveling in a truck when suddenly the truck caught fire and everyone disappeared. I wondered what the dream meant when I awakened next morning.

I analyzed the dream and decided that maybe there was some warning that must be given to my neighbor. I went to his house and asked him how everything was going. I did not want him to think I was a psychic, a prophet, a medium, or a weird person. He said that everything was fine. I asked him if he had any plans to travel, but he said no. I did not know what to say next so I went back home, but it still bothered me. If God has given this dream to me, why did He not give it to my neighbor instead? So I excused myself.

Early in the morning two days later, the earthquake hit. It was very strong and my family all went out into the garden. Half an hour later my neighbor came over to say, "I know that Los Angeles is going to be destroyed. I am going to take my family to Fresno where we will be safe." "Don't go," I said. "The earthquake is over. Your children are all fine and happy here. You do not know what dangers can exist someplace else. Nothing more will happen here now." I said everything I could think of to change his mind, but they left for Fresno anyway. Within an hour their truck had hit a pole and the whole family passed away — my neighbor, his wife, and their four children. No one survived to hear me say, "I tried to tell you."

I analyzed this occurrence. Why did I have this dream? Was it meaningless? Or did I know that this man was going to die? I did not know anything about him, and we did not have a close relationship. Why did the dream come to me?

Sometimes warnings are given to your good friends or to your neighbors because you do not have a communications line and cannot be reached. You would have been warned directly if it had been possible, but because you had not built your line of communications yet, the warning was given to someone who had built that station. I have received warnings through little girls and through grandmothers and grandfathers. I listened to them carefully. I think it is better to listen; I will not lose anything by listening.

Such guidance is given to us from the subjective worlds to guide our lives. It is given to us according to our level, according to our consciousness and purity of mind, according to our relationships, and according to the need of the world or of our life. Many people have these kind of dreams.

People also dream of disasters and nothing comes of it. This occurs because there are so many people writing and preaching about them. For example, there are so many people talking about earthquakes and saying that many parts of the earth are going to sink into the ocean. This activity builds a huge thoughtform on the astral and mental planes. Whoever tunes in to these frequencies sees these thoughtforms in his dreams. Everyone adds to them, and it becomes one giant ongoing movie which eventually affects the atmosphere of the earth.

Warning dreams can be from people who are controlled by anxiety and fear. I believe that there is real guidance from higher sources, but there are also millions of thoughtforms which are created by anxieties and fears. How then can you tell the difference between real warnings and false ones?

Telling the difference is easy. If there is no result, the warning was a false one. If you have an egg that will not hatch a chicken, the egg is not good.

If it is a warning coming from your higher consciousness, you must see the proof of its origin there. For instance, if you are warned that your house is going to be destroyed, you will see that it is cracking. There will be an objective indication of it. If there is no indication, the dream can be from your subconscious fears and anxieties. Radio and television programs and other people's thoughts are all collected on certain planes. They can come down and hit you if you are keyed into them. You must carefully notice the difference, or you will be forever running away.

When warning dreams come, I do not translate them. I just listen and watch. It is wise to be a skeptic. I do not believe something until I have tested it a hundred times. When I see that there is something I cannot reject anymore, I accept it as a theory and test it. Do not believe everything I tell you until you have tested it for yourself. It is not good to be gullible and to believe everything that people tell you. Test it. Prove it, until you see that it makes sense. When it makes sense, or your Intuition tells you that it is really good, then do it.

I analyze each contact. Each communication is educational, whether it is a mental or emotional disturbance, or a disturbance of the stomach, or a subconscious communication. If it is a warning, I take it seriously, but I do not translate it into definite fact. I watch carefully to see what is going to happen.

One night I dreamed that while I was driving my car, I had a flat tire and hit another car. When I awoke I thought, "Isn't that a stupid dream. They won't let me sleep peacefully at night." Later I had to drive somewhere, and I suddenly remembered my dream. When I went to my car and examined the tires, I discovered a big nail in my right front tire. When I pulled out the nail, the tire became flat. So I changed the tire before I went out.

A sane and logical person analyzes a warning. If he can make sense out of it, he uses it, and if he cannot, he throws it away. Maybe it is a stupid dream, because stupid dreams are very abundant. They are usually the result of an upset stomach or a spine that is out of adjustment. A spine that is not in order pinches nerves and exerts pressure in different places, creating these silly dreams. They are not really dreams. In the same way, if you are emotionally excited, in grief, or have many problems, your dreams will really be mixtures. Good contacts exist, but they cannot reach you.

Another common source of dreams is your wishful thinking. What you wish for, you see in your dreams. Your daydreams become your night dreams, in other words.

Sometimes you dream the dreams that were already dreamed in the room you are in. This happens especially in hospitals, motels, and hotels. This is a real problem for many people. The cigarette and cigar smoke and the dreams in a hotel room make it almost impossible for some people to get a good night's sleep there.

The impression of a dream stays in the atmosphere of a bedroom for a long time. When you have a dream, that dream is an impression. When that impression hits your mind, it becomes a thoughtform, a movie, or a picture. This thoughtform stays in the room for many hours, or even for centuries, according to its frequency or power.

I was in San Francisco talking with a friend who was a secret service agent. He excused himself after a while to go to a special appointment. I asked him what was so special, and he told me that a woman was going to help them find the body of someone who had been shot but could not be found. I asked him to tell me when she found it. Three hours later he called me to say that she had exactly described where it could be found, and what it would look like. It was a little girl who had been killed. Her body had been wrapped in a blanket and hidden in a garden under some leaves. A psychic had found the body.

I asked my friend how the psychic had found it. He said he did not know but that they used the psychic often at the police station and that sometimes she came and gave lectures there.

These things are happening. They are not hallucinations or "hocus-pocus." If that woman can do it, we can all be able to do this someday if we start developing ourselves. The tragedy of the human being is that he does not want to be something greater than he is now. We are satisfied with what we are. Well, make a breakthrough and enter into a higher level of consciousness. Make yourself more beautiful, more pure, and more loving.

Sometimes you do not need to sleep in order to see dreams. If your consciousness is really under your control, you can go deep into yourself and start dreaming. I had a friend in the monastery who could go into meditation and bring back information. Once he reported that a man we knew had a broken arm. I asked him how he knew and he said, "I went to him and saw that he was in agony." Then I called the man and asked him how he was. The man said that he was in great pain because he had just broken his arm.

Psychic phenomena are so tricky. I would never have believed the report unless I had called to test it and had scientifically proved it from every angle. But my friend really did leave his body, go to this man, and discover that he had broken his arm. Still, it is better to be a skeptic than to be used as a fool. Whenever you enter another dimension, you must be very careful about what you are doing and seeing.

After being very careful to discriminate whether or not it is a true guidance, you must also observe its degree of purity. Was the voice you heard clear? Were the colors in your dream pure? There are many degrees and levels.

You can dream on the astral plane and on the mental plane. There are seven senses on the astral plane and seven senses on the mental plane, but the mental plane is color and the astral plane is sound without color. If you are registering sound and color together it is a real warning for you because it is coming from higher planes. If there is no color mixed with sound, do not become too attached to it. Just keep it in mind that something may happen. These low level thoughtforms can be used for guidance by higher beings when necessary. Be alert. Alertness is always important, but sometimes people stay so "alert" that they do not sleep.

Nightmares occur when the brain is intoxicated, or sick, or the bloodstream is not pure, or there are extra chemicals in the body causing an imbalance in the system. Then you are dreaming half in the brain and half in the etheric brain. You are almost not sleeping. You are awake to some degree and asleep to some degree; that is why you get stuck and cannot go beyond that point.

Flashes of a scene, *deja vu* experiences, inconsequential dreams, and so on are the result of your state of mind. If your state of mind is really in a pure condition, then your computer will function in good order and with purpose. You must not have this confusion, shifting, and mixing. Your dreams must be clear.

We must experiment with dreams. Once when I was going to sleep, I visualized myself going to a man in his bedroom and telling him, "I really respect you." For five months he did not get it, but suddenly he called me and said, "You came to my dream last night and said that you really respected me." Something had been started now. Then I asked him to try to come to my dream and tell me something. Two nights later I picked it up.

This is how you can surpass your physical plane life and enter into a greater heritage than you have now. These abilities are within you. They are not "hocus-pocus" psychic phenomena. If a man can do them, why can't you do them too? You can have these experiences because the same Spark of the divine presence is within you, but you must cultivate it and make it bloom.

Some people say that they do not dream at all. There is no one who does not dream because dreams are contacts with the Subjective Worlds. You always have contact, but some people do not have the ability to register or record them. When you do not have the ability to translate a contact from one world to another, it seems that there is something wrong with your brain. Some nuts or screws are lacking there.

Tests have been conducted in hospitals and sleep clinics on people who have said that they never have dreams. They have been wired to monitors at night. In the morning the monitors proved that they had been dreaming all night.

When you make faces, mumble, and move in your sleep, you are dreaming. You are in contact with something, but because you do not register it, you think that you do not dream. No matter whether you register the dream or not, the influence is going to affect you because it is in your aura, even if it is not in your brain consciousness.

Higher forms of dreams come from higher planes. Some people see geometric forms, symbols, and dramas. They come from the higher mental plane. They are translated into emotional waves and forms. Then they come to the brain and become the usual pictures. They must adapt themselves. If you want to communicate a higher mental plane registration, it has to be translated into your brain consciousness.

That is how *The Unusual Court* [2] came into being. One night I was sleeping, and I found myself in a court of law. I said, "What am I doing here?" Suddenly a judge with long hair and a long beard came in and banged his gavel to begin the proceedings. A cow took the witness stand and said, "MOOOOOO. This man is killing me and eating my flesh. How long is this man going to eat us?..."

2.   Torkom Saraydarian, *The Unusual Court.*

The judge turned to the man and asked, "Is this true? Are you really eating this animal?" The man said, "Yes. I want to live." Then the judge asked, "What if the cow eats you?" This courtroom drama continued until morning.

Early in the morning I got up and wrote it down. Now it is published exactly as it happened. Maybe my love for animals triggered *The Unusual Court*, but it was a drama with meaning, beauty, and wisdom in it.

First, your consciousness starts to operate in the astral body at night. You have an astral body in which you can travel and register things. Then you must pass on to the mental body. How many million years will it take to develop these abilities? We are still so satisfied with our noses and ears! We must go farther and farther.

When you get to the next higher stage after the astral and mental planes, you reach the Intuitional Plane. Here there are no more dreams. You stand face to face with reality. You can go anywhere and talk to anyone. If his mental aura is clear, he will understand you. You can go to your Teacher and talk to him. You can even go higher and see the situation of the world. There are so many things you can do from this plane.

It is not easy to reach the Intuitional Plane. Meditation is an effort to gain consciousness on higher planes, but most of our meditations do not go farther than our nose. Real meditation is very rare. That is why meditation is called the science of thinking. When you are a thinker, you must see the results in your life of your thinking. Once you really know how to think, beyond that you can find the Intuition.

Meditation opens the door to the Intuition, but you must go beyond and beyond. Intuition is seeing the cause and the effect simultaneously in a flash.

Whatever you program into the computer of your brain will condition how it translates your dreams. The translation works according to the programming. The brain is so interesting. For example, let us say that for me a tree represents a girl, but for you the tree represents something else. My program is different from yours. This is why books on symbols and dream interpretations are confusing rather than helpful.

How do we program our brains? Our attachments, contacts, and conversations shape our program. Our wishes and desires and many other things enter our program and shape us differently. Each one's programming is different.

The brain is a very sensitive instrument. It is one of the master mechanisms that Nature gave us. If people knew what the brain really is, they would be in awe. The brain is the supreme gift of God. It must not be polluted by tobacco, dirty talk and imaginations, alcohol or drugs. It must be a clean mirror reflecting Higher Worlds.

During sleep, the human soul tries to penetrate higher planes of existence. One of the factors that hinders his journey is fear. In the memory of men are accumulated many kinds of fear — physical fears, fears related to emotions, thoughts, plans, and decisions. All these fears are also related to various symbols.

On every plane the human soul has various experiences, and these experiences are translated in the brain as dreams. It is possible that in these dreams there will be found symbols which are related to various fears. Immediately when the soul encounters such a symbol, he comes back to body-consciousness, and the dream is cut off.

Thus the association of symbols with corresponding fears brings the soul back to the physical plane. These fears are associated in the subconsciousness or lower mind any time the person breaks the law consciously and registers the experience with a wave of fear attached to it.

Fear is accumulated in the subconsciousness or in the lower mind when the person experiences destruction, violence, murder, or fearful court cases. All these experiences associate and create an electrified fence around the person. If he, in his subjective journey, touches this fence, all the power accumulated in the fence rushes on him, even through a single symbol.

For example, if the person has very negative experiences with police or he has witnessed the negative experiences of others, when he dreams of a policeman — which is a symbol — he feels a shock and the dream stops.

Thus the clearer our consciousness is from fear, the easier it will be for us to climb to higher planes when we go to sleep. The advantage of this is that when we penetrate higher in sleep, we will have greater possibilities to do the following:

    a. Repair our bodies or even heal them
    b. Expand our consciousness
    c. Receive answers to some of our questions
    d. Increase our wisdom
    e. Receive certain directions or warnings
    f. Receive strength to carry on our creative labor
    g. Deepen our foresight into coming events

When people are kept away from penetrating into higher spheres through fear, presented to them by various means, their consciousness cannot grow and they fall into vices, low pleasures, and habits. They lose the chance to renew their lives through high-level inspiration and vision.

We may say that the more deeply a nation sleeps, the higher it penetrates into lofty spheres. Healthy nations are those whose sleep is serene and not agitated by fear or a guilty conscience. Thus, before sleep one must not read frightening books or watch frightening movies to avoid association in the chain of fears and to sleep with a clear consciousness.

If a person is dedicated to service for humanity, he receives certain protection from invisible hosts who, through their psychic energy, help him advance to higher planes. The heart must be dedicated in order to draw such a protection. If the heart is full of guilt and animosity, no help comes to the person.

The impelling force toward higher spheres is the heart. The heart must be charged with psychic energy through prayers and meditation before the person goes to sleep. It is also beneficial to invoke angels of God to be with one in one's journey.[3] Once man is able to become free from subconscious associations, his life turns into a flow of wisdom, beauty, and creativity.

---

3. For specific daily prayers before sleep, please refer to booklet entitled "A Daily Discipline of Worship," and *The Psyche and Psychism*, Chapter 84.

36

Communication with the Subtle Worlds

There are many kinds of communication between the Subtle World and the physical world. There is thought communication. There are words and sentences. There are urges and impressions. There are inspirations. There are encouragements or warnings. All these communications create certain reactions and responses, but those people who do not have any idea about Higher Worlds think that all these are coming from their full stomach or their intoxicated brain.

It is very important to expect communication from the Subtle World, whether it is in a subjective or objective form. It is also important to create the proper mental, emotional, and physical states to be able to receive communication.

There are many conditions which prevent clear communication. Lack of faith, a superstitious mind, physical conditions, an agitated emotional body, and irritation are some examples. Any message received in such a state will be heavily distorted or lost.

Atmospheric disturbances, electrical storms, and sunspots hinder good communication. Radioactive materials cause heavy disturbances in the reception of any communication.

Uncleanliness of the environment or body is another negative factor in communication.

Simplicity, sincerity, and a clean heart are very good conductors of subtle messages from the Higher Worlds.

Meditation, prayer, the admiration of beauty, and gratitude highly electrify our system of receptivity.

Those who are in the Subtle World and the Fiery World want to come in contact with us for several reasons:

1. To let us know that a great future is waiting for us

2. To teach us the best way to progress and prepare ourselves for that great future
3. To warn us about the dangers ahead of us
4. To give us technical information to improve our culture and civilization
5. To create continuity of consciousness between humanity and the Higher Worlds

One must keep a spiritual diary and note every trace of any communication with the Subtle World. One will find increasing inspiration in these communications.

It has been observed that the people from the higher spheres do not waste energy repeating their calls or communications. Sometimes a communication lasts one second, and it is never repeated again. One must be very alert to grasp the message and ponder upon it perhaps for years.

There may be long intervals between communications. Sometimes the second communication may be sixty years later. Some people may complain of the long intervals, but they cannot confirm that they followed the hints of the first communication they received.

The inhabitants of the Higher Worlds do not build their temples on sand; nor do they communicate with people who will not make good use of the communication. Righteousness demands that a call must go out to everyone, but there is no law that forces the Higher Worlds to scatter their precious seeds on rocks.

Mediums, lower psychics, and channels think that they are in contact with the Higher Worlds. The truth is that they are often psychologically sick, and they are in contact with the masqueraders of the lowest astral plane.[1] There are "masters," "initiates," "guides," and "sages" in the lowest astral plane who communicate with mediums and channels. There is no doubt that mediums and channels communicate with something. There is no doubt, but the value of any communication is determined by the *source* of the communication, not the communication itself.

Mediums, lower psychics, and channels create a huge barrier on their path and continuously enter the lowest astral plane and return more defective than before.

Communication with the Higher Worlds must be done by raising ourselves into these worlds. The human soul must learn to leave his

---

1. Please refer to *The Psyche and Psychism*, especially Chapters 15 and 33 entitled "Psychism, Higher and Lower," and "Spirits and Mediums."

body to penetrate rightfully into the Higher Worlds and send his experiences to the brain as clearly as possible.

Necromancy and mediumship work in different ways. The souls of departed ones are called down to earth or forced down to earth. It is known that in ninety-nine percent of the cases of this type of communication, it is the inhabitants of the lowest astral world that can come in contact with those who use the methods of necromancy or mediumship. Higher inhabitants never want to visit the earth because of the state of their vehicles and of their consciousness. However, they like to communicate with the world if rightful communication lines are established. Rightful communication lines are thought-communication and communication in sleep when one is able to ascend into the Higher Worlds from the earth.

Obsession in any degree shows that the obsessor is a violator and, therefore, is not dependable.

It is true that very high spirits can communicate with certain people on earth. This kind of communication is not necromancy nor mediumship.

There are members of the Hierarchy living on earth in Their physical bodies, or advanced Souls Whose responsibility it is to guide or protect humanity. These people do not need mediums or channels. They can manifest and deliver Their message by creating illusionary bodies, or by building bodies out of Their thought energy.

These advanced Souls may also use the method of overshadowing. By this method, the communication lines between the soul and brain of the overshadowed one are sharpened, and the person is made capable of seeing things from the viewpoint of the soul and things as they are.

Inspiration is another method used by Great Ones. An inspiration is a current of energy which carries great ideas or visions from Higher Sources.

There are cases in which a spiritually advanced Initiate gives his physical body to a Great Soul to make it possible for Him to come in contact with the world. This saves time and energy for that Great Soul. Such cases occur in crucial periods in world history, when the Black Lodge is preparing major attacks on humanity. Such cases do not relate to any particular group or nation, but to humanity in general.

Communication with the Higher Worlds does not require a period of time as we know it. Time in the Subtle World is instantaneous. One can penetrate the Subtle World for one second and collect so much information that to express or inscribe it would require ten thousand pages. It is therefore possible to be absent from the body only for a second, but absorb vast amounts of wisdom.

Those who intend to relate to the Higher Worlds must develop a different time concept than what we have on earth. In the higher spheres it does not take time to be anywhere. It is just a matter of thinking. The higher you ascend, the deeper you understand that you can be anywhere instantaneously.

Those who come from the Higher Worlds to work on earth have the *time urge*. They cannot lose or waste a minute of their time. On one end of the pole of their being, they are still aware of the instantaneousness of the Subtle World, and on the other end they are stuck with the concept of time on earth. Instantaneousness tries to overcome time; hence they use each minute to accomplish the timelessness in time.

Mediumship delays the evolution of the beings living on the etheric and lower astral levels. This delay also costs the medium who keeps these beings busy in the worldly sphere.

Necromancy is the imposition of a human will on souls whose direction it is to move away from the earth. Bringing them to the earth for private or selfish interests not only delays their evolution but also destroys their bodies which are in the process of forming for Higher Worlds.

The Subtle World communicates through vortexes of energy. Such vortexes can be created through

1. Thought energy
2. Motion and sacred dances
3. Emotional force, desire, or aspiration
4. Purity or transmutation
5. Willpower

A vortex is a spiral sphere of energy which creates a channel for communication with the Higher Worlds. Motion or dances create a vortex, the quality of which varies according to the level of the consciousness of the participants. If a particular motion or dance is performed by great Masters, the vortex created penetrates into the Higher Worlds and transmits spiritual treasures. If these certain dances are performed by average people, they brings mass obsession from the lowest stratum of the astral plane.

Rock and roll, disco, and related dances have very undesirable movements which invite obsession by astral forces. Those who engage in such dances will sooner or later realize that they have lost their identity and are controlled by lower urges and drives and thoughts of criminal acts. Such dances can pollute a great area in a large part of a nation and eventually lead it to the path of degeneration. The music and movements in these dances create a huge, flat vortex of force, magnetic to the lower astral plane. A great amount of information can be collected by examining the lives of those who have fallen into the trap of such vortexes.

There are many other vortexes. Hierarchy is a vortex of love and compassion. Shamballa is a vortex of energy Whose spirals penetrate into the Cosmic Mental Plane. Christ is a very powerful vortex of light, love, and power, connecting humanity and Shamballa with the Hierarchy. All three of these vortexes are means of communication with the Higher Worlds and with Cosmic sources; this is to keep alive the synchronization of the worlds.

Higher vortexes exist in man as well. When chakras open, they are spiritual vortexes. The human soul is a great vortex when he is liberated. The Chalice is another vortex. Through these vortexes the human soul can communicate with the Higher Worlds. To create such vortexes one must meditate, study, render sacrificial service, and work for the purification of his threefold lower vehicles. The progress of the human soul is achieved when his bodies dissolve and vanish after he leaves them.

As we leave our physical, astral, and mental bodies, these bodies are attracted to worldly spheres. They are living corpses, and, curiously enough, they have recorded "tapes" that may run if one finds the key. Most mediums are in contact with such corpses. For long periods of time, such corpses deliver messages recorded in the "tapes" of their atoms and centers. Astral corpses are found mostly in the lowest and middle astral strata.

If the mental nature is pure, it does not permit an attack on the astral body by earthly forces. Soon, in their own sphere, the astral and mental bodies disintegrate. If the soul is very advanced, his bodies are burned immediately after he leaves them. A mental body lives a longer life if the soul cannot burn it. If it is attracted to earthly spheres, the mental body misleads people though mediums and channels.

The worst fact is that a corpse has an automatic communication system with similar corpses, and like a satellite it transmits information for these various corpses.

Inviting such corpses into our aura is a great violation of the Law of Progress. Such attachment nourishes the corpses and extends their life on earth. The delay of the decomposition of such shells is not beneficial for many reasons.

First, they pollute Space because they are on the arc of decomposition or decay.

Second, they mislead people, and in the case of mediums, create split personalities.

Third, they irritate their owners who are aware of the harmful effects of their corpses but cannot help the situation.

As on earth, so in the subtle spheres: the corpses must be cremated or burned by fire. The sooner they disappear, the better the path of the owner will be.

An advanced soul develops a ray which is used in the Subtle and Fiery Worlds to destroy his vehicles immediately after he leaves them. The ray, like a beam of energy, hits the corpses and makes them evaporate in Space.

There are also those who try to help the owners of the corpses to be cremated. Sometimes this help comes from those who live on the earth, who, because of their developed understanding, can assist the departed one by cremating the body as soon after death as possible thereby keeping the corpses away from the earth.

Detachment is a great virtue. It is also used in higher spheres. Each person who establishes a healthy communication with the Higher Worlds becomes a transmitter of greater wisdom and of new energies, which vitalize the life of the planet and create urges, aspirations, and strivings toward the Higher Worlds. Thus the betterment of life can be achieved through detachment.

Communication with the Subtle World also occurs as a result of hypnotism and posthypnotic suggestions. On the physical plane, a hypnotic suggestion takes the control into its own hands and pushes away those causes which the hypnotist thinks are undesirable. In this way the hypnotist creates an artificial and temporary unity in the psyche of the man. Sometimes these repressed causes try to find doors to escape through different communications, or they may even fight against the hypnotic suggestion if they are strong enough.

In the Subtle World a conflicting duality appears. The suggestion and the suppressed cause fight against each other to dominate the man, who cannot decide which of the two fighters has the right to own him. Sometimes the battle is so serious that the man cannot advance in the Subtle World, and he periodically swings between the fighters.

In the next incarnation this duality is born with the man, and he has a split personality; he is a psychiatric case. Thus, the post-hypnotic suggestion does not end with the death of the person. It continues on the other side of life, but the suppressed cause releases itself from the power of the suggestion and fights against it. The suggestion turns into a cause and conditions the body in the next incarnation.

The Ancients used to say that you should be careful of inviting strangers into your home; they may try to be a part of the family.

Can you imagine the confusion of a man in the Subtle World who has hundreds of hypnotic suggestions? What a battleground his life will be in the Subtle World and the physical world.

Most of our unconscious drives are the reactivation of post-hypnotic suggestions received in the past.

With great tension and distress, the Core of man periodically eliminates strangers from its field. The Core tries to solve its own problems, in its own ways, because its nature strives to be itself. The ultimate achievement of man is carried on only with his own hands and feet.

Communication with Higher Worlds becomes very difficult when a person enters into the Subtle World with heavy posthypnotic suggestions.

It is known that some people, while they are in their physical bodies, are more active in the Higher Worlds than in the lower worlds. They have highly developed psychic powers. Because of karmic reasons and environmental conditions, they have chosen to work on higher planes and do so as effectively as they would have on the physical plane.

There are also highly evolved Initiates who are engaged on earth in their daily labor and appear to be average persons. In addition, they perform very advanced labor in the Higher Worlds in many specialized fields.

Some people are aware of these facts. Others are not. Those who are aware have continuity of consciousness and are highly disciplined not to fall victim to vanity and showing off. Others, who are not aware of their subjective activities, are under the training of the Ashrams. Certain lines in their psychic network are blocked by their Master of Solar Angel, so that they work out their karma on earth, and in the meantime continue their specialized work on subtle planes without the interruption of the lower planes.

There are other reasons why these people should not be aware of their higher labor. One reason is that they may be highly specialized in a higher psychic field but still have certain weaknesses in their character. This would make them vulnerable if those in their environment knew that they were initiates and workers in subjective worlds.

Certain people know that they can think, but they cannot build a chair on the physical plane. They serve with their thinking and inspire multitudes in the Higher Worlds.

Certain people, because of their intense desire for peace and cooperation, deliver messages and work very hard in subjective levels to inspire peace in leaders and multitudes.

Those who have beautiful ideas and great aspiration to serve humanity but cannot actualize and influence people on earth, must not be discouraged. Through their thoughts and aspirations, they render great service to humanity, especially in the astral world and the Fiery World.

Certain scientists have cultivated minds in certain fields, and additionally have a highly developed psychic nature. However, they are not aware of the latter. In the Subtle World their psychic powers help them discover new formulae and new inventions, but when they awaken on the physical plane, they do not remember anything about their life in the Subtle World. In the Subtle World, these scientists may have various specializations in different fields. They may appear in the world as scientists, but in the Subtle World as politicians, artists, or even religious people. While they are physically asleep, or when they are in deep meditation, they work hard in these various fields.

Nature has many laws and many mysterious ways to arrange things, but all of it works for a Plan and for our perfection.

Some people, while they are in their physical bodies, are more active in the Higher Worlds than on the physical world. They have highly developed psychic powers, and, because of karmic reasons and environmental conditions, they have chosen to work on higher planes as effectively as they would on the physical plane.

There is also the other side of the coin. Some people actively serve on the earthly plane, but they appear useless in the subtle planes. Sometimes this is beneficial and karmically arranged to protect them from psychic attacks in the Subtle Worlds, and also to make them focus all their being on the job at hand.

Nature never leaves any talent unused. Somewhere, in some form, all is used since all talents belong to the Great Nature, even though individuals feel that their talents belong to them as personal properties.

There are also those who are completely aware of their high status in the Higher Worlds; however, they choose to live in a very low profile, though subjectively and magnetically causing substantial changes in their environment.

All worlds and planes are parts of one school. People follow different courses for different reasons, but all that they do eventually leads them to perfection. The majority of people are unaware of this fact, but the Cosmic Magnet, through the Law of Karma, pulls the Sparks toward perfection.

One can develop the ability to work consciously on subtle planes. In certain esoteric schools we are advised to take the following steps:

1. Every night before sleep one must for a few minutes think that he is going to render a service in the Subtle World, either to those who have their physical body or those who live in their subtle body.
2. Daily, during working hours, think that one is living simultaneously in two worlds; that he is in real contact with both worlds.
3. Record any experience of a spiritual nature.
4. Be careful not to use your talent, ability, or energy for your selfish interests or pleasures because immediately when you sleep your selfish desires will make you stick with the forms of your desires in the Subtle World. Many such people are like the officer who, before going to his office, used to go and get drunk and forget all about his duties.
5. Develop a keen aspiration toward beauty and service.
6. Do an evening review to clean the aura.[2]
7. Think clearly about your subjective service and go to sleep with these thoughts.

It is also very important to know how to sleep.[3]

We are told it is extremely difficult to send a voice from the Subtle World. Being in a totally different frequency, the voice from the Subtle World will not reach us, unless we have our astral ears developed and are then able to translate the voice due to an unfolded consciousness.

Again, the inhabitants of the Subtle World like to communicate with us on various occasions through their thoughts, but people on earth are not ready to receive their communications and translate them. If people work harder and develop their higher senses and higher centers, eventually a communication line will be established between the worlds, especially during sleep. When such a communication is established, new horizons and new fields of research will open for humanity.

---

2. Please refer to *The Psyche and Psychism*, by Torkom Saraydarian, Chapter 80, titled "Evening Review."
3. *Ibid.*, pp. 506-510, 537-538, for more information about sleep.

The tear glands are very mysterious glands. They register our pain, distress, and suffering and produce tears. When tears are released, the ducts block certain veins in the brain and bring the release of tensions.

The tear glands are also stimulated by our joys, ecstasy, and feelings of great achievements. When tears accumulate in this way, the ducts release them and take away the pressure caused by the joy and ecstasy affecting certain centers in the head.

During meditation, when we contact Higher Worlds or contact our Inner Source of Light, again our tear glands are stimulated. In such an instance, we see tears coming from our eyes.

When tears are analyzed, we will find that they are different in their chemical combinations. Some of them will be found to contain crystals of joy and bliss; others will contain crystals of pain, suffering, and irritation.

Many people are very interested to come in contact with the beings of the Higher Worlds. The following are some reasons why such an interest cannot be easily met:

1. Our physical, emotional, and mental bodies, as well as our entire aura must reach a special degree of purity and intensity of vibration.
2. We must be able to raise our consciousness to the level of those in the Higher Worlds.
3. We must have continuity of consciousness built firmly between our brain and the higher mind.
4. Our karma must allow us to have such an experience.

Very often great Messengers from the Hierarchy come in contact with human beings on special occasions. They exercise a great amount of caution so as not to cause any damage to those whom They contact. Their vibration is so strong that it can shatter the body of a man and cause pain, suffering, and various illnesses in him.

It is recorded that certain powerful kings had trembled like a child in the presence of a great Messenger.

Sometimes Messengers have appeared with Their physical body and sometimes with Their illusionary body. In either condition They emanate fiery vibrations, due to Their power of transmutation and the degree of Their initiation. One cannot compare having such an experience with the experiences that people have in seances, contacting apparitions or spirits. Images of the latter kind do not cause shock or strong reactions because they are ordinary shells, or corpses, animated by liars and imitators.

To prevent shocks and avoid the danger and the possibility of damaging the auras of people, the great Messengers first choose the person who can withstand Their vibration to a certain degree. Then They manifest only Their face or hand for a period of a few seconds. Such an appearance remains forever in the minds of those who experience it. The person not only passes through an unusual sensation of fear, but also through an immense degree of joy, which accumulates in his being as a perpetual source of enthusiasm and creativity.

Messengers from the Hierarchy do not appear for the sake of appearance. There must be a very serious reason to make contact. Each contact must produce a far-reaching inspiration and activity in constructive and educational ways.

In every approach They exercise a great measure of caution. For example, if a message must be given to a president of a nation, They send Their message via a person who is not aware of the content of the message.

Often They use indirect ways to reach people for various reasons.

There are many occasions in which the person is not totally qualified for the message, but the intensity and danger facing humanity can be so great that They take a risk and transmit Their message through those who do not carry Their full confidence and trust. Of course, sometimes after doing their duty, such people fall into glamors and try to use the occasion for their own advantages and egos. But the Great One considers the interest of the masses first, and then the interest of the person trapped in his own glamor. Of course, even such a person is rewarded by his karma for this service.

Often they manifest Their hand and write, for example, on the wall, as was recorded in the Bible. Or They may write letters or even correct manuscripts. To stand in the presence of Great Ones, a person must have a pure aura, not agitated with worldly interests, irritations, and problems.

The main requisite is a life dedicated to the service of humanity throughout many incarnations.

Accumulated sacrifice for the cause of humanity eventually brings us to the feet of the Great Ones.

In the future, people will be specially trained for communication with the Higher Worlds or with Great Ones. Certain virtues must be developed in them, and tested again and again, to enable them to stand in the light of the Great Ones.

There are various ways to communicate with the Higher Worlds. Let us take a few of them:

1. Through raising our standard of values and trying to live according to these standards
2. Through chanting
3. Through our developed, organized, and purified thoughts

To raise our standard of values, we need to cultivate more discipline in our life and strive toward inclusiveness and perfection.

At the present, there is confusion regarding standards. This confusion is going to continue for a long time, in fact, to such a degree that the standards of insanity and the standards of sanity will be equal. Eventually the standards of insanity will be considered to be the standards of sanity. Whenever the confusion of standards occurs, it is a sign of approaching destruction.

The shifting of values is as dangerous as the shifting of poles; it is the signal which puts the destructive forces in Nature into motion.

After destruction — just as it occurs in Nature, following a big fire — new flowers of values appear. For a cycle in time these values prevail, producing people of great spiritual achievements and with a high standard of values.

The period of shifting of the standards is a period of testing, cleansing, and selecting the real and immortal values. It is a period of giving people a new opportunity to blossom and rise into a new state of inclusive consciousness through which new communications can be established with the Higher Worlds.

It is also possible to establish communication with the Higher Worlds through **chanting**. Chanting produces energy. This energy accumulates within our aura and in our etheric centers. Such an accumulation can turn either into a source of blessing or a source of continuous disturbance, sickness, and insanity. The reason for this is as follows:

If a man is highly evolved, his aura and his centers use this accumulated energy for service and creativity. The energy creates in the centers a tension and an urge for creativity. Also, this energy unfolds his chakras a little more and creates more sublimation in them. Further, this energy heals the body and creates closer links with the Subtle World.

But if the centers are not ready, if the vehicles do not have enough purity, if the consciousness does not have the needed unfoldment, the person experiences the following reactions:

a. A feeling of additional energy for a few days, followed by a feeling of exhaustion

    b. The appearance of various weaknesses in the body and disturbances in the glands

    c. Stimulation of certain thoughtforms, leading to fanaticism

    d. A tendency to force oneself on others

    e. Inconsiderate attitudes toward the rights and values of others

It is observed that through chanting there is the possibility of obsession.

Chanting opens a channel toward the Subtle World, and if a man has a developed and synthesized consciousness, he can establish a contact with higher entities in higher levels and receive inspiration and new impressions for more creative work — provided that he knows how to chant. But if he is not evolved enough to penetrate higher levels, then lower entities try to obsess the one who chants, through the built channel.

If the one who chants is not a harmful person, he develops fanaticism, separatism, and forcefulness. He gradually loses his free will, and the entity rules his life. But if he has evil seeds in his heart, he turns into an instrument of crimes or a slave of vices.

Chanting can be a mechanical, semi-conscious, or conscious action. If it is mechanical, the reaction occurs in the physical and etheric bodies. If it is semi-conscious, the reaction is emotional, and one may expect emotional disturbances as a result, which include physical and etheric disturbances.

The effect on the mind of semi-conscious chanting can be explained by the analogy of a screw on which the threads are worn. You try to screw it, but it has no threads to grip the nut. Similarly, the mind of the chanter becomes unfocused, and it cannot stabilize itself and concentrate itself in any direction. Such a mind wanders through many teachings or directions but without the power of synthesis. Such a state of consciousness is characterized by the word "confusion."

If the chanting is a conscious action, then the response is spiritual. Conscious chanting is based on the following factors:

    a. You know the meanings of the words, and while your mouth chants, your thought is concentrated on the meaning.

    b. Your aura is pure, which means you do not have negative emotions, fanaticism, or vanity.

    c. You have a field of service through which you will use the energies evoked for helping others.

      d. You know through what center to focus and concentrate
        the flow of your chant — the heart center, the throat
        center, etc.

The third way of communication with the Higher Worlds is through our **pure thought**. In deep meditation and contemplation, if we know how to do them, we extend beams of energy toward the Higher Worlds and come in contact with higher intelligences. Actually, real samadhi or contemplation is a state in which the human soul functions in the Higher Worlds according to his evolution. Through such contact, great ideas and revelations are brought down to earth for the improvement of life. In real contemplation, the human soul leaves his physical body and functions with his mental body in higher spheres.

Those who develop pure thinking can use it in the Subtle World when they pass away.

In the Subtle World, people try to communicate with each other through their words and speech, but gradually they discover that their speech not only is obsolete but also not necessary. They begin to communicate through thought. They can create, communicate, destroy, and build through thoughts. But if thinking is not developed on the earth, they will have almost no opportunity to develop it in the Subtle World. They will be forced to depend on their verbal communication, which can seldom be adapted to the new conditions of the Subtle World.

For example, in the Subtle World people work very hard to sew dresses for themselves — of course, by using astral material — but they have no need to do so because if they can visualize the dress they want, they can create it almost immediately. But if they do not know how to think and they try to create, they create things which they cannot use. Later they will have to destroy them through their thought power. Everything they create in the Subtle World attaches to them and draws energy from them in order to continue to exist. Of course, astral forms have a period of duration, but after that they continue to exist through your thought power.

The lower levels of the Subtle World are full of ugliness because people there create according to the level of their consciousness. Like a huge field of rubbish, the trash accumulates for ages.

The stables that Hercules cleaned, by directing the rivers through them, actually refer to the three lower levels of the astral plane. In these "stables" the lower mental and astral trash had accumulated for ages, polluting not only the astral plane but also the etheric plane of the earth, and producing heavy tension in the nervous and circulatory systems of men. The rivers were the principles of the soul — Beauty,

Goodness, and Truth. It is through such "rivers" that we can cleanse our own trash accumulated for ages in our lower mental, astral, and physical nature, as individuals and as one humanity.

It is through such purification and expansions of consciousness that the Higher Worlds are found.

People sometimes think that psychic experiences, visions, and dreams are very important factors in their lives. Actually, they have no importance unless they originate from higher sources and are recorded by an unfolded and transmuted consciousness. Without an unfolded and transmuted consciousness, one cannot understand his psychic experiences; nor can he benefit from his dreams and visions, even if they drop from Higher Worlds.

It is only an expanded and transmuted consciousness that can contact the Higher Worlds, with the ability to draw benefit from all experiences recorded in the Higher Worlds. Without an unfolded consciousness, all our experiences, visions, and dreams — even our knowledge — will serve no real purpose. Unless we fully understand our experiences, dreams, and visions, they will have no value.

It is possible that one can have various psychic experiences through drugs, chanting, or other mechanical means; but these experiences cannot be translated correctly because the consciousness is dulled and darkened by the use of drugs and the disturbances of the chanting. Thus, not only are the experiences not understood, but they are also most probably misinterpreted. Every misinterpretation leads a man into wrong directions and also, in this case, increases his vanity and builds illusions in him, thus complicating the path of his future progress.

Consciousness is more important than one's own experiences, visions, dreams, and even his knowledge. Knowledge is power, and if the consciousness is not awakened, mistranslated knowledge can be used for self-destruction.

Money is power; position is power; beauty is power. But all these powers must be handled by a transmuted and developed consciousness, if they are going to serve constructive purposes and lead humanity toward greater joy, freedom, and creativity.

Communication with the Higher Worlds has many advantages. It expands and transmutes the consciousness to a great degree. It inspires the human soul and impresses him with the knowledge related to his field of labor. For example, if one is a politician, he gathers a great amount of knowledge and wisdom in that field. If he is a scientist, he sees the most advanced mechanical appliances in use in the Subtle Worlds, and he gathers precious information and formulas in his field.

If he is an artist, he sees unimaginable beauty and receives inspiration to recreate them on earth. The same process takes place in the other fields of human endeavor.

In addition, those who contact the Subtle Worlds develop a strong sense of synthesis. No matter in what field they work, they receive wisdom from all the other fields. Thus they become inclusive; they do not deny or reject, but examine and learn from any field of knowledge.

Many physicians are able to penetrate into the hospitals of the Subtle Worlds and bring down very new and advanced revelations. But unfortunately they often do not remember these visitations, or they are afraid to reveal their contacts so as not to be considered freaks. There are many cases in the medical field where certain formulas from higher realms were found in strange ways.

There have been occasions where national leaders were given advice. The Subtle Worlds closely watches us and tries to cooperate with us, if we create the right conditions.

It may seem insane to say that in the Subtle World there are also destructive weapons and pollutions. Some of the pollution in Space is the mixture of the pollution of the earth along with the pollution of the Subtle World. This pollution affects our astral bodies when we sleep and makes our communication with the Higher Worlds difficult. It is the dark forces in the lower astral plane that build hideous missiles and try to poison our atmosphere and paralyze humanity in order to prevent its evolution.

What great watchfulness is necessary to destroy the nests of evil, not only here but also in the Subtle World.

This is why the Hierarchy wants people to be warriors in spirit.

A Great One witnessed a huge explosion in the Subtle World almost fifty years ago, before our atomic and hydrogen bombs and various missiles were built. He warned humanity, but His words remained as if spoken in the desert.

People from the earth can assist warriors in the Subtle World with their prayers and invocations, and with their active participation in the battles in the Subtle World.

37

Mediums

Efforts to communicate with the dead have been exercised since the dawn of history. The methods used have been varied. There were and are advanced psychics who are able to leave their bodies and penetrate into the spheres of the "dead," or while in their bodies mentally to communicate with and see them.

There is another method through which the lower strata of the Subtle World are contacted. This is what mediumism is. In higher psychics, the centers of the subtle bodies — etheric, astral, and mental — are unfolded and synchronized with each other. In mediums, the subtle centers are not only dormant but damaged. There is a loose connection between their physical and etheric bodies, and entities from the Subtle World use the ectoplasm and lymph of the medium to come in contact with him.

When the centers are not unfolded, the cleavage between the etheric and physical bodies puts the medium in a condition in which he does not have a direction. He does not have higher connections, and he can be directed by the obsessing entity toward any direction it wants. Usually these entities direct a person toward separatism, hatred, jealousy, destruction, crimes, and fear. Such entities may give messages and instructions, but their transmissions are full of hypocrisy, lies, and distortion of facts.

When an entity chooses a medium through which to express itself, it proves it is a low level entity, like a man who chooses to live in a broken, abandoned car, full of decaying materials.

Mediums are born as mediums, but not all of them use their mediumism to attract attention or to make money. This is done by "professional" mediums. Such mediums are the slaves of certain entities, and it is very difficult to make them understand the danger they are in. If they cooperate with such advice, it is possible to cure them. This can be accomplished by making their etheric bodies connect naturally with their physical bodies.

A medium comes in contact with the astral world, not through his astral centers, but through his lymphatic system. The elements in the lymph are related to the astral plane, and the astral entities build links with the medium through the lymphatic system. We are told that the forces of darkness use the lymphatic system to remain in contact with the world.

In certain palaces the kings used to avoid lymphatic servants, in order to prevent the channeling of any astral or dark force into the palace. Because of the abundance of the lymph secretions, mediums receive transmissions but in a very distorted and sometimes reversed way.

The medium offers his ectoplasm to the visiting entities, who use that substance to be visible to human eyes or to be able to contact the medium. Ectoplasm is the element which also transmits psychic energy. If it is wasted, the medium deprives himself of psychic energy, and such a deprivation invites many fiery sicknesses in the medium. This is how the medium becomes subject to a great danger.

When a person comes in contact with the Higher Worlds through his spiritual development, his continuity of consciousness, and his naturally unfolded centers, he does not lose energy. On the contrary, he becomes charged with higher psychic energy. One can easily know if he is in contact with higher forces if the level of his energy is rising and he is becoming more creative.

It is dangerous to be around a medium because he may drain your energy to use it for his contacts. Close contact with him may open the path for obsession in your aura.

It is known that in telepathic communications mediums are the weakest because their mental centers are not developed and they lack the power of concentration. We are told that the Hierophants of Egypt did not accept mediums as their disciples. The same is true in certain Ashrams of Brahmans in India. In *Agni Yoga* we are told that, "A medium is but the inn for disembodied liars."[1]

We are told that mediums have the lowest quantity of psychic energy. Lack of psychic energy leads the mechanism of the medium into disintegration and decay.

This decay is first noticed in their moral, mental, and emotional natures, and then in their physical nature. Generally they radiate decaying materials around themselves and contaminate their surroundings.

---

1. Agni Yoga Society, *Agni Yoga* (New York: Agni Yoga Society, 1954), para. 228.

Higher sources do not use mediums to communicate with the world. They choose Mediators. A Mediator is a human being who has developed his Chalice to such a degree that Great Ones can use it to impart information to the world. Great Ones, Who are the only dependable source of wisdom and knowledge, cannot work with physical bodies, astral bodies, or even lower mental bodies. They need *temples* — Chalices — which are highly organized, pure and unfolded, to transmit Their wisdom.

The Chalice can be used only when a man passes through real transfiguration experiences. Before such an experience takes place, all psychic manifestations are highly dangerous, misleading, and unhealthy. It is after the transfiguration that a man is equipped with unfolded centers, which put him in tune with Cosmic principles and direction. He becomes a man whom Great Ones trust, and through him They work.

Most mediums bring messages from "Masters." If one has a bit of intelligence, he can immediately see how commonplace such messages are. Such formulations of messages are very easy for the disembodied spirits to fabricate. They activate, or play back, the abandoned tapes — corpses — of common people and channel them to mediums. Generally these tapes, or the astral brains of abandoned corpses, are of low-order because a high-order "tape" immediately disintegrates when the inhabitant leaves it.

We are told that a great Teacher often waits for centuries to find a Mediator to transmit a message to the world. Low-level entities do not need to wait because mediums are abundant, but Mediators are very rare.

To be a Mediator means

1. To have a record of many lives of dedicated service to the Hierarchy
2. To have highly developed purity, highly developed subtle centers, and an unfolded Chalice
3. To have a record of sacrificial lives for humanity
4. To be in a condition in which karma has been paid and cleared
5. To have a great network of right relationships with the constructive and creative forces of Existence

Such a mechanism is very rare. This is why a pure message is rare. It is like a rare diamond of wisdom.

Physical mediumship means to sit for materialization and for sensational phenomena. The entity who wants to have contact uses the ectoplasm of the medium, which is formed by nerve emanations, the lymph, and the etheric body. The entity attracts these materials and uses them as its vehicle through which it appears or produces sensational phenomena, such as playing the piano, ringing bells, or moving objects.

Such a hardening of the entity through the etheric body and the ectoplasm of the medium is very dangerous to the medium because it disturbs the network of his etheric centers, deprives him of his energy, and transmits the moral and psychic weaknesses of the entity to the medium and to the audience. When the medium continues to lend his etheric body and to lose his ectoplasm, partial or total paralysis starts in the centers and in the glands. It is noticed, for example, that after a seance the medium collapses or loses his energy to a considerable degree. Some mediums use alcohol to regain their strength, but this would eventually lead them to alcoholism.

Sometimes the entity gives energy to the medium to enable him to function, but it does not last long, and often it blows certain fuses — astral centers — in him.

A psychic who had many experiences with mediums once wrote, "Of the three mediums with whom I used to have sittings fifteen years ago, one is now blind; another died a confirmed drunkard; and the third, finding himself menaced by epilepsy and paralysis, escaped with his life only by giving up seances altogether."

There is also the phenomenon of channeling, which is widespread at this time all over the world. In channeling, a person gives his body to an entity, which uses it for lecturing, writing, or certain other activities. In such cases, the person either knows who is functioning through his mechanism, or he is not sure, or he does not know at all.

The first case is used by some advanced Individuals. They use the mechanisms, the centers, the nervous system, the brain, the etheric, astral, and mental bodies of the Mediator, which are highly developed. Because of this development, very advanced Individuals can enter the mechanism of the Mediator and use it with the person's conscious and free decision.

The second case occurs through the "medium." Entities from the lower astral plane possess his body and use it for certain ends, for example, to do any or all of the following:

1. Give a message
2. Reveal a "secret"
3. Commit a crime
4. Destroy centers of light and goodwill
5. Impart a certain "teaching"
6. Diagnose

7. Matchmake

How will one be able to discriminate between these two cases?

The first case deals with universal problems, with the destiny of the race, and with the Teaching which will lead humanity to the Path of perfection. The second case is related to personal problems. It is separative. It is done for profit or ego.

In the first case, the Mediator has a very high morality and integrity, a highly developed intellectual and intuitional capacity, and a solid sacrificial nature. Love and wisdom shine out of him, and his influence and service extend over many ages.

In the second case, the channel's morality is low and the intellect is not developed. People are manipulated and exploited in the second case. The message is very shallow and often contradictory. The followers of such mediums have no free will, and gradually they turn into robots when the astral entities complete their group obsession. Usually such groups disappear as a result of various crimes.

Higher transmission is only possible after the person goes through total transfiguration.

Lower channeling can happen to any medium. Usually such mediums live with the energy of the astral entity, but once it withdraws its presence or influence, they collapse. Such channels often share the karma of the entity obsessing them.

Many physical disturbances are inevitable when low astral entities possess a mechanism.

It is possible to communicate with the Higher Worlds through spiritual telepathy or through the method of overshadowing. In the first case, in spiritual telepathy, one can penetrate through his thought into the Higher Worlds and establish communication. In overshadowing, an advanced entity hovers over the individual, and with his energy and light he illuminates the soul of the individual.

Communication is also possible with the Higher Worlds through our Guardian Angel. This is the safest step. One must not jump into higher communication without first establishing a firm contact with his Guardian Angel.

Obsession and possession are two important words often incorrectly used. Obsession is etheric, astral, or mental inhibition. Post-hypnotic suggestion is a kind of obsession or inhibition.

Obsession on the etheric level is a mechanical habit which is the result of some distortion in the nerves and the corresponding etheric body.

Emotional obsession is an emotion caught in the astral plane which controls other emotions. Such an obsession can be local or isolated, or it can have roots in the emotional body of a society from which it derives its power. Accidents and events charged with a strong emotion can be registered like a photograph by the astral body. They serve as obsessing neuroses.

In the mental plane, obsession is an inhibited, trapped thoughtform, with or without entities attached to it.

Possession is different. Possession is done by an entity who has many obsessions and tries to occupy the nature of a man and use it partially or completely as a mechanism for his expression. Thus, a possessed person is occupied not only by an entity but also by the obsessions of the entity.

An advanced case of possession occurs when more than one entity possesses a man, all locating themselves in certain etheric, astral, and mental centers according to their levels and intentions.

There is also a kind of possession which is carried on at a distance, when a powerful person controls another person through his etheric emanations, emotions, or thoughts. Some people very easily fall victim to this kind of possession. At a distance the person controls his victims as if he were in them. Such possessions occur only if there is a karmic tie or psychological resonance between the persons. The sexual act, for example, opens the door for such possession, on any level.

People think that obsession and possession can be either good or bad, constructive or destructive. This is not true. Obsession and possession are kinds of diseases. The basic argument against them is that that which obsesses and possesses imposes itself over the person against his free will and controls him. If anyone is controlled, either by good or by evil, it does not make a difference in the long run. Even if obsession and possession are positive, they deprive a person of his divine rights of freedom and conscious evolution. No one can be beautiful, good, and just by masquerading in the role of beauty, goodness, and justice. This is why even beauty, goodness, and justice must not be imposed but evoked.

There are cases in which an advanced Master uses your body or mind for certain service, with your permission, and with your full consciousness. This is done for only a short time, during which you cooperate with Him to render His service. This is neither an obsession nor a possession.

One of the conditions of self-actualization is the existence of obstacles in our life upon the physical, emotional, and mental planes. As we confront these obstacles, we realize our own situation, our level on the Path, and our weaknesses, powers, and possibilities.

Obstacles exist as part of Nature, and in conquering them we expand our consciousness. Without the expansion of consciousness, self-actualization is impossible. Because expansion of consciousness is progressive, so is self-actualization. In whatever degree we overcome our ignorance and weaknesses, in the same degree we conquer our obstacles. Obstacles have no end. They grow as we grow.[2]

2. For further information about psychism, please refer to _Breakthrough to Higher Psychism_.

38

Lower and Higher Psychism

We do not exist only on the physical plane. We exist on many subtle planes or dimensions, the lowest of which is the physical plane. We have access to these planes through our astral, mental, and higher bodies, but this access depends upon the condition and the development of our subtle senses. No matter how undeveloped we are, we still have a contact with higher dimensions for short periods of time — consciously or unconsciously, out of the body or in the body. Except when they are impressed on us in the form of vivid dreams, we do not, most of the time, notice such contacts.

It is possible to penetrate into higher spheres consciously or mechanically. We can penetrate into higher realms through

1. Sleep. Often we do not remember our experiences while asleep. Many experiences that are not remembered are accumulated within us.

2. Drugs. Such contacts are not only violations of Nature, but they are also dangerous. The registration of the contact is distorted, misleading, and disturbing.

3. Hypnotism. Such a method creates dire consequences in the subtle mechanism of the person and eventually makes him a useless entity.[1]

4. Conscious withdrawal from the body and the lower vehicles. This method needs long preparation and discipline, a healthy body, pure emotions, a highly organized and disciplined mind, and a tolerant karma.

---

1. Please refer to Chapter 30, "The Senses and Hypnotism," *The Psyche and Psychism*.

5. Mediums. A medium is a person who can penetrate certain subtle spheres, either consciously or unconsciously, and come in contact with subtle events.

Mediums are of various kinds:

    a. There are mediums whose etheric body is loose, and they easily slide out into the astral plane. Sometimes their etheric body is not loose but burned in certain places. This allows the human soul to be *pulled away*. The pulling out is exercised by certain entities who want to occupy the person's mechanism.

If the person is pulled out from the physical body, the entities occupy the brain. If the person is pulled out from the astral body, they possess the astral body. If the person is pulled out from the mental body, they occupy the mental body. This is rare, but it is a very powerful method to bring destruction and confusion into the world: The whole current of dark forces can pour into such a medium to create disturbances, hatred, revenge, intolerance, and bigotry to slow down or stop human progress.

Many leaders in the political and religious fields have fallen into such a catastrophe. It is not really them but those who are possessing them who run the show.

Mental obsession or possession does not take place unless the person has a highly developed mental mechanism and a large amount of information regarding the field in which he is going to be used.

Astral possession is common. Physical possession also takes place very frequently and forms habits, urges and drives, and addictions. The causes for such conditions are unfortunately searched for elsewhere.[2]

    b. Mediums also come into existence when a person is under the influence of a great fear. A continuous fear causes a person to withdraw from the physical body and lives in the lower levels of the astral plane. Such a fear rends the protective network and builds an easy pathway for the human soul to enter the astral plane.

    c. The third type of medium comes into existence because of some damage done to the consciousness thread. The consciousness thread is the path of normal ascent and

---

2. *Ibid.*, Chapter 33, "Spirits and Mediums."

descent from the physical realm to higher realms and from higher realms to physical consciousness.[3]

Daily we ascend to the emotional plane through our emotions and to the mental plane through our thoughts, but normally we do not experience any event in those realms because our astral senses and mental senses are not developed enough to register events on those levels.

When the consciousness thread is damaged, we cannot descend to the physical plane or ascend from the physical plane to higher planes, and we feel trapped in the plane where we are. For a short time, we lose our continuity of consciousness with the physical, astral, and mental planes. We experience an epileptic seizure when we are stuck for a short time in the astral plane. If we are advanced, we are trapped in higher realms and suffer to return to physical consciousness. If the consciousness thread is damaged, such a damage is caused by the accumulation of all the transgressions we did against our conscience and consciousness. The higher a person is, the easier it is for him to be trapped if his consciousness thread is damaged. The Soul often acts as a jumper cable to bring the person back to his brain consciousness.

    d. A medium may also come into existence through an accident. When he is hit or falls in a certain way, his brain centers or ganglia are short-circuited or damaged, forming unnatural connections between them and centers of higher planes. Because of such connections, the medium experiences the higher planes but does not translate his experiences correctly because of lack of preparation and damage done to his nerve centers.

The medium receives messages from etheric and astral entities, but he does not have any means to verify the identity and motive of the entity who is passing him information or messages.[4]

6. Channels. Channels, on the other hand, are those used as a means of communication by mental entities or angels. Channels often act like pipes: They do not know what passes through them. Channels are used for

    a. Automatic writing
    b. Passing on the message they hear by placing it in books and other literature

---

    c. Repeating the destructive and confusing messages of dark forces

    d. Passing a pure message from higher sources

7. Mediators. These are highly developed human souls who come in contact with Great Ones existing here on earth or in higher spheres and who deliver Their Teaching to humanity. They receive the Teaching telepathically or clairvoyantly and try to present it exactly as they received it from Great Ones.

8. Creators. Creators are mediators, and in addition they function on the Intuitional Plane. They receive the Teaching from Great Ones. When there is a need, they themselves use the treasure of their Chalice and draw the Teaching from Space. They use the science of impression, and they coordinate and interpret the seeds of the Teaching they receive from Higher Sources.

9. Masterhood. Masters receive Their Teaching from the Ashram of the Ancient of Days, through Christ. They are very serious in transmitting only the part of the knowledge They are allowed to transmit. The Teaching They receive is beyond our comprehension, and it is related to higher evolution and the higher senses.

Thus, in comparison to these latter stages, a medium is in an elementary stage. He needs steady development if he wants to enter into and transmit greater light.

In general, a medium comes in contact with the astral plane. On the astral plane he can find

1. Astral entities or departed human souls
2. Astral corpses
3. Dark forces
4. Jokers, imitators, pseudo-prophets
5. Human beings from various parts of the earth who are there because they left their bodies during sleep

We must note that if a medium is in contact with the astral plane, generally he is full of glamors, or he is obsessed by the forms of his earthly desires. He is limited by his self-interest. He has fears, hatred, anger, and feelings of jealousy, revenge, and greed. His astral senses are not developed enough to allow him to work on the higher levels of the astral plane. He is influenced by the world glamors in which he lives. Such a medium is not dependable, even if he has a certain degree of clairaudience, psychometry, clairvoyance, imagination, and emotional idealism corresponding to the physical senses. The reason is that the departed human souls with whom the medium comes in contact are average human beings, even though they are free from certain limitations. They convey to the medium certain pieces of information which are not exceptional. They are able to reveal certain secrets, names, or activities to deceive the medium and his customer and give the impression that they know.[5]

First of all, they violate the law of privacy. Second, through their advice they mislead people, like an average person who tries to give medical advice to someone who has a complicated disease. Such people are not aware of the karma of people and force them to flow in certain directions, thus creating more complications in their lives. Thus, mediums violate the karma of others by giving ignorant advice and misleading people.

It is true that sometimes a departed human being reveals the place where he had hidden money or the identity of someone who committed a crime, but because of the level and psychological condition of the medium, very often such revelations are used for selfish interests.

Higher guidance is not occupied with treasures and crimes but with the expansion of consciousness and with progress on the Path.

When a medium is in contact with astral corpses, he thinks they are living human beings. They often look alive because negative forces temporarily occupy them and use their tape recordings. Our astral bodies have the registration of our entire emotional life. Once the recording is plugged into an entity, it is easy to play it back. This is why the ignorant medium thinks he is in contact with a person he knows or his client knows, as the occupied astral corpse uses the same vocabulary, manners of speech, and information as the previous owner of the body.

Once the entity in the astral corpse establishes contact with a medium and makes the one who is seeking help believe him, the entity begins slowly to misdirect them. The victim follows blindly because he thinks, "My father is giving me advice and direction," or "My mother is caring for me." It is extremely difficult to liberate such a fool from this trap.

The most horrible part of the story is that the entity occupying the astral corpse gradually comes in closer contact with the victim and eventually occupies _his_ astral body, using his "father's" or "mother's" astral body as a bridge of entrance.

A similar tragedy occurs when the medium contacts the astral corpse only, activates the recording, and draws the corpse toward him and toward his customer. Because of earthly attraction, the corpse

---

5.   _Ibid._, Chapter 14, "The Astral Senses."

sticks to them; and from that moment on, decomposition takes place in the astral and physical bodies of the medium and whoever is seeking his help, in the form of various sicknesses and crimes.

A medium can also come in contact with dark forces active on the astral plane. We are told that the astral plane is the general habitat of dark forces. During the first contact they are very sweet; they give every kind of advice until they win the heart of the medium and his customers. Gradually they put in their consciousness the seeds of hatred, malice, slander, separatism, and crimes. Once they locate themselves in a person's aura, there is little that a person can do to get away from them. They use their victims until they lose their sanity and become blind tools in the hands of the entities, or until they become exhausted and die in crimes.

There are also "jokers" in the astral plane who play with their victims. They represent themselves as masters; they know historic figures and prophecies; and the poor medium takes them very seriously and works hard to pass the prophecies to people until he realizes the disappointment of the public and feels embarrassed by all that he spoke or wrote.

Generally, such mediums are not honest enough to accept that they were fooled. They persist in continuing on their way, even if they suddenly feel that their pseudo-master has vanished in laughter. Often such mediums find a very easy way to make money, and they continue to repeat and fabricate additional lies to increase and perpetuate their income.

At this time in history, using the expectation of new revelations promised in the Scriptures, such jokers play their tricks on people. These jokers are basically not evil, but because of their disbelief in certain teachings or events they try to embarrass those who believe in such things. For example, if one is an enemy of Krishna or Hinduism, he finds a Hindu medium and fills him with such lies about Krishna's return or re-appearance that eventually everybody laughs at the concept of return as well as at the related religion and believers. Thus many jokers like to discredit the things they do not believe in.

Such jokers also do the opposite. They find a person who is a fanatic in his beliefs and make him push his beliefs with such vigor, power, hatred, and malice toward "non-believers" that eventually everybody stands away from his beliefs. In esoteric schools this is called the "bankrupting process."

A medium can also contact those human beings who are in the astral plane while they are asleep in other parts of the globe. The medium takes certain information from them. However, those who wander on the astral plane are not those from whom a wise person should take advice. When a medium contacts such human souls, generally they have nightmares and awaken because the appearance and vibration of the medium upsets them. But if there is an affinity between them, the medium tries to use the person immediately when he enters the astral plane.

There is a very serious danger in such a relationship. The medium and the human being in the astral plane sometimes attach to each other, and in his waking consciousness the victim feels that he belongs to somebody somewhere. This increases his confusion, spoils his relationship with his spouse, and causes him to appear as if unfocused.

It sometimes happens that the human soul obsesses the medium, and part of his astral body remains with the medium when the soul returns to his body. Many complicated psychological problems originate from such a relationship.

Most importantly, it must be remembered that in this stage the medium infects his victims with his glamors, vices, and negative emotions.

The next stage in which a medium works is in the lower mental plane. In the lower mental plane are found

1. Crystallized thoughtforms from ancient civilizations and cultures.
2. Crystallized thoughtforms built by bigots or fanatics found in all fields of life.
3. Manipulators and exploiters, who were in the same business while in the world. Their whole life was used to manipulate and exploit people, so they are experts in this area in any branch of human endeavor. Because of their highly developed mental body, when they die they quickly pass to the lower mental plane and continue life as it was on earth.
4. Strongly crystallized egos, who are equipped only with self-interest. Their whole mental mechanism is organized around their separative self-interest.
5. Those who are experts in many fields but use their knowledge to lead people toward destruction. For example, they impart formulas which will increase the poison and pollution on the earth.
6. Those whose intention it is to act against the Divine Plan, against Beauty, Goodness, Righteousness, Joy, and Freedom. They know how to manipulate people in order to lead them into action against these five principles.

A medium who enters such a sphere is one who is blinded by his ego and vanity. He has pride, prejudices, and separatism. He can be a good tool in the hands of those parties found in the lower mental plane. Once the medium is caught by one of these parties, he turns into a destructive force and becomes a barrier to human growth and advancement. He becomes an agent of these forces in addition to becoming an agent of very specialized dark forces in the lower mental plane.

It is true that on the lower mental plane there are good, highly organized, and morally advanced people; but these people do not come in contact with earthly mediums, as they realize that their contact can prevent their own advancement toward the higher levels of the mental plane.

7. There are also found in the lower mental plane massive thoughtforms of illusions. Illusions are distorted truths or facts which appear to be logical, but in essence are misleading and highly dangerous because those who contact them cannot get rid of them for a long period of time.

If the medium is of a high order or caliber, he must have his Rainbow Bridge built between the lower and higher mental planes. Once he is able to penetrate into the higher mental plane, he begins to develop his mental senses,[6] which are

NAME OF MENTAL SENSE	CORRESPONDENCE
Higher clairaudience	Hearing
Planetary psychometry	Touch
Higher clairvoyance	Sight
Discrimination	Taste
Spiritual Discernment	Smell
Response to group vibration	Common sense
Spiritual telepathy	Intuitive perception

Because of his level of consciousness, his unfolding senses, and the development of his higher centers, such a medium comes in contact with his Inner Watch, Who is generally called the Solar Angel or the Transpersonal Self. Once a medium is able to penetrate into the higher mental plane, he is no longer called a medium but a *Mediator*.

---

6. *Ibid.*, for additional information on this topic, Chapter 21, "The Senses on the Mental Plane"; and Chapter 49, "Higher Psychism," in *Challenge for Discipleship*.

A Mediator is one who knows how to contact a source, knows the source he contacts, and is able to understand the communication or the message and translate it accurately. One of the great differences between a medium and a Mediator is that the medium pulls down the entities to his physical plane, whereas the Mediator raises himself to the level of the entities living in the higher mental plane.

One may ask whether a person can become a Mediator before he becomes a medium. Many highly developed Mediators were mediums first, or in their past lives, but they never used their powers until they passed through total purification, or through the Transfiguration Initiation. A Mediator must have full experience of the astral and lower mental planes if he wants to help those who are stuck there. Mediators with special protection can enter these planes and serve there without being caught by the dangers present.

One may ask how to discriminate between a Mediator and a medium? There are a few signs to watch for:

1. Observe their lives. Mediators are highly virtuous and have high morals. Mediums generally violate various laws and ethics. Often many of them are caught by various vices.
2. Mediators have mastery over their physical, emotional, and mental limitations. Mediums serve their own urges, drives, personal interests, vanities, etc.
3. Mediators manifest strong psychic energy. They are capable of working long hours under disturbing conditions. Mediums are weak, non-magnetic, and pale looking. They run away from various duties and responsibilities, although sometimes they become highly violent, using their nervous energy or the energy of the astral entity they are controlled by.
4. Mediators are inclusive. They have a tendency to unify and synthesize. Mediums are generally separative and sectarian.
5. Mediators love beauty and work for beauty. Mediums do not see much difference between ugliness and beauty.
6. Mediators have a very pure sense of responsibility. Mediums in general do not have this sense.
7. Mediators are straight forward, clear, and to-the-point. Mediums are obscure and fuzzy in their thinking. Their messages are often very confusing and contradictory.
8. Mediators deal with the Teaching, with the evolving human soul and his destiny. They are impersonal and highly detached. Mediums occupy themselves with personal problems and personal interests. They like to impose themselves on others and are attached to persons and objects.

9. Mediators have a very beautiful quality of forgiveness and tolerance. Mediums maintain the memory of a painful or hurtful event for a long time, and carry feelings of unforgiveness and intolerance.

10. Mediators share and sacrifice. Mediums try to hold onto material objects, to things, and to make people serve them.[7]

These are outer signs, but the inner signs are more important and they are related to the centers, the senses and their condition, the aura, the Rainbow Bridge, etc. For example, a medium uses his sexual and solar plexus centers. A Mediator uses his heart and head centers.

A medium's etheric body is generally swollen on one side; the Mediator's etheric body is very normal, but his aura extends out for ten to twelve feet. A medium can give his astral body for the purpose of obsession, but a Mediator can give his whole personality to be used for *tulku*. Tulku means a great spirit is using the Mediator's personality, as agreed upon, and during the time of tulku the Mediator is totally conscious of whatever transpires.

Of course, certain mediums imitate such a state and fabricate certain messages, but an intelligent person can easily recognize imitation by the fruits it gives.

To be a tulku is not an easy matter. The Mediator must at least pass the Transfiguration of the personality to be able to allow a Great One to carry out through him a task for the service of humanity. Also, a Mediator must be able to focus his consciousness upon the higher mental plane and consciously work there in the light of his Watch.

A medium cannot penetrate into the higher mental plane because of the unreadiness of his mechanism and because of the karma he has built by transgressing certain subjective laws and by interfering in the personality problems of his customers.

Beyond Mediators we have creative souls or, let us say, Creators, who function on the Intuitional Plane. Mediators can also work on the Intuitional Plane for a certain length of time, but this is not their habitat. Creative souls live and function on the Intuitional Plane, and the Masters live in the Spiritual Triad.

A Mediator receives the Teaching from the Masters of Wisdom or from the *Nirvanis*, who are perfected human souls functioning on the Intuitional Plane and the higher mental plane. Mediators are free from maya, glamor, and illusion. Their etheric centers are open and

---

7. *Ibid.*, for further information on the differences between mediums and Mediators, see Chapter 15, "Psychism, Higher and Lower."

active. They are coordinated not only with the centers and senses of the astral and mental bodies but also with the petals of the Chalice. With their shining lights, their centers build various configurations, and the light of the predominating plane (where the consciousness usually dwells) flashes out strongly in rhythmic configurations.

For example, the astral plane of the medium shows this:

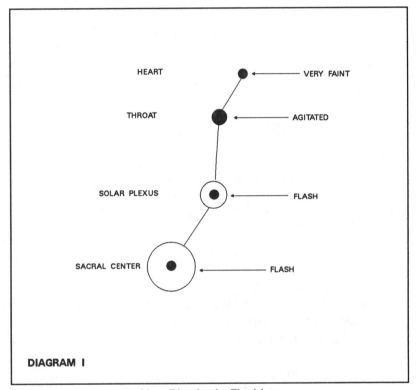

DIAGRAM I

Non-Rhythmic Flashing

This is not rhythmic flashing but occasional and irregular.

The following are found in the higher mental plane:

1. Great disciples of the Hierarchy
2. Advanced formulas related to the seven fields of human endeavor
3. Occasional visitation by Masters
4. The Watch, Who is an "Initiate of all degrees"
5. The Chalice, which contains all records of past achievements and the precious element called bliss, the elixir of life

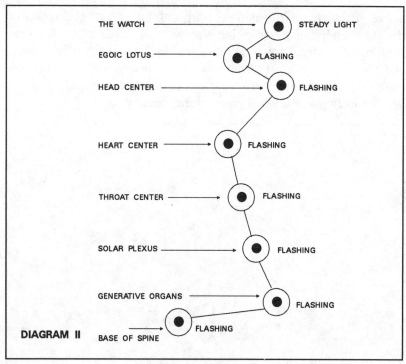

Rhythmic Flashing

Diagram II shows the rhythmic flashing of Mediators.

Actually, all the centers flash, but in relative magnitude to and under the rhythm of the main centers. The colors depend upon the rays of the Mediator.

Thus a Mediator has a great amount of freedom and many treasures to use for the benefit of humanity. Psychic powers gradually develop, life after life, if one does not violate the laws of Nature and misuse his powers. The great Teachers say that we must not use our psychic powers until we pass the Transfiguration Initiation. After that it will be safe, due to the following:

—The psychic has a purified personality.
—His ego has vanished.
—He is not running after his self-interest.
—There is no separatism in him.
—He has full knowledge of the karmic law.

How can a lower psychic or medium progress on the Path and go toward Mediatorship or Masterhood? The steps are very easy:

1. Continuous and regular meditation
2. Evening review
3. Studying the Teaching and scientific matters
4. Sacrificial service
5. Development of enthusiasm, solemnity, and the sense of global responsibility
6. Purification of the heart and motives
7. Concentration on the image of perfection

The most important item in the progress of the human soul is the ability to make a breakthrough into higher planes and function there consciously. The second important item is to watch very carefully the Law of Karma and in no way violate it. It is observed that no matter how hard one works to advance and expand his consciousness, he fails if he is violating karmic law.

The human soul cannot stop growing in the stage of the human kingdom. It has to surpass this kingdom and travel on to higher paths of expression. An ancient wise man said, "The soul of man has such a space that one will never exhaust it traveling in any direction."[8]

---

8. Heraclitus ("The weeping philosopher") c535-c475 B.C., Greek philosopher. *American College Dictionary.*

CHAPTER

39

Labor and the
Higher Worlds

The dense world and the Higher Worlds are related to each other, just as the body, emotions, and mind are related to each other. Changes occurring in any plane affect all other planes in various forms and in various intensities.

Man is very closely related to the Subtle World through his emotions, aspirations, and devotion; to the Thought World through his thoughts and knowledge; to the Fiery World through his ideas, creativity, intuition, enthusiasm, and virtues. Man affects these worlds and is affected by them more and more as he advances and his sensitivity increases.

Man lives on this earth in two ways: without a conscious plan and with a conscious plan.

The first way is the way the majority of people live: machines controlled by push buttons. These push buttons are such things as food, sex, shelter, possessions, and their supporting actions, emotions, and thoughts.

A minority of people live a life which is under a conscious plan. These people intuitively know and are aware that they are beyond the physical, emotional, and mental realms. They know they must bring refinement and changes on those three levels so that all lives existing on those levels become aware that they are not bodies but living souls.

These changes are introduced by labor. Labor is a process of giving and taking, a process of transformation and refinement, a process of rebirth and transmutation of consciousness.

Labor is an action in which the physical, emotional, and mental bodies and the human soul are involved. Through this action man spends physical, emotional, mental, and spiritual energy to introduce changes in Nature. As he gives energy and introduces changes, he receives energy in return in a variety of forms, such as money, various objects, emotional satisfaction, mental contentment, and spiritual joy.

In every act of labor one discharges a great amount of physical, emotional, mental, and spiritual energy. Prior to laboring, these energies have been latent and asleep within him. Through labor he activates them, amplifies them, and releases them into Space. Physical energy is released through action. Emotional energy is released through devotion and aspiration. Mental energy is released through concentration. Spiritual energy is released through enthusiasm and joy.

Our food, our desires, our knowledge, and our goals are transformed into action, aspiration, thought, and joy. Thus we take "crude oil" from Nature and, through a refinement process, change it into energy and fragrance. We take a part of the Universe and through our labor refine it, transform it, and give it back to the Universe, raising the level of the Universe a bit higher than before.

Like a little machine, man helps the Universe by providing it with a more precious substance to be used for more advanced work. For example, through labor your food, your desire, your knowledge, and your vision change into those energies which create a painting, a piece of music, a dance. In turn, your painting, your music, or your dance radiate high-level energy and cause refinement and transformation in their environment, thus equipping Nature with finer energies.

In every act of creative labor man brings a better part of his nature into manifestation. This means that he causes transmutation in his vehicles by radiating more refined energies from his soul and giving himself a new birth.

While Nature previously had a man of 20-degree worth, it now has a man of 200-degree worth. Nature had a horse-drawn carriage before; now it has a spaceship. Thus Nature is enriched. We are senses and organs of Nature.

There is a stage in which we cannot see, hear, or walk well. This happens during our childhood. When we grow, we have better seeing eyes, better hearing ears, and a better walk. In a similar way, Nature has now a better developed man, and with that better developed man, Nature "sees," "hears," and "acts" better.

Through labor we not only produce the energies needed for our future evolution, but we also improve and bring into perfection the vehicles through which these energies are used and by which labor is performed. Higher energies supply better vehicles for man. These energies make man a co-worker of the Plan and produce a server of the kingdom of Nature. The higher are the energies manifested, the more transformed will be the vehicles of man.

One of the most important things in labor is the motive. The motive behind labor must be inclusive, constructive, creative, and pure. If the labor is done for separative interests, for the ego; if it is destructive or criminal; if it is done to manipulate and exploit other people; then one may be successful, but his success brings him pain, suffering, and endless problems.

Labor done with wrong motives poisons Space and causes disintegration within the subtle vehicles. Then when man is ready for the flight toward the higher spheres, he will find his "spaceships," his subtle vehicles, damaged or out of order. This is why such people stay earthbound and cannot proceed on the path of their development until they return and correct all that they did wrong in the past.

Each labor must be done as a part of a great Plan and under the eye of the Great Architect of the Cosmos. Each labor must be done with enthusiasm and joy. When enthusiasm and joy accompany your labor, they act as catalysts, and your labor provides new energies to Space.

Labor done with complaint, resistance, anger, or irritation creates poison in Space. When you give transmuted and refined energy to Nature, Nature gives you health, joy, and freedom. When you give pollution or poison, Nature returns your pollution or poison in the form of emotional and mental disturbances, diseases, and problems. There is absolute righteousness in the Laws of Nature. You get back what you give.

Our labor not only affects the earthly sphere but also the Subtle World, the Thought World, and the Fiery World.

We nourish the Thought World and enrich it to a great extent with our creative thoughts and visualizations. We charge the Thought World with new, more balanced, more future-oriented, and more inclusive thoughts.

We nourish the Fiery World with our enthusiasm and with our striving. In return, these Subtle Worlds fill our Chalice with great joy, harmony, and bliss. This is why we feel so good when we perform a labor with all our heart, good intentions, visions, creative intuition, and enthusiasm. Thus each labor, instead of becoming an iron chain around our neck, becomes a path of communication with the Higher Worlds.

Labor is the best way to lead us to physical, emotional, mental, and spiritual improvement and perfection. Labor develops those characteristics in us which, life after life, bring us closer to the Plan and Purpose of the Universe. Thus we become experienced, intelligent, and conscious co-workers of Nature.

When the idea of labor is firmly established within our heart, we carry our labor through all the planes. When we pass into the Subtle

World, we continue our labor and give and take higher energies. When we pass into the Fiery World, we continue our fiery creativity and become a contributing member in the society of the Fiery World. And because of our labor, we come back into incarnation equipped with more creative energies and skills.

Nature provides all the opportunities for us when we are unfolded enough to give.

The great Law of Economy rules all transactions in the Universe. Nature does not waste any developing talents, but nourishes them and provides opportunities for them to cooperate with the efforts of the Universal Whole.

Labor is also an important element in group life. Unity in a group is achieved only through labor, a labor that is carried on with one vision, a united vision. When human beings engage in labor, they create an invisible synchronization of auras, which draws higher substances from higher planes and strengthens the unity of those who labor together with the same vision. In labor, harmony and unity are achieved and energy is utilized to build the future.

Groups of people are simply groups of different musical notes who are either in tune or out of tune. Labor tunes them together and composes melodies and songs out of them.

In labor, energy is assimilated by the co-workers. Assimilation of energy raises their level from the personality to the spiritual realms. Energy drawn in through labor changes the level of people, harmonizes them, and eventually builds a composition out of them, an organized expression of unity.

It is even observed that in some groups, the Leader forms certain committees of labor and chooses the members from those who are not in accord with each other; then he challenges them to fulfill the labor. Such a method eventually eliminates barriers and creates unity.

It is very important to develop observation, the seeing eye, to catch moments of rare beauty; moments of rare significance; moments of opportunities which never repeat themselves. Through the river of life many diamonds are carried to the ocean, and few people are able to notice them and catch them. These moments of rare beauty, opportunity, and significance are combinations of many factors. Such factors come together on rare occasions and create the special psychological moment or a world event to facilitate a needed change. Because of their rarity and because of the higher importance of these moments, one must develop observation in order to seize them.

These moments are accumulated gifts of life. They are condensed foci of wisdom. They are the lightning on the dark path of life.

Observation must be instantaneous to register them, as they manifest in a hint, in a gesture, in a drop of a tear or sweat, in a glance, in a sound, or in a moment when you least expect them. These psychological moments cannot be repeated. They are caught or lost forever. The ability to record instantaneously should be developed daily, as the moment that has passed is totally different from the present one, not only physically but also psychologically. The Cosmic Dance is an ever-moving, ever-changing symphony.

Labor, in its esoteric meaning, is a work done to cooperate with Nature and lead the whole of manifested Nature toward Transfiguration.

Individuals and groups, through their dedicated life, can create those communication lines which put the man in contact with Higher Worlds.

People do not realize yet that labor builds a link with Higher Worlds; the greater the labor, the closer the link. Those who love labor are those who have conscious or unconscious contact with the Higher Worlds. How does labor build this contact?

1. In striving to do something better, one brings into his nature and his consciousness new energies and new ideas from the Higher Worlds.
2. One awakens his higher centers, which eventually put him in contact with higher spheres.
3. As the quality of one's labor rises and the field of labor expands, he draws the attention of those who have interest in the labor and will gradually offer unconscious and conscious help to him. Thus the person establishes contact with those who subjectively supervise the labor.
4. The Plan of the Lords works out through labor, through those who in dedication offer their best to serve. In labor, one slowly realizes that he is a part of a greater labor going on upon the planet.
5. In labor, man begins to notice the invisible help given to him. For example, he sees himself doing things that he would never expect to do. He notices the increasing currents of ideas and visions, and eventually understands that he is receiving help from Above.
6. When he realizes the help given to him from Above, he tries to seek the Source.
7. As he tries to find the Source, the quality of his labor improves. The improvement of labor is a sign that the communication with the Source is getting closer.

8. Labor creates high tension. The tension of labor affects the nerve centers and glands. This makes them secrete their vapors, which offer themselves as conductors of higher contacts.
9. The refinement of the body, nerves, and glands takes place under the pressure of daily labor carried on in joy.
10. Every intelligent executive searches for laborers who are more efficient. Similarly, the executives of the Higher Worlds constantly watch those who show signs of dedicated service. When their work shows signs of greater dedication and accuracy, they raise them to higher labors.
11. As the labor goes on, the executives may pay an unexpected visit to encourage their workers. It is at this moment that a person living on earth comes in contact with one who is living in the Higher Worlds and has been supervising his work, maybe for decades or even lives.
12. Faithfulness to the labor and to the Source of inspiration paves the way for future progress.

This is how the work of the Great Architect is carried on in the Universe. There is a constant choice of better and better laborers, and a continuous promotion of those who demonstrate deeper honesty in labor, better accuracy, and self-sacrificial conduct.

40

Thinking and the Fiery World

The Path that best leads to the Fiery World is twofold. The first is the purification of life with the fire of the spirit which is in the heart. The second is thinking or meditation.

Purification prepares the mental vehicle by readying it for the fiery flight. Purification is the destruction of vices, habits, unrighteous thinking, harmfulness, hatred, jealousy, revenge, greed, fanaticism, and vanity. If these impediments are purified from our consciousness by the fire of the spirit in our heart, we will develop fiery fearlessness and will find it easy to contact or enter the Fiery World.

One must also learn *thinking*. Thinking increases the flow of the fire of the spirit into the mental body and organizes it for higher flights. The mental body, like our physical body, must grow, develop, and unfold in all its subtle parts, centers, and senses. It is through thinking that one not only nourishes his mental body but also creates communication lines with the Fiery World.

People have the impression that all human beings think; this is an incorrect idea. In fact, only a very small percentage of humanity really thinks, in the pure sense of the word.

A wise man once said that Satan "thinks" very well. Most of the so-called thinkers in the world are following the steps of Satan: They use their thinking to cheat people and to manipulate the world for their own selfish interests.

Real thinking expands the consciousness of humanity, creates right human relations, and helps people enjoy the beauties of life. Real thinking works for the past, the present, and the future of humanity. Real thinking is penetration into the Divine Mind, into the Divine Plan and Purpose of life, to create all those things that will make humanity achieve the Plan and Purpose.

Real thinking means to think in ways that always encourage the survival of humanity and spread beauty, health, happiness, and freedom. When thinking takes away our freedom, it is not thinking;

357

it is suicide. When thinking takes away our joy; it is not real thinking. Such thinking acts against Nature and against our real Selves.

It is safe to say that perhaps only ten percent of humanity exercise real thinking at this period of time. The rest of humanity "think" for their own selfish interests, at the expense of others.

There are many reasons why it is important to develop real thinking. First of all, thinking prevents you from falling into slavery — slavery of the emotions, interests, thoughts, plans, and deceptions of others as well as the slavery of your own ideas and knowledge. Thinking creates freedom.

In real thinking you can see unreality and reality. This is because thinking increases the light in your consciousness and helps you discriminate between the false and the real. Only in discriminating between the real and the unreal do you choose your own direction and gain your freedom.

Through thinking you choose the right path for yourself. No one has real direction unless he chooses his direction himself. If he follows the path or direction given by someone else, he will eventually give up that direction and search for his own inner direction, after wasting much time, money, and energy.

One day I was talking with a boy who was heavily using drugs. In trying to help him, I asked him two questions: Why are you using drugs? What will be the future effect of using drugs? I tried to make him *think* about these questions. These are two of the most important questions to ask in thinking: to find the cause and to find the future results and effects.

Actually, thinking begins with asking questions; through asking questions and looking for causes, you start thinking. Children demonstrate this fact when they are three or four years old when they constantly ask questions of their parents — "What is this, Mommy?...What is this?...How does this work?...Why?..." We are going to learn from our children; we are going to be grown-up babies and start asking questions, as much as possible.

One of my Teachers used to say that when you stop questioning, you are already dead mentally.

Whenever you sincerely question yourself, the answer is always within you. Your question is the echo of the answer that is found within the depth of yourself.

Most people read about world events in the newspaper or hear about them on television, and they are satisfied with what they read or hear. But real thinking people ask: Why did this event happen? What will the effect be on the economy, on education, in the world of science? Whenever a person asks questions, he cannot be manipulated or brainwashed; he is alert and awake.

A wise man once said that Satan is afraid of those who ask questions. In asking questions you reveal reality.

Anything created as a result of false thinking has no future. Anything created as the result of right thinking always makes your future beautiful.

Through thinking you avoid things that obscure your path and destroy your future. Thinking increases your energy and joy and makes you walk in the light instead of darkness.

Christ once said, "Search for the truth, and the truth will make you free."[1] This was not a religious statement but a philosophic and scientific piece of advice. Searching is thinking. When you find the truth — reality — you will be free because *you are reality*; you are finding your Self.

Whenever you use your thinking to find a truth, you are finding your Self. But when you use your discoveries for your own self-interests, you misuse your thinking and distort the thinking machine within you. Whenever anything in Nature is not used for its real purpose, for the purpose for which God created it, it deteriorates and degenerates. For example, listen to gossip and slander for a few days, and you will notice that your hearing is impaired.

Thinking leads you to unity and synthesis, to increasing health, and to increasing peace. Whenever you think in wrong ways, you work against these principles, and you slowly hang yourself with your own rope.

It is interesting to note that a person who uses other people for his own selfish interests hates those people if they start to think. This is because his faults and his wrong directions are revealed in the thinking of those he is using, and he can no longer make them his slaves.

Through thinking you find your success, prosperity, and health.

Once a girl told me, "I am always so nervous, and I can't find the reasons why."

I said, "Maybe there is someone you are continuously hating."

"Yes, it is true. I hate that man."

"If you are continually hating him, you will always be irritable. With irritation you create lots of poison in your system. Think about it... do you want to hate that man?"

"Yes, I do."

---

1. John 8:32

"Then you are going eventually to die in this serious condition."

A great Sage once said, "We want all the people in the world to start thinking because the salvation of humanity will come from thinking: brain thinking and heart thinking."

Brain thinking reveals things. Heart thinking points out that these revelations must be used for the benefit and the future of humanity. Thinking does not mean to create pollution and poison that will eventually kill humanity. Thinking means to eliminate all those causes that bring suffering and pain to humanity.

All the causes that separate human beings and create insanity and crime can be healed by thinking. The thinker must be an awakened human being who can see from the future to the past, from the past to the future, as well as what to do in the future, so that humanity does not repeat the things it did in the past that led it into slavery.

Through thinking you cooperate with the Creative Forces in the Universe and the laws of the Universe. Thinking is not manipulation of the principles and laws of Nature but cooperation with them. Nature is the body of a great Thinker Who created everything we have in it. Who are we to interfere with the plans of this great Thinker by playing with and distorting Nature?

The most intelligent scientists work to create poisons in order to kill various insects, but they do not stop and think that their poisons will also affect future life forms, including human beings.

Through thinking you create a higher standard of living. In order to create a true and lasting higher standard of living, you must think in terms of the good of all. If you break the laws of right human relations, you deceive and manipulate Nature, and Nature will eventually strike back and take away everything you thought you had gained.

Through thinking you solve your problems. There is no problem in the world that cannot be solved, if you think honestly and sincerely. The solution is prevented when your glamors, illusions, past hurts, and touchiness come to your mind and whisper in your ear, "Follow us; do not make us lose."

Through thinking you expand your consciousness. Consciousness is totally different from thinking; thinking expands your consciousness and makes it inclusive and future-oriented. Thinking turns your consciousness into a computer that knows the past, present, and future. The mind is the active part of the consciousness. The consciousness is the universal computer.

Thinking teaches you the language of the state of consciousness you will enter after you leave your body. When you die, you will not talk in the Other Worlds because you will not have a mouth or even a voice. In the Subtle Worlds, people communicate by thought. This means that if you do not know how to think, you will have no way to communicate with other life forms in the Subtle Worlds.

Thinking is the language of the "Country" you are going to on the other side. Through thinking you will be able to ask questions, receive answers, find direction, and penetrate into great mysteries. Real, creative thinking is penetration into greater light and finding the greater laws and principles of Nature.

There are nine steps to take to start developing thinking. **The first step is to question.** There are five questions you can use to develop your thinking: Who? When? Where? What? How? Why? These six brothers can reveal everything to you if you use them.

The second step is always to go from cause to effect and from effect to cause. If anything happens in your life, ask yourself: Why did that happen; what is the cause of that event?

The third step is to think in terms of the past and the future. For example, if you see a man drinking at the present, ask yourself: What did he do in the past that led him to this state, and what will happen to him in the future because of his drinking?

One day as a man was dying, he called his son and said, "Son, there are many traps in life, but I am going to give you one bit of advice. Follow this advice, and then later think why I gave it to you.

"If you are going to prostitutes, go after 3:00 A.M. If you are going to drink at a nightclub go after 2:00 A.M. And if you are going to gamble, be sure to gamble with the best gambler."

The son followed his father's advice. He wanted to gamble, so he found the best gambler. As they sat down to play, he noticed that the man did not even have on a decent pair of shoes. "My goodness," he thought, "if the best gambler cannot even buy a pair of shoes, why gamble?"

Then he went to a brothel. It was 3:00 A.M., and he saw the filth of the place after an evening of customers.

Then he went to a nightclub to drink. It was very late, and the only ones left were those who had passed out, who could not walk straight, or who were vomiting from too much liquor.

"Now I know why my father told me these things," thought the boy. "He is making me think and face reality, and see things from the past to the future."

The fourth step in right thinking is to go from the point of view of a part to the whole and from the whole to the part. Sometimes you fail to see reality because you do not think this way.

For example, you think only about one person, and not about the whole group. Or you think about how the group influences a man, but you do not think how the man influences the group.

Any time your thinking is limited to any one section of reality, you do not really think because you miss the interrelationship of elements. Real thinking means to increase your viewpoints.

Real thinking is multi-dimensional, not one-dimensional. Most so-called thinkers think only from the viewpoint or dimension of life on the physical plane. They do not think about the subjective life, about the future, or in terms of the future.

Have you ever thought about where your consciousness will go after your body passes away? For billions and billions of years, Nature has worked to create a consciousness in you. Why would Nature destroy that consciousness?

The fifth step to develop thinking is always to think from three angles: the physical, emotional, and mental. Ask yourself, if I do this thing, how will it affect my physical, emotional, and mental beings.

That bottle of whiskey may make your physical body really happy, but what will it do to your emotional and mental bodies? It may make your mind crazy and your emotions really negative. When you think in terms of the body only, you think in one dimension.

The sixth step is always to think in terms of energy and matter, spirit and form. You have the atom, but what is the spiritual counterpart of the atom? You may make a discovery, but then you must find the spiritual and mental counterparts of your discovery. In this way you develop abstract thinking.

The seventh step to develop thinking is to cultivate your observation. Observation means to have seeing, conscious eyes. You can play a game with yourself: Whenever you meet a person, look at his face really closely. Then when you go home, try to remember the color of his eyes, the shape of his nose, the way he smiled, even his odor. If you can remember these things, you are developing observation.

The eighth step to develop thinking is to practice concentration. Concentration means that when your mind is occupied with something, nothing else must disturb it. Concentration is the ability to use your willpower to control your mental activities.

The ninth and most important step to develop thinking is to practice meditation. It is not enough to read many books. Meditation, or scientific thinking, is the digestion of all the knowledge you gain. Meditation eventually makes you a co-worker of God — not one who asks God, "Give me a husband, a girlfriend, money, a house," but one who says to God, "What do *You* need? Tell me, so that I may help you."[2]

After meditation comes contemplation. This is an advanced step. Contemplation means direct, straight knowledge about all things. Contemplation is the flower of real thinking.

Thus, through thinking you build and organize your mental vehicles, and when you leave your body in sleep or death, you may be able to land on the shores of the Fiery World and demand admittance.

Thoughts are used in various ways. They may be

1. Verbalized or put into words
2. Symbolized or put into geometrical forms
3. Expressed as color and sound
4. Expressed as movements
5. Sent as rays of meaning, like arrows which operate in fiery realms or are directed to human minds

These latter kinds of thoughts are called "unexpressed thoughts," "silent thoughts," or "undressed thoughts." They are very direct, powerful, and instantaneous.

Thoughts that are verbalized lose their fieriness in words. Further, the words create uncertainty, due to various interpretations of them.

Thoughts expressed in geometrical forms need an interpretation and an ability to understand the meaning behind them.

Thoughts that are expressed in color and sound are more powerful, but one must know how to use color and sound to make them express the true essence of the thought. There are very few people who can read color and sound.

Thoughts that are expressed in movements are very complex and need long study and research. Once upon a time, man used this language. Animals use it very proficiently, but man cannot yet fully understand it.

Thoughts that are pure, like a beam or a ray flowing from the source to the target, are the future way of communication for mankind. One must strive to develop such thinking, which operates from the realms of the higher mind.

---

2. For more information on meditation, please refer to the following: *The Science of Meditation*; *Challenge for Discipleship*, Chapter 44; *The Psyche and Psychism*, Chapters 32, 50-69, 71-78.

In the Fiery World, communication is carried out through direct thoughts. This is why we must learn the language of fiery thinking.

We are told that in using the language of fire one must live in the light of solemnity. Solemnity can be understood here as a state of total fusion with the vision of perfection, in harmony with beauty, compassion, justice, joy, and freedom. Only in solemnity can the language of fiery thought be used and evoke direction.

To cultivate virtues and increase the fire of our soul, it is suggested that we engage in daily and regular meditation. Virtues and pure thinking can be regularly developed by meditation.

Daily meditation establishes a rhythmic pattern. Regular daily meditation creates a rhythm in the energy flow and energy reception. People talk about rhythm when they refer to music, but in essence rhythm is the impact of energy at regular intervals. It is this impact that eventually opens new ways of communication and destroys the barriers to that communication.

Rhythm is the most effective means of action in the Universe. Cycles are also rhythms.

In meditation, the flow of the rhythm of the energies of thought and the fire of the heart expand as spheres of light in Space. Each rhythm is a sphere within another sphere. The pressure of each additional sphere pushes the outer sphere farther into Space, thus forming a concentric "chain" of ever-expanding spheres. Great disturbances occur and weakness manifests when the rhythm becomes irregular or stops for long intervals. As a result, the entire sphere of energies slowly contracts and eventually disappears.

Rhythm is the power of progressive expansion.

It is these spheres of energies which function as magnetic antennas for spatial thoughts and transmit them, ring after ring, through a rhythmic procedure to the human soul.

Great is the power of rhythm. The Ancients called it the key to the closed doors of Light, Love, and Power.

However, the rhythmic flow of these spheres of light can be influenced by man-made conditions on earth. Poisonous gases and all kinds of pollution not only contaminate the Subtle World but also create those conditions in which our earth and solar system can be drastically affected. Disturbances noticed in the motion of our earth and of the other planets are the result of pollution, explosions, and human disunity. A fool will laugh at these remarks, but a true scientist is aware that our solar system lives according to the principle of balance.

Pollution, explosions, and human disunity create imbalance in Nature. Every kind of pollution affects the circulation of the subtle energies, rays, and currents in Space. Every explosion disturbs the balance of forces. Every disunity not only indirectly affects the life of the planet as a whole but also directly disturbs the forces of Nature, due to negative and malicious emanations from the emotions and thoughts of man.

Man still does not realize that a thought can either be poisonous or beneficial and fragrant. An emotion can pollute Space or cleanse it. Pollution, explosions, and disunity have brought the planet to the verge of the abyss, to the possibility of an unprecedented disaster. Typhoons, tornadoes, earthquakes, fires, and social disturbances are the effects of the accumulated pollution, explosions, and disunity. Humanity has become blind and suicidal and has trapped itself through its egocentric mind. Humanity cannot only destroy this planet; it cannot only create great catastrophes in the solar system; but it can also create a condition in the Subtle World which will be worse than the Christian hell as explained in the New Testament.

All humanity must find a way to stop war and to stop all kinds of explosive tests and war games. All humanitarians must find a way to stop the pollution of the air, if they want humanity to survive. They must emphasize one world and one humanity.

The disaster of the earth can come suddenly. The planet may be totally roasted when the gases around the earth inflame, or when the electromagnetic forces are disturbed beyond their capacity to stem a massive earthquake, submergence, or flood.

We are now in a state in which not even one shot of a gun must be tolerated. The equilibrium of the energies are very much disturbed and can bring the final disaster to our globe.

41

Subtle Emanations
and their
Effect on Life

Certain etheric and astral entities live and grow on the emanations of human beings. Human beings emanate various odors that result from blood, sweat, secretions, and radiations which originate from fear or base thoughts. Human beings also emanate various fragrances from sweet secretions and radiations which originate from joy, bliss, and ecstasy.

Man continuously feeds these entities which are always found around him. These entities either sap him and weaken him, or inspire and strengthen him.

All vices emanate malodorous gases around the body. Irritation, hatred, and anger radiate poison into the atmosphere, like gases pouring out of an exhaust pipe. We have the problem of chemical pollution as well as a subtle psychic pollution which lead the people of the world toward insanity, confusion, emotional and etheric imbalance, physical diseases, individual and mass criminal acts. Combined with chemical pollution, psychic pollution leads humanity toward chaos and destruction.

A house that is filled with the poisons of irritation, anger, fear, hatred, lust, and greed accumulates around itself the lowest kinds of entities who try to make people perpetuate these conditions to provide nourishment for them. Very often these entities follow the source of pollution and distribute the pollution to whomever the person contacts.

This psychic pollution stimulates seeds of criminal behavior in people, disturbs their mental balance, and leads to insanity.

In addition, this pollution disturbs the infected person's power of logic and reasoning and makes him irresponsible, selfish, and destructive.

One does not need to believe or reject these things. One can easily experiment and see the results.

All vices, irritation, anger, and hatred make people live against their own and others' survival.

It is these entities that eventually find their way into the etheric, astral, and mental bodies of the person and obsess or possess him.

On the other hand, virtues emanate elements which attract benevolent and highly refined entities from higher realms. These entities nourish themselves by these emanations as well as pour into the human aura higher elements of joy, elements which serve to establish communication with the Higher Worlds, and elements which nourish the subtle senses of the human being.

A virtuous man is like a spring of pure and healing water. A virtuous man radiates currents of energy which carry on their wings the elements of sanity, purity, harmony, cooperation, understanding, dedication, and striving toward the highest. A virtuous man not only inspires hundreds or thousands, but he also creates a protective net around a city and around a nation. When virtuous people increase, the whole course of a nation shifts. Prosperity, cooperation, and health increase, and the nation enters into a new cycle of unfoldment.

As an increasing number of people indulge in vices and these people take high positions in a nation, that nation will lose its vitality, sanity, prosperity, security, and health. Through such people, thousands of low-level entities will obsess those in high offices. That nation will remain in a state of pollution and in turn will continue to provide nourishment for the entities.

If history is observed through such considerations, one can easily see how nations and states prosper, or decline and fall into an abyss. The Biblical story of Lot is not a fable but a warning about the forces which carried on the work of destruction because it was not possible to find ten righteous, virtuous men.

The development or destruction of individuals follows the same path. Virtues give them wings toward the heights of achievement. Vices break their wings and make them live in the mud and dust of the world.

We are told that when these lower entities penetrate into our aura — because of irritation, hatred, malice, and vices — they can read our thoughts. One can prove from history many cases when the downfall of a country started when certain obsessed leaders, who were formerly trusted with top-secrets, gave their secrets to such entities and the entities carried them to the enemy and impressed the secrets into the enemies' minds. Very often it is not the armies and commanders who change a course of events, but entities acting through obsessed leaders.

This, of course, may sound like a fairy tale or a fabrication. But history will reveal the facts, and the future will prove them. Nevertheless, those working in responsible positions in any field will prevent harm if they reject irritation, hatred, anger, and malice.

Governments and certain organizations have many ways to check the previous record of a person who intends to work in higher positions. Of course this is necessary, but it does not guarantee against the breach of future security requirements. In the future, candidates for high positions will pass through tests that will reveal whether they can remain beyond irritation, hatred, anger, and malice.

Any action or movement influenced by irritation, anger, hatred, malice, or various other vices does not coincide with the path of success, victory, and transformation. The poison produced by these vices will attract thousands of dark entities who will eventually lead the action or movement to failure and destruction.

Certain leaders, after being obsessed by such entities, fall into the hands of mediums and low psychics who scientifically organize the downfall of the leader by messages that they impart to the leaders. This was a fact in ancient history, and this is the fact in modern history. The only safeguards for the leadership are a highly unfolded heart, purity, and creative intelligence.

42

Psychic Energy

Psychic energy is the energy of the fire existing in the human soul which energizes and charges every thought that is in harmony with the current going toward perfection. Higher thoughts are always charged by psychic energy, and one may call such thoughts currents of psychic energy.

Psychic energy is found in lofty thoughts accumulated in Space, carrying charges of the human soul. Psychic energy is found in spatial thoughts, thoughts which have originated from great Lives or Great Ones, because Their thoughts carry the energy of Their spirit.

Thus, psychic energy is everywhere. All of Space is full of psychic energy, as that Space is pervaded by the radiation of the Soul of Cosmos.

Psychic energy is inexhaustible, but one must learn how to draw it, how to transmit it, and how to accumulate it. Psychic energy can be accumulated in any object or living form, and a real magnet can be created. It can even create a magnet in and around a vision, a thoughtform, or a thought. This magnet acts exactly like a real magnet.

We are told that a metal magnet is charged by the same psychic energy. Its magnetic field is actually a psychic energy field. When consciousness is refined and transmuted, it can attract psychic energy from such magnetic fields and increase its creativity.

Actually, consciousness is a magnetic field itself. When it is transmuted and purified, it accumulates a great amount of psychic energy and transmits it to the brain and nervous system.

It is possible to use the magnetic field of a magnet by directing its energy through our thoughts. If the psychic energy in thought is strong enough, the magnetic field of the magnet follows the direction of the thought and creates an amplified current for healing work.

In its essence, will energy is psychic energy. When the consciousness focuses the psychic energy, it can manifest as a thunderbolt or lightning.

There is only One Will in the Universe. Self-will is egotistical; it is identification with matter for selfish interests. The One Will is channeled by psychic energy according to its intensity. Man has no will other than that expressed when his true Core manifests itself through his consciousness.

The One Will is the Cosmic Fire, the *Pan-Fohat*, which can only manifest through a person when he is charged with psychic energy. Man turns into a powerful magnet when the Cosmic Fire blends with the psychic energy within the field of his consciousness.

We are told that the conscious transmission and direction of psychic energy takes place when one passes through total transfiguration of his nature. This is why Holy Ones are called the "carriers of fire." When the field of consciousness is charged with psychic energy, the ascent of the soul starts.

One must remember that the field of consciousness penetrates every cell of the brain and the cavities and the glands of the head. The electricity of the consciousness flows through all our nerves. The change in consciousness creates changes in the function of the brain, the function of the pineal gland, the carotid gland, the pituitary body, the nervous system, and the other ductless glands. Thus, consciousness controls the entire mechanism of man.

An elevated consciousness even changes the secretions of the glands. Psychic energy is the creative fire, the fire that regenerates, heals, enlightens, purifies, unites, and synthesizes.

Any kind of labor done with an unselfish motive and using the heart for the purpose of advancement, enlightenment, and unity attracts psychic energy. The labor can be spiritual, mental, or physical. It can be by an individual or a group. All virtues generate, release, or attract psychic energy. Meditation, contemplation, and sacrificial service charge your aura and environment with psychic energy.

Creative labor draws a great amount of psychic energy from the human soul and from Nature, Space, and even from the Cosmic Heart.

Love, joy, and bliss are forms of psychic energy. Inspiration is a flow of psychic energy. Those people who are charged by love, joy, and bliss radiate a great amount of psychic energy to their environment and saturate any object they touch.

Psychic energy circulates and radiates continuously in the art of great creative artists. Like an electrical current, psychic energy flows in music, paintings, sculpture, writings, songs, and dances, if the creativity has originated from a highly advanced soul. Thus, true artists generate and distribute a great amount of psychic energy, spreading blessings on Nature and humanity.

People will be surprised if they discover how plants and flowers respond to objects of art, to music, songs, dances, and writings. They feel the psychic energy emanating from these art forms, and it vitalizes them, heals and charges them with energy.

It is known that plants and flowers grow and bloom in great abundance and beauty around sanctuaries and creative centers of art. The same occurs in the human constitution. Etheric and subtle flowers in the human aura bloom and flourish under the impact of the fire of psychic energy.

Psychic energy creates synthesis. Synthesis is the actualization in diversified objects of the Law of Unity. Synthesis is the Law of Harmony focused by a lofty vision. Psychic energy puts these laws into operation.

Inspiration is a form of psychic energy. Inspiration always originates from the psychic center of any conscious entity, whether it is human, superhuman, solar, or galactic. Inspiration is the flow of psychic energy charged with vision, which evokes striving and creativity and leads to victory.

Space is permeated with psychic energy. This does not mean that everyone can transmit and use this energy. The proper "wires" and "mechanisms" must be installed under proper laws to be able to have and to use this energy. Trees, plants, certain birds and animals have this wiring system and these mechanisms naturally. But human beings, even though they have more advanced wiring and mechanisms, cannot always use the treasure of psychic energy. Physical, emotional, and mental interferences act to repel the psychic energy.

For example, habits create short circuits in the psychic flow. Doubt, complaints, depression, fear, and irritation totally disperse psychic energy. Hatred changes it into poison. Vanity, illusion, unrighteousness, lies, hypocrisy, and flattery block all passages of psychic energy.

On the other hand, joy, goodwill, patience, righteousness, labor, solemnity, devotion, sincerity, and fearlessness open the channels of psychic energy.

Inspiration is the flow of psychic energy, and one must always try to keep open the channel of such a flow. Inspiration creates higher contacts, enlightenment, fusion, and expansion of consciousness. It charges the whole psychic mechanism of a person and brings the call from higher realms.

Psychic energy creates equilibrium between the fires in man and the fires in Space. It is in such an equilibrium that the flower of the soul blooms.

Trust is called the hand which opens the paths of psychic energy. Other names for trust are hope and faith. These three function together and conduct a great amount of psychic energy into a man, and especially into a group. When there is trust in a group of people, psychic energy becomes amplified to a great extent and produces a transforming and healing effect within the environment.

There are small psychic worms which, like termites, destroy the wiring of the psychic energy in the human constitution. One of these is doubt. The others are mockery, slander, servility, the tendency to use and exploit people, and flattery. Usually these worms are kept hidden under false plumage, but they destroy the channels of psychic energy and turn a man into a cave of dark entities.

Psychic energy establishes connections between etheric centers and between the human soul and Universal or Cosmic sources. As the consciousness of man expands and goes through transformation and fusion with higher spheres of consciousness, psychic energy builds the network of communication wires in Space and connects the consciousness with the distant worlds. Thus the psychic computer is built and the transformed consciousness learns how to use it in the Cosmic sense.

The consciousness of races sometimes passes through crystallizations and petrifications. Heavy shocks are necessary to break them down. Great disasters release tremendous amounts of psychic energy and cause an expansion of consciousness.

Those who survive great catastrophes usually come in contact with higher dimensions and take life seriously, which benefits their spiritual progress. Those who perish in catastrophic events usually wait for a long period of time in the subtle planes. It is seldom that they experience an expansion of consciousness. But Nature takes such steps periodically to purify Itself from the accumulations of physical and psychic pollution.

Man can periodically purify his system for better reception of spatial psychic energy. This purification is carried on through periodic renunciation, detachment, abstinence, austerity, solemnity, and sacrificial service. These correspond to the lightning and thunder in Space. The spatial dross is shattered through the sound of thunder and burned away by the fire of lightning. Man's steps to purify himself also shatter accumulated crystallizations within himself. When a man is at the level of an Initiate, he can purify his environment through the thunder and lightning of his own Intuition and Will Power.

Psychic energy can be heard as sound, seen as light, and experienced as fire. Psychic energy is even experienced as a sweet perfume, a taste, and as bliss.

A man accumulates a great amount of creative energy when he succeeds in uniting his will with the Will of the Cosmic Heart. Such a unity is achieved in consciousness and in spirit when one feels that his will is one with that Cosmic Will. Unification of the will with the Cosmic Will creates a white light which attracts creative energies like a great magnet.

The creativity of man in all domains of life depends upon this unification of wills. The creative Will in the Universe manifests through our own will according to the degree of fusion. The human soul reaches its full blooming as the degree of the fusion rises.

On the Path to the Fiery World, unification of the will of the individual with the Cosmic Will opens the Path and eliminates all obstacles and attacks of the forces of darkness. One can accomplish unification of the will if he gains freedom over his personality.

The Will of the Cosmic Heart can be sensed in silence and in renunciation of the ego. As long as the ego controls our actions, our words and our thoughts, unification with the Cosmic Will will not be possible. The Cosmic Will manifests in Beauty, Goodness, Righteousness, Joy, Freedom, in deep silence and in acts of renunciation.

The Great Ones are fused with the Cosmic Will, the Source of psychic energy.

Although it is one flow and has one main source, psychic energy can manifest in various ways as it contacts sensitive receivers. Each receiver gives a new quality to psychic energy. Thus for example, if a hundred people are exposed to the ray of psychic energy, each person may have a different expression, according to his nature, just as the light of the sun manifests in so many colors through so many various kinds of flowers.

The manifestation of psychic energy is affected by human thought, the thought mechanism, and self-will. This means that the reception of psychic energy is also affected by the thoughts, emotions, problems, and activities of the environment. We are even told that the furniture in a room, the conversations spoken in the past in that room, and the emanations of past visitors can change the quality of reception.

Psychic energy can come in one flow and can branch out in many ways, creating different colors, symphonies, and creative labor in those who receive it. It can simultaneously touch various people scattered in the world and distribute the same gift.

When psychic energy is accumulated on any object or person in various locations on the earth, it relates these objects or persons to each other through psychic communication and weaves the web of contact. Such webs are used for reception and distribution of psychic energy.

Not only are objects and human beings charged with psychic energy, but there are also superhuman entities or devas who distribute psychic energy on certain occasions, for example, during the time of meditation, group prayer, group labor, or group singing. Also, at the time of sacrificial or heroic deeds, these devas send us a special quality of psychic energy.

Psychic energy is also distributed during the time of contact with beauty in any form, during the time of creativity, prayer, and speech. Every time a person uplifts his heart and consciousness, he emanates certain colors which attract the carriers of psychic energy.

Psychic energy is also given to those heroes who, after a great sacrificial deed, feel a profound bliss in their hearts. Bliss is one of the forms of psychic energy. Joy is another one.

Psychic energy shines in the human being as a pure white flame. Once this flame comes into being, it manifests as health, strength, energy, and beauty on the physical plane. On the emotional plane, it manifests as aspiration, devotion, and calmness. On the mental plane, it manifests as striving, concentration or dedication, and enlightenment. This flame becomes the communication link between these three planes and the Higher Worlds.

When psychic energy is withdrawn from the physical plane, the person acts self-destructively. When it is withdrawn from the astral plane, the person's emotional life falls into depression and moral degeneration. When it is withdrawn from the mental plane, the person enters into confusion; he loses his direction; and he is caught in a force-field of contradictions. All these things may also happen to groups, nations, and humanity as a whole.

The flame of psychic energy keeps the light of the Higher Worlds flowing to reach the person. In the absence of psychic energy, darkness descends and spreads in all fields of human endeavor.

Psychic energy has many stages of intensity. An aspirant carries a certain voltage of it. When he enters major initiations, the charge increases considerably. When he becomes a Master, he turns into a flame. Of course, there are higher attainments in which the flame changes into lightning and into a ray and eventually into a group of rays.

43

Gratitude and the
Subtle Worlds

A great Sage once said, "The quality of gratitude is... the finest purification of the organism.... Great is the healing power of the emission of gratitude."[1]

Gratitude is an energy coming from higher realms. When a person is grateful, he emanates a kind of energy that cleans his aura and heals his body. He radiates a violet-colored energy into his aura which organizes and harmonizes all the levels of the aura and builds a bridge between him and the violet devas, who are the healing agents in this Universe.

Our life is an exact response to our consciousness. If our consciousness is lofty and beautiful, we attract a corresponding life. When we create a lofty state of consciousness, it becomes like a magnet which attracts conditions which will bring us joy, beauty, and success.

Nothing happens to us by accident. Whenever we are in those conditions which are not joyful or happy, it means that we have acted against the law of gratitude. Whenever we fall into a state of ingratitude, we inevitably fail in our life.

When you start developing gratitude, you establish a communication line between yourself and the invisible Creative Forces in the Universe. You also establish a communication line between yourself and those spiritual human beings who have the same frequency. In gratitude you expand your field of consciousness and communication.

Communication means expansion of your beingness. The greater your field of communication is, the greater you are. Communication is developed thus when you learn to express gratitude.

---

1. *Agni Yoga*, para. 31.

Gratitude slowly eliminates your ego. When you are grateful, your negativity and tensions — physical, emotional, and mental — disappear. Whenever you fail to appreciate something good someone did for you, when you start criticizing or speaking evil about that person, your ego increases; you become separative, divided within yourself. You become a tumor in the Existence. But with gratitude, this ego melts away.

The ego stands like a disturbing factor in the aura. Your ego is a psychic tumor which feeds itself on everything coming from the Creative Forces. When your ego grows too big, *you* become lost; your light becomes lost. But when your ego is dissipated, when your negativity, separatism, and fanaticism are dissipated, you create harmony in your heart, mind, and soul, and you create a harmonious relationship with all existence.

This is why gratitude is a healing agent within your system. With gratitude you dissipate all those factors that create disturbances and distortions in your aura. For example, a moment of ingratitude can cause you to fall down and hurt yourself or catch a cold. In a moment of ingratitude you lose your equilibrium and balance, and you may be forgetful.

Express gratitude before you do something, and you will see the difference in your life. This is why the Ancients recommended that we give gratitude before eating. With gratitude you assimilate the food better.

The beginning of everything must start with gratitude. A wise man used to say, "Do not open your door to go out in the morning without first giving gratitude." When you do this, immediately the Creative Forces will accumulate and assemble around you, and They will work for you.

The Creative Forces in Nature are the forces of righteousness. They want you to understand the beauty around you and give something in return through your feelings and consciousness. When you express gratitude to the Creative Forces in Nature, you give into Space a high-level substance or emanation which is like a perfume. You become like a refinery for Nature and create a substance that is very useful for the devas.

This is how we help maintain the balance, equilibrium, and righteousness in Nature.

Gratitude toward others protects you from criticism, gossip, hatred, malice, and slander.

Every time you speak ill about someone, you literally commit suicide; you cut off the Creative Forces around you and create imbalance within your system. Whenever you have negative feelings or thoughts about someone who has hurt you, immediately try to find a reason to be grateful for that person. Perhaps due to his nasty and negative attitude toward you, you have become more alert and have developed something stronger in your character.

When you develop a grateful attitude toward everyone, you protect yourself from your own negative and destructive thoughts, feelings, and words. Whenever you express any destructive thought, emotion, or word, it hurts you first before it hurts anyone else.

As you continuously express negativity, your aura weakens and loses its magnetism; you will not be successful in your life. Ugliness means to lose your magnetism, integrity, and harmony.

Gratitude makes you see beauty, acknowledge beauty, and respond in beauty.

With gratitude you relate to others in beauty. You can even raise the consciousness of others by relating to them in gratitude.

Once I went to a woman and expressed my gratitude to her, and she started to cry. She said to me, "When you expressed your gratitude to me, my heart just opened. I suddenly remembered the things I had said about you, and I felt so bad. You humiliated me, but you also uplifted me to a higher state of consciousness."

Sincerity must always stand behind your gratitude. Expressing gratitude without sincerity is like writing checks without having the money in the bank to cover them.

Gratitude creates right human relations. Right human relations are established when you start appreciating others and being grateful to them. When you build right human relations, you start to function not as individuals but as a group, a mass of people, and eventually even as one humanity; you become a spiritual army together.

Gratitude makes you realize that you yourself must become a benevolent force for others. Unless you give what you take, you cannot grow. This is a very important law. You do not have love if you are not giving love to others. You have self-respect when you respect others. Whatever you give to others, that is what you have.

When you begin to develop the spirit of gratitude, a transformation takes place in your nature. You think more about what you can do for others to prove your growing gratitude. When you give, you begin to grow.

You cannot grow until you manifest the beauty that you have within you. Your beauty manifests only by building beauty in others.

Gratitude increases in others the beauty and the willingness to give and opens in them new channels to manifest their own spiritual gifts.

For example, if someone helps you and you do not appreciate their help, eventually they will stop helping you. This is human nature. But if you say "thank you" and express your gratitude, that person will give more of himself.

When you accumulate, no magnetism is created in you. When you give back what you receive, in the form of your gratitude, you create a polarity; the energy circulates between you and the polarity created by the other person. This is a law of physics. Saying "thank you" creates circulation of energy between two people. Ingratitude disturbs this polarity.

Every time you think, speak, or act in a state of ingratitude, you build walls around yourself, and the Creative Forces of Nature cannot reach you; you break the laws of right human relations.

When there is no conscious relationship between you and others, your spirit cannot communicate with the spirit of others. You become like an island isolated in the ocean, surrounded by water, without communication with any other bodies of land. You insulate and isolate yourself and repel others.

Sometimes people think that every success they have is due to their own merit. This is incorrect. In every success and creative expression, the Higher Forces are working with you. If they are not working with you, you will never be successful.

Many creative forces are working with you, in small or large tasks, such as building your house or making a ten hour cross-country drive. Even your Guardian Angel is working with you. These invisible helpers cannot reach you if you are contaminated with the pollution of ingratitude.

Ingratitude distorts and disturbs the aura because it prevents the flow of the currents that have been received. When you do not respond with gratitude, you distort the law of giving and taking and you create psychic congestion in your aura. When your system is congested, you are not healthy or happy, and you may not even be conscious.

Joy and health come to you when you have right communication with the Creative Forces and when your aura is in harmony with these forces.

Gratitude builds communication lines between us and higher centers. We must be grateful to these higher centers.

First of all, we must be grateful to that center called the Tower, the Father's Home, or Shamballa. Shamballa is the stronghold of forces which protects this planet from the attacks of Cosmic evil.

Second, we must be grateful to the Hierarchy. It is Hierarchy Who gives all the Ageless Wisdom to this planetary humanity in the form of religion, philosophy, art, and culture. If you acknowledge Their gifts to humanity, you become a recipient of the blessings emanating from Them, and you come closer to that Center.

Third, we must be grateful to our spiritual Teacher, whoever He may be. It is our Teacher who works for us, enlightens our mind, expands our consciousness, and helps us transform our life. He deserves our heartfelt gratitude.

Fourth, we must be grateful to our parents, friends, fellow students, and our own students.

Fifth, we must be grateful for all the blessings Nature has given us.

Once I was walking in the mountains. The trees and the stream were so beautiful that I wanted to hug the trees and kiss the water. The drops of rain falling on my face were like messengers of heaven. Whenever we do not have gratitude toward someone or something, we destroy them. If we are not grateful to a beautiful stream, we will pollute it with our ingratitude. If we are not grateful for something, it means we do not understand its value. We give value to all the things we are grateful for.

Sixth, we must be grateful to those who reveal our weaknesses to us and make us strive toward perfection.

If you say, "I don't like that woman because she told me my nose is crooked," well, maybe she is right, and you should straighten your nose! But your immediate reaction is to reject that woman because she is revealing a weakness that you have.

We need such people around us who, in a loving manner, help us shape ourselves. We need such people to tell us, "My dear, you are walking crooked; don't walk like that."

Once a man I knew was walking very unevenly. I said, "Are you dancing? Can you walk straight?" He thought I was criticizing him, but I was not. Eventually he tried to improve his walk, and finally he was walking so beautifully. "If your mother were alive," I said, "she would love you!"

Seventh, we must be grateful to our Guardian Angel for guiding us down through ages. One day I was riding in the car of a friend, and a car cut in front of us. My friend slammed on his brakes and just escaped hitting the other car.

"Did you see how quick I was?" he asked me. "First say thank you to God, then to your Solar Angel, and then we will think about whether you were quick or not," I said.

This is the correct attitude to have in life. Whenever you have success in life, say thank you to the Creative Forces who helped you have that success. These Creative Forces do not need your gratitude, but They want righteousness and justice. You should acknowledge Them and fulfill the Law of Righteousness.

Eighth, we are going to be very grateful to the obstacles, pains, and sufferings in our life for letting us pay the karma we have accumulated throughout ages.

We say, "I hate that pain. I hate that suffering." But we do not realize that maybe it is better to pay this debt before it accumulates and becomes something worse. We should be grateful because our load is decreasing, and we will be able to climb more easily, with less weight on our shoulders.

Ninth, we must be grateful to the vision of the future. Without these visions, we will never be able to proceed on the path of beauty and perfection. Vision makes us feel that we can be more beautiful than we are now, that we must do something more to help humanity than we are doing now.

Develop gratitude, and you will see the changes happening in your life.

Gratitude is considered to be a bridge between the physical and the Higher Worlds. Those who climb toward the Higher Worlds are full of gratitude to all that exists. Gratitude is the peace in one's heart. Gratitude is the cause of harmony with the whole Universe. And gratitude is the wings by which one flies toward the Higher Worlds.

CHAPTER

44

Fiery Qualities

One of the factors that leads us toward greater achievements is *dissatisfaction* — dissatisfaction with the present, regarding what we are, what we do, and what interests we have. Many people fall in love with themselves and are satisfied with whatever they are and whatever they do. Such a satisfaction turns into the coffin for their soul.

Dissatisfaction creates an urge and a striving to surpass the level on which you live. It urges you to change the ways and means by which you try to serve, to change the conditions around you and create those that are favorable for your eternal progress. Dissatisfaction is the feeling that your soul needs to expand, to conquer time and space.

Dissatisfaction is the sign that your soul intuitively feels that there are other conditions in which the human soul can find greater Beauty, greater Goodness, Righteousness, Joy, and Freedom.

Dissatisfaction is the sign that you were able to penetrate into the higher astral world or the Fiery World. When you penetrate into the Higher Worlds, nothing can satisfy you any more, and this dissatisfaction propels you toward more glorious heights.

Dissatisfaction is the pull of the ideal vision, the pull of the inner subjective experiences which are often absent in the earthly life.

Dissatisfaction is the result of the decision to create a new world which is a reminder of the state of the Higher Worlds. When people are satisfied, they can no longer advance on any line of human endeavor.

Dissatisfaction is the process of replacing an outmoded way of life with one which meets new requirements of progress and success.

When the Cosmic Magnet begins to pull a human soul upward, the human soul feels dissatisfaction in life. Real dissatisfaction is not the result of ingratitude, but the effect of gratitude. The grateful man knows how much he has progressed and how much he has enjoyed life, and now he is grateful for the urge which propels him to higher levels of existence where his gratitude will be deeper. Gratitude is the feeling that one can surpass himself if he is dissatisfied with what he is at the present.

Gratitude and dissatisfaction go side by side. A grateful man looks beyond events and feels happy and thankful for all that helped him progress. Dissatisfaction directs a grateful man toward the possibility of further advancements. Gratitude turns into joy and enthusiasm through which man reaches further heights. Thus, gratitude and dissatisfaction eventually knock on the doors of the Fiery Worlds.

Dissatisfaction leads us to cultivate the fiery sense which is the sense of true direction. This sense develops as the man responds to the direction of the Cosmic Magnet in the Fiery World and, in the meantime, carefully observes the conditions of the world as the result of the Law of Cause and Effect.

Fiery qualities are those qualities which are developed in the fire of the heart. Dissatisfaction, gratitude, and the sense of direction are flowers in the Fiery World. The more fiery qualities we have, the easier our journey toward the Fiery World will be, and the richer will be the beauty of our life in any world.

People on earth expect others to give them full explanations, information about everything, and they wait for commands. They want detailed orders or instructions, and thus they are accustomed to remain passive and lazy.

In the Higher Worlds one does not waste one word, one thought, or one motion. Communication is initiated with a hint. One motion, one word, or one glance must be enough to grasp the entire chain of the message. These are just the hooks behind which extend the entire details of the hint. This is why the majority of the visitors to the Subtle World feel like strangers and for a long time cannot communicate or translate the hints.

Hints are outer beginnings of inner chains. If one has not cultivated his intuition, observation, and attention, hints pass away without leaving any impression. Most hints and signs are symbolic, and one must demonstrate direct and immediate understanding.

In the advanced strata of the Fiery Worlds, people understand each other in one glance, in one motion, or in one word. There is no set language in the Subtle World. You can use any language you want, or any word that does not belong to any language. It is the thought behind the word that makes the word meaningful to the listener. We are advised to develop pure sensitivity toward thoughts and catch the meaning by the "hooks" provided intuitively.

In the Fiery World, this symbolic language — hints, signs, and glances — are not necessary because as the thought begins to form in your mind, people "see" it immediately and respond. In the lower levels of the Fiery World one must strive to develop sensitivity to the thoughts of others and learn the language of thoughts. As the fire increases in man, the communication becomes clearer and more accurate.

In the higher Fiery World man can communicate with millions of people in one second. Thought is not restricted by Space.

Visualization in the Fiery World is a totally different action. It is the ability to *locate* the subject of interest and communicate with it instantaneously on the screen of your eyes.

The words we learn on the earthly plane have astral, fiery, and Cosmic dimensions. Thus, a mundane word has one meaning in the astral world, which is understood by the astral brain, and another dimension or meaning which is understood by the fiery brain. For example, take the word "tree." In the astral plane, it is brotherhood and symphony. In the mental world, it is a symbol of transmutation and bridging. This is why Sages throughout the centuries have suggested that we develop abstract thinking and the ability to read symbols. In the astral world, our language is worthless. In the mental world, the whole astral language is obsolete.

Another example is demonstrated by the word "home." "Home" means the house which belongs to us, which gives us shelter and protection. In the lower astral world, home is the lowest stratum. In the higher strata, home is the entire astral plane. In the Fiery World, the whole Cosmic Space is home.

This is how narrowly defined concepts tumble, along with their associated problems, and are replaced by Cosmic concepts.

Those who have already developed a fiery consciousness on earth will not have difficulty understanding the languages of the Higher Worlds. People with a fiery consciousness on earth already speak Cosmic languages. The *Vedas*, the *Upanishads*, the *Bhagavad Gita*, and the *New Testament* were written in the language of fire, and only a fiery consciousness can understand them.

The essence of communication is thought. Thought develops better if one makes an effort to read between the lines, or to hear things not stated outright.

In the future, those people who really know about the Subtle Worlds will open universities where people will go to learn about the Higher Worlds. In the future, people will understand that all life on earth must be a preparation for the journey toward higher realms.

Imagine an airplane with a final destination preceded by nine stops along the way. On each stop it "forgets" the final destination. It wastes ages at the first stop, and more time is wasted going to the next stop.

Once humanity sees the main destination, not only will they make their lives a preparation for the Subtle World, but also they will not waste time in other stations of the Higher Worlds. Each delay is painful. Each delay is a loss of opportunity. Each delay is a denial of the destined goal.

In the animal world, language is expressed by the voice and the movement of the body. In the human world, the mouth and the ear are the controlling factors. In the astral world it is the heart that speaks. In the Fiery World, the controlling factor is the eyes, which, according to the particular thought, radiate colorful and fiery rays. Thought is channeled mostly through the eyes.

When we say that thought is expressed through the eyes, we do not refer to the various types of glances but to the fiery thought energy which pours out of the eyes. The eyes control the power beams of light and use them in several ways. The most beautiful eyes are found in the Fiery World. They have a tremendous power of magnetism, penetration, transmission, and the depth of infinite Space.

The eyes have been called the mirrors of the soul. Warriors in the Fiery World are arranged according to the beauty of their eyes.

Self-denial is another fiery quality. Self-denial begins when a person feels the need of the world and tries to meet it. Of course, one must walk through the long Path of Discipleship to be able to render a better service for humanity, but such discipline turns into a joyful labor because of self-denial.[1]

A materialistic person will rejoice when he sees people living in self-denial because it may increase his own income and allow him to have power over everything possible. Such a person is not only a loser on earth but also a loser in the Subtle Worlds. For example, upon death he leaves all that he had behind him and, upon arriving in the Subtle World, he falls into the deepest poverty. Greed burns him and scorches him, and he hurries back to earth to find what he previously had. Then he finds himself in the most difficult conditions, due to the denial by the Law of Karma and because of his own identification with matter and related exploitations.

---

1. For specific information regarding discipline, please refer to *Challenge for Discipleship*, especially Chapter 7, "Discipleship and Service."

Through self-denial man not only enjoys the earthly life but also finds himself in great beauty and abundance in the Higher Worlds.

Self-denial expands his Space and the field of his communication with higher realities. In self-denial he pays his karmic debts and releases himself from the bondage of matter. He can have all that he needs, and he rejects all that he does not need. All his needs are met so that he is a better server of humanity and a better communication link between lower worlds and Higher Worlds.

Self-denial becomes very easy and painless when a man dedicates himself to the service of humanity. Through each step on that Path, his self-denial increases and eventually his ego disappears in total dedication.

Unless our ego disappears, advancement toward the Fiery World will be impossible. The ego is formed, not by fire, but by combustible materials. The ego can in some degree survive in the lower levels of the astral world but not in the Fiery World. The ego does not let the human soul expand. It limits his communications and always tends to lean toward the past.

The ego is one of the main sources of human suffering. Races have egos. Groups have egos. When one comes in contact with the Fiery World, he realizes the futility of the suffering generated by the ego.

On the Path of human progress, the ego is the worst hindrance. We are advised to dissolve this tumor before we enter into the Subtle World. There, the ego causes us extreme pain until it is dissolved by the rays of the Fiery World reaching the Subtle World.

Creative imagination and visualization are also qualities of the Fiery World. Creative imagination, in the physical plane, is a sort of recalling past memories, or projecting our desires toward the future. In the Subtle World, imagination is creativity. If you want to have an apple, you imagine an apple and you make an apple come into existence. In the Fiery World imagination is the power of duplication of any event occurring in the Subtle World, and the ability to change that event.

Events in the Subtle World are composed of astral energy. Those who develop their creative imagination on earth will be able to control events and other formations in the astral plane. A clue to this possibility is apparent if you can remember certain dreams in which you deliberately changed the events. For example, if you were falling from a cliff, you imagined that you could fly, and you did not fall. Thus you changed the event. In the Subtle World, this is a daily practice.

Visualization in higher levels of the Fiery World is also a sense which translates the objects or impressions it touches. When it further develops, it turns into the power of creativity in accordance with the Plan of the Hierarchy and in harmony with the higher archetypes.

A creative imagination and a developed power of visualization are faithful friends in the Higher Worlds. They make us understand the essence of communication and find the straight way to progress. Creative imagination and visualization build in man the seeds of genius to bloom in future incarnations.

Another characteristic of the Fiery World is unity. This is why unity is a fiery quality. Those who live, work, and think for unity are fiery people.

The physical world is characterized by cleavages and separations. The astral world is the pendulum between unity and separatism. The mental world is total unity.

If one is sensitive, he feels a certain fiery sensation in his heart in a moment of unity. This sensation is greater when the unity is more massive and on higher levels. This sensation is a taste of the Fiery World.

Those who work for unity are those who have certain contacts with the Fiery World. The light of the Fiery World makes every separative action seem ridiculous and reveals it as an anti-survival factor.

The physical world is a training school for unity. In unity, pain and loss disappear; joy and success replace them. It is deplorable that humanity has learned so little about the importance of unity.

On the Path of unity, ego and separatism must be replaced with beauty and joy. Through creative imagination one must try to recall the moments of unity in the Higher Worlds and recharge himself with the power generated in unity.

This planet was destroyed many times because man did not learn the lesson of unity.

Negativity, denial, depression, inertia, fanaticism, vanity, egoism, separatism, bigotry, and loneliness are signs of the lack of fire. When the fire departs from the personality, the personality falls into the hands of conflicting and destructive forces.

By increasing the virtues and characteristics of the Fiery World, one can heal himself. It is true that inner fire must be developed gradually so that the tissues of the subtle organs are not damaged. But fire is necessary for purification and reconstruction. Where fire is absent, impurity and destructive forces accumulate.

This is the same in any group or nation. When the fire of Spirit begins to depart, the destructive agents take their positions. They eventually undermine the group or nation through various ways and means, until nothing is left to offer the world.

45

Practical Steps
Toward the
Fiery World

The first practical step toward the Fiery World is the understanding of the nine fundamentals of life. When they are understood and lived, the Fiery World stands closer to us and opens its gates to us. These nine fundamentals of life are

Unity
Synthesis
Cooperation
Self-sacrifice
Striving
Infinity
Joy
Freedom
Beauty

This is the nine-pointed star which leads to the Fiery World. If a person continuously ponders on these year after year, he will see how the fire of psychic energy increases in him. It is not by knowledge that one achieves, but by the assimilation and living of these nine fundamentals of life.

Knowledge built upon this foundation is wisdom which spreads blessings to humanity, Nature, and into the life of the person. Without this foundation, knowledge serves greed and destruction.

One does not need detailed information to find the Path leading to the Fiery World. All information will be useless. The only way to find this Path is through the assimilation of the fundamentals of life. As one assimilates these fundamentals, the signs of the Fiery World reveal themselves increasingly until one becomes ready to enter the Fiery World.

These nine fundamentals prepare a person's mental body, develop its centers, cultivate the higher senses, and make it ready to fuse with the fire of the Fiery World without being tortured or burned by the fire. In the Fiery World these nine fundamentals will become for him nine formulas through which he will open secret gates of deeper knowledge.

The Fiery World is our greatest destination. It is the state of beauty, supreme creativity, knowingness, expansion, and the expression of all the possibilities latent in our souls. Once we understand this, we will dedicate ourselves to that goal for our entire life.

This life is a school for us, and we must graduate with honors. Every time we pass one grade and enter a higher one, we must understand that our success in higher grades is based on the work done in the previous grade. The best virtues, talents, and abilities we have in this life are the results of all the striving we did in the past. If we strive further, our future life will be more beautiful, more fruitful, and more influential. Thus, bit by bit we advance, but only if we deeply realize our destination and make all that we think, speak, and do fit into that goal.

Our present incarnation is a great opportunity for us to prepare ourselves further for the Fiery World. Each event, each crisis, each success and failure is an opportunity for us to keep our direction right and to establish spiritual perseverance, against which no force can stand.

All our problems, difficulties, failures, successes, and achievements must be observed from the viewpoint of our destination. It may be true that on many occasions we fail, but if we keep the vision of the Fiery World in our hearts, our failures will provide the fuel for a new enthusiasm to go forward with greater striving. Most of our failures can turn into stepping stones in our future adventures.

People look at the fact of death with horror instead of with great joy. People try to prolong their lives by mechanical means, instead of liberating themselves for a greater labor. Our life must be full of the expectation to enter the Fiery World.

People have no clear idea when we say astral body and mental body. Actually these are bodies like our physical body, but in a very refined state. Like our physical body, it is possible to wound our astral and mental bodies. They may have been repaired in some way, but they still carry the scars of the former wounds. They can also become sick. They can grow old and die. We are told that the mental body, like the rest of the bodies, can receive many wounds until the time when it is totally transmuted in the Fiery World.

We may enter the Subtle World with wounded and sick bodies. It is not possible to enter the Fiery World with a sick mental body, but it is possible to enter with many scars received in the battle for light. Actually, people with such scars are greeted in the Fiery World because wounds received in the battle for light, goodness, and beauty are real credentials for the Higher Worlds.

People wound the tissues of the subtle bodies through their malice, slander, hatred, bigotry, and so on. The scars of such actions remain for a long time. It is also possible to wound our subtle bodies by using them for evil purposes, or by fighting against Beauty, Goodness, Righteousness, Joy, and Freedom. When the bodies are badly wounded, they cannot function under higher pressure, and the flights toward Higher Worlds become painful and very difficult.

The fires of Space have a very curative effect on our bodies. Our bodies or vehicles live through the fire absorbed from Space and from the surrounding objects. The etheric centers and the centers in the astral and mental bodies breathe fire in and out. It is this fire that keeps the entire machine of the spirit running.

When the fires of the body are active, the body is healthy. When the higher centers are active, we manifest fiery qualities. When the Lotus is open, we manifest the virtues of the soul. When the Spiritual Triad is active, we manifest higher psychic powers similar to those which were manifested by the great disciples of the Lord.

The centers of fire in our constitution become active when the human soul begins to strive toward the Higher Worlds. Striving toward the highest is in itself a fiery breathing. It is this fire that mobilizes and synchronizes all centers to actualize our highest visions in all our daily relationships. Striving breathes in the fire of Space and breathes out that fire through all our thoughts, words, and actions, thus bringing into manifestation the fire of the Self.

Each actualization of higher visions is a manifestation of fire. When the fires of the physical body, the subtle body, and the fiery body are active, we see that the degree of assimilation of the body is the highest, the joy of the heart is the highest, and the understanding and creativity of the mind is the highest.

Fire is the foundation of health, magnetism, beauty, joy, understanding, and creativity. Those who are fiery will be able to radiate a pure sphere of light. Their auras will heal and uplift. Their auras will purify and strengthen others around them. Even the touch of a fiery person will make flowers give their best colors and fragrance.

The fire radiated from the palms or the eyes of a fiery person can disintegrate chemical formations in the body which are generally called "stones." In the future it will be possible to separate the particles of these stones and analyze them. Such an analysis will show the radiation of fire which caused disintegration. Similarly, tumors of various kinds will be dissipated by the fire of psychic energy.

Fiery persons leave traces of fire in their handwriting, on the articles they use, or on the art objects they create. In the near future, it may be possible to see or detect these fiery auras and measure their intensity and effect on human life. We are told that the Hierarchy has the instruments to measure these auras or emanations and also to see them.

As one advances toward the Fiery World, he understands more clearly that he is a warrior and that he must depend on the power of his spirit and face the dark ones alone. If his fight is unbearable, he can call on the Christ and ask His help. Of course, Christ will not come to your help if He knows that you can do it by yourself. In higher levels, the rule is that one must be left alone to battle, unless the enemy is far stronger.

Thus in the Higher Worlds, one is allowed to rejoice over his own victory achieved by his own merit, by his own fearlessness, and by his own fiery nature.

The Fiery World is surrounded by a belt of dark forces. They appear like monsters, but in reality the human Spark is far more powerful than they are, if he is fearless, daring, and striving. No enemy can stand on the Path of the spirit that feels the pull of the Cosmic Magnet. This idea must be part of our nature before we depart.

Humanity only advances through its thinking and consciousness. As long as its thinking does not change and its consciousness runs in the same grooves, it remains the same humanity. Thinking and consciousness change only if one expands his thinking toward the Higher Worlds. One must not stop in front of the grave and limit his consciousness to earthly thinking only. One must penetrate into the Subtle and Fiery Worlds. If these worlds are within the radius of his interest, he can believe that he will be able to change his thinking and his consciousness.

For ages the earthbound state of humanity — resulting in greed, possessions, and separatism — fought continuously, and now it is ready to exterminate itself. Many races have preceded us. They disappeared because they did not change their thinking and consciousness, and because their thoughts and consciousness were occupied with the interests of the earthly life.

Thinking about the Higher Worlds urges one toward perfection. Man tries to cultivate and develop his highest potentials to communicate with the Higher Worlds. Such an urge propels him toward perfection. Only in the process of perfection will one think on a planetary scale and dedicate his life to help humanity go forward toward the Higher Worlds. The Higher Worlds will never be found by our astronauts because they will always travel on the surface of the Universe. The Higher Worlds are found only by finding the higher dimensions... within oneself, and to find the higher dimensions, one must put himself on the Path of perfection, or on the Path of beauty.

As our thinking runs parallel to the lines of justice, unity, and synthesis, and as our consciousness expands toward Higher Worlds, our appearance changes in this world and in the Higher Worlds. We are told that a slave of malice, slander, cruelty, and injustice develops a dark face with a most horrible appearance. When disfiguration and degeneration reach a certain degree, he falls into an abyss until he realizes his situation and feels an urge to save himself. An abyss is a dark, fathomless sphere in Space. The love of the highest is everywhere if one awakens into that reality.

The Fiery World can be understood to a certain degree, if we observe and study the lives of fiery people who bring great improvement in the consciousness of humanity, our culture, and civilization. By observing their lives, we see how the fire inspires them to creative action, to sacrificial service, and to heroism. By observing their lives, we see how the fire strengthens them and charges them to progress in their field of service and transform life.

The Carriers of Fire prepare us for a greater life; they prepare us to live more abundantly in future incarnations; they prepare us to penetrate into the Fiery World and experience Cosmic beauty. By observing the lives of the Carriers of Fire, we can have certain ideas about their originating source.

Most of the Carriers of Fire have demonstrated joy, bliss, and ecstasy in the dark days of their lives.

Joy, bliss, and ecstasy are actually manifestations of fire. When one is charged with fire, he radiates joy. The greater the charge is, the deeper the joy. Bliss expresses itself when the fire overflows out of the soul. Ecstasy is a saturation of fiery joy. Enthusiasm is the fire of the highest centers which urges the man to strive to the highest achievement or to spread joy in greater fields.

Self-perfection runs on two roads. One can perfect himself and be the most dangerous criminal. Or he can perfect himself to be the greatest sacrificial person. The difference between these two is that one achieves self-perfection, to a certain degree, at the expense of others for his own selfish interests. The other achieves self-perfection on behalf of others, to help others transcend their level of beingness and consciousness. History shows that when people advance on selfish lines, they end in materialism, and massive destruction results. Only those who try to achieve self-perfection to help others be more successful, beautiful, and live in justice supply new life and new vision for humanity. Age after age their image turns into a source of inspiration.

Self-perfection is possible only if one devotes himself to a Great One who has already achieved a certain degree of perfection. In the Other Worlds, self-perfection proceeds in the right direction if one accepts the existence of the Hierarchy and learns how members of the Hierarchy achieved such perfection. One needs a vision toward which he can direct his steps. Against these fiery qualities there are dark forces and dark pollutions which make life miserable. For example, one of these forces is blasphemy, another is slander, and another is malice. Still others are indifference, denial, fanaticism and hypocrisy. These qualities of darkness are like contagious diseases which, when they spread, destroy nations, civilizations, and cultures.

Carriers of Fire must eventually annihilate such diseases of darkness to put the human race on the Path of self-perfection. It is the fire coming from the spirit that regenerates life and makes it a symphony of joy, bliss, and ecstasy.

Throughout the ages, the Carriers of Fire learned how to assimilate fire from Space through their lives of self-sacrifice.

One can learn the steps of assimilation of fire on a gradient scale, starting with joy. Joy assimilates fire. Admiration, ecstasy, and bliss are other signs of assimilation of fire. The purity of the vehicles is an important condition. Faith, solemnity, justice, and nobility are other ways to assimilate fire. All higher inspirations which lead to heroic actions and deeper creativity are signs of assimilation of fire.

From childhood we must learn how to teach our physical, emotional, and mental bodies to stand in the fire of the spirit and assimilate that fire. The assimilation of fire will build the path of entrance into the Fiery World.

From childhood we must also learn about the power of thought. Thoughts are very closely related to the Fiery World. Often we send thoughts to certain people, or we think about them. Certain thoughts that we have expand the consciousness, increase the light and energy, and create striving in others. Certain other thoughts lead people into corruption, disturbances, and problems. This is the reason why we must be careful of our thoughts and imagination; once a thought is released, no one can stop it.

It is possible to send great blessings in various expressions, as well as heavy poison, through our thoughts. Those who sublimate their thinking and keep it on a level of constructive frequency eventually learn how to use the fires of Space to create advancement and unfoldment. Each step toward right thinking is a step toward the Fiery World.

Before the entrance to the Fiery World, we meet the accumulated cloud of our disorderly and destructive thoughts. We have to disperse this cloud to penetrate into the Fiery World. Often people waste hundreds of years trying to disperse such a cloud. But if our creative thoughts are abundant, it is possible to disperse the cloud and win the right to penetrate the Fiery World.

As much as possible one must minimize his unworthy thoughts — those related purely to selfish pleasures, crimes, impositions, lust, greed, and revenge. All such thoughts can attack us violently whenever we attempt to cross the bridge toward the Fiery World.

There are other hindrances on the Path to the Fiery World. One of them is lower psychism — such as mediumistic activities, channeling, etc. It is very important to know that lower psychism prevents the ascension of the spirit toward the Higher Worlds because it attracts low-level forces and entities and creates many disorders in the physical, emotional, and mental mechanisms. One cannot travel on a path toward the Fiery World when he is associated with lower forces and entities. The physical, emotional, and mental mechanisms must be put on the path of refinement, integration, beauty, and health — if the human soul wants to enter into higher spheres.

If one cannot refine his mechanisms, he fails to reach his Cosmic destination. The situation in the vehicles reflects the degree of enlightenment of the human soul. If the human soul is in harmony with the Cosmic direction in all his actions, his bodies will reflect beauty, health, and strength.

Distorted vehicles, loaded with lower forces and entities, will not let the owner, the human soul, proceed on the fiery Path. Lower psychism keeps the soul entrapped in the network of low associations. Lower psychism is detrimental to the creative fires of man as it extinguishes the fires of the creative centers. The souls trapped in lower psychism cannot proceed on the fiery Path, and they return to the world with more distorted mechanisms.

Progress toward perfection is achieved through aspiration and striving. Lower psychism is a passive state. It is a state in which a channel or a medium operates. This passivity keeps the human soul static, and when he passes away, he does not have any urge to go forward.

Entities in lower levels keep their association with a lower psychic in the subtle levels, and they reincarnate with that person, resulting in one who has multiple personalities. Such people are in various stages of obsession. A confused man, a man who has no goal in life, is such a person. A man who never stands by his words and always changes his decisions is another. Still others are those who are slaves of various habits, as well as criminals and black magicians. Once a man is trapped by these low level associates, it will be very difficult for him to find the Path toward perfection, or even toward the improvement of his condition. This is why the great Sages advise us not to associate or deal with lower psychics.

Higher psychism is not obsession or possession but the result of unfoldment and perfection. It is a state wherein all the fires of the centers and senses are lit and are in synchronization with the creative fire of the Inner Core. Krishna, Buddha, Moses, Christ, and other Great Ones were higher psychics, and the Divine Fire within Them led multitudes toward the victory of the Spirit.[1]

Another hindrance on the Path to the Fiery World is fear. Fear extinguishes the fires of the centers and stops creativity, daring, and striving. Many plans and visions are lost because of fear. Fear darkens the aura and gives low entities an opportunity to exercise their evil will upon the human being.

Fear cuts the communication line between man and the fiery forces and paralyzes his creative actions. We are told that on the Path to the Fiery World one must cultivate absolute fearlessness.

The power of discrimination is another quality to cultivate on the Path to the Fiery World. This is the fire of Intuition which is expressed through the mind. We are told that one must cultivate this quality because in the Fiery World one sees things as they are in relation to the direction of the Cosmic Magnet. On the Path to the Fiery World, all that does not correspond to the direction of the Cosmic Magnet and does not express the glow of fire must be avoided or discarded. Discrimination is the ability to recognize the highest value and the direction of the Cosmic Magnet.

---

1. For further discussion of higher and lower psychism, see the following books: *Challenge for Discipleship*, Chapter 49; *The Psyche and Psychism*; *Breakthrough to Higher Psychism*.

As we go toward self-perfection and cultivate fiery qualities, the light of the spirit increasingly shines and reveals the value of all that exists around us.

The Fiery World cannot be entered unless one cultivates discrimination at a high level. Goal-fitness, harmlessness, and protection are closely related to the power of discrimination.

One needs to discriminate among his thoughts, words, and actions to place them in harmony with the highest values and with the direction of the Cosmic Magnet. In the meantime, one needs to use wisdom to be harmless and to protect those who are not yet within the light of discrimination.

In our life there are many occasions in which we feel the Guiding Hand of the Hierarchy. Those who register special impressions reaching them from the Hierarchy, and respond to them with their active aspiration, are building a thread of communication with the Fiery World. On many occasions the Hierarchy helps us pass through a dark night, but often we do not recognize the help that is given us. We are told that the Hierarchy feels great joy if we recognize the help because such a recognition draws us nearer to the Fiery World.

The Hierarchy operates within the vortex of fiery energies. It is possible to say that each member of the Hierarchy is a radioactive fire and a transmitter of the fiery rays from Space. Many human beings are subjectively guided and protected by Their assistance, but only the recognition of such assistance builds the bridge between man and the Fiery World.

46

Birthdays

In the Ageless Wisdom the process of incarnation, or taking birth, is a very important topic about which many volumes have been written. We are told that the incarnating soul follows certain laws under which it must act and come to birth. The soul, coming from subtle planes to denser planes, needs time to adapt itself, and it also is subject to certain karmic laws.

The soul can be found on astral, mental, or even on the higher planes, but it also can be found on the etheric plane. This level is where most suicides and accidental deaths stay for a while.

We are told that being born is not easier than dying. On the higher planes the soul enjoys great freedom and joy, as well as the company of advanced souls with whom it comes in contact telepathically. The soul can also freely visit places on the denser or more subtle planes as it wishes. But when the process of incarnation starts, it feels that all of its freedom and joy is being taken away and an increasing feeling of loneliness descends upon it. All of its realizations of beauty and harmony of the higher spheres is gradually lost in a mist until it is a helpless and totally imprisoned embryo in the womb.

The birth process and the process of death are much easier for those individuals who have continuity of consciousness because, for them, life is a continuum and they remain in constant contact with higher levels and with advanced souls.

The Ageless Wisdom teaches that the Cosmic Physical Plane is substantial. On whatever plane you are, that plane is real for you, just as the physical world is real to the inhabitants of this planet. All planes of the Cosmic Physical Plane are real to those who have continuity of consciousness, so nothing is lost or missed as their memory is perpetual.

A departed soul works in the subtle planes just as we work here, and they are more intensely involved with their labor than most of us are here.

In Buddhism, the law of incarnation is emphasized. At the same time, however, Lord Buddha urges us to achieve such perfection on earth that we are no longer forced to incarnate again. On the other hand, the Christian church denies the law of incarnation, but it also urges people "to be perfect as the Father is perfect" in order to escape from hell and be with the Father.

People have a deep desire to be on earth, either through living a long life or through repeated incarnation, so that they can continue their pleasures, adventures, or service. But if a person really sees the situation developing on this planet, he realizes that it will not be long before people will be eager to die and resist incarnation because this planet is not going to be a pleasant place to live.

You have a greater joy and a greater capacity to feel the bliss of the Universe in the subtle planes than in any experience you have here. Here, joy and happiness are totally limited to the five senses, but just imagine what you would experience with twenty-one senses in higher realms. Joy is amplified a thousand percent if a person is aware, if he is building the bridge between the physical and the higher planes.

As an undeveloped person dies, he loses consciousness; as he takes incarnation, he loses consciousness. He loses consciousness both times. The moment that he enters into greater light and frequency, the impact with the Higher Worlds really dulls his subtle senses. He cannot withstand the electricity or vibrations that hit him when he leaves his body. This is one way that the consciousness is dimmed. And when he is coming into incarnation, he enters into "fog," then "mud," then eventually into the "rocks" of his body. This is why we sometimes refer to our bodies as "rocks."

In both cases a person loses consciousness, except when he has developed continuity of consciousness. We must try to build this consciousness if we want to escape the tragedy of losing consciousness at birth and at death. This is one subject that great Masters and philosophers emphasize. So we need to know what continuity of consciousness is.

When you are asleep, you do not know what is happening during your sleep. When you enter into higher planes, you know nothing; you are unaware of everything. But if you build continuity of consciousness, you enter into sleep consciously. You slowly withdraw first from your physical body, then from your emotional body, and then from your mental body, and you go wherever you want as a free soul. This is why one of the characteristics of the soul is freedom. Freedom is understood as not being the slave of your bodies. But ninety-nine percent of humanity are slaves of their bodies. People do not know what happens after they sleep or after they die. In many religions when someone dies it is said, "He slept." Especially in the Old Testament, not a word is spoken about immortality. What can be found are statements like, "They slept."

It is like sleep, but actually it is death. You are dying because you do not have any kind of consciousness. Unless you have continuity of consciousness, or unless you have good karma and have performed great service, sometimes you awaken on the astral or mental planes just as if you were awakened by a nightmare. You see that you still exist but you do not know where you are or what you are. You are totally disoriented.

To overcome this kind of tragedy, you need to learn meditation. And your meditation must reach such a degree that you slowly build a bridge between the brain and the higher mind so that you learn to withdraw consciously from your body when you are sleeping. When you achieve this kind of wisdom and ability, then death will be so easy for you. At death, you will slowly withdraw from your body and enter into higher states of consciousness.

The birth process is a very important process that differs in its effects on the individual. If you are conscious, you are able to see the intricate and fascinating aspects of the process as it occurs.

According to the Ageless Wisdom, your Solar Angel, assisted by certain devas, works with a "space computer" to analyze what is recorded in your "diskettes" — your permanent atoms. Taking this information into account, and in accordance with great laws in Nature, It then determines exactly where, through whom, under what sign, in what country, and in what nationality or race you will be born. When the "computer" processes this information, a report is produced which is presented to you just before you reach the etheric plane.

After studying this report, generally you follow the suggestions that are given in it and choose your race, your country, your parents, and your date of birth accordingly. Your past karma, your affiliations, your duties, responsibilities, and future aspirations also play a great role in the choices you will make. Once you have made your choices, your consciousness begins to dim and the process of incarnation starts in dense matter.

Future visions can change past karma. Sincere and solid decisions for sacrificial service made in moments of historical crisis can have a great effect on your future life. If your karma is leading somewhere that you do not want to go because you see how much time would be wasted there, you can present a plan of sacrificial service for a race or a nation. When your intention is to live a heroic life, to help the progress of thousands, such a plan can be programmed into the computer, which will change the determinations of your past karma.

Great and advanced souls choose different lives full of dangers and suffering in order to accelerate their evolution and to pay more quickly debts accumulated in past karma.

The Solar Angel shows you a very detailed "film" of all that is going to happen to you; this film is produced by the information contained in the permanent atoms. Because you stand in the light of the Angel, you agree with the condition of life which is presented to you as your future incarnation. Three main factors are emphasized in the film:

1. The dangers waiting for you in the life to come
2. The opportunities which will be presented to you in that life
3. The karmic liabilities which must be paid and which will be very difficult — but not totally impossible — to avoid

1. Dangers. Dangers are those crucial or critical moments when two opposing forces created by you in past lives cross one another. If you use wisdom to handle these dangers, they will speed your evolution. They are huge waves upon which you surf to shore — or die beneath. In a dangerous moment it becomes possible to evoke a higher light within that is impossible to evoke at other times. Danger is a moment when you can act as a superhuman being, full of fearlessness and completely detached from any limiting conditions.

Your Solar Angel shows you these dangers, challenges you to handle them wisely, and even how to evoke the help of higher forces. We are told that giants are stepping on the summits of mountains. This is a symbolic way to express how initiates live in danger because in danger they can live closer to their ultimate goal.

2. Opportunities. Opportunities are those moments which sharpen the sword of your discrimination. To make you mature, Life presents you with choices. With right discrimination you can put the accumulated experiences and wisdom of past lives into use.

For example, a man's Solar Angel may show him three women he will encounter in his coming incarnation because of past karma. It then becomes his opportunity to choose one of them with whom to settle his karma, to have the children he wants, to create future ties that will further his future service and evolution, to cooperate with in the fulfillment of great visions, and to face his shortcomings and failures and close his account with her. Other opportunities are shown to choose various jobs in various fields of endeavor.

It is a person's task to make the right choices. This is not easy because, as a person incarnates, his vision and memory of what he was shown before birth slowly fade away, and it is his task to instinctively or intuitively choose the right marriage partner, the right job, the right place, and the right position.

For example, you may be given the opportunity to become the head of a religious order, or you could be the head of a scientific institution. If you choose the one that will be more helpful to your future incarnations and which accumulates the benefits of your past services, then you have chosen the right one.

When your Solar Angel shows you the possible opportunities, these impressions fade away and you act as if you were in darkness. There are three factors, however, which will help you make the right choices and will put you in contact with the visions of opportunity that were given to you by your Solar Angel:

a. moments of danger
b. sacrificial labor
c. meditation

It may be that you are still unable to see your vision clearly, but you will instinctively act correctly because these three factors build a communication line between your mind and the treasury where the vision has been stored.

Opportunities exercise your will and your freedom to choose.

3. Karmic liabilities. It is possible to overcome dangers or karmic liabilities and escape them. For example, your Solar Angel might show you that while traveling on the freeway there is a possibility that a drunken man will hit your car. Because of something you did in the past, the computer is programmed to seek payment from you in this form. So how can you escape this fate?

Prayers, invocations, and meditations were given to humanity for this reason. If you pray, fast, read good books, and do good things for other people, your karma will spare you and you will no longer be in danger when the predestined time comes.

M.M., speaking through His books, says that we do not know how many times daily we escape danger and we do not show gratitude to the Lord. If you take time to consider carefully those dangers from which you have been miraculously saved, you will find crucial information. For example, if you are driving and suddenly somebody cuts in front of you, you may take little notice of it. A few minutes later you turn on the rock 'n' roll and start shouting, drinking, and eating as if nothing had happened. You failed to observe that a tremendous danger passed — and you did not even express gratitude.

These are the dangers and opportunities with which you will be presented. But it is almost impossible to run away from karmic liabilities. Your Solar Angel will show, for example, that you are going to be shot and that you should be prepared. Many great leaders feel one or two hours beforehand that they are going to be shot, or that they are going to have a heart attack and pass away; or their Solar Angel reminds them in dreams. I remember very clearly when this happened to Abdullah, the King of Jordan, who was a very beautiful man. Each Friday he used to receive teachers and other people who did good works in his country. He would bless them and talk to them for half an hour or so, so that he could keep in touch with them. One day he said to the audience in general, "I will not be here with you much longer. I don't know why, but I am feeling that today, tomorrow, or the next day I will die." The next week, on his way to the mosque in Jerusalem, he was shot and killed. He knew.

Some leaders and people in higher positions feel these things; sometimes if they do not, their Solar Angel reminds them through a vision, through an accident, or through a dream. Suppose that seventy years ago when you were about to be born your Solar Angel showed you that a bridge was going to fall on you and kill you. You saw the accident; as you were going across a bridge, it fell. But during incarnation you forgot this. Let us say that you are now passing through a certain street when you see a fallen bridge. Suddenly the image of that bridge brings to mind the image you were shown seventy years ago. Something surfaces and you wonder about the complexity of your feelings. You feel shocked and you feel that something complex is going to happen. Your Solar Angel, your Guardian Angel or Christ, whatever you like to call Him, has given you a reminder through seeing this bridge that you are going to die this way, but perhaps you cannot take the hint because you were drinking that day, or angry, or for some reason you were in an unimpressionable state and were unable to interpret the message from higher realms. But your Angel will continue to try again in different ways to warn you.

This is sometimes called "symbolic reading." Symbolic reading is when you see events around you and you understand their significance. You wonder why you saw something just at the time you did, and it reminds you of something deeper. Symbolic reading is a very important sense to develop. It is sometimes called the "sense of synthesis."

Life is organized in such a way that there are no individuals; you do not have an individual life. The computer plays with all of us to create meanings and significances, phrases, sentences, and paragraphs. If you start reading Life as a single book which has many paragraphs and sentences, you will be clever enough to understand what is happening in the world through the events that are taking place in it.

This describes the process of incarnation as it happens legitimately. But there are persons who sneak into incarnation illegitimately. People also sneak into the Subtle Worlds for various reasons.

One reason for sneaking into incarnation is that these "sneakers" live close to the earth in the etheric or lower astral planes, and they try to incarnate at any opportunity. Some of them are earth-bound souls whose possessions bind them to earth. Or they can be criminals whose crimes will not allow them to go to the higher regions. "Victims" of accidents or war, those who die sudden deaths, wait in the etheric or astral planes until they incarnate or pass on to higher planes. Sneakers are those who do not obey the law, and they try to come in contact with the physical world through obsession, possession, or illegal incarnation.

When a woman becomes pregnant from rape or when she uses alcohol or drugs, a gate is opened to such people which gives them a chance to sneak in and incarnate. Generally, those who sneak in have no chance to see what awaits them in the coming incarnation; they follow only the current which has accumulated from the past. Because such currents are usually composed of the tides of revenge, hate, fear, greed, and murder, they follow the same course as far as it takes them.

This is why we are told that marriage is sacred and that conception must take place only under conditions of pure love and with an elevated consciousness. Only under such conditions can we bring in advanced sparks from higher realms who are legally entitled to incarnate.

Sneaking ones generally create trouble in their homes, living in tension with their parents. Most of the time they do not have close ties with their parents or other relatives. Sooner or later, life catches these outlaws and brings them to law and order.

Some people think that when you are born, you are totally born. But a crucial point is that when you take birth, you are only taking physical birth. Before your physical body is built, your etheric body is woven by devas and elementals. Hundreds of devas prepare your etheric body according to the recordings that you have in your permanent atoms. Permanent atoms are etheric genes; they are like recorders or diskettes. Whatever you "type" on your computer is recorded on the diskettes. The way you lived, spoke, thought, and related to others are all forms of typing which go onto your diskette. When the time comes for you to incarnate, the time has come to print what is recorded on the diskette. You push the buttons and whatever you have recorded comes out of the printer. You are exactly printed from whatever is recorded in your diskette.

The page that comes out of the printer is you; your mother is the "printer." For nine months your body was being formatted in the printer. The printer worked very hard to bring you into life within the line of the Law of Reincarnation. Everything that was printed on the paper — your body, your character, style, inclinations, and everything else that you have — is really an expression of the recording taken from the diskette. It is important to be very careful of what you type on the diskette so that when you see the printed results you do not wonder what happened, feel shame, or scream that you got something that you did not want. But you typed it yourself! This is why religions say that whatever you sow, you will reap.

You are born first on the physical plane. Current astrology is ninety-nine percent occupied with the occasion when a person is born physically. But you have not been born yet emotionally because your emotional body takes maybe another sixty years to develop after you are physically born, and you may never have a mental body at all — a condition which affects ninety percent of each generation. People have a physical body with a brain, and they may have an emotional body, but this does not mean that they have a mental body. Their brain operates like a machine which receives impressions from others and then reacts to these impressions. In our general speech we call this "thinking," but in reality it has little to do with real thinking because there is no mental body.

The mental body is a reality which can be seen. When it is formed, there is a blue vibration mixed with a lemon yellow vibration around the head and shoulders. When the spiritual body is formed, there is a green-yellow vibration. When the higher bodies are formed, the person stands in pure white light with different colors blending and dancing.

These bodies are real, but modern universities, governments, and scientists occupy themselves with creating ammunition and weapons to kill people instead of investigating these realities. These things do not matter to them now, but they will suffer very much in coming generations from their neglect.

When you are physically born, you have only physical plane consciousness. Your consciousness rises from the physical plane and focuses in the astral plane when your astral body is formed. You can tell that the astral body is formed when you can consciously withdraw from your physical body and be anywhere you want on the astral plane, just as consciously as you can on the physical plane.

This is how great disciples sometimes travel and appear to their students. They are recognized because the astral body is an exact replica of the physical body. An astrological chart prepared for an advanced person with an astral body is useless. You would have to know exactly where, when, and under what conditions the person was born astrally for the chart to be accurate. This is beyond current knowledge and experience, but in the near future clairvoyants and intuitives will be able to tell a person when his consciousness moved from the physical plane to the astral plane.

This move can be recorded and watched through the etheric centers. If a person is centered in the base of spine, sex, and lower solar plexus centers, he is born only physically. No matter what he does, it is mechanical and he cheats people. But when his center rises to the higher solar plexus center, he is born astrally. A person is mentally born when the fire starts working in his throat and ajna centers. His intuitional body is born when his heart center is completely unfolded, and his atmic body is born when the thousand-petaled lotus radiates like a rainbow.

This Teaching was given in secret Ashrams by the Great Ones, but the general public was not given this Teaching because it would not have made sense to most of those who lived two or three thousand years ago. When we try to use the Teaching that was given to the general public two or three thousand years ago and say that it is "the only way to fly," we are rejecting our own expansion of consciousness. This is what has happened to some religious people. As their answer to everything, they say, "It is written." Well, it was written — but what about all that was not written? Suppose I wrote a note to you which said, "Close the door and go." And then, when no one is around, I come and whisper in your ear, "When you close the door and go, go to the party and we will all be there." This part was not written, but it is more important than the written part, if you have ears to listen.

We must know one thing: Our subtle bodies can only be built during physical incarnation and not while we are in the higher planes. We must work very hard while we are here to build and purify our astral, or emotional body, and then to build our mental body through meditation, education, experience, discovery, and service. We must become somebody physically, emotionally, and mentally. If we succeed, we will already have twenty, fifty, or ninety percent of our bodies built when we take our next incarnation. As these bodies are built, continuity of consciousness is developed because recordings are being made simultaneously in all these three bodies which have tremendous connections to the physical brain. No experience is lost on any plane because the computer records everything. You are then born with whatever is recorded as the material of all these bodies. But the important point is first to build these bodies.

There is confusion in people's minds between emotions, feelings, and the astral body. Emotions can be strictly nervous actions, reactions, and responses — *and nothing else*. If I shout at you and you jump up and knock me down, you call it an emotional reaction, but it is just a mechanical reaction.

Feelings, emotions, and the astral body are all different. If you have a building that needs a wiring system and all the materials are there but they are just lying on the floor in a heap, the wiring system is not yet installed. You may have the materials, but your astral body, your network, is not built. When you put all the components together, it is entirely different from the heap of material.

Suppose there were fifty different words which corresponded to different feelings. You can write a word, but not have a complete sentence. As you put a few words together, you make a sentence; so, by putting together a few feelings you make an emotion. It is possible to put words together which have no real meaning. But if you put words together in such a way that they create meaning, then you have feelings, emotions, and an emotional body.

Nothing in the Universe is given to you for free. You take it by your own merit and labor. Everything that you have is given to you because of your own demand, labor, sacrifice, and striving. Do not believe that suddenly and miraculously you are going to become a genius. You will not; you have to work for it, just as you work for success in any worldly enterprise. If you want to be a lawyer, you are not going to become one effortlessly and overnight. Even if you have the highest intellect, you must go through the process.

In *The Science of Meditation*[1] I wrote that you cannot know what you are absolutely. I do not believe that it is possible to "know thyself." Who is going to know what? When you are lost completely in the

---

1. *The Science of Meditation*, by Torkom Saraydarian.

physical body, how can you know the Self? **You can only know what you are not.** If you find out exactly what you are not, there is the possibility that you will have some idea of what you are. It is like an algebraic equation with an unknown factor. **You do not know the unknown;** instead, you work with the known factors and proceed to work out the solution of the unknown — which is the Self.

First of all, ask, "Is this body really me?" For eighty years you believe that your body is you, but then suddenly it occurs to you that if you do not want your body to move, it does not — and that it stops when you tell it to. If you tell it to sit down, it obeys you. So it becomes clear that there must be something besides the body which is directing it. What is it? You do not know yet. Well, you realize that you have emotions, but you see that you also have the power to change them and to create their opposites. It becomes clear that if the emotions were the Self, then the emotions would not be obedient to you. But they are, and so you are something beyond emotions. Then there is the thinking process. You start thinking, hallucinating, visualizing, and imagining. And then you discover that you can control these things, that you can stop and start or modify your thoughts. Who is stopping your thoughts? You do not know, but you realize that there is something in you which is higher than your mind. In this manner you can start with what you are not... to try and discover what it is that you are.

Some people dwell on karma. Karma is so jumbled that only the universal computer can solve karmic problems. Our computers quickly do many things that our minds cannot do at the same level. If you begin solving an astronomical calculation by hand, you will sit for six months on a single problem that a computer could do in three minutes. And the universal computer is infinitely smarter and more complex than our earthly computers. It knows where you are going to be born, what your body will be like, and which parents you are going to have. It knows what sicknesses you are going to have because you gave them to someone else in the past. You almost cannot escape these kinds of karmic liabilities.

Doctors sometimes induce birth, but the natural ways are best. Nature is the Mother; Nature knows more than any doctor or professor. So it is best to understand what Nature is and follow Her laws and rules. Unnatural methods create "zombies" — stupid and confused people — in the world. Teen-agers are having babies, but it is not healthy or good because their bodies are not ready and they are not prepared in other ways to meet the responsibilities. They are going to make the baby suffer because a baby is not important to them.

Birthday Review

1. On birthdays, we can meditate for a few hours to receive the message of our birthday. Which is the most essential work we must do, and what is the most essential direction we must take?
2. On birthdays, we can rededicate ourselves to our Teacher, to the Teaching, and to its guidance.
3. On birthdays, we can rededicate ourselves to the labor carried on in the name of Beauty, Goodness, Righteousness, Joy, and Freedom.
4. On birthdays, we can rededicate ourselves to focus on the purpose of our life.
5. We can make firmer decisions to stay away from hatred, jealousy, and revenge.
6. On the day of our birthday, we must offer our hearts and say, "I forgive that girl, that man, that person; and God, please bless them. I don't want anything wrong now with the start of my day." Forgiveness deletes certain unwanted documents from your computer so that you do not carry messy transactions of the past with you into your new day. Express gratitude to those who have loved you; forgive those who sometimes bugged you so badly that they tested your alertness and consciousness. These people sometimes need more gratitude than others.
7. We need to ask ourselves what we are going to do and then make a decision in the light of the Most High. Pray, meditate, and then ask what you should do. Sometimes you are given a clear impression of what you need to do, and you can start right away. At other times you get the impression that nobody is going to tell you what to do, and that it is your business to decide and find out on your own. Ask your Soul, "What am I going to do during this new year?" Then make projects and plans for the year.

This is such an important thing to do on your birthday. If you follow these suggestions for a few years, you will see what a beautiful, clear life you will have. You will have to work to attain this because a beautiful life is one which is lived in self-forgetfulness, harmlessness, and right speech.

8. On the night of your birthday, light a candle and let it burn all night. Try to understand the wisdom in the candle as it burns. This is a practice that was followed in monasteries and it is a

tradition that we followed in my family. When I was a small child, I would wake up during the night of my birthday and see the beautiful candlelight and watch the shadows playing over everything. I asked my father to tell me what it meant, but he said, "Well, watch what happens when the candle is lit." I thought about it as I watched the candle and said, "There is light, and also, the candle becomes smaller and smaller as it burns." "That's just what I wanted you to see!" he replied. "The candle is the symbol of a life that is dedicated to spreading light, beauty, goodness, truth, and freedom — at the expense of yourself...."

The candle symbolizes how you will use everything you have to help others. Sometimes you run out of energy and money, but you keep going and spread the light at your own expense. You see a man who has fallen in the mud; you will be covered with mud, but you pull him out — and when he is rescued, he does not even thank you. On the contrary, he steals your wallet.

Burn a candle for your children until morning. Let them learn the meaning of the candle instead of learning how to smoke, use drugs, steal, read pornography, or indulge in all the harmful practices that are so widespread now. Teach your children to watch the candle because the candle is a reflection of their soul. As they watch it, their soul memory starts to awaken in their waking consciousness. This is the reason why we love candles.

I once read how some colorful little paper stickers in different shapes that children are given to paste on their bodies are being used by criminals to give them drugs. The children are told, "Just wet it and stick it on your face or arms," and as they lick the stickers, they ingest the drug. Such evil things are happening in our schools.

Who are the distributors, and where are the fathers and mothers of the victims? If parents were looking after their children, this nightmare could not happen. How can we protect our children? An innocent child says, "Look at these nice stickers," pastes them on his face for fun, and becomes insane. He is robbed of his mind, and later he is going to become a drug addict. Do you see what is happening in the world?

We are going to stay a thousand times more awake than those who are trying to destroy our children for profit and not tolerate such outrageous evil in our society. But it starts from the beginning when you teach your children to stand in light, love, and logic and teach them to be careful about what is happening. If you do this, then you will not have as many difficulties to worry about later.

9. The next thing to do for your birthday is to have a little seclusion. Take a few hours, a whole day, a week or even a month, if you can, and escape. Go to a cabin in the mountains, or somewhere else peaceful, and start thinking about yourself. "I am really stupid and obnoxious, you know? But I also have some very good qualities. I have made a lot of good plans, but also some that are bad for the future. How am I going to sort out this mess?" Begin to correct yourself and make plans for what you are going to do.

10. The next thing is to have a party. Some people think that birthday parties are an expression of vanity, but they are not. Great Masters have birthday parties. Christ had a birthday party attended by three kings. The New Testament did not write about it, but it was a great party. If three kings come to my birthday, what else could I want? They brought jewels, incense, and precious stones which Jesus used. His mother did not have to worry about him financially because the three kings provided everything.

The esoteric, deeper meaning is that at the time of your birthday you are susceptible and very sensitive to new impressions and inspirations. This is the secret. When you have loving friends around you who are in joy, gratitude, love, compassion and ecstasy, all of them together build an electromagnetic sphere around you through which you receive higher inspirations. Without your friends, you cannot do as much. That is why you should work to be worthy of friends who will come and express their love and good thoughts. When a good atmosphere is created, the person who is having the birthday attracts tremendous energy into the field of this magnetic tension.

It is therefore important for everyone to celebrate his birthday. Invite a few friends, prepare nice food, and be happy together. Celebrate, and slowly become worthy of and responsive to their well-being. Pray for them, bless them, love them more and more, and work for their well-being. But if you don't have friends, they do not evoke the highest sensitivity from you. They do not awaken your soul. God created societies for this reason. People who live responsibly in societies can uplift those societies and themselves.

11. On your birthday it is good to include some solitary time for sincere thoughts of gratitude. Make a list of those to whom you are grateful. Start with your parents. If they are dead, send them thoughts of deep gratitude; if they are alone, send

them a card letting them know how grateful you are for all their service, trouble, and care.

Then send gratitude to all of your Teachers, starting with kindergarten up to the present, and express deep gratitude to them. Remember to send gratitude to friends and acquaintances who helped you, especially during critical times. You can even send gratitude to people who, though they hurt you badly, taught you a great lesson or kept you alert and awake and thus protected you from falling into future mistakes.

It is wonderful to do this on your birthday to renew the network of memories and let your love and gratitude flow through the network.

12. It is also very important on the day of your birthday to have a few hours to think about your death. How are you going to shape your life in such a way that the moment you are dying will be a moment of joy in which you will have a deep feeling of accomplishment, knowing that you did everything possible to uplift and serve people? At the time of your death, all of your life-films will be shown to you. Live in such a way that you enjoy viewing your past film and enter into the Higher Worlds in joy and gratitude with a vision for a future great service and creativity.

People are equal to what they give. There are eight categories of people. When these people have birthdays, a great deal is revealed by those around them. The following are the categories:

1. Teacher
2. Father
3. Mother
4. Child
5. Co-worker
6. Sister/brother
7. Husband/wife
8. Friends

The attitude of these people toward each other is a great test — for those who come to celebrate and for those who are having the birthday.

The birthday of a person is the moment of contact for which he was born. Such a contact brings in energy at that time. After the birthday, he may express a new spirit of dedication to his labor.

If you are a soul dedicated to the Common Good of Humanity, at the time of your birthday you receive a shock from the One Who occasionally examines your "image" in the caves of the Himalayas. Such a shock can be very beneficial if it is received in joy and love and readiness to respond to it.

On your birthday, your Solar Angel blesses you and wishes that you walk on the Path of Beauty and Righteousness. On your birthday, the Life behind your birth sign and the Life of your rising sign send a call to you — if you are sensitive enough to receive the call. This call is heard by you if you feel an urge to go toward the ideals that your signs suggest.

On your birthday, there is a subjective synchronization between your karma and the configuration of the planets and your aspirations. And on this day a shock passes through your chakras, glands, and organs which creates a temporary or a lasting alignment among them.

On your birthday, a chance is given to you to have a certain expansion of consciousness. Such an expansion may lead you to take an initiation when you enter your rising sign. This is why some Teachers suggest that on your birthday you go through a tense striving and aspiration to make a conscious breakthrough which may prepare you to be ready for certain responsibilities and initiations. Then the opportunity to rededicate your life to a greater labor is opened to you.

On your birthday, it is important to try to make a contact with your Inner Guide, the Teacher, and the Hierarchy. Those who celebrate their birthdays spiritually and in solemnity prepare the path for higher evolution.

When you celebrate your birthday, the hearts of those who love you dearly and truly emanate a substance which creates a field of intense magnetism. An advanced man who is celebrating his birthday uses this substance as a magnet to draw energies from Higher Realms, shares them with his friends, and creates in them group consciousness.

Further, the leader can use provided energy to fight against destructive currents projected toward him. Cards, letters, and other hand-written notes sent to beloved ones carry great amounts of psychic energy to them. This psychic energy strengthens them, encourages them to take life more seriously, and helps them live a more beautiful life.

When the celebrant is a leader, he can use such energies in his work to provide greater service for co-workers.

What are the steps which one must take, especially on his birthday?

1. He must try to meditate and develop humility.
2. He must try to be worthy of the life which has been given to him.

3. He must try to send more love and blessings to those who have demonstrated love to him.
4. He must build a subjective line of communication, especially with those who demonstrate dedication and love, and consider accepting them as future co-workers in the labor for humanity.
5. He must build closer relationships with those who demonstrate sacrificial dedication and trust and promote them in the path of friendship.

We are told that friendship carried on for many lives with many co-workers eventually becomes a magnet which is used for higher services and labor.

It is very interesting to note that people welcome the newborn baby and his birthday with various gifts. This is very significant. Every newcomer must be greeted and welcomed by meeting his present and future needs. At the time of the birth of Jesus, three Great Ones brought very precious gifts to Him. This was a beautiful affirmation by the Hierarchy that a Great One was born, and it was also a great confirmation to His mother that the boy was a very important leader in the world. Here we see the depth of gift offering. You recognize the value of the one who is born and you prove your degree of devotion and affection by the value of your gift.

When Jesus was thirty-three years old, a prostitute brought Him a very expensive bottle of perfumed oil, knelt in front of Him and poured the oil on His feet and wiped it with her hair. Christ appreciated her so deeply that he took her into the innermost circle of His disciples, and she became one of the leaders of the Teaching of Christ. Look what happened. She demonstrated her intense aspiration and love to her Teacher by giving Him the most precious oil, and it was this offering that released her soul to spiritual realms.

Days later a third thing was offered to Him. When He was on the cross and asking in a loud voice for water, a Roman soldier offered Him a sponge full of vinegar.

Christ was very interested in offerings and gifts. One day He and a few of His disciples were secretly watching how people were making offerings in the Temple. A rich man openly displayed to everyone how much money he was putting in the offering pot. Then a poor lady who had no money came. She approached the box and, hesitating lest someone see her small offering, she put a dime into the box and went into the Temple. Christ whispered to His disciples, "Who do you think was the one who gave the most: the rich man or the poor widow?" The disciples replied, "The rich man, of course, since he put a lot of money in the box and the woman only put in a coin." "You are wrong," said Christ. "The poor woman offered the most because the rich man made his contribution out of his surplus while she, from her heart, placed all the means of living she had into the box."[2]

I remember once when I was in a mountain monastery, the ten of us who were students had a meeting about what we should give to our Teacher on his birthday. We did not have any money, but I did have two rings. The others had silver chains around their wrists and necks. Someone had an old Russian watch that was given to him by his mother. During the meeting we decided to go to a village and sell the objects we had to a goldsmith and ask him to make a silver eagle with a chain. We traveled to a far village where there was a goldsmith who knew our Teacher. When he heard our story, he said, with tears in his eyes, "All that you brought will barely cover my labor and materials, but I will do my best to make you happy for your gratitude to your Teacher." We left all our treasures and returned to the monastery.

One week before the birthday, one of us traveled to pick up the gift, but the man could not finish it and told the boy that he would have it ready on Friday afternoon — the day of the birthday. We were going to celebrate at eight o'clock that evening, so we thought we would have the gift in time. But on Thursday, a heavy snow fell. After a conference, I was appointed to go at noon and return with the gift — no matter what. When I arrived at the shop, the man was still working; when he finished, it was five thirty, the sun was setting, and I was impatient to reach the monastery.

On the trip back, I had a very difficult time in the mountains because it began to snow again. At eight o'clock, the time we all ate dinner and the celebration was to start, I knocked at the gate. One of my friends who was waiting for me in the freezing cold helped me down from the horse and took charge of it while I rushed to the hall where everybody was wondering where I was. I was covered with snow, but my friends forced me to go and give the gift to the Teacher.

I kissed his hand and offered the gift. Before looking at the gift he said, "I was so worried about you. Now I know where you were. This gift is so precious because you risked your life to bring it to me," and he hugged me for a few minutes, wetting his clothes from the snow on my coat. This was one of the happiest days of my life. Then he wanted to know all the details of how we planned everything and carried it out. One of my friends told him all we had done. He kissed all of us on the forehead and said, "This silver bird with blue eyes

---

2. Luke 21: 3-4

will always be around my neck and my blessings are within this gift."
That night we did not sleep. We went to each other's beds to tell
unending stories about how we had accomplished the giving of that
gift.

Your offerings show how deep your dedication is to the Teaching
and to the Teacher. I have received some strange gifts for my birthdays.
One was from a very pretty girl who came close to me and said, "You
know what my gift is to you?" "What?" I asked. "I fasted for four
days without a drop of water and prayed for you." I was not able to
hold my tears.

Another very precious gift was from a fourteen-year-old girl who
learned one of my compositions on the flute and played it for me as a
surprise. There was a gift from a boy who went to the old country
where my parents were living. He visited them and brought my
mother's ring to me on my birthday.

Another friend of mine went to my old monastery and brought a
lock of my Teacher's hair to me for my birthday. There was also an
old woman who came to my birthday party and brought me one of my
childhood teeth. My son went to the old country and brought back a
medallion I had won in sports.

One of my students typed a large compilation from M.M. and
presented it to me on my birthday. Once my mother sent me a
half-finished sock that I had knitted in my childhood.

But my most thrilling gift was one I received when I was nine
years old. It was night. We had eaten dinner and the cake, and I had
received the presents from my sisters, which were mostly clothing,
when Mother turned to Father and said, "Take him to the garden for
a while." My father said, "Okay. Come, let's go." I thought they were
preparing a surprise in the room for my return. Daddy took my hand
and began to walk toward the stable. After a few steps, with great joy
I began to cry. "Why are you crying?" my father asked. "I know I
have a horse." "What if it is not a horse?" "I even know exactly which
horse it is," I said. My father opened the door of the stable, and there,
in the light of an old gas lantern, I saw the shining body of a black
horse.

I jumped up and hugged my father around the neck and felt so
much love for him. Then, turning to the horse, I said, "Your name is
Blacky." The horse shook his mane and whinnied. How I wanted to
ride! Father said, "Not at night; wait until morning. The horse is tired
and needs rest." I examined and touched almost every part of the
horse. He was so gorgeous that I kissed him. Upon returning, I did
not go to the room where my mother and sisters were singing. Instead,

I went to my bedroom and tried hard to sleep deeply in order to be with my horse. All that night I rode my horse in my dreams. He was magnificent.

People are wise to celebrate birthdays. It is often in birthdays that you see the true motive of your friends and co- workers. You learn who are those who love you, who are those who will sacrifice for you. You see those who use the occasion to show off, and you see those who have a clear and pure love and appreciation for you.

Through your birthday you can create deeper concern and feelings within your friends, such as feelings of respect, appreciation, gratitude, sacrifice, and recognition of the values you have. It is good to make your friends have such feelings because it will make them more sensitive to their own values and to the values of others. All too often such precious feelings are dormant within us; they are just waiting for an opportunity to awaken and be activated.

The popular wisdom says that one must not give because he is told to give. One must not give because he has an interest in giving. But one must give if he thinks his gift will represent his love and devotion. Givingness opens his heart and he receives more than he gave.

If the recipient is a parent, a teacher or a leader, he must be indifferent to the quantity or quality of the gift but very sensitive to the state of consciousness in which the gift was given.

A leader must give such a guidance, even if people can use it against him, slandering him for self-interest. Of course, gifts have been used also for selfish purposes. For thousands of years gifts were used

1. For bribery
2. To gain confidence and then stick a knife in the back
3. To cover mistakes and errors
4. To ask for forgiveness
5. As an attraction or an invitation for sex

In ancient times, gifts were called sacrifices. Sacrifices had three qualities:

1. *Tamasic* — with dark motive
2. *Rajasic* — with mixed motive
3. *Sattvic* — with enlightened motive

Tamasic sacrifices were given in self-interest and to deceive others. Rajasic sacrifices were given for mutual benefit. Sattvic sacrifices were given as a result of devotion, dedication, admiration, and gratitude. In *The Bhagavad Gita* we read:

"Sattvic sacrifices are those which are done without expectation, as enjoined by ordinances, with a firm faith that sacrifice is a duty.

"Rajasic sacrifices are those which are done with expectation, for the sake of their fruits, and for self- glorification.

"Tamasic sacrifices are those which are done against sacred law, without faith, sacred hymns or due offerings."[3]

In the *Gita* we also read:

"The offering which is rendered to one who does nothing in return, rendered in a sense of duty, and in right place, right time and to the worthy person, such an offering is sattvic.

"But the offering which is made with the hope of return, or with expectation of future reward, or done unwillingly, is a rajasic offering.

"The offering that is done at a wrong place, at a wrong time to an unworthy person, with disrespect and with contempt, is a tamasic offering."[4]

---

3. *The Bhagavad Gita*, 17:11-13, translated by Torkom Saraydarian.
4. *Ibid.*, 17:20-22

47

The Signs of the Fiery World

Those who are in contact with the Fiery World transmit a great amount of fire into their surroundings. This fire is used in many ways, such as:

1. To purify the space where the person lives.
2. To create new orientations in people who try to regenerate their lives and direct their steps toward higher values.
3. To create purification in the Teaching. Those corruptions that entered into the Teaching to distort it and to create confusion slowly crack and vanish under the pressure of the transmuted fire.
4. To create a shield or a protective fiery field which repels psychic attacks and destroys the sendings of dark forces.
5. To create a magnetic field to facilitate the reception of higher impressions coming from the Fiery World.
6. To mobilize the energies of goodwill for the Common Good.
7. To clarify the foundations of the Teaching and inspire people to absorb and live according to the Teaching.

The Carriers of Fire are potent sources of inspiration, enthusiasm, and creativity. Wherever they go, they carry the fire of the spirit with them.

Groups and nations can be regenerated only through fire and through the Carriers of Fire. True standards and true values can only be revealed through fire. In the presence of the Carriers of Fire, one clearly sees the real values, the real principles, and the most essential fundamentals — as if in darkness a light is projected on one's path. In the presence of a fiery consciousness, one sits silently because he feels that all his questions have been dissolved and his confusion has disappeared.

Pilgrimages were established long ago so that people could go and search for those who had a fiery consciousness, or who were Carriers of Fire. Pilgrimages to the homes and sanctuaries of Great Ones was a duty and a privilege in order to come in contact with the field of their fiery energies and establish a new orientation and purification within oneself.

Pilgrimages were not easy. People used to pass through many difficulties to test their aspiration, decision, willpower, and intention to reach their destination. Thus, on the way of the pilgrimage, transmutation was already in operation because the heart of the pilgrim was already in contact with the Fiery Center.

Certain Sanctuaries and Ashrams carry a great amount of fire. Due to our modern life, people no longer visit such places before they go to their daily work. The Ancients visited Their Sanctuaries every morning and every time they had a crisis. They charged their souls, which enabled them to take the right action. At present we are dependent upon our psychologists and lawyers. No one can replace the wisdom or the advice that one receives when he opens his heart in prayer in the fiery Sanctuary. Artificial directions cannot replace the directions of the heart received from the Fiery World.

As a child I lived in a small town where many creative and influential people lived. There was an ancient Sanctuary. Every morning it was almost full. The dignitaries of the village went there, entered silently, lit a candle, and meditated or prayed for fifteen to twenty minutes. There was no crime in that village. The police were occupied all day with gardening and other domestic duties. The judge wrote novels.

It is not places of gambling and prostitution or nightclubs that can transform a nation, but Sanctuaries and Ashrams that are charged by the fire of the Higher Worlds. Once a man or a nation loses the thread of the Fiery World, the degeneration of the spirit takes place and insanity develops at the expense of the spirit.

Fiery spirits do not run after comfort or prosperity in the material sense. Rather, they strive toward perfection and choose or create those conditions which will help their unfoldment, keep them in right direction and in contact with the Fiery World, and help them live by the spiritual standards of their Souls. Fiery souls know very well that comfort does not exist in the Universe, but that joy accumulates in their hearts as they overcome the waves of darkness one by one, and thus develop greater power to radiate the beauty they have in their essence. Fiery spirits choose labor and battle rather than comfort and pleasure. They are like soldiers who are always on duty against the forces of degeneration or chaos. Their joy is the seat of labor and battle.

When people would come to study in advanced esoteric monasteries they were asked, "What are you searching for?" Sometimes the answer was, "Peace, serenity, rest." Pointing to the door of the monastery, the leader used to say, "Outside that door it is possible to find the things you wish, but not here."

All real schools of spiritual development are centers of heavy labor, tension, crisis, study, discipline, and joy. When the schools, colleges, and universities turn into centers of training so that students are prepared to reach for prosperity, success, pleasure, and luxury at the expense of others, as well as follow selfish interests, the nation loses its pillars and it collapses.

Our life is an opportunity to increase the fire in the world: the fire of transmutation, transformation, and transfiguration. All other directions will end with great failures. This is why incessant watchfulness is demanded of those who have a spark of fire in their souls from the ocean of the Fiery World. The greatest advice given to those who are preparing themselves for the Fiery World is: *"Pray and be watchful."*

Prayer is a continuous living in the presence of the Cosmic Heart. Watchfulness is the command not to let your body, emotions, and thoughts do something that disturbs the Fiery World or is contrary to the vision you have in your soul for the Fiery World. In addition, watchfulness is the following:

1. Steady obedience to the voice of your conscience
2. The ability to remember all the covenants of the Fiery World
3. The ability to catch the minutest discord in your life
4. The ability to keep your consecrated heart always pure
5. The guiding light on the Path to the Fiery World
6. The power to protect the Teaching from any attack
7. The power to protect the image of the Teacher
8. The ability to hear the call of the Hierarchy

Those who stand in the spirit of prayer and watchfulness eventually enter the Fiery World and there become creative co-workers.

We are told that if one is associated with the Fiery World for a long period of time, he gains the right to carry the message of the Fiery World and the Hierarchy to the world. The Great Ones won the right to give the Teachings and the highest Law because of association with the Fiery World for thousands of years.

The Great Ones always kept the vision of the summit in Their Hearts. While They strove toward that vision and responded to the pull of the Cosmic Magnet, the feelings of loneliness and emptiness vanished from Their lives.

The power of watchfulness is built within our hearts through thousands of years of steady and pure striving. Only those who dedicate their lives to the principles of the Fiery World become the Carriers of Fire. The Carriers of Fire contact the Fiery World through beauty. Step by step, beauty takes them to the summit. Beauty releases the innermost Self, and gradually the Self becomes a source of Beauty.

On the Path to the Fiery World, one must love beauty in any form. One must rejoice every time he contacts beauty. The admiration of beauty and the feeling of ecstasy due to beauty are major steps toward the Fiery World. Every time one identifies himself with beauty, he transforms himself. Every time one fuses himself with beauty, he meets his Self.

On the Path to the Fiery World one must walk on the path of beauty, as well as leave behind him a life of beauty. Those who leave a life of beauty behind them find a better world for themselves in the future, a world in which they can have greater contact with the Fiery World. Each seed of beauty of a past life becomes a flower in our future lives. No one can enter the Fiery World unless he leaves behind him a life of beauty.

When one dedicates himself to the Fiery World, all his thoughts, emotions, words, and actions are tested by fire. Only the most beautiful, the most essential, remains; the rest burns away. One must be careful not to be burned in the tests. Every unworthy thought, emotion, word, and action are inflammable materials. As they burn away, the centers, senses, and organs related to them burn as well. This is why we are advised not to carry inflammable materials with us into the Fiery World.

On the Path to the Fiery World, one must deny his self. Self-denial is true humility. In real humility one denies his self-interest and the interest of his separate self.

We are told that people who are separative and who feel that their self is separate from the One Self cannot enter the Fiery World. Only those who learn to live in humility can understand the meaning of the One Self.

The Fiery World is a sphere of unity and synthesis. Each separative thought or action which tries to enter the Fiery World burns away before it can enter.

Humility is a fiery quality. We are told that only self-denial and self-sacrifice can explain the depth of humility.

Heroism is self-denial; it is self-sacrifice. Heroism is the manifestation of humility. Humility is the ability to identify oneself with the greater Self. Each action carried out for the benefit of mankind is an act of heroism; it is an act of humility. It is stated that "...the pillars of a nation stand erect only on the qualities of heroism of the spirit and the heart."[1] There are many heroes working in solitude and silence for one humanity. If we are still alive on this planet, it is because of the labor of these heroes.

Humility expresses the power of beauty. Beauty manifests in heroism and in self-denial. It affirms all those creative steps which lead to the Summit. In beauty one learns to live by the principle of the most essential. After one is charged with beauty, then the power of spirit dominates all expressions of his life.

Beauty, in its essence, is synthesis. On the Path toward the Fiery World, one must manifest the spirit of synthesis. Synthesis leads us to self-denial, to humility, to heroic action, to creativity, to beauty. In every creative labor there is the spirit of synthesis.

Fire is the greatest synthesizer. The Carriers of Fire work for synthesis. The Path toward the most essential is found only in the labor of synthesis. When the Self begins to manifest through the human form, he creates synthesis. Synthesis is the reflection of the spirit in matter. Matter serves the higher laws only when involved in an act of synthesis.

One of the Paths toward the Fiery World is the spirit of cooperation. In cooperation the wholeness of beauty is manifested; the all-embracing Goodness is put into action and into manifestation. When many work for the composition of beauty, such a work is cooperation.

Humanity has yet to learn the power of cooperation. That is why revolution, war, and crime are widespread. Cooperation is one of the guides of the Fiery World. Without this guide one will never find the gates of the Fiery World. Cooperation is the crown of humility. Those who cannot cooperate for the highest good of all humanity prepare the path of the destruction of humanity.

In cooperation one actually brings the Fiery World into manifestation. Because of the lack of cooperation, we find ourselves farther from the Fiery World. The Fiery World can manifest its beauty

---

1.   Agni Yoga Society, *Fiery World III* (New York: Agni Yoga Society, 1948), para. 43.

and light only through those who have developed the spirit of cooperation with the Rays of the Cosmic Magnet, and with the rays of the flame of the heart of each human being.

Purification of human life is only possible through the spirit of cooperation. Because of the lack of cooperation, the wheels of human actions are filled with destructive elements. The entire mechanism of life has lost its integrity and harmony. The mechanism has become divided. Instead of one human mechanism, we now have thousands which work against each other. This is how time is lost, energy is lost, lives are lost, vision is lost, and the future is lost. Cooperation is the creativity of the future. Without cooperation, there will be no future.

A person's light cannot be increased by blowing out the candles of others. Cooperation is the increase of light and beauty.

It is known that self-denial and humility are the foundations of cooperation. Where the self seeks its own interests, there is no cooperation. Where the self tries to rule, there is no cooperation. The Fiery World dissolves the thought of the separative self and denounces the imposition of the self. In cooperation the One Self shines in all our actions.

Groups can become Carriers of Fire. The Fiery World manifests great signs through groups that are dedicated to the One Fire. Each member of the group must learn self-denial and realize that he exists only for the whole. Each member must realize that his labor must be harmonized to the labors of each member — for the common goal.

With these simple steps, members of a group turn into heroes, and the group turns into a flame, a potent Carrier of Fire. We are told that the will of the Higher Worlds can only manifest through a fiery group which knows how to cooperate in spirit and in labor.

Without the fire of the Higher Worlds, all that we have will be our own burden, problem, and trap. With the fire of the Higher Worlds, the abundance of all life will be ours.

These are the powerful signs on the Path leading to the Fiery World.

There are many elements with which we build. One of them is matter, in its various forms. All that is built with matter will one day disappear.

We also build using the element of emotions. The constructions built with emotions last longer than those built of matter, but sooner or later they evaporate like water. We also build with thought. Objects built with thought last still longer, but eventually a great part of them vanishes.

Those objects that are built with the element of fire exist for many eons. It is very beneficial to understand the quality of these elements and build our character or our creative forms with the element of fire. A fiery construction is a form which is built of the highest fire of spirit. Such a form reflects the highest harmony, beauty, oneness, and synthesis. It becomes a path of transmutation for all pilgrims and a channel of transmission of higher visions and higher inspirations. One must learn and know what element he builds his future with; with what element he builds his life, his relationships, and his field of labor.

It is possible to put the highest fire into all our actions. For example: music, painting, and dance which carry the highest fire last for centuries because people continuously, and for many centuries to follow, discover a new layer of fire in such works. To find a creative fire is to find a key for more life.

Fiery constructiveness builds a spiral of progressing fire through which the human soul refines himself. Every Spark in the Universe must travel that spiral of refinement. Fiery beings, and those who construct with fiery qualities, are the builders of such fiery refineries. Each day the Carrier of Fire synchronizes himself with the fiery Magnet of Cosmos. Life would never progress without such heroes. Each striving builds a new link in the golden chain of Infinity.

The Carrier of Fire always knows that he is a carrier of Cosmic Fire, and he never seeks glorification for his labor. The treasures of Space never pour through a man who tries to glorify himself for the creativity of his labor. Every moment he knows that the currents of fire are sent to him from higher centers. He knows that the Great Ones are the source of his inspirations. He realizes that the impressions reaching him have Cosmic sources. In humility, he lights torches in darkness, and if glory is given to him, he puts it on the altar of the Hierarchy with deepest gratitude. Fiery workers do not work for themselves but for the Hierarchy, for the Ones Who have brought light, love, and beauty to this world. A true worker knows that it is not he who exists but the fire, the fire of the Hierarchy and the Cosmos.

48

On the Path to the Fiery World

There are many virtues that we can develop on the Path to the Fiery World. Two of them are **kindness** and **gentleness**.

Everything that is done, spoken, and otherwise expressed in coarseness creates a barrier on your Path and the Path of others. Coarseness transmits the lower forces of your body and emotions, such as glamors, anger, fear, and jealousy. These negative forces create disintegration in the vehicles of those who are your victims. Coarseness also burns your own etheric and protective network and plants the seeds of future sicknesses. Coarseness creates a violent turbulence in the communication line between you and the Fiery World.

Thus, gentleness and kindness carry more power and more authority than coarseness. Coarseness damages and leaves scars; kindness and gentleness cure and uplift.

On the Path to the Fiery World, you become aware that any wound given to others through your own coarseness, regardless of the excuse, becomes your own wound. This is because wounding others wounds your own mental vehicle. Not many people may feel this wound, because they are very occupied with mundane problems and interests, but soon they see the weakening of the strength of their hearts and minds. In the Subtle World they can actually count their own wounds and realize that they wounded others.

In the ancient palaces, kindness and gentleness were considered royal signs, and coarseness was considered an animalistic vice.

Another virtue on the Path to the Fiery World is **tolerance.** Tolerance protects you from the traps of criticism and judgment. Tolerance frees you from the problems and involvements created by criticism and judgment. Criticism and judgment are the easiest ways to become like the one you condemn. This is a very serious phenomenon in Nature. One becomes like those he hates, criticizes, and condemns.

As one advances on the Path to the Fiery World, he becomes more careful not to criticize and judge people, and to develop deeper and deeper tolerance. Not only does he refrain from criticism and judgment, but he also discourages others from doing these things. He develops ways and means to bring others into sanity and tolerance.

Travelers on the Fiery Path have no time to judge and criticize. They strive to be examples, to uplift people to the level of beauty, to cultivate tolerance, and to protect those who are unrighteously attacked.

To be able to do all these things, you must consider the following:

1. Check to see if you are better than victims. Do a thorough examination of your motives and your life.
2. Know that people learn by their mistakes and failures.
3. Think about whether your criticism and judgment would help or not.
4. Beware of imposing your own glamors and vices on others.
5. See if you are reading your own projections into others.
6. See if you are blocking the freedom of others.
7. Think about the karmic consequences and ties.
8. See if your ego is controlling you.

Instead of condemnation, judgment, and criticism, you can try to find the causes of various things you do not like. Try to cure these things not by condemnation, judgment, or criticism but by your wisdom, beauty, love, and tolerance.

Tolerance does not mean to allow people to exploit you but to create those conditions in which the germs of many sicknesses can no longer grow. A physician does not criticize but engages himself in the art of healing. Tolerance gives people the opportunity to grow and learn.

Intolerance eventually leads to totalitarianism, and the planet becomes a prison for slaves. The Path to the Fiery World is the Path of freedom and tolerance. Intolerance makes you a bag full of vanities. You try to make yourself the ruler of the destiny of others. You impose your will on others, and eventually you become totally blind to your own weaknesses. Tolerance is the ability to see within you the things that you hate in others.

People think that tolerance is against justice and that justice can never be exercised if one is tolerant. Tolerance is the opposite of condemnation. It is the result of the understanding that first, a man is free to think the way he wants to think. Second, a man is free to believe what he wants to believe. Third, a man knows that he is not the measure of others. Fourth, he knows that there are millions of kinds of leaves, trees, and flowers, and he cannot ask them to be all of one kind. Finally, he knows that people bloom if there is no outside pressure upon them.

The Fiery World is entered through tolerance because only the mind that is trained in tolerance can understand the symphonic diversity of the Fiery World. Every intolerant person is rejected at the gates of the Fiery World because these people assert themselves instead of respecting the freedom of others.

Tolerance does not encourage crimes. A tolerant person deals with crimes as if they were real diseases. He tries not to condemn the sick but cure the disease.

Another virtue on the Path to the Fiery World is **daring**. In daring one has direction; he has the ability to measure the consequences of action; there is detachment from the limitations of the personality; and there is detachment from hindrances that would be accepted in our lives through suggestions and commands.

Every time you identify with your Real Self, you dare. Every time you identify with your hindrances and limitations, you lose the spirit of daring. Every time you follow the path of jealousy, coarseness, intolerance, and condemnation, you become weaker in spirit.

Daring is an attempt to be a spirit and radiate the powers of the spirit. Daring is an attempt to be beautiful and radiate beauty to others. Daring is an attempt to free yourself from your ego, from your self-interests and separative goals. Daring means to stand in the Creative Fire, to stand in self-sacrifice, purity, and silence.

One may ask a daring one, "How did you dare to keep silent in the chaos of condemnations and malice?"

Daring is the ability to stand above what you are. Daring is the ability to see exactly what you are. Daring is the ability to strive toward new heights and keep your balance and sanity in those heights.

Daring is the moment when you talk as a soul, act as a soul, and decide as a soul. All fiery actions are actions of daring.

Daring is the ability to reject fear, gossip, malice, and slander and seal the sources of such pollution with your nobility and detachment.

In the higher Subtle World and Fiery World one of the greatest characteristics of warriors is that they protect their co-workers. It is through daring that you become a shield for others. Daring does not let people betray their co-workers. Daring lights the flames of the heart and makes a person live in the flame of his own heart.

Daring stands for unity and synthesis because daring is the response of the human soul to the call of the Hierarchy.

Daring expresses itself in the efforts to expand the field of our service. Daring is to stand indifferent to all praise and all condemnations. Daring tries to transform the enemies into co-workers. Daring builds bridges between the present failures and the future possibilities.

Daring ones love solitude. A man of daring blesses the moments in which he can be alone for creative actions and service.

A daring one attracts fiery inspirations from the Hierarchy. A daring one knows that joy comes to us only when we expand and transmute our consciousness at the summit of any spiritual achievement.

There are many people who try to create hindrances on the path of daring ones. But all other daring ones recognize the nobility and the value of such a person and support him with great daring at his time of crisis and tension. The spirit of daring blooms in a person at the time of the spiritual defense of another daring one.

The Fiery World welcomes all daring ones because life in the Fiery World is one of continuous daring.

Another virtue on the Path to the Fiery World is **forgiveness**. Forgiveness is the ability to stand above our personality and our self-interests. It is the ability to stand away from our ego.

If any wave of revenge appears in our heart, the fires of the heart die away. No one can enter the Fiery World if he carries the dark fire of revenge in his heart because the Fiery World is unity, beauty, and harmony.

Service to our fellow man is carried out only in the spirit of forgiveness. Whoever cannot forgive someone, he is indirectly condemning himself.

Vengeance is a direct way to break the Law of Karma. Those who want to enter the Fiery World will try not to punish people but to heal them. The greatest opportunity to heal a person is the moment when you can take revenge on him, but you elect not to.

Many people find the way toward beauty only when they are forgiven. Forgiveness burns the fires of their hearts and leads them to purity. Forgiveness is not a weakness but the power of the spirit. On the Path to the Fiery World, one advances when he takes the burdens of others upon his shoulders. In the Fiery World, life is designed in a way that everyone sacrifices for each other and for the great Plan. No one needs to lose a person but, instead, to win him over after transforming that person's heart.

Another great virtue on the Path to the Fiery World is **self-givingness**. This is an advanced stage in which a person dedicates his life to the service of the world.

The opposite of self-givingness is the cult of self-service in which the person uses all and every opportunity to use people and events for his own advantage. The followers of this cult, we are told, never stop at any obstacle. They find victory at the expense of others.

On the Path to the Fiery World, such people remain in darkness, and no one guards them in that darkness. The self- serving one remains alone because things that you take from others, for your personal ends, are the same things that you lose in the Subtle World. This cult of self-servers is at the root of all the pain and suffering of humanity. It is so difficult to expose and disband them because they are everywhere, in every department of human endeavor.

Only through self- renunciation can one destroy the seeds of the dangerous cult of self-service. Self-service is a blinding cult, and those who fall into it need heroic efforts to liberate themselves. One the Path to the Fiery World, do not associate with the members of such a cult because sooner or later you will forget your destination.

The virtue of self-givingness shines like a torch on the Path to the Fiery World.

We are told that when leaving the earthly spheres, the spirit accumulates tension and power from the services he rendered to the world. Every achievement in the field of service appears to the spirit as a flower of joy and makes him proceed toward the Fiery World. Each ascent becomes possible when there is deep aspiration in the soul for further service to and adoration of the Hierarchy. We are told that such spirits are guarded by a ray which shines on their way and leads them to the Fiery World.

There are still other virtues. For example, we have the virtue called the **power of synthesis**. Such a virtue is one of the guides to the Fiery World. No one can penetrate into the Fiery World without developing the power of synthesis. The power of synthesis is the ability of the heart to fuse many currents of energies into one stream of energy. Such a power can only be developed when the spirit shines through the mind.

On the Path to the Fiery World, logic and reason are transcended by the light of synthesis. In synthesis all diversities are understood as the parts of one whole. In synthesis there is no mine and yours; all is for the whole. In synthesis there is perfect cooperation and harmony.

Fire burns away all that is not harmonious. The power of synthesis creates oneness, and only those who are one in their nature and have no cleavages within their souls enter the Fiery World.

There is another virtue which is called **creative imagination**. We are told that imagination is the reflection of the things we experienced in our past lives or in the present one.

We sometimes recall experiences we had in the Subtle Worlds. With creative imagination, memories of the experiences in the Subtle Worlds come to life.

There are also Sources in still Higher Worlds from which visions can reach our mind through impressions. Creative imagination first brings these impressions or memories into manifestation and then synthesizes them into workable formulas or wisdom.

On the Path to the Fiery World, one cannot advance if he has no creative imagination. All relationships are conducted through the power of imagination and thinking. All our needs are met through creative imagination. It is the power of creative imagination which synthesizes all our hidden memories and builds the bridges leading to the Fiery World. Creative imagination is the power to remember oneself in time and in space.

Another virtue mentioned in the Ageless Wisdom may be called the **power of unity in the Cosmos**. One must develop the power to see that all Cosmos is One; it is one whole. All that is part of the Cosmos represents one body in which every cell affects all the other cells. Once this unity is grasped, one feels himself to be on the Path to the Fiery World.

It is in the light of the understanding of such a unity that man engages himself in the service of the Cosmos. His self and his separatism vanish, and he dedicates himself with a deep sense of responsibility to serve the Cosmos. He understands that all that he thinks, speaks, and does affects the whole, and his actions either prevent the process of synthesis or work for it.

When such a virtue develops in our heart, it becomes an easy matter to renounce the germs with which the self-serving man is loaded.

The higher forces of the Cosmos cooperate with a man or with a group only when they totally fuse themselves with the idea that they are one with Cosmos. This unity allows the energy of the Cosmos to operate through a person or a group. But such a unity cannot be achieved until man demonstrates that all his actions, on all levels, are directed toward the good of all creation.

The Fiery World accepts only those who progressively fuse with the Cosmos in greater unity.

On the Path to the Fiery World, another virtue to be developed is **honesty**. Honesty is not one virtue; it is a combination of many virtues developed during thousands of years. Honesty is the ability to act, to speak, and to think in conformity with the Core of consciousness, with the directions of the Cosmic Magnet, and in harmony with the good of all beings. The acts, words, and thoughts expressed in honesty bring honor and glory to a man. An honest man inspires trust and love.

On the Path to the Fiery World, any sort of expression which is found to be below the measure of honesty will create fiery obstacles on that Path. An honest man on the Path to the Fiery World is like a man who has a valid passport to travel.

As the pressure and fire increase on the road of their ascent, the vehicles of dishonest people show signs of disintegration. Honesty keeps the subtle bodies integrated and protected. The aura of a dishonest person has the appearance of disorganized and muddy currents. These currents evaporate, burn, and disintegrate under the various kinds of pressure in Space. The vehicles of a dishonest person tremble and shake when any fiery spirit approaches them. Dishonesty is like a cracked boat in which a man attempts to cross the ocean.

On the Path to the Fiery World, we are advised to shield ourselves with the spirit of honesty. Each day presents hundreds of opportunities to test or cultivate our honesty.

An honest man must not deceive, lie, steal, or distort. He must not work for his ego. He must have right and noble motives. He must reveal his soul in all his actions. Sincerity and simplicity are component parts of honesty.

Honesty in this world produces energy which nourishes the nerves and the bones. It especially invigorates the heart. Honesty makes our aura attractive to invisible forces. Honesty creates magnetism around us and within our dwelling and attracts noble souls as our co-workers. Nobility and honesty are two pillars of the gate to the Fiery World.

Yet another virtue on the Path to the Fiery World is the **ability to see value and merit in others.** There are many people in the world who are blind to the spiritual qualities and merits of other human beings. They are only occupied with trash. On the Path to the Fiery World, one must develop his consciousness in such a way that he not only sees but also with great joy appreciates the merits, the beauty, and the spiritual qualities of other people. No one can approach the Fiery World if he has not learned to discover the merits of other people, to rejoice in their beauty, and to express gratitude for their spiritual qualities.

The inhabitants of the Fiery World are those who throughout many incarnations have developed the spirit of appreciation, joy, and gratitude for the jewels found in other human beings. The deeper one sees the merits and the values of others, the closer he comes to the Fiery World. The beauty in the human heart unfolds and blooms if that human being appreciates the beauty in others.

Criticism, belittlement, gossip, malice, slander, and treason are six brothers who always live together. They have a dark net in Space, and they catch all those souls who help them by living their lives in criticism, belittlement, gossip, malice, slander, and treason.

To see the value and merit in others is the most noble form of self-respect and the most noble way to worship the One Self in every form. On the Path to the Fiery World, one must develop the spirit of respect, admiration, and gratitude.

People assume that a fiery person is one who makes loud noises, wild gestures, imposes his will violently, controls people, and makes outrageous decisions. All these are personality manifestations which have nothing to do with the real fire.

A fiery person is one who thinks very clearly, has deep enthusiasm, and radiates energy. He speaks softly, with pure reason. He highly respects the freedom and rights of other people. He has endurance, persistence, concentration, and focus. All his words and actions are controlled, noble, and graceful. His fiery quality is his radiation of spiritual fire. He even whispers so that his voice is heard deep in your bones. Such a person has an accumulated tension in his aura which radiates sparks of psychic energy. His heart is in communion with the fires of Space, and he distributes this fire in all his actions.

Around a fiery person you feel the burning of the trash of your worries, selfish interests, vanities, hypocrisy, and deceit. His fire reveals your true picture to yourself without a remark having been made. In his fiery presence you contact your Soul and see your vision.

There is a state of consciousness in which you are in communion with the Fiery World. A *diamond thread* unites your head center with the Fiery World and transmits to you fire, psychic energy, beauty, wisdom, joy, and bliss. Those who have such a consciousness simultaneously live in both the Fiery World and the mundane world and radiate great creative power and leadership in both worlds.

Communication with the Fiery World is based on the laws of electrical currents. The whole circuit of communication breaks and communication stops in one second if a single evil thought, emotion, or act is expressed. The currents are the most sensitive energy lines. They not only create short circuits but also flames and destruction if the object of resistance is very coarse. Fiery people are the most cautious and sensitive people. They do not break the communication lines with anything unworthy of the spirit of Beauty, Goodness, Righteousness, Joy, and Freedom. It is not easy to repair broken lines. Long periods of purification, discipline, renunciation, prayer, isolation, and meditation are necessary to repair the lines and re-establish communication with the Fiery World.

At present the greatest bridge which connects the physical world, astral world, and Fiery Worlds is the Hierarchy. The Hierarchy is the Antahkarana between these three worlds. The members of the Hierarchy are active in these three dimensions. If one affiliates with Them, it will be possible for him to cross the worlds with Them. In many instances, the members of the Hierarchy lead Their co-workers into the Subtle World or the Fiery World, protecting them from the assaults of evil and from the spheres of dark accumulations.

The link between the Hierarchy and man is his Guardian Angel who, with a member of the Hierarchy, safely leads the human soul to his destination, or, if he is ready, the human soul may be lead into spatial battles. This is why it is so important that one read about the Hierarchy, aspire toward the Hierarchy, study the Teaching of the Hierarchy, and eventually build contacts with the members of the Hierarchy.

All this can be possible, we are told, through sacrificial service, meditation, and fiery living in the daily world of men.

In the Fiery World another virtue is called **broadening** or **expansion**. A traveler toward Infinity will never live in any crystallized tradition, but he will try to expand his mental horizons and come in contact with higher realities. Dogmas, doctrines, and traditions are for those who are not yet able to *think*. After one begins to think, he tries to find higher horizons in which he can exercise his growing wings.

There are many traditions which eventually turn into customs, then into habits. The traveler on the Path of Infinity will try to expand his consciousness and broaden his understanding and go beyond customs, habits, and traditions. In every age new energies operate, new inspirations are released, new visions are set. The traveler on the Path of Eternity will try to contact these new inspirations, impressions, and visions to follow the progress of Nature and not be held back for thousands of years.

It is true that there are some treasures in every tradition, but these treasures must be examined very closely to see if they fit the new and changing conditions and demands of life. They must be re-translated and adapted or totally left behind. Many traditions carry not only the limitations of their age, but they are also loaded with collective thoughtforms, which sometimes make it impossible for an average man to free himself from that tradition.

Broadening or expansion is related to one's consciousness, as well as to the field of his contact with newer and higher impressions and sources of inspirations. It is also related to the field where the new impressions and inspirations manifest and actualize. On the Path to the Fiery World, all that cannot fit new levels and new dimensions must be left behind.

Another fiery quality to be developed on the Path to the Fiery World is **persistence on all paths**. "When a disciple manifests his firmness amid storms and whirlwinds, when amidst plots and showers of stones he is not afraid to continue the designated path,"[1] then the Guiding Hand leads him toward the Fiery World. Persistence is the exercise of a concentrated will in tense dedication.

Flickering lights, or lukewarm people who change their moods, cannot continue on the Path to the Fiery World. In the smallest storms such persons change their direction. Persistence is the ability to continue in the chosen direction after the "true north" is found in the heart.

It is the power of persistence that generates energy every time man meets new obstacles and hindrances. Persistence eventually helps a man develop fiery fearlessness in all circumstances. We are told that the Fiery World is not entered unless a man is charged with pure fearlessness. Through persistence one accumulates wisdom and assimilates it in his life. Persistence brings the Real Self into manifestation in all walks of life.

Together with the virtue of persistence, we are told in the Teaching that one must develop a deep-rooted **faith in the Hierarchy**, a faith which knows that the Path given by the Hierarchy is the only path to perfection.

Christ once said, "Whenever three people unite in My name, I will be among them." This is a very important formula. On the Path to the Fiery World, if three people are united in the name of the Hierarchy, with deep respect and dedication toward each other, they

---

1.   Agni Yoga Society, *Fiery World III*, para.80.

develop a kind of power that makes their little group a source of light, a source of power, and a transmitter of the inspirations from the Hierarchy.

There is no progress toward the Fiery World except through **united labor based on the foundation of loyalty.** This is another virtue to cultivate. Loyalty must be exercised at home, in the family, in groups, and especially among co-workers. If loyalty and trust are absent, no great work can be done for the Hierarchy and for humanity.

Without loyalty and trust among co-workers and without unity in the name of the Hierarchy, all spiritual endeavors gradually degenerate and turn into corruption. This is why the core of the group is like the heart of the group. The heart must be extremely vigilant, healthy, and sensitive in order to guide the group toward the Fiery World.

When a core is founded with true co-workers, the interchange of energies between the Higher Worlds and the core takes place. Such an exchange is becoming more and more difficult because of accumulating chemical elements and poisonous gases in the atmosphere of the earth. Energies coming from higher sources will slowly become more rare, and the receiving cores will be forced to advance higher and create greater tension in order to receive them.

As the higher energies penetrate less and less into our spheres, and as beneficent Lives depart from our spheres because of pollution, the planet will enter into a dark phase which may be referred to as the stage of suicide. Most of our actions on earth already indicate that the higher guidance is less and less available and humanity is heading toward self-destruction. Unless drastic and immediate actions are taken to clean the atmosphere, the fate of our planet will be very unfortunate.

Coarseness, egoism, and conceit are three signs of degeneration of the mental body. One cannot travel toward the Fiery World if these vices are not replaced by **kindness, selflessness,** and **truth.**

The purpose of the human soul depends upon the unfoldment of the virtues. It is the virtues that cause the expansion of consciousness and create the field of service. It is the virtues that enable a man to be persistent on the Path. Only virtuous people can cooperate in the name of the Hierarchy, and only virtues increase the flow of loyalty and trust. Without the virtues of the human soul, man will not have an opportunity to survive because the lack of virtues will lead humanity into coarseness, egoism, conceit, and destruction.

We are told that **spiritual striving** is a means to achieve certain lofty states of consciousness and to accomplish great works of service.

Also it is extremely important during the crossing of the worlds. Every spiritual striving generates a special substance which changes into a stream of energy, helping the soul pass through certain strata easily and with joy. Without such an energy, one will resemble an automobile which is on the verge of consuming its last drop of gas. It is evident that it will stay wherever it stops.

Each striving creates a different kind of substance in the nerve channels and in the centers of the person. When the soul begins to leave the body, these substances immediately change into an energy which propels the soul.

Striving is composed of many elements such as courage, fearlessness, intense aspiration, persistence, the ability to sense the vision, and faith.

Striving during one's life in the physical realm nourishes the astral and mental bodies, organizes them, and makes them ready for daily and future flights.

The energies created by striving are also useful in washing away the sediments of imperil. Imperil and selfish, earthly desire and greed create certain illnesses in our subtle bodies. Most people carry such illnesses into the Subtle World and suffer the consequences. Some people can cure such illnesses before they pass away, and thus they do not contaminate the subtle spheres.

Striving is also very healing for psychic illnesses, or illnesses that are related to our etheric, emotional, and mental bodies.[2] Some people think that once the body is left behind, all psychological or emotional and mental illnesses are also left behind. This is not the case. We not only carry them with us, but we also bring them back and infect our new physical bodies.

Striving slowly cures the maladies of the subtle bodies because striving is the imposition of the rhythm of the soul upon the mechanism. This work takes time, but once the vehicles are tuned to the note of the human soul, healing progresses rapidly.

Contemporary humanity does not relate the Higher Worlds to the earthly one. This is the reason why humanity uses measures to evaluate life which are always one-sided and do not lead to synthesis and survival. The earthly life has value only because of its relation to the Higher Worlds. Without the Higher Worlds, all would end in the grave.

---

2. Psychological sickness is related to the etheric, astral, and mental bodies. Psychic sickness refers to the disturbances caused by the undue pressure of the human soul exercised upon the centers of the three vehicles — the etheric, astral, and mental.

Spiritual striving intensifies the fire of the heart. When the fire of the heart is intensified, it builds the Path toward the Fiery World. Nothing can resist a flaming heart. The heart uses all subtle energies for the flight of the soul toward the Higher Worlds and toward higher creativity.

Striving is the progressive penetration of the heart into the dimensions of the Fiery World. It is the fire of the striving heart that cures the maladies of the subtle bodies and charges them with uplifting energies. Those who lose their heart lose their future because the heart is the only door to the future.

On the Path to the Fiery World, one must protect himself with a fiery net. The protective net is woven by very subtle energies with which the human soul can come in contact. The fire of the heart is the weaver. Those whose higher centers are not unfolded, or those who are obsessed, do not have a protective net. On the Path to the Fiery World one needs to weave his protective net.

The enemies of an advanced disciple are more numerous in the Subtle Worlds than on earth, and these enemies have even more opportunities to wound the vehicles of the disciple. But when he weaves his protective net, he can repel the darts of the enemies. We are told that each blow upon the protective net is returned to the sender with a more intensified tension.

The protective net and the higher centers are nourished and protected by the fire of the heart. The protective net is woven into the finest fabric of armor through the fire of the heart and through intense aspiration and continuous striving toward the Higher Worlds.

Every time the striving reaches a certain stage of development, synthesis forms in the Chalice. Synthesis is achieved when the human soul can harmonize the treasures collected in the Chalice over thousands of years. Through great striving, the human soul orchestrates the different currents accumulated in the Chalice and composes his symphony.

The synthesis in the Chalice responds to the Cosmic creative forces. Each creative force in the Cosmos finds manifestation on earth through the synthesis achieved in the Chalice of the human heart.

The bridge between the Fiery World and the earthly world is synthesis. No great accomplishment will be possible without it. Every progressive synthesis bridges higher strata of creative forces. On the Path to the Fiery World, one can protect himself from disintegrating forces by the shield of synthesis.

It is very important to know that Christ, as the present Hierarch, holds the focus of synthesis in the Chalice of the Hierarchy. We are told that He is the Fiery King of the Spirit. On the Path to the Fiery World, His name can be used as the greatest mantram when the soul leaves the body and directs his face toward the Fiery World. Those who have already built communication with the King of Fires will be escorted to their destination by His angels and even by His presence.

Affinity with Christ and striving to assimilate His fiery principles in life build the fiery wings for the Higher Worlds. Many of those who walk the Path of the Teaching forget the King of Fire and fall into the traps of their own egos. In truth, He is the Gate and He is the Path.

On the Path of the Fiery World, one must be very cautious of the dark souls who try to pass themselves off as being light by vesting themselves in the outer trappings of light. Open enemies of light are less dangerous than those who approach us in the name of the Teaching. Wherever they go, they carry infection with them, and if they join their efforts to any labor, they eventually undermine the labor. Their mere presence invites destructive forces into those places where they work.

This is why the warriors for the light must develop pure discrimination and prevent the dark ones from entering into the holy place of their spiritual labor. These people enter with praise and flattery on their lips, with gifts in their hands, and with words of "wisdom." Try to see them for what they are because, when you affiliate with them, they will follow you into the Subtle World; and when you return to earth, they will accompany you. The following are a few of the signs that you can see in them:

—Coarseness
—Flattery
—Criticism
—Malice
—Efforts to belittle
—Ego
—Love of position

When these signs are seen, they will reveal other poisonous reptiles in their hearts. No one can enter into the spheres of the Fiery World until he is able to discern the enemies of light, freedom, and progress.

We are told that when there is intense spiritual aspiration, the psychic energy leaves crystals on the nerve channels. As the aspiration deepens, the crystals of psychic energy increase. These crystals are assimilated by the organism, and in the time of need, they supply energy to the organism and cure it if it is sick. The crystals of psychic energy melt the poisonous elements in the body. Many microbes are burned, many pollutions and poisoning are cleansed by the crystals of psychic energy.

In raising our aspiration through prayer, meditation, dedication, and sacrificial service, we not only increase our psychic energy but we also increase the crystals of psychic energy within our body. We are told that it is possible to direct these crystals toward certain organs and cure them.

Aspirations and elevation of the heart create a certain kind of heat in our system. It is this heat that makes the organs assimilate the crystals of psychic energy.

These crystals of psychic energy are used as the propelling energy for the astral and mental bodies during the subjective journey or during the transition. They also penetrate as electrical energies into the thread of the protecting network. Those who have stored a sufficient amount of psychic crystals in their system will traverse Space in joy and in victory.

During daily labor and in times of crisis, these crystals provide additional energy to fill the reservoirs of the depleted energy. The crystals of psychic energy are assimilated by the aura; they create a luminous, golden hue within the aura, which in turn charges the spoken words and thoughts.

One of the other signs of those who are on the Path to the Fiery World is **reverence for the earthly Teacher**. It is the earthly Teacher who puts in our heart the seeds of the highest aspirations. Unless this reverence is pure, sincere, and fiery, the traveler will not be allowed to benefit from the treasury of the achievements of the earthly Teacher.

Disrespectful actions, thoughts, and words about the Teacher wound the aura of the student, and gradually spiritual communication becomes impossible between them. When the thread of communication is cut, the student has failed in his life and he loses the guiding light for this incarnation because immediately when the thread is cut, he is in danger of obsession by various destructive elements. Those who betray their Teacher in thought and action will be repelled and rejected by the Fiery World.

The Teacher is the link between the student and the Hierarchy. When this link is broken, darkness takes over.

It is possible to change Teachers, but always with the advice and blessings of the former one. The student and the Teacher have a long-standing karmic tie. This tie cannot be broken without reaching a level of fulfillment and graduation.

The Great Ones do not accept a student if They find in Their spatial records that the student at one time or another betrayed his Teacher or caused great damage in His work.

It is true that earthly Teachers may have Their own weaknesses, but the student is related to the Teacher to receive His spiritual guidance, not to interfere with the Teacher's karma.

No one can respect the higher link if he has not learned to respect his first links to the light.

On the Path to the Higher Worlds, one must develop the sense of sacredness for the concept of the Teacher.

The hierarchical principle is the principle of chain and link. Teachers who are dedicated to the Hierarchy and the Teaching of the pure wisdom are for many lives the recognized links to the Hierarchy. The link carries the electrical energy of fire. Any betrayal of the Teacher cuts the flow of fire to the student, and thus the hierarchical principal is broken.

The closer we go toward our Teacher, the greater will be the flow of fire into our hearts.

The student who recognizes the principle of the Hierarchy not only respects his Teacher but also strives to bring the Teacher's visions into actualization in a practical manner. The bonds between the student and the Teacher are the most sacred bonds. The Teacher looks for his student and tries to find him, even if the student wanders in the darkness of the lower planes. The link between the student and the Teacher becomes a line of communication in eternity which eventually pulls them into greater unity, greater service, and greater cooperation in future incarnations. A worthy student eventually inherits the labor of his Teacher.

49

Fiery Baptism

Fiery Baptism takes many forms. There is the fire of pain and suffering through which one passes in gratitude and solemnity, gazing toward the door of salvation. There is the fiery baptism of conscience. Here, your whole being burns in the realization of the wrongs you have done, or of the laws you have broken.

Another fiery baptism comes to you when karma takes away all that you have collected and built.

Still another fiery baptism takes place at the moment when you withdraw yourself into the fiery beam of your Spiritual Triad and burn away all glamors and illusions hanging around your body.

There is yet another fiery baptism when you leave your body and approach the gates of the Fiery World. All the elements of your mental body which are inflammable and not worthy of passing through the gates burn away, and through an intense tension you are purified.

Fiery baptism is mostly related to the purification of the mind, or the mental body. Purification by water is related to the astral body. But remember that water is liquid fire. Purification by fire is also related to your whole nature, especially to your mental nature.

There are other fiery baptisms, such as when one stands in the presence of his Solar Angel, in the presence of his Master, in the presence of the Ancient of Days.

In such baptisms the human soul passes through an intense purification. Many hindering accumulations are burned away, helping the human soul climb toward the Fiery World.

It is important to pass through a fiery baptism to see exactly what you are and what you can be. Fiery baptism is a great gift to you, if you understand its message and accept it with gratitude. In every true fiery baptism there is a moment of expansion, vision, purification, detachment, and understanding of the inclusive nature of life. It is after the fiery baptism that permission is granted to the human soul to function in higher strata of the Higher Worlds.

Fiery baptism not only gives us the right to penetrate deeper into the treasury of Cosmic energies but also makes us ready to use these energies on behalf of the progress of one humanity. The Inner Core of man cyclically releases a powerful stream of fire to purify the sphere around him. The same occurs on planetary, solar, and galactic scales. Thus the law operates on many dimensions simultaneously to create connecting links between those who pass through a fiery baptism. It is this link which turns into a path of communication between all those who pass through the fiery baptism. The moment of fiery baptism can be a moment of being charged with Cosmic electricity. If the vehicles bear the fire without conflagration, the charge manifests as ecstasy, bliss, and joy. But if the vehicles are not ready, the charge is like a fiery hurricane which sweeps away in fiery flames all that is not fit to ascend.

He who follows his heart and his Master continuously walks in fire. All his thoughts, words, and actions are tested through fire.

Higher fires cyclically conduct the process of fiery baptism. In addition, one's karma prepares him for and leads him toward fiery baptism. When the records show that one is worthy to stand in the fire and step into the Hall of the Great Ones, the Karmic Lords or the Law prepares that man for a fiery baptism. It is after such a baptism that a new life begins for the Carrier of Fire. Karma not only opens the gate of entrance but also obliterates all burdens still hanging around the Carrier of Fire.

It is suggested that we expect such fiery baptisms and prepare ourselves for them because they will lead us to the Fiery World, where people do not live in fire but they themselves are like flames.

After each fiery baptism, one understands more deeply the mystery of *solitude*. Many ties, many links, and many bridges are burned through fiery baptism. Man experiences a new level of consciousness in the vision of great beauty that is revealed before his eyes. But, when he comes into the world of men, he feels deep in his bones that he is alone, and the silence of solitude spreads on his path.

Solitude does not mean that you are not with people or with life in general. Solitude is the feeling that very few are ready to understand you, to accept your message, to climb the difficult heights with you, and to make risky commitments. Such people are called "lions of the desert," which is where they live in their consciousness. They try to change the "deserts" into the gardens of the Lord. Such souls are increasingly hit by repeated flames of betrayal, malice, slander, and by the "showers of stones." But they continue their sacrificial service to the end. These are people who have no place to rest their heads.

When man has experienced these cyclic baptisms and he turns into a flame himself, from that point on, each of his lives becomes one fiery baptism in its entirety. [1]

Many victories on earth are registered in the Fiery World as defeats. Many defeats here are registered as victories there. The measures are different, but they are based on the law of justice. Those who destroy the reputations of others terribly disfigure their own faces in the Subtle World. Those who exploit people on earth are forced to declare bankruptcy in the Subtle World.

Through fiery baptism you eventually understand that the measures in the Subtle Worlds and in the physical world function on different scales. For example, whatever you give here becomes your savings in the Subtle Worlds. Whatever you lose here, you find there. Misfortunes here bring you fortunes there, if misfortune is understood in the right way.

Fiery baptism gives you the power to understand such measures and fill your heart with the energy of goodness. Goodness wins in both worlds. Love achieves in both worlds.

Evil committed here cuts the roots of one's existence in the Fiery World. Hatred demonstrated here locks the gates of the higher Subtle Worlds.

Fiery baptism reveals all these things to you. It demonstrates the futility of exploitation, hatred, and evil actions. Any evil action taken against anyone here on earth is an action taken against yourself in the subtle body. How deeply one must be blinded to cut the roots of his future lives!

Fiery baptism unites the fields of the Higher Worlds, prevents contradiction within a person on any level, and builds a straight line toward the Fiery World.

Fiery baptism makes us realize that one cannot ascend without the guidance of the Hierarchy. Hierarchy is the guiding star in our stormy sea. Hierarchy is the spearhead pointing toward the Cosmic Magnet. It is our Inner Guide Who awakens in us the existence of the Hierarchy. Its whole endeavor is to lead us toward the Hierarchy.

The Hierarchy on this planet holds the only gate through which one can pass toward the Higher Worlds. Fiery baptism reveals this gate to you. The fiery soul lives in harmony with the direction of the gate.

---

1. *Fiery World III*, para. 80.

Fiery baptism is also needed if one wants to see the beauty and the glory of the great Teachers and Their true value and labor in the Cosmic evolution. It is sad that, as the centuries pass, the Images of the Great Ones are deliberately distorted by people who have no interest in the transformation of life but rather an interest in damaging the positive work of Those Who seek to bring great changes to the world. A fiery purification is considered necessary to bring the essential beauty and power of these Images into the public consciousness. When the Images behind the Teaching are loaded with the ugly concepts of average, egocentric people, the Teaching itself loses its power and turns into a means of income for spiritual merchants.

It is important that before a man leaves his body he clarifies the Images of Great Ones in his heart.

Fiery baptisms also reveal the Law of Equilibrium and the need for such. Creativity on the Cosmic scale rests on this law. Those who have passed through a fiery baptism realize a new equilibrium within their being and take the needed steps which bring this state into their life. All disturbances and conflicts are the result of the lack of equilibrium. Right proportion of energies and their manifestation create equilibrium. The fire of baptism is a fire which creates equilibrium and balance in the life of the disciple.

When balance is established — between the higher and lower, energy and matter, spirit and body, science and faith — the fire once again accumulates itself to break the equilibrium and lead into a higher one. The breaking of an established equilibrium is sometimes a process of fiery baptism, leading to renunciation and intense striving in order to reach a higher equilibrium.

Fiery baptism leads us into synthesis. In this instance, one can clearly see that there is no synthesis except through fire. Synthesis is achieved through fire. Equilibrium is a fiery synthesis.

Courage cannot be achieved unless a man is ready to risk all that he has and is. It is obtained when one renounces all attachments. No one can function courageously if he clings to attachments. Fiery baptism creates courage because it eliminates all attachments. This is why without courage one cannot enter the Fiery World.

Fiery baptism makes the human soul become accustomed to spiritual difficulties. The fire of baptism makes man love difficulties because, through solving difficulties, he can find the Path of further ascent.

It is the fiery baptism that gives wings to the spirit to soar above the abyss of Space.

50

Tuning in
to the Keynote
of the Cosmos

It is very important daily to tune ourselves to the Keynote of manifestation. Every day as we think, as we speak and as we work, we identify ourselves with our expressions, and eventually we become what we think, speak and do. To return to our essence, to our Real Self, we have to key ourselves in to the Keynote of Nature. Keying in or tuning in to the Keynote of Nature will give us a new opportunity to look at the way we live. Once we tune in to that note, our thinking will change.

First of all, our ego will gradually vanish. All that is not in harmony in our life with the One Self will disappear. Ugliness will no longer exist, and selfishness will drop away. We will become a newborn child of Nature.

Great prophets and leaders used to go to the mountains, deserts, and the wilderness to tune in to that sound, the note of the Cosmos.

The Keynote of Nature is described in many ways. It is called the Silence, the Great Presence in the Universe, the primary energy, the Sound, and the *AUM*. All manifestations are the differentiations of this Cosmic note which keeps the whole manifestation in existence. Tuning in to that Cosmic note brings purity. Purity is the ability to fuse and synchronize our frequency with the Keynote or the Cosmic Sound.

On the Path to the Fiery World, one must fuse oneself, stage after stage, with the fiery Sound which sustains the whole Universe and keeps it in manifestation. The fiery Sound is the direct Path through all planes and worlds.

Tuning in to the Keynote, or the fiery Sound of manifestation, is not a form of meditation. It is not an exercise but an active fusion with the Keynote. No thought is necessary; no visualization or imagination is necessary. Tuning in takes a short period — three to five minutes of silence, deep silence without sleep. No psychic phenomena, colors, or messages will be expected but only a deep silence in which fusion will be possible.

If the fusion was successful, after the tuning in you will feel a great amount of joy and energy, an urge for creativity and service, and a transmutation of consciousness. Physically, emotionally, and mentally you will feel a great energy of healing. In the moment of fusion, your illusions, glamors, and limitations will melt away, and you will face a new clarity of mind and an open, sincere, and healthy relationship with people around you.

You can begin your fusion by tuning in to your Guardian Angel, then to the Hierarchy, then to Christ, then to Shamballa, and then to the Keynote of manifestation. Here you enter into the formless world and the silent sphere. Try to stay there and let everything go; try to feel one with the Heart of the Cosmos.

All symphonies, all melodies, and all hymns of manifestations are built upon this Keynote. Every drop of light, every spark of love, and every flower of joy spring out of this Keynote. It is this Keynote that ties together all the hearts of advancing Warriors of Light. It is this Keynote that gives them courage and daring to go forward toward the Fiery World. It is this Keynote that builds the Path toward the Cosmic Magnet.

To practice this tuning in, you can sit in a relaxed way and slowly try to focus your mind on the Source of light, love, and beauty; or try to hear the fiery sound of that Source as a note, and let the note permeate your whole nature — aligning, integrating, synchronizing, and tuning in your whole being to it. Try not to think. Very soon you will learn how to do it. But try to be regular in your practice, and, if possible, sit in the same place. You can do it many times a day; just sit, totally relaxed, and let the Presence permeate all the cells and atoms of your mechanism.

This will help you eventually to come in contact with the fiery sphere. Actually, the Presence or the Keynote is a fiery current which purifies your mechanism, and various accumulations around your being, and releases you to fuse with the fire. Remember that in your essence you are fire; you are a flame.

Through the practice of the Presence you cut your attachments with the lower levels of physical, etheric, and astral planes and tune in to the Fiery Sphere, from which originates all beauty, love, light, joy, and freedom. Thus you prepare not only your future sphere of existence but also your future creative task in the world.

The practice of the Presence is the purest form of aspiration through which the human Spark withdraws Itself from the lower worlds and orients Itself toward the dimensions of fire and beauty. Real aspiration is a process of freedom in which the human Spark expands Its radiation and harmonizes all Its bodies through the rhythm of the focus toward which It aspires.

Purification of a man or the world can be achieved only through two ways. The first is called *the sword*. The sword is the symbol of all the weapons humanity has in its hands, as well as the symbol of natural catastrophes. Thus wars, revolutions, and riots are a heavy cleansing process which is applied to humanity if it cannot use the second means of purification.

The second way is the process of tuning in to the fiery note of Nature. In other words, this process is called *fiery transmutation*. It is a process in which a man continuously aspires and strives to pay his karmic debts, to refine and purify his vehicles, and to transmute his consciousness. We are told that when a man or humanity is engaged in such a process, the fiery measures of destruction and purification will not take place.

Each step of progress toward the Fiery World increases one's sense of responsibility. The sense of responsibility awakens in a person when he realizes that his Real Self is a part of the One Self. All his life affects the life of the Sparks in every form, positively or negatively. Those individuals who forget about their responsibilities are awakened through fiery shocks. The sense of responsibility toward the One Self leads to the Path of fiery transmutation.

Accumulated in Space are millions of tons of crimes and physical, emotional, mental, and material pollutions. The Universe cannot continue to have one of its wheels stuck in the mud. This is why fiery purifications are necessary, either in the form of destructive wars or though aspiration, striving, and fiery transmutations.

The salvation of humanity will come when the world tunes in to the Cosmic note.

Progress in the physical world is made through overcoming friction or opposition. This is done through physical exertion. We are told that victory over inertia and opposing forces is achieved in the Subtle World through aspiration and spiritualization, or tuning in to the Cosmic Keynote.

In the Fiery World, progress is achieved through creative thinking. The Subtle World reflects a part of the physical world. The Fiery World contains all those currents which can regenerate the world. In the Fiery World are also found all the records of Space, and we are told that the Fiery World is the Cosmic Laboratory.

It is in the highest stratum of the Fiery World that fiery beings study the chemistry of the rays and the Cosmic forces. Higher advancement will not be possible unless people penetrate into these spheres of the Fiery World and see the blueprints of the glorious Future.

51

Sanctuaries as Bridges

There is a supreme law which states that once a form is created, it exists forever until the cause exhausts itself. Thus, once a thought is generated, once a word is spoken, once an action is taken, it exists in Space until its cause is exhausted in a great cycle of time.

Our thoughts, words, and actions are registered not only in our aura but even in our clothes, furniture, and the walls and ceilings of our house. All that we do, speak, and think is magnetically tied to us. We always live in the presence and influence of all that we have thought, spoken, and done.

These records are either of high quality or low quality. If the accumulated records are of high quality, greater opportunities will be revealed to continue our spiritual evolution. If the accumulated records are of low quality, we will find many doors closed on our path and many bridges wiped away. Opportunities for spiritual advancement will only be given to those who have higher quality records of their deeds.

Our homes and furniture accumulate the impressions of all that we do in our homes. If these accumulations are of high quality, they become magnetic to higher impressions from the Subtle and Fiery Worlds and help us in our creative efforts. But if the accumulations of impressions are ugly, criminal, dark, or of low quality, they distort the beneficent currents which could otherwise reach us. In addition, they impress our past upon our consciousness and make it difficult for us to strive toward a new future, a new life. Most houses at this time are flooded with the projections of television and the sounds of the radio. The fear, anger, greed, revenge, and hatred expressed through these programs will stay a long time in the home, conditioning one's physical and mental health. News of crimes, destructions, and wars keep the space within our home disturbed and make higher contact almost impossible.

It is wise not to dwell in places that were occupied by criminals, drug users, alcoholics, people with heavy vices, people with hatred, fear, anger, greed, and revenge, or mentally disturbed people. On the walls and ceilings of the house will be impressed their entire life's drama, and it will, in turn, gradually impress you if you do not have a strong and positively oriented aura. Living in new homes is recommended by Sages; also, moving to new locations would be very beneficial.

If Sanctuaries and Ashrams are under construction, one must very carefully choose the builders and watch their conversations during the construction. After a Sanctuary or Ashram is built, the Leaders must be so careful that no disturbing or polluting activities are carried on there. For example:

—No quarrels, anger, fear, hatred, crimes, or sexual activities must be carried on in the Sanctuary.

—No thoughts of destructive intentions must be formulated in the Sanctuary.

—No one of bad reputation must be allowed to stay there, except in public meetings.

—No polluting water, sewage, or rubbish must be allowed around the Sanctuary.

—No dead animals, trash, or rotten food must be tolerated in the Sanctuary.

—No parties, drinking, or jokes must be allowed in the Sanctuary.

The Sanctuary must be magnetized by holy and blessed objects, paintings, statues, and symbols, and with five prismatic colors.

Each Sanctuary, if charged with pure thoughts through meditations, prayers, and elevated speeches, serves as a link between the physical world and the Subtle and Fiery Worlds. A place becomes holy if it is charged by the presence of dedicated people; if it receives the inspiration, impressions, and blessings of higher sources; and if it serves the transformation of life and the transmutation of consciousness.

It is possible that Great Ones send Their messengers to inspire gatherings and lecturers and create a bridge between the higher and lower worlds. It is possible that Invisible Ones attend lectures, prayer meetings, or healing meetings to bring Their assistance.

A highly magnetized and charged Sanctuary can develop an aura for many miles around it which purifies the sphere with healing and harmonizing energies and attracts the attention of angels, devas, Great Ones, and the denizens of the Higher Worlds.

It is essential that those who are dedicated to service and to their own spiritual development live in very pure harmony with each other, leaving each other free, and never using gossip, criticism, or belittling remarks but only expressing pure love, blessings, and joy to each other. When such a core is created, the Sanctuary becomes more powerful, and its light shines all over the area.

An esoteric rule reads as follows:

> *The co-disciples must be tuned by the guru as the strings of a lute (vina) each different from the others, yet each emitting sounds in harmony with all. Collectively they must form a key-board answering in all its parts to thy lightest touch (the touch of the Master). Thus their minds shall open for the harmonies of Wisdom, to vibrate as knowledge through each and all, resulting in effects pleasing to the presiding gods (tutelary or patron-angels) and useful to the Lanoo. So shall Wisdom be impressed forever on their hearts and the harmony of the law shall never be broken.*[1]

There is another rule for disciples, which is very important to know. It states,

> *None can feel the difference between himself and his fellow-students, such as "I am the wisest." "I am more holy and pleasing to the teacher, or in my community, than my brother," etc., — and remain an upasaka. His thoughts must be predominantly fixed upon his heart, chasing therefrom every hostile thought to any living being. It (the heart) must be full of the feeling of its non-separateness from the rest of beings as from all in Nature; otherwise no success can follow.*[2]

Another rule states,

> *Meditation, abstinence in all, the observation of moral duties, gentle thoughts, good deeds and kind words, as goodwill to all and entire oblivion of Self [self], are the*

---

1. Blavatsky, H.P., *Studies in Occultism*, (London: Theosophical Publishing Society, 1946) p. 5.
2. *Ibid.*, p. 6.

> *most efficacious means of obtaining knowledge and*
> *preparing for the reception of higher wisdom.*[3]

Higher wisdom comes from higher sources to those who are ready and prepared to receive it.

It is very important that groups of people who are unified and harmonized build a group communication line between the physical world and the Fiery Worlds to bring higher assistance into the disturbed world. Only such a group, under the leadership of a dedicated Leader, can create the right atmosphere and build the right Sanctuary as a bridge between worlds.

It must be remembered that before an ideal Sanctuary is built on earth, it is first built in higher spheres by those dedicated disciples whose vision was to create a link between the worlds. It is after the subjective construction of the Temple that disciples on earth take all the steps of precaution to create the replica of the subtle Temple in the higher spheres.

Every creative action must be inspired by higher sources, if that creative action is to build a way through which man will walk toward his glorious future.

---

3. *Ibid.*, p. 7.

52

The Dance of Energy

Energy operates in three phases:

1. Origination, outpouring, related to Will
2. Formulation, related to Purpose
3. Operation, related to Plan

Origination is symbolized by the Father. Formulation is symbolized by the Son. Operation is symbolized by the Holy Spirit, or psychic energy.

Origination: Energy has no originator. Energy is the Space. A portion of Space is put in motion by a Will. Motion is considered as origination.

Formulation: This is the direction or destination, the task of the energy. Formulation is like a prism which characterizes the white light into colored beams of light. Thus, energy has a destination. Energy passes through an archetype and projects the image of the archetype in Space. That image is the Purpose. The formulated image is the Purpose of the energy.

Operation: This is carried on through programmed and progressive steps to enable it to reach its destination. These programmed steps are called plans or, as a whole, the Plan.

Energy is Space when it has no direction or no motion. When energy is put into motion or direction, then it has three characteristics:

1. flow
2. condensation
3. dissipation

Flow is the creative current. Condensation is creativity in form. Dissipation is the annihilation of form.

Flow, condensation, and dissipation form a cycle. The duration of the cycle is conditioned by the ratio of the combination of these three factors.

A cycle is a duration of time which begins with the flow and ends with the dissipation of the form. All forms in existence on any plane follow these cycles. One can see an end in a beginning, and a beginning in an end.

The perpetuation of form depends upon the voltage of the primary flow, on its accurate function on the plane, and on the power of conflicting forces which prepare the process of dissipation. If the form is kept alive against the balance of the initial flow, degeneration takes place, and the form serves a purpose which is foreign to it. We call this the violation of energy, purpose, and plan.

If the form dissipates prematurely, the energy is wasted. Wasted energy is disturbing energy in Space which blindly seeks to create forms without a plan, without being in harmony with the *basic will*.

All premature dissipations of form are sources of disturbances of the harmony in the Universe. All disturbances are felt as pain, suffering, and limitations on all planes.

If a form is kept alive in a state of integration beyond its own capacity, it serves as a runway, a landing field, for destructive forces. The cycle must not be violated. Crimes, wars, and revolutions are means to end prematurely the created forms.

On the other hand, efforts to perpetuate dying forms bring corruption in Space and into the existing forms.

The integrity of the form must be sustained naturally. "Naturally" means by the flow of energy initially put into action for that form. The dissipating elements are absorbed back into the reservoir of energy.

Wisdom is the sensitive registration of the beginning of the conception, of the duration of the form, and of the period of dissipation. It is through this wisdom that one avoids destruction, frictions, degenerating attachments, and the pain and sorrow of dissipation.

People try to know energy through thinking, but they forget that one understands energy through *feeling* it. The act of knowingness and feeling compliment each other. Feeling supplies the emotional and intuitional counterpart of the knowledge, and it is as essential as knowledge.

All thoughts, emotions, and the motions of currents are energy. Before these are captured by our thoughts, they can be captured by our feelings. For millions of years man has lived under the guidance of his feelings. Actually, his feelings have enabled him to keep closer contact with the subjective or Subtle World and thus live a more harmonious life within the cycles of his manifestations.

The mental unfoldment of man came much later and slowly disabled the centers of feeling in man. At the expense of feeling, the mental power grew and grew until it reached a state in which it almost turned into a monster.

The great center of feeling, the heart, was ignored, and the bridge of contact with the harmony of the Universe was forgotten.

The Great Ones are Those Who have kept the equilibrium between feeling and knowing.

The heart stands for the interest of universal harmony. Thought stands for the interest of the individualized form. The balance between these two is what we call equilibrium or *conscious existence*. When you see a beautiful bird singing near a flower or upon a rock, remember that it is the vibration of the primary energy. Feel it, and ponder upon it.

The flow of creativity is the period in which the human soul turns into a bridge between the subtle and the earthly spheres, between the worlds of thought and feeling.

Balance is different from equilibrium. Equilibrium is the harmony within and between the parts of a living and acting organism or form. Harmony is the exchange of energies between the parts, without disturbing the balance of the parts. Balance is the prevention of extremes and the restoration of equality of weight, power, rights, reception, and giving.

In equilibrium there is a constant progressive motion toward perfection. Every step of motion is based upon the law of balance of the factors promoting motion.

There is also a very mysterious agent in equilibrium which is called purposefulness or a goal-fitting urge. Equilibrium is achieved with the harmonious cooperation between the form, the energy, and the urge to goal-fitness for progressive unfoldment and creativity.

Balance makes each of the three factors ready for the work of equilibrium. Energy reaches its destination when the original flow, formation, and operation interact in equilibrium.

Lack of equilibrium produces confusion. Balance without equilibrium creates confusion. One must find how this happens.

Confusion is a powerful force which can agitate multitudes of forms (men or objects). Or it can create inertia or inaction. Confusion is a great political tool to hide discrepancies in the ruling power or to gain the power of exploitation. Confusion originates when you are programmed in such a way that your feelings act against your thinking and your thinking disapproves of your feelings.

Confusion disappears when thought and feeling are harmonious and in agreement. Confusion does not disappear when your thought rules your feeling.

The center of feeling, the heart, cannot restore understanding and integrity in your being, and for a long period of time the heart suffers until the mind begins to understand the source of confusion and cooperates with the heart to end the confusion.

The worth of man is conceived and reaches its flowering only when man learns to use energy in such a way that it increases harmony, equilibrium, and synthesis in space, time, and form.

53

Natural Calamities

We are accustomed to thinking that natural calamities occur on earth or only on the earthly plane. Our science has not yet penetrated into other domains. As lightning occurs on the physical plane, lightning also occurs in the astral plane; and as physically we run away or try to protect ourselves from lightning, we must take similar precautions when astral lightning and thunder occur.

For physical plane lightning we have created the lightning rod, which directs the electrical fire into the earth and prevents burning and fire. But no one has yet consciously invented certain protections for astral lightning, astral earthquakes, astral floods, astral conflagrations, and astral tornadoes. People have not yet realized that such astral calamities exist, as do physical calamities.

It is still very early to talk to people about mental catastrophes and calamities. Although the effects are clearly visible in the thinking of people, no one yet sees the causes for which the consciousness of people passes through crises.

Astral calamities are very evident if one observes the hospitals, prisons, courts, and luxurious parties which contain lust, hatred, revenge, and other destructive elements. If one is not able to protect himself from the lightning of the Subtle World, he will be hit by it, and the result will be insanity, crimes, and self-destruction through various abuses. Whenever astral floods occur, people enter mass psychoses and madness, killing and massacring each other. When astral tornadoes occur, the epidemic of fear spreads with its consequences. Whenever astral fire spreads, people either devote themselves to certain ideas, images or people, or they expose themselves to prostitution and gluttony and live an obnoxious life through the use of alcohol, drugs, and sex.

Mental calamities leave lasting effects in the form of degeneration of values and annihilation of the sense of sacredness, respect, adoration, and admiration. We also see the increase of indifference toward the needs of people, dark egotism, totalitarianism, and self-worship. Mental calamities manifest in acts of genocide, war, revolution, and massive destruction.

One may ask, "Why does man suffer because of calamities occurring on earth, in the astral plane, and in the mental plane?" The answer is very simple: The actions, emotions, and thoughts of man are responsible for all natural calamities on the three planes. It is our actions, emotions, and thoughts that evoke natural calamities. Nature reacts when wrong actions are taken, when wrong emotions are cherished, when wrong thoughts are encouraged and spread. It is our wrong thoughts, emotions, and actions that disturb the equilibrium of the three worlds simultaneously, just as, for example, a friend's wrong action can disturb us physically, emotionally, and mentally. When Nature is disturbed, the currents rush to restore the equilibrium, clearing away the factors that caused the disturbances.

Mental calamities are more widespread and have more consequences than astral calamities. Astral calamities do greater damage than physical, earthly calamities. Man is ignorant about the subtle nature, and he thinks that natural calamities are limited only to the earthly plane. Future psychologists and scientists will discover the relations between physical, astral, and mental spheres. It is only after the realization of the facts occurring on subtle levels that it will be possible to understand the causes of many events occurring on earth.

It is possible to be hit by emotional lightning; it is possible to be hit by mental lightning; but try to search for the causes which have coinciding effects upon the mundane plane. Most emotional and mental disturbances are the result of disturbances going on in the Subtle Worlds, either in man himself or on the earth in general. Emotional and mental calamities do not evaporate until they hit the physical plane and exhaust themselves in physical calamities. This is their cycle.

It is very interesting to know that natural calamities are more frequent on the mental and astral planes than on the physical plane. Those who are only focused on the physical plane see the effects of mundane calamities, but in a way they are protected from astral and mental calamities. Those who are focused in the emotional plane see the effect not only of astral calamities but also of physical calamities. Those who are focused on the mental plane can see calamities on all three planes.

If people are focused on the physical plane and do not sense astral or mental calamities, it does not mean that they do not suffer astrally or mentally. However, their suffering is mainly paid on the physical plane, or they are indirectly or directly affected by those who are caught in astral or mental storms and disturbances.

How does one escape natural calamities on the three planes? The answer is given in the Ageless Wisdom. It can be simplified as follows:

1. Think right, feel right, and act right.
2. Shelter yourself under your good deeds, loving emotions, and pure thoughts.
3. Strive for perfection, manifest beauty, work for justice.
4. Develop intuition or straight-knowledge.
5. Increase your psychic energy.
6. Strive toward the Hierarchy.
7. Cultivate joy.

With such steps you will develop an immunity and a shield to stand against natural calamities on the three planes.

Natural calamities on the three planes also come into existence when man is not ready to register, assimilate, and use energies which Nature cyclically releases. In certain cycles, the earth, the astral earth, and the mental earth release new energies in obedience to solar and galactic cycles and stimulations. If human beings are not ready for such energies, they either misuse them, or lead themselves into self-destruction, or slowly degenerate on the planet in their own pollutions and hatred. If people are ready, they can use these released energies for great scientific discoveries, social changes, emotional upliftments, and spiritual breakthroughs.

Every time Nature releases new energies, a great opportunity is given to man to build a bridge between higher and lower worlds and expand his consciousness and beingness toward higher domains. When new energies are released and humanity is not ready to absorb and utilize them, they act as natural calamities and create devastation in the human kingdom due to the unreadiness of humanity. Such events occur age after age, but humanity cannot see them because it is imprisoned in its ego, separatism, materialism, and totalitarian tendencies. Only after overcoming such "Cardinal Sins" will man become a co-worker of the physical, emotional, and mental planes.

54

Five Deaths

Man passes away through five kinds of death:

1. Physical body death
2. Astral body death
3. Mental body death
4. The death of the Chalice, after which starts the liberation of the human soul
5. Planetary body death

Our future physical bodies are built of the elements which we have produced through our present physical actions. These elements are in the form of vapor, gas, and motion activated in Space. They are related to each other by the frequency of the actor, the human soul. These elements come back to us at the time of reincarnation and are built into the physical body by the impressions imposed upon them which are found in the physical permanent atom.[1]

Every time we leave our body, these elements travel with us as our companions. If we penetrate levels where they cannot come, they wait for us at the threshold of the plane. In the future, their totality forms the *Dweller on the Threshold.*

The astral body does not disintegrate after one passes away but serves as a vehicle of contact for the human soul. If the person is really advanced, his astral body burns away almost immediately when he crosses the astral plane to the mental plane. This is the second death.

All our astral or emotional emanations are again related to us through the frequency of our human soul which generates them. They follow the person to the astral plane and stay with him for a long time until the person crosses into the mental plane (if he does). Astral

---

1. For further information on the permanent atoms, please refer to *The Science of Becoming Oneself,* Chapter 12, "The Chalice and the Seeds"; and *The Psyche and Psychism,* Chapter 89, "The Seven Principles in Man."

elements cannot penetrate into the mental plane. They wait on the threshold of the astral plane, and when the human soul begins to incarnate, these elements provide the substance for his future astral body, which is formed by the impressions found in the astral permanent atom that are forced upon these elements.

In the third death, man leaves his mental body in mental space and advances to a state of extreme joy and peace. His mental elements do not penetrate into this sphere but wait on the threshold When the human soul begins to incarnate by the pull of the Law of Karma, these elements form his mental body through the impressions found in the mental permanent atom.

Thus we see that our three bodies are the continuation of our former bodies. Whatever degree of transmutation they had reached, they continue from that point on. We carry on their transmutation to still higher levels or bring them backward into degeneration.

Some Buddhist teachers insist that the incarnating one is the sum total of his "emanations." [2] As materialists, they think that man is only a chemical combination without a core or a soul, and that *scandas*, or emanated elements, disperse and recombine and become an incarnated human being. I call this attitude "metaphysical materialism" It denies the existence of a magnet — the soul — which scatters these elements in their journey and reaccumulates them into the reincarnated human form.

During the chain of physical and astral deaths, the human soul is not yet formed in general but is a center of life-energy which he absorbs from Space and transmits to the bodies. It is only in the mental death that the soul comes into blooming. In the fourth death he gains conscious immortality.

Through their rituals and ceremonies, all ancient mysteries, brotherhoods, and religions have had one simple aim: to make the flowering of the human soul possible, or to make his existence possible. The human soul goes through the same process of conception as the human body does. He needs energy, nourishment, and the proper conditions to develop harmoniously and safely. The nourishing energy reaches the soul through the process of sublimation and transformation. Physical matter is transformed into emotional, mental, and spiritual matter and turns into the food of the soul. This sublimation and transformation is carried on through the following:

---

2. Emanations, figuratively speaking, are the result of actions, emotions, and thoughts which as a whole, according to certain Buddhists, incarnate as the human form.

—observation
—concentration
—aspiration
—meditation
—detachment
—renunciation
—discipline
—awakening
—expansion of consciousness

Crises, dangers, heavy responsibilities and labor, pressures of conscience, and virtues bring a great amount of sublimation of substance. Sacrificial services provide the highest quality food for the soul. Unless a person passes through such a process, the formation of the soul may be delayed for millenniums.

The Ageless Wisdom in all its forms provides those conditions, rules, and techniques through which man can develop his soul. It is true that once formed, the human soul never dies and is never born. It is only his vehicles that cyclically go through the states of death and life until the human soul enters the Path of liberation. This is the pure Teaching of the Enlightened One, which is distorted in the labyrinthine minds of His interpreters.

The fourth death is the final one. During this death not only are the physical, emotional, and mental bodies left behind, but the inner Chalice which holds the human soul is also destroyed. This Chalice is called the *causal body*. All the causes of birth and death are related to this Chalice, and the human soul tries throughout his life to reach the awareness of his freedom by filling the Chalice with wisdom, beauty, goodness, and joy.

When the human soul matures and no longer identities himself with the bodies and their emanations, he destroys the Chalice, liberates himself, and enters the plane of Intuition, or pure light. In this state, no causes of his actions, emotions, or thoughts reach him because throughout the ages he has learned not to create causes whose effects would pull him down to incarnation; rather, he has learned to create those causes whose effects raise him beyond any limiting and hindering elements.

In ancient times, when the knowledge of the soul was widespread and clear to people, they called the astral body the soul of the physical body. They called the mental body the soul of the astral body and the physical body. This was not a mistake because the soul was identified with the physical body and it was nothing else but the physical body. When the astral body was organized with its centers and senses, the soul inhabited the astral body and identified himself with the astral body and ruled the physical body as well as the astral body. A time came that the mental body was organized and the soul moved into it and identified with it and became the soul of the astral and physical bodies.

This is why certain people think that the soul leaves the body when the astral body leaves the body; and, when the soul incarnates, they think the astral body incarnates again because for them the astral body is the soul. But the fact is that the soul can have his independent existence when he succeeds in detaching himself from the mental body and uses the mental body as his vehicle to contact the mental world.

In ancient writings, the term *soul* was used to denote the leading principle in man in a given level of his evolution. When a Buddhist denies the soul, he does not really deny the possibility of an immortal principle in the vehicles; rather, he denies the soul identified with the vehicles.

Each body is at the same time a vehicle of a life, which is called an elemental. Physical, emotional, and mental elementals are lives, and their inclination is toward involution. The human soul has a great responsibility to use these bodies in such a way that gradually they reverse their course and begin to follow the evolutionary path. When the human soul leaves his bodies, these elementals keep their magnetic rapport with the human soul. When he begins to come to the physical plane, these mental, astral, and physical elementals succeedingly join the person in the process of incarnation.

Sometimes, because of close contacts, the elementals enter the embryo during conception and carry the parents' personality characteristics to them. It also happens that through exaggerated sexual practices one loses a great part of his elementals — physical, astral, or mental — and causes complications in his bodies, which in turn deprive him of his vitality. One who mixes with various elementals through sexual license creates nervous, emotional, and mental turbulences. This is why sexual purity has been emphasized by great Sages throughout the centuries.

The Ageless Wisdom says that when a human soul does not reach a certain level of development in a given time and breaks the law of love, his elementals can come into incarnation without him. Such incarnations are like abortions in which the personality is born in a defective form. This is why some people think that the incarnated one is the sumtotal of the accumulated *scandas* or elements produced by man while living.

When the physical body dies, the soul who is identified with the astral body survives for a short or long time in the astral plane. The time of survival is short if the body is refined; it is long if the body is coarse. When the astral body dies, the soul goes through another nightmare of death and in due time is pulled to earth for an incarnation, which occurs unconsciously if he has no continuity of consciousness. In this stage, man dies, and he is dead. He takes another body without having awareness of the process.

The mental body lives longer, and the soul has quite a good memory. But when the mental body dies, the soul is pulled to the earth; and, because of his more advanced state, he automatically chooses parents fitting to his level and to his future development.

Unless the causal body is developed, man is a victim of a state of unconsciousness in which he is not aware of himself and he does not exist for himself. When man is identified with his astral body, he is conscious only of being an astral body in an astral world. When man is identified with his mental body and he has succeeded in building his causal body, he is conscious only of being a mental body in a mental world. But when he succeeds in detaching himself from the mental body, he lives in the physical, astral, and mental worlds as a soul, not as a body.

After an Enlightened One leaves His causal body, He can again walk among men, but this time with a body of light. None of His thoughts, emotions, words, and actions create karma, but He influences people so that they can find the way of liberation.

The human soul is the flower of the Divine Spark, the Divine Spirit within the form of man. It takes thousands of years to bring such a flower into existence. It is the flowering of the Spark that forms the Individuality, the real "I." Unless this "I" or Individuality is formed, man does not have conscious existence and conscious immortality, although the spirit is always there as the core of the human mechanism.

The human soul must gain his conscious immortality by living a life of Beauty, Goodness, Righteousness, Joy, and Freedom and by paying all his debts accumulated by his wrong thinking, wrong emotions, wrong words, wrong actions, and, of course, his wrong motives.

Karmic elements, or those emanations which in their totality build our future bodies before liberation, not only exercise a magnetic pull over a traveling soul, retarding his evolution, but they also act as polluting factors in the three worlds, affecting living beings everywhere. With every thought, emotion, word and action, we spread our effect upon life as a whole, upon those who key in to our expressions, and upon those who live in the three worlds. On the other hand, after liberation all our influences spread everywhere over the earth and the subtle spheres and build new paths and bridges for the advancement of the human soul. All our expressions spread like the fragrance of the most beautiful flower, helping people develop their souls.

Nature is like a tree; "I am the tree and you are the branches."[3] Each branch brings fruit, which in its turn may become a tree. If it does not become a tree, it fertilizes the tree, and another opportunity is given to it to enter the mainstream of the tree, to bloom, be a fruit, and eventually take root and be a tree. This is the law of Nature: All individualized lives are given power to be like the Source from which they have originated.

After these four deaths, there is a fifth one which we read about in sacred literature. This is called the death of the planetary body, after which the Liberated Warrior enters the Cosmic Astral Plane. The planetary body is the sum total of the seven bodies that the human soul has gradually built. He eventually begins to function on the plane called *Adi*, or the Divine Plane.

At the Seventh Initiation, the Initiate leaves the sum total of these finest of bodies, composed of the four Cosmic Etheric Substances, and enters the Cosmic Astral Plane. No Teaching is given yet about this plane, except a few hints here and there; but one thing is clear — that the Path of Perfection is the Path leading the human Spark from one level to another level of liberation.

What kind of life can there be in the Cosmic Astral Plane? Maybe a life that is as different from our life as our life is different from the life existing in a lake. The future glory of the human soul is beyond our present level of comprehension.

There are many interesting events related to the process of death and dying. Such events may clarify the subject further, if considered carefully. For example, when some advanced human beings suddenly die or die with fear, they enter the astral plane and sleep there. Someone must awaken them and make them realize that they have already left the body and are "alive" and safe.

A man had a vivid experience of awakening a friend of his, an advanced disciple, who had been living in California. The disciple passed away but remained asleep on the astral plane. It took the man

---

3.   John 15:5

a few minutes to visit the friend and awaken him, telling him that he had already left the body and he was safe. Immediately the disciple awakened and went toward higher spheres.

When the moment of death approaches, people often withdraw to the astral plane and escape from the physical body, as if they were entering into sleep. It is this attitude that makes them sleep there until someone awakens them.

There are other cases in which the passing one enters the astral plane to sleep, but he awakens and comes back to the etheric plane to continue the things he was doing.

A woman who had died was still in her astral body and used to visit her office or prepare her bed for sleep. Once an advanced disciple visited her while she was preparing her bed. The person explained the situation to her and told her that she had left the physical body and was now in the astral body. He told her that she must not go to sleep in the astral plane but go forward into higher planes. She understood and "awakened" and passed toward higher planes. She had died in her sleep and she did not pass through the experience of dying, so it was very natural for her to go to sleep in the astral plane and awaken on the etheric plane.

People instinctively want to live longer. It is better to live as long as possible, not for the sake of living and having pleasure but for the sake of gathering more knowledge and more experience and helping people.

Our worldly lives condition the life we will have in the subtle planes. As one feels the approaching steps of death, he must consciously prepare himself and do extensive study about the states existing after death, by all possible means, avoiding every materialistic view that sees death as annihilation. He must strengthen the thought in his heart that no matter how he has lived, opportunities will be given to him to enjoy the love of God and the beauty of the Higher Worlds.

The astral body swells up and hardens as we continuously increase the astral element by our desires and by the imagination of our desires. The bigger and harder the astral body is, the longer it takes to dissolve in the astral world and release the Indweller. Thus billions of people are chained in the astral plane through their bodies hardened by numerous multicolored desires.

It is advantageous to have control upon our imagination and desires to speed our evolution on the subtle planes. The less desire we have, the less time we spend in the astral plane. Each desire built in physical incarnation must exhaust itself on the astral plane. In such a situation, man is caught in a web of desires, which, when enjoyed in the astral world, gain new energy and new momentum to repeat themselves almost endlessly, keeping the Indweller in a state of continuous enchantment and glamor.

Who wants to resign from his materialized desires? Didn't he dream and desire them night and day in the physical world? Now he has them. How will he detach himself from them?

This is how pleasure, which is the result of actualization of desire objects, keeps the man for centuries in the astral plane, forbidding him from passing toward higher levels. This prison can be broken only by listening to the advice of the *workers* on these planes, or by remembering the Teaching about glamors and tearing the veil of pleasure with the intention of going forward into a great light.

But this is not easy. Often Teachers, telepathically or by direct contact, try to help people. This is why in all the Teaching, attachment to sense objects is forbidden and detachment is presented as a great virtue. The less desire you have, the greater future you will have in the Higher Worlds and also in the physical world, when you go to another Round.[4]

Earth life is used for an important labor. This labor is to accomplish *while on earth* the transformation and death of the subtle bodies that man developed throughout centuries.

For example, on the path of earthly evolution, one must be able to die emotionally while living and, when he dies, go directly to the mental plane. But the emotional body does not die while one is living until it reaches its maturity in an earthly life. After it reaches its maturity, it is possible that it dies while the person is still living.

Then, in earthly life, not only the emotional body but also the mental body must die, and man will incarnate not with the mental body but with the intuitional body. Such a man will be a superior human being.

The etheric body also one day must die, and man will be born with an electrical body of four Cosmic Ethers. It is this body that can be resurrected any time because matter and time cannot limit such a body.

If man wants to incarnate, his electrical body of Cosmic Ethers condenses and becomes visible as a physical body. He will have the power to walk on water, be instantaneously in another location, lift

---

4. For further information regarding Rounds, please refer to *Cosmos in Man,* Chapter 1, and *The Psyche and Psychism,* Chapter 9.

himself into space, and penetrate through doors and walls. He can also become invisible or change his countenance.

There are formations that one must destroy before he is able to destroy his bodies.

For example, accumulations of glamors must be destroyed before the emotional body can be annihilated. The illusions must be destroyed before the mental body can be annihilated. Ego, vanity, and separatism are parts of the mental illusions which must be annihilated.

The incarnated period of a man has two cycles:

1. To carry the bodies to perfection
2. Slowly to annihilate the bodies to guarantee the liberation of the soul into ultimate freedom

The construction of the bodies enables a person to come in contact with the corresponding planes. When any given plane is transcended, the body corresponding to that plane is not necessary because the higher body can do all that the lower body did.

The maturity of a lower body accumulates in the higher body when the higher body is ready to take over the operations of the lower body and when it is ready to operate as the body that it is. The higher body then "swallows" the lower and makes it disappear in its own glory.

The dying process of the etheric, astral, and mental bodies takes place on earth.

The other bodies, namely the bodies built by the fourth, third, second, and first Cosmic Ethers, go through the process of disintegration in the inner globes, possibly on the fifth, sixth, and seventh globes.

There are some people who do not have emotional bodies. It is their mind that controls all their relationships. These people are found in the First, Third, Fifth, and Seventh Ray fields.

There are some who do not have mental bodies and they relate to the world as Intuitives. Some of these people are found in monasteries of every religion, in mystical orders, or in the company of higher psychics. They are very rare in the world because they do not want to waste time in world affairs, but they influence the world through their projected vision. They live in the mountains and secluded canyons or valleys of the world.

Etherically dead ones live in Higher Ashrams. They are the Immortals or Masters. Their physical bodies are formed of the substance of higher Cosmic Ethers.

We are told that periodically the fire emanating from the Galaxy facilitates the destruction of the bodies.

Periodically, certain people's astral and mental bodies are annihilated to prepare them to play various roles in Cosmos, but when such roles are fulfilled, they resume their bodies and continue their evolution. Such intervals bring credit to them, and they evolve faster than if they were left to themselves. Such souls are carried to certain planets, where mindless or emotionless people live, and they are given certain challenges to hasten their evolution.

Sometimes such people help certain devas who do not have mental or astral bodies. Often devas use them to experience earthly life.

"Mindless" people in the world act as if they were mechanical, but they do the most complicated labors. They operate under the command of a group soul who uses them in relation to certain tasks.

Some of these people feel as if some other force were operating in them, and others never realize it.

This is not the case of an entity possessing a person but rather a case of the remote control of a group soul who, because of the lack of the mental body of the person, can control it according to its own plans and needs.

There are also cases in which some people's astral and mental bodies are petrified or dead, but we are not referring to such cases. Such people still carry their petrified or dead bodies with their physical body, thereby contaminating their surroundings with certain pollutions which are the result of degenerating forces of nature attracted to their disintegrating or petrified bodies.

Usually such people do not live long but die early in their childhood, or they live in areas of great pain and suffering which often regenerates their bodies and leads them to a "normal" life.

The administrative power of Nature is a subject which will draw the full attention of people in less than one hundred years.

55

Last Rites

The last minutes of departing from the world are considered to be very important. People recognize and reinforce the importance of the last hour through various ways:

1. They administer Holy Communion to make the consciousness of the departing one fuse itself with the consciousness of Christ.
2. They administer confession, thus giving a last chance to the departing one to throw out all the trash which he still has.
3. Inspirational readings are read, describing the flight of the soul into the realms of Light.
4. Melodies, songs, and mantrams are repeated, emphasizing the immortality of the soul.
5. Music is played, incense is burned, and certain colors are used to facilitate the departure.

The Esoteric Teaching has stated that the last moments of departure are extremely important, and they condition the "stratum in which the spark will dwell and determine the succeeding life."

At the last moment, one may see all the vanities with which he was involved, but he remembers the beauty of the Higher Worlds, and with an extreme effort he pulls himself out of all his glamors. This is why, eventually, esoteric instructions will be given to humanity, to nurses and doctors, to help the departing one with a special service which will raise his heart and consciousness toward the Higher Worlds.

Even when one thinks that the consciousness of the departing one is withdrawn, in many cases one should still continue to administer the last rites because the consciousness in general is very awake, though the mechanism shows the signs of final departure.

As one lives a life of sacrificial service, develops his virtues, and strives toward spiritual heights, his etheric centers unfold and greater fire is released in the aura. It is this fire which helps the man cross the threshold and penetrate into the Higher Worlds. Every kind of deceit, dishonesty, and action against Beauty, Goodness, and Righteousness weakens the fire and makes the transition difficult and painful. By every means, one must increase the psychic energy with which he penetrates into the Higher Worlds, thus destroying all obstacles on the Path.

Each striving toward Beauty, Goodness, Righteousness, Joy, and Freedom and each sacrificial service rendered in the name of one humanity creates various precious sediments which settle on the nervous system around the etheric centers. During the transition these sediments change into fiery energy which propels the soul toward the Higher Worlds. Sometimes these sediments are called our "savings" which meets our needs in critical moments of our life.

Our subtle body needs its special food in order to grow and stay healthy. The foods for the subtle body are created by joy, ecstasy, moments of worship, admiration, love for Hierarchy, compassion, solemnity, devotion, and others. All these produce the most precious energies which feed and build the subtle body. When the subtle body is organized, is healthy and pure, the flight into the Subtle World will be easy and full of expectancy and joy.

There are also things which hurt and damage the subtle body. One of them is irritation and the resultant imperil. Others are hatred, greed, attachment, and animalistic desires which produce certain kinds of ulcers in the subtle body. Such damages must be cured by psychological, medical, or spiritual means before the man passes away because the human soul will spend much energy to heal them in the subtle planes. Besides, as the vehicles go through fires, they cause intense suffering for man.

In the Teaching we are also told about the protective net. This is a network of fiery energies which surrounds the body and protects it from various attacks. During the transition it surrounds the subtle body and protects it from many dangers and attacks of hostile forces. This shield is used in the Subtle World on various occasions. We are told that it makes a man invulnerable. Later, when man passes into the Fiery World, it slowly dissolves in the fire of the Higher World.

We are told that this protective net must be nourished continuously with the spiritual fire emanating from spiritual centers and the heart. Those who have no higher centers unfolded do not have this shield. Possessed ones also lack such a protective net. Very advanced warriors appear with their protective net, as if they were wearing a coat of armor.

A developed heart is like a rose which radiates the most wonderful fragrance in the Subtle World. Every time a developed heart enters the Subtle World, there occurs a great joy, a great festival. But when a soul enters the Subtle World with a heart whose petals are drooping and dry, people in the Subtle World feel horror. Nothing upsets them more than a dead heart.

The Cosmic Heart radiates streams of fiery energy into Space. During certain cycles these energies return to the Cosmic Heart.

Humanity uses some of these energies and lets a part of them return to Nature, instead of sending back all energies plus those which it has created. This is what Christ intended to explain when He spoke about the rich man who left some money to his servants. One of them multiplied it; another one made a few extra dollars; the third one buried the money and gave it back as it was given to him. When money is not increased, it loses value. If multiplied, as in the case of the first servant, then it increases in value. Humanity is made up of the type of men characterized by the second servant; they take more than they give. As to the third one, the judgment was severe. He was expelled from the work of the Lord.

Man is a great refinery. He can increase the amount of energy in Cosmos by aspiring and striving toward Beauty, Goodness, Righteousness, Joy, and Freedom with his creative labor. Those who increase the energy of the Cosmos will advance faster and will be the co-workers of the Cosmos. It is such people who penetrate into the higher levels of the Subtle World and soon pass into the Fiery World.

The released energies in the Cosmos must be impregnated by the fire of the human heart; they must be used in human creative labor *and multiplied.* But we are told that the majority of people do not multiply these energies, and they do not use them in their life, creating waste and disturbances in the given energies.

The karma of humanity is measured by the fertilization and multiplication of energies. Every time man "hides his talent in the earth," he is cast out from the labor of the Lord for a long period of time.

From childhood one must develop fiery striving toward any form of beauty. Also, people do not realize that in each man there exists a great beauty. Often this beauty has no form, no sound, no color; but, like a magnet, it thrills the human soul and evokes a fiery striving in him. During the moments in which one feels this beauty in his heart, tears stream from his eyes. Beauty releases a deep joy which overflows from the cup of the personality.

From a young age, children must learn to aspire toward that Innermost Beauty, which later will turn into an eagle taking the human soul to Higher Worlds.

Children must learn that we are here for a short time; that this world is not our destination; that this world is a school and a place of discipline; that this world is a place to pay our taxes or karma; that this world is a field in which we must prove our achievements. They must learn that this world is a place in which we must fertilize spatial seeds, increase the energy we receive, and give it back with an additional amount of energy; that this world is a place in which we must prove the Law of Unity in all our actions. Such a curriculum would have saved all the blood that has been shed for ages upon the earth. Such a course of study would build in each human being the golden bridge leading to the Higher Worlds.

Our subtle body is galvanized by a fluid which is generated by psychic energy when it passes through our fiery centers. The greater the development of our centers, the stronger and more organized will be our subtle body. Without psychic energy, our subtle body will be petrified or diffused, and during the transition it will not provide a good vehicle for ascent.

One of the greatest obstacles on the threshold of the transition is fear of the Subtle World. Fear paralyzes the subtle body, weakens it, and makes it very difficult for it to penetrate into the Subtle World. That is why before the transition the soul must be charged with fearlessness and deep joy.

Before transition, one must be told about the wonders and beauties of the Higher Worlds and about the beautiful people of the Higher Worlds. It is the joy, the fearlessness, and the expectations of finding beautiful people and environments that strengthen the soul and encourage him to overcome obstacles with fiery speed.

Special instructions must be prepared for those who will be in attendance during the last moments of the departing one. It is very dangerous and terrible to moan, cry, and express fear and despair in the presence of the departing one.

There are certain dates in our life when final preparation and formation of the subtle body takes place. If during this period the human soul is still identified with vices, earthly desires and negative feelings, the subtle body cannot organize itself and departs in a semi-formed or disturbed condition. Such disturbances and various debris attached to the subtle body are considered the most ugly sign for higher astral inhabitants. The astral atmosphere is polluted by such disturbances and accumulations to a considerable degree.

Sometimes dark spirits rejoice in seeing such a loaded astral body and try to possess it. Such possessions take place often in the Subtle World. Strangely enough, people reincarnate with the possessing one.

Many criminals are a result of such possessions, as well as many mediums whose hearts are dark and who have no lit candle in their souls.

The possessing one acts as a medium in order to transmit to people mixed and distorted truths, misleading them especially in the times of their heaviest crises.

Often one can observe the possessed one through the eyes of the medium who acts as a bridge between the Subtle World and the physical world.

All that man does on this planet in secret may remain so for a long time. But anything that is secretly performed on earth is a plain and clear event revealed in the strata of the Higher Worlds. Those who know how to penetrate into the Subtle Worlds will be able to see exactly the hidden layers of an act performed secretly. The things that are mysterious for us are plain facts for the inhabitants of the Higher Worlds.

Such knowledge can introduce a powerful change in our earthly life and may create better relations between human beings. Long ago the Sages told us that all that man does must be performed as if a thousand eyes were watching. Man will not have so many troubles and headaches if such advice is observed.

Certain precise steps must be taken when a person is preparing to leave his body. One of the steps is to remind the person about the many services he has done for humanity, about the many kinds of help he has given to individuals and groups. As much as possible, one must remind the departing one how much his love, his care, his words, his sacrificial deeds, his striving, his example, his thoughts, and his creative talents have helped humanity, and how they will bring greater help as the years pass. It is also important to be factual and mention specific dates and occasions when the results of his labor manifested or will manifest in the future. It may be that the departing one will show very little response, but this is not important. The departing one hears and understands more clearly than you may imagine.

The second step is to remind him about the moments of joy he had in the past — joy from Nature; from meeting new friends; from various kinds of successes, graduations, performances, creativity, publications, promotions, love, friendships, labor, cooperation, gratitude, and respect given to him in many ways. He must be reminded about the many blessings of life he has enjoyed and about the heroic and sacrificial deeds he has performed for others that gave him deep joy. When joyful moments are brought to the surface, the departing one will gather great strength for his celestial journey. Each joy will turn into a source of energy.

The third step is to encourage him to continue his striving on the same line to which he has dedicated his life. For example, one may say to the departing one:

> We know you will continue serving people in all worlds, and nothing will stop your efforts. We know you will be more creative and you will radiate your genius in the Subtle Worlds, giving them greater beauties of music, writings, light, love, joy, and Cosmic ideas. You will bring harmony and enlightenment wherever you go.
>
> We know that when you decide to return, you will bring celestial beauties to earth in new forms and new expressions.
>
> We know that you will strive toward perfection in all conditions.
>
> We know you will serve the Plan, no matter what conditions you are in. All our thoughts and love will be with you.

Of course, this responsibility must be taken by some beloved friends of the departing one and the content of the words must be adapted to the level of the departing one, but the essence must remain the same.

Another very important suggestion will be to encourage him to be fearless:

> Be fearless in all conditions because your Guide is with you; Christ is with you; the presence of the Almighty One is within you. You have no reason to fear because God is Love and His angels seek to help everyone who departs.
>
> Karma is very powerful, but above karmic law stands compassion. Nothing can overcome compassion. Do not give up when apparent obstacles and phenomena confront you. You have the power to strike even the servants of darkness. Remember they are called the "trash of the Cosmos."

The divine power within you can be put into operation the moment you leave the body. Be fearless; be courageous; be daring; be striving, and the eye of God will watch over you.

The following information concerning the type of aid that can be given at the time of passing is contained in _Cosmos in Man_.[1] We are told that the following attitudes and procedures will be helpful:

1. There should be total silence in the sick room to help the one who is passing concentrate on his experiences, and consciously release himself from the physical body. A dying person is aware of all that is happening around him, though he may not be able to let it be known by any outer sign.
2. When the physicians know that there is no possibility of recovery, they should arrange to have orange light in the room. Orange light or color helps the person focus his consciousness in the head, perhaps between the eyebrows or at the top of the head. It may also be of help to those who are advanced enough to pass away through the orifice of the head. For a less evolved person it is better to have a red light, which releases the man through the solar plexus. If he is a humanitarian, whose heart quality is evolved, it is better to use a green light.
3. Another way to help the one who is passing is to sound or chant the OM, or _Om Mani Padme Hum_, at least seven times. The one who chants must be an able man in the spiritual field, capable of guiding the dying person out of the physical plane. To awaken or clear the consciousness of the dying one, the following mantrams are highly effective:

Avira Verma Yedhi

O Self-revealing One,
reveal Thyself in me.

Lead us, O Lord,
from darkness to Light,
from the unreal to the Real,
from death to Immortality,
from chaos to Beauty.

1. _Cosmos in Man_, Chapter 19, "The Process of Death and Life After."

In so doing, we are providing him companionship with our imagination and deep love.

4. There should be no crying, no hysterical screaming; nothing but silence, peace, love, gratitude, and blessings must fill the atmosphere of the room of the dying person.

5. It is very good to repeat or read mentally the second chapter of *The Bhagavad Gita*, which is of supreme help for the dying ones.

6. It is also important to anoint the person in transition with sacred oil, putting it on the head, ajna, throat, and heart centers. It will be of tremendous help in releasing the anchorage points of the etheric body.

7. The top of the head of the dying man should be facing toward the east, and the hands and feet should be crossed. The reason for this position is related to the electrical currents of the energies controlled by the etheric body.

8. The burning of incense is good. Sandalwood is highly recommended. One great Sage states that "no incense of any other kind is permitted." Sandalwood helps to separate the nadis from the nervous system and thus release the etheric body. It not only purifies the sphere of decaying or attacking thoughtforms, but also vitalizes the mental body.

   The following aromas may also be used during the departure of the soul: *Frankincense* is very good for strengthening the subtle body as it leaves the physical body. *Rose oil* protects the astral and mental centers. *Musk oil* strengthens the astral heart center and makes it courageous in flight. *Violet* purifies the astral sphere. *Deodar oil* repels all dark forces approaching the human soul. *Eucalyptus* repels astral entities of low order.

9. Care must be taken that those close to the dying person do not express, with grief or tears, their wishes or thoughts of seeing him back in the normal physical life. Such actions may create great conflict between the dying person and the Plan of his Soul, and sometimes the dying person can be caught within the network of such thoughts and wishes. The best approach is to bless the laws of Nature and to express love and blessings at the time of the farewell.

10. In the future it will be possible to accompany the dying person to the subtle levels while he is still in his physical body. This science must be taught to all those who are related to such duties. They will be instructed on how to come out of their

physical bodies and consciously guide the person as he leaves his body. The average priests, ministers, and officials of other religions are unaware of such facts. They repeat traditional prayers or chants, or formulate their own, according to their level of experience.

11. Following cremation, sandalwood should be burned for three days in the study or private room of the departed one, and group or individual meditation should be performed there, using seed thoughts taken from the *New Testament*, *The Bhagavad Gita*, or the *Dhammapada*. The atmosphere must be charged with radiating love, blessings, and gratitude.

A great Sage has stated, "Before so very long, burial in the ground will be against the law and cremation will be enforced." Throughout ages the corpse of the human being has been buried in the earth, polluting the soil with the germs of diseases, which in turn were passed to vegetables, animals, water, and then to human beings. Cremation helps to minimize this pollution and prevent many diseases from spreading. The use of well-constructed, sealed boxes does not guarantee that germs, the tiny lives which cause disease, will not escape and pollute the soil.

A great Sage states that if we use cremation, we will be able in the next million years to stamp out syphilis and other diseases, both from the human family and from the Soul of the planet. This seems like a long time, but if we remember that we will still return to this planet many times, we will be eager to take action to clean the planet, so that we may have a better home and better living conditions in the future for the ever unfolding human soul.

Burning the body eliminates most of these viruses, and thus we create a better future for humanity.

Certain people are carriers of such viruses. During their life they are not affected because the cycle of the germination of viruses is not in action yet.

Zodiacal signs are powerful sources of energies which awaken many viruses in certain configurations with the planet.

Usually people die according to a prearranged time. Whenever they die, cremation of the body is very essential. In our bodies viruses exist which are not yet discovered by the physicians. There are viruses that sleep for years and ages until they are restimulated by certain energies which cyclically appear and bring these viruses to life.

When we bury our bodies, these germs stay in the coffin for a while. Then they travel into the earth, and if the proper cycle comes for their germination, they become active, multiply, and attack living beings, and then become known as a new kind of virus.

There is another reason for cremation. It helps to detach the subtle vehicles of the soul from the etheric body and thus release the unfolding human soul to proceed on his own way toward higher realms. Without cremation the soul is attached to the etheric body for more than six days. Occultism holds that a man is not dead until he is separated from his etheric body, after leaving his physical body behind.

We are told that the etheric body is perpetuated through mummifying or embalming. This creates a very serious problem for the developing human soul. Sometimes the etheric body is kept in existence for ages, and if the person lived a wicked life, dark forces enter into such an etheric body and use it as a distributing station for their evil intentions. The Ancient Wisdom warns that we must be very careful not to touch mummies, or to get too close to their graves or tombs because their etheric bodies can still be active and used as vehicles by dark forces.

Cremation not only eliminates such attacks but also purifies the astral plane by burning some forms of low desires seeking expression through the etheric body. Thus cemeteries, which are fields of germs polluted by psychic forces, will eventually disappear.

People will soon realize that burying the body within the grave is exactly the same as accumulating your soiled clothes in your home. "Clothes" that cannot be used any more must be eliminated and not perpetuated within marble boxes as magnets of psychic pollution.

Cremation must take place as soon as possible after a qualified physician declares that the body is *truly* dead. Some great Teachers suggest that cremation should take place within twelve hours and must be delayed no longer than thirty-six hours. The unfolding human soul rejoices when he is released from the etheric body, which subtly relates him to the physical prison in which he has acted and suffered.

We are careful not to pass our germs to others, and if we know that our clothing is contaminated with germs, we try to disinfect them by using certain chemicals or by burning them. After such an act we feel released. The unfolding human soul experiences the same feeling when his body is burned away and can in no way harm any living form.

The Services of Cremation

The body must rest in a coffin surrounded by flowers. All present must pass by and wish joy, freedom, and bliss to the soul of the person. Any tears shed must be tears of joy and blessing. Very soft music may be played and sandalwood incense may be burned.

After everyone offers his blessings, the officiant will say,

(Name), we pray that your Guardian Angel will protect you and lead you to heavenly blessings and joy. You are free now from your past sufferings and cares. All will be well for you, and all will be well for those whom you left here on earth. Let no worry or any concern tie you to earth. You are an Eternal Traveler, and your destination is the Fiery Worlds. Do not lose time at any station. Go forward toward your goal.

> _More radiant than the Sun,_
> _purer than the snow,_
> _subtler than the ether,_
> _is the Self,_
> _the Spirit within my heart._
> _I am that Self._
> _That Self am I._

The ceremony will end with all saying the _Great Invocation_, followed by _five OMs_.

Simple Memorial Service

After the body is cremated, the friends may gather together in a room or at the home of the departed one in solemnity and silence. As they sit together, they will send their love, thoughts, and good wishes to the departed one. If there is any negative emotion or thought in their hearts, they must clear it with the spirit of forgiveness and blessings.

After fifteen minutes, they can play some music or a song that the departed one used to love. They can also read some literature which the departed one used to like very much. If the departed one was an author, artist, or composer, it is better to read from a favorite book he wrote, or play his compositions, or enjoy his paintings, etc. This period may last from one to two hours.

The next period will be dedicated to his memories. Everyone must mention something good and beautiful about the departed one, about his dreams, visions, and future plans. No negative word must be spoken about the departed one. No criticism must be voiced or even thought. Only the best memories must be voiced. Then the following mantram must be said together by all present:

Dear brother (Name), we are gathered here in your memory. May the beam of Divine Light illuminate your Path. May your Guardian Angel protect you from any attack. May the blessings of Christ shine in your heart throughout your journey.

We send you our love, blessings, and courage. Try always to strive toward the Fiery World. Do not be englamored by the objects of the level where you are. Remember that the three worlds are illusions. Strive toward the highest; search for the Teacher; aspire toward Christ.

We will keep your memory in our hearts. We will keep your visions alive, and (if he was a great leader) we will follow your steps until your plans and visions are actualized in the world. We ask that you also think about us, and in our times of need we hope to receive your impressions and inspirations.

May the light of Christ shield you and inspire you to strive toward higher achievement. When your time of incarnation arrives, please obey the call to come again and meet your obligations and responsibilities on earth.

May the love of Christ surround you.

OM. OM. OM. OM. OM. OM. OM.

Then all present will adjourn silently.

This mantram must be repeated three days after the departure and also after forty days, as well as every year on the departed one's birthday for at least three years; then every seven years.

During the memorial service it is better if people dress in all white and burn sandalwood or rose incense. Rose oil is very appropriate for the occasion. A picture of the departed one can be put on a table in the room, surrounded by roses or lilies.

Observance of Memorial Day

Memorial days are observed in many countries throughout the world. In the United States, Memorial Day began during the American Civil War, when a few very distinguished women put flowers on the graves of men from both sides of the conflict who died in that war. They did this in the hope of healing the wounds of all those who were still living. This was a great healing process for all those who survived as well as for those who departed in the war.

There is a deep meaning to what those women did for the people. Spiritually they created not only a constructive communication between those who died and those who lived, but also a constructive spiritual communication between the two warring parties.

On Memorial Day, wherever we are, we can read about the Higher Worlds and the possibilities waiting for us there. On Memorial Day we can establish spiritual contact with those beloved ones who departed from the earth. This spiritual communication can bring healing for us and for those who are departed. We can also observe this day by having a one hour retreat and doing the following seven healing steps:

1. Send real love to a departed one and let him know that you still love him. You can even play music for him or read some spiritual literature that he loved. You can also put some flowers on his grave, or before his photograph if he was either cremated or has an unmarked or unknown grave.

2. Tell him how much you want to forgive him, no matter what happened between the two of you. Tell him mentally and with sincerity that you have forgiven him forever. This will release him on his journey and help him to proceed on the way of his eternal evolution.

3. Ask his forgiveness for all the bad things you did to him, for all the troubles you caused him, deliberately or accidentally. Ask his forgiveness for your negligence, lack of respect, roughness, for your inconsideration and irresponsibility, and visualize that he has forgiven you from the depth of his heart.

4. Try to pay his debts that he left behind. Suppose he borrowed six hundred dollars and was unable to pay it back. Try to pay his debts, as a son, daughter, husband, wife, friend, as much as you are able to, so that you release the departed one from his anxieties.

5. Try to see his mistakes in life in his relationships with others and promise him that you will not make these same mistakes but instead will try to develop certain virtues that he had.

This is a healing process because departed ones know their weaknesses and want their relatives, friends, sons, and daughters not to fall into the same traps.

6. In your communication, promise to take care of the ones who were left orphans or helpless in any way. Try to meet the needs of the orphans, taking care of them or making the needed

arrangements to make them continue their schooling and live a comfortable life.

Departed ones worry very much about those whom they left behind. Try to do your best to release the departed one from that worry, even by taking care of his unfinished works.

7. Try to actualize the dreams and visions that the departed one had that, for some reason, he was not able to manifest. Your father, mother, sister, brother, teacher probably had constructive and creative dreams or visions and may have spoken to you about them. Memorial Day is the day in which you can tell them that you will do your best to actualize their dream.

I knew a man who built a huge sanctuary in order to actualize his father's dream. Another built a hospital in the name of his mother. Another disciple spread the Teaching of his Teacher all over the world and published them in many languages. Still others brought freedom to their nations, actualizing the dreams of their fathers.

On Memorial Day, there should be a sacred period in which we must communicate with the departed ones and express our love and concern.

It is probable that, for many reasons, on a certain level of their journey the departed ones continuously think about us. We must take this opportunity to re-establish our communication with nobility, forgiveness, gratitude, and sacrifice.

These thoughts, released love, and blessings from the Higher Worlds may bloom on the path of our life as beautiful flowers.

Judgment Days

In esoteric literature there are three kinds of Judgment Days given:

The first Judgment Day is when the human soul leaves his body and finds himself where his thoughts, words, and actions lead him.

The Subtle World is the place of highest justice, and the Laws of Nature give you exactly in accordance with what you have been on earth. But there is no courthouse in the Subtle World. You are your own judge, and the level where you are is exactly the place you should be. You see your life on earth, and you see where you are, and you accept all conditions as righteous effects of your life. But after seeing the operation of the karmic law, you begin to accept the law and strive toward higher dimensions, knowing that such a striving is the only way for you in the Subtle World and in future incarnations.

The second Judgment Day will be at the Fifth Round,[2] where all people will pass through fiery tests either to continue their ascent or fall into pralaya, until another Solar System fits their needs. This is the Judgment Day on the planetary scale, when all humanity will face its karma.

The third Judgment Day is called the final judgment. It is related to the graduation of humanity from the earth. Those who pass such a judgment day will be able to continue their evolution on the fifth globe and develop Solar consciousness.[3]

---

2. For further information on Judgment Days see *A Treatise on Cosmic Fire*, pp. 391-393, 425-426, 705-706; and *Esoteric Astrology*, p. 231, both by Alice Bailey.

3. *Ibid.*, pp. 28-31

56

Corpses

Dissolution of astral and mental bodies can start before the physical body shows signs of dissolution. The reasons for dissolution are many; for example:

1. A heartless life
2. A life lived in fear, anger, jealousy, hatred, revenge
3. A life in which there is continuous effort to deceive others
4. A life of hypocrisy
5. A life of exploitation

are lives which accumulate vices. These five vices cause the subtle bodies to disintegrate before the physical body dies.

The astral and mental bodies often react to such states of apathy and dissolution so much that the life departs from them and man lives as a corpse. Emanations coming from such people are very contagious, and their disintegrating bodies affect those who are close to them, inducing apathy, inertia, and depression in them. Disintegrating bodies pass their qualities to others, especially through sexual intercourse.

"People in whom the primary energy has ceased its movement have been called walking corpses." [1]

Such people still live and work, but their subtle bodies affect people around them, often polluting them. Such people are very afraid of death, and that is why they hang onto material possessions.

Astral and mental corpses are used as nourishment for astral entities. These entities are attracted to blood, and they often possess people, making them shed blood so that nourishment is provided to them. Such entities are also attracted to decomposing blood and to those who eat meat or use alcohol. Mediums are often held hostage in the hands of such entities.

---

1. Agni Yoga Society, *Brotherhood* (New York: Agni Yoga Society, 1962), para. 153.

The corresponding mechanisms in the physical body of those whose astral or mental body is dead slowly decay through various forms of diseases. It will be proven one day that the cause of our physical troubles originates from ailing or dead astral or mental bodies.

A sick or polluted astral body, or a dead astral corpse, enters the astral plane when a person leaves his physical body. It is here that the danger appears in its full ugliness. The contaminated, dead or distorted astral body becomes visible to inhabitants of the astral plane, spreading ugliness, poison, and various contaminating emanations such as negative emotions.

Sometimes when the person leaves his astral body and passes on to the mental plane, the corpse floats in the astral plane for a long time. But the extreme danger begins when such corpses come in contact with human beings directly or through mediums living on the physical plane.

Astral and mental corpses sometimes spread a heavy malodor, like the smell of a disintegrating animal body. It fills the room and disintegrates, creating physical, emotional, and mental disturbances in the environment. It is sometimes absorbed by the astral bodies of others in a short period of time, affecting their entire emotional relationships with others, or injecting them with various complicated, psychological ailments.

When the human soul, or ego, leaves the physical body, he still has his astral body or his astral corpse and his mental body or his mental corpse. In the Subtle World, he is conditioned by them.

Imagine a person whose astral body is dead in the astral plane. All the centers and senses of the astral body are dead. How will he communicate with the astral world? There are certain people in the astral world called "astral vultures" who devour these astral corpses.

Sometimes a person becomes "naked." This is a term used in esoteric literature referring to those who do not have the proper "clothing" — or body — for a particular plane.

There are also entities who try to vitalize the astral corpses and impress certain post-hypnotic messages upon them, which are then passed on to those who contact corpses. There are entities which use the corpses as their "ears" to come in contact with the inhabitants of the astral and/or physical plane. To come in contact with the physical plane, they use the *ectoplasm* of certain people.

Mental corpses are less abundant than astral ones. Some mediums contact mental corpses, which are either carried on from the physical plane, or left in the mental plane when the person is ready to take a new incarnation or is ready to pass into the Intuitional Plane. If the person is leaving the mental body to pass into the Intuitional Plane, in a few hours' time the mental body turns into a fiery ball and bursts into flame, then disappears.

If the corpse is left behind by a man on the path of incarnation, it often lives for centuries in the mental plane. If it is charged by worldly, separative, destructive interests, it eventually finds its way to those people on earth who think along the same lines and either obsesses or possesses them. In general, such a visitation is accomplished by the magnetic pull of mediums or those who are occupied in necromancy.

The brains of certain people are nourished by such corpses; that is why they continue to think continually along lines of crime, genocide, horror, terrorism, and destruction, rejecting any thoughts or proposals that may bring in righteousness, truth, and peace.

Mental corpses carry within their "diskettes" various political, economic, and scientific secrets. Those who come in contact with them either think that they are becoming very smart, or they think that such an entity is a living being who can show them a prosperous and victorious way to live. It is true that they give certain good advice, but at the same time they contaminate the roots of your being.

It is important for people to know the facts about astral and mental corpses so that they avoid them after death. It is easy to be fooled by such corpses as they resemble friends, family members, even enemies. If people do not know the facts, they often come close to the corpses, thinking that they are living beings.

Sometimes a person who has recently died finds the astral corpse of his father or mother and associates with it for years, never knowing that it is a corpse. In certain regions of the world, special ceremonies attract such corpses to the physical plane for those people who enjoy astral intercourse. Once they attract the astral corpse, they contact it through drugs or a self-induced trance so that intercourse can take place. Such corpses are also used for crime. But people must experience such horrible realities to really know about them.

Children must be watched very closely up to the age of three. Children in this age group are sometimes attacked by such astral copses. An atmosphere of prayer, meditation, beauty, study, and striving can repel such corpses.

Those who are contaminated by their own dead astral or mental bodies, or by subtle corpses around them, sometimes would like to rid themselves of these bodies. To do this, they use an ugly technique called *slander*. They slander someone who is dear to them; then, once they develop irritation, malice, hatred or anger in others about the slandered person, they create a magnet in others that attracts the low-level corpses to them. Corpses can only dwell in disintegrating matter, and when slander is admitted, it creates disintegration in the system.

The interesting point is that the corpses do not actually leave the former person; they simply make him attract other corpses into his environment. This worsens the situation for all parties concerned because they begin to lose their powers of reasoning and rationality, imitating the psychology of the corpses and eventually killing their own subtle bodies in depression and through the force of hatred.

As the human soul needs to proceed on its way toward the Higher Worlds, so the elements of the astral and mental planes also need to progress in their evolution. The human soul proceeds by keeping himself focused within his own essential divinity, casting away his bodies in due time. But the astral and mental bodies must disintegrate to give their atoms a chance to evolve or be collected into their corresponding planes or reservoirs.

The delay of the departure of the human soul from his bodies is as contrary to the laws of Nature as the persistence of the bodies to exist as bodies, refusing to disintegrate. When advanced souls leave their bodies, their bodies naturally burst into flame and disperse. But those who are attached to their bodies both retard their own freedom and the release of their bodies. This is why astral and mental corpses must be burned away, by any means. Mediums and channels must not associate with them, nourish them, or attract them to earth, thus perpetuating their existence.

Advanced souls, who develop fearlessness and courage, easily leave their bodies, when the law demands, without the slightest attachment or fear. But those who worship their bodies and are not able to develop courage and fearlessness become attached to their subtle bodies after they die, as if those bodies were their only means of existence, thus delaying their own release. The more they delay, the more painful and frightening the process of leaving those bodies becomes.

It is known that mental or astral corpses intensify and become visible to certain people, often absorbing elements from their aura. In such cases, the people feel sudden fatigue or exhaustion. Such corpses are like automatons; they act like machines but severely frighten people and contaminate the environment. They sometimes appear in those locations where they committed a secret crime, in places where they were killed or vandalized, or in places where they hid a treasure or secret papers.

If the human soul is not advanced but leaves his astral body, that body floats in the astral plane like an astral "diskette." This diskette is attracted to mediums, and, like a computer, the mediums "print out" its contents, as if it were a message from the Masters. An astral "diskette" contains mostly emotional impressions, but mental impressions may also be there, though very shallow. By contacting a medium, this diskette is recharged, receiving vitality and therefore living longer as a "spook." It then slowly disintegrates, either in the environment or in the medium, or remains in the medium's astral body, causing many complicated diseases.

The mental body also has its time. When the mental body of the average person is attracted to worldly spheres because of its contents, it contacts mediums and becomes more vital, living longer and hindering the advancement of those who come in contact with it. If a mental corpse is kept alive longer than natural, it may happen that its former owner, upon taking incarnation, will attract his old mental body to himself, as well as the new mental body that Nature provides to everyone taking incarnation. Imagine the chaos that having two mental bodies would create! One would be many centuries old; the other would be totally new and conditioned for the progressive path.

Many mediums nourish such corpses, which are used as "diskettes" in their own mental computers. Such "diskettes" contain average or below average information and are unable to contribute to the advancing life of our planet.

Fools are often fascinated by the messages that they receive, and long for "secrets" that are revealed to them. No matter how many times the prophecies of such mediums prove false, they do not give up because control is held by the corpses and not by the mediums themselves.

Some lower psychics receive recordings from "diskettes" which were recorded centuries ago. They may contain prophecies of events that have already taken place.

One of my friends living in Nepal saw firsthand the making of a false prophecy regarding the destruction of a huge temple. While studying an old manuscript in a monastery, he noticed being added to the text, much after the event had occurred, that such and such temple would be destroyed at a particular period by some people. Years later, the manuscript was read by others, "proving" that the prophecy was correct, even though the so-called prophecy was added to the manuscript after the destruction of the temple!

We are told that such apparitions can be disintegrated by the willpower of advanced individuals. The destruction of such corpses also releases their former owners, wherever they may be. In various ways, the owners are tied to their "cars," and they are responsible for the accidents created with those "cars."

The less corpses we have in and around us, the better our hearts will be. The ancients warn us not to damage or kill the heart and mind before death.

The death of the subtle bodies before physical death sends various signals which appear in the victim. Some of the signs referred to in the Teaching are these:

1. The person turns irresponsible, careless, and does not admit his irresponsibility or carelessness.
2. He begins to criticize and slander the group to which he is related.
3. His eyes appear glassy.
4. He rejects cooperation.
5. He falls into coarse pleasures.
6. He may begin to think, say, and do anything he wants, giving license to himself, declaring that all he does is in the name of freedom. This is a very hidden symptom of decay of the mental body. When the mental body begins to decay, darkness increases in one's life. People in darkness feel free to do anything they want. M.M. says, "When all becomes darkened, then people fancy that everything is permitted to them." [2]
7. He feels depressed and abandons his creative abilities.
8. He enjoys treason and slander.
9. He develops certain diseases related to the nervous system.
10. He shows signs of ingratitude, unforgiveness, and irritation.

There are many other signals; if a person observes himself, he can find signals which are even more subtle.

Nature does not want the subtle bodies to disintegrate before the coarse body. This is why mental and emotional health are imperative to everyone striving toward perfection.

---

2. Agni Yoga Society, *Fiery World II* (New York: Agni Yoga Society, 1946), para. 417.

57

The Law of
Reincarnation

The Law of Reincarnation is a collective law. Many other Laws assist this Law to fulfill its destination. For example, the Law of Reincarnation is composed of

1. The Law of Attraction and Repulsion
2. The Law of Vibration
3. The Law of Synthesis
4. The Law of Karma
5. The Law of Cycles

Through the **Law of Attraction and Repulsion** the human soul locates himself in a certain area on the planet, in a certain race or nation.

Through the **Law of Vibration** he selects his parents or those with whom he will affiliate in family, group, and business circles.

Through the **Law of Synthesis** he becomes a part of a certain activity, or he creates an organization around the keynote of his soul.

Through the **Law of Karma** the physical, emotional, and mental life-events are organized; his dues are paid; and new opportunities for growth and unfoldment are given.

Through the **Law of Cycles** the duration of his life is controlled on each plane or in each form of activity.

Departed ones pass through various levels of states, or levels of existence. Some go higher to the Intuitional Plane; some remain at the etheric and lower astral planes for a long time. Some penetrate to lower or higher mental planes and come back into incarnation.

Those who lived a sacrificial life with compassion and light enter into *Rest*. The word *Rest* is not an accurate explanation of the state of consciousness where an advanced soul enters. It is better to call it the state of bliss and undisturbed happiness. In esoteric literature, it is called Devachan, which means the abode of angels — symbolically perhaps. Devachan is a state on the higher mental plane which corresponds to the Nirvanic consciousness in a still higher plane.

Devachan is more an individual state of bliss, in which all the past is left behind and the beauty of existence is realized. Nirvana is the higher correspondence of it, which is related more to group bliss than to individual.

Not every departed one can enter into Devachan, nor into Nirvana. Devachan can be entered if one is at least a second degree initiate and has a consciousness by which he is able to appreciate the Devachanic bliss.

Those who are not ready for it incarnate after hitting the lower mental plane, and this is why the less evolved one incarnates more rapidly than those who pass their time in higher regions in Devachanic bliss.

There are people who incarnate in due time and bring with them an abundance of psychic energy which manifests itself in their many creative works. Also they bring beauty, freedom, vision, compassion, righteousness, forgiveness, nobility, and magnanimity to the world because such virtues are faint reflections of the states of consciousness which people in Devachan enjoy.

Average and unevolved people do not have too much to bring down to earth, and hence they continue their evolution where they left off.

Nirvanic consciousness is open to those who are at least Fourth Degree Initiates. They can have a fair degree of awareness about it, but those who are Fifth and Sixth Degree Initiates are always in contact with or live in Nirvanic consciousness.

More advanced souls do not go to Devachan but bypass it and enter into Nirvanic consciousness, or they incarnate to continue their service for humanity and for the Hierarchy.

Such people even incarnate immediately losing no time, because nature prepares their vehicle before they pass away.

But those who are not ready to advance beyond the Devachanic state of consciousness enjoy the bliss of the Devachan.

For advanced souls the correspondence of Devachanic bliss is their sacrificial service for humanity. They enjoy almost the same bliss and joy in their sacrificial, creative, and uplifting service to humanity and Hierarchy as they would have enjoyed in the bliss of the Devachanic consciousness.

Thus, the human soul is a pilgrim wandering all over the world through many races, nationalities, colors, sexes, religions, political orientations, and careers.

Each life is recorded in the computer of Space as a succession of *lifegraphs*. A *lifegraph* is a new word by which reference is made to all recordings of our actions, emotions, words, thoughts, and motives. In subjective levels it is possible to see the *lifegraphs* which contain complete information about each of our lives on earth, as well as each life on other planes — each represented by different colors and forms. These *lifegraphs* are not actual dramas or events of our lives but the records of them, which can then be translated on the screen of our Intuition into actual life-events, just like events on our television screen.

In order to resolve racial and national problems, the problems of greed, hatred and separatism, one must study his own *lifegraph*. There he will see how he was a member of a certain race, nation, sex, color, etc., and how in succeeding incarnations he changed his course and lived in different areas as a member of different nationalities, sometimes with fanaticism, sometimes with the spirit of saturation and repulsion.

Through the study of his *lifegraphs*, one will see how much wealth he gathered in a certain life and how much he lost in another life; how much he suffered in gathering and losing; how much he enjoyed in gathering and losing. He will find the causes in his greed and perhaps be able to dissolve them.

He will find the causes of his fears. In the subjective world, one clearly sees that fear is a reaction to all actions which were taken to hurt people and which violated the Law of Love and Unity.

He will overcome his hatred and separatism once he sees that his hatred is the result of the reactions of people whom he had hurt in the past, actions which conditioned others to relate to him in such a way that they evoked hatred from him. His separatism will be dissolved once he sees that he belongs to the human race and that the attitude of separatism is a result of being wounded by the circumstances of life. Also, when one hurts others, he develops separatism.

Separatism is developed in you during those moments in which you force your thoughts and will on others, and your claims or efforts to create an image of superiority over others. The accumulated reactions from other people, or the laws of these moments, create wounds in your mental body which are translated in our common language as separatism.

In the records of *lifegraphs*, the mystery and the secrets of the problems of the world can be found. Once people begin to understand the Law of Reincarnation, they will transform their lives and their viewpoints of life.

But how can you have access to your own *lifegraphs*? The steps are as follows:

1. Purification of the physical, emotional, and mental life
2. Harmlessness
3. Study of the Law of Reincarnation; approaching it not as a curiosity or a story but as a supreme law in the Universe
4. Learning how to meditate, to pull yourself out of your crystallizations, and to enter a new dimension of contact and thinking
5. Being patient

You will come in contact with your *lifegraphs* long before you consciously realize it. The signs that you are beginning to understand your *lifegraphs* are as follows:

—The development of more tolerance
—The urge to learn more
—The urge to purify your life
—Inclusiveness
—Increasing love
—Using all your resources to uplift humanity

When these signs appear and increase in your nature, you must know that your soul is studying your *lifegraphs*, but still your brain may not be capable of being conscious of it. Be patient, and one day your eyes will open in the subjective world and you will see your *lifegraphs* with their specific symbols, colors, and sounds.

When one understands the Law of Reincarnation, he takes conscious actions to make his future lives more creative and his subjective lives more fruitful and enjoyable. We must remember that we reap whatever we sow.

Understanding the Law of Reincarnation takes away a great amount of fear from our heart during the time of transition and during the time of returning once again to earth. When this fear is eliminated, the causes of many obscure sicknesses in the world are eliminated, and the roots of many confusions and anxieties in the Subtle World are also eliminated.

In many royal houses in the Far East, the newborn baby is greeted like a king. The house is decorated with roses, jasmine, freesias, and many other flowers and fragrant bushes or plants. Colorful carpets, incense, and precious oils are spread in every corner of the house. The most inspiring singing and music are heard continuously for at least three days, day and night. Groups of people recite holy prayers and mantrams and perform deep meditations. Such efforts create a tremendously charged atmosphere into which the newborn baby is welcomed.[1]

For forty days the mother and child are kept in joy, in beauty, in ecstasy. They are surrounded by melodies, songs, and prayers and kept in an atmosphere of meditation so that the communion with the Higher Worlds is kept alive. The influence of the higher spheres penetrates into all those in the house and into the souls of the mother and child.

This was called the "ceremony of the royal welcome" for the visitor from Higher Worlds. Compare such a vision with the reality of the conditions of the contemporary woman and her childbirth.

In these royal houses the midwife and doctor were chosen by the intuition of the mother. In certain cases the mother would reject the midwife or doctor and demand the one she wanted. The physical, emotional, and mental conditions of a midwife or doctor have a lasting influence upon the newborn child. The ancients used to say that the chemistry resulting from contacts must be right in order to facilitate the blooming of the child. Certain psychic poisons are transmitted into the child by a wrongly chosen midwife or doctor. In certain cases, when the mother is unable to nurse and take care of the baby, another woman is carefully chosen to nurse and care for the baby.

A Great Sage states that a departing one is surrounded by many who welcome him, sometimes with his full consciousness. But an incarnating soul descends to earth in total psychological loneliness. Such a loneliness can be lightened by preparing the best atmosphere possible for the coming baby. The baby mostly senses the emanations of joy and beauty. Worries, anxieties, noise, fear, economic pressures, television, radio, newspapers, divorcing parents, all leave wounds in the soul of the coming child. The result is the kind of life we have in the modern world.

It is suggested that the mental, psychological, and physical health of the mother and baby will be in a much better condition if they are surrounded with beauty, joy, serenity, music, poetry, prayer, and meditation.

These seven principal factors can be arranged in a way that the mother and child are provided a psychological atmosphere in which

---

1. For further study on the relationships of mother and child, please refer to the following books by Torkom Saraydarian: *Woman, Torch of the Future*, and *Sex, Family, and the Woman in Society*.

an opportunity is granted for lofty contemplation, rest, and gratitude. Such an atmosphere helps the baby keep the link with the Higher Worlds much longer, and such a link turns into a channel of great inspiration and guidance.

In some royal houses, spiritually advanced people are invited to cast the horoscope of the baby and to watch the psychic signs and phenomena related to the mother and child. Even after the birth, certain people are designated for guidance and protection, and later for private education for the child.

It is very important that the incarnating soul is greeted in the best way possible to make him feel that he came to the right place where all his needs will be met with joy, love, and gratitude. The most important factor is to create a harmonious atmosphere for the baby, psychologically and physically. One does not need to be in a royal family to prepare a welcoming atmosphere for the child.

We are told that inharmonious conditions at home and the conflicting, disturbing actions, emotions, and thoughts of the parents and relatives leave permanent wounds in the subtle bodies of the child. These later manifest in behavior which hinders the right development of the child. The psychological condition of the nursing mother is a very important factor for the right development of the child. A Teacher once stated that "the milk of the mother must be mixed with joy and vision, and the breast-feeding must be done with singing." Lullabies of olden days contained verses from great poets which presented a vision for the future child as he was fed, or during the moment he was entering into sleep. These songs spoke of how the child was going to be healthy, beautiful, graceful, intelligent, heroic, full of talents; how he will follow the inner voice of his heart to serve people and to be an embodiment of solemnity and beauty. From the early days, a beneficial psychic atmosphere should be created around the mother and the child to make the unfoldment of a rare flower possible.

People usually do not think that the human soul is in a continuous process of birth; rather they assume that he is in a continuous process of death. Death is a release and a birth into the Subtle World. But the most interesting idea is that the child is born from the womb of the mother into the womb of the World Mother where he will go through a process of gestation until he is ready to be born into the womb of the Higher Worlds.

As there is the abortion of a fetus before being born, there are also cases of abortion during one's life. Certain souls die before their time. Certain souls are under the pressure of heavy karmic conditions and psychological disturbances. Certain nations and environments do not provide the best conditions for the growing soul. In certain areas there are massacres and butchering by acts of war and revolutions. In certain areas the "embryo" is trapped in vices and in the social network of hatred and revenge. In such conditions, the poor soul is "aborted," and he enters the Subtle World not completely formed as he was designed to be. Such souls carry with them heavy problems for humanity.

Mothers must be kept in the best condition during pregnancy, childbirth, and the time of nursing. Mother Earth must be kept in the best condition in order to receive the child and develop him in Her womb of life until he is really mature and ready to be born in the Subtle World — which is a higher womb — to develop his psychic bodies and senses.

There are also special incarnations which are prepared by the Forces of Light to bring greater light, love, and beauty to the world. The Forces of Light prepare such individuals on the subtle planes and send them toward the physical world. A Great One, referring to such events states:

"The Magnets sent by Us for Our manifestation are like the anchors of a ship tossed in the storm."[2]

Who are the Magnets? They are the Great Ones Who are sent by the Hierarchy. They are Those Who can be trusted for the labor. They are Those Who can carry the torch in spite of conditions. They are points of hope, points of trust. They are signposts for the future. Their consciousness gives refuge to thousands. They provide the sacred Path to the gates of the Hierarchy.

To meet such Magnets face to face is karmic. One must have prepared in the past and developed merit to be able to meet Them. An unprepared consciousness cracks in the fire of Their presence. A cracked consciousness is used for treason by dark forces.

The Hierarchy sends Messengers continuously to bring hope for humanity. Every Messenger is a witness of the existence of the Hierarchy, and like an anchor He makes the existence of the Hierarchy a fact to humanity. Messengers build the path for the manifestation of the Hierarchy.

Like a stormy sea, the world is in turmoil. Anchors are needed to save the ship of humanity. Every effort for stabilization and balance gives a new opportunity to humanity to progress on the Path of its

---

2. Agni Yoga Society, *Hierarchy* (New York: Agni Yoga Society, 1933), para. 117.

evolution. Without these Anchors or Magnets, humanity would be lost in the waves of the fiery ocean.

There are still deeper mysteries. It is known in esoteric Teaching that certain heroes, geniuses, kings, queens, or highly influential servers of the human race are not individuals on earth but shadows or reflections of Great Entities living in higher realms. The real individuals live in one of the four Cosmic Etheric Planes, namely the Intuitional, Atmic, Monadic, or Divine Planes. [3] They project Their image and activate it as a human being who does great heroic deeds and gives profound wisdom, art, beauty, teaching, and leadership and then fades away like a shadow when the Cause of the shadow decides to recall Its shadow.

Because such an Entity's Real Self is on higher planes, It can direct the earthly one like a pilot directing a police car from above. Usually such shadows are invulnerable and very powerful. This is why in the history of humanity there is much confusion about the Divine or heavenly origin of certain Great Ones. In one sense They are human because They have human form, and in another sense They are heavenly and Divine.

We are not referring here to etheric or astral projection but to real human forms whose Monads are in the Higher Worlds and control the bodies according to the need of the world.

In a different sense, an average person is in the same condition. His Real Self, the Monad, is far away in the sky of his higher planes, and Its shadow, the personality, lives on the physical plane, energized by the life thread coming from the Monad. In this case, the person's duty is to unite his consciousness with the Monad, achieve unity in himself, and use the personality according to the needs of the time. After man leaves his three bodies, he will either unite with his Monad (in other words, be his Self) or return to work again and again until unity with his Divine Essence is achieved.

Those who project a personality on earth and animate it from high realms are those who have achieved unity with their essence.

The Cosmic Physical Plane, which reflects all other higher Cosmic Planes, is formed of seven subplanes. Thus we have:

First ether	Adi or Divine
Second ether	Monadic
Third ether	Atmic

---

3. For information regarding the Cosmic Planes, please refer to *The Psyche and Psychism*, Chapter 7, "The Seven Cosmic Planes."

Fourth ether	Intuitional
Fifth plane	Mental
Sixth plane	Astral or emotional
Seventh plane	Concrete physical

All these planes are material planes, although some Teachers, to differentiate the subtle matter from the concrete, call the subtle matter, *substance*. Thus the higher mental Body and Intuitional or Higher Bodies are substantial.

For Higher Beings, the whole Cosmic Physical Plane is concrete substance.

Whenever the Central Spiritual Sun radiates new currents of energy, new manifestations appear. The rays emanating from the Central Spiritual Sun are finally stopped by the Cosmic Physical Plane. Here they either strive to go back or remain identified with the substance they created out of their essence.

When scientists say that all red rocks are the fossils of certain living entities, we believe them; but when the Teacher states that this planet is formed of the bodies of innumerable living Sparks, we have a difficult time believing it. In bringing their bodies together, the globe was formed. We call these Sparks, elementals.[4]

The astral plane is created by the astral elementals which took a step forward by going toward the Source. The mental elementals are those elementals which started from the physical plane and reached the mental plane. Some of these elementals came back and incarnated on the physical plane as human beings, using physical, emotional, and mental elementals as their three bodies.

Some of the Sparks did not come to the physical plane, but they turned back from the mental or Intuitional Planes and formed the kinds of evolutions which are different from the human evolution.

There is the angelic or devic kingdom, which never came to the physical plane but followed a different line of evolution and progressed toward Home. The members of this kingdom have their graded Hierarchies and various orders. However, the Law requires that, after reaching certain heights in their evolution, they must come and incarnate in the human kingdom, if they want to transcend the level of their achievements. In *The Secret Doctrine* it is stated that:

---

4. *Ibid.*, for information regarding the elementals, Chapter 17.

"...In order to become a divine, fully conscious god — aye, even the highest — the Spiritual Primeval *Intelligences* must pass through the human stage."[5]

Some great disciples knew about this. They knew that the Spark can progress on the Path of evolution, starting from the mental or higher planes, and reach states of consciousness by which It can create Its globe or even Its solar system. But if it wants to advance even more, it comes to the human level, incarnating as a human being. As we read in St. John: "And the Word became flesh and dwelt among us."[6]

The *Word* is the Solar Logos, the God of our Solar System. This is why Christians insist that God became man, in the nature of Christ. The Hindus say the same thing about Krishna. They call Him, God-incarnate. We think that there are only physical globes and solar systems; whereas the Teaching states that there are etheric, astral, and mental globes and solar systems on which live and unfold those Sparks who had either reached there from the human stage or had begun their evolution on those planes.

Evolving Sparks are divided into two main sections: After reaching the lowest sphere of matter, the first section decided to proceed on the arc of evolution. The other section opposed it. This is where the history of evil in Creation came into being.

Those Sparks who decided to remain on the physical plane were joined by all those who decided to stay on the plane they had reached. For example, those Sparks who came to the astral plane and did not want to go to the mental plane joined their earthly correspondences and thus organized a hierarchy from the lowest level of the Cosmic Physical Plane to the seventh and sixth subplanes of the Cosmic Astral Plane — where their headquarters is.

We must remember that as the physical, astral, and lower mental planes are not principles, in the same sense, neither are the Cosmic Physical, Cosmic Astral, and Cosmic Lower Mental Planes. All disturbances occurring in them are temporary and will eventually be defeated by evolutionary Sparks proceeding on to the Higher Planes from the lowest subplanes of existence.[7]

5. H.P. Blavatsky, *The Secret Doctrine*, 2 vols. (Pasadena, CA: Theosophical University Press, 1988), vol. 1, p.106.
6. John 1:14
7. For further information please refer to Chapter 28 in *The Science of Meditation*.

58

Abortion

Abortion is a crime. The human soul who left the Higher Worlds to have a new incarnation and continue his experiences in life cannot be murdered and sent back. At the moment of conception, the human soul is already attached to the physical plane, and he begins his preparation to vest himself with flesh and body. His etheric body starts to be woven from the moment of conception, and he has already broken the bridges between the physical plane and astral or Higher Worlds.

Abortion can only be allowed if the mother's life is really in danger.

Abortion can have a heavy psychological effect on the mother-to-be. The murdered soul cannot tolerate such a murder and setback in his evolution, and very often he obsesses and possesses the mother to punish her or to experience closeness to physical life.

Many mothers who have abortions pass through significant changes in their personalities. Very often they manifest signs of depression, apathy, tendencies toward crime, mental complications, and even suicidal urges. These symptoms take a few days or even a few years to appear.

The cause of these psychological complications is a deep-seated guilt feeling which the mother feels after the abortion. She may not express this feeling, but in her heart she knows she made a serious mistake killing a person who knew what blessings he wanted to bring to her and to the world. The wound left in the mother's heart by the abortion is continuously scratched whenever she sees babies or other pregnant women, or when she hears stories about abortions. Such a pressure on her heart prevents her from climbing higher ladders of evolution and causes a retardation in her spiritual growth.

Abortion encourages people to be careless and irresponsible about the most serious facts of life. There is no difference between abortion and murder; it is the same crime. On the other hand, if the mother has the baby, she can evolve more rapidly by developing the sense of responsibility and compassion, and she may slowly eradicate many weaknesses in her character as she tries to help her child. The child evokes deeper feelings in her, creativity, courage, and daring. Many young women reach psychological maturity during their pregnancy and during the years they care for their children.

Every child who comes into incarnation brings with him many blessings and talents. Every child who comes to a family is related to that family with sacred ties. Such ties cannot be broken violently because this upsets the plan of karma.

This is another very important esoteric point: Those who are coming into incarnation are usually those who have left their bodies and entered the astral plane or mental plane. When their time for incarnation comes again, they make preparations and step by step come down to the astral, etheric, and physical planes. In murdering such a person, you perform an intolerable act. Every murdered person goes directly to the level between the lower astral plane and the etheric plane and lives there as long as he would have lived on earth had he not been murdered. The sphere between the etheric and lower astral planes is the habitat of those who died by suicide, in sudden deaths, in murders and bombings, in war, etc. This is the lower hell, and the aborted soul is sent there to stay for another 70-90 years. This is why such souls are filled with hatred and revenge, and they want to hurt those who are responsible for their abortion.

We may add that abortion creates many health and emotional problems, and causes dissatisfaction and lack of normalcy in the mother's future sexual relationships.

It is true that economic and health problems sometimes create serious complications, and one does not want to make another soul unhappy; but how can one tell that the newcomer will not bring a new spirit into the family? Sometimes a family's success starts after the third or fourth child. Sometimes a family's karma is arranged so that they need the missing link to activate the wheel of success, and the new baby brings with him a great future.

Dark forces use many subtle methods to prevent the incarnation of advanced souls because one advanced soul is a powerful warrior against them. The usual method they use is abortion. They try to influence not only the mother but also her friends or parents to submit to abortion. When an abortion is performed, dark forces not only gain victory over an advanced soul, but they also create a close tie with the mother, who gradually offers herself to their service. The karma of such girls and women is deplorable.

As such women slowly enter the service of dark forces, their Souls warn them, and this warning and the pressure of the dark forces create a complicated nightmare in their heart. Often, to free themselves from such misery, they choose to die, first mentally, then emotionally, then physically. Some people do not notice how a girl who has had an abortion slowly dies first mentally, then enters moods of depression and apathy, and eventually wants to die.

Abortion is an act of destruction of the mechanisms of the soul or the human being. Abortion is not only physical but also emotional, mental, and psychic. People know about physical abortion, and conscientious ones fight against such a practice. But people do not know about emotional abortion, which is exercised daily everywhere, and there is no organization fighting against it.

As a human soul builds the physical body, he also tries to build his emotional body. The emotional body begins to develop after the birth of the physical body between the ages of seven and fourteen. The womb of the emotional body is love, joy, and harmony. If for any reason such a womb is disturbed in the family — and hatred, depression, gloom, and conflict replace the womb — the emotional nature of the soul fails to build itself and either has a premature birth or an abortion. The child will have a body but not a "heart," or emotional body. Most criminals and terrorists have had emotional abortions.

Mental abortion occurs between the ages of fourteen and twenty-one, during which time the mental body usually must be formed. The womb of the mental body is honesty, justice, light, and knowledge. If during this period the environment of the child is full of dishonesty, injustice, darkness, and ignorance, the mental body fails to develop and mental abortion takes place.

Mentally aborted children become the burdens and horrors of society. If they have emotional and physical bodies, they use the energies from them for destructive ends.

Psychic abortion is disastrous for the soul. The body of the soul is sometimes called the body of glory. This body also matures in a womb, which is formed of beauty, nobility, striving, and enthusiasm. The period of gestation is between the ages of twenty-one to twenty-eight. If during this period the person is full of ugliness, moral degeneration, inertia, and hatred, the body of glory cannot come to perfection, and psychic abortion takes place.

For such people religious and spiritual visions do not make sense. They cannot think about Higher Worlds, about the perfection of the spirit, about the Cosmic destination of man. People think that physical abortion is a crime, but the greatest crime is psychic abortion, in which the human soul loses the body of glory and appears in rags, like a beggar.

To prevent abortions, one must provide those conditions in which psychic, mental, emotional, and physical abortion will not be contemplated. As there are professionals who commit the act of abortion of the physical body, there are also specialists who try to make you have emotional, mental, and psychic abortions. Christ warned us when He said, "Be afraid of those who kill your soul."[1]

If a person is fortunate, someone acts as a womb for his emotional body — a man, a woman, a teacher, or minister; and the emotional body of that lucky one grows and matures and is born in good health. If a person is fortunate, between the ages of fourteen to twenty-one he becomes acquainted with someone who has vision, light, justice, and knowledge, and he matures and comes to perfection in that person's psychological womb.

If a person is fortunate, between the ages of twenty-one to twenty-eight he finds some group, some person, or some book in whose womb he matures and reaches perfection. This womb provides him the necessary nourishment of beauty, nobility, striving, and enthusiasm. One of the Apostles said something very significant: "My little children, of whom I travail in birth again until Christ be formed in you."[2]

It is even possible that a person's psychic body is conceived and gestated in the psychic womb of a great Saint, Teacher, or disciple, or even in the psychic womb of Christ.

Immediately when one's physical body is mature after the age of seven, he must search for an emotional womb. After age fourteen, one must search for a mental womb, if his home cannot provide it. After age twenty-one, he must look for a spiritual womb for his body of glory. In the future, groups of people will provide wombs for emotional, mental, and soul bodies, with all that is needed to nurture these bodies.

There are also different problems. It is possible that a person does not have an emotional body but was able to develop a mental body. It is also possible that a person has an emotional body but not a mental body, or maybe he has no emotional or mental body but a soul body. Of course, such conditions create an unbalanced human being who is,

---

1. Matthew 10:28
2. Galatians 4:19

for example, either all emotions or all theory, or who lives in abstraction.

A healthy human being must have all his bodies developed and matured and even integrated. Integration means that there is close synchronization between the wheels, motor, pipes, steering, and the driver. Such people are the flowers of the human race and a source of blessings for the earth.

In the past, certain monasteries, retreats, churches, and esoteric schools used to provide a womb for the soul. In the future, such a labor will be scientifically organized. Medical science will be organized to watch the growth of the baby in the womb and meet his needs until he is safely born. Similar sciences will be developed to take care of the emotional, mental, and psychic embryos and make them reach perfection and take birth.

Parallel to these sciences, certain groups will be organized on different levels to prevent emotional, mental, and psychic abortions. These groups will be equipped with subtle bodies because one cannot conceive if his womb is not ready. This means that you cannot serve as an emotional, mental, or spiritual womb if you do not have healthy and mature corresponding bodies.

Sometimes, when people are between the ages of seven and twenty-one, they find their "wombs" and dedicate their hearts to grow in those wombs; but people around them, because of their superstitions, traditions, and prejudices, give them trouble and disturb their growth and often cause abortions. Such gestation periods are very significant for the embryo, and they must not be disturbed.

What are these wombs? Certain friends, Teachers, groups, churches, and books all act as wombs for one or another subtle body of a person. For example, a child cannot conceive his emotional body in his own home if the atmosphere is full of fighting, hatred, and anger, so he tries to find a friend, a book, a Teacher, or a priest whom he loves and trusts. The child conceives his emotional body in such a womb. If he makes the right choice, his emotional body goes through gestation and eventually is born. After the birth and maturity, of course the child can stand on his own feet.

The same is true for mental conception and spiritual conception. For example, when the person passes the age of twenty-one, he becomes intuitively anxious to find a spiritual womb where he can conceive his spiritual body. Unfortunately, such wombs are very rare, and most people lack the Body of Glory. One can create his spiritual womb by dedicating himself to the Teaching of a Great One, such as Buddha, Krishna, Christ, Mohammed, or Moses. Through his faith, a person can conceive his Body of Glory and eventually have the Body of Glory. Such a conception cannot take place if it is forced or imposed by any method.

When a person passes away without an astral body (except if he is an Arhat), he merges into the astral fog of the planet and he needs many years of hard labor and lives in the astral plane to develop even the most rudimentary emotional body. If he passes away without a mental body, he remains in the astral plane and comes back to those conditions in which he is urged to search for a mental womb.

Most people do not have the Body of Glory, and they cannot pass beyond the lower mental plane. Instead, they go back to incarnation after the needed period of time. Those who build their soul body come back with many rare experiences and inspirations collected from Higher Worlds. They usually become the leaders in their own fields.

Is it possible to conceive our emotional or mental or soul bodies if we failed in the past during the required age period? We are told that Nature gives us three opportunities and these opportunities come at the following periods:

—For the emotional body, between the ages of 35-42
—For the mental body, between the ages of 42-49
—For the soul body, between the ages of 49-55

The next cycle begins at the following:
—Ages 62-69
—Ages 69-76
—Ages 76-83

It is obvious, however, that as we delay our opportunities to be conceived, we have a more difficult gestation period and a more painful birth, due to increasing problems, involvements, labor, influences, and crystallizations of the forces in our nature. This is why it is better to be "pregnant" when one is young, and never try to abort.

It should be said that if a person is using you as a womb to conceive one of his subtle bodies, then you must be a healthy womb, so that you give birth to a healthy body. This is why leaders, Teachers, friends, partners, and priests have such a great responsibility to provide a healthy gestation for a subtle vehicle. Those who fail in their responsibility become guilty of the act of abortion.

One can also refuse any conception to take place within him if he feels that he is not ready for such a responsibility. In such a case, he must gracefully direct the person to search for another womb. It is better not to accept any conception than to commit an abortion.

The incarnating ego waits in the etheric body for three to four months before entering his physical body in the womb. If abortion is done during this period, he cannot descend into the body, but he becomes trapped in the etheric body. In the majority of cases, he cannot go back to the Subtle World because he has already descended into matter. Thus the woman has an entity in her aura which manifests in various ways, causing various disturbances in her consciousness and behavior. The entity may even try to possess her.

If the incarnating ego does not understand the reason for the abortion, he expresses his dissatisfaction or despair by trying to make her pregnant again; or if he turns negative toward her, he creates psychological disturbances in her nature.

If the aborted ego stays in the etheric body of the woman for more than three months, and if through intercourse she attracts another ego into her etheric body, she may have a complicated situation. If the two egos do not agree with each other and both of them want to incarnate, they fight for the body during gestation. If there is only one body being formed, they both try to occupy it and their occupation causes various disfigurations in the embryo. But if they agree, usually two eggs are produced, and they are born as twins.

However, we must not assume that twins are *only* the result of an aborted ego waiting in the etheric level to incarnate. In the majority of cases, karmic association and the magnetism created by love invite two or more egos waiting for incarnation. In such cases, the babies are born normal.

Miscarriage is often the result of karmic complications between mother and child. In a miscarriage, the ego leaves the aura of the woman, although he is still trapped in the etheric plane. Because of certain psychic events, the ego withdraws and decides against incarnation.

A miscarriage also occurs because of the health of the mother or as the result of an accident, wrong exercises, etc. Again, however, karmic complications are a factor.

Sometimes a miscarriage occurs because the incarnating ego has an enemy or a love on the etheric plane who does not want him to leave for incarnation. In such cases, either the enemy or the love keeps the ego from incarnating, or the ego leaves by himself. For whatever reason he leaves, physiological conditions within the mother change and miscarriage occurs.

One can observe very clearly how the behavior of a woman changes after she has an abortion. In any case, it is a very gloomy setback for the ego to wait in the aura of the person and even slowly possess her to satisfy his urge to incarnate. Often such an ego leaves the mother-to-be and becomes an inhabitant of the etheric plane, until the years pass during which he would have lived had he incarnated. Then he tries for a new birth again.

For an ego coming from higher spheres to lose seventy to eighty years in the etheric plane, with its unpleasant inhabitants, is a horrible prison. Preventative actions must be taken before pregnancy for the sake of the mother's health and for the sake of the incarnating ego.

People often ask, "What about accidents which result in abortion or miscarriage? As there are accidents in the physical world, are there also accidents in the subtle planes in which the gestation is interrupted and abortion results?"

We may say that an accident is the result of many kinds of forces clashing with each other under the law which has brought these forces together at a moment when you least expect. Every accident has a cause. When you know the cause, you may then know the result; but if you do not know the cause, you do not know the result. An accident can reveal to you the result, and through the result you may know the cause.

Accidents happen when you are not conscious of what you are doing. Or accidents happen when you are fully conscious about yourself but not conscious of what is going on in your environment or in Space. Accidents will slowly vanish when we develop our intuition and become aware of what is going on, at least on this planet, which can directly affect us.

Accidents are under the influence of karmic law. Accidents can be the result of group karma or national karma. Accidents can be an attack from dark forces when you "leave your door open." When one lives closer to the higher planes and in harmony with angelic kingdoms, many accidents can be prevented.

Actually, man lives in a world of accidents, where anything can happen at any moment. But we are protected by many invisible entities and guardians. We never feel their presence except on rare or miraculous occasions. We do not express our gratitude, but the Teaching advises us to express our gratitude every evening for all those accidents that could have happened but did not.

Accidents on the emotional plane are mostly sudden attacks by dark forces who foresee the appearance of a warrior of spirit and prevent his emotional or mental birth. As the birth process on the physical plane is considered mostly a biological phenomenon, in the astral plane it is mostly a spiritual phenomenon. When negative emotions are planted or injected into the astral body by sudden attacks or other means, the gestation is stopped; abortion takes place; and the person cannot build his astral body.

The birth process of the mental body is related to thoughts. Attacks come via thought currents to frustrate the womb or the embryo and prevent gestation. Astral and mental gestation can be carried on in a healthy and protective process through moral, religious, and spiritual education. Accidents cannot approach the soul body during gestation because such a body is under the protection of the Inner Guide immediately after it is conceived.

Not only do human beings go through the unhappy process of various abortions but also nations, civilizations, and races do the same. The Lemurian and Atlantean civilizations were annihilated through abortion.[3]

The Earth is the *womb*. If the elements in the womb do not proceed in tune with the law of the womb, the Earth feels forced to abort in order not to let a beast grow in her. Our whole civilization is in danger of being aborted. There are appointed times in the time-clock of the Universe. One must not have a gestation period which is too short or too long; he must be born, or else abortion takes place. Our humanity is not yet born spiritually, and a great danger is hanging over us. May the Lord protect us from a catastrophic worldwide abortion.

---

3. Additional information regarding these civilizations can be found in Chapter 9, "The Fourth Round and the Seven Races," pp. 37-40, *The Psyche and Psychism*.

59

The Guardian Angel

Before discussing the topic of the Guardian Angel, or the Solar Angel, let us define a few words. We will begin with the definition of *Spark.*[1]

According to the Ageless Wisdom, millions of ages ago a great center of fire in Space, called the Central Fire, began to project out billions of Sparks. Throughout ages these Sparks went through forty-nine levels of density and eventually landed on the physical plane to become atoms. Imagine also a fireworks display in space with tiny little sparks going out everywhere into the Universe.

In the atom there is the Core, and that Core is the Spark. One day every atom is going to be a living form, a human being, or even a Divine Being.

When we say Spark, we mean that which is coming from the Central Fire, descending through the forty-nine levels, then, beginning from the material or physical plane, going back to the Central Core. The Spark makes a journey from that Central Fire to become matter; then, in matter, It slowly awakens and goes back to Its home. This was the secret of the parable of Christ when He said that the Prodigal Son left home and lived in the lowest levels of consciousness, but eventually he remembered his home and went back.

The word "remembering" is a very significant word. Within each human being, within each atom, within each living form, there is the secret memory of the plane from whence it emanated. This memory is a magnetic link between the Spark and the Source. Because the

---

1. For detailed information on this topic, please refer to the following books: *The Science of Meditation; The Science of Becoming Oneself; The Hidden Glory of the Inner Man; Cosmos in Man* (especially Chapter 3), *The Psyche and Psychism,* and *The Legend of Shamballa.*

Source is a great Magnet, it gradually attracts that Spark within every form and leads It back to the Central Core.

When attracted by the Magnet, the Spark is not only a Spark but also has consciousness, awareness, experience, ability, power, and progressive unfoldment. It returns to Space transfigured, like a seed transformed into an oak tree. In *The Legend of Shamballa*[2] it clearly states that every Spark is going back toward Its home. If the Spark awakens and becomes part of the vegetable kingdom, we say that the Spark is growing. Then It enters the animal kingdom and becomes the central Core of the animal. Then It enters the human kingdom and becomes a human.

When the Spark enters the mental plane, we say that man becomes a *soul*. A soul is simply a stage in the progressive development of the Spark. Then when It enters into higher levels, we say that the man becomes the *Self*.

The Self is the Spark who is Self-aware and knows where He came from and where He is going. The Self has total power over His mechanism. The Self is the unfolded Spark.

The Monad is the evolutionary expression of the human soul after the Spiritual Triad. When the human soul becomes conscious on the Second Cosmic Ether, we can say that the human soul becomes a Monad, which means he was many but now he acts as one. In the next level he will be called a Self. The Monad must sacrifice Itself in all selves to be eventually The Self.

The Self, the flower of the Spark, has power over the *mechanism*. The mechanism is the physical body, the emotional body, the mental body, and the higher bodies. The Self has total control over them. But the Spark does not have control. The Spark is controlled; the Self controls.

If you are smoking and you say, "I can't help it," who is in control? Your body is in control; your habits are in control; your hang-ups are in control. This means that you are still a Spark or a human soul, a developing human soul. A developing human soul is an advanced Spark.

But the Self is an advanced soul, just as a little boy is a boy, but when he becomes a teen-ager he is a "human soul." When he becomes a mature man, he becomes a "Self," and he has more control over his mechanism and over his environment.

---

2. *The Legend of Shamballa*, by Torkom Saraydarian.

Each atom has a Spark in it. You live in many bodies, so your mechanism has many sparks in it. You are both a *life* and *lives*. You are an advanced Spark using and controlling millions of sparks around and within your body, within your aura. You are the shining Sun in the constellation.

Actually, each man is a solar system with *millions* of stars and, at the nucleus, he is the Sun. Planets are developing so that one day they becomes Suns. But you are now the human soul or the Spark, which is the central Core of your constellation. One day you will be a real constellation, if you take care of your bodies. Billions and billions of years later, your physical, emotional, and mental atoms will come join you in Space, and you will form a constellation. This is a huge vision, but if your vision is great, you have a greater chance to grow.

There are also new Sparks continually starting out on the road and developing. One day I went to my Teacher and asked, "How many times has this whole Creation been created? How many times do the Sparks come and go?"

"That's a very good question, and I will answer you. Let's go to the seashore and rest a little, and I will talk to you."

The waves of the ocean were very, very big. My Teacher said, "Sit down here and count how many waves come." Then he left.

"This is crazy," I said, but I started to count: "One, two, three... one hundred... I don't want to count these! There is no beginning and no end to these waves!"

My Teacher came back and asked, "How many did you count?"

"Two or three hundred."

"Were there any waves before you started counting?"

"Oh," I said, "of course!"

"Well, that's the Universe. There is no beginning and there is no end. It is just like the ocean waves. One builds and comes; the next one builds and comes. You have a little idea of what God is. You think God is sitting there, smoking a pipe and judging people. God is not that. God is beyond.... He is a great love, a heart.... These words cannot express Him at all. When you say God, you must start trembling and ask, 'What is He?'"

The second term we will define is the *human soul*.

You as a Spark start to develop, and the time comes when you have expanded your consciousness and you know that you are not the physical body. This is called the first initiation. Initiation means expansion of consciousness.

At first the Spark was lost in the body; It thought that It was the body. Now It is controlling the body and It says, "The body is my car and I am the driver." This is the first initiation.

In the second initiation, the Spark does the same thing with the emotional body. It suddenly feels that the emotional body is not It; the emotions cannot control It any more. The emotions may be fighting to control It, but It definitely knows that the emotions are not It.

The Spark continues Its development and becomes a mental being. When It advances through the seventh, sixth, fifth and fourth levels of the mental plane as a mental being, we call It a human soul. The human soul is a Spark who knows that the physical, emotional, and mental bodies are not him; they are his mechanisms.

This recognition is the meaning of the human soul. The immortal being within the human form is the human soul, developing toward Selfhood.

The Spark, the human soul, the Monad, and the Self are four names for our one Inner Core, but these different names refer to different levels of development. In the level where we are identified with the physical body, we are called the Spark. In the level where we control the physical, emotional, and mental bodies, we are called a human soul. Eventually we develop further and call ourselves the Self. But throughout this development we are still the same being, just as we are the same person as a child, as an adolescent, and as an old man or woman.

Some esoteric books say that "the human soul is striving toward the Monad." This is a very misleading expression which suggests that there is a duality between the human soul and the Monad, that the human soul and the Monad are two different things. They are not.

People ask if every human being has a human soul, even if he is not conscious of being something other than his bodies. To answer, let us consider an illustration:

When you ask a question, who is asking? The mouth is not talking. *You* are talking. Who are you? We call you a human soul because you know what you are asking. If you talk with me and you don't know what we are talking about, you are a Spark, lost in the mass of the physical body. But because you know what we are talking about, we call you the human soul. You, the speaker, are using your mouth, your body, your reasoning and logic to communicate something to me. That central communicator talking with me is the human soul within you. It is you.

This is not to say that you have complete control over your body just because you know you are talking. It doesn't mean that you have control, or that you don't have control. If you don't have control but you know that your body is not you, you are becoming a human soul. But if you don't have this discrimination and you do not even think about the human soul existing or not existing, then you are lost in the body.

If you tell an average man that he has a soul, he will probably say, "What are you talking about? I am this body. That is all." He is like a man wearing his coat and insisting that he is the coat. This man is not awake.

The Spark is developing step by step, going up, and eventually becoming a beautiful flower. The beautiful flower is the Self. At the middle is the human soul. At the bottom is the sleeping god; Jacob is sleeping at the bottom of the ladder. He does not know what is going on, yet he sees the steps up toward the angels.

The Spark, the human soul, the Monad, and the Self are essentially the same. In the stage of Sparkhood, you do not have control over the mechanism. In the stage of the human soul, you have a certain amount of control. In the stage of Selfhood, you have total control.

When a king is ten years old, he does not have control of his nation; but when he becomes twenty-five, he knows more, and he has some control. When he becomes the monarch, he has total control of the kingdom that we call the human being. The Spark, the human soul, and the Monad are not different kings; they are simply different stages of the same king.

We have a certain amount of control over our bodies, emotions, and minds. We are developing human souls. But Christ has total control; Christ is a *Self*. When He died, He resurrected Himself. This is total control. Christ has power over space and time.

The tax collectors came and told Christ that He had not paid His taxes. He told St. Peter to go and catch a certain fish and he would find a jewel in its mouth to give to the tax collectors.[3] Christ had control over what came out of the mouth of a tiny fish. This is the power of the Self.

In the subjective world we are categorized as

—sleeping Sparks
—awakening Sparks
—egos
—human souls

---

3. Matthew 17:27

—Spiritual Triads
—fiery Monads
—radiant Selves

The ego is the self-bound, self-imprisoned human soul in the lower mental plane, still identified with its threefold lower vehicle.

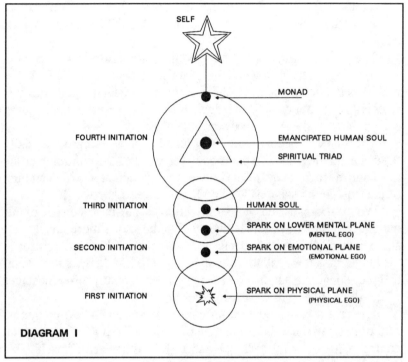

DIAGRAM I

Evolution of the Self

In the above diagram we see the Spark developing and moving from the bottom of the diagram to the top. The human soul is on the mental plane. When the mental body is mastered, the human soul functions in the Spiritual Triad and is called the Spiritual Triad. If he takes the next higher step, he will be the Monad, then the Self, and at this stage he will be able to control his whole mechanism.

You are a king, but you are enslaved in the body. You say, "Why can't I heal this body? Why can't I get rid of this body?" Then you say, "Why can't I get rid of these emotions?" You can't; you are stuck in that level for a long time.

One day you make it, and you go to the mental plane. There you have many worries and troubles. And you say, "Can't I stop this worrying?" Sometimes you can, and sometimes you can't; so you are still a slave there.

But one day you make a greater breakthrough, which started at the first initiation. You become an emancipated soul in the Spiritual Triad. You are free now, and you can control the physical, emotional, and mental lives. Then you continue going up.

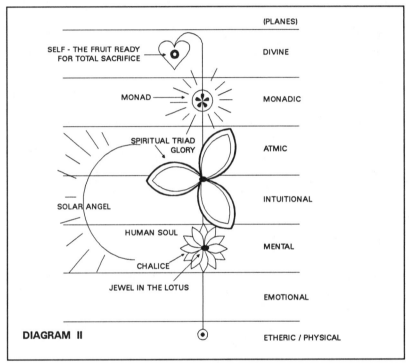

Development of the Spark

Diagram II shows the evolution of the Spark in another way. You are a seed at first. This seed is the Spark. Then you become a stem and leaves. This is the human soul stage. Eventually you are flowering and becoming your own future, or fruit. Here you become the Self.

When you are the Self, metaphorically or symbolically, you can control the whole planet. It is not easy to attain this stage, but only then are all the little lives that compose your vehicles truly unified and you become one whole.

In modern psychology the Self, the flower, is called the transcendental Self. The Solar Angel is called the Transpersonal Self.

It is when you become the Self that you realize that you are one with everyone else. In this stage, you suddenly come to the realization that all Sparks emanated from the same Source. Suddenly you realize that you are going toward that ocean and becoming one with that ocean. But the realization takes billions of years.

First you realize that you are part of that one ocean, even though you have not yet become one with the ocean; all your activities, writings, and thinking become synthetic. You start working for synthesis — for inclusiveness, oneness, unity. You go from diversity to unity.

When you are a seed, you are separative; you say, "This is mine, and that is yours." You may kill other people to take what they have because you are separative. When you become a human soul, you become more cooperative and inclusive.

When you become the Self, you become all-inclusive. You live and move and have your being in the idea of oneness. You walk on the earth and say, "This earth is me, and I am walking on it." You touch a flower and say, "This is part of me." This is why Christ said, "I am the tree and you are the branches."[4] And at the Last Supper, He turned to His disciples and said, "...that they may be one as we are one. I in them and you in me, may they be... one."[5]

But we devour each other in the name of our selfish interests. This is why we increase our suffering and pain continuously. And we call this a successful life!

Some people call the Solar Angel the conscience. Some call It the Inner Christ, the Inner Buddha. What must be understood is that the Solar Angel is a *separate being* from the human soul. It is not you, the Spark, the human soul, the Self, although many people who write and lecture about esoteric teachings have confused the Solar Angel with one or more of these names.

The term Solar Angel is given in ancient writings and in Tibetan and Trans-Himalayan Teachings. In ancient mythology the moon refers to the physical, emotional, and mental bodies. The Sun represents the spirit. The Solar Angels are beings who conquered the physical, emotional, and mental bodies and became Children of Light. Children of Light are solar lights.

These Solar Angels are not the "Sons of God" referred to in some ancient teachings. The Sons of God who came to earth and married the daughters of men are the *Kumaras*. In the first, second, and third chapters of the Old Testament, it says that the Sons of God came to

---

4. John 15:5
5. John 17:23

marry infant humanity so that it could develop. These Kumaras came and married human women and produced better children.

Where did the Solar Angels come from? How are They related to us? It is an ancient and beautiful story.

Long before our Solar System was formed, there existed the idea for its formation. The Plan[6] calls for the Solar System to be created three times. In the first Solar System, the Sparks were formed, and light or intelligence was the goal of development. In the Second Solar system, which is the present one, our destination has been to develop love and compassion. In the third Solar System, we will be developing willpower.

So three great lessons are to be learned by the Sparks during the three Solar Systems: light, love, and will, respectively. In our Second Solar System, we are going to develop love and compassion. This is why we say our God is Love. Those who fail in love will have a very difficult time in the third Solar System.

In occult literature we are told that our planet, as shown below in diagram III, has six companion globes, and these six companion globes are on different levels of density. Numbers three and five are on the etheric plane. Numbers two and six are on the emotional plane. Numbers one and seven are on the mental plane. Only our Earth, number four, became condensed and thus a solid planet.

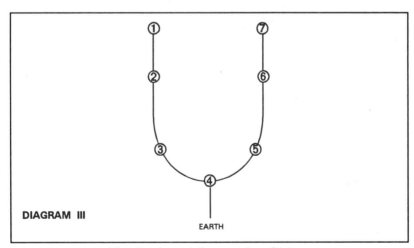

DIAGRAM III

EARTH

The Earth and Companion Globes

---

6. See *Cosmos in Man*, Chapter 24.

Let us say that number one is the mental level; number two is the emotional level; number three is the etheric level, and number four is the physical level. As the human embryo repeats the evolutionary process in the mother's womb, so our Earth repeats these stages. Our Earth becomes first mental, then emotional, then etheric, then physical.

We are living here on the fourth globe. In the evolutionary process we will rise from globe four, where we have physical bodies, to globe five, where we will have etheric bodies. When we rise to globe six, we will have astral bodies; and when we reach globe seven, we will have bodies built of thoughts.

There are planets that are yet in formation. They are still on the energy level, but they are slowly becoming materialized. Slowly they are descending to the physical level. Our planet Earth with its six companions, making a total of seven *globes*, is called a *chain*.

Seven globes make up one chain. Seven chains make up one scheme of evolution.[7]

Everything in Nature starts from unseen matter that you cannot touch. From the subtle matter it condenses and condenses, becomes visible; then slowly becomes invisible again. The symbol in diagram

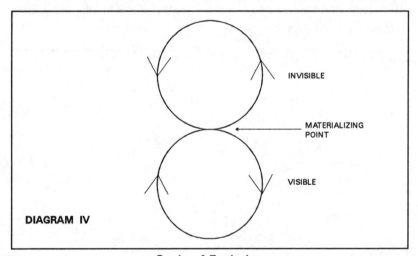

DIAGRAM IV

Cycle of Evolution

---

7. For further information see *Cosmos in Man*, pp. 25-42, and *Hierarchy and the Plan*, pp. 9-14. A *round* is the time duration within which seven Root Races develop on each round. There are seven rounds in one chain and forty-nine rounds in a scheme.

IV is an important one in the Ageless Wisdom. It starts from the invisible and goes down, gradually becoming visible. Then it becomes more and more subtle, until it reaches the stage where it becomes invisible again. The cycle of evolution is like a big figure eight.

We can also understand this symbol with the analogy of building a temple. Before you start to build, you have a picture of the temple in your mind. When you are ready to build the temple, you have the blueprint, the concrete image of your thoughtform. The temple starts from your visualization and imagination — from the invisible — then it comes down and becomes materialized. This materialized form eventually will wear out, dissolve, and enter the domain of the invisible.

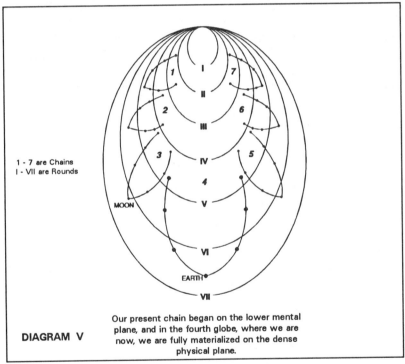

1 - 7 are Chains
I - VII are Rounds

DIAGRAM V

Our present chain began on the lower mental plane, and in the fourth globe, where we are now, we are fully materialized on the dense physical plane.

Chains, Globes, Rounds

In diagram V we see a scheme of evolution for a Planetary Logos in our second Solar System. The Ageless Wisdom tells us that there was a Sun and this Sun radiated Sparks. Some of these Sparks came to the first globe of the first chain. They started developing themselves, and as they continued to develop, they passed through each chain.

These Sparks developed in the mineral kingdom in the first chain, the vegetable in the second chain, the animal in the third chain, and became prototypes of the human kingdom in the fourth chain. However, when the mineral Sparks graduated from the first chain and entered the second chain, they did not enter as vegetables as we know them; rather, they were prototypes or blueprints of vegetables on the intuitional-mental levels.

Our forefathers in the first chain were mental beings; then they became astral beings, then etheric beings, and then physical beings. The animal Sparks passed to our fourth chain on the mental plane.

It was on the fourth globe of the fourth chain that we formed the physical body. In other words, the body that we had in the mental, astral, and etheric planes condensed and became objective on the fourth globe. Our present chain began on the lower mental plane; and in the fourth globe, where we are now, we are fully materialized on the dense physical plane.

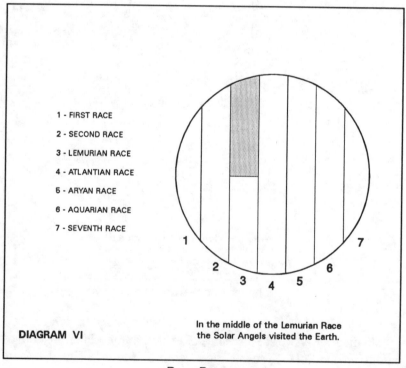

1 - FIRST RACE

2 - SECOND RACE

3 - LEMURIAN RACE

4 - ATLANTIAN RACE

5 - ARYAN RACE

6 - AQUARIAN RACE

7 - SEVENTH RACE

DIAGRAM VI

In the middle of the Lemurian Race
the Solar Angels visited the Earth.

Root Races

In each round, seven Root Races develop. In addition, sub-races branch out from the Root Races and form seven branch races of each Root Race. At the completion of one round, we have seven Root Races.

We say that the human race started in the fourth round of the fourth chain. Diagram VI shows the Root Races of our Earth, the fourth globe of the fourth chain. We are presently in the Fifth Root Race of the fourth globe of the fourth chain. The Sixth Root Race will be a more advanced Root Race, if we survive.

The term "race" in "Root Race" does not refer to people of a particular religion or racial type. The particular race depends on the development of the consciousness of the race. For example, in the humanity of the Lemurian period, the sacral center predominated and man was, for the most part, astrally oriented. In the Aryan Race, or the present civilization, the focus of consciousness of humanity is shifting from the solar plexus to the throat center. In addition, the ajna center is becoming active.

When the ajna center becomes active, it integrates the personality and makes it highly creative. We may say that the Aryan Race is characterized by mental activity and an integrated, creative personality.

We have a new race coming to the world. We are very close to the next Root Race, the Sixth Root Race, in which man will develop the heart center.

Just as big companies fail and go bankrupt, this also occurs on the Cosmic scale. We are told that our moon, the fourth globe of the third chain, was a failure. There were tremendous scientific discoveries made on the moon. They had the fastest airplanes, the best computers, and every other invention imaginable. They were far more advanced than we are. Then, for thousands of miles around the moon, pollution and inflammable gases accumulated.

Some very great Rishis saw what a disaster was coming to the moon, and with Their "spaceships" They brought some human beings and animals to the Earth. The biblical account of Noah and the Ark is a distortion of this event.

After some of the moon humanity were brought to the Earth, those who remained behind battled against each other; suddenly the atmosphere caught on fire and in one second roasted the life on the moon. This is called the disaster of the moon.

Because we came mainly from the moon race (the name of the fourth globe gives the name to the chain), we are retarded because of the materialism, anger, jealousy, hatred, and revenge we brought with us. And being affected by the failure of the moon, our Earth was not doing well up to the Third Root Race.

The center of our Solar System is the Sun. According to the Ageless Wisdom, the Sun is the body of a Great Life which radiates life energy to the entire Solar System. This Great Life is called the *Solar Logos*.

The Sun is sometimes called a great Eye that watches; It watches the forty-nine globes that form the Solar System. If this Heavenly Being sees that something is going wrong in one of the globes or chains, It takes drastic action to hasten the development of that planet or globe. Its purpose is to stimulate the Seed, the Spark, or the Life within each form, so that the Spark builds better bodies to cooperate fully with Cosmic development.

The Soul, or the life of this planet, is like the life of your body. You are a soul, and you have a body. The planet also has a body and a Soul. The planetary Soul is called the *Planetary Logos*. This is the life of the planet.

The Planetary Logos saw that humanity was not progressing according to the timetable of the Solar System. The Solar System is like a big clock with hundreds of wheels, all engaged together. If they do not run in a synchronized fashion, the entire process is retarded. At the time, humanity had passed through three and one half Root Races, but its members were still animal-like, with no mental spark. We are told that humanity was suffering greatly in its efforts to progress. The Planetary Logos informed the Solar Logos, and They planned to invite advanced entities from previous chains to further the evolution of humanity.

The Planetary Logos sent a great message into Space asking for help. The call went to the Venusian scheme, and the Lord of Venus said that He would send 105 great Kumaras (Angels or Teachers) and They would make the Planetary Life progress.

Kumaras are Ninth Degree Initiates. One of Them is called Sanat Kumara. In the Bible He is called the Ancient of Days or Melchizedek. He became the sole representative of the Planetary Logos, and with the remaining 104 Kumaras He founded Shamballa, the headquarters of the Planetary Life.[8]

Then from Shamballa, 49 (or 7 x 7) Great Ones moved closer to humanity and founded the Hierarchy. These 49 Great Ones planned and decided that humanity must be taught seven different subjects:

---

8. *The Legend of Shamballa*, pp. 29-33.

politics, education, communication, arts, science, religion, and finance. They separated into these seven different departments, and each department, with its seven Masters, contemplated day and night on the course of action. Some of them went closer to humanity to develop the fields of politics, education, the sciences, and the arts.

They opened various universities. The Great Pyramids formed one such university; the South American mystery schools were another. The Indians and the Caucasians had their own forms. In all, They put seven big schools on the planet, so that they could teach the seven branches of endeavor to humanity.[9]

When Shamballa and the Hierarchy were being formulated and organized, the Planetary Logos again sent a call into Space to those human beings who had graduated from previous Solar Systems or were waiting for incarnation. Both groups were highly advanced spirits and were called Solar Angels, Divine Flames, *Nirvanis, Manasputras,* etc.

The Solar Angels were of two main groups. One of the groups was made up of human beings from former great cycles. The other group was made up of those who were not yet human but were waiting for incarnation. This is why in esoteric literature there is a confusion about whether the Solar Angels were all human souls.

Millions of Divine Beings, or Solar Angels, came to this planet. The Great Beings were ordered to guide humanity into enlightenment by building a bridge between the Spark within the human being and his vehicles. They came in three waves.

The first wave came during the middle part of the Lemurian Age. They saw that humanity was not yet ready, so They went back.

The second wave came thousands of years later. They saw that the human mental body was just ready to take a spark. The second wave placed a spark in the human mental body. This event is recorded in all ancient literature, especially in the Greek literature in the story of Prometheus bringing fire to humanity.

When the third wave came, the Solar Angels entered the higher mental bodies of human beings, where the fire of the second wave had been placed. Immediately the mental bodies of human beings started to develop, and they began to develop thinking. The Ageless Wisdom states that when the Solar Angels entered the mental bodies of human beings, millions of human beings were shattered because they could not hold the voltage.

---

9. *Hierarchy and the Plan,* pp. 14-25.

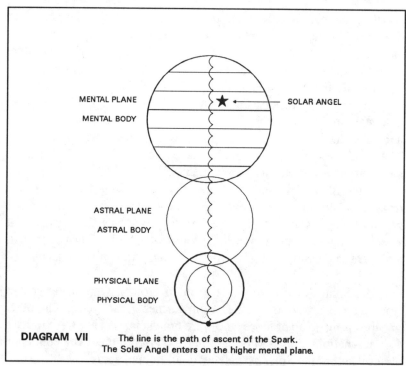

DIAGRAM VII   The line is the path of ascent of the Spark.
The Solar Angel enters on the higher mental plane.

The Spark and the Solar Angel

Eventually a large number of human beings adapted to the voltage, and the Solar Angel became the Teacher and the Guardian Angel of the human being to enable the Spark to reach Its destination. In the New Testament this event is explained in the following parable: "The kingdom of God is like leaven, which a woman took and hid in three measures of meal, until the whole was leavened."[10] The three measures refer to the three aspects of the personality — the physical, emotional, and mental bodies. The Great Beings put the spark into the minds of human beings to align and integrate their personalities. The leaven symbolizes the principle of mind which the Solar Angel (the woman) hid in the personality to leaven it.

There is confusion about how the human lower vehicles are built and who does it. In building the etheric, astral, and mental bodies, the Solar Angel, the human soul, karma, and the lower petris or elementals are all involved and all of them work cooperatively. In this labor the

---

10. Luke 13:20-21; Matthew 13:33

human soul provides the real substance or the electrical life network. The elementals give their substance to build upon it. Karma controls the form, the capacity, and the quality of the bodies. And, the Solar Angel keeps the key of cycles, of death and life and adds opportunities, possibilities, and visions for the purpose It has for the person. Thus, four factors cooperate to build the lower bodies.

It is important to understand the difference between possibilities and opportunities. The Solar Angel provides the possibilities — based on past heroic and sacrificial actions of the subject and on the contents of the Chalice. Opportunities come from people who are somewhat related to the subject, and they can provide opportunities to the subject if he is alert enough to catch them. All these affect the building of the lower bodies.

The Solar Angel is your Inner Guide Who will guide the human Spark back to Its home. The Solar Angel is your Guardian Watcher Who watches over you. When you live a life of service, love and aspiration, sooner or later you will realize that there is Someone within you watching you. You will feel this Presence — in your darkest hours, in your most dangerous moments, in sickness.

Goethe once wrote about an amazing experience he had: "Suddenly I saw an entity coming from my aura and standing in front of me. It was my Angel." There are other examples of meeting the Solar Angel in Greek mysteries. Socrates once spoke of a *daemon*: "a daemon in me, inspiring my whole philosophy." He was most probably referring to his Angel.

What are the duties of the Solar Angel?

The first duty of the Solar Angel is to pull man from the physical and emotional planes and have him focus in the mental plane so that eventually the Spark, which is the sleeping human soul, slowly liberates Itself from the physical plane and the emotional plane and becomes a mental being. Not until then can the Solar Angel communicate directly with the Spark.

The second duty of the Solar Angel is to make the human soul the master of the physical body and its physical hang-ups, the emotional body with its hang-ups, and the mental body with its hang-ups. Age after age, the Solar Angel increases the light of the human soul, just as a light focused on a seed makes that seed slowly unfold, grow, and take control of itself.

The third duty of the Solar Angel is to develop the senses of the physical body: hearing, touch, smell, sight, and taste. These senses must be developed first in the physical body; then they must be developed in the emotional body; and then in the mental body.

The Solar Angel is actually a great Teacher Who is organizing your life in such a way that you learn from every experience. Eventually you can do something. Eventually you become able to control and master the physical body, and you develop and refine your senses. You master the emotional body and develop its senses by using them constructively. Later, you master the mental body, develop its senses, and use the mental body to liberate yourself from the lower planes and go forward into the higher planes.

The fourth duty of the Solar Angel is to make the human Spark learn how to use the creative energies on the physical plane for procreation, for emotional creativity, for mental creativity, and eventually to make the human Spark a creative soul. Creativity is the radioactivity of the human Spark Who is able to unite with higher visions and express them on the physical, emotional, and mental planes.

The next task of the Solar Angel is to make the human being spread himself through three dimensions — physical, emotional, and mental — and come in contact with the planetary physical body, the planetary emotional body, and the planetary mental body. The human being enriches his experience physically, emotionally, and mentally in sharing all that exists on these planes.

The Solar Angel is not stuck with the human being; It inspires and challenges the human being while It continues Its own evolution, just as a great teacher comes and teaches in a university but in the meantime goes to a higher university to continue his own education.

Solar Angels are individual entities, just as human souls are, but very advanced. They are called Nirvanis because They were on the Intuitional Plane. The Tibetan Master states that the Solar Angels are "Initiates of all degrees." They are within us, watching us, life after life. The whole intention of the human being is to come in conscious contact with his Solar Angel.

We should look at the Solar Angel as the Master *within*, not as an exterior one. Many people say that they have met their Master, but those whom they meet are hallucinations. First, they must consciously meet their Solar Angel; then they can meet their Master. If they meet their Master before they meet their Solar Angel, it is a hallucination.

The sixth task of the Solar Angel is to help the Spark to become Itself, to become Its future. This is the science of becoming oneself.

In diagram VIII we see the relationship of the Solar Angel to the Spark. The Spark has a future — for example, to be a man. The man is the Spark and Its future. The circle is the Solar Angel.

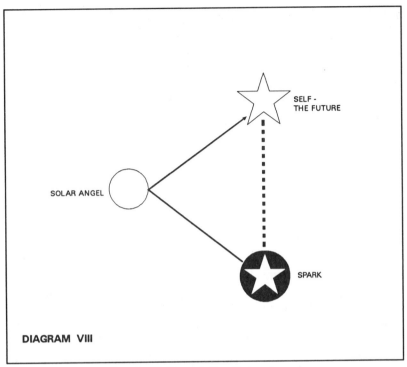

SELF - THE FUTURE

SOLAR ANGEL

SPARK

DIAGRAM VIII

Spark, Self, and the Solar Angel

The Solar Angel is a totally different entity. It is not part of you, but It is working to make you flower into the future. Just as the teacher holds the hand of a child and says, "Do this; do that," the Solar Angel helps you get up when you fall, inspires you to strive, to have courage, and to be fearless. If you are not walking in the right direction, the Solar Angel lets you hit a wall so that your nose bleeds and you realize that you are walking in the wrong direction.

There are many kinds of Solar Angels, and Their teachings are all different. But They all have the same plan for the human being — which is perfection. The Spark must go toward perfection. The Solar Angel is trying to remind us that greater Cosmic beauties await us; that we are not merely physical bodies; that greater joys and greater bliss are waiting for us if we conquer our shortcomings, hang-ups, and the wasteful way we are living; that we can surpass ourselves and unfold the Divinity living within each of us.

The Solar Angel is trying to awaken that lost Spark, your Real Self, which is identified with the body. The Spark takes another great step when It disidentifies Itself with the body and becomes identified with the emotions. If you look around you, you will find that most of humanity is identified with the emotions, with likes and dislikes. Part of humanity has released itself from the physical and emotional prisons and has entered the mental prison, but this prison is only a larger prison. There are many kinds of shrubs, trees, and games there; therefore humanity does not realize it is a prison. Only a very small portion of humanity is able to escape from these three prisons and enter the Intuitional Plane.

These steps are thoroughly explained in the *The Science of Becoming Oneself*.[11] An even smaller minority of humanity has escaped the intuitional level and entered another, greater area of consciousness, development, and relationship with Cosmos.

As the human Spark becomes able to detach Itself from the physical body, communication with and response from the Universe and Cosmos become greater. As we descend into materialization, this communication and response become limited and even reach the zero level. We become matter itself.

As we develop, unfold, and become conscious in higher states of beingness, our communication and response increase. When a great Master was speaking about the brotherhood of humanity, He said essentially, "You cannot create brotherhood within humanity by changing the government or ideologies. You can create the brotherhood of humanity only by changing the man."

How is man changed? Man is changed when he becomes the lord or master of his physical body. His physical body cannot control him. He gives the commands to his physical body. Next he completely controls his emotional hang-ups, likes, and dislikes. Then he gains complete control of his mental mechanism. He is no longer identified with his ideas and thoughts; he is beyond them. He sees them as tools and uses them, but he knows that he is not his thoughts.

There is a classic example of a man who was identified with his thoughts, ideas, and opinions. Socrates was sitting in front of his door when a philosopher came to debate with him. Socrates was so subtle, strong, and beautiful that in twenty minutes he disproved the man's ideas. When the man suddenly saw that all his ideas and crystallized thoughtforms had evaporated, he took his own life. The man was completely identified with his ideas. A man must pass this stage, also, before he can enter into direct knowledge, which in occult literature is called the intuitional level of awareness.

---

11. *The Science of Becoming Oneself*, by Torkom Saraydarian.

The seventh task of the Solar Angel is to make the human soul a citizen of the Cosmos. Eventually It takes your consciousness away from the interests of the personality, of your family, of your nation, of your race, of humanity, and makes you realize that you are a citizen of the Cosmos.

In former *manvantaras,* or creations, the majority of the Solar Angels were human beings who matured and reached the Fifth Initiation. Now They are sacrificing Their time and energy to make human seeds grow and become flowers.

Some of us were lucky enough to hear about the Guardian Angel while we were children. This idea must be taught to all children in a very beautiful way. The Guardian Angel is the Solar Angel.

Sometimes a group has a Solar Angel, an Angel who acts as the Group Angel, to inspire the group soul or the group members to be one and to be more sensitive to their own Solar Angels. This is called "amplification of the light."

Some places also have their Solar Angels. Humanity has its own Angel, and our globe has its Angel. The Solar Angel of our planet is the Entity Who is leading Venus, which is far more advanced in its evolution than our planet.

For centuries and centuries the Solar Angel within us inspires but never forces Its will upon us. The Solar Angel meditates and in meditation tries to touch the human Spark, raise Its vibration, and awaken It so that slowly It sees everything as it is. The human Spark eventually becomes a living soul instead of an imprisoned Spark.

This takes many ages. When the human Spark begins to awaken, the first great expansion of consciousness is called the *first initiation.*[12] In the first initiation the human soul, the developing Spark, suddenly realizes It is not the physical body.

Ages later, another great expansion of consciousness occurs, if the Spark really strives. This second expansion of consciousness is called the *second initiation.* It is the purification of the human heart and the human emotional responses. In Christian literature the second initiation is called the baptism, which means that emotionally a man is purified. The second initiation is related to water because water is the symbol of the emotional body in occult literature.

The third expansion, or the *Third Initiation,* comes when the human Spark enters the higher mental world and becomes illuminated

---

12. For further information regarding initiation, please refer to *Christ, The Avatar of Sacrificial Love,* Chapter 12, "Initiation."

and enlightened. Suddenly It sees that It is not the physical body, not the emotional body, and not the mind. In the Bible this event is recorded in the story of Moses going to the mountain and bringing back the Ten Commandments. On the mountain he touched his own Inner Divinity and he was enlightened. The Third Initiation is also recounted in the story of the enlightenment of the Buddha under the bodhi tree.

The fourth expansion, or the *Fourth Initiation*, is called the crucifixion because man resigns from his physical, emotional, and mental interests and enters into unity with the Great Existence within himself. In Buddhism the Fourth Initiation is called the Great Renunciation.

When the man enters the Great Renunciation, the Solar Angel leaves him so that the man will build his temple with his own hands and feet and carry on his development toward Infinity. The man has now become a *soul*. Before he was a darkened Spark; now he is a living soul.

In your daily life you can always remember that the Almighty Eye, the Great One within you, is watching you. Your Solar Angel is suffering for you so that you will eventually become divine and enter into the heritage of your spiritual glory. The Solar Angel suffers due to your delay on the Path; It is not suffering for Itself. Man lives by such a great vision and moves toward it every day. He strives to make himself better and better and tries to enter into greater light, greater sacrifice, and greater unity with humanity, the Solar System, and the Cosmos.

How do you develop contact with your Solar Angel?

The first thing you must do is purify your heart. The Solar Angel cannot directly communicate with you or reach you, even though It tries, until you purify your heart. If your heart is not purified, your aura is in a distorted and disturbed condition. When the Solar Angel sends ideas or impressions to your brain or your heart, your aura distorts them, just as the reflection of a tree on the water is distorted when the water is agitated.

Purification of the heart comes through loving more, tolerating more, being more grateful, and thinking in terms of unity and synthesis. Whenever you feel that you are doing something wrong, stop it... because you can pollute your heart. You can pollute your heart by thinking wrongly, speaking offensively, by having malice, violence, slander, or gossip in your nature.

Purification of the heart is the foundation of your contact with your Solar Angel.

Second, you must develop harmlessness in your physical actions, your emotions, thoughts, and speech. To cause harm means to hinder the flowering of the Spark of another human being. Whenever you stop life from progressing in any form, you are being harmful.

You can hurt people with your thoughts and emotions as well as with your actions. For example, you may not physically hurt a man; you may not say nasty things about him; but at night you think about killing him and you hate him in your mind. You are being just as harmful with your thoughts.

Harmlessness eventually brings the Solar Angel into your vision.

Third, you must increase your love.

Fourth, you must develop careful watchfulness over what you say. The Solar Angel cannot penetrate through the pollution created by wrong speech, or if It can, you sometimes receive Its message in reverse form.

Christ said that on the Judgment Day we will have to answer even for one nasty word that we have spoken.

Fifth, do not mix your aura with the auras of those who are polluted by criminal acts, imperil, hatred, jealousy, fear, anger, revenge, and greed. There are three ways to mix your aura with someone else's: by physically touching, by kissing, by sexual intercourse.

Intercourse totally mixes your aura with the other person's. Sometimes after intercourse you can see both auras shining with golden light; sometimes both will become so muddy and dirty that germs of future sicknesses develop in them. When people have indiscriminate sexual relations, their auras become so agitated and distorted that for ages their Solar Angel will be unable to purify the aura enough to come in contact with their Spark and help It grow.

Sexual purity is very important. It is also important to have these considerations when choosing a marriage partner.[13]

Purification of thought is the sixth important method to develop contact with your Solar Angel. To purify your thoughts you must think clearly and beautifully. Immediately when you think something evil about a person, change it and say, "I don't want to think that way. I want to think clearly and beautifully."

Do not project ugly thoughtforms. Do not think about other people as nasty, unsuccessful, stupid, or square human beings. Those pollute your mind, and when your mind is polluted you do not have the

---

13. For further information regarding this topic, please refer to *Woman Torch of the Future*, Chapter 2, "Marriage," and *Sex, Family, and the Woman in Society*.

opportunity to come in contact with that pure and radiant Entity Who is around you.

Seventh, always try to create victorious thoughts. Never accept thoughts of failure: "I am dying.... I am no good.... I am ugly.... I can't do these things." On the contrary, you should always say, "I am going to be victorious. I am going to be healthier. I am going to live. I am going to develop and unfold and become beautiful."

Just as you must think these things about yourself, you must also think this way about other people so that you do not hinder their progress with your thoughts of failure.

Eighth, live a life of sacrificial service. You work and earn a salary from your job. But can you do something else and not expect any money for it? Can you baby-sit for your neighbor who cannot pay; can you visit hospitals; can you work for other people without any expectation? Through sacrificial service, you can develop more affinity with your Solar Angel. The Solar Angel within you is the treasure house of wisdom and power. As you come closer to It, you radiate in greater dimensions.

The ninth method to develop contact with your Solar Angel is meditation.[14] Alice Bailey once wrote that the Solar Angel is in deep meditation to come in contact with the human soul. The Solar Angel meditates on how to stabilize the mental plane and how eventually to make contact with that sleeping fool who is lost in everything — in money, in greed, in hatred, in jealousy, in war, in crimes.

Start doing meditation every day — for two minutes, three minutes, five minutes. If you are regular about your meditation and conscious when you are doing it, you build a path which will eventually touch the path of your Solar Angel; you build a bridge between you and your Solar Angel. Then you will have direct contact; you will be in continuous contact with the Source of wisdom within you.[15]

For example, when you are preparing a lecture, immediately the Solar Angel will open the telecommunication path, and when you start speaking, the wisdom will flow through you. Previously, you may not have known the things you were speaking about. Now you do because the wisdom and creativity of the Solar Angel flow through you and speak.

---

14. For complete information regarding how to meditate, please refer to *The Science of Meditation*.

15. Alice A. Bailey, *A Treatise on White Magic* (New York: Lucis Publishing Company, 1974), p.xii.

The tenth step is contemplation. Contemplation is far away from us now, but we must know about it so that eventually we experience it. Contemplation is one-pointed meditation in the light of the Soul. It is not a process of knowingness; it is a process of absorption and assimilation of the light of the Solar Angel.

The eleventh method is silence, solitude, and retreat. You must become accustomed to these things. Sometimes keep silent. Go into a retreat for seven days and do not talk. Do not even think. Just keep silent. You will see how you regenerate your whole system.

The twelfth method is to aspire and strive toward the beauty of Christ. It is very important to recognize that Central Solar Angel of humanity. Christ is the Solar Angel of humanity.

Christ said something very mysterious which is explained in diagram IX. He said, "No one comes to the Father except through Me."[16] In diagram IX the Spark is the Child. The maturity of the Child is the Father; the Child becomes a Father. This means that you only

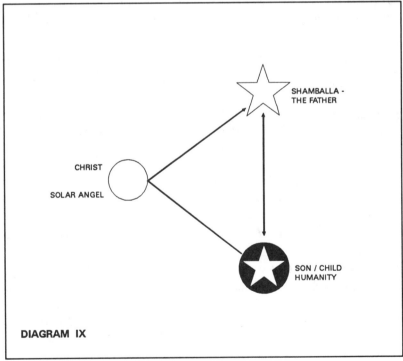

Humanity, Christ, and the Father

---

16. John 14:6-7

go to your Self through your Solar Angel. And humanity as a whole will go to its Self through its Solar Angel, through Christ.

Christ is not a Christian. Christ is the Solar Angel of humanity, and we are going to strive toward Him, no matter what religion we are.

The thirteenth way you can contact your Solar Angel is by developing your willpower. To develop your willpower means to master your body, emotions, and thoughts. If you say, "I am not going to eat today," you don't. Emotionally, establish a goal and strive for it, saying, "No matter what happens, I am going to do it." To develop your willpower you are going to swim against the currents of the contemporary life. If people are lying, you stand in the truth. If people are silly, you are solemn.

The fourteenth method is renunciation. You are eventually going to be a person who gives more than he takes — renouncing everything that you have, whatever you have collected; renouncing your vanities and pride, your showing-off. You must feel that nothing belongs to you, that it belongs to the One Life. When you renounce, you have everything.

How does the Solar Angel come in contact with the human being?

There are nine ways: The first way that the Solar Angel communicates with man is by creating certain urges and drives in him. For example, you may suddenly feel the urge to go visit your mother. When you visit her, you see that she is sick or she needs you. This is the first stage of communication with the Solar Angel.

The Solar Angel creates certain types of desires within you. When you begin to desire more and more, you start progressing, learning, and educating yourself.

The Solar Angel creates goals within you. What can you do for the nation, for a group? Can you create a big vision and try to reach that vision? The Solar Angel eventually creates that enthusiasm, that fire within you, so that you start advancing to the mental levels.

The Solar Angel contacts you through dreams. It projects certain instructive, educational dreams where you learn something. It may project help for you to pass certain dangers that you are confronting in your life. It may give you courage and strength to overcome a certain problem.

You may have thousands of these dreams, but because your emotional and mental auras are in a state of agitation, you cannot see exactly what is projected to you from your Solar Angel.

The Solar Angel contacts you through direct visions. You see something that is going to happen — a goal, a form of beauty, a person whom you are going to meet. Again, the Solar Angel shows these things, but you cannot get the message if the mirror of your aura is not clean.

The Solar Angel tries to get other people to meet you. Solar Angels communicate with each other as well. For example, a very beautiful man is looking for a really beautiful girlfriend, but he cannot find her. So his Solar Angel talks to her Solar Angel and tries to arrange a meeting. Or you go to a library and suddenly a woman appears and says, "Did you read this book?" And it was just the type of book you had been searching for.

The Solar Angel directs you, when you are ready, by direct appearance. Some great geniuses have written of the experience of meeting their Angel. There is such an example in the Bible, which people often do not notice.

St. Paul was in a prison, and his Angel came and released him from prison. St. Paul left the prison and went home. His friends were inside the home, praying for him. When he knocked on the door, a girl came and saw him through the window and ran back and told the others, "The Angel of Paul is here!" The friends of St. Paul knew his Angel. Then they checked and said, "No, it is not his Angel. It is Paul." They asked Paul how he got home and he said, "My Angel opened the bars, and I came here."[17]

You may also hear the voice of your Solar Angel. But do not hurry for this contact because there are many, many false voices that you may hear. The voice of the Solar Angel is a totally different voice from the other voices you may hear.

Eventually you meet your Solar Angel on the inner planes face-to-face, and It sits by you like a great Rishi and educates you.

With these nine methods you may come in contact with your Solar Angel. And after you meet It, something happens to you. You fall in love with this great Being. This is the meaning of the "marriage in Heaven." In esoteric language it is called "Soul-infusion." You and your Solar Angel become one.

At the Fourth Initiation when you are symbolically crucified, you may say, as Jesus did, "My Lord, my Lord, why have You forsaken me?" because it is at this point that the Solar Angel leaves you. The Solar Angel worked so hard to bring you to this renunciation, and now It leaves you alone to go on by yourself. The Solar Angel is now released for greater labor in the Cosmos.

---

17. Acts 5:19-20

Thus, the human Spark gradually blooms and reaches Its destination as a glorious being. What waits after that will be known only by those who make still higher breakthroughs with their continuous spiritual striving.

The Solar Angel uses the sophisticated computer of Space to report to the Karmic Lords whenever you break the law of Beauty, Goodness, Righteousness, Gratitude, Joy, and Freedom. Whenever you break the Law of Love and Compassion, It reports immediately.

On the other hand, your Solar Angel reports all that you do for unity, love, beauty, freedom, health...to the "Father in Heaven." We are told that our Angels see the face of the Father and report our good deeds to Him.

In the Hierarchy, we are told, every disciple has an etheric image on a special wall. This image represents his beingness and changes every time he advances or fails. As he advances, the brilliance and colors increase and attract more attention from the One Who watches the image to become aware of the disciple's progress. Every time the Great One watches the image, He transmits a great amount of energy into the person through his image. One feels this energy as enthusiasm, dedication, service, and creativity.

There is a direct communication with the mirror of the Father, with the recordings of the Karmic Lords, and with the image in the special halls of the Hierarchy. Through this image, our Master becomes aware of all that we are going through in life. This image is projected on the wall of a special hall of the Hierarchy by your Angel when you enter the Path of discipleship, and your Angel presents you to the Hierarchy as a graduate from the lower schools of life. From that moment on, you are under the watchful eyes of a Master.

Our actions on the three planes — the physical, emotional, and mental — have their specific colors. If your actions are in harmony with the Divine Plan, they usually radiate the color orange on the physical plane; your emotions radiate the color green; your thoughts radiate mostly a lemon-yellow color. Your spiritual actions radiate the colors pink or violet. Higher actions have a ruby color.

These colors continuously radiate out of you and become visible to the denizens of the Subtle World. In the Subtle World, colors are the most accurate language, which is known especially by advanced Initiates. Any advanced Initiate may read your life through the colors you project.

When an advanced Initiate radiates colors and energy, he builds forms of beauty, like rainbows and flowers. The Great Ones rejoice in seeing the process of his integration and spiritual unfoldment. An

Initiate is a walking rainbow in the Subtle World and a symphony in the Fiery World.

Your actions change into colors, sound, and geometrical forms in the Higher Worlds. This is why we are always seen under the vision of the Omnipresent Eye of the Universe.

When you are born in the Subtle World by leaving your body on the material plane, your beauty and glory increase as you ascend to higher and higher levels. Death does not exist, but birth exists. You are in a continuous process of birth. You are born in the astral world, then the mental world, then perhaps in the Higher Worlds. Then you come back and are born again into the physical world. Thus you continue, cycle after cycle, until you reach a stage where you "no more go out."

In the astral plane, the Solar Angel is again with you. In the mental plane, It is mostly visible to you. When you function on the higher mental plane, you can communicate with It face-to-face. In all states of existence you can draw It closer to you by living a life of heroic and sacrificial service and by striving for higher achievements.

Some people do not have Solar Angels. They are intellectually advanced people, but they are selfish and separative and they think only of their own interests. A person can find out whether or not he has a Solar Angel by watching his behavior. For example, if he commits a crime and does not feel the slightest reaction from his conscience and does not question himself about his actions; if the only thing that controls him is his fear; if he thinks he can escape the law, committing almost any crime, it means there is no one in him to question him.

The Solar Angel makes you feel uncomfortable when you commit crimes or hurt people's souls or hinder their progress. As you go downhill in your morality and spirituality, the Solar Angel slowly fades away after making strong attempts in various ways to warn you.

If you have a Solar Angel, you have direction. You are not an aimless wanderer, a window-shopper, but you have a constructive goal and a developing plan for Beauty, Goodness, Righteousness, Joy, and Freedom. The Solar Angel tries every means by which to inspire you in the right direction, but as you go deeper into darkness, it becomes more difficult for It to communicate with you.

Some people think that they have a Solar Angel when they feel ashamed of their evil deeds, or when they have special goals. This may be true, but when we feel ashamed, it is not because we have a Solar Angel but because our religious or moral teaching has built a standard within us. There is an automatic reaction against whatever does not agree with our standard, and we feel upset.

In addition, we often have goals that are not innate goals but goals forced upon us. Whether they are good or bad, they are not considered goals if they are forced or imposed upon us.

Before one establishes a direct communication with his Solar Angel, he is directed to a spiritual Teacher who represents his Solar Angel. The greatest transgression of a person is the moment when he tries to use the trust of his Teacher to manipulate him through giving gifts or offering love or pretending selfless service with the intention of serving his own interests, vanity, and ego. In exploiting and manipulating his Teacher, he betrays his Solar Angel and invites a dark karma on himself.

It is very interesting to notice that those who break their contact with the Solar Angel slowly develop vanity. Vanity fills the vacuum created by the absence of the Angel in their consciousness.

There is a very subtle distinction between vanity and knowing one's value. Those who have value feel and know their talents, power, and labor, and they act differently from those who have very little value. They act in self-confidence; they express firmness and directness in all their relationships.

Vain people often resemble those who have self-confidence. They *act* with a false confidence and directness, but one feels that they are showing off and imitating that they have real values. Usually those who have real values do not talk about themselves, but talk about others who have values. Vain ones talk about themselves and avoid mentioning anyone else who has values.

Vain ones do not try to improve themselves. Those who are loaded with values always feel that they need to improve themselves and progress on the Path of perfection.

Vain ones feel that they know everything and are everything, and because life occasionally makes them see their poverty, they begin to have an inner uneasiness. Then serious conflict follows. The vanity in them tries not to give up, and the awakening soul tries to see the accumulated vanity in the personality. This conflict continues for long years, with complicated psychological problems and nervous disorders. A vain one leads himself into unending problems of health and social relationships.

To cure vanity, one needs to invoke his Angel, or find a Teacher who is stern enough to break the accumulated layers of his vanity by the scientific teaching of humiliation.

Through our deeds on the three planes — physical, emotional, and mental — we may sever our connection with the Solar Angel. This has an effect on our present and future lives. We fall into prostitution, drugs, alcohol, and crimes, and through pain and suffering we eventually understand that we are not on the way leading to happiness, health, and prosperity. Once we turn our face in the right direction, the Solar Angel again begins to communicate with us.

To increase our creativity and to inspire us in the right direction, the Solar Angel contacts us at certain times and suggests that we withdraw from sex for a while or economize our sexual energy. Moral purity highly increases the power and depth of our creativity. It is known to advanced disciples that when sexual energy is sublimated and reaches the throat center, it starts to radiate into the aura, increasing the sensitivity of the aura toward higher inspirations and synchronizing one's direction to the currents of the Cosmic Heart.

Those who prepare themselves to tune in to greater missions suggested by Great Ones do not waste their energy. The Solar Angel very subtly guides your steps toward purity during certain intervals when higher currents of energies are available in Space. Usually those who turn their faces toward Home feel the presence of the Inspirer and Protector.

Some people think that they do not have an Angel because they have not had conscious communication with It. But if they become more observant, they will notice that they have been given many beautiful ideas, visions, thoughts, creative impulses; they have been protected from dangers at various times or on various occasions; they have learned great lessons through their experiences; and they have had many awakening and enlightening moments in their lives. These are all blessings of the Angel.

Wherever there is Joy, Freedom, Righteousness, Goodness, and Beauty, the Angel is present. When the Angel is present, you never feel depressed, lonely, bored, or aimless. On the contrary, Its presence turns into a radiating joy and creativity in you.

The Solar Angel is a source of creative inspiration. The closer you go to It, the greater is the current of inspiration coming from It. At times when your connection is strong, the Angel can literally pour advanced ideas and thoughts into your mind; or advanced, delightful, and inspiring music into your soul; or It may inspire you toward heroic acts. Its cooperation with you becomes so close that you feel Its presence joyfully inspiring you with creative ideas.

In an old story, a wise man is said to have advised people to have a good friend, and at the end of the story he states, "The best friend is one whom you feel but cannot touch."

60

The Intuitional Plane

According to the Trans-Himalayan Teaching, there are *Seven Cosmic Planes* which are called (from the highest to the lowest levels):

1. The Cosmic Divine Plane or Adi
2. The Cosmic Monadic Plane
3. The Cosmic Atmic Plane
4. The Cosmic Buddhic Plane
5. The Cosmic Mental Plane
6. The Cosmic Astral Plane
7. The Cosmic Physical Plane

The last Plane, the *Cosmic Physical Plane*, is divided into seven subplanes, which are in turn called (from the highest to the lowest levels):

1. First Cosmic Ether (Divine Plane)
2. Second Cosmic Ether (Monadic Plane)
3. Third Cosmic Ether (Atmic Plane)
4. Fourth Cosmic Ether (Intuitional Plane)
5. Mental Plane
6. Emotional or Astral Plane
7. Physical — Etheric Plane

According to the Ageless Wisdom, the Intuitional Plane is a very important plane at this cycle of manifestation.

We are told that our Solar System exists in the Fourth Cosmic Etheric, or in the Intuitional Plane. The Intuitional Plane is the meeting place of past, present, and future.

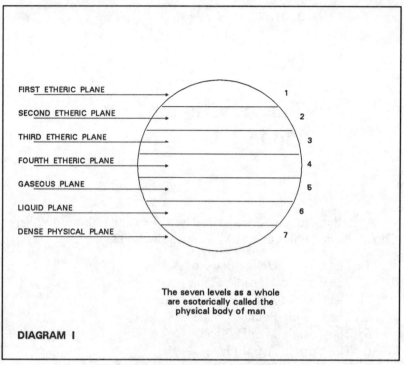

FIRST ETHERIC PLANE ⟶ 1

SECOND ETHERIC PLANE ⟶ 2

THIRD ETHERIC PLANE ⟶ 3

FOURTH ETHERIC PLANE ⟶ 4

GASEOUS PLANE ⟶ 5

LIQUID PLANE ⟶ 6

DENSE PHYSICAL PLANE ⟶ 7

The seven levels as a whole
are esoterically called the
physical body of man

DIAGRAM I

The Physical Constitution of Man

The Intuitional Plane is the sphere where man becomes a superman.[1]

The etheric body of the human being is formed of the four lower ethers. It is upon this body that the physical plane is constructed as its shadow.

The Planetary and Solar Logoi have Their etheric bodies which are build by very subtle substances. For example, the etheric body of the Planetary Logos is build of our Intuitional, Atmic, Monadic, and Divine Planes — in other words, of the four higher Cosmic Ethers.

Thus, you see that our fourth lower ether has a similar function in relation to the human being as the Intuitional body does for the Planetary Logos.

The four levels of the etheric body of the Planetary Logos correspond to our four lower etheric planes. For example:

---

1. For more information please refer to *A Treatise on Cosmic Fire*, pp. 116-125.

1. The Divine Plane, or First Cosmic Ether, corresponds to our first lower ether or first etheric plane.
2. The Monadic Plane, or the Second Cosmic Ether, corresponds to our second lower ether or the second etheric plane.
3. The Atmic Plane, or the Third Cosmic Ether, corresponds to our third lower ether or the third etheric plane.
4. The Intuitional Plane, or the Fourth Cosmic Ether, corresponds to our fourth lower ether or the fourth etheric plane.

When you examine the human constitution from the esoteric viewpoint you will see that below the fourth ether there are the gaseous, liquid, and dense physical matters. Remember that our first, second, third, and fourth ethers, plus the gaseous, liquid, and dense physical matters compose our *physical body*. The seven levels as a whole are esoterically called the physical body of man.

Similarly, the body of the Planetary Logos is built of seven elements which are of very high order. For example:

—Our Intuitional Plane, the Fourth Cosmic Ether
—Our Atmic Plane, the Third Cosmic Ether
—Our Monadic Plane, the Second Cosmic Ether
—Our Divine Plane, the First Cosmic Ether

are the etheric body of the Planetary Logos.

—Our lower mental, astral, physical planes

are as His physical manifestations.

Between the Solar Logos and the Planetary Logos, there is the difference regarding their "dense" physical bodies. The "dense" physical body of the Solar Logos is the Fourth Cosmic Ether, our *Intuitional Plane*, whereas the "dense" physical body of the Planetary Logos is our *Mental Plane*.

For the Solar Logos our mental, astral, and physical planes are unreality. For the Planetary Logos our astral and physical planes are unreality.

All of this information is given to us to make us realize that we live as cells or atoms in these Great Lives, and we can achieve a closer relationship with the Planetary and Solar Logoi by trying to raise the level of our consciousness to the higher mental plane, and from the higher mental plane to the Intuitional Plane. It is in the Intuitional Plane that we discover the gates leading us to the Higher Worlds.

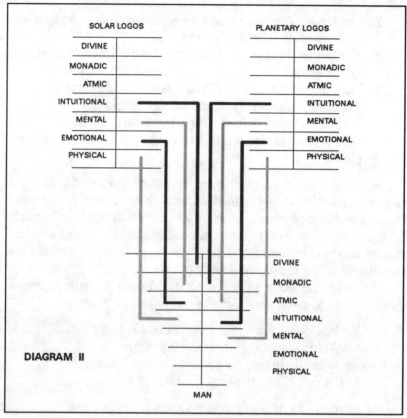

DIAGRAM II

Corresponding Planes

When we withdraw our focus of consciousness from the fourth sub-plane of the mental plane and function in the third, we enter into the domain of our Guardian Angel and penetrate into the body of the Planetary Logos. It is here that we build the Golden Bridge leading us into the body of the Solar Logos — the Intuitional Plane. After entering into the Intuitional Plane, we begin to build our own Intuitional body with the help of Angelic beings and eventually find our position in the center of the Spiritual Triad. Thus, when we build our intuitional body and transfer the focus of our consciousness from mental to the Intuitional Plane, we contact the etheric body of the Planetary Logos. We become a direct part of His etheric body and share His life forces.

In the Third Initiation, our astral body begins to fade away, and the intuitional body takes its place at the Fourth Initiation as the sentient mechanism of the person.

We can build and develop our intuitional body when we do the following:

1. Begin to express pure, unconditional love.
2. Live a life of sincerity.
3. Do sacrificial service or labor.
4. Engage in heroic actions.
5. Manifest pure creativity.
6. Have moments of ecstasy.
7. Have moments of joy and bliss.
8. Live in reality.

Unconditional love is very rare. We always have a string attached to our love. It is usually not unconditional; it is not pure. There are mixed motives behind it.

When we allow pure love to flow from our essence, we have the substance to build our intuitional body. Sublimation of sexual energy is used as the foundation of the intuitional body.

Sincerity purifies the whole aura and makes the person be as he is in his essence. It creates harmony and eliminates all those elements which cause conflict and disturbances in the aura. When the aura is harmonious and pure, it attracts the energy of the Fourth Cosmic Ether, which brings a new kind of vitality into the aura. The human soul uses this energy or element to build the intuitional body.

Sacrificial service or labor builds the intuitional body. As you engage in sacrificial labor, you draw light, love, and power from your Essence, from your Core. These elements are used to build the intuitional body.

Heroic actions are actions in which you give all that you have and all that you are without reservation. Heroic action is an action of total offering of yourself. Sacrificial labor is related to someone whom you want to help for ten, twenty, or thirty years, but heroic action is spontaneous and all-giving. Heroes not only sacrifice, but they are also victorious people in life and in death.

In sacrificial service, one still has a "precious self" or thoughts about his self. In heroic action, the self does not exist. Once a person reaches such a state of heroism, he draws intuitional energy from Space or from Those who are watching his life. The intuitional body cannot be built as long as the sense of self exists. Only heroes can walk in the presence and the glory of God, as they are dressed in the robe of glory.

Pure creativity is a process of giving form to the substance of Intuition. If the substance of Intuition is not in your creative work, your work is artificial and has no true influence on people.

Through creativity, you draw intuitional substance into your aura and subsequently use it to build your intuitional body. Creativity builds a channel from the Intuitional Plane to the mental and astral bodies and then to the human brain. It is the intuitional substance that nourishes higher centers on each plane.

Pure creativity evokes beauty. It is not dogmatic, ideological; it is not done to convert others or limit their freedom, but to evoke more freedom, joy, and striving from others.

Moments of ecstasy produce a refined element in your aura which can be used to build your intuitional body. Ecstasy is the moment when your consciousness contacts the Intuitional Plane and sees the beauty, harmony, and rhythm existing there. When your mind and brain cannot hold that experience, they go into a state of "overflow." This is expressed as an experience of extreme "giving-up." This is ecstasy, which nevertheless penetrates into your system as joy, vitality, and refreshment. Each moment of ecstasy is a moment of expansion of consciousness.

Moments of bliss are moments of contact and fusion with the Creative Will in the Universe. Such moments produce psychic energy which draws into our system intuitional substance from Space. This is why in every experience of bliss we also have an experience of expanding our consciousness, plus energy around and within us. Things which seemed impossible become easy and dissolve during moments of bliss. A moment of bliss takes us out of our ego and out of our petty problems.

When we build our intuitional body, we must also think about how to develop its five main senses. We must remember that we are born as bodies, and gradually the bodies develop their senses and keep us in contact with the corresponding planes and worlds.

The intuitional body grows like a baby grows, and its senses gradually develop. As they develop, they convey more information about the world in which the intuitional body dwells. These five senses are comprehension, healing, divine vision, intuition, idealism. They correspond to our physical senses of hearing, touch, sight, taste, and smell respectively.

On the Intuitional Plane, through *comprehension,* we understand things from all viewpoints. Comprehension is total understanding through the sound heard in the Intuitional Plane. Sound is everywhere, in all planes. As we go higher, it becomes the synthesizing agent of all that any object may convey.

Actually, all our bodies or parts of our nature manifest various sounds on all levels. Sometimes these sounds are harmonious; sometimes not. Comprehension is complete understanding of all these sounds in the key of the major, dominating sound.

For example, a person says something; this is his dominating key. But his body, emotions, thoughts, and motives say different things. Comprehension is the ability to "hear" all these and have a clear understanding of the issue — for the present and in regard to the future. Such an understanding is instantaneous and all-inclusive because the comprehension is not based on brain, logic, and reasoning.

One must have the second sense, *healing*, developed before he can spiritually heal people. This healing is related to all vehicles, not just to the physical vehicle.

Remember that all these senses are to be understood from the point of view of the light of the intuitional body, which gives them a super-sensitivity in regard to viewing reality. Thus, the sense of healing is also a sense of discovery of where the cause of the trouble is and what kind of energy must be used to annihilate the roots of it.

The sense of healing is also very sensitive to the karmic laws. It abstains if the karma of the person does not tolerate healing.

The sense of healing not only discovers the roots of trouble in the bodies but also finds the sources of pressure coming from Space or the environment. Pressure is often the cause of our problems. Pressure can originate through the presence of beauty, justice, and freedom. If the mechanism is not ready for the voltage or the pressure of beauty, justice, and freedom, it gives up under the pressure. The sense of healing discovers all this and takes the needed action to reduce the dosage of pressure and heal the vehicle.

The third sense, *divine vision*, is the eye of the human soul. In the Intuitional Plane are revealed the "beauty of divine continence" and the energy configuration or geometry, as they come and spread toward lower worlds through the prism of the intuitional body. The intuitional body is the prism of energies which distributes these energies to the centers on all lower planes, as well as to the centers of Beauty, Goodness, Righteousness, Joy, and Freedom on the planet, no matter under what name they operate. In the spiritual literature of the world, there are thousands of pages which are a record of such visions. In the future, they must be compiled from all faiths and traditions as a witness to the existence of this sense.

The fourth sense is the sense of *intuition*. It is important to know that we have the intuitional body, a sense in that body which is called intuition, and also the operation of that sense, which is called intuition. We are now talking about the sense proper.

Comprehension is related to the physical body of the Planetary Logos or the Fourth Cosmic Ether. The sense of intuition is a more advanced sense, and it is related not only to the lower planes and their objects, but also to higher planes and their objects and impressions received intuitively.

The sense of intuition penetrates the future. It is a vertical sense, not a horizontal one. It always touches higher realities and uses them for guidance on the horizontal levels.

The fifth sense, the sense of *idealism*, receives impressions and changes them into ideas and thoughtforms which evoke aspiration and striving in the hearts of human beings. For this, one must have not only a developed intuitional body but also a trained and refined mental body.

Idealism is the sense that "smells" the purpose, the right direction leading to improvement or perfection. It is only through the sense of idealism in the Intuitional Plane that the Initiate realizes the Purpose of the Highest Center.

The mental body translates ideas according to its main keynote or Ray, or according to the predominating key of the personality. Idealism presents vision on the seven fields of human endeavor, receiving its impressions from seven Cosmic sources of energy.

In the Intuitional Plane there are the following:

1. The etheric body of the Planetary Logos, formed of intuitional substance. Some people who have had certain experiences talk about light, colors, precious stones, rainbows, and energy currents just to find words to try to explain their vision of the Intuitional Plane.
2. The living forms of all correspondences that we have on the physical plane are found in the Intuitional Plane.
3. The Intuitional Plane is a place where the Planetary Logos meets and converses with the other Planetary Logoi about the Solar Plan and Their part in it.
4. Arhats, Masters, Chohans, and Angels of great power are found here.
5. All major Ashrams are on the Intuitional Plane, and all Ashrams of other planets are found on different subplanes of the Intuitional Plane. We are told that our Hierarchy, with Its

seven main Ashrams, meets in the Intuitional Plane. These Ashrams are classes in which great Masters teach the specialized wisdom of each Ray. If one can penetrate into such an Ashram by his proper merit, he absorbs the advanced Teaching and secrets of that special Ashram.

We are told that while in an Ashram, one can be charged with wisdom, power, and knowledge and bring them down to his earthly consciousness and use them for the benefit of humanity.

6. Meetings of the Great Ones are held on this plane, especially when They prepare points of crisis for humanity.

This expression is misunderstood by many. Crises are challenges to the human soul, to our essence. It is the meeting of a challenge that creates crises in our body, emotions, mind, and environment because we try to refine, organize, uplift, and transform ourselves to meet the challenge. This period of tension, readjustment, and breakthrough is called a crisis. Crises are challenges to make you beautiful, full of goodness, righteousness joy; and to be free, wise, heroic, etc.

When we truly see the beauty of the intuitional life and understand it to a certain degree, it creates a crisis in us because we try to leave behind all those thoughts, words, feelings, actions, and motives that are preventing us from reaching such a lofty level of awareness. A crisis is a period of friction and conflict between all those forces in us which want to progress and those forces which want to be attached to former values or objects. Crises occur mostly because of our crystallized inertia, attachments, glamors, illusions, vanity, ego, and the pressure of our environment. Every instance of higher wisdom creates a crisis because it mobilizes our progressive energies against those forces which tend to hold us for their own advantage.

7. In the Intuitional Plane, people realize what the essence of love is. Love is an intuitive substance of high order.

8. The Intuitional Plane is the plane of pure light. All illumination comes from the Intuitional Plane. Enlightenment is a moment of fusion with the Intuitional Plane.

9. Christ-consciousness is the light of Intuition.

10. The Planetary Logos worked very hard for millions of years and built His Intuitional body. We can also start building it on our level, which in the future will be a seed for a greater body.

11. It is said that some people appear on the Intuitional Plane with their intuitional body. You also meet your Solar Angel there, face-to-face.

When you function on the Intuitional Plane, your Solar Angel can be free and be occupied with higher works. Conversations with the

Solar Angel about your past lives will be the most interesting activity, as well as knowing all that It did to liberate you from your chains.

12. Our true heart is found in the Intuitional Plane. It is this heart that pulsates with the rhythm of the heart of the Solar Logos.

We are told that in building our intuitional body we make the foundation for the Ninth Initiation possible in the future. People have always dreamed of building spaceships. The real spaceship is our intuitional body through which, we are told, we can travel in interstellar Space and visit higher Centers of great civilizations which we have never dreamed of, even in our wildest imagination. It is only after we build the intuitional body that we are given wings in Space. Space belongs to those who have wings.

Deep down in his heart, a human being feels that Space belongs to him, but he realizes that he is a prisoner in this solar system. One day great Teachers will supervise our efforts while we sincerely try to build our wings.

61

Conscious Immortality

Conscious immortality is not a gift; it is the result of hard labor. Some people think they are immortal. It is true that all that exists will exist in some form or another, but immortality is not a mere existence. It is a conscious existence while the Awareness Unit travels from state to state without losing his continuity of consciousness.

Consciousness operates through organized bodies. Unless the bodies are organized, one cannot be conscious about his own immortality. The first body to be organized is the emotional body. If this body is organized, the person will have continuity of consciousness in the astral plane where people usually enter after death. But if the other bodies are not organized, he loses his astral consciousness when he takes another incarnation from the astral plane to the physical plane.

If the person has built the mental body, he will be consciously immortal during his astral and mental journey in the astral and mental worlds. But as on earth, so also in the subtle spheres: the consciousness of man is relative. There are people who are slightly conscious, half-conscious, seventy-five percent conscious, and fully conscious in the subtle spheres. When these people are reincarnated, they lose their continuity of consciousness and do not remember anything about life in the subtle plane or about past lives.

The next body is called the body of glory, the Chalice, or the Temple. If this is built, the person becomes consciously immortal. He consciously passes away to the Subtle Worlds and consciously incarnates and remembers many of his past lives on earth, as well as experiences in the Subtle World.

This state of awareness is also relative. If the Temple is fully completed, the consciousness is clearly uninterrupted. At the perfect completion of the Temple of Glory, the human soul becomes an Arhat who has built his continuity of consciousness and has reached immortality. It is only after reaching immortality that one is considered born in the "kingdom of gods."

The most important duty of man is to build, through everything he does, his *ark*, the symbol of the glorious body. Everything else in the Universe is useless and meaningless, except when a person begins to build his subtle vehicles. What is the use of living if one loses his soul!

To lose one's own soul means to merge into unconsciousness, into a state where there is no past, no memory, no future. This is what *death* is. One must ask himself whether he wants to die or live. To live means to have continuity of consciousness as one passes from one state to another.

Man must acquire higher bodies in order to live a conscious, immortal life. Being part of the Universe, man is always immortal. Even his bodies are immortal. They exist and never perish as elements. The human spirit is immortal, even if he is not conscious of it. The immortality we are talking about is *conscious* immortality or continuity of consciousness. Through all states and planes, the soul advances. There is no break in his consciousness once he builds the bridge between his bodies.

If a man has built the bridge between the physical and astral bodies, he passes into the astral plane without a gap in consciousness. He lives in the astral plane as a conscious entity just as he was (if he was) a conscious entity on the physical plane. But if he did not build the bridge between the astral and mental bodies, he falls into unconsciousness when his astral body dies.

What happens when the astral or mental body dies and the human soul cannot proceed to the next higher plane? He may either fall asleep on that plane until his time of incarnation comes, or he may incarnate without delay.

There are many human souls sleeping on the astral and mental planes, waiting for the hour of their incarnation. They are in their lower mental body or in the astral body, but they are not conscious. They return to incarnation with their old mental body and all its recordings, and they live a life almost identical to their former life.

If a person had begun building the bridge while on earth, he could continue building it in the astral or in the mental plane. But it must be started here on earth to be continued in the Subtle Planes. If the human soul had entered into consciousness beyond the mental plane and into the Intuitional Plane, he comes back with full memory of the life he lived in the Subtle Worlds.

Transfiguration is a graduation ceremony leading into the higher mental plane, where the person or the human soul gains consciousness. Crucifixion is another graduation ceremony leading the human soul into the Intuitional Plane. Resurrection is a ceremony which leads the human soul beyond our Cosmic Physical Plane into the Cosmic Astral Plane, where the Initiate lives as a Solar Entity.

When the human soul is born, he builds his physical, emotional, and mental bodies. After crucifixion, he begins to build his intuitional, atmic, monadic, and divine bodies. In resurrection, he leaves all these bodies and vests himself with a *solar robe*.

These robes are not the fancy of imagination. They are needed if one wants to come in contact with the life of the corresponding planes and use his robes to protect himself from electromagnetic storms, rays, and currents going on in Space, not only on the Cosmic Physical Plane but also on all other Cosmic Planes.

If the human soul has built his higher vehicles — namely, the intuitional, atmic, monadic, and divine bodies — when he incarnates, he brings them to earth with him and uses them to communicate with the corresponding planes without a gap in his consciousness. The Great Ones have such an abundant life. They live on our planet, but Their souls can soar wherever They want and live a multi-dimensional life.

Christ said, "I came to bring you life more abundant."[1] Immortality is a flame in the human soul.

There are two words which need clarification in order to understand the mystery of immortality clearly. One of them is *ego*; the other is *beingness*.

The ego, in its true sense, is part of the personality. It exists when the human soul is asleep and identified with the physical, emotional, and mental natures. Identification with the personality vehicles creates an ego who has separate interests. The ego is the human soul, identified with the vehicles.

The personality is the integration of the physical, emotional, and mental nature by the human soul identified with these three vehicles. The ego is aware of his identification with the three vehicles but is not able to detach himself; instead, he uses the vehicles for separative interests.

In the personality, the human soul is fused with the three vehicles and they are integrated. The ego thinks he is a mind and a being

---

1. John 10:10

separate from all the rest of existence. The human soul, when he progresses, identifies with the higher mental plane. He is selfless.

Soul-infusion is the stage when the human soul is identified with the Inner Light or the Solar Angel. Beyond this degree there is the Spiritual Triad, which is an electromagnetic sphere formed of light, love, and will elements. This is the birthplace of the human soul. Here the Self is called the human soul. We call man a *soul* because here he is consciously immortal and has continuity of consciousness.

Through another two steps forward, man gains his Selfhood, his permanent "I." He can now say, "I am," without a sense of separation. This takes place on the Monadic and Divine Planes.

The personality can only be changed through discipline, pain, and suffering. To change the personality means to make the human soul realize his independence and detach himself, and then bring changes into his threefold nature.

Discipline, pain, and suffering create a cleavage between the identified soul and the vehicles, and the person begins to aspire to a higher state of beingness. Discipline, pain, and suffering make a person observe. Observation is the only method by which to pull the observer out from the objects he is identified with. Once he is pulled out, for a short or long time, he begins to act, feel, and think in terms of self-interest. Here the ego is built.

The ego must be pulled out from the lower mental plane to the higher mental plane to introduce into the person's consciousness the idea of oneness and try to make him act, feel, and think more inclusively and with greater compassion.

The ego can be dissipated by developing virtues, as virtues are the rays coming from the Core of the human being which have the ability to disperse the formation called the ego. The development of virtues is carried on through meditation, study, evening review, active sacrificial service, and self-confrontation.

Once the ego is dispersed, the human soul is emancipated from the matter of the physical, emotional, and mental vehicles and is united with the Solar Angel. This is Soul-infusion, through which the human soul is conceived and born within the Spiritual Triad. It is only after one becomes a soul that he is consciously immortal, and his life and all his creative actions enter into the domain of immortality.

There are many egos, but souls are rare. Every soul brings a new influence in life and causes evolution to move on.

When the soul functions in the Spiritual Triad, he uses the energy coming from his Essence. This energy is threefold: it is the energy of will, love, and intelligence. Only those who have will can bring new currents and changes to the world. At levels below the Spiritual Triad, man has no will, which is to say, he has no free-will; he has intelligence, love, urges, drives, desires, intentions, and decisions — but not true will.

In the state of Soul-infusion, man is guided by the will of the Solar Angel. He thinks he has a will, but he does not have it. He must renounce his physical, emotional, mental, and worldly wills so that he is accepted into the energy current of the Solar Angel. For a long period of time, man must realize the nature of the will, its power, its operation, its secrets, so that he is allowed to pass to a higher level and have his own free-will. Until then, his "sword" is in its sheath. This is why symbolically one becomes a knight or a warrior after he "pulls out his sword" and is able to use it.

Sometimes the Self in Its identified stages is called Essence. For example, there is the body and the Essence, which is the identified Self, but different from the body, like a wire and the electricity in the wire. The three bodies, when integrated, are called the personality, but in the personality itself there is the Essence. In the ego, there is the Essence.

When the ego climbs into the Spiritual Triad, it becomes a soul; but the Essence of the soul is the Self. The Self is the ultimate Essence in the human stage. Behind the human Self, the Essence is the Planetary, Solar, Galactic, and Cosmic Self.

It is only the Essence that can cause changes in the vehicles, in the personality, in the ego, and in the soul, as all these *states* are vehicles.

Mechanical methods complicate the further development of the Essence. The only outside help that can be provided for the Essence is to create those conditions in which the Essence realizes its role in relation to the vehicles. All spiritual education, discipline, and meditation are ways to create right conditions for the Essence to manifest.

The Essence does not need education but only gradual release. A concealed light does not need light, but only emancipation.

Man in his Essence is omniscient, omnipotent, and omnipresent. All our knowledge must be directed toward releasing the Essence. Once It is released, all our knowledge will vanish like a patch of clouds.

Real Teachers and esoteric schools create those conditions in which the Essence is forced to act, to burst out. As long as the personality or the ego is flattered, nourished, and cherished, the Essence remains asleep. The true Teacher speaks to the Essence, not to the personality or the ego.

In the past, those who dedicated themselves to the Path were trained in the science of heroism. Many of the orders of knights and devotees of different schools were students of the science of heroism, which used to create those conditions in which the Essence would finally act. Once the Essence acts, the transmutation, transformation, transfiguration, and resurrection process begins, and the person turns his face toward his true Home.

Beingness is another very important word used in the Ageless Wisdom. Beingness is the current stage in the evolution of the awakening or releasing Self still in the chains of reincarnations. Usually, the beingness of man stays the same for a long time. The personality and the ego grow, sometimes at the expense of the beingness. Beingness only advances when the Essence awakens.

Most people need hundreds of lives to move their beingness from the physical to the astral body or from the astral body to the mental body or to higher bodies. This is why people grow in age in their bodies, but they remain children in their beingness.

Beingness, in its true sense, is achieved only while the human soul is penetrating into the Spiritual Triad.

It is there that the human soul can know, can actualize his knowledge, and periodically works as a separate entity from the personality — but keeping the personality under his ultimate control.

Thus beingness is not knowledge, is not action, but a state in which the human soul is in a process of changing into the Self.

Before a man enters into the state of beingness, he passes through various stages of pretension, imitation, showing-off, trying to be seen as different from what he is in his Essence. But when he is finished with all these games, he appears in the world of man exactly as he is in his inner world. This is the start of building beingness.

Beingness is an ever progressing state of the pure Self. There is beingness on the personality level where sincerity, purity, and synthesis manifest in all actions of the person. When the physical body for example is acting under the inspiration and control of the Self, one has beingness on that level.

Then there is a deeper beingness in the personality when the creative powers of the human soul manifest in their ultimate beauty.

Then there is the beingness in which the human soul can operate in higher planes as he does on lower planes.

Then there is also the beingness where the human soul becomes a part of Ashrams, Hierarchy, or extra planetary Centers.

In all these stages, beingness is the worth of the human soul in relation to the level on which he functions, and in relation to the laws and energies to which he responds.

Thus beingness on any given level or plane comes into being when the focus of consciousness or awareness is not only awareness or consciousness but also potentials for actualization.

He knows, and he is. His powers of actualization are a goal for his consciousness.

Beingness is the degree of existence.

People do not exist as human souls but as bodies, as emotions, as glamors, as illusions, as vanities.

The beingness is the percentage of existence, it is the level of independence of the human soul from all these identifications.

One percent liberation from the vehicles and their associates — glamors, illusions, etc. — is one percent beingness. Such a beingness does not have very many chances to survive.

Real beingness starts the moment when the human soul strives to exist.

As the beingness of a person advances, he demonstrates more leadership qualities, creativity, psychic energy, insight, and foresight, as well as the greater virtues of the Inner Watch. Beingness is advanced not by learning or accumulating knowledge but by striving to manifest or actualize greater Beauty, Goodness, Righteousness, Joy, Freedom, and sacrificial service.

Sometimes people are surprised to see the childish manner in which they act. They see how in old age they are still playing the games of children. They see how the smallest temptation defeats them, despite their possession of academic degrees and certificates. The reason is due to the fact that _their beingness_ has remained that of a child and has not grown.

It is important to watch the growth of _beingness_. In religious practices as well as in daily practices, the main item to observe is the state of one's beingness, rather than the display of exhibitionist behavior. Ashramic groups are those groups who work for the advancement of beingness and the personality in a harmonious way, until the personality becomes the _obedient servant of the Essence._

The reason humanity plays its childish games, cycle after cycle, is due to its inability to grow into maturity. After millions of years, we should be at a different level; we should at least be able to stop our war games, exploitation, pollution, crimes, greed, separativeness, and possessiveness. If one observes humanity as a whole from a high level of beingness, he will be convinced that humanity is like a nine year old child, and some nations are like seven or eight year old children in their beingness.

Our astral and mental senses have not begun to develop. Intuitional senses do not even exist. Instead we have developed powerful weapons to annihilate each other and contaminate the Earth which nourishes us, and we pollute the Space which supports our existence. Mature people would not do what humanity has done!

The progress of a human being starts when a conscious Teacher or a consciously prepared event creates a cleavage in the person and separates the observer and the object of observation. Unless such a split occurs, no progress is possible. At this time, man is the slave and prey of the flood of actions taken unconsciously, and he cannot stop this because he is identified with his own mechanical actions. Unless he is separated from the flood and put in a position to observe it and its consequences, there will be no hope for this humanity.

Disciples must increase in this world. Disciples are those who can separate themselves from their machine and observe it, control it, and use it to achieve the goal of their Essence.

We may say that the ego is a bridge which has explosives under it. All destructive actions take place on that bridge. The ego is not only destructive for others, but it is also the originator of all those actions that disturb the laws of Nature and the laws of our three personality vehicles.

Wars are the result of the cumulative tensions of egos. People think that with an atomic explosion no life will survive on this planet. Maybe no human life will survive, but insects and various animals will inherit this world which we have built, polluted, and then destroyed. This will prove that the education given to man has made him a self-destructive species, while animals and other life forms function for survival.

A bird enjoys what Nature has given him, and he sings his gratitude. The proof that we do not appreciate Nature is that we destroy it as if it were *our own* creation. It would not be surprising if animals were to go to our sophisticated offices, smell our ego, our hatred and malice on the machines we use and, sneezing, draw away from them.

When the human soul advances into the Spiritual Triad and becomes a *soul*, he respects Nature, lives according to the laws of Nature, and especially helps other life forms develop a more sensitive response to the laws of Nature. As a cell in the galactic body, every intelligent life form has three things to realize: his individual role, his place in the overall Plan, and the Purpose behind the Plan. This realization comes to us once we pass the ego level, enter the sphere of light called the Spiritual Triad, and become an immortal soul.

People must not be forced to believe in immortality. There is no immortality for a person who does not believe in it or who has no experience of it. The Teaching on immortality will only be understood by those who have some memory of their former incarnations, memories from the Subtle Worlds, or a strong faith which is based on a veiled memory.

If some criminals knew about immortality, they would think that they could take revenge on their victims in the Subtle World, and they would enter into the Subtle World with that emotion.

Some people think it is good to go to the Subtle World, so they commit suicide. Others think they should rest for a while in the Subtle World and return under more fortunate conditions to pursue their pleasures. Before people learn how to be self-forgetful, the Teaching of immortality will not change them.

Being aware of this, Buddha taught only the following fundamentals:

—How to think rightly
—How to live a righteous life
—How to renounce the ego
—How to be harmless to all beings
—How to meditate
—How to serve with self- renunciation

If these things are done, there will be no need for the Teaching of immortality; each individual on the Path would have his personal experience to guide him.

The Teaching of the Wisdom must not be forced on others or sold in the bazaars. People must come and search for it, demand it, and show an ability to understand it and use it for the transformation of their lives and for the service of humanity.

Some churches have presented the Higher Worlds to be the domain of eternal pleasure or eternal fire. Such a presentation does not convey a true meaning for the contemporary person. If he believes in hell, he lives in a hell in this life, counting his sins and expecting to burn forever. No one is sinless unless he is insane. If he believes that the Other Worlds are a place of pleasure, he retards his evolution by trying to enjoy earthly life with the expectation of unending pleasures in the Other Worlds.

Pleasure and pain have been presented as if they were eminent gods, whereas they are temporary conditions. The human soul is above pleasure and pain, and his goal in life must not be to pursue everlasting pleasures or escape pain and suffering. These are wrong goals. On earth man must learn to love, serve, and be enlightened. After that, he must begin to be interested in the life-after.

This book is not an effort to convince you about the existence of Other Worlds. If you do not have any experiences with them, you will be confused by reading this book. This book is written for those of you who *know* in your heart of the existence of the Other Worlds. It is not written to convince you about the Subtle Worlds, but to talk over things you want to know more about.

On every level of beingness, man has a corresponding consciousness. There is no end to his progress. To have consciousness does not just mean mastery over the physical, emotional, and mental natures. Actually, if the three bodies are not mastered, they can use the consciousness for their own interests and limit its expansion. The consciousness of the body, the emotions, and the mind is not the consciousness of the Essence, regardless of the stage the man is in. This is why man is always in conflict. The Essence uses its light to affect the bodies. If the consciousness of the Essence comes closer to the Inner Watch, the person has the chance to master the vehicles.

Before man can discipline and control his vehicles, he must establish contact with the Inner Watch. The Inner Watch inspires the ways by which the Essence eventually fuses the threefold consciousness of the vehicles, then fuses this with the consciousness of the Inner Watch. The next step is for the Essence to fuse his consciousness with the consciousness of the three vehicles and the Inner Watch.

As the Essence succeeds in fusion, it develops continuity of consciousness in the astral and mental planes, until the Essence locates himself as a soul in the Spiritual Triad and extends his continuity of consciousness to higher planes.

The beingness (which is the progressive stages of the Essence) experiences freedom, love, and bliss in the Spiritual Triad and — using the mental, emotional, and physical mechanisms — becomes a powerful creative source. He may create in the scientific field, in the field of art, in the field of politics, or in any field of human endeavor.

Before the beingness is focused in the Spiritual Triad as a soul, the creativity of man is not immortal.

The following diagram shows the path of the human Spark traveling up through Its Essence and identifying with higher planes, creating on each plane Its beingness.

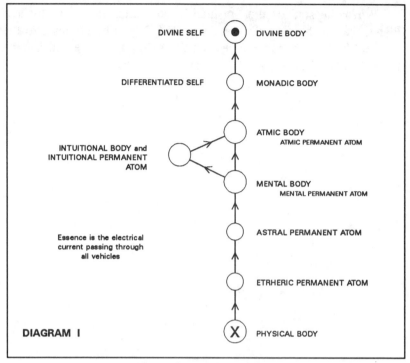

Conscious Immortality

It is this Essence that is the principle of equilibrium and harmony on all planes and levels.

One of the greatest powers in the Universe is harmony. The greatest lesson to be learned is harmony. If one wants to know what the Cosmic Self is, he must think about harmony.

The principle of harmony is everywhere and in everything. This is the Holy Spirit, the psychic energy, which shines in the darkness of all chaotic currents.

One must find ways to fuse with this principle of harmony. Every expansion of consciousness, every power is gained only in increasing harmony. Virtues are the expressions of harmony. Peace is harmony.

A thought, a feeling, a word, or an act that creates disturbances in the harmony is a seed of suffering and pain. Harmony is approached by annihilating vanity, ego, and self-will.

A harmonious person carries in himself the mighty power of the Ocean of Harmony. The chord of the Divine Harmony reverberates in Space, and each initiate composes his own melody with his chosen notes in tune with the Divine Harmony.

When the soul of the Spiritual Triad climbs into the Monadic Plane, we call him the differentiated Self. When he climbs into the Divine Plane, he becomes one with the All-Self, but he still has his Individuality. This is a great mystery.

62

The Purpose of the Human Being

People are in various stages of growth. Some are born as children and remain as such, even if they live for one hundred years. Others only reach a teen-age level in their spiritual growth. Still others become mature people.

People pass away, return, and begin once again where they left off. Some are born as children, live and depart as such, and stay children in the Subtle World. They return as children. Only a small percentage of human souls grow into adulthood in each cycle of incarnation.

It is the same in all kingdoms. The growth of the form is not the growth of the Essence. There are seeds which do not grow, due to inner and outer conditions of adversity. There are seeds which grow and turn into plants; then they dry. Only certain seeds are successful and become flowers or reach their destination.

Individual and group problems exist when people do not grow. Whenever our inner growth stops, we become problems for others and for ourselves. The Great Ones watch us from the Higher Worlds and see how much we grow in a few thousand years, or how we remain eternally as children. It is interesting to know that one can grow physically, emotionally, and mentally yet remain a child or a teen-ager in essence.

Purpose is the highest objective of a human being. All other objectives must help us reach our Purpose. Goals are steps leading to our ultimate Purpose. For example, a principal goal may be to have a house. The objectives of putting in a foundation, walls, ceiling, roof, doors, windows, etc., are all stations toward our main goal — the house.

There are goals on various levels, but through them all runs the thread of the supreme Purpose. We have personal, group, national, global, solar, galactic, and Cosmic goals. Each goal carries man toward his spiritual destination: the Purpose. The human Essence has its destiny within its Core. Destiny is different from a goal in that a goal is a step leading to destiny — the Purpose. When one realizes his destiny and takes conscious steps toward it, we say he has goals and that he is striving toward his Purpose.

This destiny must be sensed and expressed. The process of expression is just like the flowering of a seed. The lotus seed is also a lotus flower because when it is placed under a microscope, a miniature of a blossomed flower can be seen. It is considered a sacred flower for this reason, and for this reason it symbolizes the development of the human soul.

The seed of the lotus flower is first placed into mud. It spreads roots in the mud, grows through the water, and blooms in the open air.

This is the symbolic development of the human Spark. It has fallen into the physical body, which is like clay or mud. It grows through the emotional sphere or nature, which is the water. Then it grows in the mental nature, the air, and blooms in the spiritual life, which is represented by the rays of the sun.

The goal of the human being is to grow in the physical life and spread roots — which means to have a house, clothes, a car, food, etc. — and to bloom emotionally, mentally, and spiritually.

The development of the flower in any degree also appears in the Higher Worlds. For example, if a man blooms spiritually while in the physical body, his flower appears in the astral plane. If the blooming is deeper and more complete, it appears in the mental and Fiery Worlds. This is how one can enrich the gardens of the subjective worlds by unfolding his own flower. The seed unfolds on all planes and reveals the mystery, the Glory hidden in its Core. The seed becomes a flower with beautiful radiations of colors and fragrance.

The fragrance of a human flower is his influence. If the fragrance is sweet and spreads over a large area, it means the field of the influence of the man is great.

All that you have physically — money, house, food, dress, furniture — must be used in the right way, so that you can reach your Purpose. If you use your possessions in the wrong way, you cannot reach the Purpose but remain hidden in the mud.

All that you have emotionally — your love, your various feelings of joy, ecstasy, beauty, and pleasures — must be used in such a way that you move toward the blooming of your flower.

Similarly, your thoughts, plans, knowledge, and wisdom must also be used in such a way that you can grow leaves and blossom. But if you become the slave of alcohol and drugs, and do not care for your heart and body, you cannot blossom and you remain in the mire.

When you use all your physical, emotional, and mental belongings to progress in your blooming, one day the beauty that was within the seed of your soul will flower. The flower represents the harmonious development of all the spiritual qualities, as well as mental, emotional, and physical possibilities. Of course, the flowering must be repeated life after life, until it becomes the best of its kind.

We must also consider that flowering is not always a safe process. There are many dangers. We must therefore consider:

1. The condition of life and the condition of the earth as a whole.
2. The state of your inner being, conflicting forces, and inertia which make it difficult for you to bloom.
3. Certain "bugs," which can kill the flower, such as bugs of *doubt* about your future. During times of doubt, stick to your former dreams, as you would cling to a log when you are floating in the middle of the ocean.

The flowering improves life after life, reaching new standards. The miracle happens, and you see new and different flowers all around you. All these form a bouquet of flowers. This is how true spiritual groups come into being.

The stages of growth can be ascertained: if one watches the toys with which he plays; if one finds the primary interest in his life; if one discovers how much time, energy, and money he spends to run after his toys; if one discovers how much he lives for others compared to how much life is used for his separative self; and finally, if one discovers the objects of his desire, aspiration, or striving.

One can advance through observation. Observation must be directed toward our physical movements and behavior; our emotional actions, reactions and responses; our thoughts, opinions, and knowledge; our motives.

One must observe himself for a long time, if he does not wish to be trapped in judging others and developing vanities and self-pride. Vanity and self-pride are called iron traps from which one cannot free himself for a long series of lifetimes.

While one does self-observation, he must not judge and condemn himself. Through judging others and ourselves, we develop a standard beyond which we cannot pass. Our judgment and criticism become our own standards which mold our life, and we become like those we hate. Judgment, criticism, ill-feeling, malice, and slander create those elements in our aura which develop into the images or the negatives of those we hate. Once their images are developed in our aura, it is only a matter of time until we become like them. This is why we say that when one hates his enemy, he becomes like him.

The growth of a lotus seed — which spreads its roots in the mud, then rises from the stem through the water into the open air — is very symbolic. If the water is polluted, the plant cannot be healthy and bloom. The water is like our emotional aura which should be clear and pure. Negative emotions pollute our aura and prevent the growth of our Essence.

Similarly, when the air is polluted, the flower will have difficulty unfolding its beauty and spreading its fragrance. The air is like our mental aura. In a polluted mental sphere, the flower of our Essence cannot unfold.

To reach our Purpose we must make our spheres clear and healthy so that the Essence grows naturally. Physical purity brings health; emotional purity brings joy. Mental purity brings changes in our life and gives us the power to control our mechanisms.

One of the steps to help the growth of your Essence is to observe your life very objectively. Do not try to observe others at first. Instead, try to observe yourself. When you observe others and do not like the things they are doing, you develop the spirit of criticism and then the spirit of hypocrisy, thinking that you are better than they are. Once you think that you are better than other people, you fail in your goal.

How to safeguard yourself from such a danger...? The answer is to observe yourself, to watch yourself, and you will not be proud of yourself. This is the key. Once you start watching yourself, you will see there is so much to be corrected, and you will not bother yourself with the shortcomings of others.

Once again, in self-observation you must not condemn yourself. It is a great danger to do this. When you condemn others, you develop vanity, pride, and criticism. When you condemn yourself, you stop your progress because you never grow beyond the image of yourself built by condemnation.

People reach only to the level of their judgment. A barrier made by judgment is not easy to break. One can penetrate beyond such a barrier only through an intense striving. Once a person sees himself exactly as he is, he can then see others as they are.

For many, many ages people have not grown out of their spiritual childhood because they judged, criticized, and condemned — instead of understood, encouraged, and inspired. Criticism and condemnation plant the same problems in you which you hate in others, and develop those weaknesses in you which you attacked in them. Condemnation, judgment, criticism, and hatred create the chemical elements in your aura which develop the image there (like a photographic negative) which you hate in others.

The next step to make your Essence grow is to clean the dump-site of your mind. What is the dump-site? It is your mental sphere around your body. Imagine how many ugly, unhealthy, corrupt, and criminal thoughts you dump there. Can your flower unfold in such a trashy environment?

The next step is to cultivate virtues. Every month or every year try to cultivate a virtue. Virtues are ladders offered to us from Higher Worlds to make us climb toward our Real Self, toward our life goal.

The cultivation of one virtue will make it easier for you to cultivate another virtue. If you are striving to cultivate a virtue, you will notice that many obstacles begin to fight against you, or that more temptations mysteriously appear to take you away from your virtue. This is a very interesting phenomenon. The elements which are against these virtues, and which you have collected for ages, try to fight against you so as not to lose their hold on your personality. Accordingly, the outer circumstances of your life arrange themselves to correspond to the events taking place within you.

Such obstacles and temptations are also called *filters*. These filters prevent anyone from proceeding on the Path who is not worthy of it. Those who do not have enough tension of striving surrender and wander again in the shallow waters of their personality pleasures. But those who have the tension of striving use every obstacle and every temptation as a stepping stone to cross the river.

Once a young lady told me that she was thinking of stopping her daily meditation.

"Why?" I asked.

"Because every time I begin to meditate, either the telephone rings, or the children cry, or something happens out of the blue to disturb me."

"But remember," I said, "it is through confronting obstacles that we learn to control them. This is what progress is. Obstacles are challenges to our progress."

Once we learn how to face our obstacles, another mysterious thing happens. We slowly realize that we are receiving a great amount of help from life. Unexpected friends come and help us; money comes; problems dissolve; tensions melt away; enemies change into friends. Why does all this happen? The reason is that Nature is progressive. All the Creative Forces of Nature help us be successful. After one realizes this fact, he faces all obstacles with joy because they turn into a rhythm in the melody of one's life.

This is how your seed grows. You grow from the mud; you pass through the water and air; and your flower blossoms in the sunshine. All the possibilities and creative forces hidden in the seed manifest themselves. And when all the possibilities and virtues come into manifestation, you will see your True Self within your manifestation, within your flower.

The nature of life is that you cannot stop on any level of achievement. You have to bloom into your individual and divine seed. Now you must bloom as a flower in the community, in your nation, in humanity, in the Solar System, in the Galaxy, in Cosmos. This is your Purpose. For this Purpose all former achievements of your goals must be left behind. All must be sacrificed in order to reach the Purpose. Here are a number of daily disciplines to make yourself bloom:

1. Make your physical body beautiful and healthy. Do not do things which hurt your body.
2. Make your heart pure, full of compassion, kindness, and love.
3. Refrain from criticism, malice, slander, and treason.
4. Make your motives pure and your thoughts clear and beautiful.
5. Cultivate high visions about your future. Desire to be a spiritual beauty.
6. For a few minutes daily, look at a flower.
7. Develop the power of admiration.

After a while you will see how beautiful you are, and your fragrance will spread everywhere. Fragrance is your contribution to life as a whole; it is your creative influence over the life forms of the whole Existence.

63

Vision

Vision is not an apparition; vision is not sight. Vision is the future *you* which appears to you as your supreme Purpose. It exists in the Cosmic Consciousness and is reflected layer after layer into the core of your soul, into your mind, and into your brain, losing much of its beauty. At the moment when the vision hits your consciousness, you become aware of it, although whatever you are aware of is a faint reflection of your real beauty and glory. Thus vision is your supreme future "be-ness" toward which you strive through all your labor, achievements, and services throughout your eternal journey.

Vision is the image of your ultimate Purpose, reflected on the mirror of your beingness, whatever level it is on.

Every one of us has a supreme destiny. The destiny of a seed is to be a flower. The image of our destiny is concealed within our Core and is hidden in the deepest layers of Cosmic Consciousness. This vision is reflected from the highest layers of consciousness into the lower layers, and gradually it becomes dim and diffused. At this stage of vision, man no longer remembers it or is even aware of it.

At the time that one feels the vision, no matter how dim and incomplete it may be, he finds his Home. As man gets closer to his vision, he enters the path of improvement, transformation, and new spiritual achievements. The vision becomes his pole star which leads his steps toward the right direction, toward his Home through the labyrinth of his lives.

Vision is the impression in our mind of the archetypal image. Vision is the uniting thread between the three worlds and the most fiery spheres.

Vision is like a mosaic. You see it in its complexity in your highest moments of contemplation, but as your consciousness descends to earthly spheres, only a vague impression remains in your mind. Still, you sense the need to construct it, and you try to find the pieces as it is reflected in your daily strivings and labor.

You begin to feel that every piece of the mosaic is found through Beauty, Goodness, Righteousness, Joy, and Freedom. In rare moments of ascent you sense that this mosaic, which seems to be your highest destination, is a little piece in a greater and greater mosaic, which includes your own destiny as well as that of all nations.

Vision is the magnet which attracts you toward higher and higher levels of consciousness and beingness. When a man has a vision, he has a magnet toward which he progresses. That magnet evokes essential virtues and principles which are concealed in his Core. The same holds true for a nation.

Vision first appears as a spark and mobilizes the powers of your striving. Then it turns into a flame; then into a symphony; and in rare moments of your contemplation you see that the vision is the real You, the Self in all Selves. Thus, the vision comes and slowly changes and transforms you, and throughout thousands of incarnations you eventually meet your True Self, your own vision.

Man is what he thinks he is. Most of our failures, sicknesses, and problems are the result of our thinking. Vision has a magical influence upon our mind. It keeps the mind continually oriented and directed toward the future.

Imagine a teen-ager who has sensed a vision wherein he will be a world leader and bring humanity freedom, prosperity, love, joy, and unity. If this vision is really contacted and if it penetrates into his bones, imagine what kind of life he will live.

At moments when sex, drugs, and alcohol would tempt him, his vision, like an eagle, will uplift him and charge him with the energies of victory.

During times of emotional disturbances and depressions, his vision will come and tell him, "It is good; you cannot be great without experiencing such states of consciousness."

When problems, decisions, and difficulties appear, his mind will be illuminated by the vision. The vision will whisper in his ear, "To be a world leader you have to learn to solve problems. You must be schooled. Your greatness is forged in the midst of problems."

At the time of failures, he will not succumb because the vision will come and whisper to his heart, "The greatest victories are primed in defeat and failure. Hold your vision in your heart and you will conquer."

Now compare this teen-ager with another who has no vision. He does not know what he will be. Because of the lack of vision, he will fall into many traps. He will build bad karma and complicate his path.

Without a fundamental goal he will, at best, be the slave of his body, emotions, and vanities.

Two teen-agers started from the same kindergarten and went to the same school and college. One became the slave of his ego; the other became the leader of a great nation.

When the vision penetrates into the deepest layers of your heart, it makes you focused, concentrated, and enthused. As a result, you eat, drink, sleep, and work with the fire of that vision. Vision transforms your life. It transforms the life of a group, society, and nation. A man transformed by his vision becomes a beam of light, bringing vision and life wherever he goes, to whatever he does.

It is easy to read these words, but it is very difficult to actualize your vision. Once you find the thread of your vision and unite yourself with it, it becomes a transformative source of power in your life through which you conquer many difficulties.

What is the influence of vision upon your mind, emotions, body, environment? First, a man who has no vision is always confused mentally. He is in contradiction; he has no drive; he does not follow the path of construction but builds and destroys as his goals change. He does not unfold and learn deeper thinking. He does not learn concentration; thus he has no focus. The events of life control him. His mind is very shallow or crystallized in one direction or full of prejudice, superstition, and vanities.

Second, joy, which is the oil of the heart, comes into existence only with the vision of a tomorrow, of a future. What happens when you say to your child, "Tomorrow we will go to the mountains... tomorrow I will buy a bicycle for you... tomorrow you will graduate." Joy is always related to the existence of a future. Vision is the future. Whatever the condition, remind your child or friend of the vision, and you will see how you will change his heart.

Third, the physical body to a great extent is nourished by mental enthusiasm and emotional joy. When your mind thinks that in the future your body will be transformed into light and will serve a great cause, it is not likely that there will be ugly, weak, negative thoughts about your body. When your heart is in a state of joy, your body will be able to fight against germs and diseases. Thus, vision is the energy of your body.

There is a story about a warrior who made his horse jump over rivers fifteen to twenty feet wide. On the day of his father's coronation as King, the warrior found he would be late. The shortest way to reach the coronation on time was to cross an abyss forty feet wide.

A quarter of a mile before the abyss the warrior spoke to his horse, saying, "We can do it; we will arrive at the right time." The horse jumped the abyss.

When they reached the coronation his father asked, "How did you arrive so soon?"

"We jumped over the abyss of dark rocks."

"Why?"

"To see your glory."

During the coronation, when the crown was to be placed upon the king's head, the father called his son and positioned the crown upon his head instead.

"Why did you do that?" asked the Chief Justice.

"Because," the father replied, "his vision endowed him with wings. Those who have vision can magnetize a whole city, a whole nation, and create in them great cooperation and striving toward great values."

Without vision and where human dignity is lowered, weeds grow — weeds such as nightclubs, whorehouses, gambling places.

With vision people clean their lives. No nation in the world becomes great without vision. When vision is lost, disintegration sets in.

Vision comes as the result of purity of motive, striving, and service.

When one has lived many lives with pure, selfless motives in his heart; when he has striven toward improvement and has a record of selfless service; then vision appears to him. It appears when the clouds of maya, glamor, and illusions slowly fade away.

What really does the vision of perfection do? When you are always thinking about your perfection, about how beautiful you can be, about the great services you can render to humanity, your whole system programs itself accordingly and helps you reach your vision.

Those who have no vision are like cars in which the steering is out of order. The car takes you anywhere it wants.

Our minds mostly work through telepathic impressions or by the power of association, but if we have vision, we create a shield around us through which no thought can pass without invitation.

Thus vision organizes your life; it organizes all your emotions and thoughts. All that you are doing physically, emotionally, and mentally falls in line with your vision. If for any reason your actions, feelings, and thoughts are not in harmony with your vision, you feel a psychic shock; you feel unhappy, disturbed, even depressed, and you try to recover yourself and harmonize all your expressions with your real vision.

One of the most important duties of your life is to find your vision.

How do you contact your vision? The first step is the clearing of the clouds. One cannot see the sun if it is obscured by clouds. The same is true within human beings: one cannot see his vision if his mind is clouded with illusions.

Illusion is a distorted reality. Illusion is a thought about yourself which is not real or true. You have many thoughts or images about yourself that are not really you. They are distortions of your true image. When you have five, ten, or fifteen images about yourself, you are confused and you do not know which one you are.

Suppose a man is playing ten roles in a movie, and he is confused about which is the real one. He has been a king, a soldier, a priest, a butcher, a gambler. At the end he is confused, and he does not know if he even has an identity that is the real him! Such a state of confused identity builds a thick cloud of illusion in his mind, and alternately each image, separately or as a group, presents an identity. The real man is confused because he has no control over these false images.

There will be no continuity and stability in your mind as long as you are divided into many images. Contradiction in your life appears when you identify with various contradictory images of yourself.

If, without any illusion, one finds exactly what he is, he can find the way to his higher vision. To find your true image, you discard image after image, until you reach the one that is the closest to you. This game is won by losing your cards, not by adding cards to the pile you have.

We not only build images about ourselves through imagination and thinking; we also build images through our feelings and emotions. For example, if we hate someone, we build an image of a person who hates and has all the decorations of a hateful person. The same happens when we are angry, fearful, jealous, or revengeful. By these images we bury our true image under the piles of false images.

When one creates an image which is not himself, he brings cleavages into his nature. A separated nature is the source of many additional illusions. When one splits himself, he becomes weaker. He carries seven to ten heads on his shoulders, each one acting as the boss, according to psychological associations. People do not notice these things and slowly enter into the path of failure, crime, and insanity.

A hypocrite is a man who has multiple images, multiple egos. One head says one thing; the other says another. There is no unity in the person, so he is a hypocrite. Such a man says something and does something else.

Sometimes we say that man is lost. A lost man is one who does not know who he is. But if you have a vision, your false selves slowly drop away because they are not able to cope with the vision. Vision gradually sorts out all images and leaves only the one which corresponds to the vision. This is why vision creates a true identity within you. It creates balance, stability, concentration, dedication, and a steady striving toward your future.

Many mental, emotional, and physical illnesses can be cured by making people see a vision and then be the vision. When a person is not divided within himself, he is successful, healthy, happy, and creative.

In a sports activity one can never win, despite full preparation, if he has any doubt in his mind of his victory. Doubt is the sign of a split personality. In the future, people will measure the tension and integrity of each athlete. The champion will be the one who had the greatest tension regarding the vision of his victory. The second-place winner will be the one who had less tension, and so on. Those who failed will be the ones who had conflicting tensions within their system.

Doubt creates division, disunity, and disintegration. These weaken your muscles, your feelings, and your concentration. The same is true for groups, nations, and all of humanity. We can make this earth a paradise if we are united, if we synthesize all human endeavors for the good of all nations.

Glamor is an image in your aura formed when you desired any object. When your aura is surrounded with thousands of conflicting images of desires, you will have a great problem in your life. What happens when you collect many antagonistic animals in one yard? The same thing happens to a man who has many conflicting desires in his nature. For example, you desire purity, but then you develop lust. You desire justice, but all your measures are false. You desire unity, but you spread hate. This is how you bring the seeds of confusion into your mind. Thus we see that the first step is to find your vision in the process of purification from all false selves.

The second step is pure striving toward your vision. Striving is an effort to improve your life and develop all those qualities which will help you actualize your vision. Striving has four principles. If one does not consider these four principles, his striving fails. They are beauty, goodness, justice, and health. Your improvement must follow these four principles. When you apply all your striving along these four principles, you will notice that your vision is expanding and becoming all-inclusive.

The third step in contacting your vision is sacrificial service. Sacrificial service is the labor through which you give birth to your future Self. Of course, it takes time, but each expression of your future Self brings you beauty, joy, bliss, and freedom.

When you really clean your atmosphere, strive, and serve, your vision comes and shines within you and through you. You become a powerhouse of vision wherever you are. One man, one woman can change a group or a nation, if he or she sees the vision.

Not only must our individual and national vision be found, but the global vision must also be found. Everyone must find one of the pieces of the mosaic, until the whole mosaic is seen by the eyes of humanity.

But to start such a labor one must start with oneself. As you progress in finding your vision, you will set aside the toys with which you were playing. In your present consciousness, the toys are important for you, but when you transcend your consciousness, the toys will no longer interest you.

Eventually you will reach a state of consciousness in which you will slowly put away your most precious toy. Maybe that toy can be yourself.

To realize the destiny of the human being, one must go out at night when the sky is clear and watch the stars, galaxies, and constellations and contemplate.

All creation is waiting for the Sons of the Most High to enjoy, to grow, to be, and to serve in this immense manifestation.

Every Spark is striving toward that ultimate destiny. Each of us is a traveler on the Cosmic Path extending through the heavens.

In view of such a glory, we are filled with joy and bliss and with the urge to serve and liberate people from the chains of their ignorance, pain, and suffering, and we labor to help them walk the path of joy, freedom, and beauty.

The joys on this earth compared to the joys in higher realms are like fire-flies next to the Sun. Each advancement toward the Most High, toward the Source of bliss, is a revelation within your being, the Essence of the Most High, the Essence of the Supreme Bliss.

About The Author

This is Torkom Saraydarian's latest published book. Many more will be released very soon. His vocal and instrumental compositions number in the hundreds and are being released.

The author's books have been used all over the world as sources of guidance and inspiration for true New Age living based on the teachings of the Ageless Wisdom. Some of the books have been translated into other languages, including German, Dutch, Danish, Portuguese, French, Spanish, Italian, Greek, Yugoslavian, and Swedish. He holds lectures and seminars in the United States as well as in other parts of the world.

Torkom Saraydarian's entire life has been a zealous effort to help people live healthy, joyous, and successful lives. He has spread this message of love and true vision tirelessly throughout his life.

From early boyhood the author learned first-hand from teachers of the Ageless Wisdom. He has studied widely in world religions and philosophies. He is in addition an accomplished pianist, violinist, and cellist and plays many other instruments as well. His books, lectures, seminars, and music are inspiring and offer a true insight into the beauty of the Ageless Wisdom.

Torkom Saraydarian's books and music speak to the hearts and minds of a humanity eager for positive change. His books, covering a large spectrum of human existence, are written in straightforward, unpretentious, clear, and often humorous fashion. His works draw on personal experiences, varied and rich. He offers insight and explanations to anyone interested in applying spiritual guidelines to everyday life. His no-nonsense approach is practical, simple, and readily accessible to anyone who is interested in finding real meaning in life.

Torkom Saraydarian has de-mystified the mysteries of the Ageless Wisdom. He has made the much needed link between the spiritual and the everyday worlds.

Look for exciting new books and music being released by Torkom Saraydarian.

Glossary

Ageless Wisdom: The sum total of the Teachings given by great Spiritual Teachers throughout time. Also referred to as the Ancient Wisdom, the Teaching, the Ancient Teaching.

Ajna center: The center between the eyebrows; corresponds to the pituitary gland.

Akasha: Higher Cosmic Etheric substance.

Akashic Records: Existing in the Higher Cosmic Ethers, the Akashic Records are living records of all experiences and activities that have ocurred in the past, present, and future of this planet and everything in it.

All-Self: See Cosmic Self.

Ancient of Days: The ruler of Shamballa; also known as Sanat Kumara.

Ancient Wisdom: See Ageless Wisdom.

Angelic Kingdom: Refers to beings following a different line of evolution than the human family.

Antahkarana: The path, or bridge, between the higher and lower mind, serving as a medium of communication between the two. It is built by the aspirant himself. It is threefold: the consciousness thread, anchored in the brain; the life thread, anchored in the heart; and the creative thread anchored in the throat. More commonly called the Rainbow Bridge.

Arhats: Ancient term designating Fourth Degree Initiates.

Aryan: Refers to the present period of the development of the human race. The Ageless Wisdom divides human development into seven sections, called Root Races. From ancient times to the present, they have been called: Polarian Race, Hyperborian Race, Lemurian Race, Atlantean Race, Aryan Race, Sixth Root Race, and Seventh Root Race. The latter two are the future states of human development. (For more information, see *The Psyche and Psychism* by Torkom Saraydarian.)

Ashram: Sanskrit word. Refers to the gathering of disciples and aspirants which the Master collects for instruction. There are seven major Ashrams, each corresponding to one of the Rays, each forming groups or foci of energy.

Astral body: The vehicle composed of astral substance, that in which the emotional aspect of humanity expresses itself. Also known as the subtle body and the emotional body.

Astral Plane: The sixth plane of the Cosmic Physical Plane, in which the emotional processes are carried on. Sometimes called the astral or emotional world. Also known as the Subtle World or the Astral Realm or the Emotional Realm.

Atlantis: (Atlantean Epoch). The continent that was submerged in the Atlantic ocean, according to the occult teaching and Plato. Atlantis was the home of the Fourth Root Race, whom we now call the Atlanteans.

Aura: The sum-total of all emanations from all the vehicles of any living thing.

Avatar: Great Being from solar or galactic fields sent cyclically to help humanity progress; they are condensed sources and embodiments of energy.

Awareness Unit: The human soul.

Black Lodge: See Dark Forces.

Brotherhood, The: See Hierarchy.

Carriers of Fire: Great Ones who, to a high degree, manifest their spiritual Core.

Causal body: The Chalice in man; see also Lotus.

Centers: Any energy vortex found in a human, planetary, or solar body; see also chakras.

Central Magnet: The central Core of the Universe that pulls to Itself all Sparks in manifestation.

Central Spiritual Sun: The Core of the Solar System; the Sun is triple: the visible Sun, the Heart of the Sun, and the Central Spiritual Sun.

Chain: Vehicle of manifestation of a Planetary Logos; composed of seven globes on different planes of materialization, which means the Life of the planet progressively renews Itself seven times, each time producing a new and more evolved manifestation.

Chakra: Energy vortex found in each vehicle, relating to a particular part of the human body. There are seven primary chakras starting from the top of the head: (1) crown, (2) brow, (3) throat, (4) heart, (5) navel, (6) generative organs, (7) base of spine.

Chalice: See Lotus.

Chela: An accepted disciple.

Clairaudience: The ability to hear beyond the audible range of vibrations, and also the power to hear astrally, mentally, and intuitively.

Clairvoyance: The ability to see beyond the visible range of vibrations, and also the power to see astrally, mentally, and intuitively.

Continuity of consciousness: A state of consciousness in which you are aware on all levels of the mind and of the higher and lower planes simultaneously.

Core: The essence or spark of God within each being; the Monad.

Cosmic Ethers: The highest four levels of the human constitution are called (from 4 to 1) the Intuitional Plane (Fourth Cosmic Ether), the Atmic Plane (Third Cosmic Ether), the Monadic Plane (Second Cosmic Ether), and the Divine Plane (First Cosmic Ether).

Cosmic Heart: See Cosmic Magnet.

Cosmic Magnet: The invisible center of the Universe.

Cosmic Physical Plane: Refers to the totality of the seven subplanes of manifestation, from highest to lowest: Divine, Monadic, Atmic, Intuitive or Buddhic, Mental, Emotional or Astral, and Physical. Each with seven subdivisions, totaling 49 planes of manifestation.

Cosmic Planes: The seven planes of cosmic manifestation: Cosmic Physical, Cosmic Astral, Cosmic Mental, Cosmic Intuitional, Cosmic Atmic, Cosmic Monadic, and Cosmic Divine; see index for details of all planes in text.

Cosmic Self: That great Entity which pervades and sustains all things on all levels of existence.

Dark Forces: Conscious agents of evil or materialism operating through the elements of disunity, hate, and separativeness.

Deva: See Angelic Kingdom.

Devachan: A place where souls who can reach the higher mental plane after death can rest before reincarnation; the heaven referred to in the scriptures.

Disciple: A person who tries to discipline and master his threefold personality, and manifests efficiency in the field where he works and serves.

Divine Plan: See Plan.

Divine Self: See Monad.

Ectoplasm: The combined emanations of the lymph glands and the human aura. It functions as the communication line between the physical body and the subtle body.

Ego: The human soul identified with the lower vehicles (physical, emotional, and mental) and their false values.

Elementals: The lives who operate the body they inhabit; three in number: physical elemental, astral elemental, and mental elemental.

Etheric Body: The counterpart of the dense physical body, pervading and sustaining it. Formed by matter of the four etheric subplanes. The blueprint on which the physical body is based.

Etheric Centers: See chakras.

Father's Home: Shamballa, "the Center where the Will of God is known"; also, the Central Magnet.

Fiery World: Refers to the Mental Plane or above. See Higher Worlds.

Fourth Initiation: The Crucifixion Initiation during which the Solar Angel leaves and the Chalice is destroyed by the fully awakened Jewel or Core.

Glamors: Astral forms with a life of their own in the emotional body.

Globes: The evolving bodies of a planetary Life; seven globes make one chain.

Great Ones: Beings who have taken the Fifth Initiation or beyond.

Great Warrior of the Tower: Sanat Kumara.

Guardian Angel: See Solar Angel.

Hierarchy: The spiritual Hierarchy, whose members have triumphed over matter and have complete control of the personality, or lower self. Its members are known as Masters of Wisdom Who are custodians of the Plan for humanity and all kingdoms evolving within the sphere of Earth. It is the Hierarchy that translates the Purpose of the Planetary Logos into a Plan for all kingdoms of the planet.

Hierophant: The Chief Initiator.

Higher Centers: Refers to the crown, brow, throat, and heart centers or chakras, as well as to the centers in the higher bodies.

Higher Realms: See Higher Worlds.

Higher Self: Refers to the Solar Angel or Transpersonal Self. See also Self.

Higher Spheres: See Higher Worlds.

Higher Worlds: Those planes of existence that are of a finer vibration of matter than the physical plane. Generally refers to the higher mental plane and above.

Human soul: See soul.

Illusory body: A subtle body, having the appearance of the physical body, projected for the purpose of communication with the dense physical plane; same as illusionary body.

Imperil: A paralyzing poison formed of crystallizations of psychic energy mixed with anger, fear, or irritation which settles on the nerve channels.

Initiate: A person who has taken an initiation. See also Initiation.

Initiation: The result of the steady progress of a person toward his life's goals, achieved through service and sacrifice, and manifested as an expansion of one's consciousness. It represents a point of achievement marked by a level of enlightenment and awareness. There are a total of nine Initiations that the developing human soul must experience in order to reach the Cosmic Heart.

Inner Core: See Core.

Inner Guide: The Solar Angel.

Inner Lord: The Solar Angel.

Inner Presence: The Solar Angel.

Inner Watch: The Solar Angel.

Jewel, The: The Core of the human being; the Monad.

Karma, Law of: The Law of Cause and Effect or attraction and repulsion. "As you sow, so shall you reap."

Kumaras: Great Beings from other chains Who came to speed the evolution of our planet.

Law of Cause and Effect: See Karma, Law of.

Lemurian Epoch: A modern term first used by some naturalists and now adopted by Theosophists to indicate an era dealing with the period of the continent Lemuria, which preceded Atlantis. The Third Root Race.

Logos, Planetary: The Soul of the planet. The planet is His dense physical body to provide nourishment for all living forms.

Logos, Solar: The Core of the whole Solar System and all that exists in the Solar System. His purpose is to integrate, correlate and synchronize all Centers using His Light, Love, Power — like an electrical energy — to circulate within each atom through all Centers, thus revealing the Purpose for existence and challenging all forms to strive toward the highest form of cooperation.

Lotus: Also known as the Chalice. Found in the second and third mental plane (from the top). Formed by twelve different petals of energy: three love petals, three knowledge petals, three sacrifice petals. The innermost three petals remain folded for ages. They are the dynamic sources of these outer petals. The Lotus contains the essence of all of a person's achievements, true knowledge, and service. It is the dwelling place of the Solar Angel.

Lower Psychism: The ability to perceive subtle aspects of existence with the aid of the lower centers in the human body. Mediums, channels, etc. are considered lower psychics.

Lower self: The personality vehicles of the human soul. See also the self.

Magnet: See Cosmic Magnet.

Manasaputras: A name for the Solar Angels.

Manvantaras: Periods of activity or the "days" of the Eternal One.

Masters: Individuals Who had the privilege to master their physical, emotional, mental, and Intuitional bodies.

Maya: A counterpart of illusions and glamors on the etheric plane. It results in the inability of the physical, emotional, and mental bodies to respond clearly to incoming impressions.

Meditation: Technique to penetrate the mind of the planet and develop creative abilities to manifest that mind in the life of humanity. (For in-depth information, please refer to *The Science of Meditation* and *Psyche and Psychism* by Torkom Saraydarian.)

Mediumistic: A tendency of certain individuals to astral phenomena and its perception thereof. Mediumistic people can, without guidance, fall into various dangers and traps associated with the astral plane. (For more information, see *Psyche and Psychism* by Torkom Saraydarian.)

Mental Body: The vehicle composed of the substance of the mental plane in which humanity expresses itself through thought.

Mental Plane: There are seven planes through which a human being travels and which make up human consciousness. From the lowest level upward, they are called: Physical, Emotional or Astral, Mental, Intuitional or Buddhic, Atmic, Monadic, Divine. The Mental Plane itself is divided into seven levels. The first three from the bottom are numbers seven, six, and five, which form the Lower Mental Plane. Number four is the middle mind or link. Numbers three, two, and one form the Higher Mental Plane.

Mental Realms: See Mental Plane. Also known as the Fiery World.

Mental Unit: A mental mechanism in the 4th level of the mental plane which is formed of four kinds of forces, and relates man to the sources of these four forces through its four spirillae.

Mind, Higher and Lower: See Mental Plane.

Monad: See Self.

Mulaprakriti: Primordial matter.

Neophyte: An aspirant on the path of discipleship.

Nirvana: The plane of consciousness known as the Atmic Plane.

Nirvanis: A name for the Solar Angels.

Occultism: Term used to designate the Ageless Wisdom and its study. See Ageless Wisdom.

One Self: The universal Life Soul pervading all existence.

Pan-Fohat: Cosmic Fire.

Permanent Atoms: Each body of a human being has one permanent atom which is the archetype for the construction and constitution of that vehicle.

Personality: Totality of physical, emotional, and mental bodies of man.

Petals: See Lotus.

Petris: Beings on different stages of evolution from the human: lunar petris are elementals, Solar Petris are Solar Angels.

Plan: The formulation of the Purpose of the Planetary Logos into a workable program — a Plan — by the Planetary Hierarchy for all kingdoms of nature.

Planetary Soul: See Logos, Planetary.

Prakriti: Matter.

Purpose: That which the Solar Logos is intended to achieve at the end of the evolution of the Solar System. The Plan is the formulation of this Purpose for our planet only.

Race: The Ageless Wisdom divides human development into seven sections, called Root Races. From ancient times to the present, they have been called: Polarian Race, Hyperborean Race, Lemurian Race, Atlantean Race, Aryan Race, Sixth Root Race, Seventh Root Race. The latter two are the future states of human development. (For more information, see _Psyche and Psychism_ by Torkom Saraydarian.)

Rainbow Bridge: The bridge between the lower and higher mind that brings continuity of consciousness; also known as the Antahkarana.

Rishis: Great Lords of Spirit; usually refers to the seven Ray Lords of the Great Bear constellation.

Round: The wave of divine Life of a Planetary Logos as it passes through one globe of a chain.

Samadhi: Contemplation; a state in which the consciousness is awake on the Intuitional Plane.

Sanat Kumara: The physical incarnation of our Planetary Logos; He is the Lower Self, the Planetary Logos being the Higher Self; also called the Lord of the World, the Ancient of Days, the One Initiator.

Scheme: A vehicle of manifestation of a Planetary Logos composed of seven chains, each composed of seven globes.

self: The small "s" self is the sumtotal of the physical, emotional, and mental bodies of man. Commonly called the "lower self" or personality.

Self: The capital "S" Self is another term used to refer to the Core of the human being. The True Self is the developing, unfolding human soul who is trying to liberate himself, go back to his Father, and become his True Self.

Seven Fields of Human Endeavor: The expression of the Seven Rays in human evolution, each corresponding to a specific Ray. They are: Politics, Education and Psychology, Philosophy, Arts, Science, Religion, Economics and Finance.

Seven Rays: These are the seven primary Rays through which everything exists. They are pure energy, vibrating to a specific frequency and condensing from plane to plane, from manifestation to manifestation. The three primary Rays or Rays of Aspect are: The First Ray of Power, Will and Purpose; The Second Ray of Love-Wisdom; The Third Ray of Active, Creative Intelligence. There are four Rays of Attribute: The Fourth Ray of Harmony through Conflict; The Fifth Ray of Concrete Science or Knowledge; The Sixth Ray of Idealism or Devotion; The Seventh Ray of Synthesis or Ceremonial Order. These Rays indicate qualities that pertain to the seven fields of human endeavor or expression.

Shamballa: Known as the White Island, it exists in etheric matter and is located in the Gobi desert. Shamballa is the dwelling place of the Lord of the World, Sanat Kumara, and is the place where "the Will of God is known."

Solar Angels: Very advanced beings who sacrificed their life, descending from Higher Worlds to help the evolution of humanity, and guide its steps toward initiation. This happened on our planet at the middle of the Lemurian period. They are also called Guardian Angels, or Flames. See Chapter 59.

Solar Entity: A Great Being from the solar system.

Soul Awareness: The human soul's awareness of the Solar Angel or the awareness of the human soul in the Intuitional Plane.

Soul-infusion: A state in which the physical, emotional, and mental bodies are purified to a high degree and aligned with the Solar Angel so that the light of the Solar Angel can radiate through the personality in full power and beauty.

Soul: Also known as the Solar Angel.

soul: The small "s" soul is the human psyche, the Spark, traveling on the path of evolution having three powers: willpower, attraction, and intelligence to guide its development. Also known as the evolving human soul.

Spark: Human Monad fallen into matter.

Spiritual Triad: The field of awareness of the human soul. This field comes into being when the magnetic fields of the Mental Permanent Atom, the Buddhic Permanent Atom, and the Atmic Permanent Atom fuse and blend.

Subtle World: Refers to the Astral or Emotional plane.

Teaching, The: See Ageless Wisdom.

Temple of Glory: See Lotus.

Third Initiation: The total purification and alignment of the mental, emotional, and physical vehicles of the evolving human soul, leading to Transfiguration or Enlightenment.

Thousand-petaled Lotus: The head center, which takes the place of the Chalice after the Fourth Initiation.

Three-fold personality: The three vehicles of man. The combined forces and vehicles in which the evolving human soul expresses himself and gains experience during incarnation. These vehicles are the physical body, the emotional or astral body, and the mental body.

Transfiguration: The result of the action of the electric fire of the Spiritual Triad on the higher mind. The lights in the little atoms of the personality vehicles are released, and the whole personality is purified in the Third Initiation.

Transformation: The result of the action of solar fire on the astral body. The astral body comes under the influence of the Solar Angel and the Intuitional Plane.

Transmutation: The result of the action of the fire of mind on the physical body. The physical body comes under the control of the human soul.

Transpersonal Self: The Solar Angel, the Inner Guide.

Treasure House: Symbolic term for the Chalice. Also called the Treasury.

Tulku: A higher way of lending the body to a Great Being Who wants to perform some outstanding service for humanity. Such a way of lending the body requires at least a Third Degree Initiate, one who has built the Rainbow Bridge and knows what he is doing.

Twelve-petaled Lotus: See Lotus.

Upanishads: Mystical treatises forming the *Veda,* said to date approximately from the Sixth Century, B.C. *The Upanishads* are said to be the source of all six systems of Hindu philosophy.

Vedas: Consists of four collections of writings: the *Rig-Veda,* the *Sama-Veda,* the *Yajur-Veda,* and the *Athar-Vaveda. The Vedas* are the Divine Revelation of the scriptures of the Hindus, from the root *viv,* "to know," or "divine knowledge."

Bibliographic References

Agni Yoga Society. New York: Agni Yoga Society.
    Heart, 1982
    Letters of Helena Roerich, 1967.
    Infinity II, 1957.
    Supermundane, unpublished writings.
    Fiery World, vol I, 1969.
    Community, 1951.
    Agni Yoga, 1954.
    Fiery World III, 1948.
    Brotherhood, 1962.
    Fiery World II, 1946.
    Hierarchy, 1933.
Ali, Yusuf A. trans. *The Holy Qur'an.*
Bailey, Alice A. New York: Lucis Publishing Co.
    A Treatise on Cosmic Fire, 1977.
    Esoteric Astrology, 1982.
    A Treatise on White Magic, 1974.
Blavatsky, H.P. London, Theosophical Publishing Society.
    Studies in Occultism, 1946.
Blavatsky, H.P. Pasadena, Ca: Theosophical University Press.
    The Secret Doctrine, 2 vols., 1988.
Lamsa, George M., trans. Nashville, TN: Holman Bible Publishers.
    The New Testament, 1968.
Saraydarian, Torkom. Sedona, AZ: Aquarian Educational Group.
    The Psyche and Psychism, 1981.
    The Science of Becoming Oneself, 1976.
    Joy and Healing, 1987.
    Christ, The Avatar of Sacrificial Love, 1974.
    The Legend of Shamballa, 1988.
    Irritation — The Destructive Fire, 1983.
    Challenge for Discipleship, 1986.
    Sex, Family, and the Woman in Society, 1987.
    The Science of Meditation, 1981.
    The Fiery Carriage and Drugs, 1973.
    The Unusual Court, 1979.
    The Bhagavad Gita, trans. 1974.
    Cosmos in Man, 1983.
    Woman, Torch of the Future, 1980.
    The Hidden Glory of the Inner Man, 1985.
    The Legend of Shamballa, 1976.
    Hierarchy and the Plan, 1975.
    Talks on Agni, 1987.
Saraydarian, Torkom. West Hills, CA: T.S.G. Publishing Foundation, Inc.
    The Ageless Wisdom, 1990.
    Breakthrough to Higher Psychism, 1990.

Index

Other Works by
Torkom Saraydarian

The Ageless Wisdom
The Bhagavad Gita
Breakthrough to Higher Psychism
Challenge for Discipleship
Christ, The Avatar of Sacrificial Love
A Commentary on Psychic Energy
Cosmic Shocks
Cosmos in Man
A Daily Discipline of Worship
Dialogue With Christ
Fiery Carriage and Drugs
Five Great Mantrams of the New Age
Flame of Beauty, Culture, Love, Joy
Hiawatha and the Great Peace
Hidden Glory of the Inner Man
Hierarchy and the Plan
Irritation — The Destructive Fire
I Was
Joy and Healing
Legend of Shamballa
The Psyche and Psychism
The Psychology of Cooperation and Group Consciousness
Questioning Traveler and Karma
The Science of Becoming Oneself
The Science of Meditation
The Sense of Responsibility in Society
Sex, Family, and the Woman in Society
Spring of Prosperity
Spiritual Regeneration
Symphony of the Zodiac
Synthesis
Talks on Agni
Torchbearers
Triangles of Fire
Unusual Court
Woman, Torch of the Future

Next Release: **Healing in the Future**

Ordering Information

Write to the publisher for additional information regarding:

- —Free catalog of author's books and music tapes.
- —Information regarding lecture tapes and videos.
- —Placement on mailing list.
- —Information on new releases.

Additional copies of *Other Worlds*:
U.S.$27.00 for softcover; $38.00 for hardcover.
Postage within U.S.A. $3.00 for softcover, $4.00 for hardcover.
Plus applicable state sales tax.

T.S.G. Publishing Foundation, Inc.
Visions for the Twenty-First Century
P.O.Box 4273
West Hills, California, 91308
United States of America